MW01489450

The Military Commander and the Law is a publication of The Judge Advocate General's School. This publication serves as a helpful reference guide for Air and Space Force commanders, directors, and senior enlisted leaders, providing general guidance to help clarify issues and identify potential problem areas.

Disclaimer: As with any publication of secondary authority, this deskbook should not be used as the basis for action on specific cases. Primary authority, much of which is cited in this edition, should first be carefully reviewed. Finally, this deskbook does not serve as a substitute for legal advice from any judge advocate.

Editorial Note: Some of the primary authorities cited in this edition may have been rescinded, consolidated, or superseded since publication. It is imperative that all authorities cited herein be first verified for currency at https://www.e-publishing.af.mil.

Readers with questions or comments concerning this publication should contact the editors of *The Military Commander and the Law* at the following address:

THE MILITARY COMMANDER AND THE LAW

Edition Twenty 2024

THE JUDGE ADVOCATE GENERAL OF THE DEPARTMENT OF THE AIR FORCE
Lieutenant General Charles L. Plummer

COMMANDANT, THE JUDGE ADVOCATE GENERAL'S SCHOOL
Colonel James H. Kennedy III

EDITOR-IN-CHIEF
Major Jasmine A. Dixon-Sims

EXECUTIVE EDITOR
Captain Austin D. Todd

SENIOR EDITORS
Major Alexander A. Perkins
Major Clair M. Strom

COVER DESIGN AND LAYOUT EDITOR
Ms. Thomasa T. Huffstutler

SPECIAL THANKS TO

Colonel Willie J. Babor
Colonel Robin A. Donato
Colonel Brian R. Gagne
Colonel Sloan M. Pye
Lieutenant Colonel W. Sterling Anderson
Lieutenant Colonel Vicki Belleau
Lieutenant Colonel Matt Bush
Lieutenant Colonel Jasmine Candelario
Lieutenant Colonel Sara Dayton-Curran
Lieutenant Colonel Pete Ferrell
Lieutenant Colonel Jeremy Gehman
Lieutenant Colonel Andrew Kasman
Lieutenant Colonel Michelle Gregory
Lieutenant Colonel Johnathan D. Legg
Lieutenant Colonel Micah C. McMillan
Lieutenant Colonel Adam G. Mudge
Lieutenant Colonel Teah L.F. Lambright
Lieutenant Colonel Kyle A. Payne
Lieutenant Colonel Dave Routhier
Lieutenant Colonel Micah L. Smith
Lieutenant Colonel Michael G. Thieme
Lieutenant Colonel Jedediah A. Wangsgard
Major Jenna M. Arroyo
Major Ann Marie Bush
Major Alex B. Coberly
Major Grant M. Fransworth
Major Jeremy J. Grunert
Major Tawnie Gulizia
Major Kasey W. Hawkins
Major James R. Haslup
Squadron Leader Lucy Jordan
Major Craig Brunson
Major Lauren C.N. Kerby
Major Keshat S. Lemberg
Major Matthew J. Mackey
Major Courtney J. Marshall

Major Christopher D. Mitchell
Major Douglas Moquet
Major Ryan P. Payne
Squadron Leader Kate Reece
Major Nick Reyes
Major Alexis V. Sellars
Major Zachary T. Thurber
Major Kenneth Vaught
Major Justin Wier
Major Riley Widener
Major Jocelyn Q. Wright
Captain Robert "Bobby" Ritchie
Captain Clay Stubblefield
Master Sergeant N. Shereece Williams
Technical Sergent Matthew C. Thompson
Ms. Sharon Ackah
Ms. Robin Brodrick
Ms. Kristin Castiglia
Ms. Mackenzie Coy
Mr. Kurt Eberle
Mr. Stephen Eriksson
Ms. Carnita Farve
Mr. Adam Frey
Ms. Melissa Garcia
Mr. Brad Hunt
Mr. Darrel Johnson
Ms. Joanna Kieffer
Mr. Jamie E. Key
Mr. David Laws
Mr. Michael McIntyre
Mr. Tom E. Posch
Mr. J.T. Trumbo
Mr. Robert Williams
Mr. Michael Wells
Mr. Reggie D. Yager

TABLE OF CONTENTS

Chapter 5
Criminal and Military Justice 111

Chapter 6
Personnel Issues – Generally 189

Chapter 7

Personnel Issues – Military Members 243

Chapter 8

Personnel Issues – Family and Next of Kin 317

Chapter 13

Chapter 14

Chapter 15

Chapter 1
LEGAL ISSUES SPECIFIC TO THE COMMANDER

SOURCES OF COMMAND AUTHORITY

Article II, Section 2, of the United States Constitution provides the original source of command authority to the President as Commander-in-Chief. In Executive Order 12765, Delegation of Certain Defense Related Authorities of the President to the Secretary of Defense, the President delegated certain military authorities, including the authority to assign commanders, to the Secretary of Defense (SecDef).

Chain of Command

- The President and SecDef exercise authority, direction, and control of the Department of the Air Force (DAF) through two distinct branches of the chain of command: (1) an operational chain of command, flowing from the President to SecDef to the combatant commanders (CCDRs), and (2) for purposes other than operational control, a chain of command flowing from the President, to SecDef, and then to the Secretary of the Air Force (SecAF).

-- CCDRs exercise combatant command authority (COCOM) over missions and forces assigned to the combatant command (CCMD) and are directly responsible to the President and SecDef for the performance of assigned missions and the readiness of their commands. Unless otherwise directed by the President, the operational chain of command runs from the President to SecDef to the CCDR. Operational—or "warfighting"—authorities are specifically exercised by CCDRs. These authorities include operational control (OPCON), tactical control (TACON), and support.

-- Subject to the authority, direction, and control of SecDef, and subject to the authorities of the CCDRs, SecAF is responsible for the administration of DAF forces. Often referred to as "organize, train, and equip" (OT&E) authority, administrative control (ADCON) is generally regarded as a service-specific responsibility. SecAF exercises ADCON over USAF and USSF forces through their respective service chiefs and commanders. This branch of the chain of command is separate and distinct from combatant commands: it runs from the President to SecDef, from SecDef to SecAF, from SecAF to the major command (MAJCOM) and field command (FLDCOM) commanders, and then on to subordinate commanders.

The Concept of Command by Uniformed Military Personnel

- A commander is a commissioned officer who, by virtue of rank and assignment, exercises command authority over a military organization or prescribed territorial area. Commanders exercise control through subordinate commanders, principal assistants, and others to whom the commander has delegated authorities. With the exception of the USAF Academy, which is commanded by a superintendent, and school/academic units, which may be commanded by commandants, all DAF units are commanded by commanders.

-- Staff officers are not commanders. Vice, deputy, on-scene, non-unit flight, and troop commanders, while acting solely in such capacity, are staff officers and have no command functions unless otherwise specifically delegated by superior competent authority. Staff officers assist the commander through advising, planning, researching, and investigating. Subordinate officers must issue all directives in the commander's name.

-- Commanders may delegate administrative duties or authorities to members of their staff and subordinate commanders. However, delegating duties does not relieve the commander of the responsibility to exercise command supervision.

-- The authority to command is passed to an *individual*, not to a staff

- The key elements of command are authority, accountability, and responsibility. DAF commanders have four principal duties and responsibilities: execute the mission, lead people, manage resources, and improve the unit.

  -- Commanders have three mission execution responsibilities: primary mission, force readiness, and mission assurance of command and control

  -- Leading people centers on the following five principles: communication, discipline, training, development, and quality of life engagement

  -- Management of resources focuses on manpower, funds, equipment, facilities and environment, guidance, and members' time

  -- Improving the unit is a continuous process involving strategic alignment, process operations, commander's inspection program, and data-driven decisions

- Commanders must be mindful of the following constraints:

  -- Duties specifically imposed on commanders by federal law, such as the Uniform Code of Military Justice (UCMJ), shall not be delegated to staff officers

  -- Duties that have been designated non-delegable by a higher authority shall not be delegated

Command Authority over Active Duty Forces

- The commander's authority over active duty military members extends to conduct both on and off the installation

- Articles 89, 90, and 92 of the UCMJ prohibit disrespect towards, and mandate a duty to obey, superior officers

Command Authority over Reservists

- Commanders generally have administrative authority to hold reservists administratively accountable for misconduct occurring on or off-duty, irrespective of their military status when the misconduct occurred

- Commanders have UCMJ authority over reservists only for offenses committed when in military status

Command Authority over Air National Guard (ANG) Members

- ANG members ordered to active duty and placed on Title 10 status, as noted on the member's ANG Reserve Order Writing System (AROWS) orders, are assigned to the 201st Mission Support Squadron (201 MSS) for ADCON and attached to a Federal Operations/Training Mission for OPCON and Specified ADCON, except for members assigned to the ANG Statutory Tour Program who may be ADCON to the Air National Guard Readiness Center (ANGRC) or another entity. The 201 MSS commander (201 MSS/CC) is dual-hatted as the ANGRC duputy commander (ANGRC/DV).

  -- When ADCON is shared between the 201 MSS/CC and another Title 10 commander, coordination is required between the two commanders (or their designated representatives) on all disciplinary matters concerning ANG members

  -- The 201 MSS/CC, or their designated representatives, will coordinate with the ANG member's Title 32 leadership to ensure they are aware and involved, as required, on all Title 10 disciplinary matters being handled by the 201 MSS

  -- Commanders with Specified ADCON of ANG Title 10 members are required to notify the 201 MSS as soon as practical once misconduct occurs or is discovered and to communicate any planned action regarding adverse administrative actions, nonjudicial punishment, court-martial, orders curtailment, and/or early re-deployment of the member

  -- Title 32 commanders who become aware of alleged Title 10 misconduct of their members are required to notify the 201 MSS team

- Normally, when on Title 32 or state active duty status, ANG forces are under the commands of their respective governors

Command Authority over Civilians

- Commanders have certain authority over their civilian employees. Commanders and supervisors are delegated authority to take disciplinary and adverse actions against civilian employees when necessary. See Chapter 15, Civilian Personnel and Federal Labor Law, for more detail.

- The commander has less authority over nonemployee civilians on base

  -- The installation commander has authority to maintain good order and discipline and to protect federal resources

-- Where available, the Federal magistrate court program provides a means of enforcing discipline on base for civilians who commit criminal misconduct. As a practical matter, authority over civilians who commit misconduct on base may be limited to referral to the magistrate program for prosecution, detainment for civilian law enforcement officials, revocation of driving privileges, and debarment from the installation. For more information on the magistrate program refer to Chapter 5, Criminal and Military Justice. See Chapter 6, Personnel Issues – Generally, for more information on driving privileges and debarment.

-- Except in limited circumstances, a commander has no authority over civilians off base

References

· U.S. Const. Art. II, § 2
· Commanders of Combatant Commands: Assignment; Powers and Duties, 10 U.S.C. § 164
· Command: Commissioned Officers in Same Grade or Corresponding Grades on Duty at Same Place, 10 U.S.C. § 749
· Secretary of the Air Force, 10 U.S.C. § 9013
· Articles 89-92, Uniform Code of Military Justice
· *Delegation of Certain Defense Related Authorities of the President to the Secretary of Defense*, Exec. Order No. 12765, 56 F.R. 28463 (18 June 1991)
· Joint Publication 1, Volume 2, *The Joint Force* (19 June 2020)
· DAFI 36-148, *Discipline and Adverse Actions of Civilian Employees* (27 September 2022)
· DAFI 36-2907, *Adverse Administrative Actions* (14 October 2022)
· DAFI 51-509, *Appointment to and Assumption of Command* (28 December 2023)
· AFPD 51-5, *Administrative Law, Gifts, and Command Relationships* (31 August 2018)
· AFI 1-2, *Commander's Responsibilities* (8 May 2014)
· AFI 38-101, *Manpower and Organization* (29 August 2019), including AFI 38-101_ AFGM2023-01, 19 July 2023

COMMAND SUCCESSION

A commander is a commissioned officer who, by virtue of grade and assignment, exercises primary command authority over a DAF unit, and some non-units, as established by AFI 38-101, *Manpower and Organization*.

Eligibility to Command

- (1) A commissioned officer; (2) assigned or attached to the unit; (3) present for duty; and (4) otherwise eligible is authorized to command. **Note:** an officer cannot command another officer of higher grade.

- An officer is vested with command in one of two ways: either by assuming command or by appointment to command. To ensure clear lines and scope of authorities, appointment to command is preferred. An officer may be appointed to command another officer of the same grade but higher rank.

  -- A temporary assumption or appointment is used when the commander being replaced is temporarily absent and expected to resume command. Short absences do not warrant assumption of command by another officer.

  -- Assumption of command may only be by an officer assigned to the organization

- Officers cannot appoint themselves to command, and commanders cannot appoint their own successors, even for temporary absences

- There is no title or position of "acting commander"

Appointment to Command

- Appointment to command occurs by an act of the President, the Secretary of the Air Force (SecAF), or by his/her delegee(s). Unless otherwise restricted, all commanders subordinate to SecAF may appoint subordinate commanders.

- An officer assigned to an organization, present for duty, and eligible to command may be appointed to command if they are at least equal in grade to other eligible officers, without regard to date of rank. No officer may command another officer of higher grade present for duty and otherwise eligible to command.

Assumption of Command

- Legal authority to assume command is inherent in an officer's status as the senior officer in both grade and date of rank so long as the officer is assigned to the unit, present for duty, and eligible to command. No officer may assume command over another officer of higher grade or rank who is present for duty and otherwise eligible to command.

- All command succession shall be announced and recorded using G-series orders. There is no need to publish G-series orders when the original commander resumes command after a temporary absence, so long as they are still equal or senior in grade to any other officer present for duty, assigned to the organization, and eligible to command.

Limitations on Eligibility to Command and Special Rules

- Enlisted members and civilians cannot exercise command. Retired officers cannot exercise command unless recalled to active duty.

  -- Civilians may be appointed as directors to lead units and non-units. They may hold supervisory positions and provide work direction to military members and civilian personnel within their unit or defined sphere of supervision. Except as limited by law, a civilian leader of a unit is authorized to perform all functions normally requiring action by a unit commander of like position and authority.

  -- Units designated to be led by civilian directors will not have commanders, and members of the unit or subordinate units may not assume command of the unit. Thus, a succession plan for leadership of the unit should be established in the event the civilian director is incapacitated.

  -- In units with a civilian director, a competent command authority will establish procedures relating to functions that require a commander. These functions will be accomplished by attaching military members to a different unit led by a commander, or by elevating these functions to a superior command level.

  -- Units subordinate to a civilian led unit may have a military commander

- Officers assigned to Headquarters Air Force (HAF) cannot assume command of personnel, unless superior competent authority specifically directs

- Chaplains cannot assume or be appointed to command

- Students cannot command a DAF school or similar organization

- Judge Advocates may only be appointed to or assume command if expressly authorized by The Judge Advocate General. **Note:** Judge advocates may assume command as the senior officer member among a group of prisoners of war or under emergency or field conditions.

- An officer designated as a medical, dental, veterinary, medical service, or biomedical sciences officer or as a nurse may only exercise command of units whose primary mission involves health care or the health profession

- Command of Flying Units: Only Line of the Air Force officers with a current aeronautical rating may command a flying unit. The rated officer must hold a currently effective aeronautical rating or crewmember certification and must be qualified for aviation service in an airframe flown by the unit to be commanded.

  -- Certain types of organizations which have multiple missions that include responsibility for controlling or directing flying activities are considered non-flying units and may be commanded by non-rated officers

- <u>O-9 and O-10 Commanders</u>: Special rules exist for positions designated under 10 U.S.C. § 601. After the President nominates and the Senate confirms, the officer will be appointed to the command position. Actions associated with these appointments will be handled in accordance with AFI 51-509, *Appointment to and Assumption of Command,* para. 8.1.

- <u>Command of Active Duty Units by Reserve Officers</u>: Only Air Reserve Component officers on extended Title 10 active duty orders (other than for training) can command regular DAF units. "Extended active duty" is defined as a period of 90 days or more during which the officer is on active duty orders.

  -- The Commander, Air Force Forces (COMAFFOR)/Commander, Space Force Forces (COMSPACEFOR), or his/her delegate may authorize reserve component officers not on extended active duty orders to command Regular Air Force (RegAF) units operating under COMAFFOR/COMSPACEFOR's authority. This authority may be delegated no lower than commanders of Aerospace Expeditionary Wings or USSF equivalent presented space forces.

- <u>Command of Reserve Units</u>: Regular and reserve component officers on extended active duty may only command reserve units with Air Force Reserve Command (AFRC) approval

Relief of Command

- A superior competent authority may relieve an officer of command for any reason not prohibited by law or policy. An officer may be temporarily suspended, relieved of command "not for cause," or relieved of command "for cause."

  -- <u>Suspension</u>: A temporary suspension of an officer from command can occur when a superior competent authority is concerned about the officer's ability to command but a final determination has not been made on whether relief of command is warranted and/or whether relief of command should be with or without cause. During their suspension, an officer is not eligible to command.

  -- <u>Not for cause relief</u>: An assignment action where the officer's relief of command may not be used as a basis for adverse action against the officer. An officer's duty performance or potential can be addressed on the officer's performance brief.

  -- <u>For cause relief</u>: An action taken when a superior competent authority has lost confidence in the officer's ability to command due to misconduct, poor judgment, the subordinate's inability to complete assigned duties, the interest of good order and discipline, morale, the good of the organization, or other similar reasons. Relief for cause may be used as a basis to support adverse actions. See DAFI 36-2907, *Adverse Administrative Actions,* for additional requirements concerning notices of relief of command for cause.

References

- Commanders of Combatant Commands: Assignment; Powers and Duties, 10 U.S.C. § 164
- Positions of Importance and Responsibility: Generals and Lieutenant Generals, Admirals and Vice Admirals, 10 U.S.C. § 601
- Command: Retired Officers, 10 U.S.C. § 750
- Designation: Officers to Perform Certain Professional Functions, 10 U.S.C. § 9063
- Command: Commissioned Officers in Certain Designated Categories, 10 U.S.C. § 9229
- Command: Chaplains, 10 U.S.C. § 9231
- DAFI 36-2907, *Adverse Administrative Actions* (14 October 2022)
- DAFI 51-509, *Appointment to and Assumption of Command* (28 December 2023)
- DAF Form 35, *Announcement of Appointment to/Assumption of Command* (21 February 2024)
- AFI 38-101, *Manpower and Organization* (29 August 2019), including AFI 38-101_AFGM2023-01, 19 July 2023
- AFMAN 11-402, *Aviation and Parachutist Service* (24 January 2019), including AFMAN11-402_AFGM2023-01, 14 June 2023

FUNCTIONS OF THE STAFF JUDGE ADVOCATE

The Staff Judge Advocate (SJA) is the principal legal advisor to a commander and the senior legal advisor at all levels of command. SJAs and their respective staff provide the DAF, commanders, and personnel with professional, timely, and full-spectrum legal support for mission success in joint and coalition operations. Legal office staffs can include judge advocates, civilian attorneys, paralegals, and civilian support staff.

Roles and Responsibilities

- Judge Advocate General (JAG): Any United States Air Force officer designated as such by The Judge Advocate General (TJAG) who:

  -- Is a graduate of a law school accredited by the American Bar Association at the time of graduation; and

  -- Is a licensed attorney, active and in good standing, in at least one state or U.S. territory/commonwealth.

- Staff Judge Advocate (SJA): On most DAF installations, the senior judge advocate designated and assigned by TJAG to the installation commander's staff

  -- Serves as the principal legal advisor to the wing/delta commander

  -- Supervises the members of the installation's legal office

  -- The responsibilities of an Air National Guard (ANG) SJA may continue between drills. As such, ANG SJAs must be available to render legal advice to commanders, making teleworking an indispensable tool to achieve the mission

- Deputy Staff Judge Advocate (DSJA): A judge advocate who is second to the SJA in his/her functions as the wing/delta legal advisor and with supervisory responsibilities of the installation's legal office, and is designated and assigned by TJAG as such

- Assistant Staff Judge Advocate (ASJA): Other judge advocates assigned to the SJA's office. ASJAs provide the needed legal services essential for the proper functioning of the installation. In this capacity, they may perform duties such as chief of operations law, chief of military justice, chief of civil law, etc.

- Area Defense Counsel (ADC): A judge advocate performing defense counsel duties at an installation. The ADC is not affiliated with the installation's legal office and is not rated by the installation's SJA or installation commander. The ADC has an independent chain of command through AF/JA – Military Justice and Discipline, Trial Defense Division (JAJD).

- Victims' Counsel (VC): A judge advocate providing legal assistance to and representing victims of sexual assault in administrative proceedings, interviews, nonjudicial punishment, or courts-martial. The VC is not affiliated with the installation's legal office or the ADC office and is not rated by the installation's SJA or installation commander. The VC has an independent chain of command through AF/JA – Military Justice and Discipline, Victims' Counsel Division (JAJS).

Legal Domains and Functional Organization of the Base Legal Office

- In alignment with the National Security Strategy (NSS), the National Defense Strategy (NDS), and senior leadership priorities, the Air Force Judge Advocate General's Corps (JAG Corps) centers its efforts around three national security law domains: Military Justice and Discipline, Civil Law, and Operations and International Law. At the DAF-level, the JAG Corps is structured into three Directorates aligned against these domains. Leadership is at the core of all three.

-- The JAG Corps' alignment ties each legal office into the strategic framework of national security law. These legal domains reflect how legal offices are organized with the major legal functions of the JAG Corps—advising commanders, advocating and litigating, representing individual DAF service members, and informing, engaging, and partnering with stakeholders.

-- The legal office provides a wide range of legal services to the wing/delta commander and the installation. The following is a general overview of the JAG Corps' legal domains and the divisions within a typical legal office.

--- <u>Military Justice and Discipline</u>: To provide sound advice to commanders, administer fair and timely processes, ensure force readiness, efficiency, and effectiveness, and strengthen national security. Specifically, this division advises commanders on discipline, adverse administrative actions, and military justice matters, including courts-martial, nonjudicial punishment under Article 15, Uniform Code of Military Justice (UCMJ), and quality force management tools such as Control Rosters, Unfavorable Information Files (UIFs), administrative demotions, Letters of Reprimand (LORs), Letters of Admonishment (LOAs), Letters of Counseling (LOCs), and Records of Individual Counseling (RICs).

--- <u>Operations and International Law</u>: To engage legal capabilities to expand command decision options and enable the projection and employment of ready forces to defend the Nation and our allies. Specifically, this division advises commanders on operational and international law issues such as foreign criminal jurisdiction, Status of Forces Agreements (SOFAs), Rules of Engagement (ROEs) and targeting, environmental law, and trains operators and deploying personnel on law of war principles.

--- <u>Civil Law</u>: To deliver advice, advocacy, and engagement across all civil law practice areas to assert and defend DAF interests in the acquisition, operation, and protection of its people and assets. Specifically, this division advises commanders on civil law issues, including ethics, contract law, and labor and employment law. Other general civil law responsibilities include issues such as private organizations, Freedom of Information Act (FOIA) and Privacy Act releases, personnel issues, fiscal law, Commander Directed Investigations (CDIs), Line of Duty determinations (LODs), and legal assistance.

---- *Legal Assistance and Preventive Law:* Legal assistance attorneys provide advice to service members and other eligible individuals on a range of legal issues including adoption, consumer law, divorce and child custody, income taxes, the Servicemembers Civil Relief Act (SCRA), various powers of attorney, and wills and estates matters. This division also provides free notary services.

--- Leadership: To develop leaders who provide the knowledge and talent management, training, planning, resourcing, and inspection capabilities necessary to maintain readiness. Most base legal offices have three leadership positions. The SJA is the head of the office and is usually a major, lieutenant colonel, or colonel. The DSJA is typically one rank below the SJA and a Field Grade Officer. The Superintendent is the senior enlisted paralegal assigned to a legal office. The Superintendent is an E-7 or above.

References

- The Freedom of Information Act, 5 U.S.C. § 552
- Privacy Act of 1974, 5 U.S.C. § 552a
- Judge Advocate General, Deputy Judge Advocate General: appointment; duties, 10 U.S.C. § 9037
- Servicemembers Civil Relief Act, 50 U.S.C. §§ 3901–4043
- DAFI 51-101, *The Air Force Judge Advocate General's (AFJAG) Corps Operations, Accessions, and Professional Development* (20 June 2023)

PERSONAL LIABILITY OF COMMANDERS AND SUPERVISORS

Military personnel are generally immune from liability for decisions made and actions taken within the scope of their employment. However, they may be held personally liable, either civilly, criminally, or both, for actions deemed outside the scope of their employment (e.g., sexual harassment), or those that violate statutory or constitutional law.

Key Takeaways

» While uncommon, some statutes and regulations permit suing a commander or supervisor in their personal capacity. If served, immediately contact your Staff Judge Advocate (SJA).

» Professional Liability Insurance is an option for commanders and supervisors to obtain for protection against being sued in one's personal capacity

» If a commander/supervisor is sued in their personal capacity, there is a potential to obtain Department of Justice (DoJ) representation if the action was taken in the scope of his/her employment

---

Representation of Federal Employees in Civil Lawsuits

- Should you or one of your personnel be served with any summons or complaint, immediately contact your servicing SJA

    -- Representation by a Department of Justice (DoJ) attorney may be available if the employee was acting "within the scope of employment" and if providing representation would otherwise be in the interest of the United States

    -- Time is of the essence when requesting representation by a DoJ attorney and is equally important when responding to complaints or other court filings

- Professional Liability Insurance, at one's own expense, may be available to protect military commanders and supervisors against civil (not criminal) liability. Civilian employees are authorized partial reimbursement of Professional Liability Insurance under Pub. L. 104–208 § 636.

Representation of Air National Guard Members in Civil Lawsuits

- Air National Guard (ANG) personnel on duty are usually covered by the Federal Tort Claims Act (FTCA) and exempt from personal liability for actions taken within the scope of their employment. However, they are not covered by FTCA while on state active duty orders in support of a state function.

    -- ANG members served with any summons or complaint for actions taken within their scope of employment must immediately consult their SJA and forward the summons or complaint, through the appropriate channels, to the adjutant general, along with a request for representation and/or indemnification

References

· Federal Tort Claims Act, 28 U.S.C. § 1346(b)

· Representation of Federal officials and employees by Department of Justice attorneys or by private counsel furnished by the Department in civil, criminal, and congressional proceedings in which Federal employees are sued, subpoenaed, or charged in their individual capacities, 28 C.F.R. Part 50.15

· Representation of Federal Employees by private counsel at Federal expense, 28 C.F.R. Part 50.16

· Omnibus Consolidated Appropriations Act, Pub. L. 104–208 § 636 (1997)

ARTICLE 138 COMPLAINTS

Article 138, Uniform Code of Military Justice (UCMJ), gives members of the Armed Forces who believe they have been wronged by their commanding officer the right to complain and seek redress. This right extends to Regular Air Force (RegAF), United States Space Force (USSF), Air National Guard (ANG) in Title 10 active duty status, and Air Force Reserve (AFR) while in federal service, whether on active duty orders, annual training, or Inactive Duty for Training (IDT).

Key Takeaways

» Article 138, UCMJ, provides an avenue of relief for members who believe they have been wronged by their commanding officer—though many actions are prohibited from review under Article 138

» Complaints may be denied or dismissed for procedural deficiencies such as complaints that are untimely, outside of the scope of Article 138, or when the reviewing authority determines the complaint does not warrant relief on the merits

» Members are afforded an opportunity for relief in the form of an informal complaint filed with the commander who allegedly committed the wrong, and a formal complaint filed with the General Court-Martial Convening Authority (GCMCA)

Scope of Article 138 Complaints

- Matters within the scope of Article 138, UCMJ, include discretionary acts or omissions by a commander that adversely affect the member personally and are allegedly:

    -- A violation of law or regulation;

    -- Beyond the legitimate authority of that commander;

    -- Arbitrary, capricious, or an abuse of discretion;

    -- Clearly unfair or unjust (e.g., selective application of administrative standards/actions);

    -- Unlawful pretrial confinement;

    -- Deferral of post-trial confinement; or

    -- Administrative actions taken in lieu of court-martial or Nonjudicial Punishment (NJP) under Article 15, UCMJ.

- Matters beyond the scope of Article 138, include but are not limited to:

    -- Acts or omissions not initiated, carried out, nor approved by the member's commander;

    -- Submissions seeking reversal or modification of non-discretionary command actions (e.g., mandatory Unfavorable Information File (UIF) actions);

-- A challenge to a respondent commander's action on an Article 138 complaint;

-- Submissions filed on behalf of another person (however, if the petitioner is represented by an attorney, the attorney may file on behalf of the petitioner);

-- Complaints requesting disciplinary action against another person; or

-- Matters in which the petitioner may seek redress through other forums which provide the petitioner notice, the opportunity to be heard, and review by an appellate or superior authority (or reviewing authority). Examples include: NJP, performance reports, decorations, Flying Evaluation Boards (FEBs).

Article 138 Procedures for Informal Complaints

- Informal Complaint: To begin the Article 138 process, the DAF member ("petitioner") must submit an informal complaint to the commander who allegedly wronged him or her ("respondent commander")

- Member Filing Deadline (Informal Complaint): The member must file the informal complaint to the respondent commander within 90 calendar days of discovering the alleged wrong. The commander may waive the time requirement for good cause.

- Form of the Informal Complaint: Informal complaints must be submitted in writing and the petitioner must state that the informal complaint is being submitted pursuant to Article 138. All submissions must contain the following information:

  -- The petitioner's current military unit and the petitioner's military unit at the time of the alleged wrong, if different;

  -- The petitioner's current personal mailing address;

  -- The name and grade of the respondent commander;

  -- The name and contact information for any counsel representing the petitioner;

  -- A description of the facts and circumstances of the alleged wrong;

  -- A statement of the relief sought to correct the alleged wrong;

  -- All supporting evidence; and

  -- The specific law or regulation the respondent commander violated, if applicable.

- Proof Requirements: The member has the responsibility to establish a valid basis for the complaint. The complaint should allege facts that, if true, would constitute a wrong within the scope of Article 138, UCMJ, and provides sufficient evidence to properly review the petitioner's allegation against the respondent commander. It is the commander's duty to resolve whether relief is warranted, not the complainant's.

- Staff Judge Advocate (SJA) Consultation: The respondent commander must consult his/her servicing SJA before acting on the member's informal complaint

Processing Informal Complaints

- <u>Commander Initial Decision Deadline</u>: No later than 30 days after receipt of the informal complaint or application for redress, the commander must notify the member in writing that:

  -- A decision regarding the requested relief has been deferred to gather additional facts (such a notice shall be sent every 30 days until the fact gathering is complete);

  -- The requested relief is granted;

  -- The requested relief is denied, in whole or in part, because the requested relief is not warranted; or

  -- The informal complaint is dismissed because the submission is outside the scope of Article 138, UCMJ, untimely, deficient, or fails to establish a valid basis for a complaint.

- <u>Forwarding</u>: The respondent commander may forward the matter, to include all evidence obtained during the respondent commander's review, to his/her GCMCA. This action does not constitute the filing of a formal complaint.

Processing Formal Complaints

- If the respondent commander dismisses or denies (in whole or in part) the informal Article 138 complaint, the member may, within 30 days of receiving the respondent commander's written response, request GCMCA review

- If the petitioner does not receive a response from the respondent commander within 30 days of submitting an informal complaint, he/she may request GCMCA review within 60 days from the date the member submitted the informal complaint

- If the respondent commander defers the decision regarding the requested relief, the member may only request GCMCA review after 90 days from original submission of the informal complaint

- The formal complaint must be in writing and must specifically state that it is a formal complaint under Article 138, UCMJ. The member may submit the complaint directly to the GCMCA or through any superior commissioned officer.

- If the formal complaint is submitted to the immediate commander or a superior commissioned officer, that person has a duty to forward it to the GCMCA

General Court-Martial Convening Authority's Responsibilities

- A GCMCA who receives an Article 138 complaint may rely on his/her staff for assistance with investigating and/or documenting findings. However, the GCMCA cannot delegate the authority to act on formal Article 138 complaints or to respond to petitioners.

- If a petitioner submits a formal Article 138 complaint to the GCMCA without first submitting an informal complaint to the respondent commander, the GCMCA should forward the complaint to the subordinate commander who allegedly committed the wrong. Any new allegations added by a member when seeking GCMCA review will be forwarded to subordinate commanders for initial review and appropriate action.

- The GCMCA must obtain a written legal review from the servicing SJA before responding to a petitioner's formal complaint. The SJA legal review is privileged attorney work product and not releasable to the petitioner or other individuals and should be marked accordingly.

- No later than 60 days after receipt of the formal complaint, the GCMCA must notify the member that:

  -- A decision regarding the requested relief has been deferred for the completion of a proceeding or additional inquiry (such a notice shall be sent every 30 days until the fact gathering is complete);

  -- The requested relief is granted;

  -- The requested relief is denied, in whole or in part, because the requested relief is not warranted;

  -- The requested relief is warranted, but the authority to grant the relief requested resides with another GCMCA, major command (MAJCOM), or the Secretary of the Air Force (SecAF); or

  -- The complaint is dismissed because the submission is outside the scope of Article 138, is untimely, is deficient, or fails to establish a valid basis for a complaint.

- If the GCMCA believes the requested relief is warranted and the authority to grant the requested relief resides with another GCMCA, MAJCOM, or SecAF, the GCMCA should forward the complaint and the recommendation to grant the requested relief to the appropriate authority for final action

- After taking final action and notifying the member, the GCMCA will send a complete copy of the file to AF/JA – Military Justice and Discipline's Investigations, Inquiries, and Relief Division (JAJI), and will include the member's personal mailing address

References

· Articles 15 and 138, Uniform Code of Military Justice
· AFPD 51-5, *Administrative Law, Gifts, and Command Relationships* (31 August 2018)
· AFI 51-505, *Complaints of Wrongs Under Article 138, Uniform Code of Military Justice* (24 November 2020)

COMMAND INFLUENCE

Military commanders have a responsibility to maintain good order and discipline in the armed forces. While performing this role, they must remain fair and impartial in their dealings while also safeguarding the constitutional due process rights of the accused. Statements and actions taken by commanders and their staff may result in a finding of Unlawful Command Influence (UCI).

While commanders are permitted to mentor their subordinates and address behavior that is incompatible with military service and DAF policy, they cannot direct a subordinate to dispose of any particular case in any particular manner. The key is to understand what statements and actions constitute proper involvement by a commander, and what statements and actions cross the line into UCI.

Key Takeaways

» Commanders may establish and communicate those policies that are necessary to maintain good order and discipline. They are also free to pass on their experience and advice regarding disciplinary matters to subordinates.

» Commanders may not censure, reprimand, or admonish the court or any court member, military judge, or counsel, with respect to the finding or sentence adjudged by the court, or with respect to any other exercise of its functions in the conduct of a proceeding

» No person subject to the Uniform Code of Military Justice (UCMJ) may attempt to coerce or, by any unauthorized means, attempt to influence the action of any convening, approving, reviewing authority or preliminary hearing officer, or a court-martial or court members in reaching the findings or sentence in any case

» Commanders must not make comments that would imply that they expect a particular result in a given case or type of case, and commanders also cannot attempt to manipulate the court-martial process to ensure or encourage specific results

» Each commander in the chain must remain free to exercise their discretion and impose discipline without inappropriate interference from a superior commander

Permissible Command Involvement in Military Justice

- Superior commanders are permitted to establish and communicate policies necessary to maintain good order and discipline. They are also free to pass on their experience and advice regarding disciplinary matters without impacting the discretion of their subordinates in the matter. They can also withhold disposition authority for any offense, offenses, or all actions with regard to any individual or group of individuals to their level. Examples of lawful command involvement are:

  -- Withholding a subordinate commander's authority to act in an individual case or certain types of cases (offenses) and imposing punishment oneself;

  -- Obtaining information from a subordinate commander about ongoing cases, investigations, or incidents;

-- Generally discussing with subordinate commanders, officers, or supervisors matters to consider when disposing of alleged violations;

-- Consulting with subordinates regarding the disposition of an alleged offense at the subordinate's request. However, the subordinate alone must decide what disposition decision or action, if any, to take in each case;

-- "Tough talk" policy letters, talks, and briefings on issues of concern (e.g., criminal activity or a particular criminal offense) are permissible so long as they do not show an overly determined attitude or attempt to influence the finding and sentence in a particular case; and/or

-- Focusing on problem areas is permissible (e.g., characterizing illegal drug use as a threat to combat readiness). However, statements made should not advocate a particular disposition, a particular court-martial finding or sentence, and should not relate to a particular accused.

Unlawful Command Influence (UCI)

- Generally:

  -- *Convening authorities and commanders:* No court-martial convening authority, nor any other commanding officer, may censure, reprimand, or admonish the court or any member, military judge, or counsel, with respect to the finding or sentence adjudged by the court, or with respect to any other exercise of its or their functions in the conduct of a proceeding

  -- *All persons subject to the UCMJ:* No person subject to the Uniform Code of Military Justice (UCMJ) may attempt to coerce or, by any unauthorized means, attempt to influence the action of any convening, approving, reviewing authority or preliminary hearing officer, or a court-martial or court members in reaching the findings or sentence in any case

- Actual UCI: A member subject to the UCMJ (typically someone acting with the "mantle of command authority"), either intentionally or unintentionally, manipulates the court-martial process to affect the disposition of a case or drive a certain result and materially prejudices the substantial rights of the accused

- Apparent UCI: A member subject to the UCMJ (typically someone acting with the "mantle of command authority"), either intentionally or unintentionally, engages in conduct that would cause an objective observer, fully informed of all the facts and circumstances, to have significant doubt about the fairness of the proceeding and such action materially prejudices the substantial rights of the accused. The focus of apparent UCI is on the public perception of the military justice process.

- Superior commanders must not make comments that would imply that they expect a particular result in a given case or type of case, and commanders also cannot attempt to manipulate the court-martial process to drive certain results. The following actions are unacceptable:

    -- Directing a subordinate commander to make a particular disposition decision or limiting the discretion of the subordinate convening authority;

    -- Discouraging or attempting to discourage a potential witness from participating in the investigatory process or testifying at a court-martial;

    -- Influencing or attempting to influence the action of a court-martial or court members to reach a particular finding or sentence;

    -- Directly or indirectly criticizing, disciplining, or expressing disapproval of any person participating in the court-martial process (e.g., military judge, trial and defense counsel, witnesses, court members, etc.);

    -- Selecting members with the intent to achieve a particular result as to the findings or sentence (stacking the panel);

    -- Commenting on the character of the accused or victim;

    -- Establishing an inflexible policy on disposition or punishment of offenses;

    -- Publicly commenting or opining on the accused's guilt prior to trial; and/or

    -- Publicly criticizing court-martial punishments or judicial actions.

- Each commander in the chain must remain free to exercise his/her own discretion to impose discipline without inappropriate interference from a superior commander

    -- The key consideration is whether a commander is taking disciplinary action based upon that commander's own personal belief that the disciplinary action is appropriate or whether the commander is merely acquiescing to direction from a superior to impose the action

References

· Article 37, Uniform Code of Military Justice
· Rules for Courts-Martial 104 and 306 (2024)
· DAFI 51-201, *Administration of Military Justice* (24 January 2024)

SERVING AS A COURT MEMBER

At some point in your military career, you or your subordinates may be detailed to sit as members of a court-martial. Court members serve essentially the same function in a military court-martial as jurors in civilian courts. For DAF service members serving as court-martial members, that service becomes their primary duty until the court-martial concludes.

Key Takeaways

» Court members are selected by the convening authority and may only be excused from duty for good cause

» All court members have an equal voice during jury deliberations regardless of rank

» Court members listen to the evidence, arguments from counsel, and instructions from the military judge in order to make a decision as to whether an accused is guilty or not guilty and potentially on a sentence for the accused

---

Selection

- When convening a court-martial, the convening authority personally selects the court-martial panel members. The convening authority selects the "best qualified" for this duty, using factors such as age, education, training, experience, length of service, and judicial temperament. Article 25, Uniform Code of Military Justice.

- Prior to sitting as a member of a court-martial, court members are usually asked to complete a court member data sheet with personal and professional information. This data sheet provides the convening authority, and the attorneys for both sides, information about a court member's background and assists them in determining whether there is reason to object to a member's participation in the court-martial.

- Once detailed to sit on a court-martial, a member must not discuss or be a party to conversations about upcoming cases so as to maintain impartiality

Excusal

- Excusal Requests Prior to Trial: Requests to be excused from court member duty should be based on good cause and made well in advance of the dates of the court-martial. Members should not plan leave or temporary duty assignments during dates they are detailed for court member duty. Detailing to a court-martial takes precedence over all other duties unless and until properly excused.

  -- Requests should be written and forwarded by the member's commander, to the convening authority, through the installation Staff Judge Advocate (SJA). The SJA is normally delegated authority to excuse a certain portion of court members before the court is assembled.

Voir Dire

- The military judge, trial counsel, and defense counsel are all entitled to question court members to ensure impartiality. This questioning is referred to as "voir dire," and occurs prior to the court members hearing any evidence in the case.

- After voir dire, trial and defense counsel can ask the military judge to excuse any court member whose inclusion would cause the trial to be unfair or appear to be unfair. If the military judge grants a challenge to a court-martial panel member, that member is released from the court-martial and may return to his/her normal duties.

Duties at Trial – Findings

- The "findings" phase of the court-martial is the traditional "trial" portion of a case, when members hear opening statements, witness testimony, and closing arguments

   -- Court members are given an opportunity to question witnesses after the counsel have completed their questioning. Court member questions are limited by the rules of evidence, and the prosecution or the defense may object to questions from court members. The military judge will rule on any objections and ultimately decide whether the question is permitted under the rules of evidence.

- At the close of the findings phase, the military judge will provide the court members with instructions on the law

- After arguments and instructions on the law, the court members will deliberate in closed session. The court members must be convinced beyond a reasonable doubt that the evidence presented during the trial shows the accused committed the offense to find the accused "guilty." The decision of the court is called the "finding."

- The senior ranking court member is called the "president." It is the president's job to check the vote count and announce the results to the other members. The junior ranking court member collects and counts the votes during deliberations. The president announces the finding of the court in open court in the presence of the accused and counsel.

- Each member has an equal voice and vote in discussing and deciding a case. The influence of superiority in rank must not be employed in any manner in an attempt to control the independence of the members in the exercise of their own personal judgment. Service as a court member is not a rating factor to be considered on any member's performance report.

- Each member has a right to be free from harassment or ridicule based upon that member's participation as a court member. Court member deliberations are conducted in private, and each member takes an oath not to disclose any member's opinion or vote. Furthermore, no member may be compelled to answer questions about the deliberations unless lawfully ordered to do so by a military judge.

Duties at Trial – Sentencing

- If the accused is found guilty solely of offenses committed on or after 28 December 2023, the court members are excused and the accused will be sentenced by the military judge alone

- If the accused is found guilty by a panel of members of any offense committed before 28 December 2023, the accused has the option of being sentenced by the court members, or by the military judge. If the accused elects sentencing by court members, the court members will hear evidence and listen to arguments from counsel recommending a sentence and receive instructions from the military judge on sentencing procedures. The court members will then deliberate and decide on an appropriate sentence. If the accused elects sentencing by the military judge, the court members are excused.

- If the accused pleads guilty to one or more offenses committed before 28 December 2023, but decides to be sentenced by court members rather than just the judge alone, the same sentencing procedures apply as when the accused is found guilty by members

References

· Articles 25 and 39, Uniform Code of Military Justice
· Rules for Courts-Martial 501–505, 804–807, 813, 901, 911–1007 (2024)

TESTIFYING AS A COURT-MARTIAL WITNESS

You or one of your subordinates may be called to testify as a witness at a court-martial or other administrative hearing. Under the Uniform Code of Military Justice (UCMJ), both the prosecution and defense are entitled to equal access to all witnesses and evidence. No DAF member should attempt to influence the testimony of a witness or deter a potential witness from testifying for or against the prosecution or the accused.

Key Takeaways

- » Witnesses may be called at either the findings or sentencing phase of a trial
- » Witnesses generally must testify from personal knowledge (i.e., things they have observed or perceived)
- » No one subject to the UCMJ may attempt to influence the testimony of a court-martial witness

---

Overview

- Both the trial counsel and defense counsel may call witnesses during the findings portion of a court-martial to provide evidence of the offense or for a defense to the charge

    -- Witnesses are placed under oath. The witness's role is to provide truthful testimony based on personal knowledge—normally from his/her own observations. Witnesses must not hide relevant information from either side.

    -- Witnesses should not advocate for or try to "help" either side. A witness's duty is simply to honestly answer the question that is asked and allow the military judge and counsel to address any objectionable questions.

- Counsel for both sides may also call witnesses during the sentencing portion of the trial. A sentencing witness may be called to testify about the character of the accused, the impact of the offenses on a victim and/or unit, or offer an opinion about the accused's potential for rehabilitation.

    -- A witness may not testify about his/her opinion as to the appropriate specific sentence, including whether the accused should be punitively discharged

    -- When testifying about the accused's potential for rehabilitation, a witness must have sufficient knowledge of the accused in order to form an opinion. To test that opinion, opposing counsel may ask the witness questions regarding the witness' personal knowledge of the accused.

- Before trial, the attorney(s) calling the witness will discuss with the witness the types of questions they expect to ask in court. They may also discuss the questions the opposing counsel will likely ask on cross-examination.

-- The opposing attorney(s) will normally interview all witnesses before trial. If the witness is also a victim of a charged offense, the victim may decline an interview with trial and/or defense counsel.

- No one should attempt to influence the testimony of a court-martial witness, to include discouraging a witness from testifying altogether or from cooperating with counsel for either side. Immediately report any attempts to influence a witness's testimony to the legal office or to the military judge.

References

· Article 46, Uniform Code of Military Justice
· Rules for Courts-Martial 701, 703, and 1001 (2024)

Page Intentionally Left Blank

Chapter 2
QUALITY FORCE MANAGEMENT

ADVERSE ADMINISTRATIVE ACTIONS – COUNSELING, ADMONISHMENT, AND REPRIMAND

Counseling, admonishments, and reprimands are quality force management tools available to supervisors, superiors, and commanders. These tools are designed to improve, correct, and instruct military members who depart from expected standards of performance, conduct, military bearing, and integrity, on or off duty, and whose actions degrade the individual or the unit's mission.

Key Takeaway

» Quality force management tools help maintain standards and enhance mission accomplishment by correcting performance, conduct, and affording members an opportunity to respond

What Action is Appropriate

- The Basics: DAFI 36-2907, *Adverse Administrative Actions*, contains guidance on Letters of Counseling (LOC), Admonishment (LOA), and Reprimand (LOR)

  -- An LOC is the lowest level of administrative action. An LOA is more severe than an LOC. An LOR is more severe than an LOA and carries a stronger degree of official censure.

- Primary Considerations: The decision should be based primarily on two factors:

  -- *Nature of the incident:* The seriousness of the member's departure from standards should be considered before deciding the type of administrative action that is appropriate. A letter may be administered for any departure from standards. Unlike nonjudicial punishment, administrative actions are not limited to offenses punishable under the Uniform Code of Military Justice (UCMJ).

  -- *Previous disciplinary record of the member:* These tools should be considered as part of a gradual pattern of discipline in response to repeated departures from standards

Who Takes Action

- Who May Issue: Commanders, first sergeants, supervisors, and other persons in authority

- Form of the Action: May be verbal, written, or both. However, actions should usually be in writing to document the deviation as well as reinforce the importance of correcting the behavior. A verbal counseling may be recorded on a DAF Form 174, *Record of Individual Counseling* (RIC).

Initiating Action

- Standard of Proof: The standard of proof for adverse administrative actions is the "preponderance of the evidence." A preponderance of the evidence exists when it is more likely than not that the allegation(s) occurred as alleged.

- Administering Adverse Action: A written LOC, LOA, or LOR must state the following: what the member did or failed to do (cite the UCMJ article violated, if applicable), what improvement is expected, further deviation may result in more severe action, how long the member has to acknowledge the action and submit a response, as well as indicate that the member's response will become part of the record

- Attachments: Include and list as attachments all documents that serve, in part or in whole, as the basis for the action. Supporting documents include, but are not limited to, relevant statements, portions of investigations, and reports.

  -- Documents may not be released to the member without authorization from the issuing authority and must be appropriately redacted and accompanied by required markings

- Time to Respond: Provide the member with three full duty days. During this time, the member may wish to consult with an Area Defense Counsel (ADC). The member may respond prior to the expiration of the time to respond. However, the issuer of the letter should not pressure the member into responding prior to expiration of the allowed time.

- A template LOC, LOA, and LOR is attached to this section

Processing the Action

- Final Disposition: Regardless of whether the member submits a response, the issuer of the letter must inform the member within three duty days of their decision regarding final disposition

  -- If using a memorandum similar to the attachment, the issuer of the letter should fill in the date of the indorsement, strike through the inapplicable language in parentheses, and sign the indorsement

  -- After reviewing the response, the issuer may withdraw the action, downgrade the action, or leave the action as written. Withdrawing the action does not bar the issuer from taking alternate or other appropriate action.

  -- Ensure the recipient acknowledges the final disposition of the action. Once the recipient acknowledges receipt of the final disposition, the complete action becomes a finalized record. Annotate on the administrative action if the member fails to acknowledge receipt or provide a response.

Maintaining the Record

- Contents of Record: The record of the action consists of the finalized RIC, LOC, LOA, or LOR and written response submitted by the member and/or the member's defense counsel. Additional materials submitted by the member in mitigation, extenuation, or defense are not part of the record. Evidence and any other written materials considered as a basis for imposing the administrative letter are not part of the record.

- Inform Leadership: Issuer must inform the member's chain of command of the action. Send the letter with all indorsements, and any documents submitted by the member to the member's superiors or commander for information, action, or approval for entry in the member's Personnel Information File (PIF), Unfavorable Information File (UIF), or both.

- Privacy Act Requirements: LOCs, LOAs, and LORs are subject to the rules of access, protection, and disclosure outlined in AFI 33-332, *Air Force Privacy and Civil Liberties Program*. Therefore, they must contain a paragraph outlining the applicability of the Privacy Act to the document.

Adverse Administrative Actions for Reserve and Air National Guard Members

- Commanders, supervisors, and other persons in authority can issue LOCs, LOAs, and LORs to members of the Air Force Reserve and Air National Guard (ANG) who commit an offense while in civilian (non-Title 10) status. Additionally, DAFI 36-2907 applies to ANG personnel on Title 32 status except when otherwise directed by any applicable state law(s).

- When issuing an LOC, LOA, or LOR to a Reserve or ANG member, follow the procedures discussed above. However, the following exceptions apply:

  -- If the member has departed the duty area, the issuing authority may send the LOC, LOA, or LOR and supporting documents via certified mail to the member's address or best available address, and the member will be presumed to be in receipt of this official correspondence

  -- Non-extended active duty (Non-EAD) Reservists and ANG personnel have 45 calendar days from the date of receipt of the certified letter to acknowledge the notification, intended actions, and provide pertinent information before the issuing authority makes a final decision. In calculating the time to respond, the date of receipt is not counted. If the member mails the acknowledgment, the date of the postmark on the envelope will serve as the date of acknowledgment.

  -- The issuer of the LOC, LOA, or LOR has 45 calendar days from the receipt of the certified letter or personal delivery of the member's response to advise the member of his/her final decision after considering any comments submitted by the member

Reporting Demographic Information on Adverse Administrative Actions

- Upon receipt of the finalized record, the issuer's immediate commander will:

  -- Review the rank, age, gender, race, and ethnicity of both the issuer and the recipient as it is listed in their official Department of the Air Force records; and

  -- Provide this demographic data on completed actions to their servicing legal office. The following information should be reported: type of action issued; underlying offense(s); final administrative action; rank, age, gender, race, and ethnicity of the issuer and recipient; and number of prior actions received by the recipient.

Officer Adverse Information and Promotion Boards

- All LOCs related to a substantiated finding or conclusion from an officially documented investigation or inquiry, LOAs, and LORs will be filed in the Officer Selection Record (OSR) in accordance with DAFI 36-2608, *Military Personnel Records Systems*

- The FY2020 National Defense Authorization Act (NDAA) amended 10 U.S.C. § 615(a)(3) to require all services to furnish adverse information to selection boards considering regular officers for promotion to the grade of O-4 and above, and reserve officers to the grade of O-6 and above. Adverse actions, for purposes of this rule, include:

  -- Any substantiated adverse findings or conclusions from an officially documented investigation or inquiry, regardless of whether command action was taken as a result;

  -- Court-martial findings of guilt;

  -- Nonjudicial punishment (NJP) pursuant to Article 15, UCMJ;

  -- LORs;

  -- LOAs;

  -- LOCs related to a substantiated adverse finding or conclusion from an officially documented investigation or inquiry;

  -- Notices of relief of command (for cause); and/or

  -- Developmental Education removal (for cause).

- DAFI 36-2907, *Adverse Administrative Actions*, and DoDI 1320.14, *DoD Commissioned Officer Promotion Program Procedures*, establish specific policy and provide guidance associated with furnishing adverse information to officer promotion selection, special selection, federal recognition (ANG specific), and selective continuation boards

- Commanders must report all substantiated findings of wrongdoing and/or adverse information against field grade officers to SAF/IGQ in accordance with DAFI 90-301, *Inspector General Complaints Resolution*

References

- Annual Reports on Racial and Ethnic Demographics in the Military Justice System, 10 U.S.C. § 486
- Information Furnished to Selection Boards, 10 U.S.C. § 615(a)(3)
- DoDI 1320.14, *DoD Commissioned Officer Promotion Program Procedures* (16 December 2020)
- DAFI 36-2608, *Military Personnel Records Systems* (16 April 2021), incorporating Change 1, 28 September 2022
- DAFI 36-2907, *Adverse Administrative Actions* (14 October 2022)
- DAFI 90-301, *Inspector General Complaints Resolution* (4 January 2024)
- DAF Form 174, *Record of Individual Counseling* (14 October 2022)
- DAF Form 1058, *Unfavorable Information File Actions* (14 October 2022)
- AFI 33-332, *Air Force Privacy and Civil Liberties Program* (10 March 2020)

Attachment

- Sample Letter of Counseling/Admonishment/Reprimand

[Add the "CUI" banner to the footer and header of your document]

SUGGESTED FORMAT FOR LOC, LOA, AND LOR

Date

MEMORANDUM FOR [RANK FIRST M. LAST]

FROM: Organization/Office Symbol [Issuer's organization and office symbol]

SUBJECT: Letter of [Counseling/Admonition/Reprimand]

1.   Investigation has disclosed [the basis for the action, including what the member did or failed to do, citing specific incident(s) and their date(s)].

2.   You are hereby [counseled/admonished/reprimanded]! [Discuss the impact of what the member did or failed to do]. [What improvement is expected]. Your conduct is unacceptable and further deviation may result in more severe action.

3.   The following information required by the Privacy Act is provided for your information AUTHORITY: 10 U.S.C. § 9013. PURPOSE: To obtain any comments or documents you desire to submit (on a voluntary basis) for consideration concerning this action. ROUTINE USES: Provides you an opportunity to submit comments or documents for consideration. If provided, the response you submit becomes a part of the record. DISCLOSURE: Your written acknowledgment of receipt and signature are mandatory. Any other comments or documents you provide are voluntary.

4.   [For Regular Air Force, Space Force, Active Guard and Reserve, Air Reserve Component Statutory Tour members or Air National Guard members in Title 10 status (officer and enlisted)]: You will acknowledge receipt of this Letter of [Counseling/Admonishment/Reprimand] immediately by signing the first indorsement. Within 3 duty days from the date when you received this letter, you will provide your response by signing the second indorsement below. Any comments or documents you wish to be considered concerning this letter must be submitted at that time, and will become part of the record, consistent with DAFI 36-2907, *Adverse Administrative Actions*, paragraph 2.4.2.5. After receiving your response, I intend to notify you of my final disposition of this action within 3 duty days.

Controlled by: Organization/Office Symbol
CUI Category: PRVCY
Dissemination Controls: None
POC: (XXX) XXX-XXXX;
Email: XXXXX

5.   [For Air Reserve Component members not in a duty status]: You will acknowledge receipt of this Letter of [Counseling/Admonishment/Reprimand] immediately by signing the first indorsement. Within 45 calendar days from the date when you received this letter, you will provide your response by signing the second indorsement below. Any comments or documents you wish to be considered concerning this letter must be submitted at that time, and will become part of the record, consistent with DAFI 36-2907, *Adverse Administrative Actions*, paragraph 2.4.2.5. After receiving your response, you will be notified of my final decision regarding any comments submitted by you within 45 calendar days.

6.   [For officer Letters of Reprimand]: If this Letter of Reprimand is sustained, it will be placed in an Unfavorable Information File (UIF). Submit any comments or documents you wish to be considered concerning the UIF when you respond to the Letter of Reprimand.

Signature

Issuing Authority's Duty Title, Organization

[Attachment(s):

Enumerated documents as appropriate]

1st Ind to Organization/Office Symbol [of issuer], date, Letter of [Counseling/Admonishment/Reprimand]

Recipient's Rank First M. Last   Date

MEMORANDUM FOR Organization/Office Symbol [Issuer's organization and office symbol]

I acknowledge receipt and understanding of this letter on [date] at [time] hours. I understand that I have [3 duty days][45 calendar days] from the date I received this letter to provide a response and that I must include in my response any comments or documents I wish to be considered concerning this Letter of [Counseling/Admonishment/Reprimand].

Signature

Letter Recipient

2nd Ind, Recipient's Rank First M. Last   Date

MEMORANDUM FOR Organization/Office Symbol [Issuer's organization and office symbol]

I have reviewed the allegations contained in this Letter of [Counseling/Admonishment/Reprimand]. (I am submitting the attached documents in response) (I hereby waive my right to respond).

Signature

Letter Recipient

3rd Ind, Organization/Office Symbol [Issuer's organization and office symbol]   Date

MEMORANDUM FOR RECIPIENT RANK FIRST M. LAST

(I have considered the response you submitted on [date].) (You waived your right to submit a response to this action). I have decided to [withdraw the Letter of [Counseling/Admonishment/Reprimand] [sustain the Letter of Counseling/Admonishment/Reprimand] [reduce the action to a Letter of Admonishment/Counseling]. [For officers only: This Letter of Reprimand will be placed into a UIF.]

Signature

Issuing Authority's Duty Title, Organization

4th Ind to Organization/Office Symbol [of issuer], date, Letter of [Counseling/Admonishment/Reprimand]

Recipient's Rank First M. Last   Date

MEMORANDUM FOR Organization/Office Symbol [Issuer's organization and office symbol]

I acknowledge receipt of the final decision regarding disposition of this Letter of [Counseling/Admonishment/Reprimand] on [date] at [time] hours.

Signature

Letter Recipient

Note: The 1st Indorsement (Ind) is dated the same day the member receives the letter; the 2d Ind is dated within 3 duty days (or 45 calendar days for Air Reserve Component members not in a duty status); the 3d Ind should be dated within 3 duty days (or 45 calendar days) of the 2d Ind. When the first indorsement occurs on any page other than the letterhead page, it must include the citation line for the letter. In this example, the 1st Ind is the first indorsement to occur on a new page. The citation line for the indorsement memorandum consists of the indorsement number followed by the Organization/Office Symbol, SUBJECT, and date of the original memorandum. The citation line ends with the indorsement date. For administrative actions, this should be the same as the Letter of Reprimand date.

UNFAVORABLE INFORMATION FILE

The unfavorable information file (UIF) provides commanders with an official means of filing derogatory data concerning a Department of the Air Force (DAF) military member's personal conduct and duty performance. With some exceptions, the commander has discretion for what should be placed in a UIF and what should be removed. The UIF is maintained by the Adverse Administrative Actions Manager.

Key Takeaways

» The UIF is an official record of unfavorable information about an individual. It documents administrative, nonjudicial, or judicial censures of the member's performance.

» A UIF may only be established when some form of derogatory data is entered into it

» Retention time depends on the nature of the document and status of the member. Early removal is authorized under certain conditions.

Establishing a UIF

- A UIF must be established by a commander or equivalent civilian director at all levels, or by any of the other individuals listed in DAFI 36-2907, *Adverse Administrative Actions*, para 3.1. Commanders must be on G-series orders and senior to the member.

- Certain unfavorable information requires mandatory filing into a UIF. DAFI 36-2907, Table 3.2, outlines whether a UIF filing is mandatory.

- If not mandatory, the unfavorable information may be filed into a UIF at the discretion of any of the individuals listed in DAFI 36-2907, para 3.1

Contents of UIF

- A UIF must be populated with a record of unfavorable information or it ceases to exist

  -- Common UIF documents include letters of counseling (LOCs), admonishment (LOAs), and reprimand (LORs), records of nonjudicial punishment (NJP) under Article 15 of the Uniform Code of Military Justice, control roster actions, documented instances of discrimination or sexual harassment, civilian convictions, and court-martial convictions

Documenting a UIF

- The UIF is generally established with a DAF Form 1058, *Unfavorable Information File Actions*

  -- The DAF Form 1058 notifies military members of the commander's intent to establish a UIF and provides the member with 3 duty days to respond. Non-extended active duty (EAD) Reservists and Air National Guard (ANG) members will have 45 calendar days from receipt of the UIF action to provide a response.

  -- DAF Form 1058 does not need to be referred to members when UIF filing is mandatory

Retention and Disposition

- Retention time depends on the nature of the document and the status of the member (officer or enlisted). Removal of the document from the UIF is automatic at the end of the retention period. DAFI 36-2907, Table 3.2, outlines the disposition dates for all documents filed in a UIF.

- UIF establishing authorities may remove documents from the UIF early by initiating action via DAF Form 1058 or memorandum

  -- Early removal of derogatory data is not authorized if the member is still serving punishment

Access

- Only the member who has the UIF, first sergeants, rating officials, and those individuals listed in DAFI 36-2907, para 3.1, may view UIFs

  -- Military Personnel Flight (MPF) personnel, Inspector General personnel, inspection team members, judge advocates and paralegals, law enforcement personnel and investigators, Military Equal Opportunity personnel, and substance abuse counselors in the course of their official DAF duties may view UIFs with authorization from the member's commander or equivalent civilian director

Review

- All UIFs require periodic review to ensure continued maintenance of documents in the UIF is proper

- Mandatory reviews must be conducted by commanders in the following situations:

  -- Within 90 calendar days of permanent assumption or appointment to command

  -- When individuals are being considered for, among other things, promotion, reenlistment, permanent change of station, personnel reliability program duties, reclassification or retraining, or appointment or enlistment into a different component of the DAF

  -- Prior to completion of performance evaluations

  -- When Reserve and ANG members are being considered for in-residence developmental education or short courses, all Reserve assignments, statutory tours, or an active duty tour exceeding 30 days

References

· Article 15, Uniform Code of Military Justice
· DAFI 36-2608, *Military Personnel Records Systems* (16 April 2021), incorporating Change 1, 28 September 2022
· DAFI 36-2907, *Adverse Administrative Actions* (14 October 2022)
· DAF Form 1058, *Unfavorable Information File Actions* (14 October 2022)

CONTROL ROSTERS

A control roster is a "watch list" for members whose duty performance is substandard or who fail to meet or maintain Department of the Air Force (DAF) standards of conduct, bearing, and integrity, whether on or off duty. Commanders at all levels are authorized to use a control roster. They are maintained by the Adverse Administrative Actions Manager.

Key Takeaways

» The control roster is used to monitor a member's performance and/or conduct when there is a need for improvement

» There are collateral consequences to placement on a control roster, such as limited opportunity for reassignment, promotion, and reenlistment

» Regular Air Force and Space Force members may only be placed on a control roster for 6 months

Purpose

- A control roster is a rehabilitative tool

  -- Other rehabilitative tools should be considered before placing a member on the control roster

  -- A single incident of substandard duty performance or an isolated breach of standards that is not likely to be repeated should not ordinarily be a basis for a control roster action

- Control rosters assist commanders in controlling or evaluating a member's performance and provide the member an opportunity to improve that performance

  -- Placing an individual on the control roster is not a substitute for more appropriate administrative, judicial, or nonjudicial action

  -- Individuals are not shielded from other appropriate actions by virtue of being placed on the control roster

Procedure

- Control roster action is documented on a DAF Form 1058, *Unfavorable Information File Actions*

- Individuals listed in DAFI 36-2907, *Adverse Administrative Actions*, para 4.4, have the authority to add members to a control roster. Commanders must be senior to the member being placed on a control roster.

  -- Commanders may direct a performance evaluation before entering or removing the person from the control roster

-- A commander placing an officer, who is eligible for or selected for promotion, on a control roster must also decide if the officer is mentally, physically, morally, or professionally qualified for such promotion. If the commander determines that the member is not qualified, he/she should initiate a promotion propriety action.

-- A commander may not put members on the control roster who are in temporary duty (TDY) or Permanent Change of Station (PCS) status, including those enroute

- Only wing or delta commanders (or equivalent) or the issuing authority, whichever is higher in grade, may remove members from a control roster

- Regular Air Force and Space Force members, and Non-extended active duty (EAD) Reserve or Air National Guard (ANG) members on duty, acknowledge receipt of the action and have three duty days to respond

-- Any statement or document provided by the member in response to the control roster must be filed in the Unfavorable Information File (UIF). Additional materials submitted by the member in mitigation, extenuation, or defense are not a part of the record.

- Non-EAD Reserve or ANG members not in duty status have 45 days from the date of receiving the certified letter to acknowledge receipt of the action and respond. The member is presumed to have received this correspondence if it is hand delivered or delivered by certified mail to his/her address.

Duration

- Regular Air Force and Space Force: six months

- Non-EAD Reserve or ANG: not to exceed 12 months

- If the member's conduct or performance does not improve during the observation period, the commander should consider whether a more severe response is required, such as initiating an administrative discharge

- A member's time on the control roster does not stop and start for periods of TDY, ordinary leave, or change in immediate supervisor

Collateral Impacts

- Permanent Change of Station (PCS) and Permanent Change of Assignment (PCA) actions are limited

- All formal training must be canceled during the period that the member is on the control roster

- Eligibility for promotion and reenlistment is limited

- Placement on the control roster requires mandatory filing in the member's UIF

References

· DAFI 36-2608, *Military Personnel Records Systems* (16 April 2021), incorporating Change 1, 28 September 2022

· DAFI 36-2907, *Adverse Administrative Actions* (14 October 2022)

· DAF Form 1058, *Unfavorable Information File Actions* (14 October 2022)

ADMINISTRATIVE DEMOTIONS

An administrative demotion is a quality force management tool available to Department of the Air Force (DAF) commanders to help ensure a quality enlisted force. Administrative demotions are intended to place DAF enlisted members at a rank commensurate with their skill level and ability.

Key Takeaway
» Administrative demotions are not intended to be punitive and should not be used when it is more appropriate to take actions specified by the Uniform Code of Military Justice (UCMJ)

Demotion and Appellate Authorities

- Demotion Authority – Active Duty and Air Force Reserve Members:

  -- E-7 and below: Group commander or equivalent level commander

  -- E-8 and E-9: Major Command Commander (MAJCOM/CC), Field Operating Agency Commander (FOA/CC), or Direct Reporting Unit Commander (DRU/CC). This demotion authority may be delegated to MAJCOM Deputy Commander, Deputy Chief of Staff for Manpower, Personnel and Services, Numbered Air Force (NAF), or equivalent level commanders, but may not be further delegated.

    --- For Air Force Reserve members, the Air Force Reserve Command Deputy Commander (AFRC/CC) is the demotion authority for members serving in the grade of E-8 or E-9. This demotion authority may be delegated to NAF Commanders.

- Appellate Authority – Active Duty and Air Force Reserve Members: Next higher-level commander above the demotion authority

- Demotion and Appellate Authority – Air National Guard Members:

  -- Traditional Guardsmen E-1 to E-6: State Adjutant General. However, this demotion authority may be delegated to the wing, group, or installation commander

  -- Traditional Guardsmen E-7 to E-9: State Adjutant General. However, this demotion authority may be delegated to Assistant Adjutant General for Air (AAG for Air)

  -- Members on extended active duty under Title 10 orders: Director, Air National Guard, with concurrence of The Adjutant General (TAG) of the state

  -- Full-time State Active Guard and Reserve (AGR): State Adjutant General. While DAFI 36-2502, *Enlisted Airman Promotion and Demotion Programs*, does not specify a separate demotion authority for AGRs, the State Adjutant General holds the authority to initiate curtailment of AGR status for cause

Reasons for Demotion

- <u>Basis for demotion includes:</u>

  -- Officer trainee or pipeline students if eliminated from training;

  -- Termination of student status of members attending temporary duty (TDY) at DAF schools;

  -- Failure to main or attain the skill level appropriate for the grade;

  -- Failure to fulfill DAF service member, Noncommissioned Officer (NCO), or Senior Noncommissioned Officer (SNCO) responsibilities, as defined in *The Enlisted Force Structure* (16 May 2022);

  -- Failure to keep fit;

  -- For Reservists, unsatisfactory participation in statutory training requirements outlined in 10 U.S.C. § 10147, DoDI 1215.06, *Uniform Reserve, Training, and Retirement Categories for the Reserve Components*, and DAFMAN 36-2136, *Reserve Personnel Participation.*

- The basis for demotion must have occurred in the current enlistment unless the commander does not become aware of the facts and circumstances until after reenlistment

- Where appropriate, members should be given the opportunity to overcome their deficiencies prior to the initiation of the demotion action

Due Process

- The member's commander (usually his/her squadron commander) notifies the member in writing

- The member has the right to seek legal counsel and respond (orally, in writing, or both) within three duty days (30 calendar days for non-extended active duty (EAD) Reserve members and 20 calendar days for ANG members)

- Members eligible for retirement may apply for retirement in lieu of demotion. Member must apply for retirement within three duty days of receipt of the demotion notification, or the demotion will take effect on the date the demotion authority approves the demotion.

- Following the member's response, if the commander elects to continue the proceedings, the case file is forwarded to the demotion authority for action

- The demotion authority fully reviews the initiating commander's recommendation, the member's response, and the member's entire military record prior to taking action

  -- Demotion authority can do the following: (1) decline to demote the member, (2) approve the demotion recommendation, or (3) approve a greater or lesser demotion than recommended by the initiating commander. The demotion authority should request a written legal review from the Staff Judge Advocate (SJA) prior to deciding on the demotion.

- The member may appeal the decision of the demotion authority. The appeal is first reviewed by the demotion authority who can reverse his/her prior decision and restore the member's original grade. If the demotion authority does not grant the appeal, he/she must forward the case to the appellate authority without comment or recommendation.

Grades to Demote DAF Members

- The following demotions are permitted:

  -- E-2 may be demoted to E-1

  -- E-3 may be demoted to no lower than E-2

  -- E-4 through E-9 may be demoted to no lower than E-3. However, a demotion of three or more grades is only appropriate when no reasonable hope exists that the member will ever show the proficiency, leadership, or fitness that earned the initial promotion.

- Administrative demotions may trigger mandatory High Year Tenure (HYT) separations from the service. When a member is demoted, the member assumes the HYT restrictions of that grade and typically will be separated within 120 days of the effective date of the separation.

- Eligibility for promotion and reenlistment is limited

References

· Ready Reserve: Training Requirements, 10 U.S.C. § 10147
· DoDI 1215.06, *Uniform Reserve, Training, and Retirement Categories for the Reserve Components* (11 March 2014), incorporating through Change 2, 12 July 2022
· DAFI 36-2502, *Enlisted Airman Promotion and Demotion Programs* (16 April 2021), including DAFGM2023-02, 20 December 2023
· DAFI 36-2608, *Military Personnel Records Systems* (16 April 2021), incorporating Change 1, 28 September 2022
· DAFI 36-2907, *Adverse Administrative Actions* (14 October 2022)
· DAFMAN 36-2136, *Reserve Personnel Participation* (15 December 2023)
· DAF Form 1058, *Unfavorable Information File Actions* (14 October 2022)
· *The Enlisted Force Structure*, 16 May 2022

SELECTIVE REENLISTMENT PROGRAM – ACTIVE DUTY

The selective reenlistment program (SRP) is designed to ensure the Department of the Air Force (DAF) only retains and affords continued military service to enlisted members who consistently demonstrate the capability and willingness to maintain high professional standards. The program identifies members nearing the end of their current term of service and provides a process for the commander to deny reenlistment.

Key Takeaways

» Reenlistment in the DAF is not an inherent right

» DAF members may be considered for reenlistment if they meet eligibility requirements, have qualities essential for continued service, and can perform duty in a career field which the DAF has a specific need

» The SRP applies to all enlisted personnel

Standard for Denial of Reenlistment

- Commanders and civilian directors have SRP selection authority as long as no other factors barring immediate reenlistment exist

- Commanders and civilian directors may non-select any DAF member for SRP at any time

    -- A commander or civilian director's decision to render a DAF member ineligible to reenlist or ineligible for continued service can impact the member's retainability and opportunity to be selected for an assignment, promotion and/or retraining

- Commanders and civilian directors will not use the SRP to deny reenlistment when involuntary separation is more appropriate

Immediate Supervisor's Role

- Immediate supervisors are responsible for ensuring members meet quality standards

- Supervisors and commanders are notified by the Military Personnel Flight (MPF) when DAF members are nearing the end of their terms of enlistment and are subject to SRP consideration. The supervisor provides recommendations for selection or non-selection to the commander.

- SRP recommendations are made using AF Form 418, *Selective Reenlistment Program (SRP) Consideration/Denial of Continued Service for Airmen*

Commander's Role

- Commanders determine whether a member should be denied reenlistment

  -- Decisions to deny reenlistment should be based on a demonstrated lack of capability and unwillingness to maintain high professional standards. Unit commanders consider the supervisor's recommendation, the member's duty performance, and career force potential before making a decision.

  -- The commander will consider: ratings on Enlisted Performance Reports (EPRs), unfavorable information from any substantiated source, the DAF member's willingness to comply with DAF standards (fitness, dress and appearance, timeliness, etc.), the member's ability to meet required training and duty performance levels

  -- Commanders shall not consider derogatory information from a previous enlistment as a basis for denial of subsequent enlistments

  -- If a Physical Evaluation Board (PEB) found a DAF service member fit for duty, the member may not be denied reenlistment on the basis of the same condition for which the PEB made its finding

  -- Commanders may reverse their SRP decisions at any time

Appeal

- For members non-selected under SRP, the commander must discuss non-selection with the member. Specifically the commander must discuss the specific reasons for non-selection, areas needing improvement, appeal opportunity, promotion ineligibility, and the possibility of future reconsideration and selection.

- The member has three calendar days to notify the commander of whether he/she intends to appeal

- A member's appeal is due to the Military Personnel Flight (MPF) no later than 10 calendar days of notifying the commander of his/her intent to appeal

- Appellate Authorities:

  -- *Group Commander:* First Term and retirement eligible DAF service members

  -- *Wing Commander:* Second term DAF service members and those with fewer than 16 years of service at the end of their current enlistment

  -- *Secretary of the Air Force (SecAF):* DAF service members with more than 16 years of service but less than 20 years of service at the expiration of their current enlistment

- Any commander in the reviewing chain may approve a member's appeal as it is routed to the ultimate appellate authority. However, only the appellate authority has final disposition authority.

- The appeal decision is final, and the case cannot be sent to a level above the appellate authority to have the decision overturned

- A legal review is required when a member appeals SRP decisions

Collateral Impact

- SRP non-selection makes members ineligible for promotion and also automatically cancels projected promotion line numbers

- Once a member reenlists, any misconduct taking place in the earlier enlistment generally cannot be used as a basis for administrative discharge action

References

- AFI 36-2606, *Reenlistment and Extension of Enlistment in the United States Air Force* (20 September 2019), incorporating Change 1, 27 January 2021
- AF Form 418, *Selective Reenlistment Program (SRP) Consideration/Denial of Continued Service for Airmen* (12 April 2021)

SELECTIVE REENLISTMENT PROGRAM – AIR FORCE RESERVE AND AIR NATIONAL GUARD

The quality of the Air Force Reserve (AFR) and Air National Guard (ANG) depends on the quality of its enlisted members. Reenlistment in any Total Force component, to include the AFR and ANG, is a privilege and not a right. Members may be considered for reenlistment in the AFR if they meet eligibility requirements, have qualities essential for continued service, and can perform duty in a career field in which the Department of the Air Force (DAF) has a specific need.

Key Takeaways

» Commanders have significant discretion in making reenlistment decisions. In making this determination, commanders should primarily consider the member's initial eligibility and performance.

» Prior to the expiration of term of service (ETS), a commander will consider whether the member should be selected or denied reenlistment

» The selection or non-selection decision will be consistent with qualitative factors and criteria and will not be based solely on the member's career intent

---

Standard for Denial of Reenlistment

- Commanders will consider and review: supervisor recommendations, Enlisted Performance Report (EPR) rating, unfavorable information from any substantiated source, compliance with DAF standards (fitness, dress and appearance, timeliness, etc.), ability to meet required training and duty performance levels, potential, grade and skill level, aptitude, education, motivation, self-improvement efforts, training and participation, derogatory information, physical condition, medical readiness, attitude and behavior, assumption of responsibilities, and other related information

Common Factors Precluding Reenlistment

- Unsatisfactory participation, performance, attitude, military bearing, or behavior

- Currently undergoing nonjudicial punishment (Article 15) action

- Under consideration for administrative discharge

- Conscientious objectors whose religious convictions preclude unrestricted assignment

- Awaiting Surgeon General's (AFRC/SG) consideration of a physical disqualification

- Even when policy does not prohibit a member from reenlisting, the commander should carefully consider whether the member meets DAF's quality standards

Non-Selection for Reenlistment

- Commanders should contact the servicing legal office prior to notifying a member of a non-selection decision

- The commander or supervisor completes AF Form 418, *Selective Reenlistment Program (SRP) Consideration/Denial of Continued Service for Airmen*, when not selecting a member for reenlistment and notifies the member of the non-selection

- Except for physical disability or for cause, members may not be denied reenlistment if they have completed at least 18 but less than 20 years of satisfactory service for retirement purposes

Appeals of Denial of Reenlistment – AFR

- Members who have not been selected for reenlistment have a right to appeal

- Member must submit a written appeal to the Military Personnel Flight (MPF) by the next scheduled Unit Training Assembly (UTA) or 30 days after the date he/she was notified, whichever is later

- Member may appeal non-selection for reenlistment through one of two options:

  -- *Senior Rater Appeal:* Unit members may appeal to their Senior Reserve Commander for final selection or non-selection authority; or

  -- *Denial of Reenlistment Appeal Board:* A member may present their appeal to a three-person appeal board which will review all documentation and make a recommendation to the member's Senior Reserve Commander for final action.

- Under either appeal option, the ultimate decision of the member's Senior Reserve Commander is final

Appeals of Denial of Reenlistment – ANG

- Members who have not been selected for reenlistment have a right to appeal

- Member must submit a written appeal to the MPF no later than 10 calendar days (for Drill Status Guardsman, submit the appeal during the next regularly scheduled drill) from the date he/she notified the commander of his/her intent to appeal

- The member's appeal and supporting documentation are forwarded to the appellate authority. Any commander in the reviewing chain may approve a member's appeal. However, after the case file has been sent to the appellate authority and the appeal has been denied, the case file cannot be sent to the next higher authority to have the decision overturned.

References

· Enlisted Members: Retention After Completion of 18 or More, But Less Than 20, Years of Service, 10 U.S.C. § 1176

· AFI 36-2606, *Reenlistment and Extension of Enlistment in the United States Air Force* (20 September 2019), incorporating Change 1, 27 January 2021

· AF Form 418, *Selective Reenlistment Program (SRP) Consideration/Denial of Continued Service for Airmen* (12 April 2021)

OFFICER AND ENLISTED EVALUATION SYSTEMS

The single most important element needed for successful mission accomplishment is performance. The Officer Evaluation System (OES) and the Enlisted Evaluation System (EES) are the Department of the Air Force's (DAF) programs for evaluating and documenting performance. Commander involvement in the program is critical to developing and retaining a high-caliber force. The servicing Military Personnel Section (MPS) provides command support and guidance regarding evaluations.

Key Takeaway

» A properly managed evaluation system, from initial feedback to final evaluation, provides critical feedback to members, as well as to those making significant personnel decisions

---

Overview

- The DAF evaluation system is generally comprised of the Airman Comprehensive Assessment (ACA) (i.e., initial and mid-term rater performance feedback), Enlisted Performance Briefs (EPBs), Officer Performance Briefs (OPBs), Officer Performance Reports (OPRs), Letters of Evaluation (LOEs), and training reports (TRs)

- Unit commanders should encourage first-time supervisors to obtain OES/EES training within 60 days of being appointed as a rater. Additionally, the commander should encourage all unit members to receive general OES/EES training on an annual basis as needed.

Airman Comprehensive Assessment

- The first step in the evaluation of any DAF member is initial and midterm performance feedback provided to the member by his/her rater:

  -- <u>Initial Feedback</u>: within 60 days of a change in supervision

  -- <u>Midterm Feedback</u>: halfway through the member's rating period

- ACA is mandatory for all active duty members and Air Reserve Component (ARC) members in the grade of E-1 to O-6

- ACA sessions must provide realistic feedback, in the form of written comments, to improve the ratee's performance. Any behavior that may result in administrative or punitive action should be documented in a separate document.

- The rater provides the original ACA worksheet to the ratee. The rater may keep a copy for personal reference, but the ACA worksheet will not be made part of any official personnel record nor be included in an individual's Personnel Information File (PIF), **UNLESS** the ratee introduces it first or alleges that he/she did not receive required feedback or claims the sessions were inadequate.

Performance Evaluations – General Considerations

- OPBs/OPRs and EPBs are critical in nearly every personnel decision within the DAF. A poorly managed evaluation system inadequately identifies top performers and undermines confidence in the fairness of the system.

- Performance evaluations should take into account any adverse administrative or punitive actions taken against the individual during the rating period

- Disagreements between evaluators (i.e., primary rater and reviewer/higher level reviewer/senior rater) should be explained in the disagreeing rater's comments block

  -- Preceding evaluators are first given an opportunity to change the evaluation; however, they will **NOT** change their evaluation just to satisfy a disagreeing senior evaluator

  -- If, after discussion, the disagreement remains, the disagreeing evaluator marks the "non-concur" block and must provide specific comments in their block to explain each item in disagreement

Performance Evaluations – Timing

- OPBs for active duty, Air Force Reserve, and Air National Guard (ANG) officers are subject to a "static close out date" (SCOD). The SCOD is the fixed annual date that all officer evaluations will close-out for a specific grade. OPBs cannot be signed before the SCOD. OPRs for Space Force officers will be completed in accordance with timing requirements set forth in DAFI 36-2406, *Officer and Enlisted Evaluations Systems*, Table 3.3.

- EPBs are also subject to a SCOD. The SCOD is used to determine the final time-in-grade (TIG)/time-in-service (TIS) eligible pool for forced distribution allocations.

  -- Enlisted personnel in the grade of E-1 through E-3 will receive an evaluation upon completing a minimum of 36 months TIS as of the E-4 SCOD, 31 March

  -- Enlisted personnel in the grade of E-4 through E-9 will receive an evaluation as of the appropriate SCOD for their grade

  -- EPRs cannot be signed before the SCOD

Performance Evaluations – Required and Prohibited Comments

- Some specific comments or entries are required and must be included in performance evaluations. These comments should be drafted as stated in DAFI 36-2406. Slight deviations are allowed, but entries significantly deviating from the recommended format are unacceptable. These comments and entries include, but are not limited to:

  -- For a referral evaluation or training report, the evaluator must specifically detail the behavior or performance that caused the evaluation to be referred

-- Comments relating to the ratee's behavior if the ratee has been convicted by a court-martial

-- If performance feedback was not accomplished, the reason why it was not accomplished

- Certain comments are inappropriate to include in performance evaluations. These comments include, but are not limited to:

  -- Duty history or performance outside the current reporting period, except as allowed by DAFI 36-2406, para. 1.12.3

  -- Any action against an individual that resulted in an acquittal or failure to implement a recommended personnel action. This does not necessarily bar commenting on the underlying misconduct that formed the basis for the action, but consult with the servicing Staff Judge Advocate (SJA) before doing so.

  -- Race, ethnic origin, gender, age, religion, sexual orientation, or political affiliation of the ratee

  -- Participation in drug or alcohol abuse rehabilitation programs

Performance Evaluations – Referrals

- Certain comments or ratings in a performance evaluation may result in it being "referred" to the ratee for comments. An evaluator whose ratings or comments cause an evaluation to become a referral, must give the ratee a chance to comment. The following comments or ratings require referral:

  -- Comments in any evaluation, regardless of the ratings, that are derogatory in nature, imply or refer to behavior incompatible with or not meeting DAF standards of personal or professional conduct, character, judgment, or integrity, and/or refer to disciplinary actions

  -- When an evaluator marks "Does Not Meet Standards" in Section III or in any performance factor in Section IX of the OPR

  -- When an evaluator marks "Met some but not all expectations" or "Do Not Retain" in any section of the EPR

- DAFI 36-2406, para. 1.10, contains specific procedures that must be followed when referring an evaluation

  -- Officers do not require a separate Referral Memorandum

References

· Privacy Act of 1974, 5 U.S.C. § 552a

· DAFI 36-2406, *Officer and Enlisted Evaluations Systems* (4 August 2023), including DAFI 36-2406_AFGM2024-01, 17 January 2024

· DAF Form 910, *Enlisted Performance Report (AB/Spc1 thru TSgt)* (16 March 2022)

· DAF Form 77, *Letter of Evaluation* (13 February 2024)

· DAF Form 475, *Education/Training Report* (13 February 2024)

· DAF Form 707, *Officer Performance Report (Lt thru Col)* (13 February 2024)

· DAF Form 911, *Enlisted Performance Report (MSgt thru SMSgt)* (13 February 2024)

· DAF Form 912, *Enlisted Performance Report (CMSgt)* (13 February 2024)

· AF Form 715, *Officer Performance Brief (O-1 thru O-6)* (28 February 2023)

· AF Form 724, *Airman Comprehensive Assessment Worksheet (2Lt thru Col)* (13 February 2024)

· AF Form 724-A, *Airman Comprehensive Assessment Addendum* (13 February 2024)

· AF Form 931, *Airman Comprehensive Assessment (ACA) Worksheet (AB through TSgt)* (28 July 2017)

· AF Form 932, *Airman Comprehensive Assessment (ACA) Worksheet (MSgt through CMSgt)* (14 September 2017)

OFFICER PROMOTION PROPRIETY ACTIONS

Promotion is an advancement to a position of greater responsibility based on the requirements of the Department of the Air Force (DAF) and the officer's future potential. It is not a reward for past service. Commanders may recommend that the Secretary of the Air Force (SecAF) take action when an officer is not qualified for promotion by delaying the promotion or removing the officer's name from the promotion list.

Key Takeaways

» If an officer is not qualified to perform the duties of the next grade, the proper authority must take promotion propriety action before the effective date of promotion

» Commanders should consult their servicing legal office when determining if sufficient evidence exists to support a promotion proprietary action

» The AF Form 4363, *Record of Promotion Propriety Action*, and AF Form 4364, *Record of Promotion Delay Resolution,* must specify why the officer is not mentally, physically, morally, or professionally qualified to promote to the next higher grade and must include sufficient evidence as attachments to justify the recommendation

» While commanders may initially delay an officer's promotion, generally only SecAF can resolve the promotion delay action

---

Delaying a Promotion

- A commander may take action to delay a promotion if there is cause to believe that the officer has not met the requirement for exemplary conduct set forth in 10 U.S.C. § 9233 or is not mentally, physically, morally, or professionally qualified to perform the duties of the higher grade. Commanders may also delay a promotion if:

    -- Sworn charges against the officer are pending review and disposition by an officer exercising General Court-Martial Convening Authority (GCMCA) jurisdiction over the officer;

    -- An investigation is being conducted to determine whether disciplinary action of any kind should be brought against the officer;

    -- The officer's record is being reviewed by a board convened under 10 U.S.C. §§ 1181–1187;

    -- The officer is pending a criminal proceeding in a federal or state court; or

    -- The Secretary of Defense (SecDef) or SecAF is reviewing substantiated adverse information about the officer that is material to the decision to appoint the officer.

- Initiating a Promotion Delay: The officer's immediate commander initiates the promotion delay on an AF Form 4363 by notifying the officer of the intent to initiate a promotion delay

-- The AF Form 4363 is then forwarded through the servicing Staff Judge Advocate (SJA), to the reviewing commander (usually the wing commander) with a recommendation to delay the promotion before the effective date of promotion

-- The reviewing commander forwards the package to the Air Force Personnel Center (AFPC) through the servicing Military Personnel Flight. If the reviewing commander does not agree that the officer's promotion should be delayed, the action is terminated and not forwarded to AFPC.

- Effective date of Promotion Delay: The promotion delay is effective when the immediate commander notifies the officer of the delay, either verbally or in writing

- Approval Authority for Promotion Delays: The reviewing commander (usually the wing commander) approves initial promotion delays up to six months from the officer's original effective date of promotion. **ONLY** SecAF (or designee) may grant extensions up to an additional 12 months (a maximum of six months at a time) following the initial promotion delay.

- A written package should be served on the officer as soon as practicable

-- The package should include all relevant documents, which should be listed on the AF Form 4363 or 4364. It should contain a thorough statement as to why the officer is not mentally, physically, morally, or professionally ready to promote to the next higher grade.

-- If the member received adverse/administrative action for misconduct, include the substantiating documentation that the adverse/administrative action was based upon (e.g., if the officer received a Letter of Reprimand (LOR) for substantiated findings in an investigation, include the report of investigation, not just the LOR)

- Member's Response to Promotion Delay: The officer whose promotion is delayed may make a written statement in memorandum format to SecAF via the reviewing commander, in the response to the notification of initial promotion delay. After indorsement, the reviewing commander sends the memorandum electronically to AF/A1PPP for AF/JA and SAF/GC coordination, and SecAF (or designee) action.

- Authority to Terminate Promotion Delay: Commanders may initiate action to end the delay at any time by using AF Form 4364. However, generally, **ONLY** SecAF has authority to end a promotion delay.

-- Notwithstanding the commander's recommendation, SecAF may promote an officer on his/her original effective date, promote an officer with a date of rank adjustment, extend the officer's promotion delay, or remove the officer from the promotion list

-- A reviewing commander may terminate a delay **ONLY** when the delay was initiated to conduct an investigation or inquiry, and upon completion, there was no finding or conclusion that substantiated or partially substantiated any allegation and no disciplinary action of any kind (administrative, nonjudicial, or judicial) is taken against the officer

Removal from a Promotion List

- The officer's commander initiates the removal action by making a recommendation through the servicing Staff Judge Advocate to the reviewing authority (usually the wing commander) on an AF Form 4363 or, if the promotion has already been delayed, an AF Form 4364. If the wing commander concurs, the package is forwarded to AFPC through the servicing military personnel flight (MPF). The package then goes to SecAF, who must approve any removal action.

- The commander's verbal notification of removal action automatically delays the officer's promotion until SecAF makes a decision on the removal action

- If the officer is projected to promote close in time to the notification, close coordination with the servicing MPF and AFPC should also occur

- The package must contain appropriate documentation that has been served on the member. Appropriate documentation includes administrative action, judicial or nonjudicial punishment, reports of investigation, commander directed investigations, and any other documentation that supports the recommendation. The narrative portion of the AF Form 4363 or 4364 should adequately describe what led to the removal action as well.

Promotion Propriety Action Procedures

- <u>Notification to Officer</u>: The commander must inform the officer, verbally or in writing, of the promotion propriety action before the effective date of promotion

- <u>Notification in Writing is Preferred</u>: If written notification is not possible, confirm the verbal action in writing as soon as possible

- <u>Statement of Reasons</u>: The action itself must contain a clear statement stating why the officer should be removed from the promotion list, why the officer's promotion should be delayed, or why the promotion delay should be terminated. The recommendation **MUST** list the evidence that was served on the officer supporting the action. It must also show that the affected officer had an opportunity to review the information and respond to it if desired.

- <u>Officer's Response</u>: The officer should acknowledge the action and be allowed five duty days to respond. Include in the package any comment from the officer.

Not Qualified for Promotion (NQP)

- To be eligible for promotion, all officers are obliged to meet the "exemplary conduct" standard set forth in 10 U.S.C. § 9233

- The officer's immediate commander initiates the recommendation to SecAF to find the officer NQP and forwards it with appropriate coordination to the major command commander for review

- For officers meeting central selection boards, the NQP recommendation case file must arrive at AFPC before the board convenes. This recommendation is valid for only one selection board.

- Before separating a second lieutenant found NQP, an attempt should be made to retain the officer on active duty for six months from the date promotion would have occurred (unless retention is inconsistent with good order and discipline) and give the officer an opportunity to overcome any problem and qualify for promotion

- NQP should never be used in place of discharge proceedings or other appropriate disciplinary actions

References

· Removal from a List of Officers Recommended for Promotion, 10 U.S.C. § 629
· Separation of Regular Officers for Substandard Performance of Duty or for Certain other Reasons, 10 U.S.C. §§ 1181–1187
· Requirement of Exemplary Conduct, 10 U.S.C. § 9233
· Removal from a List of Officers Recommended for Promotion, 10 U.S.C. § 14310
· DAFI 36-2501, *Officer Promotions and Selective Continuation* (12 January 2024)
· DAF Form 4363, *Record of Promotion Propriety Action* (12 January 2024)
· DAF Form 4364, *Record of Promotion Delay Resolution* (12 January 2024)
· AFI 36-2504, *Officer Promotion, Continuation and Selective Early Removal in the Reserve of the Air Force* (4 August 2023)

ENLISTED PROMOTION PROPRIETY ACTIONS

Department of the Air Force (DAF) commanders are authorized to delay enlisted promotions or remove enlisted members from an approved promotion list when the commander deems it is necessary in the interests of good order and discipline.

Key Takeaways

» DAF promotion policy is to select individuals for promotion based on their potential to serve in the next higher grade

» Enlisted promotion propriety actions are a set of tools available to commanders when managing enlisted promotions

---

Non-Recommendation for Promotion

- An enlisted member is considered ineligible for promotion when non-recommended or removed from the promotion list by the promotion authority before the effective date of the promotion, commonly referred to as "redlining"

- Standard: The DAF member's behavior does not adhere to established standards

- A promotion authority can non-recommend E-3s and below in monthly increments up to six months. All other ranks are non-recommended for one specific promotion cycle at a time.

- DAF members also become ineligible for promotion under other circumstances, as outlined in DAFI 36-2502, *Enlisted Airman Promotion and Demotion Programs*, which include, but are not limited to:

  -- Placement on the control roster

  -- Serving a probationary period as part of an involuntary discharge action

  -- Pending administrative demotion action

  -- Under a suspended reduction in grade imposed through nonjudicial punishment under Article 15, Uniform Code of Military Justice (UCMJ)

  -- Disqualified from a previously awarded Air Force Specialty Code (AFSC) for cause or disqualified from a previously awarded AFSC not for cause and awaiting discharge

  -- Conviction by court-martial, or undergoing punishment or suspended punishment imposed by a court-martial, or on appellate leave

  -- Conviction by a civilian court (excluding minor traffic violations), or undergoing punishment or suspended punishment, probation, or work release program, or any combination of these or similar court-ordered conditions

  -- Failed or non-current fitness assessment as of the promotion eligibility cutoff date

Withholding of Promotion

- The immediate commander has the authority to withhold a promotion for up to one year after a member's selection for the next higher grade, but before the effective date of promotion

- Only a higher authority (wing or equivalent level commander) may approve withholding of promotions longer than one year

- Withholding a promotion is not intended to be used as a punishment or inducement for the member to conform to acceptable standards of performance. This action allows the commander to evaluate unique or unusual events so a sound promotion decision can be made.

- The reasons for withholding a promotion include, but are not limited to, when the member is:

    -- Awaiting a decision on an application as a conscientious objector

    -- Under court-martial or civilian charges

    -- Placed into the Alcohol and Drug Abuse Prevention and Treatment program (ADAPT)

    -- Under investigation or subject to an inquiry (formal or informal) that may result in action under the UCMJ or prosecution by civilian authorities

    -- When the member fails a fitness assessment after the promotion eligibility cutoff date or after having been selected for promotion (line number)

    -- When requested by the member's commander based on other reasons with prior approval from the individual's wing commander

Deferral

- A deferral is a delay in promotion for a specified period of time for members serving in the grade of E-5 through E-9

- Typically, deferral duration is for 1 to 3 months, however in some instances waivers may be submitted and approved by AFPC (see DAFI 36-2502, para. 4.2.3.1). Wing or equivalent level commanders may approve deferring promotion beyond three months to members serving in the grades of E-5 to E-7.

- A deferral action may be used to allow the commander to determine if the member meets acceptable behavior and performance standards for the higher grade. If there is clear evidence that the member is not suited to take on increased responsibilities of the higher grade because he/she does not adhere to established standards, then non-recommendation is the right course of action, not deferral.

Procedures

- When non-recommending, deferring, or withholding promotions, the commander informs the member of adverse actions before the promotion effective date

- The notification must include specific reasons, dates, occurrences, and duration of the action

- <u>Air Force Reserve</u>: AF Form 224, *Recommendation and Authorization for Promotion of Airman as Reserve of the Air Force*, is used to document promotions and non-recommendation actions

References

· Article 15, Uniform Code of Military Justice

· DAFI 36-2502, *Enlisted Airman Promotion and Demotion Programs* (16 April 2021), including DAFGM2023-02, 20 December 2023

· AF Form 224, *Recommendation and Authorization for Promotion of Airman as Reserve of the Air Force* (22 June 2012)

Chapter 3

NONJUDICIAL PUNISHMENT UNDER ARTICLE 15, UCMJ

NONJUDICIAL PUNISHMENT OVERVIEW AND PROCEDURES

Nonjudicial punishment (NJP) under Article 15, Uniform Code of Military Justice (UCMJ), provides commanders with an essential and prompt means of maintaining good order and discipline outside of the court-martial process. NJP is designed to promote positive behavior changes in service members without the stigma of a court-martial conviction.

Key Takeaways

- » NJP is designed to be an efficient means to investigate and adjudicate minor offenses under the UCMJ
- » NJP is a forum choice offered by commanders in lieu of a court-martial
- » Commanders act as finders of fact and punishment authority for the NJP process
- » Members have various due process rights with NJP, including the right to counsel, the right to review and present evidence to the commander prior to a determination on guilt, and the right to appeal

---

NJP Standards and Definitions

- <u>Determining Whether NJP is Appropriate</u>: NJP is utilized for the disposition of minor UCMJ offenses. Factors to consider for determining whether NJP is appropriate include:

  -- The nature of the offense and the circumstances surrounding its commission;

  -- The effect of the misconduct and resulting NJP on good order and discipline;

  -- The member's age, rank, duty assignment, record, and experience; and

  -- The effect of NJP on the member.

- <u>NJP Authority</u>: Generally, any commander may impose NJP for minor offenses committed by members under his/her command. Superior commanders may withhold all or part of NJP authority from any subordinate commander. Additionally, a commander may not offer NJP on a covered, known, or related offense until the Office of Special Trial Counsel (OSTC) has deferred authority over said offense(s).

- <u>NJP Timelines</u>: 80% of NJPs should be completed within 39 days from the date the offense is discovered

  -- Date of "discovery" to date of NJP offer: 21 days. "Date of discovery" means the date when any investigator (e.g., Security Forces, commander, legal office, first sergeant, supervisor) becomes aware of the offense and has identified a subject.

  -- Date of NJP offer to date of NJP completion: 18 days, with nine days for offer to punishment and nine days from punishment to legal review of the completed NJP

Procedure

- <u>Forum Choice</u>: NJP is a *forum choice* for an accused member. A commander offers NJP in lieu of a court-martial. A commander cannot force a member to accept NJP.

- <u>Staff Judge Advocate (SJA) Consultation Required</u>: Commanders must confer with the SJA prior to both initiation of NJP proceedings and imposition of punishment. The Military Justice section of the servicing legal office prepares the NJP form (AF Form 3070).

- <u>Standard of Proof</u>: Preponderance of the evidence, meaning it is *more likely than not* the member committed the offense. Commanders should consult the servicing legal office for advice on whether the standard is met for any given NJP offense.

- <u>Offering NJP</u>: A member must always be informed of the identity of the commander who will in fact make the findings and punishment decision before the member makes an election to accept NJP or demand court-martial

Accused Member's Rights

- <u>Forum Choice</u>: An accused has the right to refuse NJP and to demand trial by court-martial

  -- An accused served with NJP has 3 duty days to decide whether to "accept" NJP as the forum for their case

  -- "Accepting" NJP as the forum is **NOT** an admission of guilt, but rather a choice to allow a commander to determine guilt rather than facing trial by court-martial. After accepting NJP as the forum, the member has the right to either contest or admit guilt.

- <u>Right to Counsel</u>: Accused members have a right to, and should consult with, an Area Defense Counsel (ADC). Typically, an ADC appointment will be arranged by the member's first sergeant as soon as possible following offer of NJP.

- <u>Right to Review Evidence</u>: The accused has the right to examine all statements and evidence the commander considered in arriving at the decision to offer NJP

- <u>Right to Present Evidence</u>: The accused is entitled to present matters on his/her own behalf in defense, mitigation, and extenuation

- <u>Right to Personal Appearance</u>: An accused member is generally entitled to appear before the imposing commander, during which the accused member may present matters on his/her own behalf. There is no entitlement for the accused member's counsel to accompany the member for the personal appearance. If the imposing commander is unable to accommodate a personal appearance and alternate means (e.g., telephone, VTC) cannot be utilized, the commander may appoint a designee to receive the personal appearance. The designee must prepare a written summary of the accused member's presentation.

Commander's Findings and Punishment

- After a full and fair consideration of all matters in defense, mitigation, and extenuation, the commander must first determine whether the accused member committed the offense

- If the commander determines, by a preponderance of the evidence, the accused committed the offense, the commander must then determine what punishment to impose. Commanders must refrain from considering punishment until guilt has been determined.

- Commanders should tailor the punishment to the offense and the member. Factors to consider include the member's disciplinary history, the seriousness of the offense, and the member's willingness to accept responsibility.

Punishment Limitations

- Specific Punishment Limitations: There are limitations on certain punishments (see MCM Part 5, para 5(d)):

  -- *Restriction and Extra Duties:* If restriction and extra duties are combined, they must run concurrently and must not exceed the maximum time imposable for extra duties

  -- *Arrest in Quarters:* For officers only and cannot be combined with restriction

- Effective Dates of Punishments:

  -- *Forfeiture of Pay:* Unsuspended forfeitures of pay take effect on the date the commander imposes punishment

  -- *Reductions in Grade:* Unsuspended reductions in grade take effect on the date the commander imposes punishment. Suspended reductions also take effect on the date the commander imposes punishment.

  -- All other unsuspended punishments take effect immediately upon **notification** to the member, unless the commander provides otherwise in the punishment endorsement

Appeals

- First Appeal – Imposing Commander: Members are entitled to appeal NJP to the commander who imposed the original punishment. Members may appeal the guilty finding, the punishment, or both. This must be done within 5 calendar days after punishment.

- Final Appeal – Superior Commander: If the imposing commander does not grant the requested relief, then the next superior commander becomes the appellate authority. The appellate authority's decision is final.

References

· Article 15, Uniform Code of Military Justice

· Manual for Courts-Martial, United States, pt. V (2024), Nonjudicial Punishment Procedure

· DAFI 51-202, *Nonjudicial Punishment* (4 January 2022), including DAFGM2023-01 (21 August 2023)

· AF Form 3070A, *Record of Nonjudicial Punishment Proceedings (AB thru SSgt)* (19 March 2019)

· AF Form 3070B, *Record of Nonjudicial Punishment Proceedings (TSgt thru CMSgt)* (19 March 2019)

· AF Form 3070C, *Record of Nonjudicial Punishment Proceedings (Officer)* (28 March 2019)

SUPPLEMENTARY NONJUDICIAL PUNISHMENT ACTIONS

Supplementary nonjudicial punishment (NJP) actions provide commanders with the flexibility to alter previously imposed NJP when the member's conduct or other extenuating circumstances warrant a change. These supplementary actions include: suspension, mitigation, remission, set aside, and vacation.

Key Takeaways

» Supplementary NJP actions allow punishments to be altered in appropriate circumstances, largely to incentivize or reward positive behavior changes

» Commanders must consult with the Staff Judge Advocate (SJA) prior to taking supplementary NJP action

» Subsequent misconduct that forms the basis for a supplementary NJP vacation action may also form the basis for a separate disciplinary action

---

Initiating a Supplemental Action

- With the exception of a vacation action, supplementary NJP actions are filed with the corresponding original NJP action. Post-punishment relief may be requested by the member and may be granted by the imposing commander or successor in command. Commanders may also take supplementary action of their own volition, without a request from the member. Commanders must consult with the SJA prior to acting on any supplementary action.

Suspension

- <u>Definition</u>: Suspension postpones all or part of a punishment for a probationary period

- <u>Standard</u>: Commanders can suspend punishment at the time of imposition, thereby postponing part, or all, of a punishment for a specific probationary period as a motivational tool for the member

- Suspension of a punishment may not exceed six months

- Commanders may, at any time, suspend any part or amount of the *unexecuted* punishment imposed

    -- An *executed* punishment of reduction in grade or forfeiture may only be suspended within four months of the date of punishment

    -- When a reduction in grade is later suspended, the member's original date of rank, held before the reduction, is reinstated for the purposes of promotion. However, the date of rank for the purposes of pay is the date the commander signs the suspension. In other words, the member is not entitled to back pay.

-- If a member is under a suspended reduction in grade, the member is ineligible for promotion, promotion consideration, and testing. The member is also ineligible to reenlist but may be eligible for an extension of enlistment.

Mitigation

- <u>Definition</u>: Mitigation is a reduction in either the quantity or quality of a punishment

- <u>Standard</u>: Mitigation is appropriate when the member's subsequent conduct merits a reduced punishment, or if the original punishment was disproportionate to the offense

- With the exception of reduction in grade, only the *unexecuted* part or amount of the punishments can be mitigated:

  -- Reduction in grade may be mitigated after it has been executed. It can only be mitigated to forfeitures, and only within four months of the punishment date.

  -- Punishments involving loss of liberty may only be mitigated to less severe forms of loss of liberty (i.e., they cannot be mitigated to forfeitures or reduction in grade)

  -- When restraint on liberty is mitigated, the mitigated punishment cannot last beyond the end date of the originally imposed punishment

Remission

- <u>Definition</u>: Remission is the cancellation of any unexecuted portion of a punishment

- <u>Standard</u>: Remission is appropriate when the member's subsequent conduct merits a reduced punishment, or if the original punishment was disproportionate to the offense

- Commanders may remit punishments any time before the execution of the punishment is completed. An unsuspended reduction in grade is executed upon imposition, and therefore cannot be remitted, but under appropriate circumstances may be suspended, mitigated, or set aside.

Set Aside

- <u>Definition</u>: Set aside removes a punishment, whether executed or unexecuted. **A set aside of all punishment voids the entire NJP action** and restores all rights to the member.

- <u>Standard</u>: Set aside is appropriate when there is a question about the member's guilt or when the best interests of the DAF are served by clearing the member's record. Unlike other supplementary actions, set aside is rare and not considered a rehabilitative tool.

- <u>Time Limits</u>: Punishments should be set aside within a reasonable time (four months, except in unusual circumstances) after the punishment is originally imposed

Vacation

- <u>Definition</u>: Imposing punishment that was previously suspended

- <u>Standard</u>: Vacation of a suspended punishment is appropriate if a member violates either a condition of the suspension (specified in writing by the commander in the NJP) or any punitive article of the UCMJ

  -- A new offense may be the basis for a vacation action **and** new NJP action

  -- However, an offense warranting a vacation action does not necessarily have to be one that would otherwise warrant new NJP, nor does it have to be of the same nature as the original offense

Procedure for Vacation Actions

- The commander must notify and advise the member of the intended vacation, including:

  -- A description of the basis for the vacation (i.e., new offense or probation violation), the fact the commander is considering vacating the suspended punishment, and the member's rights during the vacation proceedings

- <u>Member's Rights during Vacation Proceedings</u>: Unlike other supplementary actions, vacation action is detrimental to the member and therefore comes with due process protections similar to NJP, namely: (1) 3 duty days to respond; (2) right to consult counsel; (3) right to submit written matters; (4) right to request a personal appearance before the imposing commander

- <u>Commander's Decision – Vacation Proceedings</u>: Following the commander's consideration of the evidence and any matters presented by the member, the commander either imposes the original punishment or terminates the proceedings

- <u>Effects of Vacation Action on Suspended Reductions</u>:

  -- If a suspension of a reduction in grade is vacated, the member's date of rank, for the purposes of promotion, will be the date the commander imposed the original punishment. For the purposes of pay, however, the date of rank will be the day the suspension is vacated. The member will not be required to return any additional pay received while holding the higher rank.

References

· Article 15, Uniform Code of Military Justice
· Manual for Courts-Martial, United States, pt. V (2024), Nonjudicial Punishment Procedure
· DAFI 51-202, *Nonjudicial Punishment* (4 January 2022), including DAFGM2023-01 (21 August 2023)
· AF Form 366, *Record of Proceedings of Vacation of Suspended Nonjudicial Punishment* (29 March 2019)
· AF Form 3212, *Record of Supplementary Action Under Article 15, UCMJ* (29 March 2019)

QUALITY FORCE MANAGEMENT EFFECTS OF NONJUDICIAL PUNISHMENT

Generally speaking, there are three main possible follow-on force management ramifications of NJP action: (1) placement of the NJP in an Unfavorable Information File (UIF); (2) placement of the NJP in a Senior Noncommissioned Officer (SNCO) or Officer Selection Record; (3) follow-on "referral" Enlisted or Officer Performance Briefs.

Key Takeaways

» All officer NJPs and enlisted NJPs with punishment exceeding 31 days are mandatory UIF entries. The remaining actions are discretionary

» Under certain circumstances, NJPs may be removed from UIFs early

» All officer NJPs must be filed in the Officer Selection Record (OSR)

» Commanders have discretion whether NJP is filed in a SNCO's Promotion Selection Record

Unfavorable Information File NJP Entries

- <u>Mandatory Entries</u>: Entry of an NJP into a UIF is mandatory for all officer NJPs. For enlisted, UIF entry is required if any portion of the executed or suspended punishment will not be completed within 31 days.

  -- Post-punishment supplementary actions to suspend a previously imposed punishment must be filed in the UIF, with the original NJP, until the suspension period is completed

  -- Actions to vacate a suspended punishment must be entered into the UIF

- <u>Discretionary Entries</u>: All other NJPs are discretionary UIF entries at the election of the imposing commander

- <u>Notice</u>: Members are entitled to notice of the action being entered into a UIF

- <u>UIF Retention Period</u>: NJP actions entered into a UIF must remain there until all punishment is completed or remitted, including any periods of suspension

  -- *Mandatory UIF:* If the commander takes no action to remove a mandatory UIF NJP action, it will remain in the UIF for two years for enlisted members and four years for officers

  -- *Discretionary UIF:* If the commander takes no action to remove a discretionary UIF NJP action, it will remain in the UIF for one year

- <u>Early Removal of NJP from UIF</u>: The commander may remove the NJP action and related documents from the member's UIF any time after the punishment or suspended punishment is completed (if removal is clearly warranted), or if the NJP is set aside

Related Administrative Actions

- In addition to NJP, commanders may take other appropriate administrative actions, including but not limited to:

  -- Control Roster action;

  -- Entry of the member into counseling or rehabilitation programs, such as the Alcohol and Drug Abuse Prevention and Treatment Program (ADAPT);

  -- Enlisted Performance Brief (EPB) comments concerning the member's underlying misconduct (referral EPB);

  -- Administrative discharge; and

  -- Removal from the personnel reliability program (PRP), withholding a security clearance, or withholding access to sensitive materials.

- NJP may also adversely affect promotion, reenlistment, and assignment eligibility

Officer Unfavorable Information File NJP Entries

- An NJP is permanently retained in the officer's Master Personnel Record Group (Correspondence and Miscellaneous Group) unless set aside in its entirety or ordered removed by the Air Force Board of Corrections for Military Records (AFBCMR)

- UIF Retention Period: Officer NJP actions are retained in a UIF for four years

  -- Early removal is only permissible after completion of all punishment. Only the wing commander or issuing authority (whomever is higher in rank) is authorized to remove an officer NJP from a UIF.

- Referral OPB/PRF Consideration: Commanders should also consider whether comments should be made in the next Officer Performance Brief (OPB) and/or Promotion Recommendation Form (PRF)

  -- Sex related offenses punished by NJP require a mandatory notation in the officer's next OPB and/or PRF

  -- A LOR, NJP, and court-martial conviction require a UIF

Officer and SNCO Promotion Selection Records

- Commanders must determine whether to place NJP in the SNCO selection record of all members in the grade of E-6 and above

- Disciplinary Actions filed in the officer OSR:

  -- LOCs: Not mandatory for a "stand-alone" mandatory if related to substantiated finding from officially documented investigation;

  -- LOA/LOR: Mandatory OSR filing;

-- NJP: Mandatory OSR filing;

-- Court-Martial: Mandatory OSR filing.

- <u>Reviewing Authority</u>: The imposing commander's decision to file an NJP in a SNCO's selection record is subject to review by the next senior Air Force commander unless the General Court-Martial Convening Authority (GCMCA) imposed the punishment

- <u>SNCO Selection Record Retention Period</u>: Retention is required for two years or until after the member meets one SNCO evaluation board. Early removal is authorized only if approved by the commander who originally placed the NJP in the selection record, or successors in command.

- <u>Officer Selection Record Retention Period</u>: Adverse information filed in the OSR will remain in the OSR for O-6 and below promotion boards indefinitely. Except for the set aside of NJP action, earlier removal of adverse information from the OSR may only be directed by the AFBCMR.

References

· Article 15, Uniform Code of Military Justice

· DoDI 1320.14, *DoD Commissioned Officer Promotion Program Procedures* (16 December 2020)

· DAFI 36-2406, *Officer and Enlisted Evaluation Systems* (4 August 2023), including DAFGM2024-01, 17 January 2024

· DAFI 36-2907, *Adverse Administrative Actions* (14 October 2022)

· DAFI 51-202, *Nonjudicial Punishment* (4 January 2022), including DAFGM2023-01 (21 August 2023)

· DAFI 36-2608, *Military Personnel Records System* (16 April 2021), incorporating Change 1, 28 September 2022

· AFI 44-121, *Alcohol and Drug Abuse Prevention and Treatment (ADAPT) Program* (18 July 2018), incorporating Change 1, 21 November 2019

· AF Form 3070A, *Record of Nonjudicial Punishment Proceedings (AB thru SSgt)* (19 March 2019)

· AF Form 3070B, *Record of Nonjudicial Punishment Proceedings (TSgt thru CMSgt)* (19 March 2019)

· AF Form 3070C, *Record of Nonjudicial Punishment Proceedings (Officer)* (28 March 2019)

Page Intentionally Left Blank

Chapter 4
ADMINISTRATIVE SEPARATION FROM THE AIR FORCE

INVOLUNTARY SEPARATION OF ENLISTED MEMBERS: GENERAL CONSIDERATIONS

Commanders and supervisors must identify enlisted members who show a likelihood for early separation and make reasonable efforts to help these members meet Department of the Air Force (DAF) standards. Members who do not show potential for further service should be discharged. Commanders must consult the servicing Staff Judge Advocate (SJA) and Military Personnel Flight (MPF) before initiating the involuntary separation of a member. DAFI 36-3211, *Military Separations* governs involuntary separations for enlisted members in the Regular Air Force (RegAF), the Air Force Reserve (AFR), and the Air National Guard (ANG). This instruction also applies to U.S. Space Force (USSF) enlisted members until such time as separate service guidance is published.

Key Takeaways

» A commander must consider the member's potential for future useful services as well as all the factors that make the member subject to discharge

» Discharges involving post-traumatic stress disorder, traumatic brain injury, and/or sexual assault may require special processing

» An administrative discharge is not a substitute for disciplinary actions

General Preprocessing Considerations

- Before initiating discharge, a commander must consider the member's potential for future service, as well as all the factors that make the member subject to discharge, including:

  -- The seriousness of circumstances that make the member subject to discharge and how the member's retention might affect military discipline, good order, and morale

  -- Whether the circumstances that are the basis for discharge action will continue or recur

  -- The likelihood that the member will be disruptive or an undesirable influence in present or future duty assignments

  -- The member's ability to perform duties effectively in the present and in the future

  -- The member's potential for advancement and leadership

  -- An evaluation of the member's military record including, but not limited to:

    --- Records of nonjudicial punishment

    --- Records of counseling

    --- Letters of reprimand or admonishment

    --- Records of conviction by courts-martial

--- Records of involvement with civilian authorities

--- Past contributions to the Department of the Air Force

--- Duty assignments and Enlisted Performance Reports (EPRs)

--- Awards, decorations, and letters of commendation

--- The effectiveness of preprocessing rehabilitation, when required

- A commander should **NOT** use an administrative discharge as a substitute for disciplinary action

- Generally, the acts or conditions on which the discharge is based must have occurred in the current enlistment. **The exceptions are:**

  -- Fraudulent enlistment, erroneous enlistment, or the interest of national security

  -- Cases in which the act or condition occurred in the immediately preceding enlistment and the commander was not aware of the facts warranting discharge until after the member reenlisted and there was no break in service

  -- Cases in which the member is being separated for failure in the fitness program and at least one instance of unsatisfactory performance is in the current enlistment. Under these circumstances, instances of unsatisfactory performance in the immediately preceding enlistment may support the basis for discharge.

- Prior to processing a member for discharge for parenthood, conditions that interfere with military service, entry level performance and conduct, unsatisfactory performance, and minor disciplinary infractions or a pattern of misconduct, commanders must give the member an opportunity to overcome deficiencies

  -- Efforts to rehabilitate may include, but are not limited to, counseling, reprimands, control roster action, nonjudicial punishment under Article 15 of the Uniform Code of Military Justice (UCMJ), change in duty assignment, demotion, additional training, and retraining, or other administrative actions

  -- It is extremely important to properly document rehabilitative efforts and keep copies of these documents

Special Processing – Members Diagnosed with or Reasonably Asserting Post-Traumatic Stress Disorder or Traumatic Brain Injury

- All enlisted DAF members being recommended for involuntary separation who have deployed overseas in support of a contingency operation or were sexually assaulted during the previous 24 months and have been diagnosed with or reasonably assert post-traumatic stress disorder (PTSD) or traumatic brain injury (TBI) must receive a medical examination. The medical examination must assess whether the effects of PTSD or TBI constitute matters in extenuation that relate to the basis for involuntary administrative separation. The medical examination is required if the member:

-- Is being administratively separated under a characterization that is not either Honorable or Under Honorable Conditions (General);

-- Was deployed overseas to a contingency operation or sexually assaulted during the previous 24 months;

-- Has been diagnosed by a physician, clinical psychologist, psychiatrist, licensed clinical social worker, or psychiatric advanced practice registered nurse as experiencing PTSD or TBI, or reasonably alleges the influence of PTSD or TBI based on deployed service to a contingency operation or a sexual assault that occurred during the previous 24 months; **AND**

-- Is not being separated under a sentence of court-martial, or other proceeding conducted pursuant to the Uniform Code of Military Justice (UCMJ).

- Members diagnosed with or reasonably asserting PTSD or TBI will not be separated until the result of the medical examination has been reviewed by appropriate authorities responsible for evaluating, reviewing, and approving the separation action, to include (if applicable): the initiating commander, administrative discharge board, convening authorities, separation authority, Air Force Review Board, and/or the Secretary of the Air Force (SecAF)

Special Preprocessing Considerations for Service Members Who Have Made an Unrestricted Report of a Sexual Assault

- DAF service members who made an unrestricted report of sexual assault and who are within one year of final disposition of his/her sexual assault allegation may request a general officer to review the circumstances of and grounds for any recommendation of his/her involuntary separation from the DAF

    -- The general officer review is conducted by the General Court-Martial Convening Authority (GCMCA) or, if the GCMCA is not a general officer, the first general officer in the member's chain of command

    -- An enlisted member entitled to GCMCA review must be notified of this right in the separation notification memorandum

    -- The member must submit his/her request for GCMCA review in writing. For officer members, the request must affirmatively assert that he/she believes the pending discharge action was initiated in retaliation for making a report of sexual assault.

    -- A member who submits a timely request to the GCMCA may not be separated until the GCMCA conducting the review concurs with the circumstances of and grounds for the involuntary separation

Characterizations of Service

- The service of a member administratively separated may be characterized as Honorable, General (Under Honorable Conditions), or Under Other Than Honorable Conditions (UOTHC)

  -- Honorable: Appropriate when the quality of the member's service generally has met Department of the Air Force standards of acceptable conduct and performance of duty, or a member's service is otherwise so meritorious that any other characterization would be inappropriate

  -- General (Under Honorable Conditions): Appropriate if a member's service has been honest and faithful, but significant negative aspects of the member's conduct or performance outweigh positive aspects of military record

  -- UOTHC: Appropriate if based on a pattern of behavior or one or more acts or omissions constituting a significant departure from the conduct expected of DAF service members. This characterization can be given only if the member is offered an administrative discharge board or if a discharge is unconditionally requested in lieu of trial by court-martial.

- A dishonorable discharge and a bad conduct discharge are punitive discharges and are authorized only as a result of a court-martial sentence

- If the sole basis for discharging a DAF member with a UOTHC service characterization is a serious offense that resulted in conviction by a court-martial that did not adjudge a punitive discharge, then SecAF must approve the service characterization. However, the following courts-martial are not authorized to impose a punitive discharge, and are thus not limited by this paragraph:

  -- Summary courts-martial

  -- Cases referred to a special court-martial by military judge alone pursuant to Article 16(c) (2)(A), UCMJ

  -- Any courts-martial where the military judge accepts a pretrial agreement or plea agreement provision whereby the accused and the convening authority agree the accused will not be sentenced to a punitive discharge

- Separation without Service Characterization: Members in entry level status will ordinarily receive an "entry level separation" without service characterization. Entry level status is defined as within **365 days** of continuous active military service.

How Characterization of Service Affects Veteran's Benefits

- The U.S. Department of Veterans Affairs (VA) provides several benefits to veterans including the GI Bill, home loan benefits, disability compensation, and other benefits. More information on the availability of veteran's benefits can be found at www.benefits.va.gov.

- To become eligible for veteran's benefits, the active duty member must have been discharged or released under conditions other than dishonorable. The term "dishonorable" is broader in the context of determining VA benefit eligibility.

- In general, to qualify for VA educational benefits (e.g., GI bill) an honorable discharge is required

References

· Members Diagnosed With or Reasonably Asserting Post-Traumatic Stress Disorder or Traumatic Brain Injury: Medical Examination Required Before Administrative Separation, 10 U.S.C. § 1177

· Article 16, Uniform Code of Military Justice

· DoDI 1332.14, *Enlisted Administrative Separations* (27 January 2014), incorporating through Change 7, 23 June 2022

· DAFI 36-3211, *Military Separations* (24 June 2022), incorporating Change 1, 20 November 2023

INVOLUNTARY SEPARATION OF ENLISTED MEMBERS: REASONS FOR DISCHARGE

Specific reasons for involuntarily separating active duty enlisted members are set forth in Chapter 7 of DAFI 36-3211, *Military Separations*. The facts and circumstances are different in each case and must be considered on a case-by-case basis. An overview of the nine broad reasons for discharge of RegAF and USSF enlisted members are below. Involuntary separations of members of the Air National Guard (ANG) and Air Force Reserve (AFR) are also governed by the provisions of DAFI 36-3211. Table 13.1 provides a comprehensive list of permissible reasons for enlisted separations for members of ANG and AFR.

Key Takeaways

» Commanders must consult with the servicing Staff Judge Advocate (SJA) and Military Personnel Flight (MPF) prior to initiating the involuntary separation of a member

» With a few exceptions, a commander is generally not required to initiate involuntary separation of a member just because a reason for discharge set out in DAFI 36-3211 exists

» Commanders must promptly either initiate discharge or seek a waiver when a member is found to have, committed sexual assault, engaged in fraudulent or erroneous enlistment, been convicted of a qualifying civilian offense, abused drugs, or engaged in certain unprofessional relationships

Mandatory Involuntary Discharge Processing

- A commander **MUST** initiate discharge processing or seek a waiver of the discharge if the reason for discharge is one of the following:

-- Fraudulent or erroneous enlistment

-- Civilian court conviction for an offense for which a punitive discharge would be authorized under the Uniform Code of Military Justice (UCMJ) **OR** civilian sentence which includes confinement for six months or more

-- Drug abuse

-- Sexual assault or sexual assault of a child

-- Unprofessional relationships with prospective members of the armed forces or new members during recruiting, entry level processing, entry level training or initial skills training

Convenience of the Government Discharges

- Discharge is appropriate when separation would serve the best interest of the Department of the Air Force (DAF) and discharge for cause is not warranted. Such separations may be based on:

  -- Parenthood, if the member fails to meet military obligations because of parental responsibilities

  -- Insufficient retainability for required training, if the cost of retraining for a brief period of service may not warrant retention

  -- Medical/Psychological conditions that interfere with military service but not rising to the level of "disabilities" severe enough to warrant medical discharge via a Medical Evaluation Board (MEB)

  -- Mental Disorders:

    --- *Documentation:*

      ---- Must be supported in writing by a report of evaluation by a psychiatrist or PhD-level clinical psychologist that confirms a diagnosis of a disorder contained in the current edition of the Diagnostic and Statistical Manual of Medical Disorders;

      ---- Must be documented in a report as so severe that the member's ability to function in the military environment is significantly impaired;

      ---- The documentation must show that prior to initiation of discharge the member has been formally counseled concerning deficiencies and afforded an opportunity to overcome them. [**Note:** The unit commander is responsible to ensure the counseling requirement has been met]; **AND**

      ---- Must include documentation from the member's supervisory chain that the condition or disorder has resulted in an adverse effect on the member's assignment or duty performance.

    --- *Special Processing:* Required for DAF service members who are currently serving or who have served in an imminent danger pay area and have been diagnosed with a personality disorder that is the basis of the discharge. Additionally, special processing is required, if the member deployed overseas in support of a contingency operation or was sexually assaulted during the previous 24 months and has been diagnosed with or is reasonably asserting post-traumatic stress disorder (PTSD) or traumatic brain injury (TBI)

      ---- The diagnosis of a personality disorder must specifically address PTSD or other mental illness co-morbidity

---- Separation **WILL NOT** be initiated if there is a diagnosis of service-related PTSD, unless the member is subsequently found fit for duty under the disability evaluation system in accordance with DAFI 36-3212, *Physical Evaluation for Retention, Retirement, and Separation*

---- The DAF Surgeon General (SG) must review the diagnosis and concur with supporting documentation prior to initiation of the separation. If the SG does not concur with the diagnosis, no further action will be taken.

- Discharge for conditions that interfere with military service is not appropriate if the member's record supports discharge for another reason, such as misconduct or unsatisfactory performance

- Service is characterized as Entry Level Separation or Honorable

- **Before recommending discharge,** commanders must ensure:

-- Preprocessing rehabilitation requirements in DAFI 36-3211, para. 7.2, have been met;

-- They have complied with all requirements of the specific DAFI paragraph authorizing discharge; **AND**

-- Circumstances do not warrant discharge for another reason.

Defective Enlistments

- <u>Enlistment of Minors</u>: A person under 17 years of age is barred by law from enlisting without parental consent

- <u>Void Enlistments</u>: An enlistment may be void because the individual is underage or for a reason other than minority

- <u>Erroneous Enlistment</u>: The DAF should not have accepted the enlistee, but the case does not involve fraud

- <u>Fraudulent Entry</u>: Involved deliberate deception on the part of the enlistee

- <u>Action Required of the Commander</u>: A commander who has information that shows an enlistment may be erroneous or fraudulent must verify the information as soon as possible

-- If the member is subject to discharge for erroneous enlistment or fraudulent entry, the commander must act promptly to recommend the member's discharge for erroneous enlistment or fraudulent entry, discharge for another reason, or a waiver of the discharge

- Authorized characterizations of service and the approval authorities are listed in DAFI 36-3211, Table 7.4

- Members approved for discharge are **NOT** eligible for probation and rehabilitation (P&R)

Entry Level Performance or Conduct

- Enlisted members in entry level status should be discharged when unsatisfactory performance or conduct shows the member is not a productive member of the DAF

- Discharge processing must start during the first **365 days** of continuous active duty

- Eligibility for discharge based on entry level performance or conduct does not preclude separation for another reason

- Before processing a member for discharge for unsatisfactory entry level performance or conduct, a commander must ensure efforts to rehabilitate the member, allowing the member the opportunity to overcome deficiencies. The commander should ensure these efforts are documented.

- Discharge under this section is described as Entry Level Separation (ELS)

- Members approved for discharge for entry level performance or conduct are **NOT** eligible for P&R

Unsatisfactory Performance

- Members should be discharged when unsatisfactory performance or conduct shows they are not qualified for service in the DAF

- Performance includes assigned duties, military training, bearing and behavior, as well as maintaining the high standards of personal behavior and conduct always required of all military members

- Unsatisfactory performance may be evidenced by any of the following:

  -- Unsatisfactory duty performance, which may include:

    --- Failure to properly perform assigned duties

    --- A progressively downward trend in performance ratings

    --- Failure to demonstrate the qualities of leadership required by the member's grade

  -- Failure to maintain standards of dress and personal appearance, other than fitness standards, or military deportment

  -- Failure to progress in military training required to be qualified for service with the DAF or for the performance of primary duties

  -- Irresponsibility in the management of personal finances

  -- Failure to meet fitness standards

- Before processing a member for discharge for unsatisfactory performance, a commander must ensure efforts to rehabilitate the member, allowing the member the opportunity to overcome deficiencies. The commander should ensure these efforts are documented.

- Service is characterized as Honorable, Under Honorable Conditions (general)

- Members approved for discharge should be considered for P&R

Failure in Drug or Alcohol Abuse Treatment

- Members are subject to discharge for failure in drug or alcohol abuse treatment if they:

  -- Are in a program of rehabilitation for abuse of drugs or alcohol and fail to complete the program due to inability, refusal to participate, or unwillingness to cooperate; **AND**

  -- Lack the potential for continued military service or need long-term treatment and are transferred to a civilian medical facility for treatment.

- Service is characterized as Honorable, General, or Entry Level

- Members approved for discharge are eligible for P&R

Misconduct Discharges

- Unacceptable conduct adversely affects military duty and may be a basis for discharge

- Types of misconduct include:

  -- Minor Disciplinary Infractions: Includes minor infractions during the current enlistment resulting in Letters of Counseling (LOCs), Letters of Admonishment (LOAs), Letters of Reprimand (LORs), and Nonjudicial Punishment (NJP) actions (DAFI 36-3211, para. 7.38)

    --- Before processing a member for discharge for misconduct consisting of minor disciplinary infractions, a commander must ensure efforts to rehabilitate the member, allowing the member the opportunity to overcome deficiencies. The commander should ensure these efforts are documented.

    --- Members approved for discharge are eligible for P&R

  -- Pattern of Misconduct: Includes misconduct more serious than that consisting of minor disciplinary infractions such as (1) discreditable involvement with military or civilian authorities, (2) conduct prejudicial to good order and discipline, (3) failure to support dependents, or (4) dishonorable failure to pay just debts (DAFI 36-3211, para. 7.39)

    --- Before processing a member for discharge for misconduct consisting of a pattern of misconduct, a commander must ensure efforts to rehabilitate the member, allowing the member the opportunity to overcome deficiencies. The commander should ensure these efforts are documented.

    --- Members approved for discharge are eligible for P&R

-- <u>Commission of a Serious Offense</u>: Includes offenses for which a punitive discharge would be authorized under the UCMJ (DAFI 36-3211, para. 7.40)

--- DAF service members are subject to discharge for misconduct based on acts of aberrant sexual behavior or acts of sexual misconduct which include but are not limited to offenses such as indecent viewing, visual recording or broadcasting, forcible pandering, and indecent exposure

--- DAF service members may be discharged for misconduct based on unauthorized absence continuing for one year or more

--- DAF service members are subject to discharge for misconduct based on acts that constitute unprofessional relationships between recruiters and potential recruits during the recruiting process or between students and faculty or staff in training schools or professional military education setting

-- <u>Civilian Conviction</u>: When the member is convicted, or there is a finding that amounts to a conviction of an offense which would authorize a punitive discharge under the UCMJ, **OR** when the sentence by civilian authorities includes confinement for six months or more (DAFI 36-3211, para. 7.41)

--- A commander must promptly initiate discharge or seek a waiver, however, **there is no time limit** for initiating discharge action, and failure to do so **DOES NOT**, at any time, constitute constructive waiver

--- It is general policy to withhold execution of discharge until the outcome of the appeal is known or the time for appeal has passed. If the appeal results in the conviction being set aside, the member may not be discharged due to civilian conviction.

--- A DAF service member whose home of record is in the continental United States (CONUS) may be discharged in absentia if he/she is in civil confinement in the CONUS or has been released from confinement in the CONUS and is absent without authority

--- A DAF service member in a foreign penal institution may not be discharged until released from confinement and returned CONUS or higher authority (Air Force Personnel Center (AFPC)) authorizes an exception

--- Members approved for discharge are eligible for P&R

-- <u>Drug Abuse</u>: The illegal, wrongful, or improper use, possession, sale, transfer, or introduction onto a military installation of any drug (DAFI 36-3211, para. 7.43)

--- This includes prescription medication, Schedules I–V Controlled Substances, 21 U.S.C. § 812. It also includes steroids and any intoxicating substance, other than alcohol or tobacco, that is inhaled, injected, consumed, or introduced into the body in any manner for purposes of altering mood or function.

- - - Commanders must act promptly when information indicates drug abuse and initiate discharge or seek a waiver of discharge processing

- - - A member found to have abused drugs will be discharged unless the member meets all the retention criteria in DAFI 36-3211, para. 7.43.4.2. The member has the burden of proving that he/she meets all retention criteria.

- - - Members approved for discharge are not eligible for P&R

-- Sexual Assault: Includes a broad category of sex offenses such as rape, sexual assault, aggravated sexual contact, abusive sexual contact, forcible sodomy, or attempts to commit these offenses. Sexual assault of a child includes rape of a child, sexual assault of a child, sexual abuse of a child, or attempts to commit these offenses. (DAFI 36-3211, para. 7.44.1)

- - - Commanders will act promptly when they have information indicating a member is subject to discharge for sexual assault or sexual assault of a child. They evaluate the specific circumstances of the offense and take prompt action to initiate discharge or seek waiver of discharge processing in accordance with applicable guidance. (DAFI 36-3211, para. 7.44.3.1)

- - - A member found to have committed sexual assault or sexual assault of a child will be discharged unless the member meets all retention criteria in DAFI 36-3211, para. 7.44.3.2.1. The member has the burden of proving he/she meets all retention criteria.

- - - Members approved for discharge are not eligible for P&R

-- Misconduct: Usually, the characterization for misconduct cases under DAFI 36-3211, paras. 7.39, 7.40, 7.41, 7.43, and 7.44 should be Under Other Than Honorable Conditions (UOTHC), but characterization may be Honorable, General, or Entry Level Separation in appropriate cases

-- The General Court-Martial Convening Authority (GCMCA), usually the Numbered Air Force commander, will approve separation for misconduct with a service characterization of Honorable or UOTHC

Discharge in the Interest of National Security

- A member whose retention is clearly inconsistent with the interest of national security may be discharged

- Discharge may only be initiated after criteria in DAFI 36-3211, paras. 7.46.1 and 7.46.2 have been met

- Discharge may be characterized as Entry Level, Honorable, General, or UOTHC

- Members approved for discharge are not eligible for P&R

Failure in the Fitness Program

- A member who does not meet fitness standards as set out in DAFMAN 36-2905, *Department of the Air Force Physical Fitness Program*, may be discharged when the failure is the result of a cause in the member's control. Note that members of the USSF who maintain satisfactory participation in the USSF's Continuous Fitness Assessment (CFA) Program trial are exempt from the Air Force Physical Fitness Program.

- The required medical examination prior to discharge must document that there is not a medical condition that would preclude the member from meeting fitness program standards

- Characterization of service is restricted to Honorable if failure in the program is the sole reason for discharge

- Members approved for discharge should be considered for P&R

Joint Processing

- In some cases, it may be preferable to cite two or more reasons as the basis for the discharge recommendation if the member's record justifies more than one basis for discharge

  -- If one of the reasons cited in the letter of notification as the basis for discharge entitles the member to a board hearing, then a hearing must be conducted unless waived by the member

  -- For determining service characterization, apply the guidance for the basis for discharge that allows the most latitude in characterizing the member's service

  -- If the separation authority directs discharge for more than one reason, the instrument or documentation direction the discharge must cited the primary reason. The separation in MilPDS is reported on that basis.

References

· Schedules of Controlled Substances, 21 U.S.C. § 812
· DoDI 1332.14, *Enlisted Administrative Separations* (27 January 2014), incorporating through Change 7, 23 June 2022
· DAFI 36-3211, *Military Separations* (24 June 2022), incorporating Change 1, 20 November 2023
· DAFI 36-3212, *Physical Evaluation for Retention, Retirement, and Separation* (22 February 2024)
· DAFMAN 36-2905, *Department of the Air Force Physical Fitness Program* (21 April 2022)

DUAL ACTION PROCESSING OF ADMINISTRATIVE AND MEDICAL DISCHARGES

"Dual action processing" refers to the simultaneous processing of an administrative and a medical discharge action. Commanders should not abandon pursuing an administrative discharge (particularly misconduct-based administrative discharges) solely because a member is also undergoing processing for a medical discharge. Instead, both processes run independently to completion. If both administrative and medical discharges are warranted, the dual action decision authority will determine which discharge to approve and execute.

Key Takeaways

» If the basis for administrative discharge **DOES NOT** authorize an Under Other Than Honorable Conditions (UOTHC) service characterization, both the administrative and medical discharge processes will run concurrently to completion. In these cases, the dual action decision authority is at the SecAF-level (see DAFI 36-3212, *Physical Evaluation for Retention, Retirement and Separation*, para. 1.5).

» If the basis for administrative discharge **authorizes an UOTHC** as a possible characterization, the dual action referral authority will decide whether the member receives dual action processing. If allowed to receive dual action processing, both processes will be completed, and the dual action decision authority will choose which discharge will be executed (see DAFI 36-3212, para. 1.7). The dual action referral and decision authority is the member's General Court-Martial Convening Authority (GCMCA) for enlisted members with less than 16 years of total active federal military service (TAFMS) at the time of discharge. The dual action referral authority for enlisted with more than 16 years and for officers is AFPC/DP2NP (or ARC/SG for ARC members) and the dual action decision authority is Secretary of the Air Force Personnel Council (SAFPC).

» Dual action processing is required when a Department of the Air Force (DAF) service member subject to discharge is also eligible to apply for retirement (20 years or more active service) or is eligible for disability separation or disability retirement

» Consult with the servicing legal office and the member's Physical Evaluation Board Liaison Officer (PEBLO) when members are potentially eligible for dual action processing

Dual Action Processing

- Cases in which a DAF member is concurrently processed for both disability evaluation and a non-disability administrative separation

- Non-disability administrative separations include second lieutenants being processed for "not qualified for promotion" and requests for retirement or discharge in lieu of court-martial

- Administrative discharge action continues if the service member is determined fit and returned for duty

Disability Evaluation Referral when UOTHC Characterization is Authorized

- DAF service members are ineligible for referral for disability evaluation process when pending separation under provisions that authorize a characterization of UOTHC **EXCEPT:**

  -- When referral is warranted as a matter of equity or good conscience

    --- Where there is a clear connection between a member's medical diagnosis and conduct. AFPC/DP2NP or ARC/SG will make a factual determination regarding this connection and make a recommendation to the dual action referral authority.

    --- When the member has been diagnosed with post-traumatic stress disorder (PTSD) and/or traumatic brain injury (TBI) based on deployed service to a contingency operation or based on a sexual assault that occurred during the previous 25 months, and the effects of the PTSD/TBI relate to the basis for administrative separation

Dual Action Authorities

- Dual Action Referral Authority (only if UOTHC characterization authorized):

  -- General Court-Martial Convening Authority (GCMCA) for enlisted members with less than 16 years

  -- AFPC/DP2NP or ARC/SG for officers and enlisted members with more than 16 years

- Dual Action Decision Authority:

  -- SAFPC for enlisted members where UOTHC characterization is not authorized

  -- GCMCA for enlisted members with less than 16 years where UOTHC is authorized and where dual action processing was approved

  -- SAFPC for enlisted with more than 16 years where UOTHC is authorized and where dual action processing was approved

  -- Secretary of the Air Force (SecAF) (or delegee) for officers

Dual Action Eligibility for Retirement

- Dual action processing is also required when a DAF member subject to discharge is also eligible to apply for retirement (20 years or more active service). Members qualified for retirement may be permitted to retire in lieu of involuntary separation. Members who are retirement-eligible must be notified at the time of the initiation of discharge for the chance to apply for retirement.

References

· DAFI 36-3211, *Military Separations* (24 June 2022), incorporating Change 1, 20 November 2023
· DAFI 36-3212, *Physical Evaluation for Retention, Retirement, and Separation* (22 February 2024)

PROCEDURE TO INVOLUNTARILY SEPARATE ENLISTED MEMBERS

Enlisted Department of the Air Force (DAF) members may be involuntarily separated through two different processes: (1) notification procedures (applicable to E-4 and below with less than six years of service), and (2) board hearing procedures (applicable to E-5 and above, members with six or more years of service, or in any case when the commander is pursuing an Under Other Than Honorable Conditions (UOTHC) service characterization). Most cases are processed using notification procedures. Administrative separation of active duty DAF enlisted members is governed by DAFI 36-3211, *Military Separations*. Involuntary separation of members of the Air National Guard (ANG) and Air Force Reserve is also governed by DAFI 36-3211.

Key Takeaways

- » Members in the grade of E-4 or below and/or with less than 6 years of total active federal military service (TAFMS) will be subject to the notification discharge procedure

- » Members in the grade of E-5 with more than 6 years of TAFMS will be eligible for the board hearing procedures

- » Members whose cases are recommended for an Under Other Than Honorable Conditions (UOTHC) service characterization will be eligible for board hearing procedures

- » Members who have been victims of sexual assault or who have been diagnosed with post traumatic stress disorder (PTSD) or traumatic brain injury (TBI) may be eligible for special processing

- » Members who have between 16 and 20 years of TAFMS are eligible for Lengthy Service Processing

- » Members who have 20 or more years of TAFMS are eligible for Retirement in Lieu of Discharge Processing

---

Preprocessing Procedures

- The type of discharge processing a member is entitled to depends upon the rank of the member, the member's years of service, and the characterization of service pursued by the commander concerned

- Medical Examination: Before the member may be discharged, a comprehensive Separation Health and Physical Examination (SHPE) is required. The medical examination must document:

  -- Any medical aspects pertaining to the reason for discharge; **AND**

  -- That the member is or is not medically qualified for worldwide service and separation.

- Special Processing – Victims of Sexual Assault:

  -- DAF service members who made an unrestricted report of sexual assault and who are within one year of final disposition of their sexual assault allegation may request a general officer to review the circumstances of and grounds for any recommendation of their involuntary separation from the DAF

    --- The general officer review is conducted by the General Court-Martial Convening Authority (GCMCA) or, if the GCMCA is not a general officer, the first general officer in the member's chain of command

    --- An enlisted member entitled to GCMCA review must be notified of this right in the separation notification memorandum

    --- The member must submit his/her request for GCMCA review in writing. In this request, the member must affirmatively assert that he/she believes the pending discharge action was initiated in retaliation for making a report of sexual assault.

    --- A member who submits a timely request to the GCMCA may not be separated until the GCMCA conducting the review concurs with the circumstances of and grounds for the involuntary separation

- Special Processing – Post-Traumatic Stress Disorder or Traumatic Brain Injury:

  -- All enlisted DAF service members being recommended for involuntary separation who have deployed overseas in support of a contingency operation or were sexually assaulted during the previous 24 months and have been diagnosed with or reasonably assert post-traumatic stress disorder (PTSD) or traumatic brain injury (TBI) must receive a medical examination. The medical examination must assess whether the effects of PTSD or TBI constitute matters in extenuation that relate to the basis for involuntary administrative separation. The medical examination is required if the member:

    --- Is being administratively separated under a characterization that is not either Honorable or Under Honorable Conditions (General);

    --- Was deployed overseas to a contingency operation or sexually assaulted during the previous 24 months;

    --- Has been diagnosed by a physician, clinical psychologist, psychiatrist, licensed clinical social worker, or psychiatric advanced practice registered nurse as experiencing PTSD or TBI, or reasonably alleges the influence of PTSD or TBI based on deployed service to a contingency operation or a sexual assault that occurred during the previous 24 months; **AND**

    --- Is not being separated under a sentence of court-martial, or other proceeding conducted pursuant to the Uniform Code of Military Justice (UCMJ).

-- Members diagnosed with or reasonably asserting PTSD or TBI will not be separated until the result of the medical examination has been reviewed by appropriate authorities responsible for evaluating, reviewing, and approving the separation action, to include (if applicable): the initiating commander, administrative discharge board, convening authorities, separation authority, Air Force Review Board, and/or the Secretary of the Air Force (SecAF)

- Completion of Enlisted Performance Report (EPR)/Letter of Evaluation (LOE): Refer to DAFI 36-2406, *Officer and Enlisted Evaluations System* for specific criteria on whether an EPR or LOE in connection with involuntary separation is needed

Notification Procedures

- If there is sufficient documentation and evidence supporting a basis for discharge, the commander serves a notification memorandum on the member. A sample of the notification memoranda is located in Figure 8.1 and 8.2 of DAFI 36-3211.

- After receiving the notification memorandum, the member has three duty days to prepare a response (see DAFI 36-3211, Figure 8.3)

- The commander considers the member's response, if any. If the commander still recommends discharge, the commander signs a recommendation for discharge to the Special Court-Martial Convening Authority (SPCMCA), who is usually the wing commander (see DAFI 36-3211, Figure 8.4).

- The servicing Staff Judge Advocate (SJA) prepares a legal review of the package

- SPCMCA reviews the package and the SJA's legal review

-- If the SPCMCA is also the separation authority, the SPCMCA determines:

--- If there is a basis for discharge;

--- If the member should be discharged;

--- If the member should be discharged, how to characterize the member's service; **AND**

--- If the member should be discharged, whether to offer Probation & Rehabilitation (P&R), if available.

-- If the SPCMCA is not the separation authority, the SPCMCA will forward the package to the GCMCA, who is usually the Numbered Air Force commander, with a recommendation concerning the above four questions

Board Entitlement

- A member recommended for discharge must be offered a hearing by an administrative discharge board if one of the following applies:

  -- The member is a Noncommissioned Officer at the time discharge processing starts (not applicable to ANG members)

  -- The member has six years or more total active and inactive service, including delayed enlistment time, at the time discharge processing starts

  -- The commander recommends a UOTHC characterization

  -- Discharge in the interest of national security is recommended. Ensure appropriate clearance to proceed.

Board Hearing Procedures

- After receiving the notification memorandum (see DAFI 36-3211, Figure 8.5), the member has seven duty days to:

  -- Request a board hearing or unconditionally waive his/her right to a board hearing (see DAFI 36-3211, Figure 8.6); or

  -- Waive the board hearing contingent upon receiving a specific type of discharge, which is called a conditional waiver (see DAFI 36-3211, Figure 8.7).

- The commander considers the member's response, if any. If the commander still recommends discharge, he/she signs a recommendation for discharge to the SPCMCA (see DAFI 36-3211, Figure 8.4).

- In cases where the member requests a board hearing, the SPCMCA reviews the recommendation for discharge and either sends the file back to the unit for further action (normally to withdraw the action or reinitiate the action using different grounds or evidence) or convenes a discharge board

- The administrative board convenes, considers all the evidence, and makes:

  -- A separate finding of fact on each allegation set out in the notification memorandum. The board's finding of fact will determine whether a basis for discharge exists.

  -- A recommendation to discharge or retain the member

  -- A recommended characterization of service if the board recommends discharge

  -- A recommendation concerning P&R (if member is eligible) if the board recommends discharge

  -- The servicing SJA prepares a legal review of the package and forwards the package to the SPCMCA

- The SPCMCA takes final action if referral to the GCMCA is not required or forwards the package to the GCMCA if referral to the GCMCA is required

- Lengthy Service Consideration: Members with more than 16 but less than 20 years of service are entitled to special probation consideration upon request and may not be separated before forwarding to the Air Force Personnel Center (AFPC) for review and processing. The final decision on a member's Lengthy Service package will be made at the SecAF level after an independent review by the Air Force Personnel Board.

- Retirement in Lieu of Discharge: Members with more than 20 years of service are entitled to request to retire in lieu of an involuntary separation. If a member requests this review, he/she may not be separated before the package is forwarded to AFPC for review and processing. The final decision on a member's retirement in lieu of package will be made at the SecAF level after an independent review by the Air Force Personnel Board.

References

· Members Diagnosed With or Reasonably Asserting Post-Traumatic Stress Disorder or Traumatic Brain Injury: Medical Examination Required Before Administrative Separation, 10 U.S.C. § 1177

· DAFI 36-2406, *Officer and Enlisted Evaluations System* (4 August 2023), including AFGM2024-01, 17 January 2024

· DAFI 36-3211, *Military Separations* (24 June 2022), incorporating Change 1, 20 November 2023

· DAFI 36-3212, *Physical Evaluation for Retention, Retirement, and Separation* (22 February 2024)

· DAFMAN 48-123, *Medical Examinations and Standards* (8 December 2020), including DAFGM2024-01, 20 February 2024

· DAFMAN 51-507, *Enlisted Discharge Boards and Boards of Officers* (27 July 2023)

PROBATION AND REHABILITATION FOR ENLISTED MEMBERS

The Department of the Air Force (DAF) program of probation and rehabilitation (P&R) allows the service to retain a trained resource while allowing enlisted members another opportunity to complete their service honorably. P&R is a conditional suspension of an approved administrative discharge for cause. In deserving cases, it allows a member to prove that he/she is able to meet DAF standards. Administrative separation of active duty DAF enlisted members is governed by DAFI 36-3211, *Military Separations*. Involuntary separation of members of the Air National Guard and Air Force Reserve is also governed by the provisions of DAFI 36-3211.

Key Takeaways

» The separation authority is also the approval authority for probation and rehabilitation (P&R)

» P&R is not available if the reason for discharge is Discharge in Lieu of Court-Martial, Fraudulent Enlistment, Entry Level Performance, certain Unprofessional Relationships, Drug Abuse, Sexual Assault or National Security

» The separation authority will set a specific period of rehabilitation between 6 and 12 months

» If a member fails to fulfill the requirements of P&R, P&R can be terminated after notice to the member and instructions to respond within seven days

P&R Considerations

- Only the separation authority can suspend the execution of a discharge for P&R

- Members who have completed at least 16 but less than 20 years of active service are entitled to special consideration upon their request and their cases are forwarded to the Air Force Personnel Center (AFPC) for review concerning probation

- P&R is appropriate for members:

  -- Who demonstrate a potential to serve satisfactorily

  -- Who have the capacity to be rehabilitated for continued military service or completion of the current enlistment

  -- Whose retention on a probationary status is consistent with the maintenance of good order and discipline

Eligibility Requirements

- Members are **NOT** eligible for P&R if the reason for discharge is one of the following:

  -- In lieu of trial by court-martial

  -- Fraudulent entry into the service

  -- Entry level performance or conduct

-- Unprofessional Relationships with Prospective Members of the Armed Forces or new members during Recruiting, Entry-Level Processing, Entry-Level Training, or Initial Skills Training

-- Drug abuse

-- Sexual assault

-- In the interest of national security

- Members must be considered for P&R if the reason for discharge is unsatisfactory performance or misconduct (except for reasons stated above)

-- The case file must show the initiating commander, board members if a hearing is involved, and separation authority considered P&R

-- If the initiating commander does not recommend P&R, he/she must give the reason for not recommending P&R

-- If the initiating commander recommended P&R and the separation authority disapproved that recommendation, the separation authority must state the reason for his/her decision

P&R Procedures

- Suspending the execution of an approved discharge is contingent on successful completion of rehabilitation

-- The separation authority sets a specific period of rehabilitation, which is not less than six months or not more than 12 months

-- The probationary period is usually served in the current unit of assignment, but reassignment to another local unit or within the major command may be authorized if warranted by the circumstances of the case

- If the decision is made to offer a member P&R, the immediate commander must:

-- Give the member information about the P&R program (DAFI 36-3211, Figures 9.1 and 9.2)

-- Counsel the member, emphasizing points listed in DAFI 36-3211, para. 9.7.2

-- Find out whether the member has enough retainability to complete P&R, and if not, try to get a voluntary request for extension of enlistment for the minimum time required

-- Require members who accept P&R to sign statements of understanding and acceptance of the terms of probation (DAFI 36-3211, Figure 9.3)

-- Ensure the terms of probation are set out in a letter from the separation authority and indorse the letter

-- Require members who refuse P&R or fail to satisfy the retention requirements to sign a statement acknowledging understanding of the rehabilitation privilege, giving the date the commander counseled the member, and acknowledging understanding of the effects of refusal to accept P&R (DAFI 36-3211, Figure 9.3)

What Happens During P&R

- The commander is the primary judge of the member's performance

    -- Commanders are not required to set up a special rehabilitation program because the member is expected to perform duties appropriate to his/her grade, skill level, and experience

    -- Promotion consideration is according to DAFI 36-2502, *Enlisted Airman Promotion/ Demotion Programs*

    -- Members are not selected for formal training while in P&R

    -- Reenlistment consideration is according to AFI 36-2606, *Reenlistment and Extension of Enlistment in the United States Air Force*

Completing P&R

- If a member successfully completes P&R:

    -- Approved discharge is automatically and permanently canceled on the date the suspension expires

    -- Separation at Expiration of Term of Service (ETS) will result in an Honorable service characterization

    -- Future failure to maintain standards may be the basis for new discharge proceedings

    -- Eligibility for reenlistment will be according to AFI 36-2606 and none of the reasons for recommending discharge that existed before P&R began may be used as a basis for denial of reenlistment

Other Command Options

- Commanders have other options during P&R, including:

    -- Canceling the probation in whole or in part where member's good conduct clearly shows goals of P&R have been met

    -- Extending the probationary period where member has made progress, but the commander is not sure rehabilitation is complete. The original probationary period and the extension together must not exceed one year, and the member must consent to the extension.

Terminating P&R

- If a decision is made to initiate vacation (termination) of the P&R, the commander notifies the member by a letter, which gives:

    -- The reason for the action

    -- The name, address, and phone number of military legal counsel (often the Area Defense Counsel)

    -- Instruction that the member may secure civilian counsel at his own expense

    -- Instruction to reply within seven workdays (rebuttal or waiver of right to rebut)

References

· DAFI 36-2502, *Enlisted Airman Promotion/Demotion Programs* (16 April 2021), including DAFGM2023-02, 20 December 2023

· DAFI 36-3211, *Military Separations* (24 June 2022), incorporating Change 1, 20 November 2023

· AFI 36-2606, *Reenlistment and Extension of Enlistment in the United States Air Force* (20 September 2019), incorporating Change 1, 27 January 2021

OFFICER SEPARATIONS

The process for officer separations is similar to enlisted discharges. However, certain key differences exist. Unlike enlisted separations, the Secretary of the Air Force (SecAF) is the approval authority for all "for cause" commissioned officer administrative discharges. The below discussion is applicable to active duty officers.

Key Takeaways

» Officer separations may be voluntary or involuntary; involuntary separations may be "For Cause" or "Not for Cause"

» If "Not for Cause," the least favorable service characterization is Under Honorable Conditions (General). If "For Cause," the least favorable service characterization is Under Other Than Honorable Conditions (UOTHC).

» SecAF or Designee action is required on all officer separations

» Special processing is required when separating officers who have filed an unrestricted report of sexual assault and some officers who are being discharged for personality or mental disorders

---

Definitions

- Non-probationary Officer:

    -- Regular officer on the Active Duty List with six or more years of active commissioned service as determined by the officer's Total Active Federal Commissioned Service Date (TAFCSD)

    -- Reserve officer with six or more years of commissioned service (inactive or active) as determined by the officer's Total Federal Commissioned Service Date (TFCSD)

- Probationary Officer:

    -- Regular officer on the Active Duty List who has completed less than six years of active commissioned service as determined by the officer's TAFCSD

    -- Reserve officer who has completed at least five years of commissioned service (inactive or active) as determined by the officer's TFCSD. Air National Guard officers do not have these distinctions and are all board-entitled pursuant to DAFI 36-3211, para. 20.2.6.

- The recommendation of a board of officers is generally required to involuntarily discharge a non-probationary reserve officer

Voluntary Separation

- Officers may apply for voluntary separation for a variety of reasons, including: completion of active duty service commitment (ADSC), hardship, pregnancy, conscientious objector status, Medal of Honor recipient, and other miscellaneous reasons

- Voluntary separations are subject to approval by SecAF. However, SecAF or designee, may disapprove applications for several reasons.

Involuntary Separations – "Not For Cause"

- Many involuntary separations are required by law (e.g., reserve officers who reach age limit, those non-selected for promotion, and officers who have reached maximum years of commissioned service or service in grade)

- Other involuntary separations include loss of ecclesiastical endorsement, failure to complete or pass medical training, nursing examinations, or nursing intern programs, and officers in health care fields who do not have required licenses

- Involuntary separations that are not for cause will normally be characterized as Honorable

Involuntary Separations – "For Cause"

- Officers may be discharged for cause for substandard performance of duty, misconduct, moral or professional dereliction, or in the interest of national security

- Officers who received education assistance, special pay, or bonus money may be subject to recoupment

- Substandard Performance of Duty:

  -- *Service Characterization:* Honorable or General (Under Honorable Conditions)

  -- *Basis:* Failure to acceptably discharge duties; failure in the Department of the Air Force (DAF) fitness program; failure to conform to prescribed standards of dress or personal appearance; inability to perform duties or meet military commitments because of family care responsibilities; drug abuse rehabilitation failure; alcohol abuse rehabilitation failure; fear of flying; mental disorders that interfere with the officer's performance of duty and do not fall within the purview of the medical disability process; failure to show acceptable qualities of leadership; failure to achieve acceptable standards of proficiency, efficiency, or effectiveness; failure to complete a course of instruction/training when participation is at government expense; substandard response to training; substandard attitude or character; unsatisfactory progress or failure in, or disenrollment from an active status skills-awarding education/training program; disqualification from Air Force Specialty Code (AFSC) or Space Force Specialty Code (SFSC)

  -- Support should include documented history of problems and efforts to correct the officer's conduct

- Misconduct, Moral or Professional Dereliction, or In the Interest of National Security:

  -- *Service Characterization:* Honorable, General, or UOTHC

  -- *Basis:* Serious or recurring misconduct punishable by military/civilian authorities; foreign court convictions; discreditable mismanagement of personal affairs; drug abuse; intentional misrepresentation/ omission of facts in obtaining an appointment or in official documents/records; culpable failure to perform assigned duties/complete required training; loss of professional status/qualifications/licensure/certifications necessary for performance of military duties; fraternization or unprofessional relationships; improper participation in political activities; failure to follow preventive medical procedures to prevent HIV transmission; acts of sexual perversion/ misconduct; sexual assault; fear of flying (rated officers); restriction of duties based on asserted moral reasons; retention inconsistent with national security; attempting to avoid deployed/hardship duty; extended confinement; unprofessional relationships with prospective/new members during recruiting/entry-level processing/entry-level training/initial skills training

Discharge Procedures

- Unit commander evaluates the information and consults with the servicing legal office

- If appropriate, the unit commander recommends discharge to the Show Cause Authority (SCA), who is usually a general officer wing commander or General Court-Martial Convening Authority (GCMCA) (e.g., Numbered Air Force commander)

- If appropriate, the SCA initiates discharge action by signing a letter to the officer notifying him/her of the discharge action

- Within 10 calendar days of receipt of the letter of notification, the officer submits evidence in response, applies for voluntary retirement (if eligible), tenders a resignation, or requests a delay to respond

- If the SCA determines no action is warranted, the action is terminated. If the SCA determines discharge action is warranted, the type of processing that occurs depends on the officer's status and the characterization recommended.

  -- Not Board Entitled: If the officer is probationary and the case does not involve a recommendation for a UOTHC service characterization, the SCA notifies the officer that the case will be reviewed by the Air Force Personnel Board (AFPB). The officer is not entitled to appear in front of or present witness testimony to the AFPB.

  -- Board Entitled: If the officer is non-probationary, or the officer is probationary and a UOTHC discharge is recommended, then the SCA notifies the officer that the officer will be required to show cause for retention before a Board of Inquiry (BOI). The officer is entitled to appear in front of and present witness testimony to the BOI.

-- <u>Air National Guard (ANG) Officer Board Entitlement</u>: ANG officers not on active duty are discharged through the withdrawal of Federal recognition process in 32 U.S.C. § 323. Withdrawal of Federal recognition pursuant to 32 U.S.C. § 323(b) automatically results in discharge from a reserve of the Air Force appointment. An ANG probationary officer category is not established by 32 U.S.C. § 323(b). All ANG officers have a board entitlement for withdrawal of Federal recognition under 32 U.S.C. § 323(b).

- SecAF (or delegee) is the final approval authority for commissioned officer separations under DAFI 36-3211

Resignations in Lieu of Further Administrative Discharge Proceedings

- When the SCA notifies an officer to show cause for retention, an officer may submit a resignation or a resignation to enlist and retire (if eligible to apply for retirement in enlisted status)

- These options should not be confused with resignations for the good of the service, which an officer may submit when facing a court-martial for alleged criminal conduct

- SecAF (or delegee) is the approval authority

Special Processing Procedures

- Special processing is required for officers who have made an unrestricted report of a sexual assault

- Special processing is required for officers being discharged for personality disorder or other mental disorder not constituting a physical disability when that officer has served or is currently serving in an imminent danger pay area; or when a member has filed an unrestricted report of sexual assault; or who has self-disclosed that they are a victim of a sex-related offense, an intimate partner violence-related offense, or a spousal abuse offense during service

References

· Withdrawal of Federal Recognition, 32 U.S.C. § 323
· DoDI 1332.30, *Commissioned Officer Administrative Separations* (11 May 2018), incorporating through Change 3, 9 September 2021
· DAFI 36-3211, *Military Separations* (24 June 2022), incorporating Change 1, 20 November 2023
· DAFI 36-3212, *Physical Evaluation for Retention, Retirement and Separation* (22 February 2024)
· DAFMAN 48-123, *Medical Examinations and Standards* (8 December 2020), including DAFGM2024-01, 20 February 2024
· DAFMAN 51-507, *Enlisted Discharge Boards and Boards of Officers* (27 July 2023)

ADMINISTRATIVE SEPARATION OF AIR FORCE RESERVE AND AIR NATIONAL GUARD MEMBERS

DAFI 36-3211, *Military Separations*, applies to total force members, officers and enlisted, unless otherwise noted. However, Chapter 13 (Enlisted) and Chapter 23 (Officer) focus on Air Reserve Component (ARC) specific bases, processing, procedure, and authorities.

Key Takeaways

» Processing requirements vary depending on a member's status—Category A (CAT A); Category B (CAT B); or Air National Guard (ANG)

» Consult servicing Staff Judge Advocate (SJA) PRIOR to initiating involuntary discharge—basis for discharge and legal sufficiency are critical to processing without undue delay

» Secretary of the Air Force (SecAF) action is required for **ALL** discharges characterized as Under Other than Honorable Conditions (UOTHC)

» Air Force Reserve Command (AFRC), Numbered Air Forces (NAFs), and Air Reserve Personnel Center (ARPC) can convene discharge boards; Wings are empowered to hold them

» Involuntary discharges for officers must be initiated by the Show Cause Authority (SCA); final decision is made at the SecAF level after an independent review by the Air Force Personnel Board (AFPB)

CAT A (Reserve Unit)

- Consult with servicing legal office prior to initiating involuntary discharge action

    -- For enlisted members, the squadron commander initiates discharge action in most cases. The recommendation is processed through the servicing legal office to the wing commander or equivalent. The owning Military Personnel Flight (MPF) processes the case through completion to the separation authority.

    -- For officer members, the Show Cause Authority (SCA) initiates discharge action. The final approval authority for involuntary separations for officers is SecAF after independent review by the AFPB.

        --- Enlisted members are notified of discharge action by a Memorandum of Notification (MON), and officer members are notified of discharge action by a Show Cause Notification Memorandum (SCNM). Each contains a description of the reason(s) upon which action is based including identification of paragraphs in DAFI 36-3211 covering each reason; the least favorable type of service characterization authorized; a recoupment statement supporting documentation; and an explanation of Respondent's rights. MON's are discussed in Chapter 8 and sample MONs are found at Attachment 10 (not board entitled) and Attachment 12 (board entitled). See Chapter 23 for information on the SCNM.

- In-person service of the MON (enlisted) or SCNM (officer) is preferred; however, if Respondent is not served in person, the notification should be sent via registered or certified mail, return receipt requested, or by first-class mail when the return receipt method is unsuccessful, to the member's address listed in the Military Personnel Data System (MilPDS)

- If notification attempts are not successful, determine whether there is another address available. Delivery to a known email address via Department of Defense (DoD) Secure Access File Exchange (SAFE) is also a good option since delivery and download can be confirmed. All attempts to serve the notification via mail should be documented and kept in the case file (see DAFI 36-3211, paragraphs 8.9.4 and 23.5 for more information regarding delivery options of the notification to ARC members).

- Enlisted members will be provided 30 calendar days to acknowledge receipt, and make elections of rights, and submit statements on their own behalf (see DAFI 36-3211, Attachments 11 or 13). Officer members shall sign and return acknowledgement of receipt within 24 hours and shall have 15 calendar days to return all other elections or request an extension of time.

- If enlisted member is not board entitled, not eligible for lengthy service consideration, and not retirement eligible, forward the entire discharge package through the servicing legal office to the discharge authority

- For enlisted members who are board entitled, have lengthy service consideration or are retirement eligible, forward entire discharge package including matters submitted by the member through command channels to the discharge authority to convene the Board (see Chapter 13, para. 13.1.1)

- AFRC and NAFs can convene discharge boards for Reserve personnel; Wings are empowered to hold discharge boards. Coordinate with AFRC/JA to determine most feasible location (see Chapter 13, para. 13.1.1).

- Additional considerations:

  -- Consider placing the member in "No Pay, No Points" status while a discharge action is pending if the commander does not want the member to continue participating

  -- Officer's may submit a tender of resignation (TOR) or if eligible, apply for transfer to the Retired Reserve, at any time before the SecAF announces the decision in the officer's case (see Attachment 20 for a sample resignation memo)

  -- A drop from the rolls of the U.S. Air Force or U.S. Space Force action may be warranted where a member (officer or enlisted) has received a civilian conviction that includes a sentence to confinement in a Federal or state penitentiary, or correctional institution. Consult your servicing legal office or AFRC/JA. SecAF approval is required.

  -- See Table 13.1 for rules on voluntary and involuntary discharge or separation for enlisted members. See Attachment 19 for rules on separation or discharge of officers. Also see AFRC/CC Delegation of Authority Memorandum for AFR members.

-- Conduct in the civilian community of a member not on active duty or active duty for training may form the basis for a UOTHC only if such conduct directly affects the performance of their military duties, and General only if such conduct has an adverse impact on the overall effectiveness of the service, including morale and efficiency (see Chapter 3, para. 3.14.1.3.7)

- Many of the requirements and procedures outlined above for CAT A Reservists likewise applies to ANG members and are also outlined in Chapter 13 and Chapter 23

- Members may be subject to recoupment for benefits or bonuses (see Attachment 18 for a sample recoupment statement)

CAT B Individual Mobilization Augmentees (IMAs)

- Discharges of IMAs are processed through the Headquarters Readiness and Integration Organization (HQ RIO)

  -- HQ RIO and its seven detachments share administrative control (ADCON) of an IMA with the IMA's active duty unit

  -- The RIO detachment commander to which an IMA is assigned, initiates the discharge process in coordination with HQ RIO and ARPC's legal office (ARPC/JA)

  -- An IMA's active duty unit commander should coordinate with the RIO detachment commander to discuss the IMA's case, gather evidence, and recommend discharge

  -- ARPC/JA reviews the case file for legal sufficiency. If legally sufficient, ARPC/JA then develops the notification package and obtains a required recommendation memorandum.

- HQ ARPC/CC is the SCA (Show Cause Authority) for officer members and the Discharge Authority for enlisted members

- HQ ARPC/CC convenes Boards of Inquiry (BOI) and discharge boards in coordination with the wing legal office that supports the IMA's unit of assignment

- For notification only IMA discharge cases, HQ ARPC/CC makes a recommendation to the SecAF-level decision authority through the Secretary of the Air Force Personnel Council (SAFPC) regarding discharge for officers and enlisted with lengthy service considerations

- For enlisted members without lengthy service considerations, HQ ARPC/CC makes the final discharge decision. However, recommendations for UOTHC service characterizations for enlisted members require forwarding to the AFPB for an independent review before SecAF-level decision.

Individual Ready Reserve (IRR)

- Members in certain specialty programs (e.g., Health Professions Scholarship Program (HPSP) and Reserve Officer Training Corps (ROTC) graduates) maintain status in the IRR pending entry onto active duty (EAD). Discharge actions for such members are processed by ARPC/JA.

- HQ ARPC/CC is the Discharge Authority to either separate or recommend to SecAF-level decision authority the separation of members of the IRR

- For cases involving potential recoupment of educational assistance or other aid, the AFPB makes a recommendation to the approval authority on discharge and whether recoupment is appropriate

Board Entitlement

- Enlisted: Recommended characterization of service is UOTHC; member is a Noncommissioned Officer; or member has six or more years of satisfactory service for retirement

- Officer: All non-probationary officers (completed six or more years of service as a commissioned officer in any of the armed forces as determined from the Total Federal Commissioned Service Date); or recommended characterization of service is UOTHC

- ANG Board Entitlement: Per DAFI 36-3211, para 8.2.2.1, the right to an administrative discharge board for Noncommissioned Officers does not apply to ANG. ANG members are only entitled to an administrative discharge board if one of the other criteria under para 8.2.2 apply. All ANG officers are board entitled (see para. 20.2.6).

References

· Reserve Officers: Limitation on Involuntary Separation, 10 U.S.C. § 12683

· DoDI 1332.14, *Enlisted Administrative Separations* (27 January 2014), incorporating through Change 7, 23 June 2022

· DoDI 1332.30, *Commissioned Officer Administrative Separations* (11 May 2018), incorporating through Change 3, 9 September 2021

· DAFI 36-3211, *Military Separations* (24 June 2022), incorporating Change 1, 20 November 2023

· DAFMAN 51-507, *Enlisted Discharge Boards and Boards of Officers* (27 July 2023)

· Delegations of AFRC/CC Authority Memorandum (28 September 2021, or current version)

Chapter 5
CRIMINAL AND MILITARY JUSTICE

INSTALLATION JURISDICTION

Installation jurisdiction refers to the type of legal authority exercised by the Department of the Air Force (DAF) over an installation. There are four main types of jurisdiction: (1) exclusive federal jurisdiction; (2) concurrent jurisdiction; (3) partial jurisdiction; and (4) proprietary jurisdiction. Depending on your installation, more than one type of jurisdiction may apply.

Key Takeaways

» Title and jurisdiction are separate concepts. In most cases, the DAF has title (legal ownership) of the land where installations reside. In a few cases, the land is leased.

» Exclusive jurisdiction means that the federal government has sole authority to enforce its laws to the exclusion of state law. As a general rule, the federal government does not want this status.

» Concurrent jurisdiction means that both the federal and state government may exercise authority over the real property in question. This is the most desirable situation.

» Proprietary jurisdiction means that the state exercises legislative authority over the land where the installation resides, and the federal government is just a tenant

Title

- Title, in relation to a military installation, is virtually the same as in a private real estate transaction. Title simply means legal ownership—the legal right to the use and possession of a designated piece of property.

- In most cases, the DAF has title to the properties on which its installations are located. However, some installations are on leased property or have portions of the base on leased property.

- The installation's civil engineer (CE) squadron maintains the deed or lease to the installation. Questions concerning title to the installation's real property should be referred to the servicing Staff Judge Advocate (SJA).

Jurisdiction

- The concept of jurisdiction is separate and distinct from that of title

- Jurisdiction includes the right to legislate (i.e., implement laws, rules, and regulations) and enforce those laws. Having title does not necessarily include legislative jurisdiction.

Sources of Legislative Jurisdiction

- Article I, Section 8, Clause 17, of the United States Constitution confers upon Congress the power to exercise legislative jurisdiction over federal property. The government can acquire the right to exercise legislative jurisdiction in three ways.

-- Purchase and Consent: The federal government purchases the property, and the state legislature consents to giving the federal government jurisdiction

-- Cession: After the federal government acquires title to property, the state may cede jurisdiction, in whole or in part, to the federal government. The federal government can later relinquish jurisdiction back to the state. 10 U.S.C. § 2683. Prior to 1940, it was presumed that jurisdiction was accepted whenever offered by the state as it was deemed a benefit. Since 1940, however, there must be an affirmative acceptance of jurisdiction before the federal government will have legislative jurisdiction. 40 U.S.C. § 3112. Check the deed to determine when the federal government acquired the property.

-- Reservation: At the time the federal government ceded property to establish a state, particularly in the western United States, it reserved some of the land as federal property. In these cases, the federal government retained legislative jurisdiction over the property. Again, check the deed.

Types of Legislative Jurisdiction

- The inquiry does not stop with determining if the federal government has legislative jurisdiction. It is also necessary to determine what type of jurisdiction it has. There are four types of legislative jurisdiction.

-- Exclusive Federal Jurisdiction: As the term implies, the federal government possesses, regardless of the method acquired, all of the authority of the state and that state has not reserved the right to exercise any authority concurrently with the federal government except the right to serve civil or criminal process. For some years now, it has been federal policy not to acquire exclusive federal jurisdiction. While at first blush this may seem odd, there are legitimate reasons for the policy. For instance, state and local authorities may be better able to deal with particular situations (e.g., child welfare services, domestic relations matters) than the federal government.

-- Concurrent Jurisdiction: Both the state and federal governments possess legislative authority. In other words, the state grants the federal government legislative jurisdiction over an area but reserved to itself the right to exercise the same authority at the same time. In the event of conflict, the federal government prevails under the Supremacy Clause of the Constitution.

-- Partial Jurisdiction: Both the state and federal government have some legislative authority, but neither one has absolute power. For instance, the state may have reserved the authority to impose and collect taxes, or it may have ceded only criminal jurisdiction over the property. Again, federal supremacy applies in the event of a conflict.

-- <u>Proprietary Jurisdiction</u>: In this case, the federal government has acquired some right or title to an area in a state but has not obtained any of the state's authority to legislate over the area. The United States is simply a tenant with no legislative authority. The federal government maintains immunity and supremacy for inherently governmental functions. The only federal laws that apply are those that do not rely upon federal jurisdiction (e.g., espionage, bank robbery, tax fraud, counterfeiting). However, the installation commander can still exclude civilians from the area pursuant to the commander's inherent authority.

References

· U.S. Const. Art. I, § 8, cl. 17
· U.S. Const. Art. VI, cl. 2
· Relinquishment of Legislative Jurisdiction; minimum drinking age on military installations, 10 U.S.C. § 2683
· Federal Jurisdiction, 40 U.S.C. § 3112
· *Greer v. Spock*, 424 U.S. 828 (1976)
· AFI 32-9001, *Acquisition of Real Property* (28 September 2017)
· AFI 32-9002, *Management of Real Property* (18 December 2020)

FEDERAL MAGISTRATE PROGRAM

The federal magistrate program provides a means of enforcing federal law on base, including civilian criminal misconduct. The availability of the program depends on the location and jurisdiction of the base, the type and location of the offense, and the status of the offender.

Key Takeaways

» Federal magistrate court is used to prosecute civilians who commit misdemeanors or petty offenses on federal property, such as military bases, with exclusive or concurrent legislative jurisdiction

» Crimes enforced through the federal magistrate program may include certain state crimes, such as vehicular or traffic laws

» Federal magistrate court is not used to prosecute military members or those who commit offenses while in a Title 10 status

» Civilian employees and civilian dependents are subject to prosecution in federal magistrate court for violations of applicable law if they occur on a military base with exclusive or concurrent legislative jurisdiction

Overview of Federal Magistrate's Court

- Federal magistrate court is a forum used to adjudicate crimes involving certain federal offenses committed on federal property. Magistrate court generally provides a more expeditious and cost-effective forum than federal district court.

- Federal magistrate court is only used to prosecute civilians; it is not used to prosecute Regular Air Force members or others who commit offenses in a federal active duty (Title 10) status. Civilian employees and civilian dependents are subject to prosecution in federal magistrate court for violations of applicable law if they occur on a military base with exclusive or concurrent legislative jurisdiction.

- Typically, offenses tried in federal magistrate court are misdemeanors, which are offenses for which the authorized penalty does not exceed one year of imprisonment

- Common offenses tried in magistrate court include traffic violations, trespassing, theft, and possession of drug paraphernalia. More serious criminal misconduct by civilians that occurs on a federal installation can be referred to the United States Attorney's Office, or, depending on jurisdiction, to state or local prosecutors.

- Only certain bases have a federal magistrate court program. To find out if your base has such a program, consult with the servicing legal office.

Role of Installation Personnel in Magistrate's Court

- Where an installation magistrate court program is established, the installation Staff Judge Advocate (SJA) should execute a Memorandum of Understanding (MOU) with the U.S. Attorney covering responsibilities and procedures for trials in federal magistrate court

- Department of the Air Force (DAF) judge advocates, when appointed by the Attorney General to act as Special Assistant U.S. Attorneys (SAUSAs), may represent the United States in federal magistrate court

Jurisdiction of Federal Magistrate's Court

- Criminal actions committed by civilians on a military installation may be handled in federal court or state court, depending upon the jurisdictional status of the installation and whether the alleged crime violated state or federal law

- Federal Statutes without Territorial Jurisdiction Requirements: Prosecuted in federal court regardless of the installation's jurisdictional status (e.g., counterfeiting, espionage, sabotage, bribery of federal officers)

- Federal Statutes with Territorial Jurisdiction Requirements: May be prosecuted in federal court if the installation where the crime occurs has exclusive or concurrent legislative jurisdiction

  -- If the federal government has only proprietary jurisdiction, federal statutes that rely on territorial jurisdiction may not be enforced in federal court. Such offenses may be prosecuted only in state court.

  -- If the federal government has exclusive jurisdiction, generally, offenses committed on an installation may not be prosecuted in state court

- State Statutes: On installations within the United States where the federal government has concurrent jurisdiction with the state, generally, state criminal law will be prosecuted in state court. However, violations of state law may be prosecuted in federal court under the Assimilative Crimes Act, 18 U.S.C. § 13.

  -- The Assimilative Crimes Act makes violating a state statute on an installation with exclusive jurisdiction a federal offense. This is available where the conduct does not otherwise violate a federal statute.

- State criminal traffic laws are expressly adopted and made applicable on military installations having concurrent or exclusive federal jurisdiction under the provisions of 18 U.S.C. § 13. In those states where violations of traffic laws are not considered criminal offenses and cannot be assimilated, DoDD 5525.4, *Enforcement of State Traffic Laws on DoD Installations*, adopts the vehicular and pedestrian traffic laws of such states and makes these laws applicable to military installations having concurrent or exclusive legislative jurisdiction.

References

· Assimilative Crimes Act, 18 U.S.C. § 13

· Installation Traffic Codes, 32 C.F.R. § 634.25

· DoDD 5525.4, *Enforcement of the State Traffic Laws on DoD Installations* (2 November 1981), incorporating through Change 3, 30 September 2020

· DAFI 36-147, *Civilian Conduct and Responsibility* (11 January 2023)

· AFI 51-206, *Use of Magistrate Judges for Trial of Misdemeanors Committed by Civilians* (31 August 2018)

COURTS-MARTIAL JURISDICTION UNDER THE UNIFORM CODE OF MILITARY JUSTICE

The Uniform Code of Military Justice (UCMJ) applies at all times and in all places to active duty military members, as well as to members of the Air Force Reserve and the Air National Guard (ANG) in federal active duty "Title 10" or "inactive duty (IDT)" status. Courts-martial jurisdiction rests upon two primary considerations: (1) commission of an offense under the UCMJ; and (2) military status of the person who committed the offense at the time the offense was committed.

Key Takeaways

» Courts-martial have exclusive power to hear "purely military offenses." Crimes that violate both the UCMJ and local criminal law may be tried by a court-martial, a civilian court, or both.

» Article 3(a), UCMJ, authorizes courts-martial jurisdiction in all cases in which the service member was subject to the UCMJ at the time of the offense and is subject to the UCMJ at the time of trial. Article 2, UCMJ, lists classes of persons who are subject to the UCMJ.

» Under certain circumstances, jurisdiction extends to members of the Air Force Reserve, Air National Guard, and Retirees

» A valid discharge from military service ends jurisdiction. A valid discharge requires receipt of a discharge certificate, a final accounting of pay, and completion of clearing processes.

Types of Jurisdiction

- <u>Military Offenses</u>: Courts-martial have exclusive power to hear "purely military offenses"

- <u>Other Offenses</u>: Crimes that violate both the UCMJ and local criminal law may be tried by a court-martial, a civilian court, or both

  -- Double Jeopardy for court-martial and civilian court prosecution of same misconduct

    --- A military member may **NOT** be tried for the same misconduct by both a court-martial and another federal court because doing so would constitute "double jeopardy"

    --- A military member **MAY** be tried for the same misconduct by both a court-martial and state or foreign court. However, as a matter of policy, if a military member was tried by a state court and jeopardy attached, regardless of the outcome, approval of the Secretary of the Air Force (SecAF) is required before proceeding with a court-martial.

  -- Host nation treaties and status of forces agreements (SOFAs) govern the exercise of jurisdiction over military members overseas for violations of foreign civilian law

Jurisdiction Over the Offense

- Courts-martial may try any offense under the UCMJ, and, in general courts-martial, the law of war

Jurisdiction Over the Person

- Article 3(a), UCMJ, authorizes courts-martial jurisdiction in all cases in which the service member was subject to the UCMJ at the time of the offense and is subject to the UCMJ at the time of trial. Article 2, UCMJ, lists classes of persons who are subject to the UCMJ.

Air Force Reserve

- Articles 2(a)(1) and 2(a)(3), UCMJ, extend courts-martial jurisdiction over reservists whenever they are in Title 10 status (i.e., inactive duty training (IDT), active duty (AD), or annual tour (AT))

- Article 2(d), UCMJ, authorizes a member of the Reserve to be ordered to active duty for nonjudicial punishment (NJP), an Article 32 preliminary hearing, or trial by court-martial

  -- When determining whether a commander has UCMJ jurisdiction over the member, the commander must determine the: (1) military status of the service member at time of the offense and; (2) military status of the service member at the time of court-martial

Air National Guard

- A member of the ANG is subject to UCMJ courts-martial jurisdiction only when in federal service

  -- ANG members are only subject to UCMJ courts-martial jurisdiction when they are in a federal duty status, often referred to as "Title 10" status

  -- When ANG members are performing state duty (state active duty or Title 32), they are subject to their state's code of military justice

  -- To ensure jurisdiction over the person, it is very important to coordinate with the local Staff Judge Advocate (SJA) when addressing ANG military justice matters

Retirees

- Courts-martial jurisdiction continues over retired Regular Air Force and Space Force personnel entitled to military pay

- Retired members should not be courts-martialed unless their conduct clearly links them with the military or is adverse to a significant military interest of the United States

- Commanders may not prefer charges against retired members without SecAF approval unless the statute of limitations is about to run out. The SJA will coordinate approval, as needed, to recall a retired member for court-martial.

Termination of Jurisdiction

- <u>General Rule</u>: A valid discharge from military service terminates jurisdiction. For a valid discharge to exist, there must be:

  -- Receipt of a valid discharge certificate;

  -- A final accounting of pay; and

  -- Completion of the clearing processes required by appropriate service instructions.

- <u>Exceptions</u>:

  -- A fraudulently obtained discharge does not terminate military jurisdiction

  -- A DAF reserve member is not, by virtue of the termination of a period of active duty or inactive duty training, "shielded" from jurisdiction for an offense committed during such period of active duty or inactive duty training

Statute of Limitations

- <u>Nonjudicial Punishment (NJP)</u>: Imposition of NJP within two years of offense

- <u>Court-Martial</u>: Preferral of charges within five years of offense

- <u>Exception</u>: There is no statute of limitation for a person charged with absence without leave or missing movement in time of war, murder, rape, sexual assault occurring on or after 26 December 2013, rape or sexual assault of a child, or any offense punishable by death

References

· U.S. Const. Amend. V

· Reserve Components Generally, 10 U.S.C. § 12301

· Army and Air National Guard of the United States: Status, 10 U.S.C. § 12401

· Articles 2, 3, and 43, Uniform Code of Military Justice

· Rules for Courts-Martial 201–204 (2024)

· *Solorio v. United States*, 483 U.S. 435 (1987)

· National Defense Authorization Act for Fiscal Year 2014, Pub. L. 113-66 (2013)

· DAFI 36-3211, *Military Separations* (24 June 2022), incorporating Change 1, 20 November 2023

· DAFI 51-201, *Administration of Military Justice* (24 January 2024)

THE OFFICE OF SPECIAL TRIAL COUNSEL

The Office of Special Trial Counsel (OSTC) is an independent prosecutorial organization for the Department of the Air Force with exclusive disposition authority over certain covered offenses committed by Airmen and Guardians. Special Trial Counsel (STC) assigned to OSTC provide expert, independent, and ethical representation of the United States, under the direct civilian control of the Secretary of the Air Force, in the investigation and trial-level litigation of offenses over which the office exercises authority.

Key Takeaways

» Congress enacted sweeping changes to military justice and command authority, creating an independent OSTC with authorities effective after 27 December 2023

» OSTC has exclusive authority to prefer, refer, defer, enter into plea agreements, withdraw, and dismiss 14 categories of "covered offenses"

» OSTC operations are integrated with law enforcement and installation legal offices in a unified investigative and prosecutorial effort that includes command input

» Commanders remain a critical stakeholder in military justice and are responsible for command climate and good order and discipline

» Installation Staff Judge Advocates remain the primary legal advisor to commanders and convening authorities at their respective installation

OSTC & the Military Justice System

- OSTC is an integrated and unified participant in the administration of military justice, partnering with commanders, law enforcement, and legal offices to ensure accountability for perpetrators of sexual assault, domestic violence, and other victim-based crimes

    -- OSTC leads a collaborative effort with law enforcement and the installation legal office to investigate and prosecute offenses under its authority. Installation judge advocates continue to serve as assistant trial counsel on covered offense courts-martial under the direction of assigned STC.

    -- Based upon statutory authority, OSTC has an important, but limited, role in the greater military justice system. While OSTC is responsible for the investigation and trial-level litigation of specified offenses listed below, installation legal office personnel remain the lead for all other military justice functions (e.g., post-trial processing, VWAP support, advising command, etc.).

Disposition Authority

- OSTC has initial disposition authority for 14 categories of "covered" UCMJ offenses, as well as known/related offenses. Command retains disposition authority for the remaining 91 categories of UCMJ offenses along with covered offenses and known/related offenses that OSTC defers back to command after exercising authority.

-- "Covered offenses" are specifically enumerated categories of UCMJ offenses established by Congress. OSTC must exercise its authority over covered offenses committed after 27 December 2023. Initial disposition authority is withheld to OSTC unless the offense is deferred to command. Covered offenses include:

- Article 117a – Wrongful Broadcast/Distribution of Intimate Visual Images
- Article 118 – Murder
- Article 119 – Manslaughter
- Article 119a – Death/Injury of Unborn Child
- Article 120 – Rape & Sexual Assault
- Article 120a – Mail: Deposit of Obscene Matters
- Article 120b – Rape & Sexual Assault of a Child
- Article 120c – Other Sexual Misconduct
- Article 125 – Kidnapping
- Article 128b – Domestic Violence
- Article 130 – Stalking
- Article 132 – Retaliation
- Article 134 – Child Pornography
- Article 134 – Sexual Harassment (Eff. 1 Jan 25)
- Inchoate offenses of any of the above offenses (attempt, solicitation, conspiracy)

-- "Known offenses" are any non-covered offense(s) alleged to have been committed by an individual accused of a covered offense. OSTC may exercise its authority over known offenses. If OSTC exercises authority over a known offense, initial disposition authority is withheld unless the offense is deferred. If OSTC does not exercise authority over the offense, disposition authority remains within command channels.

-- "Related offenses" are any non-covered offense(s) alleged to have been committed by a victim or witness to an alleged covered offense. OSTC may exercise its authority over related offenses. If OSTC exercises authority over a related offense, initial disposition authority is withheld unless the offense is deferred. If OSTC does not exercise authority over the offense, disposition authority remains within command channels.

- Commanders of accused and victims of offenses under OSTC authority may provide non-binding disposition input which OSTC must consider prior to making a disposition decision. Although the SJA remains the primary legal advisor to command, STC will be available to discuss disposition decisions.

Court-Martial Authority

- For all covered offenses, and for known/related offenses over which OSTC has exercised authority and has not deferred, OSTC has the exclusive authority to refer criminal charges for trial by general or special court-martial. In these cases, OSTC also retains exclusive authority to enter into plea agreements, withdraw or dismiss charges, and grant witnesses immunity.

- Command retains all other designated authorities, to include pretrial confinement, selection of panel members, funding of experts and witness travel, authority to direct preliminary hearings, and court-martial convening authority

Deferred Offenses

- OSTC's disposition decision is limited to: (1) preferral/referral of the offense to a general or special court-martial; or (2) deferral of the offense to command for further disposition.

- For covered, known, and related offenses under OSTC authority, command may not take action unless the offense is deferred

  -- If OSTC chooses not to prefer or refer a covered, known, or related offense for trial by general or special court-martial, then the offense is deferred back to command for further disposition. For deferred *known/related* offenses, command may take any lawful disposition action, including referral to trial by general or special court-martial.

  -- For deferred *covered* offenses, command may take any lawful disposition action, other than referral of charges for trial by general or special court-martial. Available disposition options may include nonjudicial punishment, administrative separation, and other administrative actions.

Nonjudicial Punishment after Deferral

- Command may offer Article 15, UCMJ, nonjudicial punishment for any covered, known, or related offense that is deferred by OSTC. If an accused turns down the offer of nonjudicial punishment and demands trial by court-martial, command options will be determined by whether the underlying offense is a covered offense or a known/related offense.

  -- For covered offenses, command may not refer charges to general or special court-martial, but command may seek reconsideration of the deferral decision from OSTC. If the evidence is sufficient, OSTC may then prefer and refer charges.

  -- For known/related offenses, there are no restrictions on command disposition authority, so command may prefer and refer charges without OSTC involvement

Command and OSTC

- Commanders remain a critical stakeholder in military justice and continue to be responsible for command climate and good order and discipline

- The Staff Judge Advocate will remain the primary legal advisor for command. But, in all cases, STC will be available for discussion and will work closely with the servicing legal office to ensure command is fully informed as to the status of offense investigations and prosecutions.

References

· 10 U.S.C. § 1044f enacted by § 532 of the National Defense Authorization Act (NDAA) for FY2022 Pub. L. 117-81 (27 December 2021)
· DAFPD 51-2, *Military Justice and Other Criminal Proceedings* (27 December 2023)
· DAFI 51-201, *Administration of Military Justice* (27 December 2023)

A COMMANDER'S GUIDE TO THE AIR FORCE OFFICE OF SPECIAL INVESTIGATIONS

The Office of Special Investigations (OSI) is a Field Operating Agency within the Department of the Air Force (DAF). Its mission is to identify, exploit, and neutralize criminal, intelligence, and terrorist threats in multiple domains in support of the DAF, the DoD, and the U.S. Government. OSI is the DAF's designated Military Criminal Investigation Organization (MCIO) and Military Department Counterintelligence Organization (MDCO).

Key Takeaways

- » Any DAF commander may request investigative support, but only the SecAF may direct OSI to delay, suspend, or terminate an investigation

- » OSI generally investigates major offenses, but coordination between OSI, the Security Forces Office of Investigations (SFOI), and the servicing Staff Judge Advocate (SJA) help make best use of investigative resources based upon the criminal offense(s) suspected and available manpower

- » OSI initiates investigations into **ALL** allegations of sexual assault that occur within its jurisdiction, regardless of the severity of the allegation. The allegations must be based upon credible information and have a DoD nexus.

- » Commanders must coordinate with OSI and the servicing SJA prior to reassigning a person subject to an OSI investigation or initiating a commander directed inquiry or investigation when there is an ongoing OSI investigation

- » A Report of Investigation (ROI) is provided to the decision authority upon completion of an investigation. ROIs outline information obtained through investigation and witness interviews. ROIs do not suggest or make any recommendation concerning disposition of the allegations.

- » The decision authority is required to promptly report to OSI all actions taken as a result of the investigation. The servicing legal office will provide OSI and Security Forces (SF) disposition information for inclusion in entries to appropriate national criminal indexing databases.

- » OSI records, including ROIs, must be treated as sensitive and may only be released to persons whose duties require access or as specifically provided by law or regulation (such as certain releases to Victim's Counsel). OSI should be informed any time OSI records are released. Consult with the servicing SJA prior to releasing OSI records.

OSI Organization

- OSI is a Field Operating Agency aligned under SAF/IG, which functions as an independent, centralized organization conducting unbiased investigations

- OSI's mission includes investigating allegations of criminal activity and fraud and conducting non-combat related death investigations of active-duty members, as well as counterintelligence and specialized investigative activities, counter-drug activities, protective service operations, and integrated force protection. Additionally, OSI provides training to all special agents through the USAF Special Investigations Academy (USAFSIA).

OSI Investigative Responsibilities

- Coordination between OSI, SF, and the servicing SJA is necessary to make best use of investigative resources, technical expertise, and investigative capabilities, to identify suspected criminal offenses, and to best utilize available manpower

- Generally, OSI investigates major offenses and SF investigates minor offenses. However, the OSI/CC has independent authority with the DAF to initiate criminal investigations and OSI is required to investigate **ALL** unrestricted allegations of certain sexual crimes that occur within its jurisdiction, regardless of the severity of an allegation.

Requesting OSI Investigative Service/Investigation Completion

- Any DAF commander responsible for security, discipline, or law enforcement may request investigative support, but only SecAF or DoD/IG (for DoD/IG directed investigations only) may delay, suspend, or terminate an investigation

- OSI briefs DAF commanders on the progress of investigations affecting their command as necessary and appropriate. At the conclusion of an investigation, an ROI is generated and provided to the decision authority.

  -- ROIs detail information obtained through investigation and witness interviews. ROIs do not contain recommendations or suggestions concerning the disposition of the allegations. Their purpose is to provide evidence for the decision authority to consider.

  -- The decision authority is required to provide OSI with a report of action taken, to include times when no action is taken, upon completion of an investigation. This information is used to make mandatory entries in various national criminal indexing databases.

Command Roles and Responsibilities for Supporting OSI Investigations

- Operational security (OPSEC) of OSI investigations is critical. Restrict knowledge of ongoing investigations to a strict "need-to-know" basis to avoid jeopardizing operations and the compromise of efforts to neutralize criminal or counterintelligence threats.

  -- Unauthorized release of information related to OSI sources, agents, witnesses, and investigative techniques could place persons and evidence at risk and must be avoided

-- OSI mission success and OSI agents' safety is enhanced by concealing their rank. All commanders and civilian directors are required to ensure special procedures exist to protect agents' personnel, medical, and other administrative records.

- OSI, in coordination with the servicing SJA, requests search and seizure authorizations from authorized commanders, judges, magistrates, or competent search authorities based on probable cause. Personnel must comply with the execution of an authorization as directed by the issuing authority.

Select OSI Specialized Functions

- DAF's Counterintelligence Unit:

  -- OSI is the sole DAF entity responsible for conducting counterintelligence (CI) investigations, collections, and operations. HQ OSI/JA, specifically, the National Security Law Division (NSLD), not a local or base legal office, is solely responsible for providing legal advice and support on all CI activities.

  -- OSI investigates security incidents of espionage, suspected compromise of special access information, or deliberate compromise of classified information

- Protective Services:

  -- OSI is the DAF's single point of contact for protective service operations protecting DAF members, DoD and U.S. Government personnel, and foreign dignitaries

Select OSI Policies

- Apprehension/Arrest/Detention:

  -- Apprehension is the taking of a person into custody. OSI agents may apprehend any person subject to trial by court-martial when probable cause to apprehend exists. In some circumstances, certain OSI agents may arrest civilians. However, this authority will be used judiciously and only when necessary.

- Arming:

  -- AFPD 71-1, *Criminal Investigations and Counterintelligence*, authorizes agents to carry, concealed or unconcealed, Government-issued or OSI-approved privately owned firearms

- Complaints:

  -- Complaints against OSI personnel should be referred to the OSI member's immediate supervision for thorough and expeditious investigation by HQ OSI, Office of the Inspector General's Internal Affairs Section

Release of OSI Information

- OSI records are generally Controlled Unclassified Information (CUI) and must be treated as sensitive records. Most OSI records are protected by the Privacy Act.

- The vast majority of OSI records (ROIs, policies, instructions, etc.) are not publicly releasable and must be safeguarded. OSI records may only be released/further distributed to those who have an official "need-to-know" or through the Freedom of Information Act (FOIA) process. All requests for OSI information must be processed by the servicing OSI detachment and HQ OSI/FSS/MSII. In order to avoid compromising other investigations, and unnecessary disclosure of tradecraft or law enforcement techniques, OSI should be informed any time OSI records are released for administrative actions and courts. Consult with the servicing SJA before release.

  -- Only OSI may authorize release of OSI records outside the DAF. HQ OSI/FSS/MSII is responsible for processing all FOIA and Privacy Act requests for OSI information.

  -- All media inquiries involving OSI, OSI investigations, or OSI personnel require close coordination among local and HQ OSI public affairs (PA), the servicing SJA and HQ OSI/JA, and local and OSI leadership

  -- All civilian subpoenas for OSI information or personnel must be sent to HQ OSI/FSS/MSII. HQ OSI's SJA is the release authority for such requests.

References

· Rule for Courts-Martial 302 (2024)
· Military Rule of Evidence 315 and 507 (2024)
· DoDI 5505.18, *Investigation of Adult Sexual Assault in the Department of Defense* (22 March 2017), incorporating through Change 4, 6 September 2022
· DoDM 5240.01, *Procedures Governing the Conduct of DoD Intelligence Activities* (8 August 2016)
· AFPD 71-1, *Criminal Investigations and Counterintelligence* (1 July 2019)
· AFMD 39, *Air Force Office of Special Investigations* (14 April 2020)
· AFI 71-101 V1, *Criminal Investigations Program* (1 July 2019)
· AFI 71-101 V4, *Counterintelligence* (2 July 2019)

FUNCTIONS OF THE AREA DEFENSE COUNSEL

The Area Defense Counsel (ADC) provides DAF members with free, confidential, and independent legal representation. DAF service members suspected of a criminal offense or facing an adverse administrative action receive legal advice from an experienced, certified judge advocate.

Key Takeaways

» The ADC represents DAF service members under investigation, facing adverse action, and at courts-martial

» ADCs operate outside the local chain of command and only advocate for their clients' interests

» Civilians are not entitled to ADC representation. Members of the Air Force Reserve and members of the Air National Guard (ANG) may be represented by the ADC depending on the circumstances.

» Local commands and legal offices should support the ADC mission

---

- The ADC represents DAF service members in the following areas:

  -- Courts-martial

  -- Administrative separation actions

  -- Article 32 preliminary hearings

  -- Pretrial confinement hearings

  -- Nonjudicial punishment (NJP) actions under Article 15 of the UCMJ

  -- Criminal investigations, administrative investigations, interrogations, and inquiries in which the member is suspected of misconduct, has violated the UCMJ, or faces adverse administrative action

  -- When a service member requests a defense counsel pursuant to the service member's right not to self-incriminate under Article 31, UCMJ

  -- Any other adverse administrative actions for which legal counsel is required or authorized, including but not limited to Letters of Counseling (LOCs), Admonishment (LOAs), or Reprimand (LORs), Unfavorable Information Files (UIFs), Control Rosters, referral performance reports, administrative demotions, promotion proprietary actions (PPAs), officer grade determinations (OGDs), and Flying Evaluation Boards (FEBs)

- All ADCs are assigned outside the local chain of command, operate independently of the local chain of command, and maintain an office physically separate from the base legal office to avoid conflicts of interest or command influence

  -- The ADC's responsibility is to represent the client zealously and ethically, which may include meeting with or advocating directly to commanders and unit leadership

  -- Acting as a legal representative for the client alone, the ADC is ethically prohibited from sharing any details of the representation of the client or any confidential client communications with third parties, unless the client specifically authorizes the ADC to do so

- DAF service members facing any type of investigation or adverse administrative action should be promptly referred to the ADC

  -- Civilians are not entitled to ADC representation

  -- ANG members are provided ADC representation when in Title 10 status and the command takes adverse administrative action against the member

  -- Resources permitting, reservists facing administrative discharge action that are board entitled will be represented by the ADC nearest to the location of their reserve unit. Additionally, reservists facing military criminal investigation or any other adverse administrative action will generally be represented by the ADC nearest to the location of their reserve unit.

- The ADC program requires strong command and Staff Judge Advocate support to maintain the integrity and fairness of the military justice system

  -- The ADC is available, subject to workload and client confidences, to help educate the base population on the military justice system and the ADC's function

References

· Articles 15, 31, and 32, Uniform Code of Military Justice
· DAFI 51-201, *Administration of Military Justice* (24 January 2024)

COMMAND RESPONSE TO SEXUAL OFFENSES

The legal requirements related to sexual offenses are complex. It is imperative commanders consult with their respective Staff Judge Advocate (SJA) early on for any allegation of a sexually related offense. For sex-related offenses committed after 27 December 2023, initial disposition of the offense is withheld to the Office of Special Trial Counsel (OSTC).

Key Takeaways

» The DAF's response to sexual assault is both proactive and reactive. On both fronts the DAF utilizes a multidisciplinary approach.

» The Sexual Assault Prevention and Response (SAPR) office has the lead in sexual assault prevention, but every DAF member and every agency must play a role for prevention to work

» A number of specific agencies are involved in responding to individual cases including SAPR, Family Advocacy, the Office of Special Investigations (OSI), the legal office, OSTC, medical and mental health providers, the chaplain's office, and a member's chain of command

» There are many different legal categories of sexual offenses, and this section encompasses the full spectrum

Special Considerations Unique to Sexual Offense Cases

- Authority to Investigate: Air Force OSI is the lead agency to investigate sexual allegations regardless of the severity of the offense

    -- A commander should ensure that any allegation of a sexual offense is communicated to both OSI and their respective SJA

- Disposition Authority: For offenses under command authority, by order of the SecDef, the O-6 Special Court-Martial Convening Authority (SPCMCA) is the Initial Disposition Authority (IDA) for certain sexual assault cases and all offenses arising from or relating to the qualifying incident(s)

    -- This does not prevent a squadron or group commander from preferring charges for sexual assault, but it does mean that any decision not to prefer charges based on an allegation of sexual assault will be reviewed at higher levels

    -- This does not apply to offenses committed after 27 December 2023 or for offenses otherwise under OSTC authority

- Collateral Misconduct and Safe to Report Policy:

    -- Withholding of IDA applies to all alleged offenses arising from or relating to the qualifying offense allegation(s). This includes collateral misconduct by the accused or victim.

    -- If there are allegations of collateral misconduct committed by a victim of an alleged sexual assault, the Safe-to-Report Policy dictates the IDA must determine whether the alleged collateral misconduct in question is "minor" or "non-minor"

--- If the alleged collateral misconduct is deemed minor, the victim shall not be disciplined

- Mandatory Recommendation for Discharge for Allegations of Sexual Assault: Sexual assault is incompatible with military service

  -- For offenses under command authority, if a commander believes it is more likely than not a member committed a sexual assault, they must take prompt action to initiate discharge or waiver action. Sexual assault, for the purposes of the administrative separation instruction, is defined very broadly.

  -- The member must be recommended for discharge unless the member meets all the specified exception criteria listed in the discharge regulation

  -- The initiation of court-martial charges generally takes precedence over the decision to initiate discharge, but if those charges do not ultimately proceed to court-martial, the commander is still responsible for making a discharge determination

- Discharging a Victim of a Sexual Assault: Victims have the opportunity to request the General Court-Martial Convening Authority (GCMCA) review their discharge case if the victim made an unrestricted report of sexual assault within the 12 months prior to being notified of an involuntary discharge and the victim believes the discharge was initiated in retaliation for making the unrestricted report

- Mandatory General Court-Martial (GCM) and Statute of Limitations: Specified sexual assault offenses, generally penetrative offenses, referred to a court-martial are now required to be referred to a GCM. A punitive discharge is now mandatory for a conviction of certain sexual offenses.

  -- There is no longer a statute of limitations for certain sexual assault offenses

- Victim Consultation: Victims have a number of rights under Article 6b, UCMJ

  -- In an effort to ensure victims are afforded their rights, commanders, legal offices, and OSTC are required to consult with victims of all crimes prior to taking a number of military justice related actions. Commanders should contact their legal office to ensure all victim consultation requirements are met.

- Sex Offender Registration: Federal law requires that any service member convicted in a general or special court-martial of any specified sexual offense must report for registration with the appropriate authorities in the jurisdiction in which the service member resides, works, or attends school

  -- The DoD has a separate requirement for *notifying* those jurisdictions that a military member convicted of committing certain offenses plans to reside, work, or attend school in a jurisdiction. This is triggered by the offenses listed in DoDI 1325.07, *Administration of Military Correctional Facilities and Clemency and Parole Authority*. However, it is important to note that an individual's sex offender registration requirements vary by state and may be triggered by offenses not listed in DoDI 1325.07.

Commander Response to Allegations of Sexual Assault

- Commanders notified of a sexual assault through unrestricted reporting must take immediate steps to ensure the victim's physical safety, emotional security, and medical treatment needs are met, and that OSI or the appropriate criminal investigative agency is notified

- Commanders have a role in preventing retaliation against victims and their family members, as well as witnesses, first responders, and bystanders for their role in a sexual assault case

- Commanders must ensure their subordinates are aware of the responsibility not to retaliate

- The appropriate commander should determine whether temporary reassignment or relocation of the victim or subject is appropriate; upon request, this could possibly include a permanent change of station, including an expedited transfer or humanitarian reassignment

- Commanders should consider issuing no contact or Military Protective Orders (DD Form 2873), if appropriate

- The immediate commander of the subject of a sexual assault must keep in mind that the subject is presumed innocent until proven guilty. Monitor the well-being of the alleged offender, particularly for any indications of suicidal ideation or other unhealthy attempts to cope with stress, and ensure appropriate assistance is rendered. Consult with medical and mental health providers for appropriate courses of action, as needed.

- The immediate commander of any victim who has filed an unrestricted report is required to attend monthly Case Management Group (CMG) meetings, chaired by installation leadership, to carefully consider and implement immediate, short-term, and long-term measures to help facilitate and assure the victim's well-being and recovery from the sexual assault

References

- Articles 6b, 18, 43, 56, 120, 120a, 120b, and 120c, Uniform Code of Military Justice
- DoDI 1325.07, *Administration of Military Correctional Facilities and Clemency and Parole Authority* (11 March 2013), incorporating through Change 4, 19 August 2020
- DoDI 6495.02 Volume 1, *Sexual Assault Prevention and Response (SAPR): Program Procedures* (28 March 2013), incorporating through Change 7, 6 September 2022
- DD Form 2873, *Military Protection Order (MPO)* (February 2020)
- DAFI 36-3211, *Military Separations* (24 June 2022), incorporating Change 1, 20 November 2023
- DAFI 51-201, *Administration of Military Justice* (24 January 2024)
- DAFI 90-6001, *Sexual Assault Prevention and Response (SAPR) Program* (15 July 2020), incorporating Change 1, 26 March 2021, including DAFI 90-6001_DAFGM2023-01, 29 September 2023
- AFI 71-101V1, *Criminal Investigations Program* (1 July 2019)

SEXUAL ASSAULT PREVENTION AND RESPONSE

The DAF Sexual Assault Prevention and Response (SAPR) policy and responsibilities apply to all levels of command and all DAF organizations and personnel.

Key Takeaways

» A commander must immediately contact the Office of Special Investigations (OSI) upon learning of a sexual assault, whether or not the allegation occurred within the commander's own chain of command

» Monthly Case Management Group (CMG) meetings chaired by the installation commander or deputy commander will address the holistic care of victims in unrestricted reports of sexual assault; a CMG will include the victim's commander, SAPR personnel, OSI, legal, medical, and other helping agencies

» Commanders have the authority to determine the appropriate disposition of alleged victim collateral misconduct; however, commanders should consult with the servicing legal office for the most up-to-date requirements affecting disposition of victim collateral misconduct

---

The SAPR Office

- The Sexual Assault Response Coordinator (SARC) serves as the single point of contact at an installation or within a geographic area for integrating and coordinating sexual assault victim care from an initial report of sexual assault, through disposition and resolution of issues related to the victim's health and well-being

- The SARC is responsible for: ensuring a 24 hour/day support system and response capability for all victims falling within the SAPR program; supervising SAPR Victim Advocates (VAs) and Volunteer Victim Advocates (VVAs); and assisting commanders to meet annual SAPR training requirements. The VVA program will be sunset on 30 September 2024.

- SAPR VAs and VVAs provide victims crisis intervention, referrals, and ongoing non-clinical support, including information about available options and resources, to help victims make informed decisions about their case. At the victim's request, VAs and VVAs may accompany the victim to medical examinations and investigative and counsel interviews.

SAPR Response to Sexual Assault Allegations

- The SAPR office will determine if a victim is eligible for SAPR services

  -- Regular DAF members and their dependents 18 and older and Air Reserve Component (ARC) members in Title 10 status at the time of the assault are generally eligible for services and may make both restricted and unrestricted reports of sexual assault

-- The following non-military individuals are only eligible for the unrestricted reporting option: DoD civilian employees' dependents 18 years of age and older when stationed or performing duties outside the continental United States (OCONUS) and U.S. citizen DoD-contractor personnel when authorized to accompany the Armed Forces in a contingency operation OCONUS and their employees who are U.S. citizens

-- DAF civilian employees are eligible for restricted and unrestricted reporting and will have access to the full complement of SAPR services offered to service members excluding medical entitlements or legal services unless otherwise authorized by law or policy

-- Victims sexually assaulted by their spouse, same-sex domestic partner, unmarried intimate partner, or military dependents who are 17 years-old or younger will be referred to the Family Advocacy Program (FAP)

- The SARC, VA, or VVA will meet the victim and explain reporting options

-- Unrestricted report: Made via the victim's selection of that option on DD Form 2910, *Victim Reporting Preference Statement*. SAPR personnel must refer unrestricted reports to the Air Force OSI for investigation.

-- Restricted report: Made via the victim's selection of that option on DD Form 2910. SAPR personnel will not refer restricted reports to OSI. A restricted report can be made at any time so long as a victim did not disclose the incident to law enforcement or previously make an unrestricted report regarding the same incident.

-- Independent investigations: Initiated because information about a sexual assault was disclosed to command or law enforcement from sources independent of a victim. A victim's disclosure to command or someone in the chain of command will also initiate an independent investigation because of command's obligation to report the allegation to OSI.

Expedited Transfer

- Eligible victims of certain qualifying sexual and other related offenses (violations of UCMJ Articles 120, 120c or 130) may seek an Expedited Transfer (ET), a Permanent Change of Station (PCS) or a temporary or Permanent Change of Assignment (PCA) to another location to help healing, recovery, and rehabilitation. An ET is also available to eligible victims of physical domestic violence committed by the spouse or intimate partner of the victim.

-- Upon receiving a request for an ET, the installation or host wing commander can consider potential transfer of the alleged offender instead of the victim, if appropriate. Alleged offender reassignments are handled in accordance with 10 U.S.C. § 674 and DAFI 36-2110, *Total Force Assignments*, and are not facilitated by SAPR personnel.

-- Victims under the rubric of the FAP may request an expedited transfer pursuant to DAFI 40-301, *Family Advocacy Program*

-- An ET is available to Regular DAF victims, non-prior service DAF service members performing initial skills training, and ANG and ARC members who have made an unrestricted report of sexual assault through either the SAPR program or the FAP. An ET also allows the transfer of a service member whose adult military dependent is the victim of a qualifying offense if the offense was perpetrated by another service member not related to the victim or in cases with a military nexus between the offense and dependent's status.

-- Once an ET request is made, the victim's commander (or equivalent) makes a recommendation to the host wing/installation commander for approval or disapproval; the victim's commander should base his/her recommendation upon all available information, especially that provided by OSI, and after consultation with the Staff Judge Advocate

-- If the ET request is disapproved by the wing/installation commander, the victim may appeal to the first/next general officer in the chain of command; if disapproved at this level the victim may make a final appeal to the major/field command deputy commander

Case Management Group (CMG) Meetings

- Held monthly to discuss unrestricted reports of sexual assault on the installation as well as instances of retaliation related to the report of sexual assault experienced by the victim, bystanders, and first responders (if applicable)

-- Within 72 hours of a CMG, a victim's commander will provide the victim an update regarding the investigation, ET and any other request, and command proceedings regarding the sexual assault

- The CMG will immediately form a High-Risk Response Team (HRRT) for victims who are assessed to be at high risk of harm via a safety assessment; HRRT findings must be reported to the installation commander within 24 hours of being activated

Victim Collateral Misconduct

- An investigation into the facts and circumstances surrounding an alleged sexual assault may develop evidence that the victim engaged in misconduct such as underage drinking or other related alcohol offenses, adultery, drug abuse, fraternization, or other violations of instructions, regulations, or orders. This is generally known as "collateral misconduct."

- Consult the servicing legal office for assistance in assessing available and appropriate disposition of victim collateral misconduct

References

· Temporary Administrative Reassignment or Removal of a Member on Active Duty Accused of Committing a Sexual Assault or Related Offense, 10 U.S.C. § 674

· Articles 120, 120c, and 130, Uniform Code of Military Justice

· DoDD 6495.01, *Sexual Assault Prevention and Response (SAPR) Program* (23 January 2012), incorporating through Change 5, 10 November 2021

· DoDI 6495.02, Volume 1, *Sexual Assault Prevention and Response: Program Procedures* (28 March 2013), incorporating through Change 7, 6 September 2022

· DoDI 6495.02, Volume 2, *Sexual Assault Prevention and Response: Education and Training* (9 April 2021)

· DD Form 2910, *Victim Reporting Preference Statement* (November 2021)

· DAFPD 90-60, *Sexual Assault Prevention and Response (SAPR) Program* (5 October 2022)

· DAFI 36-2110, *Total Force Assignments* (15 November 2021), incorporating Change 1, 16 November 2022, including DAFGM2023-01, 5 October 2023

· DAFI 40-301, *Family Advocacy Program* (13 November 2020)

· DAFI 51-201, *Administration of Military Justice* (24 January 2024)

· DAFI 90-6001, *Sexual Assault Prevention and Response (SAPR) Program* (15 July 2020), incorporating Change 1, 26 March 2021, including DAFI90-6001_DAFGM2023-01, 29 September 2023

VICTIMS' COUNSEL PROGRAM

The Victims' Counsel (VC) program empowers victims of sex-related offenses, domestic violence offenses, and interpersonal violence (IPV) offenses through the military legal system by allowing for a confidential, attorney-client relationship between a VC and a qualifying victim. This relationship gives victims a voice in the military justice process, providing victims with an attorney who will advocate on their behalf to protect their rights throughout the process.

Key Takeaways

- » VC program provides victims legal advice, representation, and advocacy
- » VCs represent most victims of sexual-related offenses and domestic violence offenses and provide consultation to victims of other violent offenses or workplace violence
- » Eligible victims must be informed of the availability of VC services as outlined in this section
- » If the victim requests a VC upon notification, then the individual receiving the request is required to contact their servicing VC office for further processing
- » VCs are assigned and operate independent from the local chain of command and serve as an advocate for the victim, not an advisor for commanders

Objectives of the VC Program

- The objectives of the DAF VC program are to:
  -- Provide victims of qualifying offenses with independent and privileged legal advice and representation, to include investigation and prosecution of those offenses
  -- Empower victims of qualifying offenses by providing professional and knowledgeable counsel to enable them to express their interests
  -- Provide advocacy to protect the rights afforded to victims

Overview of the VC Program

- The Special Victims' Counsel (SVC) program was implemented in January 2013
- Fiscal Year 2020 National Defense Authorization Act (NDAA), Section 548, mandated all Military Services provide legal counsel to eligible victims of domestic violence offenses
- In April 2021, the program expanded to provide legal services to IPV victims
- In November 2021, the SVC Division was renamed as the VC Division
- All DAF installations are serviced by a VC office, which may be geographically separated

Eligibility for VC Representation or Consultation

- Certain categories of victims of sexual-related offenses and domestic violence offenses are generally eligible for VC representation

-- Regular Component, Reserve Component, United States Air Force Academy (USAFA) cadets

-- Air National Guard (ANG) members, but normally referred to the National Guard SVC program

-- Dependents, Retirees, and others eligible for military legal assistance, so long as a Regular Component DAF commander may exercise jurisdiction and the victim requires legal representation for active participation in an on-going military justice investigation or process

-- For sex-related offenses only, Department of Defense (DoD) civilians not otherwise eligible for military legal assistance, so long as the subject may be prosecuted under the Uniform Code of Military Justice (UCMJ) and there is a nexus to DAF employment

- Basic military training (BMT) and technical training students who are involved in an unprofessional relationship that involves physical contact of a sexual nature with faculty or staff, if the qualifying offense occurs within the first six months of service

- DAF Regular Component victims of other violent offenses or workplace violence under the UCMJ

- Other victims on a case-by-case basis via an "extraordinary circumstances request." Eligibility for services is outlined in 10 U.S.C. §§ 1044, 1044e, and 1565b, as well as FY2020 NDAA, Section 548, along with service policies and regulations.

Notifying Victims of Availability of Special Services

- Eligible victims must be informed of the availability of VC services upon reporting the qualifying offense, before being interviewed as a victim regarding the allegation, or when seeking assistance as a victim related to the allegation from the following personnel: SARC, VA, FAP, AFOSI/SFS investigator, Victim and Witness Assistance Program (VWAP) personnel, trial counsel, defense counsel, chaplain, mental health provider, or medical provider

-- If the victim requests a VC upon notification, then the individual receiving the request is required to contact their servicing VC office for further processing

- VCs are not permitted to solicit clients; victims must request a VC

Scope of Representation

- A VC represents sexual assault victims and domestic violence victims in a confidential, attorney-client relationship, through military legal proceedings related to the offense

- Military Justice Advocacy: VCs enable victims to assert their rights under the law and applicable regulations by: advocating to commanders, convening authorities, Staff Judge Advocates, and military judges; attending interviews; representing clients at Article 32, UCMJ, preliminary hearings and courts-martial; assisting clients with post-trial submissions to the convening authority; advising clients on VWAP; assisting clients in seeking transitional compensation; and liaising with other helping agencies

- Advocacy to DoD and DAF Agencies: VCs assist clients with requests for/relating to Expedited Transfer (ET), victim's safety (e.g., Military Protective Orders (MPO)), access to medical and mental health care, workplace concerns, and military benefits

- Collateral Misconduct: VCs may represent victims accused of misconduct, in conjunction with a military area defense counsel or alone

- Advocacy to Civilian Prosecutors and Agencies: VCs may advise clients on U.S. civilian criminal jurisdiction and may provide limited advocacy regarding a client's interest to civilian prosecutors or agencies

- A VC may provide an IPV victim confidential legal advice, victim education on rights and benefits afforded to crime victims, legal consultation and referrals regarding roles and responsibilities of victims' support services, and limited advocacy

VC Qualifications

- A VC is a judge advocate certified and designated by The Judge Advocate General (TJAG) to represent the interests of victims of certain qualifying offenses

- All VCs are assigned outside the local chain of command, operate independently of the local chain of command, and maintain an office physically separate from the base legal office to avoid conflicts of interest or command influence. A VC's chain of command flows through VC districts to the Chief, Victims' Counsel Division.

- The VC's primary responsibility is to advise and zealously advocate for the client's expressed interests through the military justice process

- The VC is an advocate for the client, not an advisor for the command or legal office

References

· Legal Assistance, 10 U.S.C. § 1044

· Special Victims' Counsel for Victims of Sex-Related Offenses, 10 U.S.C. § 1044e

· Victims of Sexual Assault: Access to Legal Assistance and Services of Sexual Assault Response Coordinators and Sexual Assault Victim Advocates, 10 U.S.C. § 1565b

· Articles 6b and 32, Uniform Code of Military Justice

· National Defense Authorization Act (NDAA) FY2020, Pub. L. 116-92, § 548 (2019)

· DAFI 51-201, *Administration of Military Justice* (24 January 2024)

· DAFI 51-207, *Victim and Witness Rights and Procedures* (14 April 2022), including DAFGM2023-01, 10 October 2023

· Under Secretary of Defense Memorandum, *Safe-to-Report Policy for Service Member Victims of Sexual Assault*, 25 October 2021

· Operating Instruction, *Air Force Victims' Counsel Charter* (4 November 2021)

VICTIM AND WITNESS ASSISTANCE PROGRAM

The Victim and Witness Assistance Program (VWAP) is an installation-level program that provides guidance for the protection and assistance of victims and witnesses. It has three primary objectives: (1) to mitigate the physical, psychological, and financial hardships suffered by victims and witnesses of offenses investigated by DAF authorities; (2) to foster cooperation between victims, witnesses, and the military justice system; and (3) to ensure best efforts are made to afford victims certain enumerated rights.

Key Takeaways

- » Article 6b, Uniform Code of Military Justice (UCMJ), established certain rights for crime victims. Victims of an offense referred to a court-martial after 1 January 2019 have additional rights

- » Communications between a victim and victim liaison are **NOT** privileged under Military Rule of Evidence (M.R.E.) 514

- » Installations have responsibilities toward victims including providing information about medical and social services, assisting with restitution, and consulting victims on disposition

Overview

- The Local Responsible Official (LRO) is the installation commander or the Special Court-Martial Convening Authority (SPCMCA). The LRO often delegates LRO duties to the installation Staff Judge Advocate (SJA), who in turn appoints a VWAP Coordinator to implement and manage the requirements as part of the VWAP. The VWAP Coordinator is also responsible for conducting annual training and can serve as a victim liaison.

- A victim liaison is an individual appointed by the LRO or delegate to assist a victim during the military justice process. Communications between a victim and victim liaison are **NOT** privileged under M.R.E. 514.

- Annually, all agencies involved in VWAP (e.g., Security Forces (SF), Sexual Assault Prevention and Response (SAPR), Family Advocacy Program (FAP), etc.) are responsible for training personnel assigned to their respective agencies on their responsibilities with the program. The SJA trains commanders and first sergeants.

- Each installation should prepare and maintain a victim information packet and the same local agencies listed above should be involved in its preparation. Each identified victim or witness should be provided with that packet, which should contain DD Forms 2701-2705 (listed in references at end of section), as appropriate.

Victim Rights

- Article 6b, UCMJ, established nine rights for crime victims. These rights can be enforced by the Court of Criminal Appeals through a Writ of Mandamus.

  -- For the purposes of Article 6b and VWAP, a victim is defined as a person who suffered direct physical, emotional, or pecuniary harm as a result of the commission of an offense under the UCMJ

  -- For VWAP purposes, there is no burden of proof for these rights to apply and a victim shall be identified at the earliest opportunity after the detection of a crime

- A victim has the following rights under Article 6b, UCMJ:

  -- To be reasonably protected from the accused;

  -- To receive reasonable, accurate, and timely notice of specified hearings;

  -- Not to be excluded from any public hearing or proceeding;

  -- To be reasonably heard at specified hearings;

  -- To confer with government counsel for a proceeding;

  -- To receive restitution as provided by law;

  -- To proceedings free from unreasonable delay;

  -- To be informed in a timely manner of a plea agreement, separation-in-lieu-of-trial agreement, or non-prosecution agreement relating to the offense; and

  -- To be treated with fairness and with respect for his/her dignity and privacy.

- Victims also have several additional rights:

  -- To petition for a hearing before a military judge for relief from an investigative subpoena;

  -- To be interviewed by defense counsel only in the presence of counsel for the victim, trial counsel, or a victim advocate;

  -- To petition a military judge to require a preliminary hearing officer to comply with applicable rules;

  -- To submit supplemental materials for consideration by a preliminary hearing officer (PHO) or convening authority within 24 hours after the close of an Article 32 hearing; and

  -- In some cases, to receive a copy of the recording of all open sessions of a court-martial, a copy of the record of trial, a copy of any action taken by the convening authority, and a copy of the entry of judgment.

LRO Responsibilities to Crime Victims

- In addition to the preceding victim's rights, installation commanders have a number of specific responsibilities toward crime victims under the VWAP. These responsibilities are executed by various personnel, including law enforcement, commanders, the SJA, confinement facilities, and SAPR as applicable. Some responsibilities include:

  -- Inform eligible victims of the ability to consult with an attorney

  -- Inform victims of and assist them in obtaining medical, financial, legal, and other social services

  -- Inform victims of restitution or other relief to which they may be entitled

  -- Inform victims concerning protection against threats or harassment

  -- Provide victims notice of significant events in the military justice process

  -- Ensure victims are consulted regarding their preference as to military or civilian prosecution of an offense and consideration given to their views for each stage of a court-martial including preferral or dismissal of charges, pretrial restraint, and plea agreement

  -- If administrative action is taken, the LRO may inform the victim that "appropriate administrative action was taken." The LRO should consult with the SJA prior to revealing to the victim the specific action taken (e.g., Article 15 and/or administrative discharge) to ensure the release is not inconsistent with the Privacy Act.

  -- Safeguard the victim's property if taken as evidence and return it as soon as possible. **Note:** Additional safeguards and requirements exist for property taken as evidence in a sexual assault investigation. Consult with the servicing legal office for assistance.

LRO Responsibilities to All Victims and Witnesses

- Notify authorities of threats and assist in obtaining restraining and Military Protective Orders (MPOs)

- If a victim or witness requests, take reasonable steps to inform his/her employer of the reasons for the absence from work and assist in explaining to creditors reasons for any serious financial strain incurred as a direct result of the offense

- Provide victims and witnesses necessary assistance in obtaining timely payment of witness fees and related costs

- In cases involving adverse actions for crimes of abuse against dependents which result in the separation of the military sponsor, victims may be entitled to receive transitional compensation or payment under the Uniformed Services Former Spouses Protection Act

References

- Article 6b, Uniform Code of Military Justice
- Military Rule of Evidence 514 (2024)
- DoDI 1030.02, *Victim and Witness Assistance* (27 July 2023)
- DoDI 6400.07, *Standards for Victim Assistance Services in the Military Community* (15 November 2013), incorporating through Change 2, 6 July 2018
- DD Form 2701, *Initial Information for Victims and Witnesses of Crime* (October 2022)
- DD Form 2702, *Court-Martial Information for Victims and Witnesses of Crime* (October 2022)
- DD Form 2703, *Post-Trial Information for Victims and Witnesses of Crime* (October 2022)
- DD Form 2704, *Victim/Witness Certification and Election Concerning Prisoner Status* (March 2013)
- DD Form 2704-1, *Victim Election of Post-Trial and Appellate Rights* (March 2023)
- DD Form 2705, *Notification to Victim/Witness of Prisoner Status* (March 2023)
- DAFI 51-207, *Victim and Witness Rights and Procedures* (14 April 2022), including DAFGM2023-01, 10 October 2023

TRANSITIONAL COMPENSATION FOR VICTIMS OF ABUSE

It is the Department of Defense (DoD)'s policy to provide transitional assistance benefits, known as transitional compensation, to dependents of members who are separated for domestic abuse. Transitional compensation is an extension of benefits and/or a monetary payment for a set period of time to the abused dependents of the separated military members. Applicants initiate requests through the member's unit commander or the Military Personnel Flight (MPF).

Key Takeaways

» Transitional benefits are available to dependents of service members who are separated for dependent-abuse related offenses to help dependents transition away from the abuser

» Eligible dependents request transitional compensation through a DD Form 2698, *Application for Transitional Compensation*

» Exceptional eligibility is available through SecAF approval for dependents and former dependents who are not otherwise authorized to receive transitional compensation

» Available benefits may include monthly monetary compensation, commissary and exchange privileges, and medical and dental care

---

Eligibility for Transitional Compensation

- Dependents of a member of the armed forces who has been on active duty for more than 30 days and who, after 29 November 1993, are:

  -- Separated from active duty under a court-martial sentence resulting from a dependent-abuse offense;

  -- Administratively separated from the Regular Air Force, Space Force, the Reserve, or the Air National Guard (ANG) if the basis for separation includes a dependent-abuse offense; or

  -- Sentenced to forfeiture of all pay and allowances by a court-martial which has convicted the member of a dependent-abuse offense.

- Dependents are ineligible to receive any transitional compensation and will forfeit any further benefits if already receiving transitional compensation if they remarry, cohabitate with the member, or are found to have been an active participant in the dependent abuse

- Dependent-abuse offenses include violations of the Uniform Code of Military Justice (UCMJ) or applicable civilian criminal codes, including attempts or conspiracies to commit offenses such as sexual assault, rape, sodomy, battery, murder, and manslaughter. The facts and circumstances of each case should always be interpreted in the manner most favorable to the dependent.

- Exceptional Eligibility: 10 U.S.C. § 1059(m) authorizes the SecAF to grant transitional compensation benefits to dependents and former dependents who are not otherwise authorized such benefits. SecAF may delegate this authority to the first general officer (or civilian equivalent) in the chain of command of the member. Payments are subject to determination that the former member engaged in a dependent-abuse offense, but was allowed to separate, voluntarily or involuntarily, under other circumstances before a determination was made.

Application Procedures

- Eligible dependents request transitional compensation by completing the DD Form 2698, *Application for Transitional Compensation*

- Requests are made through the member's unit commander or through the MPF at any Department of the Air Force installation when the applicant is no longer at the installation where the member was assigned. A Victim Witness and Assistance Program (VWAP) liaison, victims' counsel, or unit representative will assist the dependent as appropriate with completing the DD Form 2698.

- The MPF commander will coordinate the package and obtain a written legal review from the Staff Judge Advocate. The installation commander is the approval authority, except in cases under the Exceptional Eligibility provision.

- Exceptional Eligibility applications are routed through the Air Force Personnel Center (AFPC) and the Military Compensation Policy Division (AF/A1PA or SF/A1PA), for SecAF's approval or disapproval, unless authority has been delegated by SecAF

- If approved, transitional compensation will last for 36 months, unless otherwise forfeited

- The statutory monthly amount for transitional compensation is adjusted every year in accordance with the Social Security Administration's annual percent cost of living adjustments, which are published in the Federal Register (10 U.S.C. § 1059(f); 38 U.S.C. § 1311(a)–(f)(4); and 42 U.S.C. § 415(i))

- Available benefits may include monthly monetary compensation, commissary and exchange privileges, and medical and dental care

- The current compensation rates can be found at the Department of Veterans Affairs website: https://www.va.gov/disability/survivor-dic-rates/

References

· Dependents of Members Separated for Dependent Abuse: Transitional Compensation; Commissary and Exchange Benefits, 10 U.S.C. § 1059

· Medical and Dental Care for Dependents: General Rule, 10 U.S.C. § 1076

· Dependency and Indemnity Compensation to a Surviving Spouse, 38 U.S.C. § 1311

· Computation of Primary Insurance Amount, 42 U.S.C. § 415

· DoDI 1342.24, *Transitional Compensation (TC) for Abused Dependents* (23 September 2019)

· DD Form 2698, *Application for Transitional Compensation* (February 2019)

· DAFI 36-3012, *Military Entitlements* (6 April 2023), incorporating Change 1, 24 October 2023

MEDIA RELATIONS IN MILITARY JUSTICE MATTERS

The DAF must balance three important societal interests when there is media interest in military justice proceedings: protection of the right to a fair trial, the privacy rights of all persons involved, and the community's right to be informed of and observe criminal proceedings. Release of information is subject to a number of legal authorities. It is critical that commanders consult with their Staff Judge Advocate (SJA) before releasing information concerning military justice proceedings.

Key Takeaways

» DAFI 51-201, *Administration of Military Justice*, contains detailed guidance concerning release of information pertaining to military justice proceedings

» Commanders must prevent the release of information that could reasonably be expected to interfere with law enforcement or judicial proceedings

» Release of extrajudicial statements concerning a proceeding is ultimately the responsibility of the convening authority for that proceeding

» If a potential extrajudicial statement is based on information contained in agency records, the office of primary responsibility for the record should also coordinate prior to its release

Providing Information and Extrajudicial Statements Generally

- DAFI 51-201 covers the rules for releasing information pertaining to military justice proceedings. It prohibits release of information that could reasonably be expected to interfere with law enforcement proceedings or deprive a person of a right to a fair trial or an impartial adjudication in a criminal proceeding.

- Extrajudicial statements are oral or written statements made outside of a criminal proceeding that a reasonable person would expect to be disseminated by means of public communication

- There are valid reasons for making certain information available to the public. Extrajudicial statements should include only factual matters—not subjective observations or opinions.

- The release of extrajudicial statements is a command responsibility. The convening authority responsible for the proceeding makes the ultimate decision. Major command (MAJCOM), field command (FLDCOM), or equivalent commanders may withhold release authority from subordinate commanders.

- Rules for release of permissible extrajudicial statements are complex and vary according to the type of information to be released and its source, the type of proceeding, and the stage of the proceeding when information is released. Any release of information is potentially subject to provisions of the Freedom of Information Act (FOIA), Privacy Act (PA), and the Victim and Witness Assistance Program (VWAP). Accordingly, it is critical that all release of information or extrajudicial statements only be made after close consultation with the servicing legal office.

Prohibited Extrajudicial Statements

- Extrajudicial statements relating to the following matters have a high likelihood of prejudicing a criminal proceeding and generally should not be made:

    -- The existence or contents of any confession, admission, statement by the accused, or the accused's refusal or failure to make a statement

    -- Observations about the accused's character and reputation

    -- Opinions regarding the accused's guilt or innocence

    -- Opinions regarding the merits of the case or the merits of the evidence

    -- The possibility of a guilty plea or other disposition of the case

    -- Information government counsel knows or has reason to know would be inadmissible as evidence in a trial

- Prior to sentencing, you should also not release facts regarding the accused's disciplinary/criminal record. Even after sentencing, do not release information about previous nonjudicial punishment or administrative actions unless they were admitted into evidence at sentencing. A statement that the accused has no prior criminal/disciplinary history is permissible.

Permissible Extrajudicial Statements

- When deemed necessary by command, the following extrajudicial statements may be made at any stage of the proceedings, subject to certain limitations (i.e., substantial likelihood of prejudice, prohibitions under the FOIA, PA, or VWAP):

    -- General information to educate or inform the public concerning military law and the military justice system;

    -- Information necessary to aid in apprehending a fugitive-accused or to warn the public of possible dangers, as well as facts and circumstances of their apprehension (e.g., time and place), after consultation with the affected law enforcement agency; and

    -- Requests for assistance in obtaining evidence and information necessary to obtain evidence.

- The following extrajudicial statements may normally only be made after a convening authority has disposed of preferred charges by directing an Article 32 preliminary hearing or referred the charges to court-martial, subject to the limitations stated above (substantial likelihood of prejudice and prohibitions under FOIA, PA, and/or VWAP):

    -- The accused's name, unit, and assignment;

-- The substance or text of charges and specifications, provided there is a statement included explaining that the charges are merely accusations and that the accused is presumed innocent unless and until proven guilty. As necessary, redact all PA and VWAP protected data from the charges and specifications to include the names of any victims;

-- The scheduling or result of any stage in the judicial process, date and place of trial and other proceedings, or anticipated dates. You may also direct them to the DAF's online Public Docket; and

-- The identity of appointed counsel, convening authorities, and reviewing authorities.

- Do not volunteer the identities of the court members or the military judge in material prepared for publication unless the convening authority's SJA determines that release would not prejudice the accused's rights or violate the members' or military judge's privacy interests

Article 32, UCMJ Hearings

- Article 32 hearings should ordinarily be open to the public

-- Access by spectators to all or part of the proceeding may be restricted by the convening authority who directed the hearing or by the preliminary hearing officer (PHO) when, in that officer's opinion, the interests of justice outweigh the public's interest in access (e.g., protecting the safety or privacy of a witness, preventing psychological harm to a child witness, or protecting classified information)

Release of Information from Records of Trial or Related Records

- Once a completed record is forwarded, the Military Justice Law and Policy Division (AF/JAJM) is the disclosure authority for all records

Reducing Tension with the Media

- Command should take positive steps to reduce tension with the media

-- Advise the media up-front of the prohibition against courtroom photography, television, and audio and visual recording, and provide an alternate location, room or office for media interviews, broadcasts, etc.

References

· The Freedom of Information Act, 5 U.S.C. § 552

· The Privacy Act of 1974, 5 U.S.C. § 552a

· Article 32, Uniform Code of Military Justice

· Rule for Courts-Martial 405 (2024)

· DAFI 51-201, *Administration of Military Justice* (24 January 2024)

· AFI 33-332, *Air Force Privacy and Civil Liberties Program* (10 March 2020), Corrective Actions applied on 12 May 2020

· AFI 35-101, *Public Affairs Operations* (20 November 2020)

· AFI 51-110, *Professional Responsibility Program* (11 December 2018)

ADVISING SUSPECTS OF RIGHTS

Commanders should not typically directly question members about alleged misconduct. Commanders shall ensure that criminal allegations involving persons affiliated with the DoD are referred to the Air Force Office of Special Investigations or Security Forces for investigation. Prior to doing the questioning themselves, commanders should contact their legal office. If a commander, or any other person subject to the Uniform Code of Military Justice (UCMJ) needs to question a member suspected of committing some form of misconduct, it is essential to follow the legal requirements of Article 31, UCMJ.

Key Takeaways

» When a commander, supervisor, first sergeant, or law enforcement suspects a DAF service member has committed an offense, they must advise the suspect of their rights under Article 31, UCMJ, before questioning the suspect or requesting a statement from the suspect

» The Article 31 advisement must include the suspected offense, the suspect's right to remain silent, and that his statements can be used at a judicial or administrative proceeding

» Failure to advise a suspect of their rights under Article 31 can result in prohibiting use of the suspect's statement, or any evidence derived from that statement, at trial or in other judicial or administrative proceedings

» When advising a suspect of rights under Article 31, the best practice is to read directly from AFVA 31-231, *Advisement of Rights*, a wallet-sized card

---

Overview

- When any person (subject to the UCMJ) with investigative or disciplinary responsibility questions or requests any statement from a DAF service member who the person suspects of having committed an offense, that person must first inform the member of their Article 31 rights

- Proper rights advisement ensures the government can use any admission or confession as evidence in a subsequent court-martial

- Admissions or confessions, and any evidence obtained as a result of those statements, made in response to a defective Article 31 rights advisement, or in the absence of a necessary Article 31 rights advisement, cannot normally be admitted as evidence at trial

When Article 31 Rights are Required

- When a person subject to the UCMJ suspects someone who is also subject to the UCMJ of an offense and starts questioning or requests any statement from that individual about the offense of which the person is suspected

- A request for a statement does not have to involve actual questions. Sometimes actions, if they are likely to elicit a response, are deemed to be enough to trigger Article 31 rights. For example, a commander declares, "I don't know what you were thinking, but I'm assuming the worst," while shrugging his shoulders and shaking his head. Even though the commander has not asked a question, his statement and actions could be deemed as likely to elicit a response.

Who Must Provide Article 31 Rights Advisements

- Military supervisors and commanders are presumed to be acting in a disciplinary capacity when questioning a subordinate. A first sergeant is also presumed to be acting in a disciplinary capacity when questioning military members. Supervisors, First Sergeants, and commanders are held to a high standard. When in doubt, consult with your Staff Judge Advocate (SJA).

What Information Must the Article 31 Rights Advisement Include

- The crime the member is suspected of committing

  -- The general nature of the offense is sufficient, but the allegation stated must be specific enough so the suspect understands what offense he/she is being questioned about

- That the member has the right to remain silent

- Consequences of making a statement (i.e., any statement can be used as evidence at a judicial or administrative proceeding)

- Although it is not necessary that the advisement be verbatim, the best practice is to read the rights directly from the AFVA 31-231, *Advisement of Rights*

- Although Article 31 does not include a right to counsel, the person reading Article 31 rights should advise the member that they may request free military defense counsel

Rights Advisement Must be Understood and Acknowledged by the Suspect

- Suspect must unequivocally and affirmatively acknowledge understanding of their rights, waive their rights, and consent to make a statement without counsel present

- The questioner cannot obtain consent by coercion, threats, or other deprivations of liberty designed to subvert the suspect's rights

- Be cautious when advising an intoxicated person of his/her rights. The individual may be legally incapable of knowingly and voluntarily waiving his/her rights.

- If a suspect hesitates over whether to assert his/her rights, the best practice is to clarify and not ask any further questions until doubt is resolved. Consult the SJA if it is unclear.

Suspect Acknowledgment and Waiver of Article 31 Rights

- When possible, obtain the waiver in writing using AF Form 1168, *Statement of Suspect*

- Have a witness present

- If, after electing to talk, a suspect changes their mind and decides to stop talking, **STOP ALL QUESTIONING**

When to Stop Questioning

- If the individual indicates a desire to remain silent, stop questioning. This does not mean, however, that you cannot give the individual orders or directions on other matters.

- If the suspect requests counsel, stop questioning immediately

  -- Inform the SJA and get advice before re-initiating any questioning

  -- No more questions can be asked until counsel is present, or there has been a sufficient break in custody (at least 14 days), unless the suspect unilaterally chooses to voluntarily reengage, without pressure or approach by government authorities

Re-initiation of Questioning Following an Earlier Invocation of Article 31 Rights

- There are three circumstances under which questioning may occur despite an earlier Article 31 rights invocation

  -- The suspect voluntarily re-initiates the questioning

  -- You are questioning the suspect about a different offense, unrelated to the previous rights advisement

  -- There has been a sufficient "break in custody" (at least 14 days) to permit the accused a meaningful opportunity to seek/consult with counsel

Documentation

- Try to get the statement in writing. A handwritten statement by a suspect is preferred, but also consider having the suspect complete the AF Form 1168 electronically.

- Whether or not the suspect makes a written statement, prepare a memorandum for record after the session ends. The memorandum should include:

  -- Where the session was held

  -- What and when you advised the suspect

  -- What the suspect said

  -- What activities took place during the questioning (suspect sat, stood, smoked, drank, etc.)

  -- What the suspect's attitude was (angry, contrite, cooperative, combative, etc.)

  -- Duration of the session with inclusive hours

References

· Article 31, Uniform Code of Military Justice

· Military Rules of Evidence 304 and 305 (2023)

· AFVA 31-231, *Advisement of Rights* (1 January 2019), certified current 1 July 2019

· AF Form 1168, *Statement of Suspect/Witness/Complainant* (1 April 1998)

CRIMINAL INDEXING

Criminal indexing entails making entries in criminal databases, detailed below, primarily for the subjects of criminal investigations. Indexing enables the rapid exchange of information between criminal justice organizations to assist with investigations and prevent firearm and ammunition sales to persons prohibited by federal law. Commanders have important responsibilities under AFMAN 71-102, *Air Force Criminal Indexing*, to ensure proper criminal indexing occurs.

Key Takeaways

» Commanders must work with their servicing legal office (JA), their local Air Force Office of Special Investigations (OSI) detachment, Security Forces (SF), and the DAF Criminal Justice Information Center (DAF-CJIC) to ensure their criminal indexing responsibilities are met

» DAF-CJIC oversees indexing across the DAF and ensures indexing compliance

» Criminal indexing may have significant consequences for individuals, as it may result in creation of permanent criminal records for them

» Failure to index when required also may have significant consequences for the DAF, including loss of access to databases or civil liability

Interstate Identification Index (III)

- A nationwide database maintained by the FBI of electronic fingerprints and criminal history record information (date of arrest, arresting agency, charges, dispositions) of persons who have been arrested

- Impact of entry: Immediate creation of a national criminal history record that may affect employment and volunteer opportunities, security clearances, and the ability to purchase or receive a firearm

- Basis for entry: A probable cause determination that the individual committed a serious offense punishable by confinement. Probable cause is defined by AFMAN 71-102 as a "determination that there are reasonable grounds to believe that an offense has been committed and that the person to be identified as an offender committed it." Non-serious offenses, enumerated in AFMAN 71-102, Atch 5, are excluded from indexing. Examples of non-serious offenses include drunk and disorderly conduct, curfew violations, and minor traffic violations.

- Expungement: Entries will be removed, upon request, if there was no probable cause at the time of indexing to believe that the offense occurred or that the person indexed committed the offense or if the offense did not qualify for indexing

- Commander's responsibilities:

-- Coordinate with OSI or Security Forces to ensure indexing is accomplished if a Commander Directed Investigation (CDI) or informal inquiry results in preferral of serious charges to a court-martial; and

-- Report administrative disposition of offenses to OSI or SF (e.g., no action, letters of counseling, reprimand or admonition, administrative discharges).

Combined DNA Index System (CODIS)

- A nationwide database maintained by the FBI of DNA specimens collected from persons under criminal investigation

- Impact of entry: Once entered, DNA is subject to comparison with other DNA profiles and used to solve crimes and link serial offenders

- Basis for entry: A probable cause determination that the individual committed a serious offense punishable by confinement. Non-serious offenses, enumerated in AFMAN 71-102, Atch 5, are excluded from indexing.

- Expungement: Entries will be removed, upon request, if current or former military members were not convicted of any offense at a general or special court-martial, if their convictions were overturned, or if they were never criminally charged (e.g., if no action or administrative action only was taken)

- Commander's responsibilities:

-- Coordinate with OSI or SF to ensure indexing is accomplished if a CDI or informal inquiry results in preferral of serious charges to a general or special court-martial

-- Indorse expungement requests by current military members to confirm whether or not they were convicted of any offense by a general court-martial (GCM) or special court-martial (SPCM)

National Instant Criminal Background Check System (NICS)

- A nationwide database maintained by the FBI of persons who are prohibited by from possessing, receiving, shipping, or transporting firearms, ammunition, or explosives, in or affecting interstate commerce

- Impact of entry: Immediate denial of ability to possess, receive, ship, or transport firearms, ammunition, or explosives

- Basis for entry: A determination that the individual met the criteria set forth in 18 U.S.C. § 922(g) or (n). Categories of prohibited persons include persons who are or have been:

-- (1) convicted of a crime punishable by imprisonment for a term exceeding one year (for military members, GCM convictions only);

-- (2) fugitives from justice;

-- (3) unlawful users of or addicted to any controlled substance;

-- (4) adjudicated as a mental defective or committed to a mental institution;

-- (5) aliens illegally in the United States;

-- (6) discharged from the Armed Forces with a dishonorable discharge or dismissal;

-- (7) renounced their United States citizenship;

-- (8) subject to a court order restraining the person from harassing, stalking, or threatening an intimate partner or the child of an intimate partner (military protection orders do not qualify);

-- (9) convicted of a misdemeanor crime of domestic violence; or

-- (10) under indictment/information for a crime punishable by imprisonment for a term exceeding one year (for military members, if qualifying charges are referred to a GCM).

- Expungement: Entries will be removed, upon request, if the criteria for entry are not met

- Commander's responsibilities:

-- Notify military members under their command via AF Form 177, *Notice of Qualification for Prohibition of Firearms, Ammunition, and Explosives,* when they are identified as meeting the criteria for entry into the NICS, and **within 24 hours**, email a copy of the completed AF Form 177 to DAF-CJIC (daf.cjic@us.af.mil) and provide a copy to the servicing legal office

-- Report all subjects who meet NICS prohibitions to DAF-CJIC **within one duty day** of commencing a CDI or informal inquiry

-- Report to DAF-CJIC when military members are adjudicated as mental defectives or committed to a mental institution

Protection Order File (POF)

- A nationwide database maintained by the FBI of civilian protection orders (CPOs) and military protection orders (MPOs) issued to prevent domestic violence, stalking, and harassment

- Impact of entry: Civilian and military authorities will be aware of existence of CPOs and MPOs. Although civilian authorities cannot enforce MPOs, they may contact military authorities in the event of off-base violations.

- Basis for entry: Issuance of CPO or MPO

- Expungement: Entries will be removed upon expiration or termination of the order

- Commander's responsibilities:

-- Report issuance, extension, modification, or termination of MPO **within 24 hours** to primary law enforcement control center (law enforcement desk, base defense operations center, or OSI)

-- Notify primary law enforcement control center **within 24 hours** upon learning of issuance of CPO

-- Advise MPO-protected persons that MPOS are not enforceable off-base by civilian authorities and to consider seeking a CPO

National Sex Offender Registry (NSOR)

- A nationwide database of individuals who are required to register in a state, territorial, or tribal sex offender registry

- Impact of entry: Immediate identification as a nationally registered sex offender; also, may impact employment or volunteer opportunities and may trigger related restrictions

- Basis for entry: Conviction of a qualifying offense under the UCMJ or United States Code; qualifying offenses include sexually violent offenses or certain offenses against minors, see AFMAN 71-102, para. 3.1., and DoDI 1325.07, *Administration of Military Correctional Facilities and Clemency and Parole Authority*, Appx 4 to Encl 2

- Expungement: Entries will be removed upon receipt by the Air Force of notification from the state, tribe or territory that the individual has registered as a sex offender or is not required to do so under state, tribal or territorial law

- Commander's responsibilities: None

Defense Central Index of Investigations (DCII)

- A DoD database of investigations conducted by DoD law enforcement activities (LEAs) and personnel security determinations made by DoD adjudicative authorities, maintained by the Defense Counterintelligence and Security Agency

- Impact of entry: Investigators may retrieve information in this database for use in criminal, security clearance, and background investigations; entry into this database is an administrative procedure that does not imply any degree of guilt or innocence and judicial or adverse administrative actions may not be taken based solely on the existence of a DCII entry, DoDI 5505.07, *Titling and Indexing by DoD Law Enforcement Activities*, para. 1.2.c.

- Basis for entry: Credible information that the subject of an investigation committed a criminal offense. Credible information is defined in AFMAN 71-102 as "information disclosed or obtained by a DoD law enforcement activity that, considering the source and nature of the information and the totality of the circumstances, is sufficiently believable to lead a trained DoD LEA person to presume the fact or facts in question are true."

- Expungement: Entries will be removed, upon request, if probable cause did not or does not exist to believe that the offense for which the person was indexed occurred or that the person indexed committed it. Probable cause is defined in AFMAN 71-102 as a "determination that there are reasonable grounds to believe that an offense has been committed and that the person to be identified as the offender committed it."

- Commander's responsibilities: None

References

· Unlawful Acts, 18, U.S.C. § 922

· DoDI 1325.07, *Administration of Military Correctional Facilities and Clemency and Parole Authority* (March 11, 2013, incorporating through Change 4, August 19, 2020)

· DoDI 5505.07, *Titling and Indexing by DoD Law Enforcement Activities* (8 August 2023)

· AFMAN 71-102, *Air Force Criminal Indexing* (21 July 2020)

· AF Form 177, *Notice of Qualification for Prohibition of Firearms, Ammunition, and Explosives* (30 July 2020)

INSPECTIONS AND SEARCHES

Military law authorizes a commander to direct inspections of persons and property under his/her command and to authorize probable cause searches and seizures of persons and property under his/her command. However, a commander who authorizes a search or seizure must be neutral and detached from the case and facts.

Key Takeaways

» Searches/seizures require probable cause, or consent, and are intended to obtain evidence for disciplinary reasons

» Inspections do **NOT** require probable cause, are usually authorized by individual commanders, and are intended for non-prosecutorial reasons

» Due to the dynamic nature of this area of the law, commanders should seek the advice of the servicing Staff Judge Advocate (SJA) office **PRIOR** to making any decisions on a search, seizure, or inspection

---

Key Terms

- Search: Examination of a person, property, or premises, for the purpose of finding evidence for use in trial by court-martial or in other disciplinary proceedings

- Seizure: The meaningful interference with an individual's possessory interest in property, usually by taking and withholding the property

- Inspection: Examinations of a person, property, or premises for the *primary* purpose of determining and ensuring security, military fitness, or good order and discipline

Searches

- A search may be authorized on the following people and things:

-- Persons subject to the Uniform Code Military Justice (UCMJ) and under the commander's command

-- Persons or property situated in a place under the commander's command and control

-- Military property or property of a nonappropriated fund instrumentality (NAFI)

-- Property in a foreign country which is owned, used, occupied by, or held in the possession of a member under the commander's command

- A search may be authorized for the following types of evidence:

-- Contraband or prohibited property (e.g., drugs, unregistered firearms)

-- Fruits of a crime (e.g., stolen property, money)

-- Evidence of a crime (e.g., bloody clothing, weapon, fingerprints, bodily fluids)

Probable Cause Searches

- As a general rule, probable cause is required before legally authorizing a search

  -- Probable cause exists when there is a reasonable belief that the person, property, or evidence sought is located in the place or on the person to be searched

  -- Probable cause may arise from your personal knowledge or hearsay/third party knowledge (or both), and may come from oral or written evidence (or both)

  -- An anonymous tip, by itself, does not justify a probable cause search, but can if it has enough indicia of reliability and specifics to indicate personal knowledge

- A search authority may orally authorize a search/seizure when exigent circumstances exist. "Exigent circumstances" means there is a reasonable belief that a delay in obtaining authorization would result in the removal, destruction, or concealment of the property or evidence sought. Probable cause is still required and it should be later recorded in writing on an AF Form 1176, *Authority to Search and Seize.*

Mechanics of a Search Request

- If you learn of information which may justify a search:

  -- "Freeze" the situation (i.e., control access to the area to be searched, if within the commander's control, so that the scene and potential evidence remain undisturbed)

  -- Immediately notify Security Forces or the Office of Special Investigations (OSI). Do not personally investigate.

  -- Coordinate with your servicing SJA

Consent Searches

- A search authorization is **NOT** required if the individual whose person or property is to be searched consents to the search

  -- Consent must be freely given and cannot result from threats, coercion, or pressure

  -- The best practice is to have a third person present as a witness when requesting consent to search

  -- Consent may be given orally or in writing. When possible, use AF Form 1364, *Consent for Search and Seizure.*

Electronic Device Searches

- To search *personal* computers, cell phones/tablets, or storage devices, a search authorization based on probable cause or consent is required

- To search *government* computers, cell phones/tablets, or storage devices, a search authorization based on probable cause might be required. Contact your servicing SJA.

- Certain electronic communications services (e.g., WhatsApp, SnapChat, Facebook Messenger, iMessage) and remote computer services (e.g., Apple iCloud, DropBox, Google Drive) require a warrant that can only be authorized by a military judge

Inspections

- Inspections are not searches, so they do not require probable cause

- Inspections may be "announced" or "unannounced"

- Inspections may be conducted personally by the commander or by others at the commander's direction

- An inspection cannot be used as subterfuge for a search/seizure

  -- The best practice is to prepare a memorandum for record concerning the purpose of the inspection to refresh memory if later called upon to testify

- Inspections must be conducted in a "reasonable manner"

  -- An inspection is "reasonable" if the scope, intensity, and manner of execution of the inspection is reasonably related to its purpose

  -- For example, if the purpose of an inspection is to look for fire hazards near office electrical outlets, inspecting the contents of the desk drawers would be unreasonable since items located in the desk drawers would not risk an electrical fire

- An examination for the primary purpose of obtaining evidence for use in disciplinary proceedings is not an "inspection." It is a "search" and, if not authorized based on probable cause, it is **illegal**.

- Examples of Lawful Inspections:

  -- Random urinalysis inspection program

  -- Unit or base-wide "dorm sweeps" or unit urinalysis "sweep" (ordered by installation or unit commander) so long as it is not done to facilitate a particularized suspicion

  -- "Operation Nighthawk" (selection for urinalysis of random individuals entering the installation in the late evening or early morning hours of a pre-designated day)

References
- Article 15, Uniform Code of Military Justice
- AF Form 1176, *Authority to Search and Seize* (1 February 2019)
- AF Form 1364, *Consent for Search and Seizure* (5 August 2019)

INQUIRY OR INVESTIGATION INTO REPORTED OFFENSES

When commanders learn of an allegation of misconduct against one of their members, commanders must ensure the allegation is properly evaluated. In cases involving a potential disciplinary action or any criminal offense, commanders should consult with the legal office.

Key Takeaways

» When a military member is accused or suspected of an offense, the member's immediate commander has primary responsibility for ensuring an inquiry or investigation is conducted

» All allegations of a sexual nature must be referred to Air Force Office of Special Investigations (OSI) for investigation

» For offenses under command authority, once the commander has all the relevant facts necessary to make a decision, he/she should consider what action, if any, should be taken, and take action in a timely manner

» For offenses under OSTC authority, commanders of the victim and the accused are entitled to provide non-binding disposition input to OSTC

Initial Investigation of Suspected Offenses

- DoD policy requires commanders at all levels to ensure that allegations of misconduct involving persons affiliated with the DoD or any property or programs under their control are referred to OSI and/or Security Forces. See DoDI 5505.03, *Initiation of Investigations by Defense Criminal Investigative Organizations*. For assistance in making this determination, commanders should consult with their servicing legal office upon learning of any criminal allegation.

- Minor Offenses: In some cases, the chain of command or first sergeant may be the appropriate authority to conduct the inquiry—this is often referred to as an informal inquiry (or a commander's inquiry). The commander may also consider a commander directed investigation (CDI) to have a neutral individual assess the situation. For assistance in making this determination, commanders should consult with their servicing legal office upon learning of any allegation of misconduct.

- Major Offenses: In more serious cases, law enforcement agents such as Security Forces investigators or OSI will conduct the investigation and report the results to the commander for disposition of the case

Disposition and Progressive Discipline Options Available to the Commander

- Once the commander has the relevant facts necessary to make a decision, he/she should consider what action, if any, should be taken, and take action in a timely manner

  -- Ordinarily the immediate commander of a person accused or suspected of committing an offense determines the appropriate initial disposition. Sexual offenses and other victim-based offenses have different disposition requirements, and disposition authority may be significantly higher or outside of the chain of command entirely. See "Command Response to Sexual Offenses" and "Office of Special Trial Counsel."

- Potential actions the commander may take include:

  -- No action

  -- Administrative action (e.g., letter of reprimand (LOR), letter of admonishment (LOA), letter of counseling (LOC), administrative demotion, removal from supervisory duties, denial of reenlistment, or involuntary discharge)

  -- Nonjudicial punishment under Article 15, Uniform Code of Military Justice (UCMJ)

  -- Preferral of court-martial charges (or forwarding of previously preferred court-martial charges)

References

- Manual for Courts-Martial, Appendix 2.1, *Disposition Guidance* (2024)
- Article 15, Uniform Code of Military Justice
- Rules for Courts-Martial 303 and 306 (2024)
- DoDI 5505.03, *Initiation of Investigations by Defense Criminal Investigative Organizations* (2 August 2023)
- SecDef Memorandum, *Withholding Initial Disposition Authority under the Uniform Code of Military Justice in Certain Sexual Assault Cases* (20 April 2012)

PREPARATION, PREFERRAL, AND PROCESSING OF CHARGES

When a commander determines a court-martial is the appropriate venue to handle alleged misconduct of a member, the commander should consult with the legal office to proceed.

Key Takeaways

» The preparation of courts-martial charges involves drafting charges and specifications with legal precision

» Preferral of charges is the act of formally accusing a military member of a violation of the Uniform Code of Military Justice (UCMJ)

» Processing the charges involves forwarding the charges and specifications to a convening authority

» An accused's right to a speedy trial—and the impact that unnecessary delay can have on the effectiveness of military justice—require charges be disposed of promptly

Preparation of Charges

- A charge states which article of the UCMJ the member is alleged to have violated

- A specification is a concise statement of exactly how the member allegedly violated the article

- Because precise legal language is required, the legal office drafts charges and specifications

  -- Charges are documented on the DD Form 458, *Charge Sheet*

Preferral of Charges

- Preferral is the first formal step in initiating a court-martial and is the act by which a person subject to the UCMJ formally accuses another person subject to the UCMJ of an offense

- Anyone subject to the UCMJ may prefer charges against another person subject to the UCMJ. For offenses under command authority, the immediate commander of an accused is ordinarily the individual who prefers charges. For offenses under OSTC authority, an STC is ordinarily the individual who prefers charges.

- Preferral requires the "accuser" (the person preferring the charge) to take an oath that he/she is a person subject to the UCMJ, that he/she either has personal knowledge of or has investigated the charge(s) and specification(s), and that the charge(s) and specification(s) are true to the best of his/her knowledge and belief

  -- An accuser is not required to believe the accused committed an offense beyond a reasonable doubt. They must only believe there is probable cause the accused committed the offense.

Processing of Charges

- Preferral does not require the presence of the accused. However, after preferral, the immediate commander must inform the accused of the charge. Notice to the accused typically occurs at the same time as preferral by the immediate commander reading the charge to the accused.

- The commander then forwards the charge with an indorsement memorandum to the summary court-martial convening authority (SCMCA). Typically, in the Department of the Air Force (DAF), the SCMCA is usually also the first SPCMCA in the chain, so the extra step of forwarding the charge from the SCMCA to the SPCMCA (if the case is not going to be tried at a Summary Court-Martial) is not required.

- For offenses under command authority, the SPCMCA can dismiss charges, return charges to a subordinate commander for alternate disposition, or take the following actions if the charges warrant a court-martial:

    -- Refer the charge to a special or summary court-martial; or

    -- Appoint a preliminary hearing officer (PHO) to conduct an Article 32 preliminary hearing.

- For offenses under OSTC authority, an STC will determine whether to dismiss the charges, defer the charges to command, refer the charge to a special court-martial, or submit a binding request to the convening authority to direct an Article 32 preliminary hearing and appoint a PHO

- The PHO completes and forwards the preliminary hearing report to the SPCMCA or STC for review, as applicable

- For offenses under command authority, the SPCMCA may then dismiss the charges or forward the preliminary hearing report along with the preferred charges to the general court-martial convening authority (GCMCA) for review and possible referral to a general court-martial

    -- The GCMCA can refer charges to a general, special, or summary court-martial, return charges to the SPCMCA for disposition, or dismiss charges

- For offenses under OSTC authority, an STC will determine whether to dismiss the charge, defer the charge to command, or refer the charge to a general or special court-martial

- Once the charge has been referred to trial, the appointed trial counsel will then formally serve the accused with a copy of the charges and specifications

- Time constraints are involved in the processing of court-martial charges. An accused's right to a speedy trial—and the impact that delay can have on the effectiveness of military justice—require that charges be disposed of promptly.

References

· Manual for Courts-Martial, Appendix 2.1, *Disposition Guidance* (2024)
· Articles 30 and 32, Uniform Code of Military Justice
· Rules for Courts-Martial 306, 307, and 405 (2024)
· DAFI 51-201, *Administration of Military Justice* (24 January 2024)
· DD Form 458, *Charge Sheet* (May 2000)

PRETRIAL RESTRAINT AND CONFINEMENT

Pretrial restraint and pretrial confinement are tools to ensure the appearance of the accused at their upcoming court-martial and/or to prevent the commission of serious misconduct by the accused while awaiting court-martial. Pretrial restraint may only be imposed when court-martial charges have been preferred or are anticipated.

> ## Key Takeaways
>
> » There are four types of pretrial restraint: (1) conditions on liberty; (2) restriction in lieu of arrest; (3) arrest; and (4) pretrial confinement
>
> » Commanders should select the least rigorous restraint necessary to assure appearance of an accused at court-martial or prevent commission of foreseeable serious misconduct pending court-martial
>
> » Before ordering any form of pretrial restraint, the commander must find probable cause exists that: (1) a violation of the Uniform Code of Military Justice (UCMJ) was committed; (2) the accused committed it; and (3) the restraint imposed is required by the circumstances
>
> » Never impose any form of pretrial restraint without first consulting the legal office because most forms of pretrial restraint trigger a speedy trial clock under Rules for Courts-Martial (RCM) 707

Who May Order Pretrial Restraint

- Officers: Only a commander in the service member's chain of command may impose pretrial restraint on an officer. This authority **MAY NOT** be delegated.

- Enlisted: Any commissioned officer may impose pretrial restraint on any enlisted member

    -- A commanding officer can delegate authority to order pretrial restraint of enlisted personnel under their command to Noncommissioned Officers (usually the first sergeant)

Pretrial Restraint Prerequisites

- Requires a reasonable belief that:

    -- An offense triable by court-martial has been committed

    -- The person to be restrained committed it

    -- Restraint is required by the circumstances

- Notice to Individual: The restrained individual must be personally notified of the nature of the offense which is the basis for the restraint and terms of the restraint. Individuals placed into pretrial confinement must also be notified of the right to remain silent, the right to counsel, the procedures involved, and how the review will occur.

- Release from Pretrial Restraint: Except as otherwise provided by RCM 305, a person may be released from pretrial restraint by any person authorized to impose the restraint

Types of Pretrial Restraint

- Conditions on Liberty: Imposed by orders directing a person to do or refrain from doing specified acts

  -- May be imposed in conjunction with other forms of restraint or separately

  -- Typical examples include orders to report periodically to a specified official, orders not to go to a certain place, and orders not to associate with specified persons

- Restriction in Lieu of Arrest: Imposed by ordering a person to remain within specified limits. Unless otherwise directed, the person will perform full military duties.

- Arrest: The restraint of a person, directing the person to remain within specified limits. Persons under arrest will not perform full military duties. The limits of arrest are normally narrower than those of restriction in lieu of arrest.

- Pretrial Confinement: Most severe type of pretrial restraint

  -- There is no "bail" in the military justice system. Therefore, placement into pretrial confinement requires a series of procedural safeguards requiring the government to demonstrate, by a preponderance of the evidence (i.e., more likely than not), that pretrial confinement is necessary under the circumstances.

Procedures Upon Entry Into Confinement

- The person to be confined must be promptly notified of the following:

  -- Nature of the offenses for which he/she is being held

  -- Right to remain silent and that any statement made may be used against him or her

  -- Right to request military counsel (at no expense) or retain civilian counsel (at their own expense)

  -- Procedures by which pretrial confinement will be reviewed

- Article 10, UCMJ, requires that "immediate steps" be taken to try the person or to dismiss the charges and release the person (usually requiring government to bring the accused to trial with reasonable diligence within 120 days)

- If the member is alleged to have committed an offense under OSTC authority, the servicing legal office must ensure the assigned STC is notified when the member is ordered into or released from pretrial confinement

Timelines Upon Entry Into Confinement

- 24-Hour Notification: If the person ordering confinement is not the confinee's commander, then the confinee's commander must be notified within 24 hours of the entry to confinement

- 48-Hour Probable Cause Determination:

  -- Within 48 hours of entry into confinement, a neutral and detached officer must review the adequacy of probable cause to continue confinement

- 72-Hour Commander Review:

  -- If confinement is continued, within 72 hours of entry into confinement, the confinee's commander must prepare a written memorandum justifying continued confinement

  -- It is not necessary to try lesser forms of restraint, but they **MUST** be considered in determining whether confinement is appropriate

    --- Convenience of the unit or suicide prevention of the accused are **NOT** valid reasons for pretrial confinement

- 7-Day Pretrial Confinement Review:

  -- Within seven days, a Pretrial Confinement Reviewing Officer (PCRO) must make written findings whether the confinee shall be released or remain confined

  -- The PCRO must review the commander's 72-hour memorandum to determine whether the requirements for pretrial confinement are met

  -- The PCRO shall consider matters submitted by the confinee, and shall allow the confinee and counsel an opportunity to appear and present a statement or evidence at the hearing

- Confinees receive day-for-day credit for pretrial confinement against any confinement adjudged by the court. Unlawful pretrial confinement, including pretrial punishment or restriction tantamount to confinement, may lead to additional credit.

- The remedy for non-compliance with pretrial confinement rules and standards can range from additional credit for each day of illegal confinement to dismissal of the charges

No Pretrial Punishment of Pretrial Confinees

- Pretrial restraint cannot be used to punish the person restrained

- Pretrial confinees may **NOT** be treated the same as sentenced prisoners, such as by being required to wear confinement uniforms, perform punitive labor, or undergo punitive duty hours

- Pretrial punishment includes public denunciation and degradation

- Commingling pretrial and sentenced prisoners, without more, is not automatically considered pretrial punishment

References

· Articles 10, 12, and 13, Uniform Code of Military Justice
· Rules for Courts-Martial 304, 305, and 707 (2024)
· DAFI 51-201, *Administration of Military Justice* (24 January 2024)

TRIAL FORMAT

A court-martial is the military equivalent to the civilian criminal trial. The process is governed by the Manual for Courts-Martial (MCM), which details military criminal procedure.

Key Takeaways

» The court-martial will consist of two major portions: (1) findings (guilty/not guilty determination) and, in the event of a conviction at findings, (2) sentencing

» In most types of courts-martial, an accused may elect to be tried by a military judge alone or by a panel of court members (the military counterpart to a civilian jury)

» All panel members must be senior in rank to the accused

» The accused is presumed innocent of all charges and specifications

Types of Courts-Martial

- Summary Court-Martial (enlisted only):

  -- The least severe court-martial. A finding of guilty at a summary court-martial is not a federal conviction.

  -- Presided over by a commissioned officer who may be a commander or a neutral judge advocate who is not affiliated with the legal office. Summary courts-martial are not typically presided over by a military judge.

  -- The accused may object to being tried in this forum

  -- Maximum authorized sentence:

    --- For enlisted members E-4 and below: one month of confinement, forfeiture of two-thirds pay per month for one month, and reduction to the grade of E-1

    --- For enlisted members E-5 and above: forfeiture of two-thirds pay per month for one month, reduction to the next lower grade, and restriction to certain limits for two months (confinement is not allowed)

- Military Judge Alone Special Court-Martial under Article 16(c)(2)(A):

  -- Presided over by a military judge alone

  -- Maximum authorized sentence: six months of confinement, forfeiture of two-thirds pay per month for six months, and reduction to E-1. A punitive discharge is not authorized.

  -- In certain circumstances, the accused may object to being tried in this forum

- Special Court-Martial:

  -- The panel is composed of four members

  -- The accused may elect trial by military judge alone

  -- Maximum authorized sentence:

    --- For enlisted members: twelve months of confinement, forfeiture of two-thirds pay per month for twelve months, reduction to the grade of E-1, and a bad conduct discharge (BCD)

    --- Officers and cadets may be sentenced up to 12 months of confinement but may not be sentenced to a dismissal by a special court-martial. For this reason, officers and cadets are rarely tried at a special court-martial.

- General Court-Martial:

  -- The panel is composed of 8 members (12 members in capital cases)

  -- Maximum authorized sentence at a general court-martial depends on the offense(s) charged and can include death or life without the possibility of parole, total forfeiture of a member's pay and allowances, reduction to E-1 for enlisted members, and a dishonorable discharge for enlisted members or a dismissal for officers

Findings

- Findings is the first part of the trial, during which it is determined whether the accused is guilty or not guilty

- An accused may plead guilty or not guilty. If the accused is charged with multiple offenses, he/she may plead guilty to all, some, or none of the offenses.

- Guilty Plea:

  -- Following an accused's plea of guilty, the military judge questions the accused under oath to make sure he/she is, in fact, guilty and understands the meaning and effect of pleading guilty to the specific offenses

  -- If the military judge accepts the guilty plea, the accused will then be sentenced by the military judge or a panel of members, whichever the accused elects

- Not Guilty Plea:

  -- Forum Choice:

    --- Enlisted Accused: An enlisted accused may elect trial by one of the following: (1) military judge alone; (2) all officer members; or (3) mixed panel of officer and enlisted members (at least one-third enlisted members included on the court-martial panel, all of whom must be senior in rank to the accused)

    --- Officer Accused: An officer accused may elect trial by one of the following: (1) military judge alone; or (2) officer members (all of whom must be senior in rank to the accused)

- The accused is presumed innocent of all charges and specifications

  -- The prosecution proceeds with its case first, calling witnesses and presenting evidence. The prosecution must prove the accused's guilt beyond a reasonable doubt in order to secure a conviction.

  -- Once the prosecution has finished, the defense has an opportunity to present its case. An accused has an absolute right to remain silent and has no obligation to present evidence. The accused may choose to testify or present evidence in his/her defense.

  -- If the defense presents a case, the prosecution may offer evidence or call witnesses in rebuttal. If the prosecution puts on a rebuttal case, the defense may offer additional evidence or call witnesses in surrebuttal.

  -- In non-capital cases with members, three-fourths of the members, voting by secret written ballot, must concur in any finding of guilty. In capital cases with members, three-fourths of members must still concur in any finding of guilt. However, for the death penalty to be adjudged, unanimity is required with regard to both the relevant finding(s) of guilt and any alleged aggravating factor(s).

Sentencing

- Sentencing is the second part of the trial if a member is found guilty of any offense during the findings portion. In this stage, an appropriate punishment is determined.

  -- Unlike many civilian courts, sentencing normally occurs immediately following findings

  -- In non-capital cases, the sentence is decided by a military judge alone

  -- Sentencing is an adversarial process that usually includes the presentation of evidence and may involve witnesses

    --- The prosecution may present matters in aggravation, show lack of rehabilitative potential in society, and rebut evidence the accused presents

--- The defense may present matters in extenuation to explain the circumstances surrounding the commission of the offense and/or matters in mitigation to lessen the punishment to be adjudged by the court-martial

--- As in the findings portion of trial, the accused also has an absolute right to remain silent and present no evidence during sentencing. In addition, the accused may elect to make a statement that is not offered under oath, known as an "unsworn statement."

--- A crime victim of an offense of which the accused has been found guilty has the right to be reasonably heard at sentencing, which can include an unsworn statement

-- In capital cases, a unanimous vote of panel members is required to sentence an accused to death

- After consideration of all matters in aggravation, extenuation and/or mitigation, and the sentencing criteria and parameters applicable to a particular offense or offenses, a military judge will sentence the accused within the discretion of the court-martial

References

· U.S. Const. Amend. V.

· Article 16(c)(2)(A), Uniform Code of Military Justice

· Rules for Courts-Martial 201, 501, 705, 903, 910, 913, 918, 921, 1001, 1002, 1003, 1004, 1006, 1301, and 1303 (2024)

· DAFI 51-201, *Administration of Military Justice* (24 January 2024)

CONFIDENTIALITY AND PRIVILEGED COMMUNICATIONS

In the military, only certain communications are recognized as privileged and therefore protected from disclosure. Privileges are narrowly construed. Privilege may be waived by the privilege holder, which occurs when the privilege holder voluntarily discloses or consents to disclosure of any significant part of the matter or communication. For guidance regarding whether a privilege applies in a particular circumstance, commanders should consult their servicing legal office.

Key Takeaways

» The law recognizes privilege can apply to communications made to clergy, attorneys, mental health care providers, spouses, victim advocates, and, sometimes, communications made for the purpose of drug abuse treatment

» The Military Rules of Evidence (M.R.E.) do not recognize a medical physician-patient privilege. Disclosure of medical records and communications to physicians are governed by Health Insurance Portability and Accountability Act (HIPAA).

» Communications to clergy, mental health care providers, victim advocates, and attorneys are privileged only when the communications are made to such a person acting in an official capacity

Communications to Clergy

- A person has a privilege to refuse to disclose and to prevent another from disclosing a privileged communication by the person to a clergyman or to a clergyman's assistant in their capacity as a spiritual advisor, if such communication is made as a formal act of religion or matter of conscience

- The privilege extends to the chaplain's or clergyman's staff

Attorney-Client Privilege

- Privilege applies to all information divulged to an attorney who represents a person, including an Area Defense Counsel, Victims' Counsel or legal assistance attorney, except with respect to some future crimes or frauds and other limited exceptions

- Communications between a commander and Staff Judge Advocate are privileged only when the commander is acting as an agent or official of the Department of the Air Force (DAF) and the commander's interests in no way conflict with those of the DAF

- The privilege extends to non-lawyer members of the attorney's staff

Physician-Patient

- The Military Rules of Evidence do not recognize a medical physician-patient privilege

Medical Records

- Military medical records are the property of the Department of Defense

- Information in the health record is personal to the individual and will be properly safeguarded pursuant to HIPAA

- Commanders or commanders' designees may access members' military medical records, but only to the extent necessary to ensure mission accomplishment

Psychotherapist-Patient Privilege

- A limited privilege exists between patients and psychotherapists

    -- Generally, the limited privilege protects only confidential communications which are made to a psychotherapist (or assistant) for the purpose of diagnosis or treatment of the person's mental or emotional condition in cases arising under the Uniform Code of Military Justice (UCMJ). The privilege does not necessarily extend to diagnoses and treatments contained within medical records.

    -- Exceptions include: (1) when the patient is dead; (2) the communication is evidence of child abuse or neglect, or in a proceeding in which one spouse is charged with a crime against a child of either spouse; (3) when the psychotherapist believes that a patient's mental or emotional condition makes the patient a danger to any person, including the patient; (4) when the communication clearly contemplates future commission of a fraud or crime; (5) when necessary to ensure safety and security of military personnel or property; or (6) law or regulation imposes a duty to report the information

- Under DAFI 51-201, *Administration of Military Justice*, communications between a patient and a psychotherapist (or assistant) made for purposes of facilitating diagnosis or treatment of the patient's mental or emotional condition are confidential and must be protected against unauthorized disclosure

- A limited privilege also exists under the Limited Privilege Suicide Prevention (LPSP) Program under DAFI 51-201, which applies to communications made after notification of an investigation and placement into the LPSP program

DoD Safety Privilege

- The deliberations, opinions, recommendations, and conclusions of safety investigators and any evidence from witnesses and contractors given under a promise of confidentiality are privileged and not releasable outside DoD safety channels

- These investigations are conducted solely for DoD mishap prevention purposes and access is highly restricted even within DoD and the DAF

Victim Advocate-Victim Privilege

- A limited privilege exists between victim advocates and victims of sexual or violent offenses

  -- Generally, the limited privilege protects only confidential communications between a victim and a victim advocate or between the victim and DoD Safe Helpline staff, for victims of sexual or violent offenses in a case arising under the UCMJ, made for the purpose of facilitating advice or supportive assistance to the victim

  -- Exceptions include, but are not limited to: (1) when the patient is dead; (2) federal/state law or service regulations impose a duty to report; (3) when the victim advocate believes that a victim's mental or emotional condition makes the victim a danger to any person, including the victim; (4) the communication clearly contemplated the future commission of a fraud or crime; (5) when necessary to ensure safety and security of military personnel or property; or (6) disclosure is constitutionally required

Drug/Alcohol Abuse Treatment Patients

- AFI 44-121, *Alcohol and Drug Abuse Prevention and Treatment (ADAPT) Program*, grants limited protections for DAF members who voluntarily disclose personal drug use or possession. Those protections do not include any future drug abuse.

  -- Such disclosure may not be used as the basis for UCMJ action or for the characterization of service in a discharge proceeding

  -- A member must disclose their drug abuse before the use is discovered or the member is placed under investigation. The member may not disclose after he is ordered to give a urine sample as part of the drug testing program in which the results are pending or have been returned as positive.

- Federal law protects medical records pertaining to drug and alcohol abuse

Marital Privilege

- A spouse may elect not to testify against the accused if a valid marriage exists at the time the spouse is to provide testimony (testimonial privilege)

- A spouse may prevent testimony by the other spouse (or ex-spouse) regarding private communications made during the marriage even if the marriage has been dissolved at the time of testimony (marital communications privilege)

- Neither privilege (testimonial or marital communications) applies when one spouse is charged with a crime against the person or property of the other spouse, child, or children of either spouse, if the marriage is a sham as determined by state law, or if the spouses are co-conspirators in a crime

Medical Quality Assurance Privilege

- 10 U.S.C. § 1102 generally restricts access to information emanating from a medical quality assurance program activity. Release is authorized "[t]o an officer, employee, or contractor of the Department of Defense who has a need for such [information] to perform official duties."

Family Support Center Program

- Family Support Center (FSC) staff should neither state nor imply that confidentiality exists

- The FSC Director will notify the appropriate authority when a DAF member constitutes a potential danger to self, others, or could have an impact on the mission

References

· The Privacy Act of 1974, 5 U.S.C. § 552a

· Confidentiality of Medical Quality Assurance Records: Qualified Immunity for Participants, 10 U.S.C. § 1102

· Confidentiality of Records, 42 U.S.C. § 290dd-2

· Rule for Courts-Martial 706 (2024)

· Military Rules of Evidence 302, 501–514 (2024)

· *United States v. Weber Aircraft Corp.*, 465 U.S. 792 (1984)

· DoDI 6025.18, *Health Insurance Portability and Accountability Act (HIPAA) Privacy Rule Compliance in DoD Health Care Programs* (13 March 2019)

· DoDI 6055.07, *Mishap Notification, Investigation, Reporting, and Record Keeping* (6 June 2011), incorporating through Change 2, 11 June 2019

· DAFI 36-2710, *Equal Opportunity Program* (18 June 2020), incorporating DAFGM2023-02, 23 December 2023

· DAFI 36-3009, *Military and Family Readiness Centers* (4 November 2022)

· DAFI 51-201, *Administration of Military Justice* (24 January 2024)

· DAFI 91-204, *Safety Investigations and Reporting* (10 March 2021)

· AFI 33-332, *Air Force Privacy and Civil Liberties Program* (10 March 2020), Corrective Actions applied on 12 May 2020

· AFI 44-121, *Alcohol and Drug Abuse Prevention and Treatment (ADAPT) Program*, including DAFGM2024-01, 3 January 2024

· AFI 51-110, *Professional Responsibility Program* (11 December 2018)

POST-SENTENCING MATTERS

Many courts-martial sentences do not go into effect automatically. All sentences of courts-martial are subject to post-trial review by the convening authority and appellate review by applicable military authorities. In the event of a court-martial conviction and sentence, the accused has the right to submit post-trial matters to the convening authority for clemency consideration. Further appellate review of the accused's case is determined by the severity of the sentence. Finally, in the event of a court-martial conviction and sentence involving a victim, the victim is also entitled to submit post-trial matters for the convening authority's review.

Key Takeaways

» Subsequent to court-martial and after the military judge prepares a Statement of Trial Results, the victim, the accused, and defense counsel should receive a copy of the Statement of Trial Results

» Both the victim and the accused can submit clemency matters to the convening authority. The victim's submission must be presented to the accused.

» After the convening authority receives clemency matters, the convening authority will consult with the Staff Judge Advocate (SJA) before taking action or deciding to take no action on the accused's findings or sentence

» The Entry of Judgment will be prepared by the military judge, and will reflect the results of the accused's court-martial as well as the convening authority's decision to take action or no action on the findings and sentence

Statement of Trial Results and Submissions by the Accused and Victim

- Following a court-martial, the military judge prepares and signs a Statement of Trial Results (STR). This should take place on the day the sentence in the case is announced. The STR summarizes the findings and sentence of the case and is provided to the accused's immediate commander, the convening authority, and, in cases of confinement, the confinement facility. The accused, defense counsel, and victims(s) will also receive the STR.

- Within 10 calendar days (seven calendar days for summary courts-martial) of the sentence being announced, the accused and victim(s) in a case have an opportunity to submit clemency matters to the convening authority for the convening authority's consideration as to whether to approve findings of guilt or to approve or disapprove all or part of the sentence

  -- Accused and victim(s) may also request an extension of time of up to 20 days to submit clemency matters

  -- Accused and victim(s) may also waive his/her right to submit clemency matters

- Trial counsel shall make reasonable efforts to inform a crime victim of the right to submit a statement and the manner in which it may be submitted

- The accused may submit any clemency matters that may reasonably tend to inform the convening authority's exercise of discretion under the clemency rules. The matters must be in writing but cannot include matters that relate to the character of a crime victim unless they were admitted as evidence at trial.

- The victim may submit any clemency matters that may reasonably tend to inform the convening authority's exercise of discretion under the clemency rules. The matters must be in writing but cannot include matters that relate to the character of the accused unless they were admitted as evidence at trial. The crime victim is entitled to only one opportunity to submit matters to the convening authority.

  -- In a case where a crime victim submits matters, the accused shall be given five (5) days from the receipt of those matters to submit any matters in rebuttal. The issues are limited to those raised in the crime victim's submissions.

Convening Authority Action

- After the court-martial is over, depending on the nature of the offenses and the punishment, the convening authority has limited authority to take "action" on the findings or sentence

- The convening authority is required to consult with the SJA or legal advisor before taking action on the findings and/or sentence of a court-martial. The convening authority must also review matters timely submitted by the accused and victim(s) (if applicable) and may consider other matters (to include the STR and evidence introduced at the court-martial) before taking action.

- After considering such matters, the convening authority may take no action on the findings and sentence if all the convicted offenses occurred after 1 January 2019. If no action is taken, the convening authority's SJA or legal advisor shall notify the military judge that no action was taken.

- If one of the convicted offenses occurred before 1 January 2019, the convening authority is required to take "action" on the sentence. If action is taken, the convening authority's decision should be in writing and include a statement explaining the reasons for the action. The convening authority's SJA or legal advisor shall forward the written action to the military judge.

  -- Taking "action" should be one of the following post-trial actions: approve, disapprove, commute, or suspend the sentence in whole or in part

- In general and special courts-martial, after the convening authority action or notification that no action was taken, the military judge will complete an "Entry of Judgment" which terminates the trial proceedings and initiates the appellate process. The "Entry of Judgment" reflects the result of the court-martial as modified by any post-trial action, rulings, or orders.

Effective Date of Court-Martial Punishments

- <u>General and Special Courts-Martial</u>: Generally, the sentence takes effect when the judgment is entered into the record by military judge ("Entry of Judgment")

- <u>Summary Courts-Martial</u>: Takes effect when the convening authority takes action

- <u>Exceptions in General and Special Courts-Martial</u>:

  -- *Punitive Discharge:* Not effective unless and until approved after appellate review

  -- *Confinement:* Effective immediately unless deferred (i.e., delay the effective date). Deferment ends when the military judge enters judgment into the record (Entry of Judgment) unless otherwise stated by the convening authority.

  -- *Reduction in Grade:* Effective 14 days after announcement of the sentence or the date on which the sentence is approved by the convening authority (summary court-martial only) unless deferred

  -- *Forfeiture of Pay and Allowances:* Effective 14 days after announcement of the sentence or the date on which the sentence is approved by the convening authority (summary courts-martial only) unless deferred or waived. Forfeitures cannot be deferred or waived if the member's ETS date has passed. There are a number of rules that impact the deferment and waiver of forfeitures and these rules address adjudged and automatic forfeitures.

    --- *Automatic Forfeitures:* An accused automatically forfeits pay and allowances, up to the jurisdictional limits of the court-martial, during any period of confinement if the adjudged sentence includes death, a punitive discharge, or any sentence to confinement for more than six months. The jurisdictional limit at a general court-martial (GCM) is total forfeiture of a member's pay and allowances, and the limit at a special court-martial (SPCM) is forfeiture of two-thirds pay per month for 12 months.

    --- *Waiver of Automatic Forfeitures:* In addition, when taking action, the convening authority may lessen the impact of "automatic" forfeitures of pay by "waiving" them for up to six months. A convening authority may only waive mandatory forfeitures in cases where the accused has dependents. The waived forfeitures are for the benefit of the accused's dependents and are paid directly to the dependents.

- <u>Restriction and Hard Labor Without Confinement</u>: Effective upon Entry of Judgment and executed concurrently

References

· Articles 57, 58a, 58b, 60, 60a, 60b, and 60c, Uniform Code of Military Justice
· Rules for Courts-Martial 1101–1114 (2024)
· *United States v. Emminizer*, 56 M.J. 441 (C.A.A.F. 2002)
· *United States v. Brubaker-Escobar*, 81 M.J. 471 (C.A.A.F. 2021)
· DAFI 51-201, *Administration of Military Justice* (24 January 2024)

Page Intentionally Left Blank

Chapter 6
PERSONNEL ISSUES – GENERALLY

TOTAL FORCE: AIR RESERVE COMPONENT

Regular Air Force and Space Force, Air National Guard (ANG), and Air Force Reserve (AFR) service members work together as a team in air, space, and cyberspace worldwide. Together, the AFR and ANG make up the Air Reserve Component (ARC). The ARC's mission is to provide combat ready forces to the Department of the Air Force (DAF) whenever needed.

ARC Personnel Categories

- Ready Reserve: Includes the Selected Reserve and Individual Ready Reserve (IRR) who are available to be involuntarily ordered to active duty in time of war or national emergency, pursuant to 10 U.S.C. §§ 12301 and 12302

  -- *Selected Reserve:* Those units and individuals within the Ready Reserve approved by the Joint Chiefs of Staff as essential to initial wartime missions that they have priority over all other reserve components. It includes Traditional Reservists (TRs), Individual Mobilization Augmentees (IMAs), Active Guard Reservists (AGRs), and Air Reserve Technicians (ARTs).

  -- *IRR:* Individuals who have had training and previous experience in the Regular component or the Selected Reserve and still have a military service obligation

  -- Includes all ANG (including Inactive National Guard)

- Active Guard Reserve (AGR): Reservists on full-time active duty for the primary purpose of organizing, administering, recruiting, instructing, or training Reserve Component units. AGRs may also perform other duties prescribed in 10 U.S.C. § 12310(b) to the extent that the performance of those duties does not interfere with the performance of their primary AGR duties. AGRs do not usually mobilize, as they are the steady force that stays to organize, administer, recruit, instruct, or train others.

- Standby Reserve: Pool of trained individuals (other than those in the Ready Reserve or Retired Reserve) who could be ordered to active duty only in time of war or national emergency

- Retired Reserve: Reservists who have at least 20 years of service and are either waiting to turn 60 years of age to collect retirement pay (nicknamed a "Gray Area" retiree) or are over age 60 and receiving retirement pay

- Regular Active Duty Retired: May be ordered to active duty by the Secretary of the Air Force (SecAF) if deemed necessary for the national defense

Air Force Reserve

- AFR is an integrated Total Force partner in every DAF core mission, providing combat-ready forces to fly, fight, and win. In addition to the categories discussed above, participating reservists hold a duty status.

- <u>Types of Reserve Personnel Duty Status</u>:

  -- *ART:* Members are full-time federal civil service employees of a DAF reserve unit and serve in dual roles as both civilians and Reserve service members. The primary purpose of ARTs is organizing, administering, instructing, or training of the Selected Reserve or the maintenance and repair of supplies or equipment issued to the Selected Reserve or the armed forces. ARTs may perform certain additional duties prescribed in 10 U.S.C. 10216(a)(3) to the extent that the performance of those duties does not interfere with the performance of the primary duties.

  -- *TRs (CAT A):* Members assigned to stand-alone reserve units

    --- Required to perform 14 days of Annual Training (AT) and 24 days during Unit Training Assemblies (UTAs) in Inactive Duty Training (IDT) status (each UTA day counts for two IDTs, for a total of 48 IDTs required)

  -- *IMAs (CAT B):* Members augment, and are attached to, active component and government agency missions and are rated by active component or government agency supervisors

    --- Required to perform 12 days of IDT per year (two IDT periods per day for a total of 24 IDTs) and 12–14 days of AT, in a Title 10, active duty status per year

    --- IMAs may volunteer for additional active duty orders or be mobilized to fill DAF mission requirements

  -- *Participating Individual Ready Reservist:* Participate for points only that are applied toward retirement

Air National Guard

- ANG members have a dual role based on the Militia Clause of U.S. Constitution, Article 1, Section 8

  -- <u>Federal Role (Title 10)</u>: Mission is to maintain well-trained, well-equipped units available for prompt mobilization under Title 10 of the United States Code during war and national emergencies

  -- <u>State Role (Title 32)</u>: Mission is to provide trained, organized, and disciplined units and individuals to protect life, property, and preserve peace, order and public safety within the state or territory by providing emergency relief support, search and rescue, support to civil defense authorities and counterdrug operations

-- There are also National Guard Title 32 technicians and Title 5 employees who are federal civilian employees. The Title 32 technicians must be members of the state ANG in addition to their federal civil service (dual status technicians). The primary purpose of Title 32 technicians is organizing, administrating, instructing, or training of the National Guard and the maintenance and repair of equipment/supplies issued to the National Guard or the armed forces. Title 32 technicians may also perform certain additional duties as prescribed by 32 U.S.C. 709 to the extent that the performance of those duties does not interfere with the performance of their primary duties. Military membership is not required for Title 5 employees.

- ANG Required Training: 24 days of IDTs (two IDTs per day for a total of 48 IDTs) and 15 days of Annual Training (AT) service per year

Administrative and Disciplinary Action

- Air Force Reservists:

-- Reservists are subject to the Uniform Code of Military Justice (UCMJ) in active duty and IDT status

-- Address questions of alleged misconduct or administrative actions to include separation and/or demotion involving IMAs to their respective active duty Staff Judge Advocate (SJA) and the Headquarters Readiness and Integration Organization (HQ RIO) legal advisor located at Headquarters Air Reserve Personnel Center (ARPC)'s legal office (ARPC/JA). ARPC/JA advises the Individual Reservist's (IR) HQ RIO Detachment Commander and the RIO/CC. The active duty commander and HQ RIO Detachment Commander share administrative control (ADCON) over the IR.

-- Address questions about alleged misconduct involving Traditional Reservists and ARTs to their reserve unit's SJA who coordinates with their respective Numbered Air Force legal office (NAF/JA) and HQ AFRC/JA

-- If deployed, look to member's activation orders for guidance

- ANG Members:

-- Misconduct of ANG members is governed by the member's status at the time of the alleged misconduct. ANG personnel are only subject to the UCMJ when "in Federal service" (Article 2(a)(3), UCMJ), although they may be subject to their particular state military justice code at other times. The member must be in Federal service when disciplinary action is taken under the UCMJ. ANG members may be subject to administrative action even when not in Federal service. Consult the local SJA before initiating disciplinary or administrative actions against ANG members.

-- Activation orders show if member is in Title 10 (Federal) or Title 32 (state) status and where they are assigned for administrative control/operational control

-- If in Title 10 status, contact the local SJA, who will coordinate with the 201st Mission Support Squadron's legal office (201 MSS/JA)

-- If in Title 32 status, contact the local SJA, who will coordinate with the member's home unit SJA (unless orders direct otherwise)

-- If in military technician status, contact the local SJA, who will coordinate through member's home unit (if in military status) or the applicable State Human Resources Office (if in civilian status)

References

· U.S. Const. Art. I, § 8

· Reserve Officer Personnel Management Act, 10 U.S.C. §§ 10141–10154

· Reserve Forces Revitalization Act of 1996, 10 U.S.C. §§ 10215–10218

· Reserve Forces Act of 1955, 10 U.S.C. §§ 12301 *et seq.*

· National Guard, 32 U.S.C. §§ 101–908 (2004)

· Article 2(a)(3), Uniform Code of Military Justice

· DoDI 1215.06, *Uniform Reserve, Training, and Retirement Categories for the Reserve Components* (11 March 2014), incorporating through Change 2, 12 July 2022

· DAFI 36-3211, *Military Separations* (24 June 2022), incorporating Change 1, 20 November 2023

· DAFMAN 36-2114, *Management of the Air Force Reserve Individual Reserve (IR) and Full-Time Support (FTS) Programs* (24 May 2021)

· DAFMAN 36-2136, *Reserve Personnel Participation* (15 December 2023)

· ANGI 36-2001 *Management of Training and Operational Support within the Air National Guard* (30 April 2019)

AIR NATIONAL GUARD DUTY STATUS

Members of the Air National Guard (ANG) may serve in various federal missions during their career, but upon completion of any active duty tour, they are reassigned to their state. The ANG has three basic types of statuses.

State Active Duty (SAD)

- Application: When activated by the state for a purely state function

- Benefits: Member's pay and benefits are provided by the state and there is no federal military pay or retirement benefits

  -- Servicemembers Civil Relief Act (SCRA): Members on SAD orders are not covered under SCRA. Members may be covered under their state equivalent of SCRA.

  -- Department of Veterans Affairs (VA) benefits: Members on SAD orders may not be entitled to certain benefits administered by the VA. Members may be entitled to special state health benefits.

  -- Uniformed Services Employment and Reemployment Rights Act (USERRA): USERRA applies to SAD if: (1) duty is for 14 days or more; **and** (2) duty is in support of a national emergency declared by the President under the National Emergencies Act; **or** (3) the duty is in support of a major disaster declared by the President under Section 401 of the Stafford Act. Additionally, the member's state may have an equivalent to USERRA under state law.

- Liability: The state is responsible for addressing any personal claims of loss by members while in SAD status. This often manifests in workers compensation claims under state law for injuries suffered while on SAD. The state may also be liable to the federal government for loss or damage to equipment caused by the member including a requirement to reimburse the federal government.

- Discipline:

  -- *Criminal:* Members are not subject to the Uniform Code of Military Justice (UCMJ) while on SAD. However, members must adhere to state military justice codes (sometimes called "militia codes") and may be court-martialed under state law. They are subject to prosecution by a civilian jurisdiction which can include federal prosecution. A member can potentially be subject to prosecution under state law or the state military code, **and** also federal law because the sources of authority are considered separate "sovereigns." Thus, double jeopardy protections may not apply.

  -- *Adverse Administrative Actions:* Some DAF instructions may not apply to members on SAD. Consult with the Staff Judge Advocate (SJA) regarding applicability of DAF instructions and state alternatives.

Title 10

- Applicability:

  -- Voluntary non-training temporary duty assignments: With the consent of the member and governor under 10 U.S.C. § 12301(d)

  -- Voluntary extended active duty in the Regular DAF: With the consent of the member and governor but with a defined end date under 10 U.S.C. § 10211 and 10 U.S.C. § 10305

  -- Involuntary for **specific contingencies** or **emergencies**: "Call-up" or mobilizations under 10 U.S.C. § 12301(a), § 12302, and § 12304

- Benefits: All federal benefits and pay (but may be limited based on tour length)

- Liability: The federal government is responsible for addressing any personal claims of loss by members while in Title 10 status. The federal government may be liable to claimants for loss incurred by the actions of the member.

- Discipline:

  -- *Criminal:* Members must adhere to the UCMJ and may be court-martialed under federal law while in Title 10 status. They are subject to prosecution under civilian jurisdiction, including federal prosecution. However, because the UCMJ and civilian federal courts get their authority from the same "sovereign" (the federal government), double jeopardy protections will prevent prosecution in both fora. See Chapter 1, Sources of Command Authority, for additional guidance and requirements concerning disciplinary actions.

  -- *Adverse Administrative Actions:* All adverse administrative action DAF instructions apply to members in Title 10 status. Some actions like demotions may not be effectuated upon the member's return to the state. This may result in the member reverting to the higher grade. Consult with your SJA and coordinate with the member's state commanders to determine appropriate action. See Chapter 1, Sources of Command Authority, for additional guidance and requirements concerning administrative actions.

Title 32 ("Traditional," Full-time Duty, and Active Guard Reserves)

- Applicability:

  -- Drill Status Guardsman (i.e., "Traditional Guardsmen") perform duty via Inactive Duty Training (IDT) in monthly "drills" (Unit Training Assemblies (UTAs)) and in Annual Training (AT)

  -- Active Guard Reservists (AGRs) are on full-time status with a specific charter to organize, administer, recruit, instruct, or train National Guard members under Title 32

  -- Technicians are "federal technicians" employed by the National Guard under 32 U.S.C. § 709 to meet the day-to-day needs of maintaining the force. They are federal employees, but the law authorizes state Adjutant Generals (and their subordinate chain of command) to supervise them. Their benefits and disciplinary actions are determined by their employment agreement and are often quite different from other military members. Consult your SJA and civilian personnel office (CPO) before initiating any administrative and/or disciplinary action, change in their employment, or change in their working conditions.

- Benefits: Similar federal benefits and pay to Reg DAF members for an equivalent period of service, including the potential to earn a federal retirement pension. Duty under Title 32 is not covered under the SCRA and may not gain entitlement to certain VA benefits. Members may be covered under the state equivalent of SCRA and may be entitled to special state health benefits. Consult with the member's SJA for details.

- Liability: Even though the command and control of Title 32 members flow through the state, their duty is ultimately federal. Thus, the federal government is responsible for addressing any personal claims of loss by members while in Title 32 status. This often manifests in Line of Duty determinations for injuries suffered while in training.

- Discipline:

  -- *Criminal:* Title 32 members are not subject to the UCMJ. They must adhere to state military justice codes (sometimes called "militia codes") and may be court-martialed under state law. They are subject to prosecution under civilian jurisdiction, including federal prosecution. A member **can** be subject to prosecution under state law/military code **and** federal law because the sources of authority are considered separate "sovereigns." Thus, double jeopardy protections may not apply.

  -- *Adverse Administrative Actions:* Reference DAFI 36-3211, *Military Separations*, DAFI 36-2907, *Adverse Administrative Actions*, and other AFIs as they apply to Title 32 status members unless otherwise directed by state law

Table 6.1: Air National Guard Duty Status Quick Reference Guide

Common situations and the rules that apply based on duty status.

Situations	State Active Duty (SAD)	Title 32	Title 10
Command and Control	Governor	Governor	President
Location of Duty	Determined by State Law	Territory of the U.S.	Worldwide
Funding	State	Federal	Federal
Mission Types	Determined by State Law	Training and other federally authorized missions	Overseas Training and Federal missions
Duties may include law enforcement on civilians	Yes	Yes	No
Military Discipline	State Military Code	State Military Code	Uniform Code of Military Justice (UCMJ)
Adverse Administrative Action	IAW applicable DAFIs	IAW applicable DAFIs	IAW applicable DAFIs but demotions may not be permanent
Indemnity from Accidents	State	Federal	Federal

References

· Policies and Regulations: Participation of Reserve Officers in Preparation and Administration, 10 U.S.C. § 10211

· Air Force Reserve Forces Policy Committee, 10 U.S.C. § 10305

· Reserve Components, 10 U.S.C. §§ 12301–12304

· Technicians: Employment, Use, Status, 32 U.S.C. § 709

· Uniformed Services Employment and Reemployment Rights Act, 38 U.S.C. §§ 4301–4335

· DoDI 1215.06, *Uniform Reserve Training, and Retirement Categories for the Reserve Components* (11 March 2014), incorporating through Change 2, 12 July 2022

· DoDI 1235.12, *Accessing the Reserve Components (RC)* (7 June 2016), incorporating Change 1, 28 February 2017

· DAFI 36-2619, *Active Duty Operational Support (ADOS) – Active Component Man-day Program* (25 November 2019), incorporating Change 1, 13 April 2023

· DAFI 36-2907, *Adverse Administrative Actions* (14 October 2022)

· DAFI 36-3211, *Military Separations* (24 June 2022), incorporating Change 1, 20 November 2023

· ANGI 36-101, *Air National Guard Active Guard and Reserve (AGR) Program* (21 April 2022)

AIR FORCE RESERVE ACTIVE GUARD AND RESERVE CURTAILMENTS

The Air Force Reserve Active Guard and Reserve (AGR) Program is established by DoD policy and implemented in DAFMAN 36-2114, *Management of the Air Force Reserve Individual Reserve (IR) and Full-Time Support (FTS) Programs*. The AGR career program provides an AGR with opportunities for promotion, career progression, retention, education, and professional development. This program may lead to regular retirement after attaining the required years of active federal military service.

- Initial entry into the AGR program is by individual application for selection assignment

- Voluntary Curtailment: A voluntary release from an AGR tour is referred to as a curtailment

  -- AGRs may request curtailment of an AGR tour based on position realignment, personal hardship, retirement, or other valid reason

  -- AGRs submit a curtailment request through the chain of command to arrive at the Air Reserve Personnel Center's (ARPC) Assignments Division (ARPC/DPAA) (O-5 and below) or the Air Force Reserve Senior Leader Management Office (AF/REG) (O-6) at least 120 days prior to and no more than 365 days before the requested date of separation (DOS)

  -- Curtailment requests for the purpose of retirement must be received by ARPC/DPAA (O-5 and below) or AF/REG (O-6) no later than 60 days prior to the requested permissive temporary duty assignment (TDY)/terminal leave start date but not less than 120 days before the retirement date

- Involuntary Curtailment: Commanders considering involuntary curtailment should use all quality force management tools available prior to initiating an involuntary curtailment

  -- Depending on the nature of the involuntary curtailment, commanders should consider discharge in lieu of involuntary curtailment

  -- Commanders should consult with ARPC/DPAA (O-5 and below) or AF/REG (O-6) and their servicing legal office to determine if an involuntary curtailment is appropriate

  -- Air National Guard Instruction (ANGI) 36-101, *Air National Guard Active Guard Reserve (AGR) Program*, provides guidance on voluntary and involuntary curtailment actions involving Title 32 AGR members. Additionally, most states have their own state supplement which can change the career service timeline of an AGR member. As such, commanders should consult their state's Staff Judge Advocate regarding state specific requirements.

References

· DoDI 1205.18, *Full-Time Support (FTS) to the Reserve Components* (5 June 2020)

· DAFI 36-2110, *Total Force Assignments* (15 November 2021), including DAFGM2023-01, 5 October 2023

· DAFMAN 36-2114, *Management of the Air Force Reserve Individual Reserve (IR) and Full-Time Support (FTS) Programs* (24 May 2021)

· ANGI 36-101, *Air National Guard Active Guard Reserve (AGR) Program* (21 April 2022)

REASSIGNMENT TO THE INDIVIDUAL READY RESERVE

The Individual Ready Reserve (IRR) is a manpower pool consisting of individuals who have had some training and who have served previously in the active component or in the Selected Reserve. Members may voluntarily participate in training for retirement points and promotion, in accordance with DAFI 36-2110, *Total Force Assignments*. Transfers to the IRR may be voluntary or involuntary.

Voluntary Reassignment to the IRR

- Members who no longer desire to actively participate in the Air Force Reserve (AFR) may request to be reassigned to the IRR

- Commanders **MUST** deny "voluntary" requests for reassignment to the IRR when discharge is more appropriate

- Application: Members request reassignment to the IRR by submitting DAF Form 1288, *Application for Ready Reserve Assignment*, or a personal letter to the unit commander or to the Readiness Integration Organization (RIO) detachment commander for the Individual Mobilization Augmentee (IMA) program

  -- As part of completing DAF Form 1288, members must certify that they either have or have not received an Unfavorable Information File (UIF) within the last two years (enlisted) or five years (officers). If the member has had a UIF during this period, the last five Officer Performance Reports (OPRs) or Enlisted Performance Reports (EPRs) must accompany the assignment request.

- Approval Authority:

  -- Wing commander or equivalent (unit program) or the RIO detachment commander (IMA program) is the approval authority for voluntary requests

  -- In the unit reserve program, any commander in the chain of command may disapprove a request for reassignment and must notify the member with the reasons for disapproving the request

  -- In the IMA program, the RIO detachment commander may disapprove a request for reassignment and must notify the member with the reasons for disapproving the request

  -- Approved requests for voluntary reassignment from the unit or IMA program must have an effective date of change of strength accountability not earlier than 6 months from the date requests are approved. See DAFI 36-2110 for waiver authorities to this provision.

Involuntary Reassignment to the IRR

- Involuntary reassignment to the IRR from the Ready Reserve for cause is generally inappropriate

  -- Use involuntary reassignment only as a last resort

  -- Initiate involuntary reassignment for cause or derogatory reasons only after all appropriate disciplinary and/or administrative actions have been taken and documented

  -- Consider exceptions to these policies on a case-by-case basis

- Involuntary reassignment is not a substitute for discharge. If administrative discharge is warranted, process in accordance with DAFI 36-3211, *Military Separations*.

- Appropriate Situations: Some potential situations where involuntary reassignment may be appropriate include (but are not limited to):

  -- *Unexcused Absences:* In the unit reserve program, if a member has nine or more unexcused absences from Unit Training Assemblies (UTAs) in a 12-month period, commanders should reassign the member to the IRR if not discharging the member

  -- *Failure to Meet Fitness Standards:* Members of the IRR maintaining an unsatisfactory fitness level after a second 90-day period are referred to the commander of the unit of assignment or attachment for appropriate action per DAFMAN 36-2905, *Department of the Air Force Physical Fitness Program*

  -- *Health Assessment Non-compliance:* Failure to comply with requirement for reserve component periodic health assessment

  -- *Whereabouts Unknown:* Member not immediately available but not missing in action

- Evaluation: Unit commander (or RIO detachment commander) will examine and evaluate any information received that indicates a member should be considered for involuntary reassignment

- Memorandum of Notification: If a commander determines grounds exist to warrant initiation of involuntary reassignment action, a Memorandum of Notification (MON) is sent to the member. DAFI 36-2110 includes the information that must be provided to the member.

  -- *Personally Deliver:* When feasible, the MON should be personally delivered

    --- Delivering official must obtain a written acknowledgement of receipt

    --- If member refuses to acknowledge receipt, the delivery official makes an annotation to that effect on the receipt, including the date and time of delivery of the notification. The receipt should be kept in the case file.

  -- *Certified Mail:* When personal delivery is not feasible, the unit should send the MON by certified mail, return receipt requested, to the member's last known address

--- If attempts to deliver the MON by certified mail are unsuccessful, send the MON by first-class mail

--- If the member resides outside the United States, an equivalent form of notice may be used

-- *Undelivered:* If postal service returns the MON without indicating a more current address, file the returned envelope in the case file

--- If an address correction is received from the postmaster or if a returned envelope discloses a more current address, update the record, and send the MON to the member at that address

--- If all attempts to deliver the MON by certified and first-class mail are unsuccessful, complete the Affidavit of Service

- Review:

-- *Member:* Member must be allowed 15 calendar days after receipt of the MON to consult with legal counsel and submit statements or documents on his/her behalf. If the member fails to submit statements or documents during this period, the case may proceed based on the information available, without further notice to the member.

-- *Commander:* The commander reviews any matters submitted by the member and determines whether to continue involuntary reassignment action

- Determination:

-- If the commander elects to continue the involuntary reassignment action, the case file must be processed through the servicing Staff Judge Advocate and chain of command to the approval authority

-- The approval authority reviews the case to determine whether the facts are properly substantiated

-- The approval authority then approves or denies the reassignment and notifies the member

- It is in the best interest of both the Department of the Air Force and the member to process the case as expeditiously as possible. Commanders should monitor the process to ensure cases are processed without undue delay.

References

· DAFI 36-2110, *Total Force Assignments* (15 November 2021), including DAFGM2023-01, 5 October 2023
· DAFI 36-3211, *Military Separations* (24 June 2022), incorporating Change 1, 20 November 2023
· DAFMAN 36-2136, *Reserve Personnel Participation* (15 December 2023)
· DAFMAN 36-2905, *Department of the Air Force Physical Fitness Program* (21 April 2022)
· DAF Form 1288, *Application for Ready Reserve Assignment* (23 May 2019)

INSTALLATION BARMENT

Installation commanders have broad authority to control activities on their installations, including the authority to remove or exclude any person whose presence on the installation is unauthorized or disrupts good order and discipline. This authority enables a commander to fulfill his/her responsibilities to protect personnel and property, and to ensure the successful, uninterrupted performance of the Department of Defense's (DoD) mission. The terms debarment, barment, and barred are often used interchangeably to mean that an individual is no longer permitted access to a specific DoD installation.

Key Takeaways

» Installation commanders may deny access to the installation with a barment order

» People barred from an installation should be notified in writing that they are prohibited from entering the installation

» Anyone entering an installation after receiving notice of barment is subject to prosecution under 18 U.S.C. § 1382

Who is Subject to Barment

- Members of the armed forces are not normally barred. Service members being involuntarily separated may, in conjunction with their discharge, be barred from their former place of duty if their presence would be prejudicial to good order and discipline.

- Non-affiliated civilians may be barred from a military installation

- Dependent family members and retirees **may not** be completely barred from an installation. They must be granted access to the installation to receive any medical or dental care they are entitled (statutory right under 10 U.S.C. §§ 1074 and 1076).

- Civilian employees may be barred, but they should be placed on forced leave with the intent to take removal action if being completely barred

    -- Otherwise, the employee may still be entitled to collect a salary

    -- Check with the Civilian Personnel Office (CPO) to determine if the local collective bargaining agreement, should one exist, contains additional due process requirements

- Salespersons and businesses may be barred for misconduct. Misconduct may lead to barment of a single agent or an entire firm.

- Contractors may be barred for misconduct. Contractor employees with security clearances are not entitled to greater protection from barment. Actions to bar contractors must be coordinated with the local contracting office.

Procedural Requirements

- A person who is barred from an installation should be notified, in writing, that they are prohibited from entering the installation. The notification (called a "barment letter") should state the reason for and period of the barment. It should also include an exception for access to medical or dental care if the person subject to barment is entitled to such care.

- The barment is for the specific installation and does not prohibit access to other military installations not subject to the control of the issuing installation commander

- Determining the barment period is a matter of discretion

  -- Commanders should consider the individual, the reason for the proposed barment, and the need for good order, discipline, and security. The bottom line is what is reasonable given all the circumstances.

  -- Length of the barment period should be stated in the barment letter. The commander may bar an individual for a specific length of time or, in appropriate cases, the barment may be permanent.

- Individuals can ask the installation commander to lift the barment at any time, regardless of whether the barment is for a set period or permanent

- A copy of the barment letter should be hand-delivered to the individual. If the individual is unavailable, the letter will be sent by certified mail to ensure a record of receipt.

- An individual who enters an installation after receiving notice of barment from the installation commander is subject to federal criminal prosecution under 18 U.S.C. § 1382. Maximum penalty for violation of the law is six months confinement and a fine.

References

· Medical and Dental Care for Members, Certain Former Members, and Dependents, 10 U.S.C. §§ 1074, 1076

· Entering Military, Naval, or Coast Guard Property, 18 U.S.C. § 1382

· Penalty for Violation of Security Regulations and Orders, 50 U.S.C. § 797

· Installation Entry Policy, Civil Disturbance Intervention and Disaster Assistance, 32 C.F.R. § 809a.1-a.5

· DoDI 5200.08, *Security of DoD Installations and Resources and the DoD Physical Security Review Board (PSRB)* (10 December 2005), incorporating through Change 3, 20 November 2015

· DoDM 5200.08V3_AFMAN 31-101 V3, *Installation Perimeter Access Control*, Guidance Memorandum 2023-01 (5 June 2023)

DRIVING PRIVILEGES

Driving on a military installation, whether in a government motor vehicle (GMV) or a privately owned vehicle (POV), is a privilege granted by the installation commander. This authority may be delegated to the deputy installation commander (CD), mission support group commander (MSG/CC), or other appropriate official not occupying a law enforcement, investigative, or other position raising the appearance of a conflict of interest.

Key Takeaways

» Driving on a military installation is a privilege granted by the installation commander

» Driving privileges may be suspended or revoked due to intoxicated driving or other traffic violations

---

Operating a POV on the Installation

- A person must do the following to drive on a Department of the Air Force installation:

  -- Lawfully be licensed to operate motor vehicles in appropriate classifications and not under suspension or revocation in any state or host country

  -- Comply with all laws and regulations governing motor vehicle operations on the installation

  -- Comply with installation vehicle registration requirements

  -- Possess, while operating a motor vehicle, and produce upon request the following:

    --- Proof of ownership or state registration, if required by state or host nation

    --- A valid state driver's license (or host nation/status of forces agreement license)

    --- A valid vehicle safety inspection sticker, if required by state or host nation

    --- Documents that establish identification and status of cargo and vehicle occupants, when appropriate

    --- Proof of valid insurance

    --- Operators of GMVs must have proof of authorization to operate the vehicle

Implied Consent

- When operating a motor vehicle on a military installation, a driver is deemed to have given implied consent in several areas:

  -- Consent to test for the presence of alcohol or drugs in their blood, on their breath, and in their urine, provided there is a lawful stop, apprehension, or citation for any impaired driving offense committed while driving or in physical control of a motor vehicle on a military installation

  -- Consent to the removal and temporary impoundment of their POV if it is illegally parked, interfering with military operations, creating a safety hazard, disabled by accident or incident, abandoned, or left unattended in a restricted or controlled access area

Suspension

- An installation commander can administratively suspend or revoke installation driving privileges

  -- A suspension of up to six months may be appropriate if a driver continually violates installation parking standards or habitually receives other non-moving vehicle violations

  -- The installation commander is authorized to immediately suspend installation driving privileges pending resolution of an intoxicated driving incident under any of the following circumstances:

    --- Refusal to take or complete a lawfully requested chemical test for the presence of alcohol or other drugs in the driver's blood

    --- Operating a motor vehicle on or off the installation with blood alcohol content (BAC) of 0.08 percent by volume or higher, or more than the applicable BAC level in the local civilian jurisdiction, whichever is applicable

    --- Receipt of an arrest report or other official document showing an intoxicated driving incident occurred

Revocation

- An installation commander will immediately revoke driving privileges for a period of not less than one year in any of the following circumstances:

  -- Person is lawfully apprehended for intoxicated driving and refuses to submit to or complete tests to measure blood alcohol or drug content

  -- Conviction, nonjudicial punishment, or a military or civilian administrative action resulting in the suspension or revocation of a driver's license for intoxicated driving

Procedures

- A point system is used on-base to provide a uniform administrative process to supervise traffic offenses impartially. Points are assessed for violations of motor vehicle traffic regulations for on-base offenses and for on and off-base traffic offenses involving GMVs. Certain procedural guidelines apply before an individual's driving privilege may be suspended or revoked.

  -- An individual has the right to a hearing before a designated hearing officer. The individual must be notified of his/her right to a hearing, but it is only held if the individual requests it within the prescribed time period.

  -- A suspension for a driving while intoxicated offense may be effective immediately if based on reliable evidence. Such evidence can include witness statements, a military or civilian police report, chemical test results, refusal to complete chemical testing, video tapes, written statements, field sobriety test results, or other evidence.

- Civilian offenders may be prosecuted in federal magistrate court for on-base traffic offenses. However, jurisdiction is dependent upon the installation where the offense occurred.

- If an Air National Guard (ANG) base is co-located with a Regular Air Force (RegAF) installation, the authority to grant and deny driving privileges and establishment of driving rules rests with the RegAF installation commander (or designee). If an ANG base is not co-located with a RegAF installation, the ANG installation commander holds the authority and responsibility of granting and denying driving privileges and creating and enforcing driving rules.

Reference

· DAFI 31-218, *Motor Vehicle Supervision* (10 December 2021), including DAFGM2021-01, 10 December 2021

ARMY AND AIR FORCE EXCHANGE SERVICE AND COMMISSARY BENEFITS

Although Department of Defense (DoD) directives and inter-Service regulations govern exchange and commissary benefits, installation commanders may exercise some discretion in granting, suspending, or revoking privileges of patrons who abuse these privileges. The installation Force Support Squadrons work with the Army and Air Force Exchange Service (AAFES) and DeCA (Commissary) managers to maintain a positive retail environment and ensure military families are adequately supported.

Key Takeaways

» Exchange and Commissary benefits are important elements of our military benefits

» CONUS and OCONUS installation commanders have considerable discretion in approving patron benefits for classes of users other than uniformed service members

» Commander's remedies for abuse of privileges include suspension and revocation of Exchange and Commissary patron benefits

» Installation commanders should have open channels of communication with AAFES and Commissary facilities managers to ensure the needs of military families are met

---

Exchange

- <u>AAFES</u>: The establishment of an exchange is authorized by the Department of the Army and Department of the Air Force (DAF) at any federal or state installation and other locations where DoD military personnel are assigned

- An exchange may be established at other locations, such as state-operated National Guard installations or Reserve Training Centers, provided it is cost-effective

Exchange Privileges

- Unlimited exchange privileges extend to all uniformed, retired, and other personnel (such as Medal of Honor recipients) and their dependents

- Unlimited exchange privileges extend for two years to involuntarily separated service members under other than adverse conditions

- Unlimited exchange privileges may be extended to government departments or agencies outside the DoD when:

  -- Local commander determines the desired supplies or services cannot be conveniently obtained elsewhere; and

  -- Supplies or services can be furnished without unduly impairing the service to exchange patrons.

- Limited exchange privileges extend to some government civilian employees and to others, such as members of foreign military services visiting a military installation

- In non-foreign OCONUS areas (e.g., Alaska, Hawaii, and Puerto Rico), the responsible commander may extend limited or unlimited privileges to other personnel or organizations if it is in the best interest of the mission of the command concerned

- Exceptions involving patron privileges are based on alleviating personal hardships and may only be granted by the Secretary of the Army or Secretary of the Air Force upon request by the appropriate installation commander through command channels

- All honorably discharged veterans may utilize the AAFES online catalog service to purchase goods

Abuse of Exchange Privileges

- Exchange patrons are prohibited from abusing privileges, including:

  -- Purchasing items for purposes of resale, transfer, or exchange to unauthorized persons;

  -- Using exchange merchandise or services in the conduct of any activity to produce income (**Note:** for-profit businesses operating out of base housing may not compete with AAFES even if they do not use exchange merchandise or services in their operations); and

  -- Theft, intentional or repeated presentation of dishonored checks, and other indebtedness.

Commander Actions when Abuse of Exchange Privileges Occurs

- When an abuse of privileges occurs, the commander will take prompt disciplinary and other appropriate action, such as revocation or suspension of exchange privileges

  -- Commanders may revoke exchange privileges for any period deemed appropriate, except the minimum period of revocation is six months for shoplifting, employee pilferage, and intentional presentation of dishonored checks

  -- The individual concerned will be provided notice of the charges and the opportunity to offer rebutting evidence

  -- On appeal, the commander who revoked the privileges, or the next higher commander, may reinstate exchange privileges for cogent and compelling reasons

Commissary Privileges

- The DoD operates commissaries as an integral element of the military pay and benefits system and as an institutional element to foster the sense of community among military personnel and their families. The intent of patronage is to provide an income benefit through cost-savings on food and household items necessary to subsist and maintain the household of the military family.

- Authorized Patrons:

-- Several classes of individuals are authorized commissary privileges by regulation, including active duty and their dependent family members, retired personnel and their dependent family members, reservists, and others

-- At overseas locations, military commanders or Secretaries of military departments may extend commissary privileges to certain individuals and groups of individuals, provided it is without detriment to the ability to fulfill the military mission

- Restrictions on Purchases:

-- Authorized personnel may not sell or give away commissary purchases to individuals or groups not entitled to commissary privileges

-- Personnel are prohibited from using commissary purchases to support a private business. However, patrons may use their commissary privileges to support limited charitable endeavors (e.g., preparing a meal for their place of worship or a homeless shelter).

-- Sanctions for violating restrictions on purchases range from temporary suspension or permanent revocation of commissary privileges to appropriate action under regulation, Uniform Code of Military Justice (UCMJ), or federal or state law

Appointing Agents for Authorized Users

- An installation commander is authorized to extend exchange and commissary privileges to the agent of an authorized user. Appointment typically occurs when the authorized user is unable to exercise their privileges on their own behalf. This often occurs when a custodial parent is not an authorized patron, but the non-custodial parent is a DAF service member.

References

· DoDD 5124.02, *Under Secretary of Defense for Personnel and Readiness* (23 June 2008)

· DoDI 1330.17, *DoD Commissary Program* (18 June 2014), incorporating through Change 2, 14 September 2018

· DTM 21-003, *Access to Morale, Welfare, and Recreation, Category C Online Activities, DoD Commissaries, and Military Service Exchange* (12 April 2021), incorporating through Change 2, 19 April 2023

· DAFI 34-110(I), *Army and Air Force Exchange Service Operations* (23 January 2024)

SUBSTANCE ABUSE

Drug abuse, alcohol misuse, and other wrongful uses of substances that affect mood or function negatively impact behavior, duty performance, and physical and mental health and are incompatible with Department of the Air Force (DAF) standards.

Key Takeaways

» Drug abuse is incompatible with military service and all DAF service members who abuse drugs, even once, are subject to discharge for misconduct

» Military members and civilian employees who self-identify as having issues with drugs or alcohol may avoid certain negative consequences for their behavior

» The Alcohol and Drug Abuse Prevention and Treatment (ADAPT) program is focused on prevention and comprehensive clinical treatment of members with substance abuse issues

» Commanders should encourage members to seek help for problems with drugs or alcohol without fear of negative consequences

---

Unit Commanders and Supervisor Responsibilities

- Evaluate potential or identified abusers through the evaluation process of DAFI 44-121, *Alcohol and Drug Abuse Prevention and Treatment (ADAPT) Program*. The provisions of this instruction also apply to Air National Guard (ANG) members when eligible for DoD medical services.

- Provide appropriate incentives to encourage members to seek help for problems with drugs or alcohol without fear of negative consequences

- Command involvement is critical to a comprehensive treatment program, as well as during aftercare and follow-up services

ADAPT

- The ADAPT program attempts to identify and assist military members with drug problems, but the focus of the ADAPT program is prevention and clinical treatment

  -- ADAPT staff members evaluate all members suspected of drug or alcohol abuse to help the commander understand the extent of the substance abuse problem and to determine the patient's need for treatment and the level of care required

  -- Except in cases of self-identification, personal information provided by the member in response to assessment questions **MAY** be used against the member for Uniform Code of Military Justice (UCMJ) actions or considered for characterizing service in an administrative discharge

Referrals to ADAPT

- Positive drug test results **mandate** a substance abuse evaluation

- Self-Identification:

  -- Military members who voluntarily disclose prior drug use or possession are granted limited protections. Such disclosure may not be used against the member in UCMJ actions or in characterizing an administrative discharge so long as they:

    --- Are seeking treatment and voluntarily disclose evidence of personal drug use or possession to the unit commander, first sergeant, ADAPT staff member, or a military medical or mental health professional; **and**

    --- Have not previously been apprehended for drug involvement, placed under investigation for drug abuse, ordered to give a urine sample as part of the drug-testing program in which the results are still pending or have been returned as positive, advised of a recommendation for administrative separation for drug abuse, or has entered treatment for drug abuse.

  -- DAF members with alcohol abuse problems are encouraged to seek assistance from their commander, first sergeant, ADAPT staff member, a military medical professional, or mental health professional

    --- Self-identification is reserved for members who are not currently under investigation or pending action as a result of alcohol-related misconduct

- Commander Referral: A unit commander will refer all service members for assessment when substance use or misuse is suspected to be a contributing factor in any misconduct or any other incident, such as deteriorating duty performance, excessive tardiness, absenteeism, misconduct, or unacceptable social behavior

- Incident to Medical Care: Medical personnel must notify a member's unit commander and the ADAPT program manager when a member is observed, identified, or suspected to be under the influence of drugs or alcohol, receives treatment for any injury or illness that may be the result of substance abuse or is suspected of abusing substances

Mandatory Administrative Discharge Processing for Drug Abuse

- Pursuant to DAFI 36-3211, *Military Separations*, drug abuse is incompatible with military service and members who abuse drugs one or more times are subject to discharge for misconduct

- Drug Abuse Includes:

  -- Wrongful use of prescription medication;

  -- Any Controlled Substance in Schedules I, II, III, IV, and V of 21 U.S.C. § 812; and

  -- Any intoxicating substance, other than alcohol, introduced into the body in any manner for purposes of altering mood or function.

- Generally, a member found to have abused drugs will be discharged unless the member can prove that they meet required retention criteria in DAFI 36-3211

Civilian Employees

- The Air Force Drug Demand Reduction Program, which includes the Air Force Civilian Drug Testing Program, is designed to achieve a drug-free workplace, consistent with Executive Order 12564, Drug-Free Federal Workplace

- Similar to military members, civilian employees who self-identify for illicit drug use are provided a "safe haven" from disciplinary action if they:

  -- Voluntarily identify themselves as a user of illicit drugs prior to being notified of the requirement to provide a specimen for testing or being identified through other means (e.g., drug testing, investigation);

  -- Obtain and cooperate with appropriate counseling or rehabilitation;

  -- Agree to and sign a last chance or statement of agreement; and

  -- Thereafter refrain from illicit drug use.

- Commanders should consult with the Civilian Personnel Office (CPO) and/or the legal office if they suspect a civilian employee's poor performance, discipline, or conduct may be caused by drug abuse

References

- Controlled Substance Act, 21 U.S.C. § 812
- DAFI 34-107, *Alcoholic Beverage Program* (5 July 2023)
- DAFI 36-3211, *Military Separations* (24 June 2022), certified current as of 20 November 2023
- DAFI 44-121, *Alcohol and Drug Abuse Prevention and Treatment (ADAPT) Program* (18 July 2018), incorporating Change 1, 21 November 2019, Corrective Actions applied on 19 December 2019, including DAFGM2024-01, 3 January 2024
- DAFMAN 44-197, *Military Drug Demand Reduction Program* (5 September 2023)

PRIVATE ORGANIZATIONS

Private Organizations (PO) are non-Federal entities recognized by the installation commander, per AFI 34-223, *Private Organizations Program*, to operate on the installation because they will contribute to the morale, welfare, and quality of life of assigned Department of the Air Force (DAF) service members and their families. POs are usually formed around a specific special interest (e.g., snowmobiling, golfing) or to support a specific DAF unit or activity. POs may be chapters of larger non-Federal entities.

Key Takeaways

» POs are allowed to operate on the installation because they contribute positively to the quality of life of the installation community. However, their activities cannot prejudice or discredit the DAF.

» POs must undergo annual financial review with the Force Support Squadron (FSS) and have specific financial controls based on their cash holdings

» POs may engage in continuous retail operations or occasional fundraising events (three per quarter) with installation commander permission

» POs may form around a specific racial, ethnic, national origin or religious interest, but may not restrict membership to any particular class

Definitions

- A PO is a self-sustaining special interest group, set up by individuals (DAF service members and family) acting exclusively outside the scope of any official position they may have in the DAF

- POs are **NOT** any of the following:

  -- Federal entities, and should not be treated as such;

  -- Nonappropriated fund instrumentalities (NAFIs), nor are they entitled to the sovereign immunities and privileges given to NAFIs or the DAF;

  -- "For us, by us" (FUBU) fundraising entities as defined in DAFI 36-3101, *Fundraising*;

  -- Unofficial unit-affiliated activities, (although such activities whose current assets exceed a monthly average of $1,000 over a 3-month period must apply to the installation for PO recognition); or

  -- Organizations not considered POs covered by AFI 34-223 but are also governed by specific Department of Defense (DoD) directives and instructions such as scouting organizations, military relief societies, banks or credit unions, Red Cross, and United Service Organizations (USO).

Establishing a Private Organization

- A PO must submit a written constitution and bylaws to the FSS and legal office

- POs must be approved in writing by the installation commander or designee when they determine a PO will make a positive contribution to the quality of life of base personnel

    -- Authorization may be withdrawn if the PO prejudices or discredits the United States government, conflicts with government activities, or for any other reason or just cause

- A PO must resubmit certification every two years or when there is a change in the purpose, function, or membership eligibility of the PO

Operating Rules

- POs must prevent the appearance of an official sanction or support by the DoD

    -- POs may not use the seals, logos, or insignia of the DoD or DAF

    -- POs operating on an Air Force or Space Force installation may use the name or abbreviation of the DoD, DAF, or installation in the PO name if the status of the PO is unambiguous and there is no appearance of official sanction or support by the DoD

        --- POs promptly display the following disclaimer on all print and electronic media mentioning the PO: "THIS IS A PRIVATE ORGANIZATION. IT IS NOT A PART OF THE DEPARTMENT OF DEFENSE OR ANY OF ITS COMPONENTS AND IT HAS NO GOVERNMENT STATUS."

- Service members may not perform activities for a PO while in an official duty status

Financial Controls

- POs must be self-sustaining, primarily through dues, contributions, service charges, fees, or special assessments of their members

- POs must use budgets and financial statements

- FSS Resource Management flight chiefs review each PO annually to ensure financial statements, documents, records, and procedures are in order

- POs with certain levels of gross annual revenue must undergo audits and financial reviews at the PO's own expenses

- POs will not engage in activities that duplicate or compete with Army and Air Force Exchange Service or Morale, Welfare, and Recreation programs

Private Organization Fundraising

- POs are prohibited from conducting games of chance, lotteries, or other gambling activities, except in very limited circumstances such as certain types of raffles (for further guidance on raffles see AFI 34-223, para. 10.20, and the Joint Ethics Regulation)

- The installation commander or designee approves PO continuous thrift shop sales operations and occasional on-installation events for fundraising purposes. Occasional fundraising is defined as not more than three (3) events per calendar quarter.

- POs will not sell or serve alcoholic beverages on DAF installations with very limited exceptions (see AFI 34-223, para. 10.14, for further guidance)

- POs must have liability insurance unless waived by the installation commander

  -- Insurance should be required unless the PO's activities are negligible in risk

  -- PO members are jointly and severally personally liable for the obligations of the PO

- POs desiring tax-exempt status must file an application with the IRS and state taxing authority

- POs may not directly solicit cash donations for their organization on base

Private Organizations and Staff Office Support

- Installation legal offices should not provide legal advice to prospective and currently recognized POs

  -- However, legal advisors may assist POs by identifying guidance on formation, certification, annual financial reports, dissolution, and other provisions, particularly in the case of DAF-affiliated POs on a joint base where another Military Service is the lead component

- POs may not unlawfully discriminate in hiring practices or membership policies on the basis of age (over 40 years old), race, religion, color, national origin, disability, ethnic group, or gender (including pregnancy, gender identity, and sexual orientation)

- Religiously oriented POs may be authorized on installations if:

  -- Requests by similar organizations are also approved;

  -- Authorization is for non-exclusive use of government facilities;

  -- No sign or insignia or other organizational identification is placed on or inside government facilities except when the organization's activities are in progress;

  -- Membership is not restricted to members of the religion involved; and

  -- Installation staff chaplain coordinates on the request.

Logistical Support to Private Organizations

- The use of government equipment and systems for other than official purposes is limited

- Government communication systems may be used to inform DAF members of PO events of possible interest to the unit and its families

  -- However, official communication systems should not be used to advertise PO fundraiser and membership events, unless the primary purpose of the communication is for a purpose other than the PO's fundraising effort, such as to inform DAF members of a local event of possible interest (e.g., sale of alternate lunch option in unit parking lot)

- POs must furnish their own equipment, supplies, and other materials with limited exceptions

- Logistical support to POs may be permitted if the installation commander determines the request meets the test under JER 3-211 (Logistical Support of Non-Federal Entity Events)

- POs in overseas areas may be able to request additional logistical support. Always consult the Staff Judge Advocate for such requests.

References

· DoD 5500.07-R, *Joint Ethics Regulation* (30 August 1993), incorporating through Change 7, 17 November 2011

· DAFI 34-107, *Alcoholic Beverage Program* (5 July 2023)

· DAFI 36-3101, *Fundraising* (25 October 2022)

· AFI 34-223, *Private Organizations Program* (13 December 2018)

POLITICAL ACTIVITIES, FREE SPEECH, DEMONSTRATIONS, OPEN HOUSES, AND EXTREMISM

> ### Key Takeaways
>
> » Commanders must balance members' constitutional right of free expression with the responsibility to execute the mission and protect good order and discipline
>
> » Military members are prohibited from actively participating in extremist activities
>
> » While military members are encouraged to carry out their rights and responsibilities of citizenship, they are prohibited from engaging in certain political activities

Commander Responsibilities

- Commanders have the inherent authority and responsibility to execute the mission, protect resources, and maintain good order and discipline. This authority and responsibility includes placing lawful restrictions upon participation by Department of the Air Force (DAF) members in certain dissident and protest activities, including demonstrations.

- Commanders balance this inherent command responsibility with individual DAF members' constitutional right of free expression. Commanders preserve members' right of free expression to the maximum extent possible, consistent with good order, discipline, and national security.

- To properly balance these interests, commanders must exercise prudent judgment and should consult with their Staff Judge Advocate (SJA). In appropriate cases, commanders may find it advisable to confer with higher authorities before initiating action to restrict manifestations of dissent.

Extremism

- Extremist activities are inconsistent with the responsibilities of military service and can be prohibited even in some circumstances in which such activities would be constitutionally protected in a civilian setting

    -- Military personnel are prohibited from <u>actively participating</u> in <u>extremist activities</u>

        --- The term "extremist activities" is defined within DoDI 1325.06, *Handling Protest, Extremism, and Criminal Gang Activities Among Members of the Armed Forces*, Enclosure 3, para. 8.c.(1)

        --- The term "active participation" is defined within DoDI 1325.06, Enclosure 3, para. 8.c.(2)

- Commanders should remain alert for signs of future extremist activities. Commanders should intervene early, primarily through counseling, when observing such signs even though the signs may not rise to the level of active participation or threaten good order and discipline, but only suggest such potential

- Upon a credible report or suspicion of extremist activities, commanders **WILL** notify the appropriate Military Criminal Investigative Organizations, counterintelligence organizations, command security manager, legal office, and the Insider Threat Hub

Publication of Personal Writing Matters

- DAF members may not distribute or post any unofficial printed or written material within any DAF installation without permission of the installation commander

- DAF members may not write for unofficial publications during duty hours or use government resources, even off-duty

Controlling or Prohibiting Demonstrations and Protests

- Commanders may also take measures to control or prevent demonstrations and protest activities within the installation

  -- Demonstrations or related activities on a DAF installation may be prohibited if:

    --- They interfere with mission accomplishment; or

    --- They present a clear danger to loyalty, discipline, or morale of service members.

  -- No one may enter a military installation for any purpose prohibited by law or regulation, or reenter an installation after having been barred by order of the installation commander

  -- DAF members are prohibited from participating in demonstrations when they are on duty, when they are in a foreign country, when they are in uniform, when their activities constitute a breach of law and order, or when violence is likely to result

Political Activities by Members of the Department of the Air Force

- It is DoD policy to encourage DAF members to carry out their rights and responsibilities of United States citizenship. While on active duty, however, members are prohibited from engaging in certain political activities in order to maintain good order and discipline, and to avoid conflicts of interest and the appearance of improper endorsement in political matters.

- DAF service members may register to vote and express personal opinions on political candidates and issues, but not as a representative of the Armed Forces

- For a list of permitted and prohibited political activities, see DAFI 51-508, *Political Activities, Free Speech and Freedom of Assembly*, paras. 2.3 and 2.4

- The Hatch Act, 5 U.S.C. §§ 7321-7326, governs political activities of Department of Defense (DoD) civilian employees. Among other restrictions, the Hatch Act prohibits most ("Less Restricted") employees from engaging in political activities (activities directed at the success or failure of a political party, candidate for partisan political office, or partisan political group) on-duty in a federal workplace, while wearing a government uniform, or official insignia, and while using a government vehicle.

Open House Requirements and Responsibilities

- An open house where the general public is invited onto the installation does not, in and of itself, cause the installation to lose its status as "closed" for the purposes of limiting political or ideological speech. "Closed" means that non-DoD personnel are not permitted to enter without express permission of the Commander. The base is not a public forum for protests or demonstrations, or other ideological expression.

  -- Open houses are for local community relations and are accomplished primarily through aerial demonstrations. Commanders retain the authority to restrict political or ideological speech or demonstrations on the installation during an open house.

  -- Commanders should prohibit demonstrations inside an installation that could result in interference with the mission or present a clear danger to loyalty, discipline, or morale of military forces

    --- If a demonstration or unauthorized activity begins to take place during an open house, commanders and Security Forces should be ready to respond immediately

  -- If a person or group attempts to engage in political or ideological expression or demonstrations on an installation, the commander may escort the offending party or parties off the installation, and issue a barment letter, the violation of which can subject the offender to criminal penalties

  -- An installation loses its status as "closed" for the purposes of preventing political or ideological speech or demonstrations **ONLY IF** the commander allows political or ideological speech or demonstrations to occur or by abandoning control over the installation or parts of it

  -- Installation commanders should be careful about whom they invite onto the installation and what they allow those people to do. It is important to work closely with the SJA to plan open houses so that potential problems can be prevented and to solve free speech issues should they arise.

References

- The Hatch Act, 5 U.S.C. §§ 7321–7326
- DoDD 1344.10, *Political Activities by Members of the Armed Forces* (19 February 2008)
- DoDI 1325.06, *Handling Protest, Extremist, and Criminal Gang Activities Among Members of the Armed Forces* (27 November 2009), incorporating through Change 2, effective 20 December 2021
- DAFI 51-508, *Political Activities, Free Speech and Freedom of Assembly of Air Force Personnel* (24 March 2023)
- AFMAN 10-1004, *Conducting Air Force Open Houses* (23 August 2018)

RELIGIOUS ISSUES IN THE DEPARTMENT OF THE AIR FORCE

Issues involving religion have an inherent potential to generate media, advocacy group, and political attention quickly. Resolution of religious issues, such as accommodation requests, religious speech or practices in a duty context, and potential religious endorsement, is always highly dependent on the facts and circumstances and seldom amenable to simple, bright line, "one-size-fits-all" rules. It is essential that commanders consult their staff chaplains and judge advocates when religious issues arise.

Key Takeaways

» Leaders at all levels must balance constitutional protections for free exercise of religion with the constitutional prohibition against governmental establishment of religion

» Commanders must ensure their words and actions cannot reasonably be construed as official endorsement or disapproval of any faith, belief, or absence of belief

» Follow the provisions of DAFI 52-201, *Religious Freedom in the Department of the Air Force*, when reviewing and analyzing requests for religious accommodation

Constitutional Basis

- <u>First Amendment</u>: "Congress shall make no law respecting an establishment of religion, or prohibiting the free exercise thereof …"

  -- *Establishment Clause:* Provides that the government is prohibited from exercising preference for one religion over another, or religion over non-religion

  -- *Free Exercise Clause:* Provides constitutional protection for religious speech and practices (but does **NOT** absolutely protect all religious expression under all circumstances)

General Principles for Leaders

- Leaders at all levels must balance constitutional protections for free exercise of religion with the constitutional prohibition against governmental establishment of religion

- Commanders must ensure their words and actions cannot reasonably be construed to be officially endorsing or disapproving of, or extending preferential treatment for any faith, belief, or absence of belief

  -- Commanders must be sensitive to the potential for real-world military implications when religion and official business intersect. Context is critical and commanders should exercise caution before engaging in activities in the military setting that would leave a reasonable observer with the impression that the commander is endorsing, sponsoring, or inhibiting religion.

  -- Not all members of the command will share the commander's beliefs and may feel alienated or marginalized when their commander espouses a particular religious belief or preference for one religion

-- Some may question whether they will be viewed with impartiality or with disfavor if they do not agree with their new commander's religious views

Religious Expression in the Workplace

- DAF service members may permissibly engage in voluntary discussions of religion, even if conducted in uniform, to the same extent that they may engage in comparable private expression about subjects not related to religious issues, where it is clear that the discussions are personal, not official, and they are free from coercion or appearance of coercion

- A DAF member may share his/her faith or invite another co-worker to attend his/her place of worship as long the member respects the views and requests of the co-worker

- Restrictions on such expression must be based on generally applicable content-neutral factors, such as whether the expression would disrupt mission accomplishment or would have an adverse impact on good order and discipline. Additionally, restrictions on religious-related expression are appropriate if the member's expression can reasonably be attributed to the DAF, thus constituting an impermissible endorsement.

- When religious expression is directed towards other DAF members, the speaker must refrain from such expression when a member asks that it stop or otherwise demonstrates that it is unwelcome

- Leaders should be mindful that subordinates could perceive their religious expression as coercive, even if it is not intended as such. Consequently, commanders and supervisors should be mindful of the supervisor and subordinate relationship during such discussions.

Prayer

- As a general rule, prayer constitutes protected religious expression. However, in official circumstances, or when superior/subordinate relationships are involved, superiors must be sensitive to the potential that personal religious expressions may appear official or coercive.

- Public prayer must not endorse, or appear to endorse, religion

  -- Prayer may not be part of routine official business (e.g., staff meetings)

  -- If a chaplain is asked to pray at an official event, the choice of prayer is in the discretion of the chaplain as long as the prayer does not state or imply any DAF endorsement of a specific religion

- Leaders should avoid leading prayers at official functions. Any prayers should be led by a chaplain, if possible, or another DAF member.

- Religious content/prayer is acceptable as an exercise of free exercise in ceremonies that are primarily personal to the honoree, such as retirements or promotion ceremonies. If a commander is the presiding official for the event, the commander could ask to have the "emcee" announce that the religious content/prayer is at the request of the honoree.

- Attendance at National Prayer Breakfast activities in uniform is neither prohibited nor encouraged (i.e., it is left to attendee's discretion)

Religious Displays

- Displays of religious articles are permissible in government offices where it is clear that the articles are personal and are not used to promote a specific religious belief to office members

- Supervisors may restrict all posters regardless of content, or posters of a certain size, in private work areas, or require that such posters be displayed facing the employee, and not on common walls. However, a supervisor is not permitted to specifically single out religious posters (e.g., the Ten Commandments) for either negative or preferential treatment compared to other posters.

- Context is critical. While the Ten Commandments may be permissible in the employee's cubicle, religious displays have the potential to send a message of endorsement of particular religious beliefs.

- Commanders and others in leadership positions must be sensitive to the nature, extent, and circumstances of their religious displays

Official Communications

- Chaplains at all levels of command are encouraged to work with Public Affairs (PA) to generate communication plans for the dissemination of information for chapel-sponsored religious services, activities, or events

- As part of this communication plan, PA will recommend appropriate internal and external communications channels

  -- Distribution of information about chapel-sponsored services, activities, or events, should be consistent with the tools commanders use to inform DAF members and their families about other command programs or events (e.g., Morale, Welfare and Recreation (MWR), Military and Family Readiness Center (M&FRC), Sexual Assault Prevention and Response (SAPR), etc.)

- Commanders at all levels who are considering personally disseminating information about chapel-sponsored religious services, activities, or events, should balance constitutional protections for their own free exercise of religion—including individual expressions of religious beliefs—with the constitutional prohibition against governmental establishment of religion. Commanders should ensure their words and actions cannot reasonably be construed to be officially endorsing, disapproving of, or extending preferential treatment for any faith, belief, or absence of belief.

  -- For example, a commander may disseminate the installation chapel's schedule of events for the month and encourage attendance at events/activities that are open to all DAF members (and their dependents), of all faith groups and belief systems

-- However, a commander may not endorse or encourage attendance at an activity or event that is limited to members of a single faith, especially if the commander is also a member of that faith

Accommodation of Religious Practices

- The DAF places a high value on the rights of its members to observe the tenets of their respective religions or to observe no religion at all

- Pursuant to DoDI 1300.17, the DAF will approve an individual's request for accommodation of a religious practice unless the request would have an adverse impact on readiness, unit cohesion, good order and discipline, health, or safety

- Commanders and supervisors must fairly consider requests for religious accommodation. Except in the case of immunization or medical practice, DAF members requesting accommodation will continue to comply with directives, instructions, and lawful orders from which they are requesting accommodation unless and until the request is approved.

- Religious expression in the DAF is governed primarily by the Free Exercise Clause, the Religious Freedom Restoration Act (RFRA), DoDI 1300.17, *Religious Liberty in the Military Services*, provisions of AFI 1-1, *Air Force Standards*, and DAFI 52-201, *Religious Freedom in the Department of the Air Force*

- RFRA provides broad protection for religious liberty and provides the government shall not substantially burden a person's exercise of religion unless the burden is:

    -- In furtherance of a compelling governmental interest, and

    -- Is the least restrictive means of furthering that compelling governmental interest.

- Follow the required processes and procedures in DAFI 52-201 in reviewing and acting on religious accommodation requests. Consult your Staff Judge Advocate (SJA) regarding any questions pertaining to the analysis of such requests.

Outside Advocacy Groups

- Interest group advocates (including lawyers) seeking a particular resolution of a religious issue of which they have become aware might call commanders directly, advising that the law "requires" the commander to adopt a specific position. If this happens, commanders should consider the following guidelines:

    -- Commanders should avoid sounding sympathetic or agreeable to the group's pronouncements

    -- Threats of adverse publicity or litigation are to be expected. Commanders should inform PA and their SJA of the identity of the caller and the nature of the call (including the requests and demand of the caller) and advise the caller that such consultation will occur.

-- Commanders should not take unilateral action (i.e., action without first consulting SJA and/or PA) to do what the caller is requesting or demanding

-- Commanders may thank the caller for bringing the matter to their attention but should not make any promises to investigate or take action within a specific time frame

-- Commanders who believe a follow-up response is required should make that known to their SJA, PA, and chaplains, but should disengage themselves from further communication with the advocacy group

References

· U.S. Const. Amend. 1
· Religious Apparel: Wearing While in Uniform, 10 U.S.C. § 774
· The Religious Freedom Restoration Act of 1993 (RFRA), 42 U.S.C. §§ 2000bb *et seq.*
· DoDI 1300.17, *Religious Liberty in the Military Services* (1 September 2020)
· DAFI 36-2903, *Dress and Personal Appearance of Air Force Personnel* (29 February 2024), Corrective Actions applied on 13 March 2024
· DAFI 52-201, *Religious Freedom in the Department of the Air Force* (23 June 2021)
· AFI 1-1, *Air Force Standards* (18 August 2023)
· AFI 35-101, *Public Affairs Operations* (20 November 2020)
· AFI 48-110, *Immunizations and Chemoprophylaxis for the Prevention of Infectious Diseases* (7 October 2013), certified current 20 May 2023

SOCIAL MEDIA AND ELECTRONIC COMMUNICATION

Social media includes, but is not limited to, weblogs, message boards, video sharing, streaming, and other media sharing sites. The rules for use of social media can be divided into two categories: official use (use by the Department of the Air Force to conduct official Air Force and Space Force duties) and personal use. In its official capacity, social media is a tool that allows the Department of the Air Force to conduct outreach with the general public, as well as for Airmen and Guardians—military and civilian—to interact personally with friends, family, the media, elected officials, and strangers.

Key Takeaways
» Look to AFI 35-101, *Public Affairs Operations*, regarding guidance on official use of social media
» Look to AFI 1-1, *Air Force Standards*, regarding guidance on the personal use of social media

Official Use

- Official use of social media must comply with all DoD and Department of the Air Force guidance as outlined in DoDI 5400.17, *Official Use of Social Media for Public Affairs Purposes*, and AFI 35-101, *Public Affairs Operations*, Section 5D

- Before expanding an organization's social media presence on a new social media platform, the site must have been vetted through the Defense Information Systems Agency's DoD Application Vetting Environment

- Any official use of social media must be approved by a Department of the Air Force Public Affairs Office (PA) and follow policies established by the Secretary of the Air Force Office of Public Affairs (SAF/PA)

- Official Department of the Air Force social media presences must be registered on the websites: https://www.defense.gov/Resources/Register-a-Site/; https://www.digitalgov.gov/services/u-s-digital-registry/; and https://www.af.mil/AFSites/SiteRegistration.aspx. Closed social media sites will not be accepted in the registry.

  -- Federal-compatible Terms of Service (TOS) agreements may modify or remove problematic clauses in standard TOS agreements and allow federal employees to legally use these tools. Before deciding to use a social media tool (e.g., Facebook, Instagram, Twitter, etc.), organizations should seek the advice of an Air Force or Space Force social media team for an updated list of federal-compatible services.

- Air Force and Space Force official social media sites may not contain any non-public information or link to any site that contains non-public information

  -- DoDI 5400.17 requires local PA officials and social media managers to establish communication plans to ensure information posted to social media has been reviewed and cleared for release

- All Air Force and Space Force official social media sites should have the organization's patch or logo, a link back to the organization's .mil website, and a .mil email address on their pages to verify that they are a valid Air Force or Space Force page

- Official Air Force and Space Force social media will not link to offensive or unrelated commercial material

  -- No surveys may be conducted via official social media without prior approval

- All Air Force and Space Force official social media sites must contain disclaimers, comment policies, and privacy policies. Contact your local PA office for sample disclaimers and comment policies.

- Comments received on Air Force and Space Force official social media sites must be moderated for topic and language, as outlined in the comment policies. Direct or private messaging on Air Force and Space Force official social media sites should be conducted with care, and direct or private messages may not be sent if they automatically expire (e.g., Snapchat).

- All Air Force and Space Force official social media posts and comments received must be maintained in accordance with Air Force and Space Force records retention guidelines

Personal Use

- Generally, the Air Force and Space Force views personal websites and blogs positively, and it respects the right of Airmen and Guardians to use them as a medium of self-expression, even if their status as Airmen and Guardians is apparent

- Personal social media accounts should not be used to conduct official business, with exceptions for emergencies and other critical mission needs, when official communications capabilities are unavailable, and when it is in the interests of Air Force or Space Force to do so

- For Airmen and Guardians with official social media accounts, DoDI 5400.17 requires distinctions to be made between their official and personal online personas. All Airmen and Guardians must ensure their personal social media accounts avoid use of DoD titles, insignia, uniforms, or symbols in a way that could imply official endorsement of the content.

- Social media and electronic communication generally encourage informal, sometimes intimate, and at times adversarial interactions. Military members and civilian employees must remember that, generally, actions prohibited in person are not otherwise condoned or tolerated through social media or electronic communication.

  -- The use of social media and other forms of communication that allow communication with a large number of people brings with it the increased risk of magnifying operational security lapses. Classified, Controlled Unclassified Information (CUI), and other official DoD information and documents are prohibited from being posted on social networking services or transmitted via non-DoD email accounts without proper authority.

-- Airmen and Guardians' obligation is to maintain appropriate communication and conduct with officer and enlisted personnel, peers, superiors, and subordinates (to include civilian superiors and subordinates). This is applicable whether communicating via a social networking service or other forms of communication, such as email, instant messaging, or texting.

-- Airmen and Guardians must avoid offensive and/or inappropriate behavior on social networking platforms and through other forms of communication that could bring discredit upon the Air Force or Space Force or that would otherwise be harmful to good order and discipline, respect for authority, unit cohesion, morale, mission accomplishment, or the trust and confidence that the public has in the United States Air Force or United States Space Force

-- Airmen and Guardians who provide commentary and opinions on internet blogs that they host or on others' internet blogs, may not place comments on those blog sites, which reasonably can be anticipated, or are intended, to degrade morale, good order, and discipline of any members or units in the U.S. Armed Forces, are Service-discrediting, or would degrade the trust and confidence of the public in the United States Air Force

-- When expressing personal opinions on social media sites where members can be identified as an Airman or Guardian, they should make clear that they are speaking for themselves and not on behalf of the Air Force. While service members may generally use their rank and service even when acting in their personal capacity, they should not do so in situations where the context may imply official sanction or endorsement of their personal opinions.

-- Airmen and Guardians should recognize that social network "friends" and "followers" may potentially constitute relationships that could affect determinations in background investigations and periodic reinvestigations associated with security clearances

-- If Airmen/Guardians violate federal or state laws and regulations and policies through inappropriate personal online activity, or any other form of communication, they may be subject to disciplinary action

References

· DoDI 5400.17, *Official Use of Social Media for Public Affairs Purposes* (12 August 2022), incorporating Change 1, 24 January 2023
· DoDI 8170.01, *Online Information Management and Electronic Messaging* (2 January 2019), incorporating Change 1, 24 August 2021
· AFI 1-1, *Air Force Standards* (18 August 2023)
· AFI 35-101, *Public Affairs Operations* (20 November 2020)

SPECIAL EDUCATION LEGAL ASSISTANCE
TO EXCEPTIONAL FAMILY MEMBERS

Public schools are required by the Individuals with Disabilities Education Act (IDEA) to provide a Free and Appropriate Public Education (FAPE) to children whose education is impacted by their disabilities. Legal assistance attorneys can help families navigate special education challenges for students with disabilities.

Key Takeaways

» Students whose educational performance is adversely impacted by their disabilities are entitled to a free and appropriate public education

» Individualized Education Programs (IEPs) and Section 504 Plans are the vehicles used to capture the unique needs of a child with a disability

» Subject to Staff Judge Advocate (SJA) approval, legal assistance attorneys can attend IEP meetings and similar administrative hearings

» IDEA and Section 504 provisions are applicable to schools receiving federal funds. Private schools are generally not subject to the provisions of the IDEA or Section 504.

» Legal assistance attorneys can help families navigate special education issues for students with disabilities. Families with exceptional family members should reach out to their local legal office for assistance with special education disputes.

Federal Laws Governing Special Education

- IDEA is the Federal Law that governs the identification and eligibility of children with disabilities, and the provision of special education to those students who qualify

- The Rehabilitation Act of 1973, Section 504, prohibits discrimination against people with disabilities, in programs that receive federal financial assistance such as public schools

- The Family Education Rights and Privacy Act of 1974 (FERPA) provides that parents or eligible students have the right to inspect and to review the student's education records maintained by the school. They also have the right to request that a school correct records they believe to be inaccurate or misleading.

- The Americans with Disabilities Act (ADA) prohibits discrimination solely on the basis of disability, in employment, public services, and accommodations. Title III of the ADA expressly lists "a nursery, elementary, secondary, undergraduate, or postgraduate private school, or other place of education" as a public accommodation.

Applicability of Federal Special Education Laws

- IDEA generally applies to all public schools, including Department of Defense Education Activity (DoDEA) Schools. The law requires schools to conduct eligibility testing and evaluations to identify children in need of special education and related services. In coordination with the parents, an IEP is then developed and implemented to meet the child's unique educational needs.

- Section 504 provisions generally apply to all public schools, including DoDEA Schools. This program covers a broader range of disabilities than IDEA and provides accommodations in the classroom, around the school building, and transporting children to and from school.

- The ADA is not conditioned upon the receipt of federal funding and therefore applies to public and private schools. Under the ADA, a private school must accommodate any individual who has a physical or mental impairment that substantially limits one or more major life activities.

The Special Education Process

- Generally, the special education process begins when a parent suspects their child may be experiencing challenges with the educational curriculum and requests an evaluation

- When a child has been found eligible for special education services under IDEA, the vehicle that is used to capture that agreement is called an Individualized Education Program (IEP). The IEP and other disability related documents represent an agreement with a State or Federal agency and should reflect the parents' understanding of what the organization has offered to provide.

- When a child with an IEP starts at a new school during the school year, the gaining school must continue to provide a FAPE, including services comparable to those described in the IEP, until the new school adopts the current IEP, conducts any necessary evaluations and/or develops a new IEP if appropriate and consistent with Federal and State law. IEP decisions should be made in consultation with the parents.

- By federal law, IEPs must be reviewed annually. Evaluations must be done tri-annually. If a secondary disability is suspected, the school would have reason for an earlier re-evaluation. Parents can also request evaluation earlier than the federally prescribed tri-annual period. The school may consider the parent's requests, but they do not have to act on them.

- Section 504 of the Rehabilitation Act specifically designates plans or approaches for students with disabilities, including life-threatening allergies, asthma, epilepsy, and diabetes, to protect against discrimination in education. Plans can be targeted at provisions such as accessibility, nutrition blocks, time for testing and completion of class work.

Assistance in Special Education Matters

- Families have multiple avenues of support in special education matters, including:

  -- <u>School Liaisons (SLs)</u>: SLs provides special education support, guidance, and resources for families;

  -- <u>Exceptional Family Member Program (EFMP) Family Support Coordinators (FSCs)</u>: FSCs assess EFMP families for community needs and provide local, state, and federal resources to help improve quality of life; and

  -- <u>Legal Assistance</u>: Legal assistance attorneys assist families to understand special education laws and to advocate for the rights of their children. Subject to SJA approval, legal assistance attorneys can attend IEP meetings and similar administrative hearings. Further information on special education and special education legal services can be found on the EFMP's website, https://daffamilyvector.us.af.mil/.

Educational Reassignments

- The EFMP can provide reassignment when a DAF service member is assigned to an area and a new medical, special education, related service, or early intervention need arises for which the needed services are not available within the assignment locale

- Legal Assistance may help to resolve educational disputes and avoid reassignment requests

References

· The Family Educational and Rights and Privacy Act, 20 U.S.C. §§ 1232 *et seq.* (2002)
· Individuals with Disabilities Education Act, 20 U.S.C. §§ 1400 *et seq.* (2004)
· Section 504 of the Rehabilitation Act of 1973, 29 U.S.C. §§ 794 *et seq.*
· Prohibition of Discrimination by Public Accommodations, 42 U.S.C. § 12182
· DoDI 1315.19, *Exceptional Family Member Program* (23 June 2023)
· DAFI 36-2110, *Total Force Assignments* (15 November 2021), incorporating Charge 1, 16 November 2022, including DAFGM 2023-01, 5 October 2023
· AFI 51-304, *Legal Assistance, Notary, Preventive Law and Tax Programs* (22 August 2018)
· DAF Family Vector website, https://daffamilyvector.us.af.mil/membersite/

RECORDS MANAGEMENT, FREEDOM OF INFORMATION ACT, PRIVACY ACT, AND CIVIL LIBERTIES COMPLAINTS

Commanders are required to properly maintain and dispose of records (when required) created under their command. Any Air Force record can be requested by the public, and can only be released, or withheld, under specific federal law or other legal authority, such as a court order. Federal law also protects from improper use or public release the personal information of individuals that the Air Force collects and maintains on individuals in order to accomplish their missions. Airmen and Guardians can file complaints to their commander alleging a violation of their constitutional civil liberties, which must be addressed by the command.

Key Takeaways

» Appropriate records management is a commander's responsibility

» Air Force records can only be withheld from public release according to specific federal laws

» Information collected about Airmen and Guardians and records kept on them can only be used and shared within the DoD and outside the DoD according to federal law. Records must be properly secured to prevent unauthorized access.

Records Management

- The Federal Records Act of 1950, and as amended, requires all federal agencies to properly store, maintain, and, when required, either destroy (when no longer needed), or permanently archive with the National Archives and Records Administration, all records, in whatever format (paper, electronic, to include email and text, video, and photographic), the federal agency creates in order to accomplish its mission(s)

-- In the Department of the Air Force (DAF), this is a command/commander responsibility. The DAF Records Officer within SAF/CN (Office of the Chief Information Officer) provides records management guidance to commander appointed personnel, who are charged with the responsibility for managing their command's records.

Freedom of Information Act (FOIA) of 1966

- The FOIA requires federal agencies to disclose its records to any member of the public upon written request. The basic goals of the FOIA are to ensure an informed public, to serve as a check against corruption, and to hold the government accountable.

-- No requested record can be denied under the FOIA unless one of nine (9) specific FOIA exemptions apply, or other appropriate legal authority, such as a court order, permits denial. FOIA Initial Denial Authorities at the HQ, major command and base level are specifically appointed to make release decisions for records created and controlled at these different levels of command.

-- The nine exemptions protect from release matters such as personally identifiable information, sensitive government information, such as classified information or controlled unclassified information, or information that another federal law prohibits from being publicly released

Privacy Act of 1974

- The Privacy Act (PA) has the opposite purpose of the FOIA. It is designed to protect from improper use, or public release, the personal information of individuals that federal agencies maintain in order to accomplish their missions. The PA also controls a federal agency's ability to collect information about individuals.

  -- A federal agency cannot share or use the PA record of an individual without consent of the individual, unless one or more of twelve (12) specific PA exemptions apply. PA exemptions include using PA records whenever necessary for an agency's internal official use purposes; releasing records as required under the FOIA; or other required releases of information, such as to Congress.

  -- Examples of some of the over 250 different types of PA records the DAF maintains on individuals include criminal investigative records, disciplinary and other personnel records, and medical records

Civil Liberties Complaints & Reporting

- DAF service members can file complaints with various DAF investigative entities when they believe a constitutional civil liberty under the U.S. Constitution has been denied to them. These civil liberties include those under the First Amendment (speech, religion), Second Amendment (right to bear arms), and Fifth Amendment (right to due process).

  -- DoD requires that civil liberty complaints handled through the Commander Directed Investigation process be reported bi-annually to DoD (April and October). This data is captured at all command levels by servicing legal offices and are sent to the Office of The Judge Advocate General.

References

- Freedom of Information Act, 5 U.S.C. § 552
- Privacy Act of 1974, 5 U.S.C. § 552a
- The Federal Records Act of 1950, 44 U.S.C. §§ 3101, *et seq.*
- DoD 5400.11-R, *Department of Defense Privacy Program* (14 May 2007)
- DoDM 5400.07_AFMAN 33-302, *Freedom of Information Act Program* (27 April 2018)
- AFI 33-322, *Records Management and Information Governance Program* (23 March 2020), incorporating Change 1, 28 July 2021
- AFI 33-332, *Air Force Privacy and Civil Liberties Program* (10 March 2020), Corrective Actions applied on 12 May 2020

DELIVERY OF MILITARY PERSONNEL TO CIVILIAN AUTHORITIES FOR TRIAL

The Department of the Air Force (DAF) expects military personnel, employees, and family members to comply with court orders issued by federal, state, and local authorities. Upon the issuance of a warrant or court order to testify, commanders must cooperate with civilian authorities to ensure the appearance of DAF service members facing felony-level criminal charges.

Key Takeaways

» Commanders will cooperate with civilian authorities and act promptly to ensure delivery of DAF service members facing felony criminal charges

» Personnel may not use military service to avoid prosecution by civilian U.S. authorities

» The DAF has the authority to deliver military members to civilian custody. DAF-affiliated civilians may face administrative consequences for failure to comply with court orders.

» Military members may be placed in pretrial restraint or detention pending delivery to civilian authorities. However, consult with the servicing legal office before doing so.

» DAF policy is to request criminal jurisdiction of military members from civilian authorities if the underlying offense is also an offense under the Uniform Code of Military Justice (UCMJ)

Compliance with Court Orders to Testify

- DAF service members, civilian employees, and family members are expected to comply with orders issued by a federal, state, or local court unless non-compliance is legally justified. This applies equally to members stationed outside the United States. DAF members who fail to comply with civilian court orders may face adverse administrative action, including administrative separation.

- DAF officials will ensure members, employees, and family members do not use assignments or officially-sponsored residences outside the United States to avoid complying with valid court orders. Failure of a family member located outside the United States to comply with a court order may be the basis for withdrawal of command sponsorship from the family member.

Procedure: Delivery of Military Personnel Located Outside the United States

- In general, members stationed outside the United States who are charged with, or convicted of, any felony or unlawful removal of a child from the jurisdiction of the legal custodian will be expeditiously returned for delivery to civilian authorities. Commanders must act on requests to return military members within 30 days of receipt. Commanders should consult their servicing legal office prior to taking action. Similarly, the servicing legal office must consult with the Military Justice Law and Policy Division (AF/JAJM) on all requests.

- Approvals must come from a general court-martial convening authority (GCMCA), an installation commander who has been delegated the authority by a GCMCA, or The Judge Advocate General (TJAG)

- Denials must come from the Under Secretary of Defense for Personnel and Readiness (USD(P&R)) in felony cases or certain child custody offenses. TJAG may deny all other requests.

Procedure: Delivery of Military Personnel Located Within the United States

- Requests for, and delivery of, military personnel located within the United States generally follow the same procedures outlined above for the return of members outside the United States, with the exception of involvement by the USD(P&R)

  -- The requirement to follow this procedure is only necessary when the military must play a role in the delivery of the member. For example, a request from civilian authorities to access an installation to arrest the member would trigger this requirement, but an off-base arrest made without any military involvement would not.

Commander Responsibilities and Authority

- Commanders must take the following action when acting on return requests:

  -- Inform the requesting authorities of the member's travel itinerary, port of entry, and estimated date and time of arrival at least 10 days before the member's arrival;

  -- Provide the member an Instruction Letter (DAFI 51-205, *Delivery of Personnel to United States Civilian Authorities for Trial and Criminal Jurisdiction Over Civilians and Dependents Not in the United States*, para. 3.4.2.3). Commanders should consult with their servicing legal office to obtain the Instruction Letter, which is located on the Virtual Military Justice Deskbook; and

  -- Execute an Acknowledgement and Agreement Letter with the requesting civilian authorities (DAFI 51-205, para. 3.4.2.4). Commanders should consult with their servicing legal office to obtain the Acknowledgement and Agreement Letter, which is located on the Virtual Military Justice Deskbook.

- Commanders may restrain or confine a military member whose delivery has been requested by civilians if the commander determines there is probable cause that the member committed the charged offense, and that restraint or confinement is necessary. However, military pretrial restraint procedures and requirements under Rule for Courts-Martial 305 apply in any situation where a military member is restrained or confined.

Initial Actions Following Report of Service Member Arrest by Civilian Authorities

- When a commander receives notice that a member of his/her command is charged with a crime or detained by civilian authorities, the commander should contact the civilian authorities, inform them the person is a military member, and gather the following information:

-- The charge(s) against the member;

-- The facts and circumstances surrounding the charged offense(s); and

-- The level of the criminal offense (i.e., misdemeanor or felony).

- **DO NOT** take the following actions:

-- State/imply the DAF will guarantee the member's presence at subsequent hearings; or

-- Post bond for the member or personally guarantee any action by the member.

Release of Criminal Jurisdiction by Civilian Authorities to Military Authorities

- When a military member commits an offense off base in violation of both civilian and military law (e.g., rape, robbery, murder), the member is subject to prosecution by both civilians and the military

- While separate civilian and military prosecutions for the same offense is permissible, DAF policy is that it will only prosecute under the UCMJ if the civilians do not take jurisdiction of the case. As a matter of policy, the DAF, generally through the applicable Office of Special Trial Counsel district office for covered, known, and related offenses under Articles 1(17) and 24a, UCMJ, or the installation staff judge advocate's office for all other offenses, will request criminal jurisdiction from civilian authorities if the underlying offense is also an offense under the UCMJ.

Civilians Associated with the DAF

- Commanders ordinarily do not have authority to compel civilian compliance with court orders but will strongly encourage civilians associated with their organizations to comply with valid orders of federal and state courts. Failure to comply may result in adverse administrative action against civilian employees and withholding of official command sponsorship for military dependents, where appropriate.

References

· Articles 1(17), 14, and 24a, Uniform Code of Military Justice

· Rule for Courts-Martial 305 (2024)

· DoDI 5525.09, *Compliance with Court Orders by Service Members and DoD Civilian Employees, and Their Family Members Outside the United States* (23 April 2019)

· DoDI 5525.11, *Criminal Jurisdiction Over Civilians Employed by or Accompanying the Armed Forces Outside the United States, Certain Service Members, and Former Service Members* (3 March 2005)

· DAFI 51-205, *Delivery of Personnel to United States Civilian Authorities for Trial and Criminal Jurisdiction Over Civilians and Dependents Not in the United States* (19 January 2023)

· DAF Form 2098, *Duty Status Change* (12 July 2022)

CITIZENSHIP FOR MILITARY MEMBERS

The Immigration and Nationality Act (INA) provides naturalization options for United States military members and certain veterans of the military. Foreign nationals who are serving or have served in the U.S. military may pursue naturalization through peacetime military service (8 U.S.C. § 1439), through military service during a period of hostilities (8 U.S.C. § 1440) or naturalization may be pursued posthumously for members who served during a designated period of hostilities (8 U.S.C. § 1440-1).

Key Takeaways

» Non-citizen service members can become U.S. citizens through their military service

» Service members needing assistance with the naturalization process should contact their local legal office for legal assistance

---

Naturalization through Peacetime Service

- A member who has served honorably in the U.S. Armed Forces at any time may be eligible to apply for naturalization under Section 328 of the INA (8 U.S.C. § 1439). The military community refers to this as "peacetime naturalization."

- In general, an applicant for naturalization based peacetime service must:

    -- Have served honorably in the U.S. Armed Forces for one year, or periods aggregating one year;

    -- Be a lawful permanent resident at the time of your naturalization interview;

    -- Be able to read, write, and speak English (unless qualified for a waiver/exception);

    -- Demonstrate knowledge of U.S. history and government (civics);

    -- Demonstrate good moral character for at least five years prior to filing the application until the time of his/her naturalization;

    -- Have an attachment to the principles of the U.S. Constitution and be well disposed to the good order and happiness of the United States during all relevant periods under the law; and

    -- Have continuously resided in the United States for at least five years and have been physically present in the United States for at least 30 months out of the five years immediately preceding the filing date of the application, **UNLESS** the applicant has filed an application while still in the service or within six months of an honorable discharge. In the latter case, the applicant is not required to meet these residence and physical presence requirements.

Naturalization through Qualifying Service During Periods of Hostilities

- Members of the U.S. Armed Forces who serve honorably during specifically designated periods of hostilities are eligible for naturalization under Section 329 of the INA (8 U.S.C. § 1440). Although the INA allows a service member's citizenship application to be accelerated for active service, this does not apply to Air National Guard service unless the unit is federally recognized as a reserve component of the U.S. Armed Forces.

- In general, an applicant for naturalization based on service during a period of hostilities must:

    -- Have served honorably in an active duty status during a designated period of hostilities and, if separated from the U.S. Armed Forces, have been separated honorably;

    -- Have been lawfully admitted as a permanent resident **OR** have been physically present in the U.S. or certain territories at the time of enlistment, reenlistment, or induction;

    -- Be able to read, write, and speak basic English;

    -- Demonstrate knowledge of U.S. history and government (civics);

    -- Demonstrate good moral character for at least one year prior to filing the application until the time of his/her naturalization; and

    -- Have an attachment to the principles of the U.S. Constitution and be well disposed to the good order and happiness of the United States during all relevant periods under the law.

- An applicant who files based on military service during hostilities is exempt from the general naturalization requirements of continuous residence and physical presence

- The designated periods of hostilities include: 2 August 1990 – 11 April 1991 (Persian Gulf Conflict), and 11 September 2001 to the present (Executive Order 13269, 3 July 2002). **Note:** The current designated period of hostilities will terminate when the President issues an Executive Order terminating the period.

Application Processing

- Service members must apply for naturalization through United States Citizenship and Immigration Services (USCIS). Service members are not charged filing or biometrics fees associated with the naturalization process.

- Service members who fail to obtain citizenship during their initial enlistment may not be eligible for reenlistment (see AFI 36-2606, *Reenlistment and Extension of Enlistment in the United States Air Force*, para. 5.11.13).

- Every military installation should have a designated point of contact to assist members with completing Form N-400, Application for Naturalization, and Form N-426, Request for Certification of Military Naval Services. The forms may be accessed at https://www.uscis.gov.

- Authority to certify honorable service (via USCIS Form N-426) is with the first commanding officer in the grade of O-6 or higher within the individual's chain of command. These commanding officers may re-delegate certification authority to officers serving under their direct supervision in the grade of O-6 and may not delegate any further.

-- Honorable service cannot be certified if the member is the subject of any pending disciplinary actions, pending administrative actions or proceedings, or is the subject of a law enforcement or command investigation. Additionally, honorable service cannot be certified if the member has not completed all screening and suitability requirements as defined by the Office of the Under Secretary of Defense (OUSD) for Personnel and Readiness (P&R)'s 13 October 2017 Memorandum titled Certification of Honorable Service for Members of the Selected Reserve of the Ready Reserve and Members of the Active Components of the Military or Naval Forces for Purposes of Naturalization.

--- Please note that the minimum time service requirements in this memorandum have been rescinded following a court order in the case of *Ange Samma v. DoD et al*, 486 F. Supp. 3d 240 (D.D.C. 2020)

References

· Immigration and Nationality Act (INA), 8 U.S.C. §§ 1101 *et seq.*

· Naturalization through Service in the Armed Forces, 8 U.S.C. § 1439

· Naturalization through Active Duty Service […] Periods of Military Hostilities, 8 U.S.C. § 1440

· *Ange Samma v. DoD et al*, 486 F. Supp. 3d 240 (D.D.C. 2020)

· DoDI 5500.14, *Naturalization of Aliens Serving in the Armed Forces of the United States and of Alien Spouses and/or Alien Adopted Children of Military and Civilian Personnel Ordered Overseas* (4 January 2006)

· AFI 36-2606, *Reenlistment and Extension of Enlistment in the United States Air Force* (20 September 2019), incorporating Change 1, 27 January 2021

· OUSD (P&R) Memorandum, Certification of Honorable Service for Members of the Selected Reserve of the Ready Reserve and Members of the Active Components of the Military or Naval Forces for Purposes of Naturalization (13 October 2017), as amended by OUSD (P&R) Memorandum, Compliance with Court Order in Case of *Ange Samma v. DoD*, 31 August 2020 (see also SAF/MR Memorandum, Compliance with Court Order in Case of *Ange Samma v. DoD*, 3 September 2020.

· USCIS: https://www.uscis.gov/military/military

· USCIS Military Help Line: 877-247-4645

Chapter 7
PERSONNEL ISSUES – MILITARY MEMBERS

THE DEPARTMENT OF THE AIR FORCE URINALYSIS PROGRAM

The purpose of the Department of the Air Force (DAF) urinalysis program is to assist commanders ensure their troops are mission ready by deterring DAF members from using illegal drugs and other illicit substances. DAFMAN 44-197, *Military Drug Demand Reduction Program*, sets forth procedures regarding Drug Demand Reduction (DDR) activities for Department of the Air Force personnel.

Key Takeaways

» The Air Force Drug Testing Laboratory (AFDTL) can test for the presence of all drugs on the Department of Defense (DoD) standard drug testing panel. For a list of the current DoD standard testing panel, contact the AFDTL Legal Advisor.

» Each sample must undergo at least two tests before it may be considered positive: (1) screen and (2) confirmation

» Upon receipt of a positive test report, regardless of type of test (with the exception of post-mishap toxicology results), the unit commander should immediately contact the servicing legal office

» Commanders' options following a positive drug testing result depend in great part on the basis for the testing. Authorized actions are outlined in Table 9.1 of DAFMAN 44-197.

» Upon notification of a positive urinalysis test, law enforcement from the Office of Special Investigations (OSI) or Security Forces (SF) will schedule an interview with the service member. Do not advise the service member of the test result in advance of the interview.

Air Force Drug Testing Laboratory (AFDTL)

- The AFDTL can test for all drugs on the DoD standard drug testing panel. For a list of the current DoD standard testing panel, contact the AFDTL legal advisor.

- The AFDTL uses a DoD-prescribed combination of analytic techniques to determine whether specimens are positive for various drugs

  -- Each sample must undergo at least two tests before it may be considered positive: (1) screen and (2) confirmation

  -- Screen Test: Conducted using immunoassay testing, with occasional directed screen testing using liquid chromatography/tandem mass spectrometry (LC-MS/MS)

  -- Confirmation Test: Conducted using gas chromatography/mass spectrometry (GC/MS) or liquid chromatography tandem mass spectrometry (LC-MS/MS)

Urinalysis Testing Collection Basis

- The installation DDR office facilitates urinalysis drug testing. The Staff Judge Advocate (SJA) inspects the DDR program's regulatory compliance quarterly using the checklist provided by AFDTL.

- In addition to the random drug testing program, there are five common situations that may justify urinalysis testing: consent, probable cause, commander directed, inspection, and medical care. Each of these has its own legal considerations for when it can be taken and how it can be used, so consult with the servicing SJA before determining which to use.

- Consent:

  -- A Commander who suspects a subordinate of having used drugs in violation of the Uniform Code of Military Justice (UCMJ), may not question the member about such use without first informing the member of the offense he/she is suspected of having committed and advising the member that he/she does not have to make a statement and that any statement made may be used as evidence against him/her in a trial by court-martial. Article 31, UCMJ. Commanders are not required to give these Article 31, UCMJ, rights if they limit their question to asking the member to consent to drug testing. However, evidence that a member was read these rights may be used to help demonstrate that any consent obtained was voluntary on the part of the member.

  -- When practicable, consent should be obtained in writing, using an AF Form 1364, *Consent for Search and Seizure*

- Probable Cause:

  -- To have probable cause, there must be a *reasonable* belief that illegal drugs, or drug metabolites, will be present in the individual's urine

  -- Requires a search and seizure authorization from a neutral and detached commander with authority over the person being searched to seize a urine specimen

- Commander Directed:

  -- Appropriate where the member displays strange, bizarre, or unlawful behavior or where the commander suspects or has reason to believe drugs may be present but probable cause does not exist

  -- Results obtained through commander-directed tests can be used as a basis for administrative discharge but cannot be considered when characterizing the member's service upon discharge

  -- Results can be used to support administrative actions such as Letters of Reprimand (LORs) and promotion propriety actions, but **CANNOT** be used to take UCMJ action, such as courts-martial or nonjudicial punishment

- Inspections:

  -- Sometimes called a "unit sweep," an entire unit or part of a unit may be inspected. Individual members **MAY NOT** be targeted for an inspection.

-- Urine specimens may be ordered and collected as a part of an inspection under Military Rule of Evidence 313(b). The primary purpose of an inspection is to determine and ensure the security, military fitness, or good order and discipline of the unit.

-- Coordinate inspections with the installation Drug Demand Reduction Program Manager (DDRPM). Do not announce the inspection in advance to those being inspected. Inspection testing is the best deterrent available against drug abuse.

- Medical Care:

-- A urine specimen collected as a part of a patient's medical treatment (for a valid medical purpose), including a routine physical, may be subjected to urinalysis drug testing

-- Members may not be disciplined under the UCMJ when they legitimately self-identify for drug abuse and enter the Alcohol Drug Abuse Prevention and Treatment Program. See AFI 44-121, *Alcohol and Drug Abuse Prevention Treatment (ADAPT) Program*, for more information.

- Special Considerations:

-- Specimens collected as a result of aircraft incidents/accidents must be collected by the military treatment facility laboratory. DDRPMs and/or DTPAMs may assist with collection of these specimens upon request. See DAFMAN 91-223, *Aviation Safety Investigation and Reports*.

Positive Results

- Upon receipt of a positive test report, the unit commander should **immediately** contact the SJA

- Commanders' options following a positive drug testing result depend in great part on the basis for the testing. Authorized uses of positive test results in administrative actions are outlined in Table 9.1 of DAFMAN 44-197.

- Authorized administrative actions following a positive drug test result include, but are not limited to, Letters of Counseling (LOCs)/Letters of Admonishment (LOAs)/Letters of Reprimand (LORs), denial of re-enlistment, removal from the Personnel Reliability Assurance Program status, removal from duties involving firearms, and suspension of security clearance

- Upon notification of a positive urinalysis test, OSI or SF investigators will schedule an interview with the service member. Do not advise the service member in advance of the interview of the positive test result.

References

· Article 31, Uniform Code of Military Justice

· Military Rule of Evidence 313 (2024)

· AFI 44-121, *Alcohol and Drug Abuse Prevention Treatment (ADAPT) Program* (18 July 2018), incorporating Change 1, 21 November 2019, Corrective Actions applied on 19 December 2019, including DAFGM2024-01, 3 January 2024

· DAFMAN 44-197, *Military Drug Demand Reduction Program* (5 September 2023)

· AF Form 1364, *Consent for Search and Seizure*, 5 August 2019

· Quarterly and Annual DDR Inspection Checklist, October 2023

UNPROFESSIONAL RELATIONSHIPS AND FRATERNIZATION

Unprofessional relationships and fraternization are detrimental to good order and discipline. AFI 36-2909, *Air Force Professional Relationships and Conduct*, sets out a detailed discussion of Department of the Air Force policy concerning unprofessional relationships and fraternization.

> ## Key Takeaways
>
> » Familiar relationships within a supervisory chain are at high risk for becoming unprofessional, as are familiar relationships between officers and enlisted members generally
>
> » Retaliation is a form of unprofessional relationship that also includes maltreatment and ostracism
>
> » Commanders and supervisors must take corrective action as soon as possible when an unprofessional relationship develops, beginning with counseling and orders to cease behavior

Overview

- Professional relationships are essential to the effective operation of all organizations. The nature of the military mission requires confidence in command and adherence to orders that may result in inconvenience, hardships, or, at times, injury or death.

- Personal relationships become matters of official concern when they adversely affect or have the reasonable potential to adversely affect the Air Force or Space Force by eroding morale, good order, discipline, respect for authority, unit cohesion, or mission accomplishment

Unprofessional Relationships

- Unprofessional relationships, whether pursued on or off duty, are those relationships that detract from the authority of superiors or result in—or reasonably create the appearance of—favoritism, misuse of office or position, or the abandonment of organizational goals for personal interests

- Unprofessional relationships can exist between officers, between enlisted members, between officers and enlisted members, and between military personnel and civilian employees or contractor personnel

- Certain kinds of personal relationships present a high risk of becoming unprofessional

  -- Familiar relationships in which one member exercises supervisory or command authority over another member

  -- Shared living accommodations, vacations, transportation, or off-duty interests on a frequent or recurring basis in the absence of any official purpose or organizational benefit

- Tailored rules for unprofessional relationships exist in the recruiting, training, and education environments. These rules draw very specific lines for types of activities a recruiter and recruit or trainer and trainee can participate in, locations where they may not be at the same times, and limitations on personal interaction.

  -- Additionally, Article 93a, Uniform Code of Military Justice (UCMJ), prohibits sexual activities (any "sexual act" or "sexual contact" as defined by Article 120, UCMJ) with military recruits or trainees by persons in positions of special trust. Consent to the sexual act or sexual contact by the recruit or trainee is not a defense.

- All military members share responsibility for maintaining professional relationships, but the senior member in a personal relationship bears primary responsibility

Fraternization

- Fraternization is a unique form of unprofessional relationship. It exists when a relationship between an officer and an enlisted member puts the enlisted member on terms of military equality with the officer resulting in prejudice to good order and discipline or discredit upon the armed forces.

- AFI 36-2909 specifically prohibits officers from engaging in the following activities with enlisted members and may be prosecuted under Articles 92, 133, and/or 134 of the UCMJ, with reasonable accommodation for married members or members related by blood or marriage:

  -- Gambling

  -- Lending money, borrowing money, or otherwise financially involved

    --- An exception exists for infrequent, non-interest-bearing loans of small amounts to meet exigent circumstances (e.g., an individual who forgets his/her wallet or purse and cannot pay for lunch at a unit function)

  -- Sexual relations or dating

    --- When evidence of fraternization exists, the fact that an officer and enlisted member subsequently marry does not preclude appropriate command action based on the prior fraternization

  -- Shared living accommodations, except when reasonably required by military operations

  -- Personal business enterprises or soliciting, except as permitted by DoD 5500.07-R, *Joint Ethics Regulation* (JER)

Retaliation

- AFI 36-2909 prohibits retaliation against an alleged victim or other member of the Armed Forces for reporting a criminal offense. The term retaliation includes *retaliation*, *ostracism*, and *maltreatment*.

- Retaliation against individuals who report criminal offenses is unlawful and erodes good order and discipline, respect for authority, unit cohesion, and, ultimately, mission accomplishment

- Commanders and supervisors at all levels bear responsibilities to ensure compliance with prohibited retaliation policies

- Retaliation may be prosecuted under Article 132, UCMJ, or state equivalent military code

Command and Supervisory Responsibilities

- A commander or supervisor must take corrective action if unprofessional relationships develop or reasonably creates the appearance of, regardless of whether the unprofessional relationship actually causes degradation of morale, good order and discipline, or unit cohesion. Failure to take corrective action may lead to punishment of the commander or supervisor.

  -- Orders, in writing, should be issued to cease the relationship or the conduct

  -- Disciplinary action should normally be the least severe necessary to terminate the unprofessional aspects of the relationship

  -- Counseling is often an effective first step in curtailing unprofessional relationships. However, the full spectrum of administrative actions should be considered.

  -- Nonjudicial Punishment (NJP) should be considered in more serious cases

  -- Referral of charges to a court-martial is only appropriate in aggravated cases

References

· Articles 92, 93a, 132, 133, and 134, Uniform Code of Military Justice

· DoD 5500.07-R, *Joint Ethics Regulation* (30 August 1993), incorporating through Change 7, 17 November 2011

· DoDI 1304.33, *Protecting Against Inappropriate Relations During Recruiting and Entry Level Training* (28 January 2015), incorporating Change 1, 5 April 2017

· AFI 36-2909, *Air Force Professional Relationships and Conduct* (14 November 2019)

HAZING

Department of Defense (DoD) policy recognizes the adverse effects hazing can have on morale, operational readiness, and mission accomplishment. Hazing is prohibited and should never be tolerated.

Key Takeaways

» Hazing is a form of harassment where service members or DoD employees injure or create the risk of injury toward another service member or DoD employee for the purpose of group affiliation

» Hazing can be physical, psychological, written, verbal and/or nonverbal conduct

» Hazing jeopardizes combat readiness and weakens trust within the organization

» Commanders must investigate all allegations of hazing and take appropriate action to prevent it

---

Definitions

- Hazing is a form of harassment where service members or DoD employees physically or psychologically injure or create a risk of injury to other service members or DoD employees for the purpose of affiliation with a particular group. Affiliation often includes initiation, admission, change in status or continued membership with the group. Hazing does not have a proper military or other governmental purpose even if takes place in connection to military service. Hazing can be conducted in person or through use of electronic devices or communication, including social media.

- Hazing is evaluated by a reasonable person standard and includes, but is not limited to, the following:

  -- Physically striking another person or threatening to do the same

  -- Oral or written berating of another person for the purpose of belittling or humiliating

  -- Encouraging another person to engage in illegal, harmful, or dangerous acts

  -- Playing abusive or malicious tricks

  -- Branding, handcuffing, duct-taping, tattooing, shaving, greasing, or painting another person

  -- Subjecting another person to excessive or abusive use of water

  -- Forcing another person to consume food, alcohol, drugs, or any other substance

  -- Soliciting, coercing, or knowingly permitting another person to solicit or coerce acts of hazing

- Promotion ceremonies carry a unique risk of hazing. Hazing includes pressing any object into another person's skin, regardless of whether it pierces the skin, such as "pinning" or "tacking on" of rank insignia, aviator wings, jump wings, diver insignia, badges, medals or any other objects. DoD hazing policy does not prohibit tapping a promotee's cloth rank insignia on the member's sleeves during the traditional "tacking on" portion of the enlisted promotion ceremony. However, local commanders may provide more restrictive guidance on this issue in consultation with the Staff Judge Advocate.

- A military member or DoD employee may still be responsible for an act of hazing even if there was actual or implied consent from the victim and regardless of the grade/rank, status, or service affiliation of the victim

- Hazing does not include properly directed command activities that serve a legitimate purpose or the requisite training activities required to prepare for such activities (e.g., administrative corrective measures, extra military instruction, or command-authorized physical training)

- Hazing is prohibited in all cases, including off-duty or in "unofficial" celebrations and unit functions and settings

Command Action

- Commanders and Senior Noncommissioned Officers (SNCOs) must promptly and thoroughly investigate all allegations of hazing and take appropriate action if a hazing allegation is substantiated

- A commander's options begin with counseling and reprimands and extend to court-martial for serious cases that involve assault, aggravated assault, maltreatment of subordinates, etc.

- Commanders must evaluate all activities that appear to be an initiation or "rite of passage" to ensure that the dignity and respect of all members are maintained

Punitive Regulations and the Uniform Code of Military Justice (UCMJ)

- There is not a punitive Uniform Code of Military Justice (UCMJ) article that directly deals with hazing, and the Department of the Air Force does not have a specific punitive regulation that addresses it. However, commanders may pursue disciplinary action under the UCMJ for dereliction of duty and the underlying misconduct, such as assault, battery, maltreatment of subordinates, etc.

References

- DoDI 1020.03, *Harassment Prevention and Response in the Armed Forces* (8 February 2018), incorporating through Change 2, 20 December 2022
- DAFI 36-2710, *Equal Opportunity Program* (18 June 2020), including DAFGM2023-02, 27 December 2023
- AFI 1-1, *Air Force Standards* (18 August 2023)

PERSONAL FINANCIAL RESPONSIBILITY

Department of the Air Force (DAF) members are expected to timely and properly satisfy financial and family obligations. Failure to do so can result in administrative or disciplinary action and/or their debt being paid involuntarily through garnishment or involuntary allotment.

Key Takeaways

» DAF members are required to provide financial support to their dependents. The amount of support that must be provided is determined by use of the formula set forth in Figure 4.1 of DAFI 36-2906, *Personal Financial Responsibility*.

» The DAF cannot resolve debt claims or require members to pay a debt without a civil judgment/court order

» DAF service members have a statutory right to file for bankruptcy. However, doing so may affect their eligibility for a security clearance.

Commander's Responsibilities

- Review and assess the basis of any allegation of financial irresponsibility and respond to complainants within 15 days for Regular Air Force and Air Force Reserve and 60 days for Air National Guard. Complainants should be provided attachments 2 and 3 of DAFI 36-2906, which address involuntary allotments of a member's pay, if appropriate;

- Advise member and complainant that the Department of the Air Force has no authority to arbitrate disputed cases of nonsupport or personal indebtedness. **DO NOT** provide information to the complainant regarding administrative or disciplinary action contemplated or taken against the member;

- Refer members with demonstrated financial irresponsibility to the appropriate base agency for assistance (normally the Military and Family Readiness Center (M&FRC) and legal assistance at the installation legal office); and

- Consider whether administrative or disciplinary action is appropriate for continuing financial irresponsibility.

Financial Support to Dependents

- DAF service members are required to provide financial support to their spouses and children and must comply with financial support provisions of court orders or written support agreements. DAFI 36-2906, Chapter 4, outlines the required amount of financial support in the absence of a court order or financial support agreement.

- DAF can terminate or recoup the Basic Allowance for Housing (BAH) with dependent rate allowances for those failing to provide adequate financial support to a family member

- Members who fail to support their dependents or who falsify support documentation can be subjected to disciplinary or administrative action

Child Support and Alimony Payments

- Complainants seeking alimony or child support from a military member can either secure an allotment or provide a garnishment order to the Defense Finance and Accounting Service (DFAS) and receive a portion of the payment directly. Complainants who are eligible for legal assistance may consult the legal office for assistance.

- Commanders should ensure the military member involved in these processes has access to a legal assistance attorney if they are not already represented by a civilian attorney

Third Party Allotments

- Creditors whose bona fine efforts to collect a debt from a military member have failed can secure an involuntary allotment to satisfy a final judgment from a court. The DAF has no authority to resolve disputed claims or to require members to pay a private debt without a civil judgment.

- Complainants who attempt to serve DAF with documents should be referred to DFAS. When a request for involuntary allotment is received, DFAS notifies the member and the member's commander.

- See Chapter 10, "Ensuring the Fair Handling of Debt Complaints Against Service Members" for additional information on creditors and debt collectors

Bankruptcy

- Filing for bankruptcy protection in federal court is a statutory right of all citizens and does not provide a basis for adverse action. However, filing for bankruptcy may affect a member's security clearance. Service members may consult with the M&FRC as well as the installation legal office for limited assistance with personal bankruptcy.

References

· Protection Against Discriminatory Treatment, 11 U.S.C. § 525
· Servicemembers Civil Relief Act, 50 U.S.C. §§ 3901–4043
· Articles 123a and 134, Uniform Code of Military Justice
· DoD 7000.14-R, *Financial Management Regulation*, Volume 7A, (May 2023)
· DoDI 1344.09, *Indebtedness of Military Personnel* (1 February 2022)
· DD Form 2654, *Involuntary Allotment Notice and Processing* (December 1999)
· DAFI 36-2906, *Personal Financial Responsibility* (23 August 2023)

CIVILIAN JURY SERVICE BY MILITARY MEMBERS

When a Department of the Air Force (DAF) member on active duty receives a summons to state or local jury duty, the member should inform his/her immediate commander, who will consult with the installation's Staff Judge Advocate (SJA). For the purpose of jury service, "active duty" includes full-time duty in the active military service, full-time training, annual training, active duty for training, and attending a service school while on active military service.

Key Takeaways

» Members on active duty may be exempt from State or local jury duty under certain circumstances

» Members who receive a summons to State or local jury duty should inform his/her immediate commander, who will consult with the installation's SJA

» Certain members are categorically exempt from jury service, while other members are only exempt where the commander has determined that the jury duty would interfere with military duties or adversely affect readiness

---

Exemption from Jury Service

- <u>Categorical Exemption</u>: All general officers, commanders, operating forces (forces whose primary missions are participating in and supporting combat), personnel in a training status, and personnel stationed outside the United States are categorically exempt from serving on a State or local jury

- <u>General Exemption (Not Categorical)</u>: For all other personnel, the member's commander determines whether jury duty would unreasonably interfere with military duties or adversely affect the readiness of a unit, command, or activity to which the member is assigned

Air National Guard Command Note

- <u>State Law Disqualification</u>: Many state laws categorically disqualify members in the active service in the armed forces of the United States from jury service. However, many states define active military service of the United States in such a way as to exclude Air National Guard members not serving in a Title 10 status. Consult with your SJA for state-specific applicability.

Procedures

- If the member is categorically exempt, the immediate commander or designee notifies the issuing state or local official by written notice (complying with the format in AFI 51-301, *Civil Litigation*, para. 2.8.3.4)

- If the member is generally (not categorically) exempt, the immediate commander decides whether jury duty would unreasonably interfere with military duties or adversely affect the readiness of a unit, command, or activity to which the member is assigned

  -- The commander may consider, among other factors, the travel time that would be required of a member between his/her duty location and the place where the jury duty would be served, the potential effect such travel time would have on the member's ability to return to productive military duties, and the possible length of time the member would be away from the unit if selected for jury duty

  -- If jury duty would not unreasonably interfere with military duties or adversely affect the readiness of a unit, command, or activity, the member must perform jury duty

  -- If the immediate commander decides jury duty would unreasonably interfere with military duties or adversely affect the readiness of a unit, command, or activity, the immediate commander requests approval of the exemption from the Special Court Martial Convening Authority (SPCMCA); the SPCMCA may then decide whether:

    --- Exemption is **inappropriate** and instruct the member to comply with the jury summons; or

    --- Exemption is **appropriate**, and direct the immediate commander to send a written notice of exemption to the issuing state or local official (complying with AFI 51-301, para. 2.8.3.4). The SPCMCA's determination is final.

Fees and Reimbursement

- Time spent by military members on jury duty service should not be charged against them as leave, nor should pay or entitlements be deducted for the period of jury service

- Military members are not entitled to keep any fees for jury service. Any fees should be made payable to the U.S. Treasury and turned in at the local finance office.

- Military members may receive and keep reimbursement from the state or local jury authority for expenses incurred in the performance of jury duty, such as transportation costs or parking fees

References

· Members: Service on State and Local Juries, 10 U.S.C. § 982
· DoDI 5525.08, *Service Member Participation on State and Local Juries* (7 January 2021)
· AFI 51-301, *Civil Litigation* (2 October 2018)

HUMAN IMMUNODEFICIENCY VIRUS

Human Immunodeficiency Virus (HIV) is a viral disease involving the breakdown of the body's immune system. The Department of the Air Force (DAF) tests all members for HIV, medically evaluates all active duty diagnosed members, and educates members on means of prevention. Medical experts believe the nonsexual, person-to-person contact that occurs among co-workers within the workplace does **NOT** pose a risk for transmitting the virus.

Key Takeaways

» All DAF military members are screened for HIV infection every two years

» Per DoD policy, service members who have been identified as HIV-positive, are asymptomatic, and have undetectable viral loads are not automatically restricted from deploying or commissioning solely due to their HIV positive status

» Air Force policy limits the use of information obtained during epidemiological assessments in administrative actions and disciplinary actions

» Upon notification of laboratory evidence of HIV infection, the unit commander must issue an order to follow preventive medicine requirements

» DAF civilian employees are not generally tested for laboratory evidence of HIV; HIV infection is considered a disability with protections afforded individuals against discrimination

HIV and Military Members

- All active duty and Air Reserve Component (ARC) personnel are screened for HIV infection every two years, preferably during their Preventive Health Assessment (PHA). Additionally, ARC personnel must have a current HIV test within two years of the date called to active duty for 30 days or more.

- An active duty member who tests positive for HIV is referred to the HIV Medical Evaluation Unit, located in the Joint Infectious Disease Service of the San Antonio Military Medical Center (SAMMC) for medical evaluation and to determine status for continued military service

  -- Members with laboratory evidence of HIV infection who are able to perform their duties may not be separated solely on the basis of laboratory evidence of HIV. An active duty member with laboratory evidence of HIV determined to be fit for duty will be allowed to serve in a manner that ensures access to appropriate medical care.

  -- HIV-infected members on flying status must be placed on duty not involving flying (DNIF) status pending medical evaluation or a waiver determination. Waivers are considered using normal procedures established for chronic diseases.

-- Due to a permanent federal court injunction, *Harrision v. Austin*, 597 F. Supp. 3d 884 (E.D. Va. 2022) and updated DoD policy, dated 6 June 2022, service members testing positive for HIV are not automatically referred to the Disability Evaluation System (DES) but are generally retained with an assignment limitation code. Likewise, a service member with laboratory evidence of HIV, who is asymptomatic and has an undetectable viral load, is not considered non-deployable solely because they are HIV-positive. Decisions on deployability are made on a case-by-case basis. A service member with laboratory evidence of HIV currently cannot be discharged solely on the basis of ineligibility to deploy.

-- Per DoD policy, dated 6 June 2022, the presence of HIV or laboratory evidence of infection is not, in and of itself, disqualifying for certain covered personnel seeking a commission (including Academy cadets, contracted Reserve Officers' Training Corps (ROTC) cadets, and other participants in in-service commissioning programs). Such individuals are evaluated on a case-by-case basis.

Limitations on Use of Information

- DAF policy strictly safeguards results of positive HIV testing as set forth in Attachment 10 of AFI 44-178, *Human Immunodeficiency Virus Program*

-- In accordance with DoDI 6485.01, *Human Immunodeficiency Virus (HIV) in Military Service Members*, the privacy of a service member with laboratory evidence of HIV infection is protected consistent with the Health Insurance Portability and Accountability Act (HIPAA) and the Privacy Act

-- Very limited release within the DAF is permitted on a "need-to-know" basis only (e.g., unit commanders should not inform First Sergeants and/or supervisors unless a determination is made that those individuals truly need to know)

- Laboratory test results confirming HIV infection may not be used as the sole basis for separation of a member or as an independent basis for any adverse administrative or disciplinary action, including punitive action under the Uniform Code of Military Justice (UCMJ)

- Information obtained from a member during, or as a result of, an epidemiological assessment interview **MAY NOT** be used to support any adverse personnel action against the member

Order to Follow Preventive Medicine Requirements

- After a member is informed that he/she has tested positive, the member's unit commander will be notified expeditiously

- The unit commander will issue an "Order to Follow Preventive Medicine Requirements" to the HIV positive member. An example order may be found in AFI 44-178 at Attachment 13. For unit assigned reservists, this order is issued only after the member's immediate commander determines the member will be retained in the Selected Reserve.

- A service member who knows he/she is HIV positive but violates an order to follow preventive medicine requirements can be punished under the UCMJ for violation of the order, including engaging in the following conduct:

  -- Failing to inform sexual partners of HIV status

  -- Failing to use proper methods to prevent transfer of body fluids during sexual relations

  -- Failing to inform emergency health care personnel of HIV status

  -- Donating blood, sperm, tissues, or organs

HIV and Air Force Civilian Employees

- The DAF does not test its civilian employees for HIV, except for those civilian employees (appropriated or nonappropriated) selected for assignment overseas who will be screened for HIV infection pursuant to host nation requirements. Civilian employees are also tested for occupational exposures (e.g., civilian medical providers).

- HIV infection is considered a disability under federal civil rights laws, and discrimination on the basis of physical or mental disability is prohibited

References

· *Harrison v. Austin*, 597 F. Supp. 3d 884 (E.D. Va. 2022)
· DoD Regulation 5400.11-R, *Department of Defense Privacy Program* (14 May 2007)
· DoDD 6485.02E, *DoD Human Immunodeficiency Virus (HIV)/Acquired Immune Deficiency Syndrome (AIDS) Prevention Program (DHAPP) to Support Foreign Militaries* (6 December 2013), incorporating Change 1, 1 June 2018
· DoDI 6130.03-V1, *Medical Standards for Military Service: Appointment, Enlistment or Induction* (6 May 2018), incorporating through Change 4, 16 November 2022
· DoDI 6130.03-V2, *Medical Standards for Military Service: Retention* (4 September 2020) incorporating Change 1, 6 June 2022
· DoDI 6485.01, *Human Immunodeficiency Virus (HIV) in Military Service Members* (7 June 2013), incorporating through Change 2, 6 June 2022
· DoDM 6025.18, *Implementation of the Health Insurance Portability and Accountability Act (HIPAA) Privacy Rule in DoD Health Care Programs* (13 March 2019)
· AFI 44-102, *Medical Care Management* (17 March 2015), including AFGM2022-01, 5 September 2023
· AFI 44-178, *Human Immunodeficiency Virus Program* (4 March 2014), certified current 28 June 2016
· SecDef Memorandum, *Policy Regarding Human Immunodeficiency Virus-Positive Personnel Within the Armed Forces*, 6 June 2022
· DHA-PI 6485.01, *Guidance for the Identification, Treatment, and Care of Human Immunodeficiency Virus (HIV) among Persons Infected with HIV* (10 December 2021)

IMMUNIZATIONS

Service members are required to take certain vaccinations to remain mission ready and deployable. Vaccines are administered to personnel on the basis of military occupation, the location of a deployment, duty station, health status, travel plans, or other mission requirements. Unless granted an accommodation or exception, a member's refusal to take a required vaccine may result in adverse administrative actions, up to and including involuntary administrative discharge. Violation of a lawful order to receive a required vaccine is punishable under the Uniform Code of Military Justice (UCMJ) or state equivalent military code.

Key Takeaways

» Service members can be mandated to take fully licensed vaccines. If a vaccine is authorized for emergency use, a Presidential waiver may be required before the vaccine can be mandated.

» An order to comply with a vaccine mandate is a lawful order enforceable under the UCMJ

» Service members may request a religious accommodation or medical or administrative

Vaccine Mandates

- A vaccine under an Emergency Use Authorization (EUA) and not yet fully licensed by the U.S. Food and Drug Administration (FDA), which requires that individuals be informed of an option to accept or refuse the vaccine, generally may not be mandated for service members absent a waiver by the President

Enforcement

- Commanders are responsible for the accomplishment of the military mission and the protection of the health and readiness of the force. Commanders must ensure military and nonmilitary personnel under their command receive required immunizations and chemoprophylaxis. Orders for military members to comply with vaccine requirements are lawful and enforceable under the UCMJ.

-- If a member indicates he/she will refuse or has refused a required vaccine, the commander should ascertain why the member is reluctant, provide the member with appropriate education to ensure the member understands the purpose of the vaccine, and refer the member to the appropriate subject matter expert (e.g., concerns about vaccine safety should be referred to the supporting medical organization; concerns about the threat should be addressed by intelligence personnel; etc.)

-- If the member is still reluctant to take the vaccine after receiving additional education, send the member to the Area Defense Counsel for an explanation of potential consequences of refusal

- Following appropriate counseling, commanders should again order the member to take the vaccine. If the member continues to refuse, the commander should consult with their servicing Staff Judge Advocate for appropriate action.

 -- On 10 January 2023, SecDef rescinded the COVID-19 vaccine mandate for the DoD, pursuant to section 524 of Pub. L. 117-263, James M. Inhofe National Defense Authorization Act for Fiscal Year 2023

- For the purposes of vaccination, medical personnel will not administer medical care against a patient's wishes. If a military member refuses to receive a vaccine, commanders are limited to administrative enforcement only.

Religious Accommodation

- Members may seek a religious accommodation to a vaccine mandate, which must be processed in accordance with the procedures found in DAFI 52-201, *Religious Freedom in the Department of the Air Force*

Medical and Administrative Exemptions

- Members may seek a medical exemption based on a medical contraindication to a specific immunization in accordance with AFI 48-110_IP, *Immunizations and Chemoprophylaxis for the Prevention of Infectious Diseases*. Health care providers determine whether a medical exemption is appropriate based on the health of the individual and the nature of the specific immunization.

- Members may seek an administrative exemption in accordance with AFI 48-110_IP or other applicable guidance. For example, an exemption may be appropriate for a service member within 30 days or fewer of service remaining, or, in the case of deployment (mobility) immunizations, for a member within 180 days of separation or retirement.

References

· Emergency Use Products, 10 U.S.C. § 1107a
· James M. Inhofe National Defense Authorization Act for Fiscal Year 2023, Pub. L. 117-263 § 524 (2022)
· DAFI 52-201, *Religious Freedom in the Department of the Air Force* (23 June 2021)
· AFI 48-110_IP, *Immunizations and Chemoprophylaxis for the Prevention of Infectious Diseases* (7 October 2013), certified current 20 May 2023
· AFMAN 48-105, *Public Health Surveillance* (11 October 2023)
· SecDef Memo, *Rescission of August 24, 2021 and November 30, 2021 Coronavirus Disease 2019 Vaccination Requirements for Members of the Armed Forces*, January 10, 2023

COMMAND DIRECTED EVALUATIONS

Commanders or supervisors who have concerns about a member's safety or fitness for duty may direct the member to the mental health clinic for an involuntary Command Directed Evaluation (CDE) in accordance with DoDI 6490.04, *Mental Health Evaluations of Members of the Military Services* and AFI 44-172, *Mental Health*. Members may also self-refer to mental health care at any time under the Brandon Act.

Key Takeaways

» Commanders and supervisors should encourage help-seeking behavior and may make non-mandatory recommendations for service members to seek care from a Mental Health Provider (MHP)

» Commanders or supervisors with concerns about safety, fitness for duty, or significant changes that might be attributable to a mental status change can order a CDE

» A commander or supervisor shall not refer a member for a CDE in reprisal for making a protected communication

» Under the Brandon Act, service members may request a referral for any reason or on any basis and are not required to provide a reason or basis to request and receive a referral

---

Commander/Supervisor Responsibilities

- Commanders or supervisors may make informal, non-mandatory recommendations for service members to seek care from MHPs when circumstances do not require a CDE based on safety or mission concerns

- Commanders or supervisors may order a CDE for a variety of concerns, including fitness for duty, safety, occupational concerns, and significant changes in behavior or performance that may be attributable to potential mental status changes

  -- Supervisors and individuals who exercise supervisory authority over a service member due to the member's current or temporary duty assignment can be either a commissioned officer in or out of a member's official chain of command, or a civilian employee in a grade level comparable to a commissioned officer. Supervisors are authorized, due to the impracticality of involving an actual commanding officer in the chain of command, to direct a mental health evaluation.

  -- When possible, MHPs will assist the commander or supervisor in determining whether to direct a CDE

- Emergency CDEs: A commander or supervisor shall refer a member for an emergency CDE as soon as practicable when: the member intends to or is likely to cause serious injury to himself or others, the facts and circumstances indicate the member's intent to cause such injury is likely, and the commander or supervisor believes the member may be suffering from a severe mental disorder

-- Commanders or supervisors ordering an emergency CDE must remember safety is the first priority and take appropriate precautions. Commanders will report the circumstances and observations that led to the emergency CDE to the MHP.

-- A senior enlisted member may be designated to order emergency CDEs for enlisted service members. Officers that are senior in rank may be designated to order emergency CDEs for commissioned officers.

- Non-Emergency CDEs: When the commander or supervisor determines a non-emergency CDE is required, they must (1) advise the member there is no stigma associated with seeking mental health services, (2) refer the member to a MHP with name and contact information, and (3) tell the member the date, time, and place of the scheduled CDE

CDE Procedures

- CDEs are conducted in accordance with DoDI 6490.04. The MHP provides a written assessment to the commander or supervisor including duty limitations; recommendations for further monitoring, evaluation, and/or treatment; guidance on how to assist the member's treatment; and recommendations for continued military service.

- CDEs may not be conducted in embedded settings, as set forth in AFMAN 48-149, *Flight and Operational Medicine Program (FOMP)*

Brandon Act – The Commander/Supervisor Facilitated Referral Program

- Service members can initiate a referral process for a mental health evaluation through a commanding officer or supervisor who is in a grade above E-6 on any basis, at any time, and in any environment, including CONUS, OCONUS, deployed, TDY, or leave

-- A referral under the Brandon Act differs from a command-directed or independent referral in several ways. A Brandon Act referral is initiated by the service member to their commander/supervisor, while a command-directed mental health referral is initiated by a commander or supervisor and is mandatory. An independent self-referral is handled completely by the member themselves.

- Service member patient rights and confidentiality are protected as much as possible, in accordance with requirements for confidentiality of health information under HIPAA and applicable privacy laws and regulations

- The commanding officer or supervisor will refer a service member to a mental health provider for a mental health evaluation, as soon as possible, following a request by the service member

-- Commanding officers or supervisors in a grade above E-5 will ensure measures are in place so a service member under their command understands the procedures to request a referral for a mental health evaluation

- Mental health providers will conduct the mental health evaluation as soon as possible and provide necessary clinical care. Mental health providers will assess the service member's medical readiness for duty with specific consideration for mental health, risk of harm to self or others, symptom severity, prognosis for return to duty, and risk of decompensation, aggravation, or further injury if participation in occupational activities continues.

Involuntary Inpatient Admissions

- Military Medical Treatment Facilities (MTFs): At bases where the MTF has an inpatient psychiatric unit, a member will be involuntarily admitted for inpatient evaluation and/or treatment only when a qualified provider determines the member has, or likely has, a severe mental disorder or poses imminent or potential danger to self or others and outpatient treatment is not appropriate

    -- A qualified official must review the admission within 72 hours to determine whether continued involuntary hospitalization is clinically appropriate. The member must be notified of the purpose of the 72-hour review and the right to legal representation by a judge advocate or an attorney of the member's choosing at the member's expense.

    -- Members must be afforded the right to contact a friend, relative, chaplain, attorney, any office of Inspector General (IG), or anyone else the member wishes as soon after the admission as the member's condition permits

- Civilian Facilities: In the case of referral for an involuntary admission at a base where there is no military inpatient psychiatric unit, a member can be admitted to a civilian facility through the processes established by state law, which often differ from DoD standards. In a foreign country, applicable host nation laws must be followed when involuntary admission to a host nation facility is required.

Command Notification

- MHPs are prohibited from notifying a service member's commander when the member voluntarily obtains mental health care or substance misuse education services, unless the member authorizes the disclosure or one of the following exigent circumstances are met:

    -- The provider believes there is a serious risk of harm to self, others, or a specific military operational mission

    -- The member is in the Personal Reliability Program (PRP) or another pre-identified special program

    -- The member is admitted or discharged from any inpatient mental health or substance use disorder treatment facility

    -- The member is experiencing an acute mental health condition, a substance misuse induced condition, or is engaged in an acute medical treatment regimen that impairs their ability to perform assigned duties

-- The provider has determined that the member requires treatment for a substance misuse disorder

-- The mental health services were obtained as the result of a CDE

- Certain special circumstances, as determined on a case-by case basis by a healthcare provider at the O-6 or GS-15 level or above, as detailed in DoDI 6490.08. In making a disclosure, healthcare providers may release only the minimum amount of information necessary to satisfy the purpose of the disclosure as set forth in DoDI 6490.08.

Prohibited Practices

- A commander or supervisor may not refer a member for a CDE as a reprisal for making a protected communication or restrict the member from lawfully communicating with the member's attorney, the IG, or other authority about the referral

References

- Brandon Act, Pub. L. 117-81, "The National Defense Authorization Act for Fiscal Year 2022," December 27, 2021
- DoDI 6490.04, *Mental Health Evaluations of Members of the Military Services* (4 March 2013), incorporating Change 1, 22 April 2020
- DoDI 6490.08, *Command Notification Requirements to Dispel Stigmas in Providing Mental Health Care to Service Members* (6 September 2023)
- DTM 23-005, *Self-Initiated Referral Process for Mental Health Evaluations of Service Members* (5 May 2023)
- DAFI 40-301, *Family Advocacy Program* (13 November 2020)
- AFI 44-121, *Alcohol and Drug Abuse Prevention and Treatment (ADAPT) Program* (18 July 2018), incorporating Change 1, 21 November 2019, Corrective Actions applied on 19 December 2019, including DAFGM 2024-01, 3 January 2024
- AFI 44-172, *Mental Health* (13 November 2015), certified current 23 April 2020
- AFMAN 48-149, *Flight and Operational Medicine Program (FOMP)* (13 October 2020), incorporating through Change 2, 19 October 2022

LIMITED PRIVILEGE SUICIDE PREVENTION PROGRAM

Those who are under investigation are much more likely to commit suicide than other military members. Commanders who have concerns that a member under their command who is facing disciplinary action may be at risk of suicide should encourage the member to seek mental health treatment or may direct the member to the mental health clinic for a Command Directed Evaluation (CDE) in accordance with DoDI 6490.04, *Mental Health Evaluations of Members of the Military Services*. The Limited Privilege Suicide Prevention (LPSP) program affords protections beyond the psychotherapist-patient privilege (Military Rule of Evidence (M.R.E.) 513) so as to encourage at-risk members facing disciplinary action to receive timely mental health treatment.

Key Takeaways

» The objective of the LPSP program is to facilitate timely mental health treatment for Department of the Air Force (DAF) members facing disciplinary action who are at risk of suicide

» DAFI 51-201, *Administration of Military Justice*, is the governing instruction for the program and provides guidance for commanders and others to facilitate mental health treatment for those members who, due to the stress of being under investigation, pose a risk for suicide

» The LPSP program operates in conjunction with the guidance on CDEs as well as the psychotherapist-patient privilege under M.R.E. 513, and the protections afforded under the Health Insurance Portability and Accountability Act (HIPAA)

Eligibility and Procedures

- Eligible Members: The LPSP program applies to Department of the Air Force members who have been officially notified (written or oral) that they are under investigation or suspected of violating the Uniform Code of Military Justice (UCMJ). **Note:** LPSP program only applies to ANG members when activated under Title 10 active duty.

- Initiation: An eligible member enters the LPSP program when the member receives treatment or care from a Mental Health Provider (MHP) subsequent to the notification that triggers eligibility. The treatment or care may be the result of a CDE, on the member's own initiative, or a continuation of ongoing or previous treatment.

- Duration: The enhanced protections offered by the LPSP program continue until the member is no longer receiving mental health treatment or until the investigation and subsequent disciplinary action, if any, is closed. Matters disclosed while the member was in the LPSP program retain the enhanced protections of the LPSP program.

Limited Protection

- Members in the LPSP program are granted limited enhanced protection with respect to information revealed in, or generated by, their clinical relationship with MHPs. Any such information may not be used in any existing or future UCMJ action or when weighing the characterization of the member's service in an administrative separation. However, the enhanced protections **do not apply to**:

  -- The use of the information as evidence for impeachment or rebuttal purposes in any proceeding in which information generated by and during the LPSP relationship was first introduced by the member concerned

  -- Disciplinary or other action based on independently derived evidence

References

· Health Insurance Portability and Accountability Act, Pub. L. 104–191

· M.R.E. 513 (2024)

· DoDI 6490.04, *Mental Health Evaluations of Members of the Military Services* (4 March 2013), incorporating Change 1, effective 22 April 2020

· DoDM 6025.18, *Implementation of the Health Insurance Portability and Accountability Act (HIPAA) Privacy Rule in DoD Health Care Programs* (13 March 2019)

· DAFI 51-201, *Administration of Military Justice* (24 January 2024)

· DAFI 90-5001, *Integrated Resilience* (25 January 2019), incorporating Change 1, effective 21 October 2021, including DAFI90-5001_DAFGM2023-01, 2 August 2023

· AFI 41-200, *Health Insurance Portability and Accountability Act (HIPAA)* (25 July 2017), certified current 10 April 2020

· AFI 44-172, *Mental Health* (13 November 2015), certified current 23 April 2020

HEALTH INSURANCE PORTABILITY AND ACCOUNTABILITY ACT

The Health Insurance Portability and Accountability Act (HIPAA) Privacy Rule provides safeguards for individually identifiable health information held by medical providers, insurers, and facilities. This type of protected information is typically referred to as protected health information (PHI). The rule permits certain uses and disclosures, even without the individual's authorization.

Key Takeaways

» HIPAA protects health information held by health care entities from unlawful use or disclosure. HIPAA does not apply to health information held by military commanders.

» Where health information of a service member is needed to accomplish the military mission, there is generally a way to obtain it from a health care entity consistent with HIPAA

» When a commander receives health information regarding a member under his/her command, the information remains subject to the Privacy Act

Background

- The Department of Defense (DoD) has implemented the HIPAA Privacy Rule through DoDM 6025.18, *Implementation of the Health Insurance Portability and Accountability Act (HIPAA) Privacy Rule in DoD Health Care Programs*

- HIPAA's Privacy Rule applies to organizations that meet the definition of "covered entities." Covered entities generally include healthcare providers, healthcare facilities such as medical treatment facilities (MTFs), and health plans such as TRICARE.

  -- Effective 30 September 2021, pursuant to 10 U.S.C. § 1073c, the Defense Health Agency (DHA) is responsible for the administration of every MTF. Requests for PHI from MTFs will generally be handled by DHA personnel with legal advice from DHA's Office of General Counsel.

  -- Commanders are generally not considered "covered entities." This means that health information possessed by a commander, even if received from a "covered entity," is not protected by HIPAA, though it remains protected by the Privacy Act of 1974.

- Certain records that might be considered quasi-medical have been determined by the DoD to not be subject to HIPAA. For example, the DoD drug testing program is not subject to HIPAA. DoDM 6025.18, para. 1.1.b. contains a comprehensive list of health-related records and activities in the DoD to which HIPAA does not apply. HIPAA does not apply to health information in employment records.

Permissible Disclosures

- Under HIPAA, even without the individual's authorization, an MTF may disclose PHI for certain purposes when certain requirements are met as outlined in DoDM 6025.18, Section 4.4. Some specific provisions which allow for such disclosures include:

  -- As required by law (includes requirements in DoD and DHA publications, as well as Department of the Air Force service level regulations and instructions to the extent consistent with DoDM 6025.18)

  -- For public health activities

  -- Victims of abuse, neglect, or domestic violence

  -- For judicial and administrative proceedings

  -- For certain law enforcement purposes

  -- To avert serious and imminent threats to health or safety

  -- For "specialized governmental functions," including the proper execution of the military mission

- <u>Accounting of Disclosures</u>: The MTF must document most disclosures of PHI, including who received the information, when, and for what purpose. The MTF must maintain the accounting for six years and provide the information upon the patient's request.

- <u>Minimum Necessary Rule</u>: When HIPAA allows a use or disclosure of PHI, MTFs are typically required to provide only the minimum amount of information necessary to satisfy the intended purpose of the disclosure

Command Access to Information

- Under the "specialized government functions" provision, commanders can access PHI of Armed Forces personnel (not including dependents or civilian employees) for activities deemed necessary by appropriate military command authorities to assure the proper execution of the military mission. This rule generally permits disclosures for fitness for duty purposes.

  -- For example, commanders may need PHI related to readiness, such as vaccinations or profiles, or to verify the whereabouts of subordinates, such as confirming the service member was at the MTF

- Under the "minimum necessary" rule, any release of PHI must be limited in scope to what the commander actually needs to accomplish the mission

  -- For example, if a member has a foot injury that precludes prolonged standing, the MTF may disclose PHI to the commander related to the foot injury because it impacts the duties the member can be assigned. The MTF could not disclose the member's dental records or other information unrelated to the foot injury because that would exceed the minimum necessary.

- There is no "blanket rule" concerning disclosure of PHI to commanders. In each case, the nature and extent of PHI needed should be fully articulated in the request.

- Only commanders and their designees can access PHI. AFI 41-200, *Health Insurance Portability and Accountability Act (HIPAA),* provides that a commander's designee includes deputy/vice commander and first sergeant. If the commander wishes to designate any other individual as an authorized recipient of PHI, the commander must do so in writing.

- A commander's access to information may be further limited by other law or DoD policy, such as confidentiality for sexual assault victims, DoD policies on reducing the stigma of mental health treatment, or other applicable policy

References

· Privacy Act of 1974, 5 U.S.C. § 552a

· Administration of Defense Health Agency and military medical treatment facilities, 10 U.S.C. § 1073c

· Health Insurance Portability and Accountability Act, Pub. L. 104–191

· DoDI 6025.18, *Health Insurance Portability and Accountability Act (HIPAA) Privacy Rule Compliance in DoD Health Care Programs* (13 March 2019)

· DoDI 8580.02, *Security of Individually Identifiable Health Information in DoD Health Care Programs* (12 August 2015)

· DoDM 6025.18, *Implementation of the Health Insurance Portability and Accountability Act (HIPAA) Privacy Rule in DoD Health Care Programs* (13 March 2019)

· DD Form 2870, *Authorization for Disclosure of Medical or Dental Information* (November 2003)

· AFI 41-200, *Health Insurance Portability and Accountability Act (HIPAA)* (25 July 2017), certified current 10 April 2020

· AFMAN 41-210, *Tricare Operations and Patient Administration* (10 September 2019), incorporating Change 1, 22 June 2021

PERSONNEL RELIABILITY PROGRAM

The Personnel Reliability Program (PRP) ensures only designated persons who demonstrate reliability are certified to perform specified duties associated with U.S. nuclear weapons systems, nuclear command and control (NC2) systems, material equipment, and special nuclear material (SNM). PRP is a critical link in nuclear surety by determining an individual's fitness for PRP duties.

Key Takeaways

» Individuals on PRP are personally responsible for continuous monitoring and evaluation of their reliability, as well as situations that may impact the reliability of others in the unit and have a duty to report to the PRP monitor and or certifying official

» Certifying officials judge the reliability of each individual identified for PRP based on personnel security investigations, review of personnel and health records, position qualification requirements and a personal interview

» Members may be removed from PRP duties through suspension or decertification

Responsibilities

- Wing Commanders are generally the reviewing official (RO) and are responsible for the wing PRP

  -- ROs are responsible for review of all permanent decertification case files started by subordinate units. ROs also ensure base PRP meetings are conducted quarterly at the wing level.

- Group and unit commanders, who control or have access to nuclear weapons, weapon systems or critical components are generally the certifying officials (COs)

  -- COs certify and initiate decertification for their personnel. They may delegate this duty in writing to their vice/deputy in limited instances such as TDY/extended absence.

  -- COs and their delegates must be certified in a PRP category equal to, or higher than, the personnel they are certifying

- Individuals in the PRP are subject to continuous evaluation of their reliability and are responsible for complying with the intent of PRP at all times, even while away from their duty station (e.g., leave, TDY, etc.)

  -- Individuals must also monitor others in the unit PRP for reliability and have a duty to inform supervisors, the unit PRP monitor, and/or certifying official of situations that may affect reliability

  -- Individuals must inform the unit PRP monitor and/or CO of medical and mental health treatment that may affect an individual's reliability and submit documentation to the Competent Medical Authority (CMA)

PRP Certification Requirements

- COs judge the reliability of each individual identified for PRP based on personnel security investigations, review of personnel and health records, position qualification requirements, and a personal interview

- Personnel assigned to PRP must be dependable; mentally alert; technically proficient commensurate with their respective duty requirements; flexible in adjusting to changes in the working environment, including the ability to work in adverse or emergency situations; have good social adjustment, emotional stability, personal integrity, sound judgment, and allegiance to the United States; and have a positive attitude toward nuclear weapons duty

- Initial certification also requires verification of security clearance eligibility

    -- Critical position: Initial certification for critical positions must have Top Secret eligibility completed within the last five years and favorably adjudicated

    -- Controlled position: Initial certification for a controlled position must have Secret eligibility or a higher investigation that was completed within the last five years and favorably adjudicated

PRP Suitability Factors/Potentially Disqualifying Information

- In determining suitability for PRP duties, any of the following traits or conduct is potentially disqualifying information (PDI):

    -- Personal conduct involving questionable judgement, untrustworthiness, unreliability, dishonesty, or unwillingness to comply with rules or regulations;

    -- Emotional, mental, and personality disorders; negative financial habits or circumstances; a history or pattern of criminal conduct;

    -- Substance or drug misuse and improper or illegal involvement with drugs; perpetrator of sexual harassment or assault;

    -- Noncompliance with security regulations; and

    -- Misuse of information technology systems.

Removal from PRP

- Members may be removed from PRP duties through suspension or decertification

- Suspension immediately removes an individual from PRP related duties, initially up to three months, without starting decertification action. The CO may extend the suspension up to one year, in three-month increments.

    -- After one year, if the reasons or conditions for suspension still exist and impact reliability, the individual will be decertified

-- The CO makes the final decision and can return an individual to PRP duties at any point during the suspension timeframe

-- A CO who is suspended may perform PRP administrative functions

- <u>Mandatory Decertification or Disqualification Occurs When:</u>

-- The individual is diagnosed with an alcohol use disorder and subsequently fails a required after-care program or fails to participate in the prescribed rehabilitation program or treatment

-- The individual is involved in trafficking, cultivation, processing, manufacture, or sale of any controlled substance or illegal drug, including cannabis-based products

-- The individual has ever used a drug that could cause flashbacks

-- The individual is diagnosed with a severe substance use disorder

-- Loss of confidence by the certifying official in the reliability of the individual

-- The individual's security clearance has been revoked

- Within 15 workdays of decertification, the CO will advise the individual, in writing, of the reasons for decertification and of the requirement for review by the reviewing official

References

· DoDM 5210.42, *Nuclear Weapons Personnel Reliability Program* (13 January 2015), incorporating through Change 4, 9 May 2022
· DoDM5210.42_AFMAN 13-501, *Nuclear Weapons Personnel Reliability Program (PRP)* (19 September 2018), including AFGM2023-01, 23 August 2023
· DAFI 91-101, *Air Force Nuclear Weapons Surety Program* (26 March 2020), incorporating Change 1, 6 April 2022
· AFI 31-117, *Arming and Use of Force by Air Force Personnel* (6 August 2020)

FIREARMS PROHIBITIONS

The Brady Handgun Violence Prevention Act of 1993, Pub. L. 103-159, which amended the Gun Control Act of 1968, 18 U.S.C. § 921 *et seq.*, prohibits certain persons from possessing, receiving, shipping, or transporting firearms, ammunition, or explosives, in or affecting interstate or foreign commerce. It also requires initiation of a background check before firearms may be purchased or received.

Key Takeaways

» Felony convictions, domestic violence convictions, and drug abuse are several of the categories prohibiting firearms possession

» The length of prohibition ranges from one year, to event-dependent, to permanent

» Commanders, Staff Judge Advocates (SJA), and law enforcement personnel are responsible for properly notifying members of qualifying prohibitions and then reporting the notification, both within 24 hours of occurrence

» Commanders have specific responsibilities to ensure that government-owned firearms and ammunition are not issued to personnel with qualifying domestic violence convictions

» Persons prohibited by the Brady Act from possessing, receiving, shipping, or transporting firearms, ammunition, or explosives are entered into the National Instant Criminal Background Check System (NICS)

Air Force Implementation

- Commanders are responsible for notifying personnel of certain qualifying prohibitions, identified in AFMAN 71-102, *Air Force Criminal Indexing*, Table 4.1, within 24 hours of the occurrence, utilizing the AF Form 177, *Notice of Qualification for Prohibition of Firearms, Ammunition, and Explosives*

  -- Within 24 hours of serving the AF Form 177 on personnel who qualify for prohibition, commanders must email the AF Form 177 to the DAF Criminal Justice Information Center (DAF-CJIC) at daf.cjic@us.af.mil

  -- DAF-CJIC enters personnel into the NICS upon receipt of the AF Form 177

- Commanders may permit prohibited personnel to possess, receive, ship or transport government-owned weapons for official government business, IAW 18 U.S.C. § 925(a)(1)

  -- However, personnel with qualifying domestic violence convictions may not possess, receive, ship, or transport government-owned weapons, ammunition, or explosives for official government business, IAW 18 U.S.C. § 925(a)(1) and DoDI 6400.06, para. 9.2.b

Qualifying Prohibitions

- 18 U.S.C. §§ 922(g) and (n) detail the categories of persons prohibited from possessing, receiving, shipping, or transporting firearms, ammunition, or explosives

- Categories resulting in permanent prohibition:

  -- Persons who have been convicted in any court of a crime punishable by imprisonment for a term exceeding one year (for military members, convictions at a general court-martial (GCM) only)

  -- Persons who have been discharged from the United States Armed Forces with a dishonorable discharge or dismissal

  -- Persons who are aliens illegally in the United States

  -- Persons who have renounced their United States citizenship

  -- Persons who have been convicted of a misdemeanor crime of domestic violence (MCDV) (except those convicted of one MCDV based on a dating relationship between the subject and victim, in which case the initial prohibition is 5 years and will convert to permanent in the event of a subsequent conviction of any MCDV)

- Categories resulting in temporary prohibition:

  -- Persons who are unlawful users of, or addicted to, any controlled substance: one year prohibition from date of qualifying event

  -- Persons who are under indictment/information for a crime punishable by imprisonment for a term exceeding one year (for military members, includes referral to a GCM of charges punishable by imprisonment for a term exceeding one year): terminates at the conclusion of trial; does not prohibit possession of currently held firearms or ammunition

  -- Persons who are subject to a court order restraining the person from harassing, stalking, or threatening an intimate partner or the child of an intimate partner (military protection orders do not qualify): terminates upon expiration of the court order

- Categories resulting in indefinite prohibition:

  -- Persons who are fugitives from justice: prohibition ends upon termination of fugitive status

  -- Persons who have been adjudicated as a mental defective or have been committed to a mental institution: prohibition terminates upon court order declaring person to be mentally competent or releasing them from commitment

Lautenberg Amendment to the Gun Control Act, 18 U.S.C. § 922(g)(9)

- A qualifying domestic violence offense is defined by 18 U.S.C. § 921(a)(33) as an offense:

  -- That is a misdemeanor (generally punishable by imprisonment for one year or less);

  -- That has, as an element, the use or attempted use of physical force, or threatened use of a deadly weapon; and

  -- That was committed by a current or former spouse, parent, or guardian of the victim, by a person with whom the victim shares a child in common, by a person who is cohabiting with or has cohabited with the victim as a spouse, parent, or guardian, by a person similarly situated to a spouse, parent, or guardian of the victim, or by a person who has a current or recent former dating relationship with the victim.

    --- The term "dating relationship" is defined by 18 U.S.C. § 921(a)(37) as a relationship between individuals who have or have recently had a continuing serious relationship of a romantic or intimate nature based on the length and nature of the relationship and the frequency and type of interaction between the individuals involved in the relationship

- Per DoD policy (DoDI 6400.06, para. 9.2.), the prohibition of the Lautenberg Amendment applies to any domestic violence conviction at a GCM, special court-martial, or civilian court, of a misdemeanor or felony (generally punishable by imprisonment for more than one year); the prohibition does not apply to summary courts-martial or nonjudicial punishment

- Qualifying domestic violence offenses include violations of Articles 120, 120b, 128, and 128b, Uniform Code of Military Justice (UCMJ), as well as qualifying offenses under the United States Code

- Commanders are responsible for ensuring personnel are informed of the Lautenberg Amendment and its requirements, IAW DoDI 6400.06, para. 9.4.a., including:

  -- Notice that personnel have an affirmative, continuing obligation to inform their supervisors of qualifying domestic violence convictions;

  -- The required use of the DD Form 2760, *Qualification to Possess Firearms or Ammunition*, to obtain information regarding qualifying domestic violence convictions; and

  -- Posting of notices about the Lautenberg Amendment and its requirements in all facilities where firearms, ammunition, or explosives are stored, issued, or disposed.

- Personnel convicted of qualifying domestic violence offenses may work with major military weapons systems or crew-served military weapons and ammunition (e.g., tanks, missiles, aircraft), IAW DoDI 6400.06, para. 9.3.c.

- Once personnel are found to have a qualifying domestic violence conviction, or if there is credible information to believe they have a qualifying conviction, steps should be taken IAW DoDI 6400.06, para. 9.3.d., to:

-- Immediately retrieve all government-issued firearms and ammunition from the individual;

-- Suspend their authority to possess government-issued firearms and ammunition; and

-- Advise them to surrender, transfer, and dispose of privately-owned firearms, ammunition, and explosives.

References

· Gun Control Act of 1968, 18 U.S.C. §§ 921 *et seq.*

· Brady Handgun Violence Prevention Act, Pub. L. 103-159

· Articles 120, 120b, and 128, Uniform Code of Military Justice

· DoDI 6400.06, *DoD Coordinated Community Response to Domestic Abuse Involving DoD Military and Certain Affiliated Personnel* (15 December 2021), incorporating through Change 2, 16 May 2023

· DD Form 2760, *Qualification to Possess Firearms or Ammunition* (March 2023)

· AFMAN 71-102, *Air Force Criminal Indexing* (21 July 2020)

· AF Form 177, *Notice of Qualification for Prohibition of Firearms, Ammunition, and Explosives* (30 July 2020)

CONSCIENTIOUS OBJECTION TO MILITARY SERVICE

Even when the draft made military service an obligation, Congress recognized that certain individuals and groups hold convictions against the use of force in any form. Members may still apply for administrative separation or reassignment based on certain sincerely held moral, ethical, or religious beliefs.

Key Takeaways

» Members may be granted administrative separation or reassignment of duties due to conscientious objection

» Beliefs must be based on a moral, ethical, or religious belief and must be firm, fixed, sincere, and deeply held

» Applicants have the burden of proof to establish a claim of conscientious objection by clear and convincing evidence

General Policies

- A conscientious objector (CO) is a person who is opposed to participation in war **in any form** or the bearing of arms, based on sincerely held morals, ethical, or religious beliefs, or a combination of such beliefs

- The objection to war must be all-inclusive, not to specific wars and conflicts or based solely on considerations of policy, pragmatism, expediency, or political views

- COs are classified as either Class 1-O, which is a person who sincerely objects to participation in combatant and non-combatant military training and service in war in any form, or as Class 1-A-O, which is a person who sincerely objects to only participation in combatant military training and service, but whose convictions will permit him or her to serve in non-combatant status

- Administrative discharge by the Secretary of the Air Force (SecAF) prior to completion of term of service is discretionary based on the facts of each case

- Applicants for CO status who are awaiting disposition of their case should be assigned to duties that conflict as little as possible with their beliefs. Applicants must comply with the normal requirements of military service and perform duties they are assigned to include active duty or transfer orders in effect at the time of the application or subsequently issued.

Application Procedures

- Applicants have the burden of proof to show they meet CO status, and they must establish the following by clear and convincing evidence:

  -- They oppose participation in war in any form or the bearing of arms;

  -- Their belief is firm, fixed, sincere, and deeply held;

  -- Their belief is based on a moral, ethical, or religious belief, or a combination of such beliefs; and

  -- The nature or basis of their claim falls under the definition of conscientious objection in DAFI 36-3211, *Military Separations*.

- Applicants generally submit their applications to the servicing Military Personnel Section (MPS)/Career Development Element. Applicants in the Air Force Reserve (AFR) or Air National Guard (ANG) that are not serving on extended active duty (EAD) submit their applications to their immediate commander. See DAFI 36-3211, Chapter 29, for information that should be included.

- The MPS notifies the unit commander, reviews the personnel records of the applicant for pertinent information, and counsels the member about the effect of a CO determination on Veteran's Administration (VA) entitlements. MPS also schedules interviews with a chaplain and a psychiatrist.

- A chaplain personally interviews the applicant to determine sincerity and depth of conviction against war. The chaplain must submit a written report detailing conclusions but does not make any recommendation concerning the application.

  -- An appropriately credentialed mental health professional interviews the applicant to determine the presence of any mental disorder warranting medical or administrative disposition. Again, no recommendation on the application is made.

- For active duty and AFR non-EAD members, the Special Court-Martial Convening Authority (SPCMCA) appoints a judge advocate as an Investigating Officer (IO) to interview the applicant under oath, assemble all the relevant material, and interview other witnesses. For ANG non-EAD members, the wing or group commander exercising control over the servicing ANG/MPS appoints the IO.

- Guidelines for approving or disapproving applications are found in Chapter 29 of DAFI 36-3211. Generally, the reviewing authorities must find:

  -- For conscientious objection (1-O) classification, the applicant's moral and ethical beliefs oppose participation in war in any form and that the applicant holds these beliefs with the strength of traditional religious convictions;

-- For assignment to noncombatant training and service based on conscientious objection (1-A-O), the applicant's moral and ethical beliefs objects to participation as a combatant in war in any form, but their convictions are such as to permit military service in a non-combatant status;

-- Conscientious objection must be the primary controlling factor in the applicant's life; **AND**

-- The applicant sincerely holds this belief, including through the applicant's conduct, outward manifestation of their belief, thinking, and lifestyle.

- The commander who appoints the IO makes a recommendation before forwarding the file up the chain of command. For ANG cases, the Director or Deputy Director, Air National Guard, and judge advocates are required to review and make a recommendation on all conscientious objector applications. Final decision for all applicants regarding conscientious objector status is made at the SecAF level after an independent review by the Air Force Personnel Board (AFPB). (DAFI 36-3211, para 29.4.1.1).

- Members determined to be COs, either 1-O or 1-A-O where further service is not desired by the Air Force or Space Force, will be processed for administrative discharge according to the applicable Department of the Air Force instruction, for convenience of the government as the basis for separation

References

· DoDI 1300.06, *Conscientious Objectors* (12 July 2017)
· DAFI 36-2023, *The Secretary of the Air Force Personnel Council (SAFPC)* (3 June 2022)
· DAFI 36-3211, *Military Separations* (24 June 2022), incorporating Change 1, 20 November 2023

PHYSICAL FITNESS PROGRAM AND PHYSICAL FITNESS ASSESSMENTS

The goal of the Department of the Air Force (DAF) Physical Fitness Program is to motivate all members to participate in a year-round physical conditioning program that emphasizes total fitness, to include proper aerobic conditioning, muscular fitness training, and healthy eating. An active lifestyle will increase productivity, optimize health, and decrease absenteeism while maintaining a higher level of readiness. Commanders and supervisors must incorporate fitness into the DAF culture by establishing an environment for members to maintain physical fitness and health to meet expeditionary mission requirements. The Physical Fitness Assessment (PFA) provides commanders with a tool to assist in the determination of overall fitness of their military personnel. The program promotes the primary physical fitness components of cardiorespiratory endurance (aerobic), body composition, muscular strength, muscular endurance, and flexibility of each DAF member.

Unit/Squadron Commander's Duties

- The unit/squadron commander's duties are outlined in DAFMAN 36-2905, *Department of the Air Force Physical Fitness Program*, and include, but are not limited to, the following:

  -- Establishing an environment that supports, encourages, and motivates a healthy lifestyle through optimal physical fitness and nutrition and ensures compliance with DAFMAN 36-2905

  -- Establishing and enforcing the unit's physical fitness program and ensuring appropriate administrative action is taken in cases of non-compliance

  -- Appoint, in writing, individuals to conduct PFAs in support of the Fitness Assessment Cell (FAC), appoint Physical Training Leaders if unit physical training is implemented, and appoint a Unit Fitness Program Manager (UFPM)

  -- The Air Reserve Component (ARC) Commander must promote and support unit physical fitness programs as mission requirements and resources allow. Additionally, they must appoint the installation's Fitness Information Manager (FIM) and FAC Manager. The FIM should be a Noncommissioned Officer or Senior Noncommissioned Officer of any Air Force specialty code appointed by the installation commander, ARC wing commander, or equivalent.

Physical Fitness Standards

- Members will receive a composite score of 0 to 100 based on component scores for aerobic fitness (60 points max), muscular strength (20 points max), and core endurance (20 points max). Effective December 2020, the DAF permanently removed the waist measurement from the PFA.

- The following fitness levels are determined by a member's composite score:

  -- <u>Excellent</u>: All component minimums met and member scores at/above 90. DAF service members in this category will test at least annually (12 months from prior excellent score).

-- <u>Satisfactory</u>: All component minimums met and member scores 75 to 89.99

--- Regular Air Force (RegAF), Air Force Reserve (AFR), and Air National Guard (ANG) members on Title 10 Statutory Tour and Title 32 Active Guard/Reserve (AGR) who obtain a satisfactory score on a PFA shall test every six months (twice a year)

--- ANG Title 32 Drill Status Guardsmen (DSGs) must complete an official PFA at least annually and must be tested by the last day of the 12th month following the previous satisfactory test

-- <u>Unsatisfactory</u>: One or more component minimum not met and/or member scores less than 75 total points

--- RegAF, AFR, and ANG (Title 10 Statutory Tour or Title 32 AGR) Airmen and Guardians who fail to attain a passing PFA score must retest within 90 days (180 calendar days for Title 32 DSGs)

--- Although members may voluntarily retest before the end of the 90-day reconditioning period (180 calendar days for Title 32 DSGs), retesting is not recommended for a minimum of 42 calendar days (90 calendar days for ANG Title 32 Drill Status Guardsmen) to allow sufficient time for reconditioning

--- Members wishing to test earlier than the 42 calendar days (90 calendar days for ANG Title 32 DSGs) must obtain their commander's approval

- Commanders may grant exemptions from the various components of the PFA in accordance with DAFMAN 36-2905, Table 4.1. Airmen and Guardians with exemptions prohibiting them from performing one or more components of the PFA will be assessed on the remaining components.

- DAF service members with pregnancies lasting 20 weeks or more are exempt from PFA for 12 months after discharge from the hospital upon completion of pregnancy (delivery, miscarriage, etc.). The member must test by the last day of the 13th month. Pregnancy-related exemptions apply to the PFA and do not exempt the member from participating in an approved physical fitness program.

Fitness Improvement Program

- The fitness improvement program (FIP) targets nutritional and exercise behavior changes necessary to improve a DAF service member's health and fitness utilizing various intervention options

- FIP is mandatory for all DAF service members with an unsatisfactory PFA score and is available for any member who wishes to improve their overall health and fitness. DAF service members and their commanders select an option such as BE WELL online and Military OneSource Health Coaching as appropriate to their fitness improvement needs and/or desires.

- RegAF, Title 10 Statutory Tour, Title 32 AGR, and AFR/AGR Airmen and Guardians must start the FIP within 10 duty days of their unsatisfactory PFA. Title 32 DSGs and Traditional AFR personnel are required to accomplish FIP within 60 calendar days of the unsatisfactory PFA.

Diagnostic Fitness Assessments

- Diagnostic PFA: A non-attribution assessment aimed to provide feedback and help Airmen and Guardians identify and improve any problem areas. Diagnostic PFAs will follow the same standards and procedures for an official PFA. In other words, a diagnostic PFA is an unofficial PFA conducted under official conditions.

- DAF service members with a current PFA on file (regardless of score or exemption status on last PFA) and not presently exempt may voluntarily complete a diagnostic PFA no later than 16 calendar days in the month their current PFA is due. Members who are not current are not eligible to take a diagnostic PFA.

- DAF service members may attempt at least one but no more than three diagnostic PFAs per calendar year. Commanders must allow members the opportunity to take at least one voluntary diagnostic PFA each year.

- DAF service members will be notified of their overall score after completing the diagnostic PFA

    -- If the result is a passing score (satisfactory or excellent), the service member must elect to accept or decline the result

    -- Only after a service member elects to count the diagnostic PFA will the results be recorded in MyFitness

    -- DAF service members may not be directed to make a diagnostic PFA official

Administrative and Personnel Actions

- Members are expected to always comply with DAF fitness standards. When members fail to comply with those standards (receive an unsatisfactory PFA score), they potentially render themselves to adverse action. Commanders should consult with their servicing Staff Judge Advocate before taking such action.

- Prohibited Actions:

    -- Commanders may not impose nonjudicial punishment solely for failing to achieve a satisfactory fitness score

    -- While units may perform unofficial practice tests for diagnostic purposes, commanders will refrain from taking adverse action based on the results of these tests

    -- A member is not subject to adverse personnel action for inability to take the PFA if the member is on a 365-day PFA exemption that has been validated by the military treatment facility

- Authorized Actions: DAFMAN 36-2905, Attachment 6, contains guidance on mandatory and optional administrative and personnel actions for members failing to meet fitness standards on one or more PFAs, with options covering the full range of administrative tools for progressive discipline. The guidance contained in Attachment 6 is illustrative, non-binding selected guidance includes:

  -- Unit commanders will consider adverse administrative action upon a member's unsatisfactory fitness score on an official PFA. If adverse administrative action is not taken in response to an unsatisfactory fitness score on an official PFA, unit commanders will document in the member's fitness case file as to why no action is being taken. The lack of such commander documentation does not discount the testing failure as a basis in support of administrative discharge action.

  -- As appropriate, unit commanders will document and take corrective action for a member's unexcused failure(s) to participate in the fitness program such as failing to accomplish a scheduled PFA, failing to attend a scheduled fitness appointment, failing to complete mandatory educational intervention, or failing to maintain the required documentation of exercise while on the fitness improvement program

  -- Enlisted DAF members failing to have a current/passing PFA score at the Promotion Eligibility Cut-Off Date (PECD) are ineligible for promotion. Likewise, commanders should consider delaying the promotion of officers who fail to have a current/passing PFA at his/her projected date of promotion.

  -- It is within a commander's discretion to document within an Enlisted Performance Brief (EPB) or Officer Performance Brief (OPB) a referral for a non-current/failing PFA at the evaluation close-out date, or EPB Static Close-Out Date (SCOD)

  -- Unit commanders **MUST** make a discharge or retention recommendation to the separation authority (enlisted DAF members), show cause authority (officers), or appropriate discharge authority for Air Force Reserve and Air National Guard members when an individual remains in the Unsatisfactory fitness category for a continuous 12-month period or receives four unsatisfactory PFA scores in a 24-month period. For ANG Title 32 members (DSG), unit commanders must make a discharge or retention recommendation to the appropriate discharge authority when the member receives four unsatisfactory fitness assessment scores within a 36-month period. However, prior to initiation of discharge action, a military medical provider must rule out medical conditions precluding the member from achieving a passing score. If the sole reason for an administrative separation is for failure to meet physical fitness standards, then only an honorable characterization may be given. As with administrative separation of other bases, administrative separations of officers are approved at the SecAF level after an independent review by the Air Force Personnel Board (AFPB).

References

· DAFI 36-2502, *Enlisted Airman Promotion and Demotion Programs* (16 April 2021), incorporating Change 1, 17 June 2022

· DAFI 36-3211, *Military Separations* (24 June 2022), incorporating Change 1, 20 November 2023

· DAFMAN 36-2905, *Department of the Air Force Physical Fitness Program* (21 April 2022)

UNAUTHORIZED ABSENCE

Most forms of unauthorized absence, from simply being late for work (failure to go) to an extended absence without leave, are punishable under Article 86, Uniform Code of Military Justice (UCMJ), while desertion is punishable under Article 85, UCMJ. Department of the Air Force service members who intend to abandon their military duties permanently are classified as deserters. Aside from disciplinary actions, there are certain requirements and considerations a unit must satisfy when handling cases involving an unauthorized absence.

- When an unauthorized absence is discovered, it is important to note the date and time

    -- Failure To Go: An absence of fewer than 24 hours is classified as a "failure to go" for administrative purposes

    -- Absence Without Leave (AWOL): When the member's absence continues longer than 24 hours and fewer than 30 days, the member's unit must change the member's administrative status to "absence without leave"

    -- Deserter: If a member has been absent for more than 30 consecutive days, the member's unit must change the member's administrative status to "deserter"

    -- Taking these administrative steps **WILL NOT**, standing alone, prove the member has committed an unauthorized absence in violation of any UCMJ article

    -- The administrative steps will affect pay and allowances and put the service member's name in a database to support apprehension efforts of military and civilian law enforcement authorities

    -- Duty Status Whereabouts Unknown: Regardless of the reason for the absence, if the commander's initial investigation reveals the possibility of an involuntary casualty and there is insufficient evidence to make a determination that the member is missing or deceased, a status of Duty Status-Whereabouts Unknown (DUSTWUN) may be appropriate. Consult DAFI 36-3002, *Casualty Services*, the Military Personnel Flight (MPF), and the servicing Staff Judge Advocate (SJA) for advice in such cases.

    -- For ANG cases: The specific action you take against an absent ANG member will depend on whether the ANG member is on active duty, full-time national guard duty (AGR), annual training (AT), or is merely missing a regularly schedule unit training assembly (UTAs). If the ANG member is absent from AT or UTAs, or is an AGR, you should check with your unit SJA for guidance on any state military code, regulation or policy governing Unsatisfactory Participation and AWOL. For ANG members on Title 10 active duty, follow RegAF guidance and 201 MSS notification.

Commander Responsibilities

- Under DAFI 36-3802, *Force Support Readiness Programs*, Chapter 8, and in accordance with the FY2022 National Defense Authorization Act (Pub. L. 117-81), if the member reasonably appears to be absent without authority, the commander on G-series order must undertake the following actions:

-- Immediate Actions:

--- Notify the relevant military criminal investigative organization regarding the requirement to enter all relevant information into the Missing Persons File of the National Crime Information Center (NCIC) database

--- Notify local law enforcement agencies with jurisdictions in the immediate area of the military installation

--- Contact MPF and inform them of the member's status

--- Consult with the servicing SJA to determine whether the member's status should be changed to "deserter"

---- Criteria include duty or travel restrictions, access to top secret or other qualifying classified documents, request for asylum or residence in a foreign country, uncompleted action for a previous AWOL, escaped prisoner, under investigation for UCMJ violation or awaiting trial at a general court-martial, believed likely to commit violent acts or harm oneself or others, or evidence of intent to remain away permanently

--- Evaluate the case to determine whether the casualty services provisions of DAFI 36-3002 applies

-- After 24 Hours of Absence: Prepare an DAF Form 2098, *Duty Status Change*, changing the absentee's status to either AWOL or deserter as appropriate, and forward it to MPF, with a copy to the local finance office. Consult the servicing SJA.

-- On the 3rd Day of Absence: Prepare and forward a 72-hour inquiry to the Security Forces Squadron (SFS) and MPF and re-evaluate whether DAFI 36-3002 applies

--- If the member is administratively classified as a deserter, the commander prepares, signs, and distributes DD Form 553, *Deserter/Absentee Wanted by the Armed Forces*, and changes the member's duty status within 24 hours of the decision to place the member in deserter status

-- On the 10th Day of Absence: Prepare and forward letters to the next of kin and allotment payees, and provide copies of these letters to MPF

-- On the 31st Day of Absence:

--- Ensure processing of DD Form 553 (MPF will assist in preparation) and decide (with the assistance of SFS and MPF) to whom DD Form 553 should be sent

--- Initiate AF Form 2098 changing status from AWOL to deserter

--- Notify MPF of the member's continued absence and retrieve dependent ID cards as required by AFI 36-3026V1_IP, *Identification Cards for Members of the Uniformed Services, Their Eligible Family Members, and Other Eligible Personnel,* Table 8.3, when member is placed in deserter status. Dependents lose medical benefits and shopping privileges in accordance with AFI 36-3026V1_IP, Table 9.2.

--- Consult with SJA about filing court-martial charges

--- Prepare 31st day status report

-- <u>On the 60th Day of Absence</u>: Notify SFS and MPF of the member's continued absence, obtain updated input from SFS and prepare and forward the 60-day status report

-- <u>On the 180th Day of Absence</u>: Military Personnel Data Systems (MilPDS) program automatically drops absentee from the unit rolls. Commander notifies SFS of status change and consults with SJA concerning other options and/or requirements.

- Military law enforcement personnel and commissioned, warrant, petty, and Noncommissioned Officers may apprehend absentees and deserters. Civil officers authorized to arrest offenders under federal and state laws may arrest a deserter and deliver the offender into the custody of the Armed Forces. These civil officers may also arrest absentees at the request of military and federal authorities.

- United States authorities may apprehend absentees and deserters in foreign countries only when an international agreement with the country authorizes it or under an agreement with proper local authorities that does not violate an existing international agreement. Always consult the SJA in these cases.

References

· National Defense Authorization Act (NDAA) for Fiscal Year 2022, Pub. L. 117-81 § 548 (2021)
· Articles 85 and 86, Uniform Code of Military Justice
· DoDI 1325.02, *Desertion and Unauthorized Absence or Absence Without Leave* (26 October 2021)
· DD Form 553, *Deserter/Absentee Wanted by the Armed Forces* (November 2021)
· DAFI 36-3002, *Casualty Services* (4 February 2021)
· DAFI 36-3802, *Force Support Readiness Programs* (9 January 2019), incorporating Change 1, 21 November 2021
· DAFI 51-201, *Administration of Military Justice* (24 January 2024)
· DAF Form 2098, *Duty Status Change* (12 July 2022)
· AFI 36-3026 Volume 1, *Identification Cards for Members of the Uniformed Services, Their Eligible Family Members, and Other Eligible Personnel* (4 August 2017), including DAFGM2024-01, 16 January 2024

LINE OF DUTY DETERMINATIONS

A Line of Duty (LOD) determination is a finding made after an investigation into the circumstances of a member's injury, illness, disease, or death. The finding determines: (1) whether the illness, injury or disease existed prior to service (EPTS) and, if so, whether an EPTS condition was aggravated by military service; (2) whether the illness, injury, disease, or death occurred while the member was absent without authority; and (3) whether the illness, injury, disease, or death was due to the member's misconduct or willful negligence. On the basis of the LOD determination, the member or their next of kin may be entitled to benefits administered by the Department of the Air Force (DAF) or exposed to liabilities.

Key Takeaways

» An LOD determination is a finding made after an investigation into the circumstances of a member's injury, illness, disease, or death

» An LOD determination must be initiated for any death and certain injuries

---

Use of the LOD Determination

- An LOD determination may impact the following:

  -- Disability, retirement, and severance pay

  -- Forfeiture of pay

  -- Extension of enlistment

  -- Veteran benefits

  -- Survivor Benefit Plan

  -- Basic Educational Assistance Death Benefit

  -- Medical benefits and incapacitation pay for members of the Air Reserve Component

Limits on Use of an LOD Determination

- An LOD determination shall not be used as a basis for disciplinary actions

- An active duty member cannot be denied medical treatment based on an LOD determination. Further, an LOD determination does not authorize recoupment of the cost of medical care for active duty members. Reserve component members will be financially responsible for medical expenses in accordance with DoDI 1241.01, *Reserve Component (RC) Line of Duty Determination for Medical and Dental Treatments and Incapacitation Pay Entitlements*.

When an LOD Determination is Required

- An LOD determination must be initiated on an AF Form 348, *Line of Duty Determination,* when the following occurs:

  -- Death of a member: In every case involving the death of a member in any duty status, to include travel to and from a duty station

  -- An injury involving likelihood of a permanent disability

  -- An injury or disease involving alcohol or other drugs

  -- A self-inflicted injury

  -- An injury or disease possibly incurred during a period of unauthorized absence

- An injury or disease possibly incurred during a course of conduct for which charges have been preferred under the Uniform Code of Military Justice (UCMJ); or the state military code for ANG members

- For members of the Air Reserve Component (ARC), an LOD determination must also be made when:

  -- The member incurs or aggravates an illness, injury, or disease, or receives any medical treatment while serving in any duty status, regardless of the member's ability to perform military duties

  -- The member dies, or incurs, or aggravates an illness, injury or disease while traveling directly to or from the place at which duty is performed

  -- The member dies, or incurs, or aggravates an illness, injury or disease while remaining overnight immediately before or between successive periods of inactive duty training (IDT), at or in the vicinity of the site of the IDT, if the site is outside reasonable commuting distance from the member's residence

  -- Members have up to 180 days after completion of their current duty status to report their medical conditions for a LOD determination, absent special circumstances. After 180 days have passed, the avenue for addressing previously unreported illness, injury, or disease is through the DVA.

Possible LOD Determinations

- <u>In Line of Duty (ILOD)</u>: Means the illness, injury, disease, or death was not due to the member's misconduct and occurred when the member was in an authorized duty status

- <u>Not In Line of Duty (NILOD)</u>:

  -- *NILOD – Not Due to Member's Misconduct:* Follows a formal investigation that determined the member's illness, injury, disease, or death occurred while the member was absent without authority, but neither the absence nor any misconduct were the proximate cause of medical issues

-- *NILOD – Due to Member's Misconduct:* Follows a formal investigation that determined the member's illness, injury, disease, or death was proximately caused by the member's misconduct. If the member's illness, injury, or disease occurred prior to service, in a non-duty status, or while the member was absent without authority, and was proximately caused by the member's misconduct, the case should be finalized as NILOD – Due to Member's Misconduct.

- Existed Prior to Service (EPTS):

-- *Existed Prior to Service-Service Aggravation (EPTS-SA):* Means a condition is aggravated when the member was in a qualified duty status, and the illness, injury or disease worsened over and above its natural progression due to trauma or the nature of military service

-- *Existed Prior to Service – Not Service Aggravated (EPTS-NSA):* Follows an investigation that determined, by clear and unmistakable evidence, the member's illness, injury, disease, or underlying condition existed prior to the member's entry into military service with any branch or component of the Armed Forces or between periods of such service, and was not service aggravated

Standard of Proof for LOD Determinations

- Active duty members and reserve component members in a qualified status are presumed In the Line of Duty (ILOD). The burden of proof is on the government to prove NILOD using the appropriate standard of proof outlined below. For reserve component members on orders for less than 30 days the burden is on the government to prove NILOD by a preponderance of the evidence.

- A preponderance of the evidence is defined as the greater weight of credible evidence

- When determining whether a preponderance of evidence exists, all available evidence must be considered, including:

-- Direct evidence based on actual knowledge or observation of witnesses

-- Indirect evidence, such as facts or statements from which reasonable inferences, deductions, and conclusions may be drawn to establish an unobserved fact, knowledge, or state of mind

-- Accepted medical principles, based on fundamental deductions, consistent with medical facts that are so reasonable and logical as to create a reasonable certainty that they are correct

- Preponderance of Evidence: Is not determined by the number of witnesses or exhibits, but by all the evidence and evaluating factors such as a witness' behavior, opportunity for knowledge, information possessed, ability to recall, as well as related events and relationship to the matter being considered. In other words, a factfinder may choose to believe a single credible witness over several witnesses the factfinder does not find credible.

- NILOD – Not Due to Member's Misconduct or EPTS-NSA Determination: The standard of proof used is **clear and unmistakable evidence** for active duty members and reserve component members on orders for more than 30 days

  -- Clear and unmistakable evidence means undebatable information that the condition existed prior to military service or if increased in service was not aggravated by military service. In other words, reasonable minds could only conclude that the condition existed prior to military service from a review of all the evidence in the record. It is a standard of evidentiary proof that is higher than a preponderance of the evidence and clear and convincing evidence.

- NILOD – Due to Member's Misconduct: The standard of proof used is **clear and convincing evidence**

  -- Clear and convincing evidence is defined as evidence indicating that the thing to be proved is highly probable or reasonably certain. It is a burden of proof that is higher than a preponderance of the evidence but lower than clear and unmistakable evidence.

Types of Processing for LOD Determinations

- Administrative LOD are permissible when a military medical provider sees a member under any of the below circumstances, he/she makes an administrative determination that the member's condition is ILOD. This determination is final, and no further action is required.

  -- As a hostile casualty (other than death)

  -- As a passenger in a common carrier or military aircraft

  -- The injury, illness or disease clearly did not involve misconduct, abuse of drugs or alcohol, or self-injurious behavior

  -- The injury or illness is simple, such as a sprain, contusion, or minor fracture, and is not likely to result in permanent disability

  -- For ARC, the medical provider may make an administrative determination to document a minor condition as ILOD if there is no likelihood of permanent disability, hospitalization, or requirement for continuing medical treatment

- Informal LOD: Are permissible when an administrative determination is not appropriate. The commander investigates the circumstances of the case to determine if the member's illness, injury, disease, or death occurred while the member was absent without authority, is due to the member's own misconduct or EPTS.

- Interim LOD (ARC Only): May be made to establish initial care and treatment for ARC members pending a final LOD determination. An Interim LOD determination should not be made if clear and unmistakable evidence shows an EPTS condition or that the member's misconduct was the proximate cause of the illness, injury, or disease.

- Formal LOD: Are made by higher authorities based upon a thorough investigation conducted by a specially appointed disinterested Investigating Officer (IO), in the grade of O-3 or above and senior to the member being investigated

  -- Required to support a determination of NILOD unless the condition was EPTS-NSA

  -- The immediate commander may also recommend a Formal LOD determination when the member's illness, injury, disease, or death occurred under strange or doubtful circumstances or under circumstances the commander believes should be fully investigated

  -- Follow guidance in DD Form 261, *Report of Investigation Line of Duty and Misconduct Cases*

LOD Determination Processing for Sexual Assault Cases

- A member who has incurred an injury, illness, or disease as a result of sexual assault while performing active duty service or IDT must have his/her LOD processed in accordance with DoDI 6495.02, Volume 1, *Sexual Assault Prevention and Response: Program Procedures*

- The LOD determination process will vary depending on whether the member elects unrestricted or restricted reporting

LOD Determinations for Specific Situations

- See DAFI 36-2910, *Line of Duty (LOD) Determination, Medical Continuation (MEDCON), and Incapacitation (INCAP) Pay*, Attachment 2 for guidance on common LOD situations

References

· DoDI 1241.01, *Reserve Component (RC) Line of Duty Determination for Medical and Dental Treatments and Incapacitation Pay Entitlements* (19 April 2016)

· DoDI 6495.02, Volume 1, *Sexual Assault Prevention and Response: Program Procedures* (28 March 2013), incorporating through Change 7, 6 September 2022

· DD Form 261, *Report of Investigation Line of Duty and Misconduct Status* (25 March 2021)

· DAFI 36-2910, *Line of Duty (LOD) Determination, Medical Continuation (MEDCON), and Incapacitation (INCAP) Pay* (3 September 2021), incorporating Change 1, 28 September 2022, including DAFGM2023-02, 17 November 2023

· AF Form 348, *Line of Duty Determination* (16 October 2020)

· AF Form 348R, *Line of Duty Determination for Restricted Report of Sexual Assault* (20 October 2015)

DISABILITY EVALUATION SYSTEM

The Disability Evaluation System (DES) is the mechanism for determining fitness for duty because of disability. The Secretary of the Air Force may retire, or separate service members who, because of a disability, are unfit to perform the duties of their office, grade, rank, or rating, and ensures fair compensation to members whose military careers are cut short due to service-incurred or service-aggravated medical conditions. Department of the Air Force service members, to include active duty, Guard, Reserve, Air Force cadets, and basic military training (BMT) trainees, who are facing medical separation, can all be referred into the DES.

Key Takeaways

» Disability evaluation begins only when examination, treatment, hospitalization, or substandard performance results in referral to an Airman Medical Readiness Optimization (AMRO) Board for medical screening

» When notified, a commander must provide a statement describing the impact a member's medical condition(s) has on his/her ability to accomplish unit missions

» For those members eligible for the Limited Assignment Status (LAS) program, a memorandum from the service member's commander is required

» Commanders must inform the Physical Evaluation Board Liaison Officer (PEBLO) of any pending administrative or unfavorable action arising before or during a service member's DES processing

Commander's Role and Responsibilities

- The member's immediate commander must provide a statement via AF Form 1185 describing the impact of the potentially unfitting medical condition(s) on the member's ability to perform assigned military duties in-garrison and in a deployed location

  -- AFI 36-3212, *Physical Evaluation for Retention, Retirement and Separation*, contains a detailed Commander's Impact Fact Sheet, Attachment 3

  -- Commanders should consult with the member's primary care provider (PCM) to address any questions or concerns regarding the member's ability to perform assigned military duties

- Commanders must ensure members are available to attend all required DES-related appointments

- A commander may assist a member in getting their case recalled by the Military Treatment Facility commander. A recall is appropriate when there is a major change in the member's condition, or a new condition is discovered.

DES Phases

- Disability evaluation begins when examination, treatment, hospitalization, or substandard performance results in referral to a pre-DES screening review process. The referral decision authority Air Force Personnel Center Medical Retention Standards (DPMNR), AFRC/SGO (AFR), or NGB/SGPS (ANG) can either return the member to duty or refer the member into the DES. ARC members with a medically disqualifying condition that is not compensable under the DES may elect referral to the PEB for fitness determination only (Non-Duty Disability Evaluation System (NDDES)).

- Service members referred into the DES proceed through the Integrated Disability Evaluation System (IDES) process unless an exception for the Legacy Disability Evaluation System (LDES) applies

  -- IDES is the joint DoD/VA process by which DoD determines whether ill or injured Service members are fit for continued military service, and the DoD and VA determine appropriate benefits for Service members who are separated or retired for disability through a single set of disability ratings provided by the VA

  -- LDES is the process by which the Military Treatment Facility Commander or designee (O-6 or GS-15 equivalent or higher) may direct members into LDES by election of the service member, for compelling and individualized reasons, or when the member fails to submit a VA disability claim. Service members approved for LDES may only apply for veterans' disability benefits through the VA Benefits Delivery at Discharge Program or upon attaining veteran status.

  -- NDDES is the Air Force process to determine whether an ARC service member with a nonduty related condition is fit for continued military service. Disability ratings are not assigned.

Medical Evaluation Board (MEB)

- The MEB marks the first official phase of the DES

  -- If the MEB determines the service member has a potentially unfitting condition(s), the MEB forwards the case to the Physical Evaluation Board (PEB) at the Air Force Personnel Center (AFPC)

  -- If the MEB determines the service members condition meets medical standards and is not unfitting, the MEB returns the service member to duty

  -- An "unfitting" condition prevents the member from performing the duties of their Air Force specialty code (AFSC), deploying, or taking a full-component physical assessment; or the condition represents a health risk or imposes unreasonable requirements on the military to safeguard the member or others

  -- The MEB normally consists of two or three physicians who determine whether the member has any medical issues that could make him or her unfit for continued military service. In all mental health cases, one of the three physicians must be a psychiatrist or psychologist.

Physical Evaluation Board (PEB)

- The PEB marks the second phase of the DES. The PEB is further divided into the Informal Physical Evaluation Board (IPEB) and the Formal Physical Evaluation Board (FPEB).

  -- The IPEB consists of two board members (one physician and one personnelist) who adjudicate cases based on a records-only review

  -- The FPEB consists of three board members (one physician and two personnelists), one of whom serves as the board president. For ARC cases, one of the FPEB board members must be an ARC member. The FPEB hearing convenes in a closed-door session with the board members, the service member whose case is under appeal, and his/her counsel. The service member has the right to call witnesses to testify on his/her behalf.

  -- The IPEB and FPEB generally recommend one of the following four outcomes: return to duty, medical retirement, discharge with severance pay, or return without action for further processing

  -- Service members have the right to appeal an unfit determination from the IPEB to the FPEB

The Air Force Personnel Board

- Service members also have the right to appeal their results from the FPEB to SAFPC for an FPEB Appeal

  -- The FPEB Appeal Board consists of three board members (one physician, one personnelist, and one legal advisor)

  -- The service member can request either a virtual hearing or records review

  -- The decision of the FPEB Appeal Board is final

- Members who believe the decision of the FPEB Appeal Board represents an error or injustice may appeal the decision to the Air Force Board for Correction of Military Records following separation from service

Limited Assignment Status (LAS)

- Service members found unfit for duty by the PEB may apply for continued military service in a permanent limited duty status

- To be eligible for LAS, members must meet the following criteria:

  -- Have 15 or more but less than 20 years active service or deemed combat wounded;

  -- Possess qualification in a needed skill or shortage AFSC;

  -- The unfit medical condition must be essentially stable;

-- The ability to function in a normal military environment without adverse effect on member's health or the health of others, and without need for excessive medical care; and

-- Commanders must provide a retention recommendation for LAS applications.

Dual Action Processing

- A Dual Action is a case wherein a DAF service member is concurrently processed for both disability evaluation and non-disability involuntary administrative separation

    -- Commanders must inform the PEBLO of any pending administrative or unfavorable action arising before or during the member's DES processing

    -- Commanders should inform their servicing legal office of a pending disability evaluation concerning a member who is also pending involuntary administrative separation

Office of Disability Counsel (ODC)

- RegAF and ARC judge advocates, civilian attorneys, and paralegals work at the ODC

    -- The ODC's mission is to deliver prompt, professional, independent legal counsel to fit, ready warriors determined to return to the mission and to ill, injured, and wounded Airmen and Guardians facing medical separation from military service

    -- Prior to referral into the DES, the ODC can provide general information to assist members in understanding any applicable rights and responsibilities. As members progress through the DES phases, the ODC can provide more specific advice aimed at developing a strategy to reach desired outcomes, such as being returned to duty, medical retirement, or receiving a medical discharge with severance pay.

    -- The ODC provides representation primarily at the FPEB and at SAFPC in instances of an FPEB appeal. The ODC also assists with appeals of Veterans Affairs (VA) ratings for any unfitting condition(s).

Rights of Airmen and Guardians

- The law requires government legal representation be made available for all members in the DES

    -- A member who is pending an MEB or PEB may contact the ODC for consultation concerning their rights and elections

References

· DoDI 1332.18, *Disability Evaluation System (DES)* (24 February 2023)

· DAFI 36-3212, *Physical Evaluation for Retention, Retirement and Separation* (22 February 2024)

· DAFI 36-2910, *Line of Duty (LOD) Determination, Medical Continuation (MEDCON), and Incapacitation (INCAP) Pay* (3 September 2021) incorporating Change 1, 28 September 2022, including DAFGM2023-02, dated 17 November 2023

· DAFMAN 48-108, *Physical Evaluation Board Liaison Officer (PEBLO) Functions: Pre-Disability Evaluation System (DES) and Medical Evaluation Board (MEB) Processing* (5 August 2021)

· DAFMAN 48-123, *Medical Examinations and Standards* (8 December 2020)

PROFILES AND DUTY LIMITATIONS

Service members may develop injuries, illnesses, or disabilities that impact their ability to perform military duties or deploy. Profiles and Duty Limiting Condition (DLC) procedures have been developed to ensure maximum utilization and readiness of personnel, while preserving members' health and minimizing risk of further injury or illness.

Key Takeaways

» Healthcare providers should promptly notify commanders when a service member's health or ability to accomplish the mission is at risk due to health concerns

» DLCs that restrict mobility for 365 consecutive days or 365 cumulative days in a three-year period will trigger review by the Airman Medical Readiness Optimization (AMRO) for potential referral to the Disability Evaluation System (DES)

» Healthcare providers may disclose limited medical information to commanders to inform of a member's fitness for duty. Consult servicing legal representative for specific guidance.

Responsibilities

- Healthcare Providers:

-- Determine at each encounter whether service members are able to perform duties required by their Air Force Specialty Code (AFSC), deploy, meet medical retention standards, and perform fitness assessments

-- Use AF Form 469, *Duty Limiting Condition Report,* to promptly notify commanders when a service member's health or ability to accomplish the mission is at risk due to health concerns. Include specific recommendations regarding duty limitations and/or restrictions for service members.

-- DAF medical providers will render the final authority on deployment, medical retainability and physical limitation recommendations made from non-military treatment facility medical consultations

- Commanders:

-- Ensure unit and individual medical readiness

-- Ensure unit service members are available for and complete examinations including required follow-up studies and final disposition in a timely manner

-- Ensure appropriate medical and occupational duty restrictions are relayed to supervisors while protecting sensitive health information

-- Because commanders must know whether their subordinate members are fit for duty, the Health Insurance Portability and Accountability Act (HIPAA) allows for limited disclosures of health information to commanders in some circumstances, including fitness for duty determinations

-- Commanders may consult with the medical unit's Senior Profiling Officer to appropriately utilize personnel with DLCs. An assessment based on operational risk to personnel assigned to a unit is critical to maintaining unit readiness at the highest degree possible.

-- Commanders may disagree with a health care provider regarding a service member's mobility restriction. To do so, commanders must contact the installation's Chief of Aerospace Medicine (MDG/SGP) within seven duty days of receipt of the mobility restricting AF Form 469. The MTF must then re-adjudicate and resubmit the profile to the commander, within an additional seven duty days. If the MDG/SGP and unit commander still disagree after the re-adjudication, the profile will stand, as it is a medical recommendation, and the commander can choose to accept the recommendation or not.

- DAF Service Members:

-- Report any new medical condition, or any change in medical status, to the appropriate medical provider at the time of onset

-- Must attend all scheduled medical appointments as directed and inform unit supervisor of required follow-up evaluations and appointments

-- Must make all attempts to resolve medical conditions in a timely manner, including, but not limited to, attendance at all appointments, active participation in rehabilitation, and using medications as prescribed

-- Report all medical or dental treatment obtained through civilian sources to the primary care team

-- When a service member's failure to comply with medical assessment requirements renders the Air Force Medical Service (AFMS) unable to determine the current medical status, the following actions will be deferred: clearance actions for deployment; PCS; retraining; attendance at service academies or professional military education (PME); military personnel appropriation (MPA) or Reserve Personnel Appropriation (RPA) orders; or any other orders status to include medical continuation (MEDCON) orders (ARC)

Duty Limiting Conditions (DLC)

- A DLC is a medical condition which impairs, restricts, and/or prevents the military member from performing at least some requirements of military service or duties expected to be part of the member's AFSC or a current or projected assignment

- DLCs annotated on an AF Form 469 must be reviewed for appropriateness and accuracy at every appointment/clinical encounter between the service member and a provider. Additionally, at a minimum, the AF Form 469 must be re-validated and renewed or revised at each preventative health assessment. A service member may only have one active AF Form 469 at a time.

- Any one of three circumstances trigger special review by the Airman Medical Readiness Optimization (AMRO) board and potential referral to the Disability Evaluation System (DES): (1) a DLC that restricts mobility for 365 consecutive days; (2) any DLC that restricts mobility for 365 cumulative days in a three-year period; or (3) a DLC that may be considered unfitting for continued military service

Fitness Restrictions (FR) and Fitness Assessment Exemptions (FAE)

- If a service member has a medical condition affecting fitness, but not impacting mobility, retention, or AFSC duties, the provider who initially assesses the condition will generate an AF Form 469

- <u>Permanent Profiles</u>: May only be for fitness; require approval at the AMRO board prior to signature; require a note from the orthopedist or other appropriate specialist documenting medical condition is permanent, not likely to improve, and recommends avoiding specific fitness activities; and require annual validation during Preventative Health Assessment (PHA) review

  -- Permanent profiles may have multiple fitness restrictions without necessarily requiring further DES processing, so long as the member can still perform required actions for duty and deployment

- If the service member has a valid AF Form 469 and changes duty locations, the Form 469 is valid at the gaining installation for FRs and FAEs

References

- DoDM 6025.18, *Implementation of the Health Insurance Portability and Accountability Act (HIPAA) Privacy Rule in DoD Health Care Programs* (13 March 2019)
- DAFMAN 48-123, *Medical Examinations and Standards* (8 December 2020)
- AFI 48-133, *Duty Limiting Conditions* (7 August 2020)
- AF Form 469, *Duty Limiting Condition Report* (31 January 2020)

OFFICER GRADE DETERMINATIONS

The Secretary of the Air Force (SecAF) can retire regular and reserve officers in a lower grade than their highest grade held if their service has not been "satisfactory." This authority has been delegated to the Director, Air Force Review Boards Agency for those in the grade of colonel and below. General officer cases require SecAF resolution, with or without referral to a formal Officer Grade Determination (OGD) Board. Contact AF/JAJI – Investigations, Inquiries, and Relief for guidance on general officer cases.

Key Takeaway

» OGDs are required where an officer's conduct or record raises questions as to the quality of his/her service in a particular grade

---

Process

- When an officer applies for retirement, any commander in the officer's chain may initiate an OGD if there is evidence the officer's service in their current grade has been less than satisfactory

  -- In making the "satisfactorily held" determination, consider the nature and length of the officer's improper conduct, the impact the conduct had on military effectiveness, the quality and length of the officer's service in each grade at issue, past cases involving similar conduct, and the recommendations of the officer's command chain. A single incident of misconduct can render service in a grade unsatisfactory despite a substantial period of otherwise exemplary service.

- A commander **MUST** submit an OGD if the officer has:

  -- Applied for retirement in lieu of judicial or administrative separation;

  -- A conviction by court-martial;

  -- A conviction by a civilian court for misconduct which did (or would) result in a mandatory comment and referral in the member's next Officer Performance Brief (OPB), training report (TR), or Promotion Recommendation Form (PRF), in accordance with DAFI 36-2406, *Officer and Enlisted Evaluations Systems*;

  -- Received nonjudicial punishment pursuant to Article 15, Uniform Code of Military Justice, or a Letter of Reprimand, since the officer's last promotion; or

  -- Been the subject of any substantiated adverse finding from an officially documented investigation, proceeding, or inquiry (except minor traffic infractions), regardless of the command action taken against the officer (if any), since his/her last promotion.

- A commander **MAY** submit an OGD in other cases if he/she believes an OGD is appropriate

- At the time an officer applies for retirement, the commander will review the officer's record to determine if any of the above conditions exist. If, based on that review, one of the above conditions exists, the commander initiates an OGD.

  -- The commander must notify the officer that an OGD is being initiated and why

  -- All information relevant and material to the determination of "satisfactory service" must be provided

  -- The officer is given 10 business days to respond

- All commanders within the officer's chain of command, up to and including the MAJCOM/FLDCOM, will make a recommendation regarding the officer's retirement grade

- For retirement in lieu of judicial or administrative separation, the officer is considered on notice that he/she is subject to an OGD based on that administrative or judicial action. The officer's commander is not required to separately notify the officer of the OGD unless the commander intends to add or consider evidence that was not already provided to the officer during the underlying administrative or judicial action.

- OGD packages, including matters and documents submitted by the member, are forwarded through the MAJCOM/FLDCOM to the Air Force Personnel Center (AFPC), which sends the case file to the Secretary of the Air Force Personnel Council (SAFPC) for decision

- Any questions concerning officer misconduct, reporting requirements, or the appropriate administrative or judicial response to misconduct should be addressed through the servicing Staff Judge Advocate or MPF

References

· Regular Commissioned Officers, 10 U.S.C. § 1370

· Officers Entitled to Retired Pay for Non-Regular Service, 10 U.S.C. § 1370a

· DAFI 36-2023, *The Secretary of the Air Force Personnel Council (SAFPC)* (3 June 2022)

· DAFI 36-2406, *Officer and Enlisted Evaluations Systems* (4 August 2023), including AFGM2024-01, 17 January 2024

· DAFI 36-3203, *Service Retirements* (29 January 2021), incorporating Change 1, 13 October 2023

TATTOOS/BRANDS, BODY PIERCING, AND BODY ALTERATION

DAFI 36-2903, *Dress and Personal Appearance of Department of the Air Force Personnel*, governs the use of tattoos, body piercing, and body alterations by Department of the Air Force (DAF) members. Failure to abide by these instructions may subject DAF service members to prosecution for violation of a lawful general regulation under Article 92 of the Uniform Code of Military Justice (UCMJ). Additionally, commanders retain authority to be more restrictive for covering tattoos, body ornaments, and personal grooming based on legal, safety, sanitary, or foreign country cultural reasons.

Key Takeaway

» DAFI 36-2903 governs the use of tattoos, brands, body markings, body piercing, and body alteration/modification by members both on and off duty

» Members who violate the policy are subject to administrative action and/or prosecution under Article 92, UCMJ

Tattoos, Brands, or Body Markings

- Commanders will use the provisions in DAFI 36-2903 in determining the acceptability of tattoos, brands, and body markings displayed by members in uniform

  -- A tattoo is defined as a picture, design, or marking made on the skin or other areas of the body by staining it with an indelible dye, or by any other method, including pictures, designs, or markings only detectable or visible under certain conditions (such as ultraviolet or invisible ink tattoos)

  -- A brand is defined as a picture, design, or other marking that is burned into the skin or other areas of the body. Body markings are pictures, designs, or other markings as a result of using means other than burning to permanently scar or mark the skin.

- Authorized: Tattoos, brands, or body markings are authorized on the chest and back, arms, legs, feet, hands, and neck

  -- Authorized hand, arm, leg, neck, and ring tattoos can be exposed/visible while in any uniform

  -- Chest and back tattoos will not be visible through any uniform, or visible while wearing an open collar uniform

  -- Cosmetic tattooing (for men or women), when directed by qualified medical personnel to correct a medical condition, illness, or injury. Also permitted for women if done to apply permanent facial makeup and for men if for permanent cosmetics for scalp only to create a natural hair appearance.

- Unauthorized: Tattoos, brands, or body markings anywhere on the body that are indecent or obscene, commonly associated with gangs or extremist/supremacist organizations, or that advocate sexual, racial, ethnic, or religious discrimination are prohibited in and out of uniform

  -- Tattoos, brands, or body markings with unauthorized content that are prejudicial to good order and discipline, or the content is of a nature that tends to bring discredit upon the Air Force or Space Force are prohibited both in and out of uniform

  -- Likewise, other than those authorized in DAFI 36-2903 and above, tattoos, brands, or body markings are prohibited on the head, face, tongue, lip, eyes, and scalp

  -- Airmen and Guardians may not simply cover up tattoos, brands, or body markings with bandages or make-up in order to comply with this policy

Tattoo Removal/Alteration Policy

- DAF members who have or receive unauthorized content tattoos, brands, or body markings are required to initiate tattoo, brand, or body marking removal and alteration. At the commander's discretion, members may be seen on a space and resource available basis, in a Department of Defense (DoD) medical treatment facility for voluntary tattoo, brand, or body marking removal. When DoD resources are not available, members may have the tattoo, brand, or body marking removed or altered at their own expense outside of DoD medical treatment facilities. Permissive TDY is not authorized for this purpose; therefore, travel is at member's expense.

  -- Members who fail to remove or alter unauthorized tattoos, brands, or body markings in a timely manner will be subject to appropriate administrative and disciplinary actions. The requirement to comply with DAF guidance is not negated by an inability to obtain removal at government expense. The member is ultimately responsible for complying with DAF guidance, while supervisors and commanders are charged with enforcing standards via appropriate actions.

Body Piercing

- Earrings:

  -- Male DAF service members are not authorized to wear earrings while in uniform or in civilian attire for official duty but are authorized to wear earrings in civilian attire while off duty on a military installation

  -- Female DAF service members may wear small (not exceeding 6 mm in diameter) conservative (moderate, being within reasonable limits; not excessive or extreme) round or square white diamond, gold, white pearl, or silver earrings as a set with any uniform combination. If member has multiple holes, only one set of earrings are authorized to be worn in uniform and will be worn in the lower earlobes. Earrings will match and fit tightly without extending below the earlobe unless the piece extending is the connecting band on clip earrings.

- <u>On official duty in uniform or civilian attire (on or off a military installation)</u>: With the exception of earrings for females (see above), all members are prohibited from attaching, affixing, or displaying objects, articles, jewelry, or ornamentation to or through the ear, nose, tongue, eyebrows, lips, or any exposed body part (includes visible through clothing)

- <u>Off duty in civilian attire, on a military installation</u>: With the exception of earrings (see above) and when in areas in/around military family and privatized housing, DAF members are prohibited from attaching, affixing and/or displaying objects, articles, jewelry, or ornamentation to and/or through the ear, nose, tongue, eyebrows, lips, or any exposed body part (includes visible through clothing)

Body Alteration/Modification

- Members are prohibited from altering or modifying their bodies if the alteration is intentional and results in a visible, physical effect that disfigures, deforms, or otherwise detracts from a professional military image

- Examples include, but are not limited to, tongue splitting or forking, tooth filing, and acquiring visible, disfiguring skin implants, and gouging (piercing holes large enough to permit light to shine through)

References

· DAFI 36-2903, *Dress and Personal Appearance of Department of the Air Force Personnel* (29 February 2024), Corrective Actions applied on 13 March 2024

· SPFGM2023-36-01, *Space Force Guidance Memorandum Establishing U.S. Space Force (USSF) Dress and Appearance Standards* (8 November 2023), Corrective Action, 30 November 2023

RETALIATION

Retaliation is punishable under Article 132, Uniform Code of Military Justice (UCMJ), or AFI 36-2909, *Air Force Professional Relationships and Conduct*. Retaliation against individuals who report criminal offenses or make protected communications is unlawful and erodes good order and discipline, respect for authority, unit cohesion, and mission accomplishment.

Key Takeaway

» Military members shall not retaliate against an alleged victim or other military member who makes, or is planning to make, a protected communication or reports a criminal offense

» Protected communications include communications to a Member of Congress or an Inspector General (IG), or complaints/disclosures of a violation of law or regulation

» Retaliation is a broad term that includes retaliation, ostracism, and maltreatment, all of which are punishable under AFI 36-2909

» Commanders and supervisors must take appropriate action when they believe retaliation has occurred and may be held responsible for failing to act in certain circumstances

Overview

- Retaliation is a categorical term that includes retaliation, ostracism, and maltreatment

  -- Pursuant to Article 132, UCMJ, the offense of retaliation is focused upon the abuse of otherwise lawful military authority for the purpose of retaliating against any person for reporting, or planning to report, a criminal offense or for making, or planning to make, a protected communication. It is also focused on the use of military authority for the purpose of preemptively discouraging any person from making a criminal report or protected communication.

  -- Article 132, UCMJ, specifically prohibits taking adverse personnel actions, or withholding favorable personnel actions, for unlawful purposes

    --- Personnel Action: Any action taken on a service member that affects, or has the potential to affect, that person's current position or career. Examples include promotion, disciplinary or other corrective action, transfer or reassignment, performance evaluations, decisions concerning pay, benefits, awards or training, relief and removal, separation, discharge, referral for mental health evaluations, and any other personnel action defined by law.

      ---- A significant change in duties and responsibilities inconsistent with the service member's grade may also constitute a personnel action

-- Pursuant to AFI 36-2909, Chapter 5, retaliation may also take the form of ostracism or maltreatment

--- Ostracism is wrongfully excluding a military member from social acceptance or membership in, or association with, a group of which such member was a part, or a reasonable person would conclude wanted to be a part, with the intent to do any of the following: (1) inflict emotional distress on the military member; (2) discourage reporting of a criminal offense or sexual harassment; or (3) otherwise discourage the due administration of justice concerning a criminal offense or sexual harassment

--- Maltreatment is treatment by another, that, when viewed objectively under all the circumstances, is cruel, abusive, or otherwise unnecessary for any lawful purpose, that is done with the intent to discourage reporting a criminal offense, or otherwise discourage the due administration of justice

---- If the maltreatment is done to a subordinate, the perpetrator may be punished under Article 93, UCMJ

Protected Communications

- Preemptively discouraging any person from making a protected communication is a form of retaliation

- There are two types of protected communications:

-- A lawful communication to a member of Congress or an Inspector General (IG)

-- A communication to a covered individual complaining of or disclosing a violation of law or regulation (including sexual harassment or unlawful discrimination) or reporting gross mismanagement, gross waste of funds, an abuse of authority, or a substantial and specific danger to public health or safety

--- Covered individuals include (but are not limited to): a Member of Congress, an IG, a member of a Department of Defense (DoD) audit, inspection, investigation, or law enforcement organization, any person or organization in the chain of command, a court-martial, or any other person or organization designated pursuant to regulations for such communications

Command Actions in Response to Retaliation

- Commanders, supervisors, and first sergeants, at all levels, have the authority and responsibility to ensure subordinates do not retaliate against an alleged victim or other military member who reports a criminal offense. Commanders, supervisors, and first sergeants have a duty to prevent retaliation and may be held accountable for failing to act in appropriate cases.

- Commanders, first sergeants, and supervisors should evaluate cases involving retaliation or allegations of retaliation to determine if they involve a reprisal for making a protected communication or an attempt to restrict someone from making a protected communication. If so, the allegation must be immediately referred to the Inspector General Complaints Resolution Program.

- As soon as practicable, the alleged victim, or other military member who is believed to have been retaliated against, will be informed that command is aware of the suspected act or acts or retaliation, and that the alleged offenders have been ordered to cease from engaging in any further retaliation

- The individual retaliated against will be advised to report any further acts of retaliation

References

- Articles 93 and 132, Uniform Code of Military Justice
- DAFI 90-301, *Inspector General Complaints Resolution* (4 January 2024)
- AFI 36-2909, *Air Force Professional Relationships and Conduct* (14 November 2019)

NO CONTACT ORDERS AND MILITARY PROTECTIVE ORDERS

Commanders may issue two kinds of protective orders: "no contact orders" and Military Protective Orders (MPOs). "No contact orders" can be issued by commanders, first sergeants, and other members senior in rank to the recipient of the order. They are issued to temporarily stop communications between two or more parties who are involved in a dispute that does not rise to the level of a criminal investigation or to safeguard the investigative process in a criminal matter. MPOs may only be issued by a commander (an officer on G-series orders) and are typically issued to protect a person from a subject during criminal investigations and prosecutions (usually to stop spousal, child, or intimate partner abuse).

Key Takeaways

» No contact orders and MPOs are directed towards military personnel and prohibit them from having communication or physical contact with a particular person or persons

» Only a commander may issue an MPO

» MPOs must be completed on a DD Form 2873, *Military Protective Order*

» No contact orders should be in writing with a written receipt from the recipient. A verbal no contact order should only be given in exigent circumstances and should be reduced to writing as soon as possible.

» Protective orders cannot preclude a member from contacting defense counsel and cannot preclude defense counsel from contacting potential witnesses as part of an investigation

Standard

- Reasonably necessary to ensure the safety and security of persons within a command or to protect other individuals from persons within the command

Purpose

- To protect others, safeguard the investigative process, or prevent continuing misconduct (e.g., prevent continued contact between parties accused of unprofessional relationships in violation of AFI 36-2909, *Air Force Professional Relationships and Conduct*, or fraternization in violation of Article 134, UCMJ)

  -- Most often used to protect victims of domestic violence, child abuse, or crime victims from contact with the accused pending investigation or court-martial

  -- If a victim of sexual assault requests either a no-contact order or MPO, the commander may either issue the order or deny the request. If the request is denied, the reasons must be documented and forwarded to the installation commander as the final approval authority.

Scope

- MPOs/no contact orders must be tailored to meet the specific needs of an individual victim. Limitations may include, but are not limited to:

  -- Prohibiting communication or physical interaction

  -- Refrain from contacting, harassing, or touching certain named persons

  -- Do, or refrain from doing, certain acts or activities

  -- May also include provisions to remain a specific distance away from protected persons and/or locations

- MPOs/no contact orders **MAY NOT** preclude the defense counsel of a member from contacting a potential witness as part of counsel's investigation in a pending case

Duration

- No contact orders should state the term length, be limited in duration, and may be renewed as circumstances warrant

- MPOs do not expire but may be modified or rescinded by the commander

- The subject of the MPO may request a review of that MPO from the issuing commander

Form of Protective Orders

- No contact orders should be in writing with a receipt confirmed in writing by the recipient. Verbal no contact orders should only be issued under exigent circumstances and should be put into writing as soon as possible after issuance.

- Commanders must use DD Form 2873 when issuing an MPO

Relationship of Military Protective Orders to Civilian Protective Orders

- MPOs can be issued in conjunction with, or in addition to, Civilian Protective Orders (CPOs) (a.k.a. Restraining Orders) issued by civilian courts. Commanders will advise MPO protected persons that MPOs are not enforceable by civilian authorities, so protected persons may want to pursue a CPO off-base in addition to an MPO. Civilian authorities also may not enforce no contact orders; therefore, it may be prudent to advise no contact order protected persons of the availability of a CPO.

- Civilian court issued restraining orders have the same force and effect on a military installation as they would have within the jurisdiction of the court that issued such orders

- The terms of a no contact order/MPO should not be less restrictive than the terms of a CPO. However, a commander may issue a no contact order/MPO with terms that are more restrictive than those in the CPO to which the member is subject.

- Violations of a CPO are enforceable in the civilian court that issued the order. The military may pursue administrative or disciplinary action for violations of CPOs/MPOs/ no contact orders.

- MPOs must be entered into the National Crime Information Center (NCIC) database to ensure that civilian law enforcement agencies are aware of the MPO and can notify military authorities if violations of the MPO occur off-base

Enforceability

- Violation of a no contact order or an MPO may be punishable under the UCMJ, including under Articles 90 and 92

References

- Civilian Orders of Protection: Force and Effect on Military Installations, 10 U.S.C. § 1561a(a)
- Duration of Military Protective Orders, 10 U.S.C. § 1567
- Mandatory Notification of Issuance of Military Protective Order to Civilian Law Enforcement, 10 U.S.C. § 1567a
- Articles 90 and 92, Uniform Code of Military Justice
- Rule for Courts-Martial 304
- DoDI 6400.06, *DoD Coordinated Community Response to Domestic Abuse Involving DoD Military and Certain Affiliated Personnel* (15 December 2021), incorporating through Change 2, 16 May 2023
- DoDI 6495.02, Volume 1, *Sexual Assault Prevention and Response: Program Procedures* (28 March 2013), incorporating through Change 7, 6 September 2022
- DD Form 2873, *Military Protective Order* (March 2021)
- DAFI 51-201, *Administration of Military Justice* (24 January 2024)
- AFI 36-2909, *Air Force Professional Relationships and Conduct* (14 November 2019)
- AFMAN 71-102, *Air Force Criminal Indexing* (21 July 2020)

Page Intentionally Left Blank

Chapter 8
PERSONNEL ISSUES – FAMILY AND NEXT OF KIN

FAMILY ADVOCACY PROGRAM

The mission of the Department of the Air Force (DAF) Family Advocacy Program (FAP) is to build healthy communities by implementing programs and policies for the prevention and treatment of domestic abuse, child abuse and neglect, and Problematic Sexual Behavior in Children and Youth (PSB-CY). The FAP enhances DAF readiness by promoting family and community health and resilience through prevention services, maltreatment intervention, and research and evaluation.

Key Takeaways

> » FAP helps promote healthy families, healthy communities, and resilience of service members and their families

> » Commanders must report incidents of domestic abuse to military law enforcement and FAP

> » Commanders must report any credible information or reasonable suspicion of child maltreatment to FAP

> » Command participation is critical to the success of the DAF FAP

Applicability of FAP to Air Force Reserve and Air National Guard

- Air Force Reserve Command (AFRC):

 -- The AFRC does not maintain a FAP. Reserve service members and their families, when not eligible for care in a military treatment facility (MTF), are routinely managed by civilian social services agencies in conjunction with civilian law enforcement agencies.

- Air National Guard (ANG):

 -- The DAF FAP provides services to ANG members when they are serving in a Title 10 or Title 32 status and are not in the dual status Technician Program. When a member who is suspected of domestic abuse or child maltreatment is in the Technician Program, the case will be considered by the ANG installation unit Director of Psychological Health for information and referral. Consult with the servicing Staff Judge Advocate to determine applicability.

Command Responsibilities

- Domestic Abuse: Commanders are required to refer any incident of domestic abuse reported or discovered independent of law enforcement to military law enforcement or the appropriate criminal investigative agency and to FAP. Adult victims of domestic abuse have two reporting options:

 -- *Unrestricted Reporting:* Allows the victim to report an incident using chain of command, law enforcement, or FAP for clinical intervention and pursuit of command or criminal investigation

-- *Restricted Reporting:* Allows an adult victim to report an incident to a domestic abuse victim advocate (DAVA), FAP, or any health care provider for the purpose of receiving medical care and supportive services without triggering the investigative process or notification to the victim or alleged offender's command

- Child Maltreatment: Commanders are required to report any credible information or reasonable belief of suspected child maltreatment to FAP

- Commanders direct suspected active component offenders to FAP for assessment. If the Central Registry Board (CRB) determines that an incident meets criteria for maltreatment or abuse, the commander directs the active component offender to complete recommended treatment.

- Commanders ensure no-contact orders and Military Protective Orders are issued in accordance with DAFI 51-201, *Administration of Military Justice*

FAP Structure and Key Elements

- The ultimate responsibility to implement FAP rests with the installation commander. The MTF service commander administers and monitors the installation FAP.

- Family Advocacy Committee (FAC): The FAC is an independent forum to address installation implementation of FAP. The FAC coordinates local policies, agreements and procedures with installation agencies and community partners to ensure the safety of victims of domestic abuse and child maltreatment, alleged offenders, family members and the community at large. The FAC includes multidisciplinary members of the installation community as set forth in DAFI 40-301, *Family Advocacy Program*.

- Central Registry Board (CRB): The CRB is the DAF Incident Determination Committee (IDC) for the FAP. This multidisciplinary team makes administrative determinations regarding whether an alleged domestic abuse or child maltreatment incident meets DoD criteria, requiring entry into a central registry database for substantiated incidents. Membership is determined by the FAC, as set forth in DAFI 40-301. Squadron Commanders attend and serve as voting members for incidents involving members of their squadron.

- Clinical Case Staffing (CCS): The CCS is the forum for clinical management of domestic abuse and child maltreatment cases; the CSS makes recommendations for each new or open domestic abuse or child maltreatment case. The CCS is chaired by the Family Advocacy Officer (FAO) and includes FAP staff and relevant healthcare personnel.

- Child Sexual Maltreatment Response Team (CSMRT): This multidisciplinary team is activated immediately upon receipt of a child sexual abuse allegation to manage the initial response, minimize the risk of trauma to the victim and family, and ensure coordinated decision making and case management. Membership is in accordance with DAFI 40-301.

-- The CSMRT also addresses PSB-CY, defined as behavior initiated by someone under 18 that involves sexual body parts in a manner that deviates from normative and typical behavior and is developmentally inappropriate or potentially harmful

- <u>High Risk for Violence Response Team (HRVRT)</u>: This multidisciplinary team is activated when there is a threat of immediate and serious harm to family members, unmarried intimate partners, FAP staff, or command in relation to FAP incidents. The HRVRT addresses safety issues and risk factors to develop and implement a coordinated plan to manage the risk. Membership is as set forth in DAFI 40-301.

Managing Child Safety in Foreign Locations

- At foreign locations, host nation laws apply to all civil matters; host nations generally maintain jurisdiction of cases where the welfare of a child is a risk, unless otherwise agreed upon in a Status of Forces Agreement (SOFA), Memorandum of Agreement (MOA), or other treaty or international agreement

- DAF defers to host nation authorities unless emergency conditions require immediate action to protect a child from an imminent risk of death or serious bodily harm. In such cases, the installation commander may direct separation of the child and the alleged offender for up to 48 hours. See DAFI 40-301, Attachment 5, for further guidance.

References

· DoDI 6400.01, *Family Advocacy Program* (1 May 2019)
· DoDI 6400.03, *Family Advocacy Command Assistance Team (FACAT)* (25 April 2014), incorporating Change 1, 3 April 2017
· DoDI 6400.06, *DoD Coordinated Community Response to Domestic Abuse Involving DoD Military and Certain Affiliated Personnel* (15 December 2021), incorporating through Change 2, 16 May 2023
· DoDI 6400.10, *DoD Coordinated Community Response to Problematic Sexual Behavior in Children and Youth* (30 December 2021)
· DoDM 6400.01, Vol. 1, *Family Advocacy Program (FAP): FAP Standards* (22 July 2019)
· DoDM 6400.01, Vol. 2, *Family Advocacy Program (FAP): Child Abuse and Domestic Abuse Incident Reporting System* (11 August 2016)
· DoDM 6400.01, Vol. 3, *Family Advocacy Program: Clinical Case Staff Meeting and Incident Determination Committee* (11 August 2016), incorporating Change 1, 16 July 2021
· DAFI 40-301, *Family Advocacy Program* (13 November 2020)
· DAFI 51-201, *Administration of Military Justice* (24 January 2024)

CHILD CUSTODY AND THE MILITARY

Child custody laws vary by state, but generally employ a "best interest of the child" standard. Courts will usually look at many factors in determining the child's best interests. Military members will likely need assistance in navigating court proceedings and managing substantial stress and emotions. Service members should be aware of state and federal laws that protect their custodial interests and prohibit using military service as a sole factor in deciding custody.

Key Takeaways

» If a Department of the Air Force (DAF) service member is going through a child custody dispute, they should be encouraged to seek advice from an attorney

» A court may consider the possibility of deployments in drafting alternative visitation arrangements, but military service cannot be the sole factor considered regarding custody

» DAF service members with unresolved custody disputes may suffer complications with their court proceedings if consideration is not given to military requirements such as a permanent change of station (PCS)

» Commanders must ensure all DAF service members establish a Family Care Plan choosing individuals that would in fact be able to care for children in an emergency

» At a minimum, Airmen and Guardians should support dependents as required by DAFI 36-2906, *Personal Financial Responsibility*

State Jurisdiction

- The Uniform Child Custody Jurisdiction and Enforcement Act (UCCJEA), limits jurisdiction in child custody cases to the child's home state. Forty-nine states and the District of Columbia, Guam, Marianas Islands, and the U.S. Virgin Islands have adopted the UCCJEA; while Massachusetts, Puerto Rico, and American Samoa have not. Courts of any UCCJEA state will enforce the child custody rulings of courts in other UCCJEA states.

  -- The "home state" is defined as the state where the child has lived for six consecutive months (or since birth if the child is less than six months old) prior to the commencement of the custody proceedings

  -- If state jurisdiction cannot be established as described, then it can be established by (1) "significant connections" with the child and one parent; **AND** (2) "substantial evidence concerning the child's care, protection, training, and personal relationships." If more than one qualifies, then the states must agree which will assume jurisdiction.

-- <u>Continuing Exclusive Jurisdiction</u>: The state that makes the initial custody determination maintains jurisdiction for modifications unless the court determines that the child, the child's parents, and any person acting as a parent no longer have a significant connection with the state or until any state determines that the child, the child's parents, and any person acting as a parent no longer reside in the decree-granting state

-- **Note:** A child's relocation for the duration of a parent's deployment could result in a change of jurisdiction

-- <u>Emergency Jurisdiction</u>: A court in a state other than the home state may assume temporary jurisdiction when a child is (1) present in the state; and (2) has been abandoned or subjected to or threatened with mistreatment or abuse

Best Interest of the Child Standard

- Courts will usually make custody decisions based primarily on the child's best interest. Factors the court may consider include, but are not limited to:

-- Child's age, gender, mental/emotional/social development, comfort in their home, school and community, degree of emotional attachment of the child to each parent, or child's preference (for children over ages 12–14 in most states)

-- Physical, emotional, social, and financial stability of each parent, history of domestic violence or child abuse, involvement with the child and willingness to cooperate with the other parent

Deployment as a Factor in Determining Custody Arrangements

- The effects of deployment are often considered by the courts as one of the factors in determining the best interest of the child. Several laws were enacted to help ensure custody is not determined solely based on the issue of deployment or the threat of deployment. For instance:

-- Nearly every state has laws addressing custody and visitation of deployed parents, including 16 states that have adopted the Uniform Deployed Parents' Custody and Visitation Act (UDPCVA). The key aspects of the UDPCVA are that it forbids consideration of military service as a negative factor in determining custody, and that a "military absence" of a military parent won't be used to deprive that state of custody jurisdiction.

-- The UDPCVA also allows delegation of a deploying parent to petition for delegation of parenting time to a third-party adult with whom the child has a close relationship (such as a stepparent or grandparent) rather than to the non-deploying parent. Some non-UDPCVA states have laws with similar provisions (e.g., Arizona, Illinois, and South Carolina).

-- The Servicemembers Civil Relief Act (SCRA) also limits a state court's consideration of a member's deployment as the sole factor in determining the best interest of the child

-- Despite these prohibitions, parents with primary custody should consult with a lawyer in developing their Family Care Plan prior to a deployment. In some states, courts have found that long absences due to deployments are a "change in circumstances" warranting a change in primary custody.

Mobility as a Factor in Determining Custody Arrangements

- The impact that a change to a child's environment (e.g., frequent PCS moves) has on a child's well-being is also likely to be considered by individual judges and guardians ad litem in determining the best interest of the child. While states are prohibited from discriminating against service members in making custody decisions, service members should be aware of this and make efforts to dispel myths judges may have about military service and highlight the benefits.

- While PCSs can disrupt a child's life, it also gives them unique and profound opportunities to live and experience different cultures and learn about the world around them. Each child handles the stressors of military life differently and the individual needs of the child need to be considered.

- Commanders should encourage members to take advantage of the many resources available to support military families, including mental health services, child development centers, outdoor recreation and recreational sports leagues, religious services, Military and Family Readiness Centers, military treatment facilities, and other base activities. Service members should highlight these resources to their counsel and judges to ensure these are considered when making custody decisions.

-- DoDI 1342.19_AFI 36-2908, *Family Care Plans*, requires certain service members to plan for contingencies in the care and support of dependent family members

-- The following service members, including civilian employees who are members of the Department of Defense (DoD) Civilian Expeditionary Workforce, shall develop and submit a family care plan on an DAF Form 357, *Family Care Certification*

--- Single parents and service members who have primary responsibility for dependent family members

--- Dual-service member couples with dependents and married service members with custody or joint custody of a child whose non-custodial biological or adoptive parent is not the current spouse of the service member, or who otherwise bear sole responsibility for the care of children under the age of 19, or for others unable to care for themselves in the absence of the member

-- Service members, particularly those with primary custody, should consult with their attorney to consider what impact their Family Care Plan could have on their custody arrangement

Child Support

- Child support issues also fall under state law and are determined by state courts

  -- Military members who are going through a divorce or custody determination should document the support believed to be provided

  -- In accordance with DAFI 36-2906, *Personal Financial Responsibility*, military members will provide financial support to spouses, children or other relative for which the member receives allowances for support. Military members must comply with a written support agreement or court order to provide support, but absent that, commanders will use a pro-rata share equation to calculate the support required for a service member's dependents.

  -- DAFI 36-2906, Figure 4.1, contains the pro-rata share formula below for determining the financial support required of service members. See DAFI 36-2906 for more details on how to complete this calculation and to see various exceptions.

References

· Servicemembers Civil Relief Act, 50 U.S.C. §§ 3901 *et seq.*

· Uniform Child Custody Jurisdiction and Enforcement Act (citation varies by state)

· Uniform Deployed Parents' Custody and Visitation Act (citation varies by state)

· DoDI 1342.19_AFI 36-2908, *Family Care Plans* (10 March 2023)

· DAFI 36-2906, *Personal Financial Responsibility* (23 August 2023)

· DAF Form 357, *Family Care Certification* (20 June 2023)

FAMILY MEMBER MISCONDUCT

Installation commanders are often called upon to resolve difficult problems arising from family member misconduct. The installation commander is responsible for maintaining good order and discipline and protecting Department of the Air Force (DAF) resources. However, the installation commander may have little authority when it comes to punishing civilians. Nonetheless, there are certain actions available to address family member misconduct.

Key Takeaways

» Installation commanders have several options for allegations of family member misconduct, up to and including barment

» Where criminal actions occurring on a military installation will be prosecuted depends on whether the base jurisdiction is exclusive federal, concurrent, or proprietary

» Early return of dependents from a foreign country based on family member misconduct may be authorized under certain conditions

Commander Responsibilities and Options

- <u>Administrative Actions</u>:

  -- *Suspend or revoke privileges*

    --- Driving suspension may be mandatory in certain circumstances (e.g., drunk driving)

    --- Base Exchange (BX)/Commissary

    --- Morale, Welfare, and Recreation (MWR) facilities

  -- *Terminate military family housing*

    --- Requires 30-days written notice

    --- Department of the Air Force pays for the move, but partial dislocation allowance is not payable

  -- *Barment*

    --- 18 U.S.C. § 1382 makes it a crime to enter the installation after being barred

    --- Barment should be in writing, setting forth the specific reasons for barment

    --- Barment may be permanent or for a period of time

    --- Barment must still provide access to medical treatment if authorized and available

- Criminal Actions:

  -- Where criminal actions occurring on a military installation will be prosecuted depends upon the legislative jurisdiction of the base

  -- If the base is under exclusive federal jurisdiction, family members may be prosecuted in federal magistrate court. In most cases, at least one of the attorneys in the legal office serves as a Special Assistant United States Attorney (SAUSA) and handles these prosecutions in coordination with the local United States Attorney's Office.

  -- If the base has concurrent jurisdiction, either federal court or state court may be the proper forum for prosecuting family members. Consult with your servicing Staff Judge Advocate (SJA) for guidance on prosecuting civilians for offenses committed on a military installation.

  -- If the base has only proprietary jurisdiction, which means that the state retains law enforcement duties, the state has the authority to prosecute family member misconduct (involving only state crimes) occurring on the installation. Any family member misconduct should be referred to the local authorities for prosecution.

  -- Some installations have established programs for handling juvenile misconduct. These programs go by a variety of names such as Juvenile Correction Board, Youth Misconduct Board, Juvenile Intervention Council, etc. These boards consider cases of misconduct committed by juveniles (unmarried non-military persons under the age of 18 years old) and recommend to the installation commander how to handle the matter. Although participation in the program is voluntary, juveniles who choose not to participate may be subject to other actions to include, but not limited to, barment from the base.

- Early Return of Dependents (OCONUS):

  -- Table 5-20 of the Joint Travel Regulation (JTR) specifies the eligibility and allowances for the early return of dependents when a command sponsored dependent of a member stationed in a foreign country becomes involved in an incident that is any of the following:

    --- Embarrassing to the United States

    --- Prejudicial to the command's order, morale, and discipline

    --- Facilitates the conditions in which the dependent's safety can no longer be ensured due to adverse public feeling in the area or due to force protection and antiterrorism considerations

    --- Requires the dependent to register as a sex offender under the laws of any jurisdiction

References

· Entering Military, Naval, or Coast Guard Property, 18 U.S.C. § 1382

· Joint Travel Regulations (JTR) – Uniformed Service Members and DoD Civilian Employees (1 December 2023)

· DoDM-5200.08_Volume 3_AFMAN 31-101_Volume 3, *Installation Perimeter Access Control* (27 February 2020)

· DAFI 36-3026, Volume 1, *Identification Cards for Members of the Uniformed Services, Their Eligible Family Members, and Other Eligible Personnel* (1 June 2023), including DAFGM202401, 16 January 2024

· AFI 32-6000, *Housing Management* (18 March 2020), including DAFGM2023-01, 12 June 2023

· AFI 51-206, *Use of Magistrate Judges for Trial of Misdemeanors Committed by Civilians* (31 August 2018)

ON-BASE FAMILY HOUSING

Congress established the Military Housing Privatization Initiative (MHPI) in 1996 with the goal to improve the quality of life for service members. The Fiscal Year 2020 National Defense Authorization Act (NDAA) created the MHPI Tenant Bill of Rights. These 18 rights are codified in 10 United States Code (U.S.C.) § 2890, and military commanders should generally be aware of them.

Key Takeaways

» The Tenant Bill of Rights was established to ensure safe, quality, and well-maintained living conditions and communities as well as fair treatment of tenants by privatized housing companies

» The Formal Dispute Resolution process provides tenants a means for resolving disputes with privatized housing landlords. The installation commander serves as the deciding official.

» Military tenants and their dependents are entitled to the assistance of a legal assistance attorney for privatized housing issues

---

Tenant Bill of Rights

- The goal of the MHPI Tenant Bill of Rights is to ensure safe, quality, and well-maintained living conditions and communities as well as fair treatment from private partners (privatized housing companies) that operate and maintain privatized housing. The Tenant Bill of Rights contains eighteen rights, such as the right to reside in a housing unit with working fixtures, appliances, and utilities, and the right to a written lease with clearly defined rental terms.

Formal Dispute Resolution Process

- The MHPI Tenant Bill of Rights provides for a standardized Formal Dispute Resolution Process for active duty, activated Guard/Reserve, and their dependents who are on the lease, to resolve disputes with privatized housing companies

  -- In order to utilize the Formal Dispute Resolution Process, tenants must first attempt to resolve the dispute through the Informal Dispute Resolution Process, working directly with the privatized housing company

  -- If the Informal Dispute Resolution Process is unsuccessful, the tenant may elect to submit a written request for Formal Dispute Resolution in accordance with the lease. The Military Housing Office (MHO) receives all Formal Disputes. The installation commander serves as the "deciding authority" and must appoint a neutral investigator to investigate the tenant's claims.

-- Under certain circumstances, tenants can request that their rent payments be held in a separate account (known as "Rent Segregation") pending resolution of the dispute. The MHO makes this determination.

-- Tenants are not required to utilize this process before seeking remedies through civilian courts

Termination from Privatized Housing

- Tenancy may be terminated by the privatized housing company if a member/tenant does not abide by the terms of the signed tenant lease

- Military members and their dependents are entitled to legal assistance from the base legal office regarding issues related to privatized housing

References

· Rights and Responsibilities of Tenants of Housing Units, 10 U.S.C. § 2890

· AFI 32-6000, *Housing Management* (18 March 2020), including DAFGM2023-01, 12 June 2023

· SAF/IEI Formal Dispute Resolution Implementation Guidance, 29 June 2021

AIR FORCE CHILD AND YOUTH PROGRAM

Installation commanders are required to mandate appropriate facilities, funding, and manpower to operate the child and youth programs (CYPs) on their installation. The goal of the CYP is to assist Department of Defense (DoD) personnel in balancing duty and family life obligations by providing family services for youth from birth to 18 years of age. These services take the form of child development centers (CDC), family childcare (FCC) homes, school age care (SAC), and youth programs.

Key Takeaways

» AF/A1 and the AF Services Center manage the Department of the Air Force (DAF) Child and Youth Program enterprise including child development center, school age care, and family child care homes

» Airmen and Guardians have a variety of childcare options available on the installation that meet their family's needs, duty location, and best fit for their child(ren)

» When waiting times exceed needs or families prefer off-installation care, the contracted Child Care Aware of America can arrange placement and fee assistance for community resources

» Unlicensed on-base childcare providers that routinely provide more than ten (10) hours of childcare will be investigated by the Child and Youth Program and Force Support Squadron Commander or designee

---

Eligibility

- Eligibility for CYP services is contingent on the status of the sponsor. Eligible patrons are outlined in AFI 34-144, *Child and Youth Programs*, and DAFI 34-101, *Air Force Morale, Welfare, and Recreation (MWR) Programs and Use Eligibility*. Generally, eligible children and youth have sponsors who are:

  -- Active duty military and Coast Guard members;

  -- DoD civilian employees;

  -- Air National Guard or Reserve members on active duty orders or inactive duty training status;

  -- Surviving spouses, and *loco parentis* guardians of youths that would otherwise be eligible;

  -- Combat related wounded warriors in an active duty status;

  -- Gold Star spouses of military members who die from a combat-related incident;

  -- DoD contractors with specific contractual eligibility; and

  -- In the case of unmarried, legally separated parents with joint custody or divorced parents with joint custody, children or youth are eligible for childcare only when they reside with the eligible sponsor at least 25% of the time in a month.

- Children and Youth Program services may be available to those who do not qualify for the above categories on a case-by-case and space-available basis

  -- Space-available patrons must make way when space is needed for the above listed groups

- Community based fee assistance programs are available to families who do not have access to installation programs. For example, assistance is available through the Child Care Aware of America website at https://www.childcareaware.org.

Child Development Programs

- CDC: Provides care to children from six weeks to five years of age

- SAC: Provides care to children and youth from five to 12 years of age

- FCC: Provides care to children and youth from two weeks to 12 years of age. Childcare is provided in certified homes located on or off the installation. FCC likewise provides nontraditional childcare needs (e.g., nights, weekends, unique childcare).

  -- All on-installation childcare is subject to regulation by AFI 34-144 and must be certified by the installation Mission Support Group Commander

  -- Uncertified, regular (more than 10 hours per week), on-installation childcare will be investigated by the installation FCC Coordinator, accompanied by the Force Support Squadron (FSS) Commander or designee. An unannounced visit will be made to individuals living in government-owned housing or privatized housing. The individual will be provided a written request to complete the certification procedures and cease providing care until they become certified. The Security Forces Squadron (SFS) will be contacted if there are suspected violations of law.

Certification of FCC Homes

- Not issued until the applicant provides evidence required for liability insurance

- Valid for no more than 12 months

- Must comply with most restrictive of state, local and/or Department of the Air Force requirements

- Inspected for fire, safety, first aid, liability insurance, and criminal background checks

- Random, unannounced visits by FSS personnel occur on a monthly basis

References

- DoDI 6060.02, *Child Development Programs (CDPs)* (5 August 2014), incorporating through Change 2, 1 September 2020
- DAFI 34-101, *Air Force Morale, Welfare, and Recreation (MWR) Programs and Use Eligibility* (7 March 2022)
- AFI 34-144, *Child and Youth Programs* (2 July 2019)

SUMMARY COURT OFFICER

For deceased Department of the Air Force (DAF) active duty members and other entitled individuals, the DAF collects, safeguards, and promptly disposes of their personal property and effects. The installation commander appoints a summary court officer (SCO) to perform these duties in accordance with DAFI 34-160, *Mortuary Affairs Program*. For deceased Department of Defense (DoD) civilians, see AFI 36-809, *Civilian Survivor Assistance*.

Key Takeaways

» The SCO works with the Mortuary Officer and the family member that the decedent named to direct disposition of the personal property and effects and arrange shipment

» If the decedent did not name a Person Authorized to Direct Disposition (PADD), AFI 34-501 provides a default list of family members to fulfill this role

» SCOs must use good judgment and tact as they may have to work with off-base landlords or decide what personal effects/property may cause undue grief to survivors

» If DAF service member is missing in action for at least 30 days, the installation commander will appoint a SCO to inventory and take possession of property/effects

Definitions

- Personal Effects: Any personal item, organizational clothing, or equipment physically located on or with the remains. Some examples of personal effects include eyeglasses, jewelry, wallets, insignia, and clothing.

- Personal Property: All of the other personal possessions of the decedent. Some examples of personal property include household goods, mail, pets, personal papers, and privately owned vehicles.

Prioritized List of Recipients to Receive Personal Property and Personal Effects

- Surviving spouse or legal representative

- Children in order of age. If the recipient is a minor, forward the property as instructed by the minor's surviving parent, guardian, or adopting parent.

- Parents in order of age. If parents are divorced or legally separated and the divorce or legal separation occurred while the deceased was a minor, then the recipient is the custodial parent. In a shared custody arrangement, the custodial parent is the parent who had physical custody at the time the deceased reached the age of majority or entered the military.

- Siblings in order of age

- Next of kin of the deceased. If there are several persons equal in relationship to the deceased, the oldest is the recipient.

- A beneficiary named in the will of the deceased. Where there are several primary beneficiaries, the oldest is the recipient.

Handling and Disposing of Personal Effects

- The Mortuary Officer (MO) must inventory and document all personal effects using DD Form 1076, *Record of Personal Effects of Believed to Be (BTB) Deceased.* The inventory sheet must accompany the personal effects at all times and a copy should be maintained in the case file. The MO must also clean the personal effects and lock them in a secure area.

- SCO collects and returns all issued organizational clothing and individual equipment to the member's squadron commander

- Once the MO ensures the authorized recipient has been officially notified of the death, the MO asks the authorized recipient to provide instructions for disposing of the personal effects

- MO may only destroy personal effects after receiving written authorization by the authorized recipient and any such destruction must be documented on the DD Form 1076. Mortuary personnel do not have the authority to arbitrarily destroy or discard personal effects.

Handling and Disposing of Personal Property

- SCO obtains property disposition instructions and the name, telephone number, and address of the authorized recipient ("Person Authorized to Direct Disposition (PADD)") from the MO

- SCO corresponds with the authorized recipient at least once a week about progress in resolving property matters and annotates all correspondence in a log of events

- SCO alerts organizations on base to make a claim for any unpaid debts. Alternatively, the SCO may accomplish the base-wide notification via email. In all cases, the SCO should coordinate with the installation Public Affairs office for message release.

- SCO inventories all property on DD Form 1076

  -- Promptly gathers the uniform and clothes needed for burial and gives to the MO

  -- Collects organizational clothing and equipment for turn in

  -- Removes any questionable items and determines the disposition of this property based on criteria set forth in AFI 34-160, para. 13.15.4. Generally speaking, questionable items are those with no intrinsic or sentimental value, unfit to forward to the authorized recipient, or inflammatory items which could cause further grief.

  -- Coordinates with the Travel Management Office (TMO) to arrange shipment and/or storage of household goods and personal property

    --- Even if TMO or a Household Goods (HHG) contractor packs/ships the personal property, the SCO is responsible for the items to be shipped in an orderly and respectful manner and properly received by the intended recipient

- The servicing legal office provides guidance to the SCO on disposition of personal property and reviews the summary court file for legal sufficiency

  -- Generally, SCOs have no authority to inspect and remove the decedent's property from off-base quarters, but with the concurrence of both the landlord and a Power of Attorney from the PADD, SCO may settle security deposit claims and arrange for the final transportation of personal effects and personal property

For Missing, Detained, and Captured Persons

- The MO secures and holds the property for at least 30 days or until the member's status is changed from missing to detained, captured, or the member returns

- If, after 30 days, (1) the missing member's status is changed to detained or captured, or (2) there is no change in status, the installation commander will appoint a SCO to secure, inventory, and give or ship the property to the authorized recipient

- If the missing member returns, the property is released to the member

- SCO secures, inventories, and disposes of the property to those authorized to receive it in the event of the member's death

References

· Disposition of Unclaimed Property, 10 U.S.C. § 2575
· Disposition of Effects of Deceased Persons by Summary Court-martial, 10 U.S.C. § 9712
· DoDD 1300.22, *Mortuary Affairs Policy* (30 October 2015), incorporating Change 2, 2 September 2021
· DAFI 34-160, *Mortuary Affairs Program* (3 March 2022)
· DAFI 36-167, *Civilian Survivor Assistance* (18 April 2023)
· DAFI 36-3002, *Casualty Services* (4 February 2021)
· DD Form 1076, *Record of Personal Effects of Believed to Be Deceased* (August 2015)

Chapter 9
LEGAL ASSISTANCE

OVERVIEW OF LEGAL ASSISTANCE PROGRAM

The armed services may, in accordance with 10 U.S.C. § 1044, provide legal assistance to eligible beneficiaries in connection with their personal civil legal affairs. Legal assistance is governed by AFI 51-304, *Legal Assistance, Notary, Preventive Law, and Tax Programs*. The legal assistance program supports and sustains command readiness and enhances resiliency for eligible clients.

Key Takeaways

» Legal assistance can only be provided to eligible clients; see below for more details, but primarily active duty service members, Air Reserve component members (in certain statuses), retirees, and dependents

» Legal assistance is provided for personal civil matters; not matters for third parties, commercial enterprises, criminal matters, or other matters excepted below

» The legal assistance program gives priority to solving mobilization and deployment related legal issues—that is, a member's legal issues that could negatively affect command readiness

» Legal assistance can be provided in a large variety of legal areas; however, certain clients will still have to be referred to more specialized offices, another government agency, or a private attorney for assistance

Eligibility for Legal Assistance

- The following individuals are generally eligible for legal assistance services (see AFI 51-304 for more details):

-- Active duty members, including reservists and guardsmen on federal active duty under Title 10 of the U.S. Code, and their dependents who are entitled to an ID card

-- Air Reserve component members performing Active Guard/Reserve (AGR) tours

-- Members of reserve components (not otherwise covered) under a call or order to active duty for more than 30 days. The period of eligibility equals to twice the length of the order to active duty. Dependents entitled to an ID card are eligible during the same time period.

-- Members entitled to retired or retainer pay or equivalent pay and former members of reserve components entitled to retired pay under 10 U.S.C. § 12731. This includes members receiving retired pay as a result of retirement due to permanent disability or placement on the temporary disability retired list. **Note:** "Gray Area" reservists are not entitled to legal assistance (e.g., those who have retired, but are not yet entitled to retired pay under 10 U.S.C. § 12731).

-- Civilian employees stationed outside of the United States and its territories, and their family members who both reside with them outside of the continental United States (OCONUS)

-- Reservists and National Guard members not in Title 10 status, but subject to federal mobilization in an inactive status, are eligible for only mobility/deployment related legal assistance

-- DoD civilian employees deploying to or in a theater of operations for contingencies or emergencies shall be furnished assistance with wills and powers of attorney

-- Foreign military personnel assigned to the United States under official orders for purposes of combined missions with the United States or for training programs sponsored by the United States. Assistance will be limited to matters involving the interpretation or application of United States domestic law pertinent to the person's relocation and requirement to be present in the United States (e.g., landlord-tenant, consumer affairs, driver's license, customs, tax relief, and similar assistance).

-- Estate representatives for members who die on active duty or as a result of an injury or disability that resulted in retirement from active duty

- Staff Judge Advocates (SJAs) may authorize legal assistance to persons not specifically identified above as an eligible beneficiary in unique situations where a military obligation is relevant to the legal problem

Legal Assistance Services Provided

- The following legal topics may be addressed as resources and expertise permit:

  -- Wills, living wills, powers of attorney, and notary services

  -- Family law, to include adoptions, dependent care issues, child custody, domestic relations, and financial responsibilities

  -- Servicemembers Civil Relief Act (SCRA) and Uniformed Services Employment and Reemployment Rights Act (USERRA)

  -- Consumer law, to include bankruptcy, consumer fraud, identity theft, illegal lending practices, and vehicle leases

  -- Immigration/naturalization law

  -- Tax assistance

  -- Assistance to victims of crime, including domestic violence victims

  -- Landlord-tenant and lease issues, including privatized housing

  -- Exceptional Family Member (EFM) matters, such as special education disputes between a service member and a local school district

  -- Other issues deemed connected with personal, civil legal affairs

- Referral: Due to the scope and limitations of the program, as well as the particular needs of the client, the legal office may refer clients to other resources, such as a civilian attorney (through the local bar referral service), Area Defense Counsel (ADC), Victim's Counsel (VC), chaplain, equal opportunity (EO) counselor, military personnel flight, family advocacy, the family support center, or available free or "pro bono" legal services

Preventive Law

- Each base will have a preventive law program, with a focus on educating members on preparing for mobilization and deployment, seeking timely legal advice, the consequences of signing legal documents, and maintaining vigilance to identify and avoid legal/financial scams

- Education programs are designed to allow Airmen and Guardians to focus on mission requirements and reduce the time and resources needed to correct legal problems that occur

Matters Specifically Outside the Scope of the Program

- The following are generally outside the scope of legal assistance:

    -- Issues involving personal business or commercial enterprises. **Exception:** legal assistance may be provided to service members business owners if related to the SCRA.

    -- Criminal issues. **Exception:** advice to the victim of a crime.

    -- Official matters in which the Air Force or Space Force has an interest or is involved in the investigation or final resolution (e.g., reports of survey)

    -- Legal issues or concerns raised on behalf of third parties, even if the third party is eligible for legal assistance

    -- Issues involving private organizations

    -- Representation in a civilian court or administrative proceeding. **Exception:** In certain circumstances under AFI 51-304's Expanded Legal Assistance Program (ELAP) and for EFM clients, with SJA concurrence, represent clients at Individualized Education Program (IEP) or other administrative meetings.

    -- Drafting or reviewing for legal sufficiency real estate sales or closing documents, separation agreements, divorce decrees, transfer on death deeds, inter vivos trusts, and other types of pleadings prepared for off-base court proceedings unless the SJA determines an individual attorney within the office has the expertise to do so

Attorney-Client Relationship

- Air Force attorneys establish an attorney-client relationship with their legal assistance clients and, as such, any information or documents received from or relating to a client are considered privileged and confidential

- Privileged information may be released only with the client's express permission, pursuant to a court order, or as otherwise permitted by the Air Force Rules of Professional Responsibility

References

· Legal Assistance, 10 U.S.C. § 1044

· Age and Service Requirements, 10 U.S.C. § 12731

· Servicemembers Civil Relief Act, 50 U.S.C. §§ 3901 *et seq.*

· DoDI 1350.04, *Legal Assistance Matters*, 3 February 2022

· AFI 51-304, *Legal Assistance, Notary, Preventive Law, and Tax Programs* (22 August 2018)

· ANGI 51-504, *Air National Guard Legal Assistance Program* (20 November 2014), certified current 25 February 2019

NOTARIES

Many important documents are required by law to be notarized. Notarization demonstrates that a person with notary authority—that is, a notary public—confirmed the identity of the person signing the document and witnessed the signature. It can also confirm, if required, that the person made an oath as part of executing the document. Notary services are available to eligible service members, dependents, and some civilian employees, under Title 10 of the U.S. Code, as part of the military legal assistance program.

Key Takeaways

» Notarization demonstrates that a person with notary authority confirmed the identity of the person signing the document and witnessed the signature

» Members of the armed forces, other persons eligible for legal assistance, and persons serving with the armed forces outside of the United States are eligible for notary services

» Department of the Air Force members with notary authority include judge advocates, civilian attorneys, and enlisted paralegals. Others may be appointed as notaries at locations where no judge advocate is assigned.

Eligibility for Notary Service

- Personnel eligible for military notary services are:

    -- Members of any of the uniformed services;

    -- Other persons eligible for legal assistance under 10 U.S.C. § 1044 or other regulations of the Department of Defense (DoD), to include AFI 51-304, *Legal Assistance, Notary, Preventive Law, and Tax Programs*;

    -- Persons serving with, employed by, or accompanying the armed forces outside the United States, Puerto Rico, Guam, and the Virgin Islands; and

    -- Other persons subject to the Uniform Code of Military Justice (UCMJ) outside the United States.

Persons with Notary Authority

- Under 10 U.S.C. § 1044a, state laws, AFI 51-304, and ANGI 51-504, *Air National Guard Legal Assistance Program*, the following individuals have the general powers of a notary public and of a consul of the United States in the performance of all notary acts:

    -- All judge advocates, including reserve judge advocates when not in a duty status

    -- All civilian attorneys serving as legal assistance attorneys

    -- Air National Guard (ANG) judge advocates and paralegals while performing duty under Title 10 or Title 32 or if qualified as a notary public under state law

-- ANG judge advocates and paralegals, even when not in a duty status, have the general powers of a notary public in the performance of all notarial acts

-- ANG commanders may name civilian employees to serve as notaries as part of their official duties provided they qualify under the laws of the state where they will serve

-- Other civilian employees (e.g., paralegals) must qualify as a notary under state laws

-- All civilian paralegals serving at a military legal assistance office if supervised by a military legal assistance counsel. A military legal assistance counsel is a judge advocate or a civilian attorney serving as a legal assistance officer.

-- Enlisted paralegals on active duty or performing inactive duty training

-- Commissioned officers or master sergeant and above stationed at geographically separated units (GSUs) or remote locations where no judge advocate or paralegal notary is assigned, and who have been designated in writing by the GSU's servicing general court-martial convening authority's Staff Judge Advocate (SJA) and received proper training

References

· Authority to Act as Notary, 10 U.S.C. §§ 1044, 1044a
· DoDI 1350.04, *Legal Assistance Matters*, 3 February 2022
· AFI 51-304, *Legal Assistance, Notary, Preventive Law, and Tax Programs* (22 August 2018)
· ANGI 51-504, *Air National Guard Legal Assistance Program* (20 November 2014), certified current 25 February 2019

WILLS AND POWERS OF ATTORNEY

Wills and powers of attorney (POAs) are useful legal documents for members to manage their personal and financial affairs. A will is an instrument by which a person, known as a "testator," provides for the disposition of his/her property after death. A POA is a document by which a person (the "principal") authorizes another person (the "agent") to conduct specific acts on their behalf. Commanders should emphasize to their Airmen and Guardians the importance of preparing wills and POAs, especially prior to deployment.

Key Takeaways

» Wills are an important tool to ensure loved ones are properly cared for after death; they can be used to distribute property to specific people and name a guardian for minor children

» POAs enable a person to name an agent to act on their behalf. While highly useful, POAs also can be abused—choose trustworthy agents, and tailor the POA to the specific situation/needs.

Wills

- Though it must be a free and voluntary act by the service member, **ALL commanders** should encourage their Department of the Air Force service members to make a will. Even if a testator has little property, settling affairs with a will ensures the testator's wishes are honored after death and is often easier for the family.

- A will is particularly important for the following:

  -- Personnel with minor children. The court will generally follow the designation of a guardian for the children in a will, which often alleviates confusion and family disputes about the parents' intention concerning the care of their child. Personnel with special needs children may require advanced estate planning advice to ensure the children are properly cared for and that any inheritance received does not disqualify or remove the special needs child from government programs.

  -- Personnel with business interests or high-value estates. On a case-by-case basis, it may be advisable for members with business interests or substantial estates to seek outside counsel for a more comprehensive estate plan.

  -- Personnel in a subsequent marriage or with blended families where either spouse comes to the marriage with children from a prior relationship

  -- Personnel who are divorced or widowed

- State law dictates the requirements for making a valid will. These laws vary widely from state to state. For this reason, service members should seek the services of the base legal office and avoid "do-it-yourself" will programs.

- If a service member dies without a will, his/her property will be distributed according to state law, and the result can sometimes be unexpected

- A will remains in effect until changed or revoked by the testator

- Certain life events may impact provisions in a testator's will, such that it would be advisable to create a new will. A testator should review his will periodically and consider updating it, especially with these changed circumstances:

  -- The birth, death, or change in circumstances of any person affected by the will;

  -- The marriage or divorce of the testator; or

  -- A substantial change in the testator's estate.

Powers of Attorney (POA)

- A POA is a document that enables a person (the principal) to grant someone else the authority to act as their legal agent, or "attorney-in-fact." These documents are available at all base legal offices and can be particularly important for mobilizing personnel.

- Third parties (e.g., banks and businesses) may be unwilling to accept the authority granted within a POA. Additionally, granting an agent overly broad powers increases the risk that the agent will abuse the authority given to them in the document. Therefore, to minimize the risks of rejection and abuse, it is usually best to choose a trustworthy agent and tailor the POA to the given situation and/or the specific act and/or location (e.g., bank) required of the agent. Some financial institutions may require use of their specific POA forms.

- Although copies are usually acceptable, it is best to provide the agent with the original, executed POA in order for them to perform the authorized acts

- To revoke a POA before its expiration, personnel may retrieve the original document (and any known copies) and destroy it or execute a revocation of a POA and give a copy to any person that might deal with the person who has the original POA

- There are several types of POAs, as described below:

- General POA:

  -- Gives comprehensive authority over virtually all legal and some non-legal affairs. Basically, the attorney-in-fact can do anything the principal could do.

  -- Because the authority granted is so expansive, this type of POA should only be used if a special POA will not suffice and if the agent is completely trustworthy. A person with a general POA could cause serious financial or legal problems for the principal because of the vast and comprehensive authority given.

  -- Many banks and realtors will not accept a general POA for the purchase or sale of real estate and instead require a special POA containing the legal description of the property and the actions authorized

- Special POA: Grants limited authority to accomplish specific transactions, such as buying/selling real estate or a car, usually for a limited time period

- Durable POA:

  -- Remains effective, notwithstanding the principal's incapacity. A general or special POA may be made "durable" with appropriate language.

  -- Allows the agent to make decisions and manage the affairs for the incapacitated person for the duration of their incapacity

- Springing POA: Becomes effective only upon the occurrence of a specified event, such as the principal's incapacity. This will require proof that the specified event has occurred (e.g., doctor's opinion of incapacity) in order for the agent to be able to use the POA.

- Healthcare POA:

  -- Gives the agent the authority to make decisions for medical purposes, including a decision regarding terminating or limiting medical care in appropriate cases

  -- The Healthcare POA is sometimes found in an Advance Healthcare (or Medical) Directive, which might also include a Living Will (in which the principal would express their end-of-life treatment preferences, should they become terminally ill)

- 10 U.S.C. §§ 1044b–d respectively, provide for the execution of military POAs, military advance medical directives, including "living wills," and military testamentary instruments or "wills." These documents, though executed by military legal assistance practitioners, will be given the same legal effect as documents prepared and executed in accordance with the laws of the state concerned.

  -- Military living wills are not enforceable in states that do not recognize living wills

References

· Military Powers of Attorney, 10 U.S.C. § 1044b

· Advance Medical Directives of Members and Dependents, 10 U.S.C. § 1044c

· Military Testamentary Instruments, 10 U.S.C. § 1044d

· DoDI 1350.04, *Legal Assistance Matters*, 3 February 2022

· AFI 51-304, *Legal Assistance, Notary, Preventive Law, and Tax Programs* (22 August 2018)

· ANGI 51-504, *Air National Guard Legal Assistance Program* (20 November 2014), certified current 25 February 2019

TAX ASSISTANCE PROGRAM

Tax Assistance programs are command programs designed to provide free tax assistance and filing services to eligible beneficiaries. When resourced and managed properly, an active and well-publicized program can enhance morale and help beneficiaries address some of the unique income tax aspects associated with a military lifestyle. The size and scope of each program may vary from base to base, depending on mission requirements, geographical location, availability of resources, and the unique needs of the local community.

Key Takeaways

» Installation commanders, in consultation with the Staff Judge Advocate (SJA), have discretion to decide whether and what type of tax assistance program to host

» Options for tax assistance programs include traditional full-service, self-service kiosks, or referrals to other programs

» Commanders consider mission requirements, availability of resources, impact on morale, and other factors in determining what type of program to host

Tax Assistance Programs

- The installation commander, in consultation with the SJA, has the flexibility to decide, based on the needs of the installation and available resources, which of the following program(s) is best for eligible beneficiaries. If circumstances warrant, the commander may also elect to not have an installation tax program.

- Full-Service Tax Assistance Program:

-- Full-service programs are supervised by the SJA and staffed by legal office personnel, as well as volunteers, under the Internal Revenue Service (IRS) Volunteer Income Tax Assistance (VITA) program

-- Tax assistance personnel are trained by and use the IRS' electronic filing resources

-- VITA programs are separate and distinct from the legal assistance program; attorney-client privilege does not apply to the preparation of income tax returns

- Free Tax Preparation Services:

-- Without endorsing any non-federal service or entity, the base legal office will make available a listing of off-base and electronic tax assistance options, such as Military One Source's free MilTax online preparation and filing service (https://www. militaryonesource.mil/financial-legal/taxes/miltax-military-tax-services/) and the IRS Free File Alliance, which is a group of private-sector tax preparation companies that provide free online tax preparation and electronic filing only through the IRS.gov website (https://www.irs.gov/e-file-providers/about-the-free-file-alliance)

-- Service members using these free tax services can still utilize base legal assistance services should they have any specific tax questions or issues. Additionally, Military One Source MilTax provides free tax consultation from tax professionals via their website or telephone (1-800-342-9647) or for OCONUS service members call 800-342-9647 or 703-253-7599.

Decisional Factors

- When deciding which program to establish, commanders and their SJAs should consider factors that may impact the availability and sustainability of the program such as:

  -- Competing mission requirements;

  -- Availability of local volunteer support;

  -- Availability of IRS software and training support;

  -- The negative impacts to program continuity (e.g., loss of future IRS support, loss of future volunteer support, loss of institutional knowledge) should the installation want to continue the program at a later date;

  -- Budgetary constraints;

  -- Impact on base morale;

  -- Demand for tax services;

  -- Availability of free online filing services and other nearby VITA programs accessible for all beneficiaries; and

  -- Availability of other professional filing services near the installation.

  -- Additionally, commanders and SJAs for commands serving in a host or supporting role-on joint bases are advised to review support agreements for any provisions regarding the tax program

Eligible Beneficiaries

- Eligible beneficiaries include active duty service members, dependents, retirees and their dependents, and others who are entitled to legal assistance services under AFI 51-304. SJAs can limit eligible beneficiaries for the tax program (e.g., personnel in the grade of E-6 and below).

- SJAs may also extend services, as resources allow, to federal civilian employees to the extent permitted by the IRS VITA program

References

· Legal Assistance, 10 U.S.C. § 1044

· AFI 51-304, *Legal Assistance, Notary, Preventive Law, and Tax Programs* (22 August 2018)

· IRS Free File Alliance: https://www.irs.gov/e-file-providers/about-the-free-file-alliance

· Military One Source: https://www.militaryonesource.mil/financial-legal/taxes/

Chapter 10
CIVIL LAW RIGHTS AND PROTECTIONS OF MILITARY PERSONNEL

EQUAL OPPORTUNITY AND TREATMENT

The federal government has enacted statutes to ensure equal opportunity (EO). The Department of Defense (DoD) and Department of Air Force (DAF) anti-discriminatory policies protect military members and civilian employees through a bifurcated system where military members present complaints to executive department forums only and civilian employees file complaints before an administrative forum or federal court after exhausting their administrative remedies.

Key Takeaways

» DAFI 36-2710, *Equal Opportunity Program* (18 June 2020), sets out the Air Force Military Equal Opportunity (MEO) program for processing informal and formal discrimination complaints made by military members

» DAF policy is clear: "zero tolerance" for any kind of unlawful discrimination or harassment

» Commanders are responsible for ensuring an environment free of unlawful discrimination and harassment and ensuring all such allegations are investigated

» MEO serves as focal point for discrimination complaints brought by military members, but the nature of the complaint determines which agency conducts the investigation

Department of Air Force Policy

- The DAF policy is to conduct its affairs free from unlawful discrimination and sexual harassment, and to provide equal opportunity and treatment irrespective of race, color, religion, sex (to include pregnancy, gender identity, and sexual orientation), national origin, age (40 or older), disability, genetic information, or prior equal employment opportunity (EEO) activity (reprisal)

- Commanders are required to conduct an investigation into allegations of discrimination based on sexual harassment when a report is made. Commanders must take appropriate administrative or disciplinary action to eliminate unlawful discrimination and sexual harassment.

Department of the Air Force Equal Opportunity Program

- Chapter 4 of DAFI 36-2710, *Equal Opportunity Program*, sets out the DAF MEO program for processing informal and formal discrimination complaints made by military members

-- The DAF policy is clear: "zero tolerance" for any kind of unlawful discrimination or harassment. Discrimination in the MEO context is any unlawful action that denies equal opportunity to persons or groups based on their race, color, sex, national origin, religion, or sexual orientation.

- Such discrimination includes, but is not limited to:

  -- Insults, printed materials, visual materials, signs, symbols, posters, or insignias that infer negative statements pertaining to protected status (e.g., race, religion); sexual harassment; discrimination by an individual that bars or deprives a person of a right or benefit; and/or institutional practices that deprive a person or group of a right or benefit

- The MEO office is the office of primary responsibility for the DAF EO programs and handles most discrimination complaints brought by military members

Unit Commander's Responsibilities

- Commanders are responsible for ensuring an environment free of unlawful discrimination and harassment and ensuring all such allegations are investigated

Complaint Processing Procedures

- MEO serves as focal point for discrimination complaints brought by military members, but the nature of the complaint determines which agency conducts the investigation

  -- MEO complaints against senior officials, consisting of officers in the grade of O-7 select and above, ANG colonels with a certificate of eligibility, and members of the senior executive service (SES), must be immediately referred to Secretary of the Air Force Official Inquiries Directorate (SAF/IGS)

  -- EO must notify the installation commander and local Inspector General (IG) when there is an MEO complaint against an officer in the O-6 grade, an officer who has been selected for O-6, or a civil service employee in the grade of GS-15, and the installation commander must notify the Complaints Resolution Directorate at both the major command (MAJCOM/IGQ) and Secretary of the Air Force levels (SAF/IGQ)

- Complaints involving criminal activity such as assault, rape, or child abuse must be referred to the Air Force Office of Special Investigations or Security Forces Squadron. The EO specialist will notify the Sexual Assault Response Coordinator in sexual assault cases.

- Complainants may use the informal complaint process, which includes alternate dispute resolution (ADR)

- When the MEO office investigates a complaint of discrimination, it is called a complaint clarification. Base-level MEO personnel conduct clarifications of formal complaints.

  -- The purpose of clarifications is to determine whether a formal complaint is supported by a preponderance of credible evidence (the term "preponderance" requires the evidence to show the complaint is more likely true than not). Credible evidence is believable, confirmed, and corroborated evidence. If a clarification results in a determination that an alleged violation occurred, the case must be forwarded through the offender's servicing Staff Judge Advocate (SJA) and the complainant's commander for appropriate action.

- Both the complainant and the subject of a formal EO complaint may appeal the findings upon completion of the complaint clarification. All appeals must be in writing.

  -- Commanders are not required to withhold command action pending an appeal. Findings rendered pursuant to command action under the Uniform Code of Military Justice (UCMJ) are not subject to appeal through MEO channels.

  -- Installation commanders, MAJCOM/CVs, and Air Force Review Boards Agency (SAF/MRB) are authorized to decide appeals of formal complaints of discrimination in MEO cases

Air Force Reserve and Air National Guard Considerations

- See DAFI 36-2710, paras. 4.13 and 4.14, for complaint processing guidance involving Air Force Reserve members while on Regular Air Force duty status (including while on Title 10 orders), Active Guard/Reserve personnel, Air Reserve Technicians (ARTs) and AGRs under Title 32, and ANG personnel serving under Title 10 of the United States Code. For Title 32 Air National Guard complaints, process complaints using CNGBM 9601.01, *National Guard Discrimination Complaint Process.*

Performance Evaluation Reports and Assignments

- Rating and reviewing officials must consider membership in groups espousing supremacist causes or advocating unlawful discrimination in evaluating and assigning military members. While membership in such groups is not prohibited, members who join groups espousing supremacist causes or advocating unlawful discrimination may not be suited to hold certain positions if their views conflict with EO and Treatment Program guidelines. Rating and reviewing officials must document serious or repeated deviations from DoD and DAF directives prohibiting discrimination.

Reprisal/Whistleblower

- DAF members are protected from reprisal for making, preparing, or attempting to make, a complaint of unlawful discrimination or sexual harassment to certain personnel pursuant to DAFI 90-301, *Inspector General Complaints Resolution.* Reprisal complaints are referred by EO to the installation IG.

References

· Classification of Positions Available Above GS-15, 5 U.S.C. § 5108

· Equal Employment Opportunity Act of 1972, Pub. L. 92-261, as amended, 42 U.S.C. §§ 2000e *et seq.*

· The Rehabilitation Act of 1973, as amended, 29 U.S.C. §§ 701 *et seq.*

· 1978 Amendments to the Age Discrimination in Employment Act, 29 U.S.C. §§ 621 *et seq.*

· Title VII of the Civil Rights Act of 1964, 42 U.S.C. §§ 2000e *et seq.*

· The Civil Rights Act of 1991, Pub. L. 102–166, as amended, 42 U.S.C. § 2000e

· DAFI 36-2710, *Equal Opportunity Program* (18 June 2020), including DAFGM2023-01, 20 July 2023

· DAFI 90-301, *Inspector General Complaints Resolution* (4 January 2024)

· AFPD 36-27, *Equal Opportunity (EO)* (18 March 2019)

· CNGBI 0402.01, *National Guard Alternative Dispute Resolution* (24 July 2015)

· AF Form 1587, *Military Equal Opportunity Formal Complaint Summary* (30 August 2010)

· AF Form 1587-1, *Military Equal Opportunity Informal Complaint Summary* (23 August 2010)

THE INSPECTOR GENERAL COMPLAINTS RESOLUTION PROCESS

The inspector general (IG) is the "eyes and ears" of the commander to be alert to issues affecting an organization's productivity and morale. The IG complaints resolution program is a leadership tool to resolve issues affecting the Air Force or Space Force mission promptly and objectively. A successful complaint resolution program (CRP) is designed to enhance the organization's discipline, readiness, and warfighting capability. IGs use fact-finding methodologies to seek out systemic issues affecting the organization.

Key Takeaways

» There are five resolution paths for complaints presented to IGs. Most do not result in IG investigations. Often, complaints are referred to command.

» IG investigations focus primarily on allegations of reprisal and restriction

» Only IGs can investigate allegations of reprisal and restriction

» IGs will encourage complainants to resolve their issues at the lowest level first

» Commanders must provide a copy of the completed report and all exhibits to their local IG, along with final copies of all disciplinary and administrative actions resulting from the investigation

---

The IG CRP

- An IG complaint analysis will result in one of five resolutions paths

  -- Referral, including referral to a commander to address the identified issue. If the IG refers a complaint to a commander, the commander will determine how best to address it and then will inform the complainant of the actions they took.

  -- The other resolution paths are a transfer of the issue to another IG; an assist (e.g., an IG makes a phone call on the complainant's behalf); dismissal of the complaint; or investigation

- The IG CRP should not be used for

  -- Matters normally addressed through other channels unless there is evidence those channels mishandled the matter or process

  -- See DAFI 90-301, *Inspector General Complaints Resolution*, Table 3.7, for an outline of agencies that have programs for redress of complaints. The information in the table is not all-inclusive. IGs will advise complainants of the appropriate entity to address their complaint.

IG Investigations

- IG investigations are distinct from other investigations, such as commander directed investigations (CDIs)

- An investigating officer (IO) investigates pursuant to DAFI 90-301 when appointed, in writing, by the appropriate appointing authority (usually a wing commander)

- The Air Force Hand-Off Policy requires the IO to engage in a person-to-person hand-off with the commander/director or designee for all subjects and suspects in investigations at the conclusion of their interview

Reprisal (Whistleblower Protection) Complaints

- Reprisal occurs when a responsible management official (RMO) takes or threatens to take an unfavorable personnel action, or withholds or threatens to withhold a favorable personnel action on a military member, for making or preparing to make, or being perceived as making or preparing to make, a protected communication

  -- *Example:* A major files a complaint of gender discrimination by her squadron's Director of Operations with the Equal Opportunity (EO) Office. The major's commander finds out and reprises against her by issuing her a letter of reprimand for a minor offense.

- Reprisal is a violation of 10 U.S.C. § 1034 (The Military Whistleblower Protection Act), and DoDD 7050.06, *Military Whistleblower Protection*, and may result in disciplinary action under the Uniform Code of Military Justice (UCMJ), Articles 92 or 132, or applicable civilian directives or instructions

- AF IGs never investigate allegations of reprisal brought by civilian or contractor employees. Only DoD IG and the Office of Special Counsel investigate such complaints. However, AF IGs do investigate allegations made by a military member that a civilian employee engaged in reprisal.

Restriction Complaints

- Restriction is preventing or attempting to prevent members of the Armed Forces from making or preparing to make lawful communications to Members of Congress and/or an IG

  -- *Example:* A commander tells his unit there should not be any problems to report to the IG during an inspection, and that he knows the IG and will find out who made any negative comments

- Engaging in restriction is a violation of 10 U.S.C. § 1034 and DoDD 7050.06, and may result in disciplinary action under the UCMJ, Article 92

Miscellaneous Considerations

- The potential that an action a commander takes could result in an IG complaint should never dissuade a commander from taking timely and appropriate corrective and preventative actions, when done for legitimate mission-related reasons

- Commanders should coordinate with their Staff Judge Advocates for effective legal guidance on these issues

References

· Protected Communications: Prohibition of Retaliatory Personnel Actions, 10 U.S.C. § 1034

· Articles 92 and 132, Uniform Code of Military Justice

· DoDD 7050.06, *Military Whistleblower Protection* (17 April 2015), incorporating Change 1, 12 October 2021

· DoD Inspector General, Guide to Investigating Military Whistleblower Reprisal and Restriction Complaints (18 April 2017)

· DAFI 90-301, *Inspector General Complaints Resolution* (4 January 2024)

· DAFI 90-5001, *Integrated Resilience* (25 January 2019), incorporating Change 1, 21 October 2021, including DAFGM2023-01, 4 August 2023

· DAFPD 90-3, *Inspector General* (3 February 2021), including DAFPM2023-01, 12 December 2023

· AFI 38-101, *Manpower and Organization* (29 August 2019), including AFGM2023-01, 19 July 2023

· AFI 71-101, Volume 1, *Criminal Investigations Program* (1 July 2019)

· SAF/IGQ Inspector General Guide for Investigating Officers (December 2020)

PROHIBITION ON SEXUAL HARASSMENT

Prevention is the best tool to eliminate sexual harassment (SH) in the workplace. The Department of the Air Force (DAF) leadership (military and civilian) at every level must take steps to prevent SH from occurring and take immediate action to investigate and resolve all civilian employee and service member SH complaints.

Key Takeaways
» A supervisor/commander who condones any form of SH is engaging in SH
» Service member SH may constitute criminal misconduct under Article 134, Uniform Code of Military Justice (UCMJ)
» Commanders will communicate to civilian employees and service members that SH is not tolerated, provide SH prevention training, ensure an effective complaint process, and take immediate action to investigate/resolve all SH complaints (72 hour/14-20 day requirements)
» Commanders who substantiate SH complaints have many disciplinary/administrative options

Overview

- The DAF defines SH as an action involving unwelcome sexual advances, requests for sexual favors, and other verbal or physical conduct of a sexual nature:

  -- When submission to such conduct is made either explicitly or implicitly a term or condition of a person's job, pay, or career;

  -- Submission to or rejection of such conduct by a person is used as a basis for career or employment decisions affecting that person; or

  -- Such conduct has the purpose or effect of unreasonably interfering with an individual's work performance or creates an intimidating, hostile, or offensive working environment.

- Workplace conduct may be actionable as "hostile work environment" harassment even if it does not result in concrete psychological harm to the victim; rather, it need only be so severe or pervasive that a reasonable person would perceive, and the victim does perceive, the work environment as hostile or offensive. Workplace is an expansive term.

- Further, the act constituting sexual harassment can occur at any location, regardless of whether the victim or accused is on or off duty at the time of the act. Physical proximity is not required, and the acts may be committed through online or other electronic means.

- Any person in a supervisory or command position who uses or condones any form of sexual behavior to control, influence, or affect the career, pay, or job of a military member or civilian employee is engaging in SH. Any military member or civilian employee who makes deliberate or repeated unwelcome verbal comments, gestures, or physical contact of a sexual nature in the workplace is also engaging in SH. When a military member engages in such misconduct *and* the misconduct is prejudicial to good order and discipline or of a nature to bring discredit upon the armed forces, it may constitute criminal conduct under Article 134, UCMJ.

Types of Sexual Harassment

- Quid Pro Quo (or Tangible Employment Act): SH occurs when an employee suffers or is threatened with some kind of employment injury for refusing to grant sexual favors, or is promised some sort of tangible job benefit in exchange for sexual favors

- Hostile Work Environment: Created when a supervisor, co-worker, or someone else with whom the victim encounters on the job engages in a series of acts which are so severe or pervasive as to alter the terms and conditions of employment. This may include words, actions, or conduct that is perceived as sexual in nature. Examples include, but are not limited to, discussing sexual activities, unnecessary touching, commenting on physical attributes, displaying sexually suggestive pictures, using demeaning or inappropriate terms, using sexually profane gestures or language, etc. Once again, the sexual harassment need not occur in the work center to create a hostile work environment so long as the harassment alters the terms and conditions of employment.

- Command Attention to SH Must Include: Publishing DAF zero tolerance policies, ensuring avenues of communication and complaint for civilian employees and military members are well publicized throughout the unit, ensuring military members experiencing SH have access to and are referred to the Sexual Assault Prevention and Response (SAPR) office for victim advocacy support, providing training on preventing SH, ordering a fair and impartial investigation promptly when a complaint alleging SH by a military member or civilian employee is received. As of 27 December 2023, federal law requires the commander to appoint an independent investigator to investigate these complaints) and seeking advice from the equal opportunity (EO) office, the Staff Judge Advocate (SJA), and the civilian personnel office (CPO), as appropriate, before taking action against offenders.

Commander's Inquiry – Military or Civilian Complainant

- A complainant may elect a commander directed investigation (CDI) and/or the military equal employment opportunity (MEO) process for military complainants and/or the equal employment opportunity (EEO) process for civilian employees

- Upon receipt of the complaint, 10 U.S.C. § 1561 requires that, within 72 hours, the commander forward the complaint or a detailed description of the allegation to the general court-martial convening authority (GCMCA), begin the investigation, advise the complainant of the investigation's start, and provide available victim support resources. Commanders are responsible for ensuring the CDI is completed no later than 14 days after commenced. The commander must submit the final investigative report to the local SJA office for a legal review.

- The commander shall submit an investigation progress report to the GCMCA within 20 days of its initiation and every 14 days thereafter until complete. The commander shall submit a final report on the investigation's results, including a report of any action taken resulting from the findings. The complainant will be notified of the investigation's completion, his/her appeal rights, and provided a copy of the investigative report.

Complaint Processing – Military Complainant

- EO is the office of primary responsibility for the DAF EO programs and has primary responsibility for handling sexual harassment complaints. Generally, a formal complaint filed by a military member will generate an investigation by EO personnel (called a clarification) designed to determine the facts and cause of the EO incident, whether it is substantiated, assess its severity and effect on morale, good order, and discipline, and develop recommendations concerning the incident's classification and appropriate corrective action. If substantiated, the commander will provide a summary of any action(s) taken in response to the Installation Equal Opportunity Office. An appeal is available regarding a clarification's findings.

Complaint Processing – Civilian Employee Complainant

- Pre-Complaint: The EEO counselor advises the complainant of their rights and obligations, places all allegations in the pre-complaint process regardless of merit or timeliness, and attempts to resolve the situation between parties within 30 days. If unable to resolve the situation, the complainant is advised that they may file a formal complaint.

- Formal Complaint: The complaint is evaluated by the EEO Director for full/partial acceptance or dismissal. If accepted, the installation EEO Director requests an investigator from the Investigations and Resolutions Directorate (IRD) within 30 days of the formal complaint's filing.

-- IRD will investigate the complaint and send a report of investigation and complaint file to the installation EEO Director and the Air Force Civilian Appellate Review Office (AFCARO). AFCARO will provide the complainant a redacted copy of the report of investigation. After receiving the report, the complainant must elect an Equal Employment Opportunity Commission hearing or a Final Agency Decision (FAD) by AFCARO. Following the issuance of either the FAD or the Administrative Judge's ruling, the complainant may appeal to the Equal Employment Opportunity Commission or file suit in federal court. Complaint resolution through settlement or other alternative dispute resolution processes can be discussed at any time in the process.

Command Options to Address Substantiated Complaints of Sexual Harassment

- Commanders who find military members engaging in sexual harassment have numerous disciplinary and administrative options, including counseling, admonishment, reprimand, nonjudicial punishment, administrative discharge, and court-martial. Commanders who find civilian employees have engaged in sexual harassment should base any charges drafted for disciplinary action on the offensive acts themselves rather than charging "sexual harassment," since this is a term of art requiring various elements of proof. The conduct can be addressed using procedures described in DAFI 36-148, *Discipline and Adverse Actions of Civilian Employees*.

References

· Complaints of Sexual Harassment: Investigation by Commanding Officers, 10 U.S.C. § 1561

· Title VII of the Civil Rights Act of 1964, as amended, 42 U.S.C. §§ 2000e *et seq.*

· Article 134, Uniform Code of Military Justice

· Federal Sector Equal Employment Opportunity, 29 C.F.R. Part 1614

· DoDD 1350.2, *Department of Defense Military Equal Opportunity (MEO) Program* (4 September 2020), including Change 1, 20 December 2022

· DoDI 1020.03, *Harassment Prevention and Response in the Armed Forces* (8 February 2018), incorporating through Change 2, 20 December 2022

· DAFI 36-148, *Discipline and Adverse Actions of Civilian Employees* (27 September 2022), incorporating Change 1, 31 August 2023, certified current, 31 August 2023

· DAFI 36-701, *Labor-Management Relations* (14 November 2019), incorporating Change 1, 10 November 2021, certified current 10 November 2021

· DAFI 36-2710, *Equal Opportunity Program* (18 June 2020), including DAFGM2023-02, 27 December 2023

· DAFI 90-301, *Inspector General Complaints Resolution* (4 January 2024)

SERVICEMEMBERS CIVIL RELIEF ACT

The Servicemembers Civil Relief Act (SCRA) provides a wide range of protections for service members whose duties might interfere with certain civil obligations and proceedings. Congress regularly amends the act with the goal of allowing service members to focus on the military mission first.

Key Takeaways

» SCRA provides a wide range of protections for service members. Such protections include allowing a service member to terminate a lease due to permanent change of station or deployment and reducing pre-service interest rates to a maximum of 6%.

» Other protections for service members include that civil procedures can be put on hold (or "stayed") in certain circumstances, service members and their spouses can keep their state of residency for taxation and voting purposes, and evictions of service members are generally prohibited without a court order

Overview

- SCRA applies to civil matters, **NOT** criminal matters

- SCRA provides protections for active duty members, reservists on federal active duty, and members of the National Guard on federal orders for a period of more than 30 days

- SCRA also provides certain benefits and protections to dependents of service members, and, in certain instances, to those who co-signed a loan for, or took out a loan with, a service member

- SCRA generally covers the time period on active duty. However, some provisions apply to pre-service obligations (e.g., vehicle leases entered prior to entry on active duty) or to the period following active service.

- Service members should contact a legal assistance attorney at the installation legal office for advice and assistance in these situations

Most Common and Relevant Provisions

- Eviction: SCRA prohibits eviction of a service member and dependents from rented housing without a court order. For this provision to apply, the rent cannot exceed a cap set each year. This cap is generally set high (e.g., the cap for 2023 is $9,106.46).

- Liens (Storage and Towing Companies): A person holding a lien on a service member's property or effects may not foreclose or enforce any lien on the property or effects without a court order during any period of military service and for 90 days thereafter

- <u>Landlord-Tenant Lease Termination</u>:

  -- A service member may unilaterally cancel a residential lease, without fees, upon entering service or if they receive permanent change of station orders, separation/ retirement orders, or deployment orders for more than 90 days

  -- To terminate a residential lease, the service member must submit a written notice and a copy of his/her military orders, or a letter from a commanding officer, to the landlord. If the service member pays rent on a monthly basis, once he/she gives proper notice, then the lease will terminate 30 days after the next rent payment is due.

- <u>Vehicle Lease Termination</u>:

  -- A service member may cancel a pre-service lease for a motor vehicle if they receive orders bringing them onto active duty

  -- A service member may cancel any motor vehicle lease (pre-service or signed during service) for deployment orders for 180 days or more, or permanent change of station (PCS) orders to a location outside of the continental United States (OCONUS), or PCS orders from Alaska or Hawaii to any location outside of those states

  -- Early termination fees are prohibited

- <u>Other Leases and Contracts</u>: Subject to certain procedural requirements, service members are permitted to cancel telephone, internet/cable, gym and home security contracts upon receipt of military orders to relocate for a period of not less than 90 days to a location that does not support the contract. In limited situations, dependents can do the same.

- <u>Maximum Rates of Interest</u>: The interest rate on a service member's pre-service consumer debt or mortgage obligation must be capped at 6%, including most fees, unless the creditor shows that the ability of the service member to pay interest above 6% is not materially affected by reason of their military service

- <u>Professional License Portability</u>: Subject to specific criteria, a service member or spouse with a professional license may retain the use of that license when military orders force them to move outside the jurisdiction covered by the license. Licenses to practice law are specifically excepted. Department of Justice Fact Sheet: https://www.justice.gov/d9/2023-07/doj_scra_license_portability_fact_sheet.pdf.

- <u>Stay of Proceedings</u>: Courts have the discretion to delay a civil court proceeding (**NOT** criminal) when the requirements of military service prevent the service member from either asserting or protecting a legal right. The courts will look to whether military service materially affected the service member's ability to take or defend an action in court.

- <u>Taxation – Service Members and Dependents</u>: A service member's state of legal residence may tax military income. Service members and dependents do not lose legal residence solely because of a transfer pursuant to military orders. For example, if a member is a Virginia resident and is moved to a base in California, the service member does not lose Virginia residency, nor will he/she be subject to pay California state income tax on his/her military pay. Under SCRA, service members and spouses may elect to use one of three states for taxation purposes: the service member's state of residence or domicile, the spouse's state of residence or domicile, or the permanent duty station of the service member.

- <u>Child Custody</u>: A state court is prohibited from considering a service member's deployment as the sole factor in determining the best interests of the child, though this provision does not create a federal right of action

SCRA Application to ANG Service Members

- Certain provisions of SCRA apply to service members in Title 32 state status called to duty for 31 days or more in response to a national emergency declared by the President and supported by federal funds

- **Note:** Many states have statutes or regulations that provide benefits similar to those afforded by SCRA, even if SCRA itself does not apply

References

· Servicemembers Civil Relief Act, 50 U.S.C. §§ 3901– 4043

· Department of Justice, Servicemembers and Veterans Initiative: https://www.justice.gov/servicemembers

UNIFORMED SERVICES EMPLOYMENT AND REEMPLOYMENT RIGHTS ACT

The Uniformed Services Employment and Reemployment Rights Act (USERRA) encourages non-career military service by entitling service members to return to their civilian employment upon completion of their military service with the seniority, status, and rate of pay that they would have obtained had they remained continuously employed by their civilian employer. USERRA also prohibits discrimination based on present, past and future military service.

Key Takeaways

» USERRA prohibits discrimination against military members by their civilian employers, prospective employers, or temporary employers

» Service members are eligible for protection of the jobs, title, pay, and seniority by their pre-service employer for a period of up to 5 years if they comply with notice requirements

» Members returning from an activation period must request reinstatement within a specified period of time depending on the length of their activation

» Employers cannot take adverse action, deny promotions, retention, or any benefits against a person because they enforce their rights under USERRA

» Parties may benefit from contacting the U.S. Department of Labor (DoL) or the Employer Support for the Guard and Reserve (ESGR) for questions or to help mitigate disputes

Overview

- USERRA covers nearly all employees, including part-time and probationary employees, and it applies to virtually all U.S. employers, regardless of size. USERRA prohibits employment discrimination against a person on the basis of past military service, current military obligations, or intent to serve. An employer must not deny initial employment, reemployment, retention in employment, promotion, or any benefit of employment to a person on the basis of a past, present, or future service obligation. In addition, an employer must not retaliate against a person because of an action taken to enforce or exercise any USERRA right or for assisting in an USERRA investigation.

  -- It protects members in the Department of Air Force (DAF), Army, Navy, Coast Guard, Marine Corps, the Commissioned Corps of the U.S. Public Health Service, Army National Guard, and the Air National Guard

  -- "Service" includes performing duty on a voluntary or involuntary basis. It includes active duty, inactive duty for training, initial active duty for training, full-time National Guard duty, certain periods of State active duty, as well as absences due to fitness for duty examinations for such duty or injuries streaming from military duty.

Eligibility Criteria

- To have reemployment rights in a civilian job (including temporary jobs) following a period of uniformed service, a person must meet the following criteria:

  -- Must have given advance notice to the employer that they were leaving the job for service in a uniformed service, unless such notice is impossible or unreasonable or otherwise prevented by military necessity

  -- The cumulative period of service does not exceed five years with the same employer. The federal government is considered the same employer.

    --- Most periodic and special Reserve and National Guard training, most service in time of war or emergency, and involuntary extensions on active duty do not count toward the five-year limit, and other exempted periods of service as expressed in the Memorandum from the Assistant Secretary of the Air Force, *Civilian Reemployment Protections for Department of the Air Force Military Personnel* (27 January 2022)

  -- Must have reported back to the civilian job in a timely manner or have submitted a timely application for reemployment

  -- Not been separated from service with a disqualifying discharge or under other than honorable conditions

Table 10.1 USERRA Return to Work or Apply for Reemployment Timeline*

Period of Military Duty	1-30 Days of Service	31-180 Days of Service	181 Days or more of Service
Return to Work /Apply for Reemployment	By the beginning of the first regularly scheduled work period after the end of the calendar day of duty, plus time required to return home safely and an eight-hour rest period. If this is impossible or unreasonable, then as soon as possible.	Apply within 14 days following completion of Service. If this is impossible or unreasonable through no fault of the employee, then as soon as possible	Apply within 90 days following completion of service

* Service-connected injury or illness: Reporting or application deadlines are extended for up to two years for persons who are hospitalized or convalescing.

Entitlements

- People who meet the eligibility criteria under USERRA have seven basic entitlements:

  -- Prompt reinstatement to employment position, meaning, as soon as is practicable under the circumstances of each individual

  -- Accrued seniority and status, just as if the person had been continuously employed

    --- This is the "escalator principle," requiring each returning service member to be reemployed in the position the person would have occupied with the same seniority they would have enjoyed had the person remained continuously employed

    --- The "status" the person would have attained if continuously employed includes location, opportunity to work during the day instead of at night, and the opportunity to work in a department or at such times when there are better opportunities to earn commissions or to be promoted

  -- Immediate reinstatement of civilian health insurance coverage, even if the member did not elect to continue it during service

  -- Employees are entitled to non-seniority rights and benefits at the time they left for military service, and to those rights and benefits that became effective during their service and that are provided to similarly situated employees on furlough or leave of absence

  -- Training or retraining and other accommodations necessary to update a returning employee's skills so he/she has the ability to perform the essential tasks of the position

    --- For employees who become disabled or have existing disabilities aggravated during services such that they are no longer "qualified employees," the employee must be reemployed in: (a) a position equivalent in seniority, state, and pay to the escalator position, or (b) a position nearest in approximation consistent with the circumstances of the employee's case

  -- A reemployed employee shall not be discharged without cause:

    --- For one year after the date of reemployment if the person's period of military service was for 181 days or more

    --- For 180 days after the date of reemployment if the person's period of military service was for 31 to 180 days

    --- Persons who serve 30 or fewer days are not protected from discharge without cause. However, they are protected from discrimination because of military service/obligation.

-- USERRA prohibits both discrimination and reprisal. This means an employer may not deny initial employment, reemployment, retention, promotion, or any benefit of employment because of a person's military service or application to serve. In addition, an employer may not take adverse employment action against a person because they either exercise a right, testify or assist in an investigation under USERRA.

Assistance and Enforcement

- The Veterans' Employment and Training Service (VETS) within the United States DoL will assist persons claiming rights under USERRA, including persons claiming rights with respect to the federal government as a civilian employer. They can be reached at 1-866-237-0275 or at https://www.dol.gov/agencies/vets/programs/userra/fileaclaim.

- The Office of Employer Support of the Guard and Reserve (ESGR) will also assist service members in enforcing USERRA. They can be reached at 1-800-336-4590 or through their website at https://esgr.mil/USERRA/USERRA-Contact.

- The Office of Special Counsel (OSC) (https://osc.gov) also enforces USERRA violations for federal employees at claimants' request once the claimant has exhausted the Department of Labor process

References

· Uniformed Services Employment and Reemployment Rights Act, 38 U.S.C. §§ 4301– 4335

· Regulations Under the Uniformed Services Employment and Reemployment Rights Act of 1994, 20 C.F.R. Part 1002

· Civilian Employment and Reemployment Rights for Service Members, Former Service Members, and Applicants of the Uniformed Services, 32 C.F.R. Part 104

· DoDI 1205.12, *Civilian Employment and Reemployment Rights for Service Members, Former Service Members and Applicants of the Uniformed Services* (24 February 2016), incorporating Change 1, 20 May 2016

· Memorandum from the Office of the Assistant Secretary of the Air Force, *Civilian Reemployment Protections for Department of the Air Force Military Personnel* (27 January 2022)

· Department of Labor: https://www.dol.gov/agencies/vets/programs/userra

UNIFORMED SERVICES FORMER SPOUSES' PROTECTION ACT

In 1982, Congress passed the Uniformed Services Former Spouses' Protection Act (USFSPA) to provide financial protections to certain former spouses of service members. Generally, USFSPA allows state courts to divide military disposable retired pay as marital property upon divorce and provides certain additional benefits to former spouses.

Key Takeaways

» State courts can divide a service member's retired pay as part of a divorce

» These court orders can be enforced by the Department of Defense (DoD) when specific requirements are met

» Former spouses can apply for payments directly from the DoD through the Defense Finance and Accounting Service (DFAS)

» A service member can elect to include a former spouse on their Survivor Benefit Plan (SBP) or it can be part of the divorce settlement

Overview

- The USFSPA accomplishes several things:

    -- It recognizes the right of state courts to distribute disposable military retired pay to a former spouse if a former spouse was awarded a portion of a member's military retired pay as property in their final court order

    -- "Disposable retired pay" is retired pay minus the amount of disability pay, unless the service member is receiving concurrent payments

    -- It provides the DoD a method of enforcing court orders such as final decrees of divorce, dissolution, annulment, and legal separation, and court-ordered property settlements incident to such decrees. The pertinent court order must provide for the payment of child support, alimony, or retired pay as property, to a former spouse.

    -- To apply for payments under the USFSPA, a former spouse must submit a DD Form 2293, *Application for Former Spouse Payments from Retired Pay*, a copy of the applicable court order certified by the clerk of the court, and a few other documents, to DFAS. An application checklist and access to DD Form 2293 is available at https://www.dfas.mil/Garnishment/usfspa/apply/.

- An un-remarried former spouse may retain a military ID card and associated commissary, exchange, medical benefits if they meet the 20/20/20 rule. The 20/20/20 rule requires at least twenty years of marriage, at least twenty years of military service by the sponsor, and at least twenty years of overlap of the marriage and the military service. There are additional protections such as the 20/20/15 rule, which would allow medical benefits for one year after the termination of the marriage.

Division of Retired Pay as a Marital Asset or Community Property

- Retired pay as property awards must be expressed as a fixed dollar amount, a percentage of disposable retired pay, a formula, or a hypothetical

- An award of a percentage of a member's retired pay is automatically construed under the USFSPA as a percentage of disposable retired pay (gross retired pay less authorized deductions)

  -- Final court orders, after 23 December 2016, issued to service member prior to retirement, limit disposable income to "the amount of the basic pay payable to the member for the member's pay grade and years of service at the time of the court order" and increased by the cost-of-living granted to military retirees from divorce to the date the member retires

Enforcement of Court Orders

- The 10/10 Rule: For a former spouse to receive their share of retired pay directly from DFASS, the member and former spouse must have been married to each other for 10 years or more during which the member performed at least 10 years of military service creditable towards retirement eligibility

- Court orders dividing disposable retired pay as property are only enforceable by DFSAS if the state court had jurisdiction over the member by reason of (1) the member's domicile in the territorial jurisdiction of the court, (2) the member's residence in the territorial jurisdiction of the court (other than because of military assignment), or (3) the member's consent to the jurisdiction of the court (which some states may assume based on the member's participation in the proceedings)

- The 10/10 Rule and the jurisdictional requirement do not apply to enforcement of child support or alimony awards under the USFSPA Survivor's Benefit Plan (SBP)

- A member may elect to provide coverage under the SBP for a former spouse who was originally a "spouse" beneficiary under SBP, provided the parties were divorced after the member became eligible to receive retired pay

- A court can order a spouse to provide SBP coverage for a non-service spouse, but to be effective, it must be served on DFAS within one year after the divorce. A former spouse can submit his/her own request to DFAS—this is known as a "deemed election request."

Maximum Payment Amount

- The maximum that DFAS can be ordered to directly pay to a former spouse under the USFSPA is 50% of a member's disposable retired pay

- If a state court awards the former spouse more than 50% of the member's disposable pay, the former spouse must rely on the state court to enforce payment of the amount above 50%

- In cases where there are payments both under the USFSPA and pursuant to a garnishment for child support or alimony, the total amount payable cannot exceed 65% of the member's disposable earnings for garnishment purposes

References

· Definitions, 10 U.S.C. § 1072
· Uniformed Services Former Spouses' Protection Act, 10 U.S.C. ch. 71 § 1408
· Former Spouse Payments from Retired Pay, Procedures, 32 C.F.R. Part 63.6
· DoD Financial Management Regulation (FMR) 7000.14–R, Volume 7B, Chapter 29, *Former Spouse Payments from Retired Pay* (February 2023)
· DD Form 2293, *Application for Former Spouse Payments from Retired Pay* (April 2018)
· Defense Finance and Accounting – Former Spouses' Protection Act:
https://www.dfas.mil/Garnishment/usfspa/apply/

ENSURING THE FAIR HANDLING OF DEBT COMPLAINTS AGAINST SERVICE MEMBERS

Service members have the same legal rights under state and federal law as civilian consumers. It is important for commanders to understand that both law and Department of Defense (DoD) policy make a distinction between dealing with third party "creditors" with whom the debt originated, and "debt collectors" who are in the business of collecting debts for another person or business.

Key Takeaways

» Commanders should consult DAFI 36-2906, *Personal Financial Responsibility*, for procedures on how to respond to a creditor's allegations that a service member has a delinquent debt

» Debt collector communications and interactions are regulated by the Fair Debt Collection Practices Act (FDCPA)

» Service members facing harassment from a debt collector or otherwise needing assistance should contact their local legal office for legal assistance

Overview

- The Fair Debt Collection Practices Act (FDCPA) is a federal law that regulates how debts may be collected. The FDCPA regulates debt collection agencies and attorneys and does not apply to original creditors.

  -- A creditor is defined as a person or entity to whom or to which a debtor owes money. Most major creditors, particularly credit card companies, have adopted collection policies that do not violate federal law. Original creditors are also regulated by state laws which may closely follow the FDCPA.

  -- Debt collectors are in the business of collecting debts that are owed to creditors. This includes individuals, collection agencies, lawyers who collect debts on a regular basis, and companies that buy delinquent debts and then try to collect them. Debt collectors are strictly limited in how they conduct their activities under both the FDCPA and state law.

- As opposed to the general prohibition on debt collectors contacting the chain of command (detailed further below), creditors can contact the chain of command about a service member's debt. Specific procedures for commanders to address cases alleging a service member's delinquent financial obligations are outlined in DAFI 36-2906, *Personal Financial Responsibility*. This instruction contains the process by which a creditor can request an involuntary allotment of pay.

  -- Under DoD policy, the chain of command's assistance in indebtedness matters shall not be extended to creditors who have not made a bona fide effort to collect the debt directly from the member, whose claims are patently false and misleading, or whose claims are obviously exorbitant

Debt Collector Communications with the Chain of Command

- Debt collectors are generally *prohibited* from contacting third parties—including commanders and first sergeants—without a court order or the debtor's prior consent given directly to the debt collector. This is because the debt collector should be dealing directly with the service member/debtor. There are two limited exceptions to this rule:

  -- First, a creditor, or debt collector can call and ask for the member's contact information, but they are not permitted to identify themselves as someone calling regarding a debt

  -- Second, if the member/debtor gave a creditor or debt collector written permission after the debt was created

- Under these exceptions, debt collectors may only contact the command section and may only do so once. Absent these circumstances, a debt collector should not be contacting the chain of command.

Debt Collector Communications with the Service Member/Debtor

- A debt collector is allowed to directly contact and communicate with a debtor, but the FDCPA limits where, when, and how these communications may occur. The FDCPA prevents debt collectors from several illegal actions. These include but are not limited to:

  -- Harassing the alleged debtor or others, including threats of violence, use of obscene language, and repeated or continuous phone calls;

  -- Debt collectors cannot contact the alleged debtor at unusual hours, such as before 0800 or after 2100;

  -- Continuing to contact the debtor after receiving a notice from the debtor to cease all communication; and

  -- Revealing the debt to third parties.

Remedies for Affected Service Members

- If a debt collector has violated the law, the debtor has the right to sue the collector in state or federal court within one year of the date the law was violated

- Any problems in dealing with debt collectors should be reported immediately to the base legal office. Additionally, service members may contact the Consumer Financial Protection Bureau (CFPB), the state Attorney General's Office, and the Federal Trade Commission (FTC) for further assistance.

- In accordance with the Fair Credit Reporting Act (FCRA), service members have the right to dispute a debt listed on their credit report, and to request a free copy of their credit report (the official federal website is: https://www.AnnualCreditReport.com)

- Service members should consult with a legal assistance attorney before making payments to a debt collector and to find out more about their rights under applicable law

Third Party Allotments

- Creditors whose bona fide efforts to collect a debt from a military member have failed can secure an involuntary allotment to satisfy a final judgment from a court. The DAF has no authority to resolve disputed claims or to require members to pay a private debt without a civil judgment.

- Complainants who attempt to serve DAF with documents should be referred to DFAS. When a request for involuntary allotment is received, DFAS notifies the member and the member's commander.

References

· Fair Credit Reporting Act, 15 U.S.C. §§ 1681 *et seq.*

· Fair Debt Collection Practices Act, 15 U.S.C. §§ 1692 *et seq.*

· DoD 7000.14-R ("DoD FMR") Volume 7A, Chapters 41–43, "Garnishments and Other Involuntary Allotments" (January 2023) "Discretionary Allotments" (April 2022), and "Nondiscretionary Allotments" (October 2023)

· DoDI 1344.09, *Indebtedness of Military Personnel* (1 February 2022)

· DAFI 36-2906, *Personal Financial Responsibility* (23 August 2023)

· AFMAN 65-116V1, *Defense Joint Military Pay System Active Component Financial Management Flight Procedures*, Chapter 57, Allotments of Pay (23 October 2019)

Chapter 11
CIVIL LAW ISSUES

COMMERCIAL ACTIVITIES

As a general rule, DoD installations are not routine forums for commercial activities by service members, their family members and others. Some commercial sales can be made during a scheduled interview between the Airman/Guardian and the vendor. There are also rules for commercial businesses operated out of base housing, but they can be authorized with oversight. Lastly, due to prohibitions on gambling, raffles are other games of chance are strictly controlled.

Key Takeaways

» Commercial solicitations on the installation (e.g., investment counseling, insurance sales) have been subject to past abuse so specific appointments are required

» Door-to-door commercial solicitations are not permitted in base housing

» Home-based businesses can be operated out of base housing with Housing Office approval, but must comply with state, local, and host nation licensing requirements and tax laws

» Games of chance are generally only allowed in approved Club gaming activities, except that recognized private organizations can utilize raffles as fundraising events

Permitted On-Base Commercial Solicitation

- On-base solicitation is a privilege, not a right, granted at the discretion of the installation commander. Personal commercial solicitation on an installation will be permitted only if the following requirements are met:

-- The solicitor is duly licensed under applicable laws;

-- The installation commander permits it; and

-- A specific appointment has been made with the individual concerned and conducted in family quarters or other areas designated by the installation commander.

Prohibited On-Base Commercial Solicitation

- Certain solicitation practices are prohibited on military bases including, but not limited to:

-- Soliciting personnel who are on-duty

-- Soliciting any kind of mass audience, e.g., commanders call or town hall

-- Soliciting in housing areas without an appointment

-- Soliciting door-to-door

-- Implying DoD sponsorship or sanction

-- Soliciting members junior in grade

-- Procuring or supplying roster listings of DoD personnel

-- Use of official ID cards by active duty members, retirees, or reservists to gain access for purposes of commercial solicitation

Operating Businesses from Base Housing

- Housing occupants may operate business enterprises while living in base housing limited to the sale of products and personal services, minor repair service on small items, limited manufacturing of items or tutoring

  -- Members must request permission in writing to conduct the commercial activity from the housing office

  -- Home-based businesses should not present unreasonable burdens on installation services (e.g., U.S. Post Office, commercial Wi-Fi, Pass & ID Office)

  -- Home-based businesses should not compete with Army and Air Force Exchange Service (AAFES)

  -- Occupants must meet local government licensing requirements, agreements, and host country business practices before requesting approval to operate a private business

Games of Chance

- Bingo and Monte Carlo (Las Vegas) events are authorized in accordance with Enclosure 3 of DoDI 1015.10, *Military Morale, Welfare, and Recreation (MWR) Programs*. However, games of chance must not otherwise violate local civilian laws. International agreements apply overseas.

- Cash prizes may be awarded for bingo. Play-in bingo programs should be limited to eligible patrons, their family members, and guests.

- Only non-monetary prizes may be awarded for Monte Carlo events. Play-in Monte Carlo events should be limited to Club members and their adult family members, members of other clubs exercising reciprocal privileges and their adult family members, and adult guests.

  -- Once a participant purchases a money substitute for a Monte Carlo event, no reimbursement can be made for any unused portion, and money substitutes may not be used to buy resale items, including food and beverages

Raffles

- Installation-recognized private organizations may hold occasional and infrequent raffles, which must be approved in advance by the installation commander, with the Staff Judge Advocate's advice. Such raffles count towards the private organization's allowable limit of three on base fundraisers per quarter. Raffles must not otherwise violate local civilian laws.

  -- Raffle prizes cannot be strictly monetary in nature

References

· DoD 5500.07-R, *Joint Ethics Regulation* (30 August 1993), incorporating through Change 7, 17 November 2011

· DoDI 1000.15, *Procedures and Support for Non-Federal Entities Authorized to Operate on DoD Installations* (24 October 2008)

· DoDI 1015.10, *Military Morale, Welfare, and Recreation (MWR) Programs* (July 6, 2009), incorporating Change 1, 6 May 2011

· DoDI 1344.07, *Personal Commercial Solicitation on DoD Installations* (30 March 2006)

· DAFI 34-101, *Air Force Morale, Welfare, and Recreation (MWR) Programs and Use Eligibility* (7 March 2022)

· DAFI 36-3101, *Fundraising* (26 October 2022)

· AFI 32-6000, *Housing Management* (18 March 2020), including AFI32-6000_DAFGM2022-01, 8 March 2022

· AFI 34-223, *Private Organizations Program* (13 December 2018)

OFF-LIMITS ESTABLISHMENTS

The establishment of off-limits areas is a function of command. It may be used by installation commanders to help maintain good order and discipline, health, morale, safety, and welfare of service members. The establishment of off-limits areas is also intended to prevent service members from being exposed to or victimized by crime-conducive conditions. Armed Forces Disciplinary Control Boards (AFDCBs) advise and make recommendations to commanders on the establishment of off-limits areas.

Key Takeaways

» Installation commanders may place a civilian establishment or area off-limits to military members after receiving a recommendation from the AFDCB

» In emergency situations, commanders may declare establishments or areas temporarily off-limits

» Military members who enter off-limits establishments or areas are subject to disciplinary action

Armed Forces Disciplinary Control Boards

- AFDCBs are established under the provisions of AFI 31-213, *Armed Forces Disciplinary Control Boards and Off-Installation Liaison and Operations*

  -- AFDCBs must meet quarterly

  -- AFDCBs may recommend the installation commander place a civilian establishment or area off-limits to military members

  -- The AFDCB is usually composed of a president and voting members, appointed by the commander, and representatives from various base functional areas, such as law enforcement, Staff Judge Advocate, equal opportunity, public affairs, chaplains, consumer affairs, health, and environmental protection

- To place an establishment off-limits, the installation commander must attempt to work with civic leaders or officials to correct adverse conditions. If that does not work, the AFDCB normally must then:

  -- Notify the proprietor of the offending establishment, in writing, of the alleged condition or situation requiring corrective action;

  -- Specify in the notice a reasonable time for the condition or situation to be corrected; and

  -- Provide the proprietor the opportunity to present any relevant information to the board.

- If the AFDCB recommends an establishment be placed off-limits, the installation commander makes the final decision

    -- A decision to place an establishment off-limits may be appealed to the next higher commander after exhausting any local appeal rights

    -- The establishment remains off-limits until the decision is overturned or the commander determines adequate corrective action has been taken

Emergency Situations

- In emergency situations, commanders may declare establishments or areas temporarily off-limits to personnel of their respective commands. Follow-up action must be taken by AFDCBs as a first priority.

Commander Disciplinary Options

- Members who enter off-limits areas or establishments are subject to disciplinary action under applicable Service regulations and the Uniform Code of Military Justice (UCMJ). Family members of service members and others associated with the Service or installation should be made aware of off-limits restrictions.

- Do not post off-limits signs or notices on private property

- In areas outside of the continental United States, off-limits and other AFDCB procedures must be consistent with existing status of forces agreements

References

· Off Limits Establishments and Areas, 32 C.F.R. § 631.11

· AFI 31-213, *Armed Forces Disciplinary Control Boards and Off-Installation Liaison and Operations* (27 July 2006), certified current 5 July 2018

UNIT UNOFFICIAL ACTIVITIES/UNIT SOCIAL FUNDS

Unit social funds, coffee/flower funds, booster clubs, and similarly named unit-controlled unofficial activities are acceptable when determined to be an unofficial (but still federal) activity with limited assets. Activities that do not meet monetary thresholds to remain as unit unofficial activities must transition to become private organizations (i.e., non-federal entities recognized by the installation commander to operate on the base).

Key Takeaways

» Unit unofficial activities are unofficial federal entities that commanders can form for various purposes (such as organize a holiday party or manage a conference "landing fee")

» If the monetary holdings of unit unofficial activities become too excessive, the entity must transition to an AFI 34-223, *Private Organizations Program*

» Commanders can also decide for tactical reasons to transition unit unofficial activities to a private organization (e.g., to allow the entity to engage in off-base fundraising)

» Since they are federal entities, unit unofficial activities can be supported by Airmen/ Guardians on duty time and their efforts supported with use of official communications

---

Overview

- Assets may not exceed a monthly average of $1,000 over a three-month period. Unofficial activities may temporarily exceed these limits if the substantial majority (>75%) of their raised funds are to be expended within a six-month period on a unit social event (e.g., holiday party).

- The $1,000 average monthly limit may be increased by $100 for every 50 unit members over 300 members, to a maximum of a $5,000 monthly average

- Inventory of unit memorabilia items for sale are not counted towards the $1000 limit

- When assets exceed the above figure, the unofficial activity must either become a private organization, discontinue its operations, or reduce its assets below the asset threshold

- Unofficial activities will:

  -- Maintain a two-person accountability system for all cash transactions; and

  -- Submit a basic annual financial report to the unit commander detailing income and expenditures throughout the year.

- Installation and unit commanders must carefully review the status of all such unofficial activities operating on their installation and ensure their compliance with all applicable rules and regulations

- Such unofficial activities are not meant to become permanent slush funds

  -- Intended to allow group monetary collections for social events (e.g., holiday parties and unit picnics)

-- May also be used to collect landing fees (volunteer contribution of pro rata personal funds) to pay for refreshments and/or meals and unit-hosted conferences and symposia

-- Installation and unit commanders may maintain unofficial activity checking accounts year-round, but the permanent account balance should ideally be the minimum necessary to keep the account open per the financial institution's rules

- No such fund can duplicate or compete with an installation nonappropriated fund revenue-generating activity

- Unofficial activities may not engage in frequent or continuous resale activities

-- Unit commanders must make a tactical decision whether to transition their unofficial activities to installation-recognized private organizations (POs)

--- POs are subject to lawsuits and installation commanders may require private organizations to purchase liability insurance in an amount adequate to cover potential liability arising from their activities. In addition, individual members of the unit/squadron could incur personal liability if not insured. Furthermore, PO events, generally, may not advertise through official communication systems (like those unofficial activities may use). However, unlike unofficial activities, POs have much broader latitude to raise funds, both on and off-base.

-- Unofficial activities must comply with all federal, state, and local laws governing such activities, including federal tax laws

- Unofficial activities may not sell alcoholic beverages, solicit funds, operate amusement or slot machines, or conduct games of chance, lotteries, raffles, or other gambling-type activities

References

· DoD 5500.07-R, *Joint Ethics Regulation* (30 August 1993), incorporating through Change 7, 17 November 2011
· DAFI 36-3101, *Fundraising* (26 October 2022)
· AFI 34-223, *Private Organizations Program* (13 December 2018)

COMMANDER DIRECTED INVESTIGATIONS

Commanders at all levels of the Department of the Air Force (DAF) may conduct investigations of individuals, programs, and processes which fall under their authority. DAFMAN 1-101, *Commander Directed Investigations*, sets out the requirements commanders must follow when directing investigations.

Key Takeaways

» Commanders must always consult with their Staff Judge Advocate before directing any inquiry or investigation

» Commanders are prohibited from conducting investigations into allegations of reprisal and restriction

» Only DAF Official Inquiries Directorate (DAF/IGS) will investigate non-criminal allegations against senior officials

» A Commander Directed Investigation (CDI) is one tool a commander has when an Inspector General (IG) refers a complaint to him/her

» Commanders must notify their local IG upon initiation and completion of all CDIs concerning an officer

Inherent Authority to Investigate

- Commanders who have assumed or were appointed to command in accordance with AFI 51-509, *Appointment to and Assumption of Command*, and AFI 38-101, *Manpower and Organization*, have inherent authority to order CDIs to investigate people and matters under their command

- Others authorized to direct CDIs include Air and Space Staff directors, senior Air and Space Force officers assigned to non-units, and civilians leading organizations designated as a unit in accordance with AFI 38-101, *Manpower and Organization*. Civilians leading directorates are not permitted to direct investigations. The same is true for non-senior officers in such positions.

Subject Matters Appropriate for a CDI

- Reasons a commander may want to conduct a CDI:

  -- To investigate systemic or procedural problems

  -- To investigate a matter related to an individual's conduct or responsibility

- Commanders are **prohibited** from conducting investigations into allegations of reprisal and restriction. Commanders must immediately report all allegations of reprisal or restriction to the DAF, Officer of the Inspector General, Complaints Resolution Directorate (DAF/IGQ) through the local IG.

- Commanders are permitted to investigate allegations of retaliation (Article 132, Uniform Code of Military Justice (UCMJ)). Commanders should discuss such allegations with their Staff Judge Advocate and IG before engaging in such an investigation.

- Commanders shall refer allegations of criminal conduct involving persons affiliated with DoD, or property and programs under their control, to Security Forces, Air Force Office of Special Investigations (AFOSI) or local law enforcement as soon as possible

CDI Process

- Commanders **MUST** notify DAF/IGQ when they initiate any investigation concerning an officer. Commanders will do so through their local IG. They must do the same upon conclusion of the investigation as well as provide a copy of the completed report and any evidence to their local IG.

- Per DAFMAN 1-101, the Air Force Hand-Off Policy requires the Investigating Officer (IO) to engage in a person-to-person hand-off with the commander for all uniformed subjects and suspects in investigations at the conclusion of their interview. The IO should do this for civilian subjects as well.

- If the IO substantiated any allegations and the Appointing Authority (AA) concurs with the findings, the AA provides the subject(s) an opportunity to address the substantiated allegations via a tentative conclusion letter (TCL)

- Once the CDI is complete and the AA signs off on the Report of Investigation (ROI), he/she notifies the complainant and subjects of the results. The commander can use any of the information found during the investigation in any administrative action against an individual.

References

- DAFI 90-5001, *Integrated Resilience* (25 January 2019), incorporating Change 1, 21 October 2021, including DAFI90-5001_DAFGM2023-01, 2 August 2022
- DAFMAN 1-101, *Commander Directed Investigations* (9 April 2021)
- DAFI 90-301, *Inspector General Complaints Resolution* (4 January 2024)
- AFI 38-101, *Manpower and Organization* (29 August 2019), including AFGM2023-01, 19 July 2023
- AFI 51-509, *Appointment to and Assumption of Command* (14 January 2019), including DAFI51-509_DAFGM2023-01, 10 February 2023
- AFI 71-101, Volume 1, *Criminal Investigations Program* (1 July 2019)

ACCEPTANCE OF VOLUNTEER SERVICES

Installation commanders and other officials of the Federal Government are permitted to accept voluntary (i.e., gratuitous) services, in support of certain quality of life programs. Volunteers are considered unpaid employees of the Federal Government in terms of many privileges and protections.

Key Takeaways

- » Volunteer services may be accepted in support of Morale, Welfare and Recreation (MWR) programs and other quality of life programs
- » Volunteers may be provided training and other employee-type benefits and protections as part of their official duties
- » Volunteers must sign a DD 2793 which acknowledges that they will not seek compensation from the U.S. Government in return for their volunteer services
- » Certain functional programs have specific authority to accept volunteer services

General Considerations

- Acceptance of gratuitous services (when the provider agrees in writing and in advance to waive any right to compensation) is always permissible in emergencies involving the safety of human life or the protection of property

- Acceptance of gratuitous services may pose other issues, such as conflicts of interest, liability for damages or injuries both to and by the provider, or the illegal augmentation of another appropriation

- Government employees may not waive their rights to statutory entitlements. This issue may arise in connection with civilian employees and uncompensated overtime.

- Seek the counsel of a Staff Judge Advocate any time free services are offered, unless you know they are specifically authorized by law

Types of Permissible Volunteer Service

- Military services are also specifically authorized by law to accept certain voluntary services in support of certain Department of Air Force (DAF) programs, including medical, dental, legal, religious, family support, library, and MWR programs

    -- All volunteers must sign the DD Form 2793, *Volunteer Agreement for Appropriated Activities or Nonappropriated Fund Instrumentalities*

- Volunteers providing services under authorized programs are considered federal employees only for purposes of compensation for work-related injuries, tort claims for damages or loss, maintenance of records, and conflicts of interest

    -- The volunteer must have been acting within the scope of the accepted services

-- The volunteer will most likely be entitled to Department of Justice representation should he/she be named in an action filed under the Federal Tort Claims Act (FTCA)

-- A volunteer may not hold policy-making positions, supervise paid employees or military personnel, or perform inherently governmental functions, such as determining entitlements to benefits, authorizing expenditures of government funds, or deciding rights and responsibilities of any party under government requirements

-- Volunteers may be used to assist and augment the regularly funded workforce, but may not be used to displace paid employees or in lieu of filing authorized paid personnel positions

Employment of DoD Volunteers

- Volunteers may be provided training related to their duties

- Volunteers may be provided official email access using the Volunteer Logical Access Credential (VOLAC) program

  -- Volunteers may be provided access to Personally Protected Information (PII) if it is required for their duties and they are given proper training

- Properly licensed volunteers may use government motor vehicles (GMVs) if required for their duties (**note:** additional training by the installation Logistics Readiness Squadron (LRS) may be required)

- Volunteers may be reimbursed for minor miscellaneous expenses they incur in the course of their duties

- Volunteers may use childcare services in the installation Child Development Center (CDC), space permitting, during the period of their duties

Volunteers in Specialized DAF Programs

- Federal agencies are specifically authorized by law to accept voluntary services provided by student interns as part of an established educational program

- Volunteer legal assistance services may be accepted in accordance with 10 U.S.C. § 1044

- Military services are statutorily authorized to accept services of Red Cross volunteers

  -- Pursuant to a Memorandum of Understanding between the DoD and the Red Cross, Red Cross volunteers are generally considered government employees for purposes of the protections of the FTCA when acting in the scope of the services accepted by the DoD

- Volunteers accepted per 10 U.S.C. § 1588 are also generally considered government employees for purposes of the protections of the FTCA when acting in the scope of their official duties

References

· Legal Assistance, 10 U.S.C. § 1044

· Authority to Accept Certain Voluntary Services, 10 U.S.C. § 1588

· Federal Tort Claims Act, 28 U.S.C. § 1346(b)

· Limitation on Voluntary Services, 31 U.S.C. § 1342

· DoDD 1000.26E, *Support for Non-Federal Entities Authorized to Operate on DoD Installations* (2 February 2007)

· DoDI 1100.21, *Voluntary Services in the Department of Defense* (27 March 2019)

· DAFMAN 17-1304, *Identity, Credentialing and Access Management* (18 August 2021)

· DD Form 2793, *Volunteer Agreement for Appropriated Fund Activities or Nonappropriated Fund Instrumentalities* (March 2018)

· DAFI 36-3026, Volume 2, *Common Access Card (CAC)*, Attachment 12 (24 January 2023)

· AFI 51-306, *Administrative Claims For and Against the Air Force* (14 January 2019), incorporating through Change 3, 5 May 2021

· Memorandum of Understanding between the United States Department of Defense and the American Red Cross (March 2009) located at https://www.jcs.mil/Portals/36/Documents/Doctrine/Interorganizational_Documents/mou_arc2009.pdf

Page Intentionally Left Blank

Chapter 12
THE AIR FORCE CLAIMS PROGRAM

PERSONAL PROPERTY CLAIMS

The Military Personnel and Civilian Employees Claims Act (PCA) is a gratuitous payment statute. It is not insurance coverage and is not designed to make the United States a total insurer. Payment does not depend on tort liability or government fault. Congress passed the PCA to lessen the hardships of military life, and, within approved guidelines, to compensate proper claimants for property loss or damage.

Key Takeaways

- » Claim must be incident to member's service
- » Notice of all loss and/or damage or complete claim must be submitted to the transportation service provider (TSP) within 180 days of delivery
- » Claim must be submitted within 9 months to be eligible for full replacement value (FRV). Claims submitted after 9 months but within two years are subject to depreciation.
- » The TSP's maximum liability for FRV is $75,000 or $6.00 times the net shipment weight

Requirements under the Statute

- The loss or damage must be incident to the member's service

- The loss or damage cannot be recoverable through private insurance (limited exceptions)

- The claim must be substantiated

- The Air Force must determine that the member's possession of the property was reasonable or useful under the circumstances

- The loss or damage must not have resulted from negligence of the claimant

FRV Program Processing Guidelines

- FRV applies to household goods (HHG) shipments picked up on or after 1 October 2007

- Members may first claim FRV for damaged or lost household goods directly with the carrier

- The claim must be substantiated

- If a member cannot reach an acceptable settlement with the carrier on certain items, the member can file a claim with the Claims Service Center (CSC) for the disputed items only

  -- Standard depreciation rules will apply. The CSC will assert an FRV claim against the carrier, and, if recovery is successful, will pass it on to the member.

- If a member has a significant loss under FRV, they should be aware that the carrier's maximum liability is $75,000 or $6.00 times the net weight of the shipment

FRV Program Filing Deadlines

- Claimant must file the Notice of Loss/Damage After Delivery in the Defense Personal Property System (DPS) Claims Module, placing the carrier on notice that additional loss or damage has been found within 180 days after delivery. Notice can also be provided via email or U.S. Postal Service.

- The claimant must file a claim directly with the carrier within nine months. If the claimant fails to file during this time, they may file a claim with the carrier or the CSC within two years, but standard depreciation rules will then apply.

Defense Personal Property System

- A claimant files a Loss/Damage Report After Delivery within 180 days after delivery (DPS replaced DD Form 1840R and DD Form 1851)

  -- If the member cannot file the Loss/Damage Report After Delivery due to computer or other technical issues, the member should contact the CSC for guidance

- The claimant must file a claim in DPS within nine months of delivery. If dissatisfied with the carrier's offer, the claimant can transfer the items/file a claim with the CSC.

Statute of Limitations and Other Important Time Periods:

- A claim for a sum certain must be presented by the member (or authorized agent) within two years from the incident date or delivery date. FRV is only available if filed within nine months.

- The two-year statute may be extended, for good cause, during time of war. The CSC will determine whether good cause exists to extend the timeline.

- Damage for privately owned vehicles (POVs) is noted on DD Form 788 at the port

  -- If additional damage is discovered after leaving the Vehicle Processing Center (VPC), but within 48 hours of vehicle pickup, the member should contact the VPC and report the additional damage

Proper Claimants

- Active duty Air Force and Space Force military personnel

- Retired or separated Air Force and Space Force military personnel who suffer loss or damage resulting from the last entitled storage or movement of their personal property

- Air Force and Space Force civilian employees paid from appropriated and nonappropriated funds (NAF). Claims filed by NAF civilian employees are paid from NAF funds.

- Air Force Reserve (AFR) and Air National Guard (ANG) personnel when performing federally-funded active duty, full-time ANG duty, inactive duty for training, and ANG technicians serving under 32 U.S.C. § 709

Payable Claims

- <u>Government-sponsored transportation or storage under orders</u>: Examples include household goods and unaccompanied baggage shipments, shipped vehicles, mobile homes and contents in shipment, and, in some circumstances, personally procured moves, luggage and hand-carried property

- <u>At quarters and other authorized locations</u>: Examples include fire, explosion, hurricane, theft, and vandalism in continental United States (CONUS) base housing or at overseas quarters either on or off-base

- <u>Privately owned vehicles</u>: Examples include damage in shipment, theft or vandalism to parked cars, damage or loss during TDY where POV is authorized, and paint over-spray

Non-Payable Claims

- <u>Uniform Items</u>: Uniform items damaged while performing normal duties are not payable

    -- Uniform item claims must be investigated and any payment must be supported by facts. There should be no negligence or lack of due care on the claimant's part.

- <u>Real Property</u>: Real property includes land and whatever is permanently erected, growing upon or affixed to land (i.e., fixtures)

    -- Real property damage can occur when origin or delivery agents are in your residence packing or delivering your household goods

References

- Military Personnel and Civilian Employees' Claims Act (PCA), 31 U.S.C. §§ 3701, 3721, 32 U.S.C. § 709
- DoDD 5515.10, *Settlement and Payment of Claims Under 31 U.S.C. 3701 and 3721, "The Military Personnel and Civilian Employees' Claims Act of 1964"* (24 September 2004), certified current 31 October 2006
- DD Form 788, *Private Vehicle Shipping Document for Automobile* (September 1998)
- AFI 51-306, *Administrative Claims for and Against the Air Force* (14 January 2019), incorporating through Change 3, 5 May 2021
- Air Force Claims Service Center, https://claims.jag.af.mil/

DISASTER CLAIMS

The Air Force Claims Service Center (CSC) and base legal offices work together when a disaster strikes to ensure Airmen, Guardians, and their families receive compensation for personal property that is lost or damaged incident to service.

Key Takeaways

» Request for a disaster claims team must come from wing or installation commander

» Emergency payments can be made within 96 hours

» Claims must be filed with available insurance coverage before filing with CSC

» Claims must be filed with CSC within 2 years of disaster date

Disaster Claims Team

- A team from AF/JA – Civil Law and Litigation Directorate, Claims and Tort Litigation Division, is available to assist base legal offices in large disasters. The disaster claims team will deploy to the disaster location at the request of the wing or installation commander.

- The CSC, with Defense Finance and Accounting Services (DFAS) support, can make emergency payments within 96 hours by electronic funds transfer (EFT)

  -- Alternatively, the CSC can provide the wing accounting liaison officer an emergency funding document to make cash payments, if needed

- If deployed, the team, along with base legal personnel, will inspect and document damaged property, and assist members with filing claims

  -- Claims must first be filed with any available insurance coverage. Claims filed against the Air Force and Space Force are secondary.

- Affected Airmen, Guardians, and their families have two years from the date of the disaster to file their claims

References

· Military Personnel and Civilian Employees' Claims Act (PCA), 31 U.S.C. §§ 3701 & 3721

· DoDD 5515.10, *Settlement and Payment of Claims Under 31 U.S.C. 3701 and 3721, "The Military Personnel and Civilian Employees' Claims Act of 1964"* (24 September 2004), certified current 31 October 2006

· Air Force Claims Service Center, https://claims.jag.af.mil/

TORT CLAIMS

Dependents, retirees, and nonaffiliated civilians may file claims related to accidents or injuries they have suffered. Service members may file claims for property damage or for injuries arising from medical malpractice that occurs in military treatment facilities. Commanders should refer potential claimants to the servicing Staff Judge Advocate's office and should not make any promises or implications that their claim will be approved.

Key Takeaways

» Tort claims are claims arising from alleged negligent or wrongful acts or omissions of government personnel while acting within the scope of their office or employment

» Generally, to receive compensation, an injured person or entity must present a signed written request for payment of a specific amount of money (claim) within two years of the accident or incident

» Installation legal offices accept, investigate, and adjudicate most tort claims alleging $25,000 or less in losses. Higher headquarters handles claims for more than $25,000.

» Tort claims payments do not come from local funds

Introduction

- Under certain circumstances, federal law subjects the United States to liability for property damage, personal injuries, and death that result(s) directly from the negligent or wrongful acts/omissions of government personnel acting within the scope of their employment

- Federal law authorizes the United States to pay for property damage, personal injuries, and death that directly result(s) from "noncombat activities" of United States armed forces

- Normally, to receive compensation, an injured person or entity must present a signed written request for payment of a specific amount of money (claim) within two years of the accident or incident to the agency that created the loss, personal injury, or death

- In some cases, denial of a claim or failure to resolve a claim within six months after it is presented creates a right to sue the United States in federal district court

- Installation legal offices work with AF/JA – Civil Law, Claims and Tort Litigation Division (JACC), to receive and process claims against the Air Force or Space Force and help defend the Air Force or Space Force when claims are litigated

Claims and Claimants

- Torts claims are claims arising from alleged negligent or wrongful acts or omissions of government personnel while acting within the scope of their office or employment

- Airmen and Guardians who cause damages or injuries while acting within the scope of their employment are protected from personal liability. "Scope of employment" generally means they are doing their assigned jobs, not performing personal errands. Common tort claims include car accidents involving government motor vehicles (GMV) or rental cars while on official business, slips and falls on base, barrier or bollard accidents, medical malpractice, or aircraft accidents.

- Claimants may be individuals, organizations, or companies that have suffered loss

Payable Claims

- Claims must demand a specific amount of money, be signed by the claimant or authorized agent, and allege damage to real or personal property, personal injury, or death. Damage must be a direct result of a negligent or wrongful act or omission of government personnel acting within the scope of employment.

  -- Government personnel include Air Force and Space Force military and civilian employees, Civil Air Patrol members performing Air Force or Space Force assigned missions, and Air National Guard military members when in federal status

- A negligent act occurs when a person's failure to exercise the degree of care considered reasonable under the circumstances results in an unintended injury to another party, as determined by the state law where the incident occurred

- The legal office determines, preliminarily, whether an employee acted within the scope of employment and whether a negligent act or omission occurred

  -- Liability is determined by the law of the state where the alleged negligent act or omission occurred or, for claims arising in foreign countries, by the legal standards controlled by United States military regulation or policy, or applicable international agreements

- In rare cases, the loss, injury, or death may be payable even if there is no negligence. This typically happens when the mishap involved conduct that is uniquely military in nature short of combat (noncombat activity). Explosive Ordnance Disposal (EOD) operations and military training maneuvers (including training flights) fall under this category.

  -- If the claim is from a service member or the service member's representative, alleging medical malpractice that occurred in a covered military medical treatment facility, the claim may be payable if the injury or death is the result of negligent care by a military, civilian DoD employee or personal services contractor

- Some forms of claims are specifically excluded by statute and not payable. These include, but are not limited to, claims for intentional torts (acts the person intends to commit), such as assault, battery, false imprisonment, false arrest, malicious prosecution, abuse of process, libel, slander, misrepresentation, deceit, or interference with contractual rights.

Processing and Payment

- Payment for claims does not come from local funds. It comes from either a central AF fund or the U.S. Treasury.

- Installation legal offices accept, investigate, and adjudicate most tort claims alleging $25,000 or less in losses, except for personal injury and medical malpractice tort claims. Claims above $25,000, for personal injury, at CONUS locations are forwarded immediately to JACC. All claims arising out of medical malpractice CONUS and in Alaska and Hawaii, are forwarded immediately to JACC.

- JACC investigates and takes final action on all medical malpractice claims arising within the United States. At USAFE and PACAF bases outside the 50 states, base legal offices investigate medical malpractice claims under the Military Claims Act (MCA) and forward the claims files to JACC with the full investigation and recommendation for final adjudication.

- Final action is taken by mailing the denial of claim or, when applicable, denial of a reconsideration request. In certain cases, claimants may sue the Department of Air Force within six months after final action is taken on the claim. Six months of no action may be deemed a denial by the claimant and the claimant can file suit. Suits are filed in federal district court. The Department of Justice (DoJ) defends the Air Force or Space Force in litigation. JACC works with the installation legal office to help DoJ defend litigation.

References

· Military Claims Act, 10 U.S.C. § 2733

· Medical Malpractice Claims by Members of the Uniformed Services, 10 U.S.C. § 2733a

· Foreign Claims Act, 10 U.S.C. § 2734

· International Agreement Claims Act, 10 U.S.C. §§ 2734(a), 2734(b)

· Federal Tort Claims Act, 28 U.S.C. §§ 1346(b), 2401, 2671–2680

· National Guard Claims Act, 32 U.S.C. § 715

· H.R.2500, National Defense Authorization Act for Fiscal Year 2020, 116th Congress (2019–2020)

· AFI 51-306, *Administrative Claims For and Against the Air Force* (14 January 2019), incorporating through Change 3, 5 May 2021

AVIATION CLAIMS

Aviation claims occur in a variety of ways including, but not limited to, claims arising from aircraft crashes, range operations, falling objects, jet blasts, low overflights, and sonic booms. These claims can involve the Regular Air Force, Regular Space Force, Air Force Reserve (AFR), Air National Guard (ANG), Aero Club, and Civil Air Patrol (CAP) personnel and aircraft.

Key Takeaways

» Aviation Claims may be processed under the Federal Tort Claims Act (FTCA), Military Claims Act (MCA), or National Guard Claims Act (NGCA)

» Base settlement authority is limited to $25,000 and can only be used for claims involving property damage

» Adjudicating ANG and CAP claims depends on the aircrew's status

---

FTCA Claims

- Claims are most commonly resolved under the FTCA and are resolved in accordance with the state law where the mishap or negligence occurred. If the claim is not resolved, the claimant may bring a lawsuit in federal district court. The claimant will need to provide proof of negligence, causation, and damages.

- Base settlement authority is limited to $25,000 and can only be used for claims involving property damage

MCA and NGCA Claims

- If the mishap results from noncombat activities, claims may be adjudicated under the MCA, or possibly the NGCA. There is no requirement to show negligence by the United States.

- Base settlement authority is limited to $25,000 and can only be used for claims involving property damage

- Advanced payments may be possible for extraordinary circumstances where urgent need is demonstrated

Sonic Boom Damage

- The location of the claimant's property in relation to the sonic boom is critical to determining liability

- Broken window glass, cracked stucco and drywall, and fallen items in a house are generally the most common types of damage. A sonic boom is unlikely to cause significant structural damage, such as cracked foundations or sidewalks, without causing other damage.

Low Overflight Damage

- Noise alone generally does not cause damage to property

- Noise may damage a claimant's health and may startle animals, leading to stampeding cattle, horses, or other animals

- Claims alleging loss of property value due to noise from repeated low overflights are not usually payable under any tort claims statute. The remedy is generally a "takings" claim under the Constitution's Fifth Amendment due process clause.

AFR and ANG Claims

- AFR crewmembers have the same status as Regular Air Force and Regular Space Force personnel

- When adjudicating ANG claims, it is important to determine the status of crewmembers of ANG personnel involved in the mishap

- The United States is only liable for the negligence of ANG crewmembers performing federal duties under Title 10 or certain duties under Title 32 at the time of the incident. The United States is not liable when an ANG member is performing duty for the state.

- ANG claims may also be settled pursuant to the NGCA (32 U.S.C. § 715) for death, personal injury, or property damage arising out of the authorized noncombat activities of the ANG

Aero Club Claims

- Aero Clubs are operated as nonappropriated fund instrumentalities (NAFIs) of the United States

- The *Feres* doctrine generally bars Regular Air Force, Regular Space Force, ANG, and AFR **military members** from receiving compensation under federal claims statutes for death or injuries arising out of their participation in Aero Club activities. Such participation is incident to their military service.

- The Federal Employees' Compensation Act (FECA) generally bars Department of Air Force **civilian employees** from receiving compensation under federal claims statutes for death or injuries arising from their participation in Aero Club activities

- The FTCA recognizes third-party claims arising from the negligence of Aero Club employees or military members working in their official capacity

- Aero Club claims under the FTCA are investigated and adjudicated by the same settlement authorities as other FTCA claims. However, settlement of Aero Club claims are paid from nonappropriated funds and administered by the Air Force Installation and Mission Support Center (AFIMSC) located at Joint Base San Antonio-Lackland, Texas.

CAP Claims

- CAP is a federally-chartered, nonprofit civilian corporation under 36 U.S.C. § 40301. It is also a volunteer civilian auxiliary of the Air Force under 10 U.S.C. § 9492 when performing missions assigned by the Air Force. The United States is not liable for third party claims arising out of CAP activities when CAP is acting in its nonprofit status.

- The Air Force is authorized to use the services of the CAP for certain noncombat programs and missions of the Air Force that have been approved as Air Force Assigned Missions (AFAMs). AFAM approval authorities are laid out in DAFI 10-2701, *Organization and Function of the Civil Air Patrol.*

  -- Typical AFAMs include support of homeland security, search and rescue, disaster relief, and counter-narcotics reconnaissance flights

  -- The FTCA recognizes third-party claims arising out of activities of CAP while performing AFAMs

References

· Federal Employees' Compensation Act, 5 U.S.C. §§ 8101 *et seq.*

· Military Claims Act, 10 U.S.C. § 2733

· Civil Air Patrol, 10 U.S.C. § 9492

· Federal Tort Claims Act, 28 U.S.C. §§ 1346(b), 2671–2680

· National Guard Claims Act, 32 U.S.C. § 715

· Organization, 36 U.S.C. § 40301

· *Feres v. United States*, 340 U.S. 135 (1950)

· DoDI 1400.25-V810_DAFI36-150, *Injury Compensation* (9 December 2022)

· DAFI 10-2701, *Organization and Function of the Civil Air Patrol* (17 June 2021)

· AFI 51-306, *Administrative Claims For and Against the Air Force* (14 January 2019), incorporating through Change 3, 5 May 2021

INTERNATIONAL AND FOREIGN TORT CLAIMS IN FOREIGN COUNTRIES

Congress enacted the International Agreement Claims Act (IACA), Foreign Claims Act (FCA), and Military Claims Act (MCA) for consideration of claims alleging wrongful death, personal injury and/or property damage by U.S. Armed Forces personnel in foreign countries. Claims are payable only if meritorious, that is, they are factually substantiated and payment is consistent with applicable law.

Key Takeaways

» For tort claims arising in foreign countries, DoDI 5515.08 is the starting point for determining which military department has responsibility for the claim

» Nominal solatia under 10 U.S.C. § 2242 is not authorized as compensation for payable or non-payable tort claims and is justified as a claim-investigation expense only with proof of custom

» Geographic combatant command Staff Judge Advocates (COCOM SJAs) and their service component command SJAs provide guidance on international agreements and claims under such agreements arising in their respective areas of responsibility (AORs)

» FCA (if IACA is inapplicable) may provide compensation to inhabitants of foreign countries incurring tort damages in their country or another foreign country; payment exclusions apply

» MCA (applicable worldwide) may provide compensation to inhabitants of the United States incurring tort damages in foreign countries; payment exclusions apply

Single Service Claims Responsibility

- Responsibility for processing tort claims arising in foreign countries is vested with the Departments of the Army, Navy, and Air Force

    -- In DoDI 5515.08, the Department of Defense General Counsel (DoD/GC) lists the countries for which these three military departments exercise exclusive claims responsibility for DoD tort claims

    -- Some countries are not assigned. Claims arising in unassigned countries should be processed by the Army, Navy, or Air Force command whose activity or personnel allegedly caused the claim.

Solatia

- A solatium payment is a nominal payment made immediately to a victim or victim's family to express sympathy when local custom exists for such a payment

- Solatia under 10 U.S.C. § 2242 is not compensation for tort damages and, in countries for which the Air Force has claims responsibility, is limited to Japan, where U.S. military regulation governs the practice

IACA Claims

- The IACA is not available as a source of compensation unless the United States is party to an international agreement (IA) providing for "cost sharing of claims" against the United States

  -- Article VIII, Paragraph 5(e) of the *Agreement Between the Parties to the North Atlantic Treaty Regarding the Status of their Forces* (NATO SOFA) exemplifies "cost-sharing of claims." (Total claim payout is made by the United States and one or more other Parties to the SOFA).

- The timeliness of such claims is determined by the receiving state (host nation) law, but no IACA claim, even if timely, may be paid for combat-related damages

- All conditions governing the adjudication and payment of the claim under the IA and IACA must be satisfied

- Geographic COCOM SJAs and their service component command SJAs provide guidance on IAs applicable to their respective areas of responsibility (AORs)

FCA Claims

- Congress disallows payment of FCA claims not presented within 2 years of accrual (incident occurrence) and claims arising from enemy or U.S. actions in combat

  -- However, an FCA claim arising indirectly from combat and based on an aircraft accident or malfunction while preparing for, going to, or returning from a combat mission may be considered under 10 U.S.C. § 2734(b)(3)

- Proper claimants under the FCA include foreign nationals, foreign businesses, foreign governments, U.S. expatriates residing abroad (not connected with U.S. Government service), and U.S. corporations with a place of business inside the country where the claim arose

- For favorable FCA payment consideration, the investigation must show damages were caused, negligently or wrongfully, by U.S. Armed Forces personnel or caused by noncombat activities of the U.S. Armed Forces (see AFI 51-306, *Administrative Claims for and Against the Air Force* "Terms")

- The Secretary of the Air Force has promulgated AFI 51-306, *Administrative Claims*, and 32 C.F.R. Part 842, *Administrative Claims* (Subpart E) to implement Department of the Air Force policy under the FCA

  -- AFI 51-306, Attachment 2, identifies FCA Settlement Authorities

  -- 32 C.F.R. § 842.55 lists extensive FCA payment exclusions

MCA Claims

- Congress disallows payment of MCA claims not presented within 2 years of accrual

- Proper claimants under the MCA are primarily citizens and inhabitants of the United States (present abroad as tourists or U.S. Government employees, dependents, or contract employees)

  -- U.S. military and civilian personnel are not proper claimants for injury or death incident to their service

- MCA claims arising in foreign countries require a showing that damages were caused, negligently or wrongfully, by U.S. Armed Forces personnel acting in the scope of their employment or caused by noncombat activities of the U.S. Armed Forces

- The Secretary of the Air Force has promulgated AFI 51-306 and 32 C.F.R. Part 842 (Subpart D) to implement Department of the Air Force policy under the MCA

  -- AFI 51-306, Attachment 2, identifies MCA Settlement Authorities

  -- 32 C.F.R. § 842.40 lists extensive MCA payment exclusions

References

· International Agreement Claims Act, 10 U.S.C. § 2734a

· Foreign Claims Act, 10 U.S.C. § 2734

· Military Claims Act, 10 U.S.C. § 2733

· Advance Payments Act, 10 U.S.C. § 2736

· Authority to Use Appropriated Funds for Certain Investigations and Security Services, 10 U.S.C. § 2242

· Administrative Claims, 32 C.F.R. Part 842

· DoDD 5515.3, *Settlement of Claims Under Sections 2733, 2734, 2734a, and 2734b of Title 10, United States Code* (27 September 2004), certified current 31 October 2006

· DoDD 5515.9, *Settlement of Tort Claims* (19 April 2004), certified current 31 October 2006

· DoDI 5515.08, *Assignment of Claims Responsibility* (30 August 2016)

· AFI 51-306, *Administrative Claims For and Against the Air Force* (14 January 2019), incorporating through Change 3, 5 May 2021

PROPERTY DAMAGE TORT CLAIMS IN FAVOR OF THE UNITED STATES

The Department of the Air Force (DAF) has the right under federal law to collect claims for damage to its property through someone's negligence or wrongful act. Claims on behalf of the United States for property damage by a tortfeasor require the base to be proactive and aggressively look for these claims, which are known as "G claims" or "government claims".

Key Takeaways

» The Air Force has a right to collect claims for damage to its property caused through someone's negligence or wrongful act

» Legal office claims personnel need the cooperation of installation units responsible for property to identify potential claims and to collect evidence of the damage done to Air Force property

» Monies collected from G claims are not typically returned to the unit for use but instead are deposited in different accounts based on what property was damaged by the tort

» The repair in kind collection method may be used to avoid spending unit funds on repairs to damaged property

Introduction

- Installation legal offices should aggressively assert claims against a tortfeasor for loss or damage to government property. Cooperation with installation units responsible for property is key to a successful program. This includes Civil Engineering, Transportation, and Security Forces.

- To successfully pursue a G claim, claims officers must collect evidence that shows a tort (negligent or wrongful act) was committed and that Air Force property was damaged. This evidence typically consists of police reports, completed SF-95s (Claims for Damage, Injury, or Death), witness statements, photographs of the incident site and damaged property, and detailed invoices generated by qualified repair technicians.

- Due to fiscal laws, monies collected from G claims are not typically returned to the unit for use but instead are deposited in different accounts based on what property was damaged by the tort

- However, the repair in kind collection method may be used to avoid spending unit funds on repairs. Under this process, instead of paying the Air Force for damages, a tortfeasor can pay a repair technician directly for repairs made to the damaged Air Force property. This collection method comports with federal spending laws and directly compensates the unit whose property was damaged.

Identifying, Investigating, and Asserting G Claims

- Air Force Instruction 51-306, *Administrative Claims for and Against the Air Force*, para. 7.2, directs Air Force personnel to promptly assert claims against all tortfeasors or other responsible parties (such as an insurance company) for loss of or damage to government property, if the loss or damage is for $100 or more

- Claims officers should establish lines of communication with installation units that monitor and maintain Air Force property, including but not limited to Civil Engineering, Transportation, Logistics Readiness (to include Morale, Welfare and Recreation programs), and Security Forces

- Personnel in these units should be trained by claims officers to identify government claims and to collect and preserve the evidence needed to pursue the claim

- Once evidence of a tort and invoices for repair have been compiled, a claims officer notifies the tortfeasor of the claim and requests payment. The tortfeasor is offered an opportunity to rebut the claim in writing or through the offering of additional evidence.

- Once a tortfeasor accepts fault for damaging Air Force Property, the tortfeasor can pay the entire amount claimed outright, establish a payment plan, or pay a repair technician directly (repair in kind) for repairs made to the damaged property

Collecting and Depositing G Claims Payments

- If a tortfeasor agrees to make payment, claims personnel deposit collections in the following manner:

  -- Deposit collections for loss, damage, or destruction to Air Force or Space Force family housing, caused by abuse or negligence, to the DoD military family housing management account

  -- Deposit collections for loss, damage, or destruction to other real property to the appropriate funds account of the organization responsible for the repair, maintenance, or replacement of the real property. These funds may not be reused without their appropriation by Congress.

  -- Deposit collections for loss, damage, or destruction to property of an Air Force or Space Force industrial fund or other revolving funds account to that account

  -- Pay or deposit recoveries involving nonappropriated fund instrumentality (NAFI) property to the appropriate NAFI

  -- Deposit all other collections for which there is no statutory exception to the U.S. Treasury miscellaneous receipts account

- If a tortfeasor refuses to make payment, claims personnel should forward the case file to the DAF Headquarters, Claims and Tort Litigation Division (HQ USAF/JACC) for potential collection through the U.S. Treasury's Cross-Servicing Administrative Offset Program. Under this program, the U.S. Treasury will garnish funds payable to the tortfeasor (such as tax refunds) until the full claim is satisfied.

References

· Damage to Real Property: Disposition of Amounts Recovered, 10 U.S.C. § 2782 Military Family Housing Management Account, 10 U.S.C. § 2831

· Custodians of Money, 31 U.S.C. § 3302

· Money and Finance: Claims, 31 U.S.C. § 3701

· Federal Claims Collection Act, 31 U.S.C. §§ 3711–3719

· AFI 51-306, *Administrative Claims For and Against the Air Force* (14 January 2019), incorporating through Change 3, 5 May 2021

MEDICAL COST REIMBURSEMENT CLAIMS

The Air Force and Space Force may recover the cost of providing medical care to active duty, reserve (in certain situations), and retired military members and their beneficiaries who are injured as a result of negligent conduct of third parties under the Federal Medical Care Recovery Act (FMCRA) and for all care covered by a third-party payer under the Coordination of Benefits statute (COB). The Air Force and Space Force may also recover lost wages if a military duty member is unable to work because of the injuries they sustained from the accident.

Key Takeaways

» If an active duty, reserve, or retired military member is injured because of someone else's negligence, the United States may recover the cost of their medical care

» If a military member is unable to work because of their injuries, the United States may recover their lost wages as part of the claim, and this money goes back to the unit the member was assigned to at the time of the accident

» A military member's chain of command should refer military members to the closest legal office and/or Medical Cost Reimbursement Office when they learn of these types of incidents

---

FMCRA Claims

- Under this statute, the government's recovery is predicated on circumstances creating tort liability

  -- Usually, the elements of negligence: duty, breach, causation, and damages—must be present before considering the assertion of an FMCRA claim

  -- The FMCRA applies even in no-fault jurisdictions. Where a system of tort liability has been replaced by a no-fault system, the government may pursue an FMCRA claim as a third-party beneficiary.

  -- Any defenses available under state law that may negate tort liability, such as contributory negligence, may be interposed to defeat the government's claim. However, state procedural defenses cannot be interposed to defeat the claim.

  -- In general, a federal statute of limitations of three years applies

  -- Since the United States has an independent statutory right of recovery, a release signed by the injured party is usually not effective in extinguishing the government's claim

- All successful collections for treatment provided by a military treatment facility (MTF) are deposited into the Operations and Maintenance (O&M) account of the MTF rendering treatment. Collections for active duty pay are deposited to the O&M account of the unit to which the injured member was assigned at the time of the injury. Recoveries for treatment paid by the Defense Health Agency (DHA), previously known as TRICARE, are returned to the Defense Health Program (DHP).

Coordination of Benefits (COB) Claims

- Congress allows MTFs to pursue recovery from statutorily defined plans

  -- These include health insurance policies/plans, auto insurance providing for medical treatment, workers' compensation coverage, and similar plans, policies, and programs

  -- The COB statute makes the United States a third-party beneficiary under such plans

  -- In general, a federal statute of limitations of six years applies

- Successful recoveries of medical expenses are deposited directly into the treating MTF's O&M account. COB has been extended to allow recovery of payments made through DHA. Medical expenses paid for by DHA are deposited into the DHP.

Collection of Medical Cost Reimbursement Claims

- These claims are collected either by overseas base legal offices or one of eight Medical Cost Reimbursement Program ("MCRP") regional offices within the United States. The MCRP offices are located at:

  -- Joint Base McGuire-Dix-Lakehurst, New Jersey

  -- Joint Base Langley-Eustis, Virginia

  -- Eglin Air Force Base, Florida

  -- Wright-Patterson Air Force Base, Ohio

  -- Joint Base San Antonio-Lackland, Texas

  -- Offutt Air Force Base, Nebraska

  -- Nellis Air Force Base, Nevada

  -- Travis Air Force Base, California

- Collections are generated from reports of injuries to covered personnel from MTFs, medical treatment providers, Security Forces (SFS) blotters, and notice from the injured party's chain-of-command. If commanders or first sergeants become aware of an injury to an active duty, reserve, or retired military member and/or their beneficiaries caused by a negligent act, the chain of command should promptly notify the base legal office for guidance on how to process this information and/or advise the injured party to contact the closest MCRP office.

References

· Collection from Third-Party Payers, 10 U.S.C. § 1095

· Federal Medical Care Recovery Act, 42 U.S.C. §§ 2651–2653

· AFI 51-306, *Administrative Claims For and Against the Air Force* (14 January 2019), incorporating through Change 3, 5 May 2021

ARTICLE 139 CLAIMS

Under Article 139, Uniform Code of Military Justice (UCMJ), commanders may direct collection and pay a claim for property that military personnel willfully damage or wrongfully take, if the claim results from riotous, violent, or disorderly conduct.

Key Takeaways

» Commanders may direct collection and pay a claim for property that military personnel willfully damage or wrongfully take

» Claims under this provision must be submitted within 90 days of the date of the incident, unless the commander determines good cause for a delay

» Commanders appoint a board of officers to investigate Article 139 claims

» After reviewing the Board's recommendations, commanders assess an amount against each offender and direct Defense Finance and Accounting Service (DFAS) to withhold the specified amount from each offender's pay

Scope of Article 139 Claims

- Assertable Claims:

    -- Property claims only, not personal injury or wrongful death

    -- Must involve willful misconduct, not performance of legally authorized duties; and must arise from riotous, violent, or disorderly conduct, not conduct involving simple negligence or, for example, bad checks or private indebtedness

- Article 139 claims are entirely separate and distinct from disciplinary action taken under any other article of the UCMJ, or any other administrative action that may be appropriate

- Proper Claimant:

    -- Any individual, to include military and civilian, business entity, state, territory, local government, or nonprofit organization may file an Article 139 claim

    -- An appropriated fund, nonappropriated fund instrumentality, or any other component of the United States government may not file an Article 139 claim

Procedures

- The claim must be submitted to an appropriate commander

- The appropriate commander is the officer exercising Special Court-Martial Convening Authority over the offender

- Claims must be submitted within 90 days of the date of the incident, unless the commander determines good cause for a delay

- Examples of good cause for delay may include deployment, a claimant who does not know the identity of the tortfeasor, or the claimant's reasonable lack of knowledge of the ability to file an Article 139 claim

  - Initially, the claim may be presented orally, but it must be written and state a sum certain before final action may be taken

- The claim should be submitted to the commander of the military organization or unit of the alleged offending member or members. However, it may be presented to the commander of the nearest military installation to be forwarded to the appropriate commander for jurisdiction. Commanders who receive Article 139 claims that are not under their jurisdiction should forward it promptly to the appropriate command.

- The appointing commander appoints a board of officers to investigate the claim

- A board of officers may consist of one to three commissioned officers. After evaluating all available evidence, which may include interviewing the individual against whom the claim was asserted (in accordance with the rights afforded by Article 31, UCMJ, and the right to counsel), the board:

  - Determines if the claim falls under Article 139, UCMJ

  - Identifies the offender(s)

  - Determines liability and damages

- The board may recommend:

  - Assessing damages against the identified service member (deducting from the assessment any voluntary or partial payments already made)

  - Assessing damages against members who were present during the incident, if authorities cannot individually identify the offenders

  - Disapproving the claim

- After the board completes its review, it forwards the claim to the Staff Judge Advocate for a legal review prior to action by the appointing commander

Action by the Appointing Commander

- Determine if the claim falls under Article 139, UCMJ

- Assess an amount against each offender, but not more than the board's recommended amount

- Forward the board's report to the appropriate commander if it is determined that one or more offenders are in a different command, since only the commander of an offender may order payment of the claim under Article 139, UCMJ

- Direct the DFAS office to withhold the specified amount from each offender's pay to pay the claimant

- Notify the offender and claimant of the action taken

Appeals and Reconsideration

- The commander's action may not be appealed by the claimant or the offender

- The commander who originally ordered the assessment may reconsider and change the decision if the findings later prove to be wrong, even if the offender is no longer a member of that command

- A successor in command may change or cancel the assessment only based on newly discovered evidence, fraud, or obvious error of law or fact

References

· Articles 31 and 139, Uniform Code of Military Justice

· AFI 51-306, *Administrative Claims for and Against the Air Force* (14 January 2019), incorporating through Change 3, 5 May 2021

LIABILITY FOR DAMAGE TO RENTAL VEHICLES

Vehicles rented on government orders are for official use only. The use of a rental vehicle on government orders for other than official purposes places a member at risk of personal liability for damage to the rental car. A member avoids personal liability if they were authorized a rental vehicle and were using the vehicle for an official purpose while acting within the scope of the member's employment. When members rent vehicles through channels other than Defense Travel System (DTS), the fund cite used to pay for the TDY will have to pay for any damage to the rental car. This can be tens of thousands of dollars if the rental car is totaled.

Key Takeaways

» Damage to rental cars will be paid from unit TDY funds if proper procedures are not followed

» When renting a vehicle pursuant to an authorization on orders, it is mandatory to obtain the rental vehicle through the commercial travel office (CTO)

» Under the Defense Travel Management Office (DTMO) negotiated agreement, a rental car company assumes the entire risk of loss/damage to the rental vehicle up to the policy limits

» For the rental company to assume risk under the DTMO negotiated agreement, travel orders must reflect that a rental vehicle is authorized

» After an accident, call and report the accident to the rental car company and the government travel card (GTC) company

Introduction

- Generally, a member avoids personal liability for damages to, and caused by, a rental vehicle they were driving, if the member was authorized a rental vehicle and was using the vehicle for an official purpose while acting within the scope of employment

- "Official purposes" is a standard in the Joint Travel Regulation (JTR) and is used to determine whether a renter will be reimbursed for damage to a rental vehicle

  -- Official purposes include transportation to and from duty locations, lodging, dining facilities, drugstores, barber shops, places of worship, and similar places required for the traveler's subsistence, health, or comfort

  -- Even with these official purposes, there are limits. For example, a member who drives a significant distance past numerous restaurants to have dinner with a family member or friend is no longer on official purpose and risks personal liability if they are involved in an accident.

- "Scope of employment" is based on the law of the state in which the accident occurs and is the legal standard under the claims statutes that will be used to determine whether the United States will defend a renter in a lawsuit

DTMO Rental Vehicle Agreement

- If a rental car is authorized on orders but not covered by the DTMO agreement, any damage to the rental car is likely going to be paid from the fund cite that paid for the travel. It is important that renters do all within their power to ensure the DTMO agreement applies to their rental agreement. They do this by renting vehicles through DTS and selecting the preferred vendors offered in their itinerary.

- When renting a vehicle pursuant to an authorization on orders, it is mandatory to reserve the vehicle through DTS. If unavailable, reserve the vehicle through the CTO. DTS and CTO will first attempt to reserve a vehicle from a company participating in the Defense Travel Management Office (DTMO) negotiated agreement.

- Major rental car companies subscribe to a Memorandum of Understanding (MOU) with DTMO. Under the agreement, the rental car company is responsible for the entire risk of loss of or damage to the rented vehicles with a few rare exceptions. The rental car company also provides the government and traveler with up to $300,000 in liability coverage if the government driver causes damage or injury to another vehicle.

- In order for the rental company to assume risk under the DTMO agreement, travel orders must reflect a rental vehicle is authorized, the member must be using the rental vehicle for an official purpose and acting within the scope of the member's employment. The vehicle must not be misused or recklessly operated. Drag racing, off-roading, driving while intoxicated, or the vehicle being stolen due to misplacing the keys are examples of situations where the rental company is not responsible for the loss or damage.

Liability for Damages to the Rental Vehicle and to Others

- There are four different situations involving rental car liability: (1) rented on orders pursuant to DTMO agreement; (2) rented on orders not under the DTMO agreement; (3) personal rental vehicle on official temporary duty (TDY); and (4) rented pursuant to an umbrella contract

  -- (1) When a vehicle is rented by a member who is on orders pursuant to the DTMO negotiated agreement, the rental company provides coverage as described above

  -- (2) When a vehicle is rented by a member who is on orders but not under the DTMO agreement, the GTC carries limited coverage for damage to the rental car. Strict deadlines apply for reporting the damage. It is important that a renter report damage to the GTC as quickly as possible after the damage has been discovered.

    --- While there are some exceptions, the GTC collision coverage generally covers collision or rollover, theft-related charges, vandalism, windshield damage due to road debris, and loss of use and towing charges due to covered damage

--- If the GTC does not provide coverage, the loss or damage to the vehicle is a reimbursable expense under the JTR. The member claims reimbursement on their travel voucher and it is paid from the fund cite that funded the travel. For damage to another vehicle, property, or personal injury, the United States will defend the driver so long as the driver was acting within the scope of employment.

-- (3) When a member rents a vehicle while TDY but that rental was not authorized on their orders, the member is personally responsible for damage to the rental vehicle. For damage to another vehicle, property, or personal injury, the United States will defend the driver if the driver was acting in the scope of employment.

-- (4) When a vehicle is rented pursuant to an umbrella contract, the DTMO agreement is not applicable. Claims for damage to rental vehicles under contract are settled under contractual provisions as claims against the contract.

--- Unlike vehicles rented on a GTC; a financial liability investigation may be required for damage to a vehicle rented under a government contract

--- For damages to another vehicle or property, the United States will defend the driver if the driver was acting in the scope of employment

In Case of Accident

- Call the rental company and report. If rented on a GTC, call the travel card company and report immediately. Notify the police. If the police respond, get a copy of the accident report or find out how to get a copy later.

- If someone else is injured in the accident and the renter is TDY at or near a base, the renter should inform the base legal office of the accident. If renter is not near a base, he/she should contact their base legal office upon return.

- Inform the Staff Judge Advocate immediately if the renter becomes aware of a lawsuit filed regarding a vehicle rented by an Air Force or Space Force member/employee while on TDY orders, even if the United States is not a named party in the suit

- Never admit liability or make payment assurances at the site of an accident

References

· Exclusiveness of Remedy, 28 U.S.C. § 2679
· Federal Acquisition Regulation (FAR) §§ 28.312, 52.228-8
· Joint Federal Travel Regulations (JTR), https://www.defensetravel.dod.mil/Docs/perdiem/JTR.pdf Defense Transportation Regulation (DTR) DoD Regulation 4500.9-R-Part I, Passenger Movement (May 2016), including changes through 14 January 2021
· AFI 51-306, *Administrative Claims for and Against the Air Force* (14 January 2019), incorporating through Change 3, 5 May 2021
· Defense Travel Management Office, https://www.defensetravel.dod.mil/index.cfm

FINANCIAL LIABILITY INVESTIGATIONS: REPORTS OF SURVEY

Commanders at all levels are responsible for not only the personnel in their unit, but also for all assigned equipment and property under their control. Occasionally some of that equipment may be lost, damaged or destroyed. Depending on the type of item(s) that are lost or damaged, a financial liability investigation (formerly known as a report of survey (ROS)) might be required to investigate and document the circumstances and determine the appropriate corrective actions.

Key Takeaways

» The primary purpose of the financial liability investigation is to determine financial liability for the loss, theft, damage, or destruction of government property

» A financial liability investigation is mandatory when sensitive, classified, or leased property, real property, or government-owned equipment with a value of $5,000 (with evidence of negligence or abuse) has been lost, damaged, destroyed, or stolen

» Procedures for conducting a financial liability investigation are found in DoD 7000.14-R, Department of Defense Financial Management Regulation (DoD FMR), Volume 12, Chapter 7, *Financial Liability for Government Property Lost, Damaged, Destroyed, or Stolen*

Purpose

- Note that the information discussed below does not apply to nonappropriated fund assets. Nonappropriated fund assets are governed by the procedures outlined in Chapter 8 of AFMAN 34-202, *Procedures for Protecting Nonappropriated Fund Assets*.

- The primary purpose of the financial liability investigation is to determine financial liability for the loss, theft, damage, or destruction of government property. This purpose is accomplished by:

  -- Investigating the cause of loss, damage, or destruction of property and determining if it was attributable to an individual's negligence or abuse

  -- Assessing monetary liability or relieving individuals from liability if there is no evidence of negligence, willful misconduct, or deliberate unauthorized use

  -- Providing documentation to support adjustment of accountable records

  -- Providing commanders with case histories to enable them to take corrective action to prevent recurrence of the incident

Mandatory Financial Liability Investigation

- A financial liability investigation is mandatory when the following have been lost, damaged, destroyed, or stolen:

  -- Sensitive, classified, or leased (capital lease) property regardless of initial acquisition cost

  -- Real property

  -- Government-owned equipment where there is evidence of negligence or abuse, and the equipment has an initial cost (value) of $5,000 or more

Non-Mandatory Financial Liability Investigation

- For all other losses, commanders have discretion to conduct a formal financial liability investigation when the circumstances warrant it (e.g., when the loss, damage, destruction or theft of small amounts of property occur frequently enough to suggest a pattern of wrongdoing)

- Additionally, commanders may use other investigations or inquiries such as a Commander Directed Investigation (CDI) to augment a financial liability investigation

Liability Thresholds

- Before moving into the process itself, it is important to be aware of the amount of financial liability Air Force and Space Force members may be expected to repay. These amounts vary depending on the nature of the items affected by the loss/damage. In most cases, the liability threshold is limited to the full amount of the loss, damage, or destruction, or up to one month of the member's basic pay, whichever is less.

The Financial Liability Investigation Process

- The first step to initiating a financial liability investigation is for the appointing authority to appoint an investigating officer (IO) to determine the facts. Some of the investigative processes are highlighted below.

  -- At a minimum, the IO will answer the following six questions:

    --- What happened?

    --- How did it happen?

    --- Where did it happen?

    --- When did it happen?

    --- Who was involved?

    --- Was there any evidence of negligence, willful misconduct, or deliberate unauthorized use or disposition of the property?

- Based on the facts gathered, the IO makes findings and recommendations on the issue of liability of the person(s) involved

- The financial liability investigation is forwarded for legal review

- Upon legal review, the investigation and IO's recommendations are reviewed by the appointing authority, who determines liability

- If liability is approved, the appointing authority informs the subject(s) of the determination and gives him or her an opportunity to provide a rebuttal

- The approving authority then reviews and considers the rebuttal and makes a second determination as to liability

- If the member is held liable, the approving authority sends the financial liability investigation to the financial manager to process for collection

- The final paperwork then goes to the equipment custodian to write off the property

Processing Times

- As lost, damaged, or destroyed property has an impact on the Air Force, Space Force, and the individual(s) liable, the Air Force and Space Force have established the following timelines for initiation and completion of a financial liability investigation:

  - Within 10 days from the date of the discovery of the loss, the unit's supervision will conduct the initial inquiry (not a formal investigation) and gather data to determine whether the situation warrants a more formal investigation

  - Within 11 days from the date of the discovery of the loss, the appointing authority will appoint an IO if a formal financial liability investigation is required or desired, and obtain a case number

  - The financial liability investigation should generally be completed within 90 days of the date of the discovery of the loss

  - Additional timelines for each step of the investigative process may be found in the SAF/FMF *Reports of Survey Program Policy Memorandum*, dated 9 November 2018

References

· DoD 7000.14-R, *Department of Defense Financial Management Regulation* (DoD FMR), Volume 12, Chapter 7, *Financial Liability for Government Property Lost, Damaged, Destroyed, or Stolen* (January 2021)

· AFI 23-101, *Materiel Management Property* (22 October 2020), including DAFI23-101_DAFGM2021-01, 8 July 2021

· AFMAN 23-122, *Materiel Management Procedures* (27 October 2020), including DAFMAN23-122_DAFGM2022-01, 2 August 2022

· AFMAN 34-202, *Procedures for Protecting Nonappropriated Fund Assets* (25 June 2019)

· SAF/FMF Memorandum, *Reports of Survey Program – Policy Memorandum* (9 November 2018)

Chapter 13
FISCAL AND CONTRACTING ISSUES

FOUNDATIONS OF FISCAL LAW

In Fiscal Law, any expenditure of funds requires Congress to have authorized and appropriated funds. The commander must have affirmative authority to use funds for a particular purpose. The three pillars of affirmative authority are purpose, time, and amount.

> ### Key Takeaways
>
> » Congress controls the expenditure of public funds through authorizations and appropriations
>
> » Expenditures that violate Congress' authorizations and appropriations can result in personal criminal and civil liability

Purpose

- Funds may be expended only for the purpose intended by Congress. However, not every expenditure is required to be specified in an appropriations act. There is a three-part test to determine whether an expenditure is a "necessary expense" and meets the purpose of a particular appropriation:

  -- The expenditure must be necessary and incident to the purposes of the appropriation;

  -- The expenditure must not be prohibited by law; and

  -- The expenditure must not otherwise fall within the scope of another more specific appropriation or statutory funding scheme.

- Examples of common issues regarding questionable expenses (i.e., items that are generally for personal use/convenience):

  -- <u>Bottled Water</u>: Typically a personal expense, with some exceptions for disasters and locations where no potable water exists

  -- <u>Clothing</u>: Typically a personal expense with limited exceptions

  -- <u>Payment of Fines and Penalties</u>: Typically a personal expense unless the individual was directed to incur the fine or penalty, or a fine or penalty was imposed on the agency itself

  -- <u>Food</u>: Typically a personal expense with some exceptions for certain situations involving training, conferences, and award ceremonies

Time

- An agency may obligate funds only within the time limits applicable to the appropriation

  -- <u>Bona Fide Needs Rule</u>: Generally, government agencies may not purchase supplies or services unless there is a bona fide (good faith) need for the supply or service in the fiscal year in which the supplies or services are to be purchased

-- <u>For Supplies</u>: Exceptions to the default rule are allowed if lead-time is required to either produce or deliver the supply, or to maintain normal/customary stock levels of a supply

-- <u>For Services</u>: The bona fide need does not arise until the services are rendered and must be funded with funds current as of the date the services are performed. For severable services (such as lawn maintenance), DoD agencies may obligate funds current at the time of contract award to finance the contract so long as the period of performance does not exceed one year (which may cross fiscal years). For non-severable services (such as the results of a longitudinal healthcare study), the DoD must fund with dollars available for obligation at the time the contract is executed. Performance of such a contract may cross fiscal years.

Amount

- An agency must obligate funds within the amounts appropriated by Congress

The Antideficiency Act (ADA)

- The ADA was originally enacted by Congress to prevent the federal government from making expenditures in excess of the amounts that Congress appropriated and includes the possibility of criminal, civil and administrative penalties. Under the ADA, unless authorized by law, an officer or employee of the U.S. Government may **NOT**:

-- Make or authorize an expenditure or obligation exceeding an amount available in an appropriation

-- Involve the government in a contract or obligation for the payment of money before an appropriation is made

-- Make or authorize an expenditure or obligation exceeding an apportionment, or the amount permitted by regulations

-- Accept voluntary services for the United States or employ personal services, except for emergencies involving the safety of human life or the protection of property

- Officials can correct a potential ADA violation using the proper funds to pay the obligation if the following conditions are met:

-- Proper funds were available at the time of the erroneous obligation;

-- Proper funds were available at the time of correction for the agency to correct the erroneous obligation; and

-- Proper funds were available the whole time between the erroneous obligation and correction.

References

· Contracts for Periods Crossing Fiscal Years, 10 U.S.C. § 3133

· Appropriations, 31 U.S.C. § 1301(a)

· Antideficiency Act, 31 U.S.C. §§ 1341 *et seq.*

· Limitations on Expending and Obligating Amounts, 31 U.S.C. § 1341

· Limitations on Voluntary Services, 31 U.S.C. § 1342

· Reports on Violations, 31 U.S.C. § 1351

· Balances Available, 31 U.S.C. § 1502(a)

· Prohibited Obligations and Expenditures, 31 U.S.C. § 1517(a)

· *United States v. MacCollom*, 426 U.S. 317 (1976)

· DoD 7000.14-R, *Department of Defense Financial Management Regulation (DoD FMR)* (December 2022), https://comptroller.defense.gov/FMR/

· Principles of Federal Appropriations Law – U.S. Government Accountability Office (GAO), 3rd and 4th eds. ("The Red Book"), https://www.gao.gov/legal/appropriations-law-decisions/red-book

· DAFMAN 65-605, Volume 1, *Budget Guidance and Technical Procedures* (31 March 2021)

· DAFI 65-601, Volume 1, *Budget Guidance and Procedures* (22 June 2022)

· AFI 65-601, Volume 2, *Budget Management for Operations* (29 January 2021)

FOUNDATIONS OF CONTRACT LAW

The Department of Defense (DoD) relies heavily on contractors to deliver necessary supplies and services to the warfighter. Therefore, it is imperative that acquisition professionals, attorneys, and commanders work together to protect the integrity, precision, and reliability of the acquisition process.

Key Takeaways

» Warranted contracting officers are the only individuals authorized to obligate government funds

» When an unauthorized commitment cannot be ratified, the individual who inappropriately committed government funds is the one responsible for paying the bill

---

Contracting Authority

- Generally, commanders do not have contracting authority

- Commanders nonetheless have a duty to ensure personnel are informed of proper contracting authority

    -- Normally, only contracting officers (COs) who have been delegated authority by the head of an agency in the form of a "warrant" have the authority to enter into contracts on behalf of the U.S. Government

    -- Government Purchase Card cardholders (with limited monetary thresholds) have limited contract authority that has been delegated from senior contracting officials

Unauthorized Commitments

- An "unauthorized commitment" is when an individual without contract authority enters into a commitment to accept supplies or services. Once discovered, unauthorized commitments may be "ratified" by a person with contract authority, thereby allowing for government payment.

- To be eligible for ratification, an unauthorized commitment must meet the seven criteria set forth at Federal Acquisition Regulation (FAR) 1.602-3(c). The commander of the individual's organization must ensure the CO is provided a report of the circumstances surrounding the unauthorized commitment, including a statement on corrective actions taken to prevent a recurrence of the event, and a description of disciplinary action taken or an explanation of why no action was taken.

- Any unauthorized commitments that are not ratified are the sole financial responsibility of the individual making the unauthorized commitment and are not the financial responsibility of the government

References

· Federal Acquisition Regulation Subpart 1.6, *Career Development, Contracting Authority, and Responsibilities*

· Federal Acquisition Regulation Subpart 1.602-3, *Ratification of Unauthorized Commitments*

· Department of the Air Force Federal Acquisition Regulation Supplement Subpart 5301.6, *Career Development, Contracting Authority, and Responsibilities*

· Department of the Air Force Federal Acquisition Regulation Supplement Subpart 5301.602-3, *Ratification of Unauthorized Commitments*

· DAFMAN 64-119, *Nonappropriated Fund Contracting Procedures* (30 August 2023)

ACQUISITION PLANNING AND MARKET RESEARCH

Acquisition planning and market research are required for all acquisitions to ensure that the Department of the Air Force obtains what it needs in the most effective, economical, and timely manner possible. Commanders must ensure sufficient capability to manage and oversee the contracting process from start to finish. Acquisition planning should begin as soon as the agency identifies its needs. Wherever possible, agency personnel should avoid issuing requirements on an urgent basis, or with unrealistic delivery or performance schedules, as these generally restrict competition and increase prices.

Key Takeaways
» Determining whether a function is inherently governmental is an important part of acquisition planning
» Government employees must perform Inherently Governmental Functions (IGFs)

Inherently Governmental Functions (IGFs)

- Contractors are specifically prohibited from performing IGFs

- IGFs are functions so intimately related to the public interest as to mandate performance by government employees. IGFs include activities that require either the exercise of discretion in applying government authority, or the making of value judgments in making decisions for the government.

- Federal Acquisition Regulation (FAR) 7.503(c) provides a list of examples of IGFs

- Contracting Officers, supported through the acquisition process with legal advisors, should be able to avoid awarding contracts that involve IGFs. However, if after awarding a contract, monitoring reveals that contractors are performing IGFs, Air Force and Space Force personnel must reestablish control over these functions by strengthening oversight, in-sourcing the work to government employees, refraining from exercising options under the contract, or terminating all or part of the contract.

- Determinations of IGFs are made by the manpower analysts following DoDI 1100.22, *Policy and Procedures for Determining Workforce Mix*

References

- Planning and Solicitation Requirements, 10 U.S.C. § 3206
- Contractor Performance of Acquisition Functions Closely Associated with Inherently Governmental Functions, 10 U.S.C. § 4508
- Public-Private Competition Required Before Conversion to Contractor Performance, 10 U.S.C. § 2461
- Guidelines and Procedures for Use of Civilian Employees to Perform DoD Functions, 10 U.S.C. § 2463
- Planning and Solicitation Requirements, 41 U.S.C. § 3306
- Federal Acquisition Regulation Part 7, *Acquisition Planning*
- Federal Acquisition Regulation Part 10, *Market Research*
- Defense Federal Acquisition Regulation Supplement Subpart 207.5, *Inherently Governmental Functions*
- Defense Federal Acquisition Regulation Supplement PGI Subpart 207.105, *Contents of Written Acquisition Plans*
- Office of Federal Procurement Policy Policy Letter 11-01, *Performance of Inherently Governmental and Critical Functions* (12 September 2011) (technical correction made by FR 20397, 19 April 2010)
- Office of Management and Budget Circular A-76, *Performance of Commercial Activities* (29 May 2003)
- DoDI 1100.22, *Policies and Procedures for Determining Workforce Mix* (12 April 2010), incorporating Change 1, 1 December 2017
- AFI 63-138, *Acquisition of Services* (30 September 2019)

COMPETITION IN CONTRACTING

The Competition in Contracting Act requires the government to achieve competition when selecting contractors to perform services or provide supplies.

Key Takeaways
» Full and open competition is required unless an express exception applies
» When an exception to full and open competition is used to procure a requirement, the contracting officer must document their justification and approval in the contract file

The Competition in Contracting Act

- The Competition in Contracting Act (CICA), 10 U.S.C. § 3201, requires "full and open competition through the use of competitive procedures" unless an express exception applies. To fulfill competition requirements, the procuring office will advertise the requirement, request quotes, bids, or proposals, and select an awardee based on the solicitation's evaluation criteria.

- CICA has two categories of exceptions, allowing limited competition and sole-source awards:

  -- *Limited Competition:* "Full and open competition after exclusion of sources" allows the procuring office to limit the sources from which it seeks competition

  -- *Sole Source Awards:* Made through "other than full and open competition" and will require a written justification and approval (J&A) identifying the specific exception

- Contract Modifications: A modification to an existing contract will violate CICA when the changes are beyond the scope of the original contract and a sole source award has not been justified

- Unsolicited Proposals: Commanders may potentially receive an unsolicited proposal from a business, apart from (not in response to) any solicitation from the government. Because receipt of unsolicited proposals often creates a risk of unintended exposure of proprietary information, the Department of the Air Force has established regulations prescribing procedures and standards for safeguarding and evaluating unsolicited proposals. CICA requirements are not waived for unsolicited proposals.

References

· The Competition in Contracting Act, 10 U.S.C. § 3201

· Federal Acquisition Regulation Part 2, *Definitions of Words and Terms*

· Federal Acquisition Regulation Part 6, *Competition Requirements*

· Federal Acquisition Regulation Subpart 15.6, *Unsolicited Proposals*

· Defense Federal Acquisition Regulation Supplement Part 206, *Competition Requirements*

· Department of the Air Force Federal Acquisition Regulation Supplement Part 5306, *Competition Requirements*

· Department of the Air Force Federal Acquisition Regulation Supplement MP5306.502, *Air Force Competition and Commercial Advocacy Program*

· Department of the Air Force Federal Acquisition Regulation Supplement MP5315.606-90, *Receipt, Evaluation, and Disposition of Unsolicited Proposals*

ACQUISITION PROCESS

"Acquisition process" describes how the Department of the Air Force purchases supplies and services and is subject to the rules contained in various Federal, Department of Defense, and Department of the Air Force regulations.

Key Takeaways

» Simplified acquisition procedures can be used for purchases under the simplified acquisition threshold

» Acquisitions above the simplified acquisition threshold generally use negotiated procurement procedures

---

Micro-Purchases

- A micro-purchase is a government purchase of supplies or services which in the aggregate, for the Department of Defense (DoD), does not exceed a specific threshold, currently set at $10,000, except for:

  -- Construction, when the value is $2,000

  -- Nonprofessional Services, when the value is $2,500

  -- Support of contingency or chemical/biological/radiological/nuclear (CBRN) recovery/defense operations (excluding construction), the threshold is $20,000 inside the United States and $35,000 outside the United States

- The DoD is directed to use the government purchase card (GPC) to pay for purchases valued at or below the micro-purchase threshold. **Note:** splitting a larger purchase into smaller segments to stay under the micro-purchase threshold is **NOT** allowed.

Simplified Acquisition Procedures

- Simplified acquisition procedures allow the contracting officer (CO) to reduce the amount of time required to procure supplies and services below the simplified acquisition threshold, and to create or utilize more efficient ordering methods. The current simplified acquisition threshold is $250,000.

  -- For support of contingency or CBRN recovery/defense operations (excluding construction), the threshold is $800,000 inside the United States and $1.5 million outside the United States

  -- Acquisitions under the simplified acquisition threshold are reserved exclusively for small businesses

  -- The government's policy is to procure commercial products and services when possible

Negotiated Procurement

- An agency can obtain the best value in negotiated acquisitions by using any one or a combination of source selection approaches

- Most Federal acquisitions over $250,000 use negotiated procurement. Often, this is accomplished by using either the lowest-priced technically acceptable approach, where requirements are well defined and risks are low, or a best-value trade-off where the Department of the Air Force may select a higher priced offer because the offeror has superior past performance or technical skill.

References

· Micro-Purchase Threshold, 10 U.S.C. § 3573

· Simplified Acquisition Threshold, 41 U.S.C. § 134

· Federal Acquisition Regulation Subpart 2.1, *Definitions*

· Federal Acquisition Regulation Part 12, *Acquisition of Commercial Items*

· Federal Acquisition Regulation Part 13, *Simplified Acquisition Procedures*

· Federal Acquisition Regulation Subpart 13.2, *Actions at or Below the Micro-Purchase Threshold*

· Federal Acquisition Regulation Part 15, *Contracting by Negotiation*

· Federal Acquisition Regulation 15.101, *Best Value Continuum*

· Defense Federal Acquisition Regulation Supplement Part 213, *Simplified Acquisition Procedures*

· Defense Federal Acquisition Regulation Supplement Part 215, *Contracting by Negotiation*

· Department of Defense Source Selection Procedures (20 August 2022), (https://www.acq.osd.mil/dpap/policy/policyvault/USA000740-22-DPC.pdf)

· DoDI 5000.02, *Operation of the Adaptive Acquisition Framework* (23 January 2020), incorporating Change 1 (8 June 2022)

· DAFI 64-117, *Government Purchase Card Program* (19 May 2022)

CONTRACT ADMINISTRATION

Contract administration includes everything after contract formation.

Key Takeaways
» The Government can make contract changes unilaterally and bilaterally
» The contracting officer generally resolves disputes that arise during contract performance

Inspection, Rejection, and Warranties

- Standard contract clauses normally give the government the right to inspect supplies and services before acceptance, reject supplies and services that fail to conform to the contract, and demand the contractor provide supplies and services that comply with the contract. Some supply contracts contain warranties, which allow the government, after acceptance, to demand the contractor repair or replace defective supplies or demand the contractor remit a portion of the paid price.

Contract Changes (Modifications)

- Contract changes or modifications are any additions, subtractions, or modifications to the terms of the contract, such as work or performance time required by a contract. Only a contracting officer (CO) may modify a contract. Contract modifications are of two types:

  -- Unilateral: The CO directs a change to the contract. The contractor must comply with the change, but may be entitled to additional compensation or time.

  -- Bilateral: Both the CO and the contractor agree to modify the contract

Terminating a Contract for the Convenience of the Government

- A termination for convenience (T4C) occurs when the government terminates, fully or partially, a contract because termination is in the government's best interest

  -- The government and the contractor may mutually agree to the terms and conditions, including a term for the contractor to release all claims against the government

  -- If the government and the contractor cannot agree, or no negotiations occur, the contract and Federal Acquisition Regulation (FAR) outline a process for the contractor to submit a settlement claim to the CO

  -- This process, and its resolution, vary depending on the type of contract involved and other circumstances

  -- If the contractor disagrees with the CO's final decision on settlement, the contractor may appeal that decision to the Armed Services Board of Contract Appeals (ASBCA) or the U.S. Court of Federal Claims (COFC)

Terminating a Contract because of a Contractor's Failure to Perform

- A termination for default (T4D), or termination for cause for commercial contracts, occurs when the government terminates a contract because the contractor has failed, without excuse, to perform the contract. If the CO believes the contractor's action or inaction is endangering performance of the contract, the CO usually must provide the contractor written notice of the issue and give the contractor a reasonable amount of time (at least 10 days) to "cure" the issue. This is called a cure notice.

- The CO will issue a final decision and the contractor may appeal to the ASBCA or COFC

Resolving Government and Contractor Disputes

- If a contractor believes they are entitled to additional money, time, or other relief, the contractor may demand, in writing, to the government CO, that relief. That demand is called a claim.

- If the government believes that the contractor is entitled to additional money, time, or other relief, the CO will issue a final decision asserting a right to that relief

- After a claim is submitted, the CO has 60 days to issue a written final decision, or if the claim exceeds $100,000, identify a firm date by which a final decision will be issued. If no final decision is issued, the contractor may treat the claim as denied and appeal the denial.

- All COs' final decisions, including decisions regarding claims, must be sent to the Air Force Judge Advocate General's Corps Contract Law Field Support Center (AF/JACQ) for review, via your servicing legal office

References

· Federal Procurement Policy – Division C, 41 U.S.C. §§ 3101–4714
· Contract Disputes, 41 U.S.C. §§ 7101–7109
· Federal Acquisition Regulation Part 43, *Contract Modifications*
· Federal Acquisition Regulation Part 49, *Terminations of Contracts*
· Department of the Air Force Federal Acquisition Regulation Supplement Subpart 5333.2, *Disputes and Appeals*
· Department of the Air Force Federal Acquisition Regulation Supplement Part 5349, *Termination of Contracts*
· *Torncello v. United States*, 681 F.2d 756 (Ct. Cl. 1982)
· Rules of the United States Court of Federal Claims (31 July 2023), https://www.uscfc.uscourts.gov/rcfc
· Rules of the Armed Services Board of Contract Appeals (21 July 2014), https://www.asbca.mil/Rules/rules.html

COMMUNICATIONS WITH INDUSTRY/INTERFACING WITH CONTRACTORS

Department of Air Force (DAF) leaders are expected to engage with industry groups and commercial entities to help ensure we maintain our ability to rapidly innovate and stay ahead of our adversaries. However, such engagement efforts by DAF personnel must comply with federal laws and regulations on procurement and ethical conduct.

Key Takeaways

» Avoid engagements that appear to give a particular company exclusive access

» Only share publicly available information

Overview

- Meetings are generally permitted subject to the following guidelines:

  -- The nature and types of information shared or obtained during these meetings must not provide the commercial entity with an unfair competitive advantage

  -- Avoid the appearance you are providing exclusive access to a particular company or group. The government must allow equal access to industry.

  -- Avoid meeting with industry with less than two government employees

  -- Do invite the Contracting Officer to attend meetings with Industry (when possible).

  -- Allow industry to provide information on their capabilities that would be of interest to the DAF

  -- Focus discussions on topics the DAF can discuss and share publicly with any interested party. Avoid discussing proprietary or procurement-sensitive information. If it arises, you are legally obligated to protect it from disclosure to third parties. Do not discuss ongoing procurements or litigation.

  -- Do not invite other contractor personnel into the meeting

  -- In partnering with industry representatives, government staff, including industry liaisons, should balance the Federal Acquisition Regulation (FAR) Subpart 9.5 requirements to limit conflicts of interest and to ensure that agencies do not inadvertently reduce the field of competition by precluding a potential offeror from participating in a future procurement. Senior DAF leaders work with the Secretary of the Air Force's Office of Public Affairs (SAF/PA) to ensure your comments align with the DAF's strategic themes and messages.

- DAF leaders should generally decline invitations to speak to a non-federal entity's internal audience

References

- Trade Secrets Act, 18 U.S.C. § 1905
- Federal Acquisition Regulation Subpart 9.5, *Organizational and Consultant Conflicts of Interest*
- Federal Acquisition Regulation Subpart 15.201, *Exchanges with Industry Before Receipt of Proposals*
- DoD 5500.07-R, *Joint Ethics Regulation* (30 August 1993), incorporating through Change 7, 17 November 2011
- Deputy Secretary of Defense Memorandum, *Engaging with Industry* (2 March 2018)
- Office of Federal Procurement Policy Memorandum, *"Myth-Busting #4" – Strengthening Engagement with Industry Partners through Innovative Business Practices* (30 April 2019)

CONFLICTS OF INTEREST (PERSONAL AND ORGANIZATIONAL)

The Federal Acquisition Regulation (FAR) requires government business to be conducted in a manner above reproach and, except as authorized/required by statute or regulation, with complete impartiality.

Key Takeaways
» Contracting officers are required to mitigate, neutralize, or eliminate possible conflicts of interest before award
» Conflicts of interest can be personal or organizational

Personal Conflicts of Interest (PCIs)

- Department of Air Force (DAF) employees (military and civilian) are prohibited from participating personally and substantially (e.g., making a decision, giving advice, or making a recommendation) in any government matter that would have a direct and predictable effect on the financial interests of any of the following:

  -- The employee, employee's immediate family, or general partner

  -- An organization for which the employee serves as an officer, director, trustee, general partner, or employee

  -- A company or organization with which the employee is negotiating for employment or has an arrangement for future employment

    --- DAF employees also should not participate in a particular government matter if the employee believes a reasonable person with knowledge of the facts would question his/her impartiality unless the employee's supervisor and ethics counselor determine that the government's interest outweighs the appearance of a conflict

Organizational Conflicts of Interest (OCIs)

- OCIs are situations where, because of other activities or relationships, a contractor or potential contractor is unable or potentially unable to render impartial assistance to the government, in a situation of impaired or potentially impaired objectivity, or has an unfair competitive advantage

- The three types of OCIs are:

  -- Unequal access to non-public information

  -- Biased ground rules

  -- Impaired objectivity

References

- Acts Affecting a Personal Financial Interest, 18 U.S.C. § 208
- Personal and Business Relationships, 5 C.F.R. § 2635.502
- Federal Acquisition Regulation Subpart 3.104, *Procurement Integrity*
- Federal Acquisition Regulation Subpart 9.5, *Organizational and Consultant Conflicts of Interest*
- Federal Acquisition Regulation Subpart 9.508, *Examples of Organizational Conflicts of Interest*

CONTRACTORS AUTHORIZED TO ACCOMPANY THE U.S. ARMED FORCES

Contractors often support military forces overseas, including in contingency environments. There are two types of contractors who support these overseas contingency operations: those with "Contractors Authorized to Accompany the Force (CAAF)" status and those without this status (non-CAAF).

Key Takeaways

» CAAF personnel have letters of authorization

» CAAF cannot perform inherently governmental functions (i.e., combat)

Contractors Authorized to Accompany the Force (CAAF)

- CAAF are contractor personnel, including all tiers of subcontractor personnel, who are authorized to accompany the force in applicable contingency operations and have been afforded CAAF status through a letter of authorization (LOA)

- CAAF generally include U.S. citizens and third-country national contractor employees not normally residing within the operational area whose area of performance is in the direct vicinity of U.S. forces and who routinely are co-located with U.S. forces, especially in non-permissive environments. CAAF status does not apply to contractor personnel in support of contingencies within the boundaries and territories of the United States.

- Contractors are generally responsible for providing their own logistical support. However, in austere, uncertain, and/or hostile environments where the contractor cannot obtain adequate support at a reasonable cost, the Department of Defense (DoD) may provide limited support (force protection, emergency medical care and basic human needs) to CAAF to ensure continuation of essential contractor services.

International Law and Contractor Legal Status

- CAAF may support military operations if the force they accompany designates the contractors as CAAF and provides CAAF with an appropriate identification card pursuant to the Geneva Conventions

- If captured during armed conflict, CAAF are entitled to prisoner of war status

- CAAF must comply with applicable international law, including the law of war. Subject to the application of international agreements, CAAF must comply with applicable host nation and third country nation laws.

- CAAF remain subject to U.S. laws and regulations and may be subject to prosecution under the Military Extraterritorial Jurisdiction Act of 2000 (MEJA) and the Uniform Code of Military Justice (UCMJ)

- Basic law of war training is required for all contractor personnel supporting U.S. Armed Forces deployed outside the United States. Advanced law of war training is required for private security contractors, security guards in or near areas of military operations, and interrogators, linguists, interpreters, or guards who will come into contact with enemy prisoners of war, retained persons, detainees, terrorists, or detained criminals.

- Contractors who engage in activities governed by the law of war are required to implement effective programs to prevent violations of the law of war. CAAF are required to report violations of the law of war as well as gross human rights violations.

- CAAF may provide communications support, transport munitions and other supplies, perform maintenance functions for military equipment, and provide logistic services such as billeting and messing. Like all contractors, CAAF may not perform inherently governmental functions such as combat.

Medical Issues

- CAAF must provide medically and physically qualified personnel

- The Secretary of Defense may direct immunizations as mandatory for CAAF performing DoD essential contractor services

- Generally, CAAF must provide their employees medical care at CAAF's expense, unless the contract requires government provided care or in emergency situations such as resuscitation, stabilization, prevention of loss of limb or eyesight

Individual Protective Equipment

- Generally, contractors shall be required to provide their employees all life, mission, and administrative support necessary to perform the contract

- When necessary and directed by the geographic combatant commander (CCDR), the contracting officer (CO) will include language in the contract authorizing CAAF and selected non-CAAF to be issued military individual protective equipment (IPE)

Uniforms

- CAAF are responsible for providing their own personal clothing, including casual and work clothing required by a particular assignment

- Generally, commanders shall not issue military clothing to CAAF or allow the wearing of military or military look-alike uniforms. However, CCDRs (or a subordinate Joint Force Commander (JFC) deployed forward) may authorize certain CAAF personnel to wear standard uniform items for operational reasons. This authorization shall be in writing and always maintained by authorized CAAF personnel. Care must be taken to ensure, consistent with force protection measures, that the CAAF personnel are distinguishable from military personnel using distinctive patches, arm bands, nametags, or headgear.

Force Protection and Weapons Issuance

- CCDRs must develop a security plan for protection of those CAAF personnel (and non-CAAF personnel) in locations where there is not sufficient or legitimate civil authority and the commander decides that it is in the interests of the government to provide security because of any of the following:

  -- The contractor cannot obtain effective security services;

  -- Such services are unavailable at a reasonable cost; or

  -- Threat conditions necessitate security through military means.

- CAAF personnel may be armed for individual self-defense, on a case-by-case basis, **ONLY IF**:

  -- It is determined that military force protection and legitimate civil authority are deemed unavailable or insufficient;

  -- It is authorized by the CCDR; and

  -- It does not violate applicable U.S., host nation, and international law, relevant status of forces agreements (SOFAs) or international agreements, or other arrangements with local host nation authorities.

- Commanders should consult with their Staff Judge Advocate prior to authorizing the arming of CAAF. If weapons are authorized:

  -- The government shall ensure completion of weapons familiarization, qualifications, and briefings on the rules regarding the use of force;

  -- Acceptance of weapons by CAAF personnel shall be voluntary and permitted by the defense contractor and the contract; and

  -- These CAAF personnel must not be otherwise prohibited from possessing weapons under U.S. law.

Security Services

- If consistent with applicable U.S., host nation, and international law, and SOFAs or other international agreements, a defense contractor may be authorized to provide security services provided they are not performing an inherently governmental function, and are limited to providing a defensive response to hostile acts, or to demonstrated hostile intent

- Whether a particular use of contract security personnel to protect military assets is permissible is dependent on the facts and requires legal analysis

  -- Requests shall be reviewed on a case-by-case basis by the appropriate Staff Judge Advocate to the CCDR (or designee)

-- Contractors shall be used cautiously in contingency operations where major combat operations are ongoing or imminent. In these situations, contract security services will not be authorized to guard U.S. or coalition military supply routes, military facilities, military personnel, or military property except as specifically authorized by the CCDR.

References

· Persons Subject to the UCMJ, 10 U.S.C. § 802

· Military Extraterritorial Jurisdiction Act, 18 U.S.C. Chapter 212

· Defense Federal Acquisition Regulation Supplement Subpart 225.3, *Contracts Performed Outside the United States*

· Private Security Contractors Operating in Contingency Operations, 32 C.F.R. Part 159

· DoDD 2311.01, *DoD Law of War Program* (2 July 2020)

· DoDI 3020.41, *Operational Contract Support* (20 December 2011), incorporating Change 2, 31 August 2018

· AFI 51-401, *Law of War* (3 August 2018)

· AFI 64-105, *Contingency Contracting Support* (1 October 2020)

Page Intentionally Left Blank

Chapter 14
ETHICS ISSUES

STANDARDS OF ETHICAL CONDUCT

Every employee must be aware of and comply with the Standards of Ethical Conduct for Executive Branch Employees and the *Joint Ethics Regulation* (JER). Department of Defense (DoD) employees shall not engage in any commercial or professional activity that places them in a position of conflict between their private interests and the public interest of the United States. To preserve the public confidence in the Air Force and Space Force, even the appearance of a conflict of interest must be avoided.

Key Takeaways

» The primary authorities for ethical conduct in the DoD are the Standards of Conduct (which apply to the Executive Branch) and the JER

» There are substantial restrictions on the acceptance of gifts from outside sources and gifts given between DoD employees (especially those from a subordinate employee to a senior employee)

» DoD personnel may participate in non-Federal entities (including the management thereof) so long as those activities are completely separate and apart from their official duties

» All DoD personnel should be sensitive to situations where a conflict of interest (financial or organizational) can arise between their official duties and their personal activities

Duty to Avoid Conflicts of Interest

- DoD personnel shall not use sensitive government information to further a private gain for themselves or others if that information was obtained by reason of their DoD position and is not generally available to the public

- Personnel may obtain further clarification of the standards of conduct and conflict of interest provisions by consulting with their servicing legal office or ethics counselor

- Commanders must emphasize that resolution of a conflict of interest must be accomplished as soon as practicable

- The JER imposes annual financial reporting requirements for officers in the grade of O-7 or above and other government officials, such as commanding officers and procurement officials, to assist in identifying potential conflicts of interest

Prohibited Activities under the Standards of Conduct and the *Joint Ethics Regulation*

- Active duty members are prohibited from making personal commercial solicitations or solicited sales to DoD personnel junior in rank at any time (on or off-duty, in or out of uniform), particularly for insurance, stocks, mutual funds, real estate, or any other commodities, goods, or services

- DoD personnel may not engage in unauthorized gambling with subordinates, or while on-base or on-duty

- DoD personnel may not solicit or accept any gift, including entertainment or anything of value, given by any person or company, which is engaged in procurement activities or does business with any agency of the DoD (including contractors), or that was given because of one's official position. There are numerous exceptions to this rule, so, if offered a gift, consult the ethics counselor—normally your organization's Staff Judge Advocate.

- DoD personnel may not solicit contributions for gifts to a superior, except voluntary gifts or contributions of nominal value (not to exceed $10) on special occasions like marriage, birth/adoption of a child, transfer (permanent change of station or assignment), or retirement. Birthdays and promotions are not considered special occasions.

Restrictions on Activities involving with Non-Federal Entities

- Active duty military or civilian personnel may not use their grade, title, position, or organization name in connection with activities performed in their personal capacities

- Explicit or implied endorsement of a non-federal entity, event, product, service, or enterprise is prohibited

  -- DoD employees must not use their official capacities and titles, positions, or organization names to suggest official endorsement or preferential treatment of any non-federal entity except those listed in JER § 3-210, such as the Combined Federal Campaign and the Department of the Air Force Assistance Fund

- Accepting employment outside of the DoD is prohibited if it interferes with or is not compatible with the performance of government duties, or if it might discredit the government

- DoD employees may not participate in their official DoD capacities in the management of non-federal entities unless pursuant to a federal statute and with authorization from the DoD General Counsel

- DoD employees may, however, serve as DoD liaisons to non-federal entities when appointed by the head of the DoD component command or organization who determines there is a significant and continuing DoD interest to be served by such representation. Liaisons serve as part of their official DoD duties, under DoD component memberships, attend meetings of the non-Federal entity on official time and using official travel, and represent only DoD interests to the non-federal entity in an advisory capacity.

References

· Standards of Ethical Conduct for Executive Branch Employees, 5 C.F.R. Part 2635
· DoDD 5500.07, *Standards of Conduct*, (29 November 2007)
· DoD 5500.07-R, *Joint Ethics Regulation* (30 August 1993), incorporating through Change 7, 17 November 2011
· U.S. Department of Defense Standards of Conduct Office, https://dodsoco.ogc.osd.mil/

FINANCIAL DISCLOSURE FORMS

The Department of Defense (DoD) currently uses two different financial disclosure forms—the Office of Government Ethics (OGE) Form 450 (Confidential Financial Disclosure Report) and the OGE Form 278e (Public Financial Disclosure Report). The Code of Federal Regulations (C.F.R.) describes who must file, outlines the required contents in these reports, and specifies filing times.

Key Takeaways

» General Officers and Senior Executive Service personnel are required to file a Public Financial Disclosure Report (OGE 278e) on an annual basis

» Specified O-6/GS-15 and below personnel (including installation commanding officers and certain acquisition positions) are required to file a Confidential Financial Disclosure Report (OGE 450) on an annual basis

» OGE 278e filers are also required to file a monthly OGE 278-T transaction report on the purchase, sale or exchange of stocks and securities

» Public Financial Disclosure Report filers are also required to file a Termination Report at the end of covered assignments

Financial Disclosure Report Systems

- The form an individual must use depends on the rank or grade and responsibilities of that individual. Most Department of the Air Force personnel are not required to file a financial disclosure report.

- Office of Government Ethics policy requires OGE 278e filers to use the Integrity.gov electronic filing system, unless electronic filing is not practically possible, such as in certain deployed or remote locations. DoD policy requires OGE 450 filers to use the Financial Disclosure Management (FDM) online reporting system.

- Both systems use the most current OGE forms and build upon prior years' inputs to reduce duplication of effort. However, OGE 278e filers are also required to file monthly OGE 278-T periodic transaction reports within Integrity.gov system. Contact your servicing Staff Judge Advocate (SJA) to determine whether these online systems are available at your location.

Confidential Financial Disclosure Report (OGE 450)

- Persons required to file this form include:

  -- Commanding officers, heads and deputy heads of all installations or activities, if the military member is O-6 and below, or if a civilian is GS-15 or below, are required to file an OGE 450. Commanders, heads, and deputy heads who are general officers or senior executive service employees file the OGE 278e report exclusively.

-- All military members (O-6 and below) and all civilian employees (GS/GM-15 and below) when their duties require them to participate personally and substantially in taking an official action for contracting or procurement, or if their supervisor determines such a report is necessary to avoid an actual or apparent conflict of interest

- Specific requirements for this report are set forth in Chapter 7 of the *Joint Ethics Regulation* (JER), including:

  -- The report must provide sufficient information about the individual, as well as the individual's spouse and dependent children, such that an informed judgment can be made regarding compliance with conflict-of-interest laws

  -- No disclosure of amounts or values is required in this report

  -- This report must be filed within 30 days after assuming a covered position and annually thereafter

- Annual reports are submitted to the servicing SJA no later than 15 February for the preceding calendar year

Public Financial Disclosure Report (OGE 278e)

- Persons required to file this form include:

  -- Regular and Reserve officers whose grade is O-7 or above

  -- Members of the Senior Executive Service

  -- Civilian employees whose positions are classified above GS/GM-15 or whose rate of basic pay is fixed at or above 120% of the minimum rate of basic pay for a GS/GM-15

- Specific requirements for the content of this report are set forth in Chapter 7 of the JER

  -- Generally, this report is far more detailed in content than the OGE 450

  -- Although specific amounts are not required on the report, individuals must indicate the value of assets within both a given range and type of asset

  -- General officers must report a mortgage on their personal residence

- This report must be filed within 30 days after assuming a covered position

- Annual reports must be filed between 1 January and 15 May and cover the preceding calendar year

- An individual must also file a termination report within 30 days after terminating a covered position unless, within 30 days, the individual assumes another covered position

  -- Termination reports may be filed up to 15 days prior to the termination date, provided that the individual agrees to update the report with any changes

- Late reports are subject to a $200 penalty, absent an approved extension

Periodic Transaction Report (OGE 278-T)

- An OGE 278-T must be filed by OGE 278e filers who conduct the sale, purchase, or exchange of stocks, bonds, and other securities held by the filer, the filer's spouse, or dependent children, with a transaction value exceeding $1,000

   -- The filer is later able to use the OGE 278-T reports when building their annual OGE 278e incumbent report, Schedule B (Transactions)

- OGE 278-Ts are filed monthly (usually by the 15th of every month); negative reports not required

- Reports are considered late (subject to the $200 penalty), absent an approved request for an extension, if they are filed more than 30 days after they are due (i.e., 30 days after notification of a covered transaction or 45 days after the actual covered transaction)

References

- 5 C.F.R. §§ 2634.201–2634.205
- DoD 5500.07-R, *The Joint Ethics Regulation* (30 August 1993), incorporating through Change 7, 17 November 2011
- U.S. Department of Defense Standards of Conduct Office, https://dodsoco.ogc.osd.mil/
- Financial Disclosure Management System, https://www.fdm.army.mil
- Integrity.Gov Office of Government Ethics Electronic Filing System, https://integrity.gov
- OGE 278e, OGE 278-T and OGE 450 forms are available at https://www.oge.gov/

GIFTS TO THE DEPARTMENT OF THE AIR FORCE

Like most Federal agencies, the Department of Defense (DoD) has a General Gift Statute (10 U.S.C. § 2601) which allows for the acceptance of gifts of funds, personal property, and real property to the agency for support of DoD programs and operations. Acceptance levels depend on the value of the gift offered. The DoD gift statute does not allow for acceptance of gratuitous services in most situations. The DoD does have a volunteer statute (10 U.S.C. § 1588) for support of certain programs.

Key Takeaways

» Unlike gifts to individual DoD employees which are governed by the *Standards of Conduct*, gifts to the Department of the Air Force are accepted under the DoD General Gift Statute

» Installations and higher headquarters may accept gifts of funds, personal property, and real property for support of programs and operations. Gifts for distribution to individual Airmen/ Guardians may also be accepted by the DAF when appropriate.

» The governing AFI provides certain factors to be considered when deciding whether to accept a gift. Certain situations may dictate that a gift (or the condition that a donor places upon its use) should be rejected.

» The DoD also has a statute governing the acceptance of volunteer services for certain programs (such as family support and morale, welfare, and recreation activities)

Accepting or Rejecting Gifts

- The Secretary of the Air Force is the authority who may accept conditional gifts of personal property (tangible or intangible) and real property. The General Counsel may accept any gift of personal property. The Assistant Secretary of the Air Force for Installations, Environment, and Energy (SAF/IE) may accept any gift of real property. Gifts may not be solicited.

- See AFPD 51-5, *Administrative Law, Gifts, and Command Relationships*, and Chapter 2 of AFI 51-506, *Gifts to the Department of the Air Force from Domestic and Foreign Sources*, for a listing of all Air Force gift acceptance authorities. Installation commanders may accept gifts of funds and personal property up to $5,000 (regardless of other delegations).

- Types of Gifts: *Unconditional* gifts have no conditions attached to them. Conditional gifts have specific conditions tied to their acceptance (e.g., "a gift of $15 million to construct a new library wing at the United States Air Force Academy").

- Gifts may be rejected for any of the following reasons:

  -- Acceptance involves expending funds in excess of amounts appropriated by Congress;

  -- The offered item is extremely dangerous or in poor taste;

-- Acceptance of the gift would raise a serious question of impropriety in light of the donor's present or prospective business relationships with the Air Force or Space Force;

-- The cost of acceptance and maintenance is disproportionate to any benefit; and

-- Acceptance would not be in the best interest of the Air Force or Space Force.

Gifts for Distribution

- AFI 51-506, Chapter 7, governs gifts that are received for distribution to individual Airmen and Guardians

- These types of gifts must be used for health, comfort, convenience, or morale. Examples include playing cards or personal electronic devices for deployed Airmen and Guardians. Products containing tobacco, alcohol, cannabis, or nicotine are **NOT** acceptable gifts.

Recognition of Donors is Limited

- Receiving commanders may send an appropriate letter of thanks; do not grant special concessions to donors, and do not initiate publicity for donors

- If the gift itself is worthy of a press release (e.g., new United States Air Force Academy library wing) then the release may discuss the fact of the gift and the identity of the donor without emphasis

- At the discretion of the appropriate commander or gift acceptance authority, donors may be invited, present, and identified at a ribbon-cutting or similar ceremonial public event. However, such events shall not be planned or conducted solely to commemorate acceptance of a gift or acknowledge donors. Appropriated funds may not be used to fund travel, lodging, or donor expenses to be present at such events.

Gifts of Voluntary Service

- 10 U.S.C. § 1588 and DoDI 1100.21 permit the acceptance of limited gifts of volunteer services, such as: medical services, dental services, nursing services, or other health-care related services; services to be provided for a museum or a natural resources program; and programs administering services to members of the armed forces and their families, including family support, child development and youth services, library and education services, religious services, employment assistance to spouses of military members, and morale, welfare, and recreation services

- Volunteers must complete a DD Form 2793, *Volunteer Agreement for Appropriated Fund Activities & Nonappropriated Fund Instrumentalities*

- Voluntary legal services may be provided and/or accepted in accordance with 10 U.S.C. § 1044 and AFI 51-110, *Professional Responsibility Program*

References

· Legal Assistance, 10 U.S.C. § 1044

· Authority to Accept Certain Voluntary Services, 10 U.S.C. § 1588

· General Gift Funds, 10 U.S.C. § 2601

· DoDI 1100.21, *Voluntary Services in the Department of Defense* (27 March 2019)

· DD Form 2793, *Volunteer Agreement for Appropriated Fund Activities & Nonappropriated Fund Instrumentalities* (March 2018)

· DAFI 34-101, *Air Force Morale, Welfare & Recreation (MWR) Programs and Use Eligibility* (7 March 2022)

· DAFI 36-3009, *Military and Family Readiness Centers* (4 November 2022)

· AFI 51-110, *Professional Responsibility Program* (11 December 2018)

· AFI 51-506, *Gifts to the Department for the Air Force from Foreign and Domestic Sources* (16 April 2019)

· AFPD 51-5, *Administrative Law, Gifts and Command Relationships* (31 August 2018)

ACCEPTANCE OF GIFTS OF TRAVEL

A non-federal entity (NFE) may gift the cost of an employee's travel to the Air Force or the Space Force, pursuant to 31 U.S.C. § 1353, to allow employees to attend a "meeting" (e.g., meetings, conferences, speaking engagements, and events where the employee receives a public service award from the NFE).

Key Takeaways

» A NFE may fund an employee's travel where the employee is attending in their official capacity a meeting, conference, or similar event

» The gift acceptance authority must carefully consider whether the circumstances of the offer, and the benefits offered, are appropriate

» In certain circumstances, the employee might be able to accept travel benefits more expensive than what could be accepted through government-funded travel arrangements

» In rare circumstances (usually involving awards ceremonies), an NFE can also fund the travel of a spouse to accompany the employee

Processing Gifts of Travel Benefits

- Use of 31 U.S.C. § 1353 travel benefits are only for official, non-local travel. This authority **CANNOT** be used for a "widely attended gathering" or for permissive TDYs.

- Allowable costs include transportation, lodging, meals, and conference registration fees

- Approval level for acceptance of travel benefits is at the "highest practical administrative level" (typically the first General Officer/Senior Executive in the chain of command) and such travel benefits should be approved in advance of employee travel

- A travel payment from a NFE shall not be accepted if the approval authority determines that acceptance would cause a reasonable person to question the integrity of Air Force or Space Force programs or operations

- Unit travel funds are used to pay any expenses not covered by the offer from the NFE

- Meetings can include musical and sporting competitions where the employee is a participant in the competition

Travel Payments

- In-kind provision of travel, lodging, and meals is preferred, as NFE funds should not pass directly through employee's hands

- In the continental United States (CONUS), the cost of lodging provided may exceed the authorized per diem rate if similar lodging is provided to all other attendees/speakers. Outside the continental United States (OCONUS), the cost of lodging provided may not exceed the Department of State area per diem rate.

- If the NFE offers travel on a commercial airline, the employee may accept travel in coach class. Travel in a premium class of seating (e.g., business class), that is not first class, may also be accepted if similar NFE-funded air travel is provided to all other attendees/speakers. Travel in first class is not permitted unless the conditions exist that would authorize the U.S. Government to purchase a first-class ticket for the employee.

- Accepted travel benefits must be reported to the Air Force Ethics Office (SAF/GCA) on the semi-annual OGE Form 1353, *Semiannual Report of Payments Accepted from a Non-Federal Source*

Spouse Travel

- An NFE may also pay for travel for employee's spouse if: spouse attendance supports the Air Force or Space Force mission or will substantially assist the employee in carrying out their official duties; the spouse will attend a ceremony where the employee is to receive an award or honorary degree from an NFE related to their official duties; or the spouse participates in substantive programs related to Air Force or Space Force programs/operations

References

· Acceptance of Travel and Related Expenses from Non-Federal Sources, 31 U.S.C. § 1353

· 41 C.F.R. Part 304

· AFI 51-506, *Gifts to the Department of the Air Force from Domestic and Foreign Sources* (16 April 2019)

· OGE Form 1353, *Semiannual Report of Payments Accepted from a Non-Federal Source* (2013)

GIFTS TO SUPERIORS

To avoid the appearance that a supervisor is being improperly influenced, the *Joint Ethics Regulation* (JER) include several guidelines concerning gifts to superiors.

Key Takeaways

» As a rule, Department of Defense (DoD) employees should not accept gifts from subordinates or those receiving less pay

» Gifts (appropriate in value) may be given from an employee, or group of employees, to a senior employee on occasions of personal significance

» DoD has a special ethics rule that gifts given from a group of employees to a departing senior employee should not exceed $480. This rule is usually used for permanent change of station (PCS) gifts and retirement gifts.

» All gifts must be truly voluntary, and requests to contribute to a group gift should ask for not more than $10. Employees are free to voluntarily donate more than that amount.

Gifts to Superiors

- Generally, Air Force and Space Force personnel **MAY NOT**:

    -- Directly or indirectly give a gift to a superior

    -- Solicit a contribution from other DoD personnel for a gift to a superior

    -- Make a donation for a gift to a superior

    -- Accept a gift from subordinate personnel

- Exceptions to the general rules prohibiting gifts to superiors or their solicitation:

    -- On occasions where gifts are traditionally given or exchanged, items having an aggregate market value of $10 or less, such as food items or minor mementos, may be given

    -- On occasions of personal hospitality at a residence, appropriate gifts of a reasonable value (e.g., $15 bottle of wine) may be given to superiors and accepted from subordinates

    -- On occasions of personal significance (e.g., marriage, birth of child) or on occasions that terminate the superior-subordinate relationship (i.e., retirement, separation, or permanent change of station (PCS)):

--- Employees may solicit a contribution for an appropriate group gift for a unique occasion, provided, however, that contributions must not exceed $10 per person (the aggregate of individual voluntary contributions are subject to an overall cap of $480). However, a voluntary contribution of a nominal amount for food, refreshments, and entertainment for the superior, the personal guests of the superior, and other attendees at an event to mark the occasion for which a group gift is given may be solicited as a separate, voluntary contribution not subject to the $10 limit.

--- The general rule is that a DoD employee **MAY NOT** accept a gift that exceeds $480 in value from a group that consists of one or more subordinates to the honoree. Further, if an individual donates to more than one donating group, then the donating groups will be considered one donating group, and the combined value of their gifts must be $480 or less.

--- Donating groups should be defined by reasonable and rational parameters and are usually related to the structure of the overall organization and individual units within that organization. There is no limit on the number of donating groups.

--- A superior employee receiving a gift valued at more than $480 may not "buy down" the gift (i.e., pay back the money in excess of $480)

--- Under all circumstances, gifts must be truly **voluntary**

References

· Gifts to Superiors, 5 U.S.C. § 7351

· 5 C.F.R. §§ 2635.301– 2635.304, 3601

· DoD 5500.07-R, *Joint Ethics Regulation* (30 August 1993), incorporating through Change 7, 17 November 2011

GIFTS FROM OUTSIDE SOURCES

Subpart B of the *Standards of Ethical Conduct for Executive Branch Employees* establishes the general rule that gifts from outside sources should not be accepted. This prohibition stems from the core ethics principle that the federal government should not show preferential treatment toward any particular non-federal entity (NFE). Subpart B also creates an intricate system of exemptions and exceptions from the general no-gift rule.

Key Takeaways

» The general rule of 5 C.F.R. 2635 Subpart B is that Department of the Air Force employees should not accept items of value from prohibited sources (i.e., contractors) or items given because of an employees' official position

» There are various exemptions from the definition of a gift that reflect business realities, such as the ability to accept mementos of appreciation and modest refreshments

» Recognized gift exceptions may allow more substantive gifts to be accepted, such as gifts from family members or discounts offered to all military members

» Even an otherwise acceptable gift should be declined if acceptance could lead to public concerns about the employee's integrity or impartiality

General Gift Rule

- Department of Defense (DoD) employees (military and civilian) are beholden to the same standards of ethical conduct as other employees of the executive branch, including restrictions on gifts from outside sources/NFEs. Because public service is a public trust, DoD employees must not abuse their official position for private gain—to include using public office to acquire gifts from NFEs which are improper/illegal (e.g., bribes/kick-backs) or create the appearance of impropriety.

  -- General Rule: The *Standards of Ethical Conduct for Executive Branch Employees* prohibit DoD employees from soliciting or accepting a gift from an NFE if it is offered **because** of the employee's official position. Similarly, DoD employees may not solicit or accept a gift from a "prohibited source" (e.g., an NFE engaged in or seeking to engage in business with the defense agency, seeking official agency action, is regulated by the agency, or whose interests may be substantially affected by the employee's duty performance or nonperformance).

  -- Values-Based Decision-Making: Every DoD employee has a responsibility to place loyalty to the Constitution, laws, and ethical principles above private gain. **For this reason, and in an abundance of caution, employees should decline otherwise permissible gifts if they believe that a reasonable person with knowledge of the relevant facts would question the employee's integrity or impartiality as a result of accepting the gift.** Factors to consider are the value of the gift, the timing of the gift, the identity of the donor, and any potential access the gift may provide the donor.

--- For example, a DoD official conducting a visit to a prospective contractor's production facility and home office should not accept a proffered free lunch (valued at $15) even though this meal may otherwise be acceptable under the 5 C.F.R. 2635.204(a) $20 gift exception because the optics of the situation dictate that the DoD official remain completely neutral and objective with regards to the contractor

Exemptions and Exceptions

- Definition of Gift: A gift is considered anything of value, regardless of whether the thing of value is tangible or intangible (such as discounts or memberships). Additionally, gifts to DoD employees' dependents will be considered gifts to the DoD employee.

  -- Items not considered gifts include modest items of food and non-alcoholic refreshments, opportunities/benefits available to all military personnel, greeting cards, and other items with negligible intrinsic value and intended primarily for presentation

  -- The acceptance of a meal as part of giving an official speech is not considered a gift, provided the meal is integral to the event itself (i.e., making a keynote speech during a dinner event, compared to providing opening remarks at a conference and sticking around solely for a free lunch)

  -- Exceptions to the General Rule Against Accepting Gifts: There are numerous exceptions to the general prohibition against accepting gifts. Common exceptions include: prizes/discounts/incentives open to the public or all DoD employees without regard to official position; the $20/$50 rule (DoD employee may accept a non-cash gift valued at up to $20 per occasion, per source, and no more than $50 per year from the same source); gifts based on a family/personal relationship or an outside business relationship (including the spouse's employer); and the widely attended gathering rule.

- These and the many other gift exceptions require a fact-specific analysis and legal review to ensure that a gift may be accepted without creating the reasonable appearance of impropriety or possibly violating criminal statutes. As such, gift issues should be discussed as early as possible with the servicing Staff Judge Advocate or ethics counselor.

References

- 5 C.F.R. § 2635, Subpart B
- 5 C.F.R. § 3601.103
- DoD 5500.07-R, *Joint Ethics Regulation* (30 August 1993), incorporating through Change 7, 17 November 2011
- U.S. Department of Defense Standards of Conduct Office, https://dodsoco.ogc.osd.mil/

FOREIGN GIFTS

The Constitution prohibits persons holding an "office of profit or trust" for the United States from accepting gifts from foreign "personages or governments" without consent of Congress. Congress has consented to accepting and retaining gifts under certain conditions and when following specified procedures.

Key Takeaways

» The offering of gifts from foreign governments (and their officials) is a common scenario for Department of the Air Force officials who work with foreign counterparts or in overseas locations

» Foreign gifts of less than "minimal value" may be accepted by the individual recipient as a personal gift

» Recipients of foreign gifts of more than "minimal value" should be retained and the recipient should make a recommendation disposition to and/or request disposition instructions from the Office of the Administrative Assistant to the Secretary of the Air Force (SAF/AA)

» Recipients who desire to retain a foreign gift of more than "minimal value" (except firearms) may pay the U.S. Government the fair market retail value of the gifted item

Foreign Gifts Generally

- The general prohibition against accepting foreign gifts applies to military members, civilian employees, consultants, and their spouses or other dependents. This includes retired and reserve component members, regardless of duty status, Air National Guard members, when federally recognized, and their spouses and dependents.

- No Department of Defense (DoD) employee may request, or otherwise encourage, the offer of a gift from a foreign government or their agents and representatives

- Small table favors, mementos, remembrances, or other tokens bestowed at official functions, and other gifts of minimal value received as souvenirs or marks of courtesy from a foreign government (e.g., plaques or paper certificates), may be accepted and retained by the recipient

- "Minimal value" is currently defined as not exceeding $480 in retail value. "Minimal value" is based on the Consumer Price Index and changes every three years. The value of the gift is the item/items' retail or fair market value in the United States. If multiple gifts are offered on the same occasion, they will be aggregated when determining value.

- For all foreign gifts, the person receiving the gift should make a written record describing the circumstances of the gift, including the date and place of presentation, identity and position of the donor, description and value of gift, and means by which the value was determined

- For gifts equal to or less than "minimal value," the recipient may retain the gift for their personal use including destruction or re-conveyance of the gift as desired

Foreign Gifts of more than Minimal Value

- DoD employees shall refuse the offer of a gift greater than "minimal value" unless refusal would cause offense, embarrassment, or otherwise adversely affect foreign relations. The donor should be advised that U.S. law prohibits persons in service of the United States or their dependents from accepting the gift.

  -- However, refusal requires Department of State approval, coordinated through the Office of the Administrative Assistant to the Secretary of the Air Force (SAF/AA)

  -- If the employee accepts a gift greater than "minimal value" because its refusal is likely to offend or embarrass the donor or adversely affect foreign relations, the gift becomes U.S. property and must be reported to the Air Force and Space Force

  -- Further, the employee may purchase a foreign gift (from the U.S. Government) if the employee desires by paying full retail value (with the exception of firearms)

- For gifts of more than "minimal value," consult the guidance in AFI 51-506, *Gifts to the Department of the Air Force from Domestic and Foreign Sources*, and make a recommendation as to the disposition of the gift (e.g., display in a unit's common area). Gifts of more than "minimal value" (with the exception of firearms) may also be donated to charitable non-federal entities, including installation-recognized private organizations. Firearms may not be purchased from the U.S. Government by the recipient.

References

· Receipt and Disposition of Foreign Gifts and Decorations, 5 U.S.C. § 7342

· 41 C.F.R. § 102-42.10 (2019)

· DoD 5500.07-R, *Joint Ethics Regulation* (30 August 1993), incorporating through Change 7, 17 November 2011

· DoDD 1005.13, *Gifts and Decorations from Foreign Governments* (19 February 2002), incorporating Change 1, 6 December 2002, certified current 21 November 2003

· AFI 51-506, *Gifts to the Department of the Air Force from Domestic and Foreign Sources* (16 April 2019)

HONORARIA

Federal employees are often professional experts in their functional field and may be invited to give speeches, teach, or write articles within that field of expertise. Department of the Air Force (DAF) employees may not be dually compensated for their official duties and may not receive any type of payment for such communications that are directly related to their official position. DAF employees may engage in "outside" speaking/teaching/writing and accept honoraria for doing so.

Key Takeaways

» DAF employees may not accept any form of compensation for speaking, teaching, or writing for non-federal entities (NFE) if related to their official position or duties

» DAF employees may accept compensation for outside speaking, teaching, and writing not directly related to their official duties, even if it relates generally to their unit's area of responsibility

» If a DAF employee negotiated specific compensation, such speaking, teaching, and writing would be off-duty employment. If the compensation is in the nature of a gift from the NFE, it is considered honoraria

» Military members may use their grade and service when speaking, teaching, or writing in a personal capacity, but the member must use a verbal or written Department of Defense (DoD)/DAF disclaimer

General Rules

- Federal employees may accept the payment of money or anything of value for a speech, teaching, or writing **unrelated** to their official duties, assuming there are no statutory or regulatory prohibitions

- An honorarium is generally defined as a payment given to someone, such as a consultant or a speaker, for which custom or propriety forbids any fixed payment or price be set

- In the context of the *Joint Ethics Regulation*, honoraria are considered compensation for a lecture, speech, or writing, and involve the payment of money or anything of value

- Federal employees may accept compensation for a lecture, speech, or writing based on the employee's field of individualized expertise (rather than official duties or agency operations), even if that field is generally within the agency's area of responsibility

- Use of a military member's grade and military service is acceptable (e.g., as part of an introduction), but requires a disclaimer (either written or verbal) that the views being expressed are those of the speaker/writer and do not necessarily represent the views of the DoD or DAF

- Although travel reimbursement for a speech related to official duties may be accepted by the agency under certain circumstances (see Gifts of Travel), a fee or other direct compensation for speaking for such an engagement **MAY NOT** be accepted

- Although 18 U.S.C. § 209 generally prohibits an employee from receiving compensation from an outside source for an activity undertaken as part of the employee's official duties, compensation for speaking, teaching, and writing has been viewed as falling outside the scope of § 209 because payments are merely gratuitous and are not intended to compensate for government services

References

· Salary of Government Officials and Employees Payable Only by United States, 18 U.S.C. § 209

· Teaching, speaking, and writing, 5 C.F.R. § 2635.807

· DoD 5500.07-R, *Joint Ethics Regulation* (30 August 1993), incorporating through Change 7, 17 November 2011

USE OF GOVERNMENT MOTOR VEHICLES

Government Motor Vehicles (GMVs) are closely controlled because of their easy accessibility, high visibility, and potential for misuse. Whether owned or leased by the U.S. Government, GMVs should only be used for official purposes. Decisions regarding authorized GMV use/support must be resolved in favor of strict compliance with controlling guidance and with special consideration for avoiding negative public perception. For detailed guidance concerning GMV use for various situations, please consult Chapter 2 of AFMAN 24-306, *Operation of Air Force Government Motor Vehicles.*

Key Takeaways

» Use of GMVs is subject to close scrutiny and substantiated misuse has severe consequences. GMVs should not be assigned based on grade, prestige, or personal convenience.

» Use of domicile-to-duty (DTD) transportation must be specifically approved by Secretary of the Air Force (SecAF) and Congressional notification is required

» Commanders with permanently assigned GMVs to facilitate 24/7 communications must not take the GMV to a personal residence to avoid the perception of DTD utilization

» Use of GMVs by permanent party personnel is limited to official purposes and does not include many morale and social events

GMVs assigned to MAJCOM/FLDCOM, NAF, and Wing/Delta Commanders

- Major or Field Command, Numbered Air Force, and Wing/Delta Commanders may be assigned telecommunication-equipped GMVs to facilitate overall responsibility for operations or installation security needing 24/7 emergency communication support. This approval authority is extended to Operations Group Commanders responsible for ongoing flight operations.

- Permanently assigned GMV authority is not the authority for DTD transportation. Such GMVs should **NOT** be taken to the employee's residence for routine stops or parked in locations that facilitate partial DTD transportation, or the appearance of such use.

- As a general rule, GMVs should not be assigned based on grade, prestige, or personal convenience

Domicile-to-Duty Transportation

- DTD transportation, per 31 U.S.C. § 1344, is only authorized for:

-- SecAF, Chief of Staff of the U.S. Air Force (CSAF), and Chief of Space Operations (CSO)

-- Field work (e.g., recruiters and medical officers performing outpatient service away from military treatment facility)

- Intelligence, counterintelligence, protection services, or law enforcement duty

- Exigent circumstances—namely, highly unusual circumstances that present a clear and present danger, emergency situations, or other compelling operational considerations

- SecAF is the approval authority for DTD transportation. Congress must be notified, in certain circumstances, when DTD transportation is authorized.

National Capital Region (NCR)

- Washington Headquarters Service has an Operating Instruction that governs GMV usage and reflects the ready availability of public transportation in the NCR

- GMV usage to Commercial and Military Air Transportation Terminals is **only permissible if the** terminal is in an area where other modes of travel will not meet mission requirements (e.g., taxi/rideshare not available or parking insufficient)

Permanent Party GMV Usage

- Travel to command picnics, holiday parties, or similar events is not authorized

- Travel to retirement and change-of-command ceremonies is authorized **only** for official participants (e.g., the retiree, the incoming/outgoing commanders, or the presiding official)

- Travel to off-base sustenance is limited to situations when traveling between different installations for duty purposes

Temporary Party GMV Usage

- Transport to/from off base lodging, restaurants & other sustenance is acceptable

- Only reputable non-adult themed restaurants are permitted

- Transport to/from entertainment/recreation locations is acceptable only when the locations are on base

References

· Passenger Carrier Use, 31 U.S.C. § 1344
· Adverse Personnel Actions, 31 U.S.C. § 1349(b)
· DoDD 4500.09E, *Transportation and Traffic Management* (27 December 2019), incorporating Change 1, 21 October 2022
· DoDI 4500.36, *Acquisition, Management, and Use of Non-Tactical Vehicles* (1 February 2023)
· DoDM 4500.36, *Acquisition, Management, and Use of Non-Tactical Vehicles* (7 July 2015), incorporating Change 1, 20 December 2018
· Washington Headquarters Services (WHS) – Serviced Components Administrative Instruction (AI) 109, *Use of Motor Transportation and Scheduled DoD Shuttle Service in the Pentagon Area* (31 March 2011), incorporating through Change 2, 22 February 2022
· AFI 24-301, *Ground Transportation* (22 October 2019)
· AFMAN 24-306, *Operation of Air Force Government Motor Vehicles* (30 July 2020)

USING GOVERNMENT FUNDS: MEMENTOS/GIFTS AND OFFICIAL REPRESENTATION FUNDS

Federal law requires that appropriated funds not be used to purchase gifts for military members, employees, or private citizens unless specifically authorized by law. The only authority to use Air Force or Space Force appropriated funds for gifts is through Official Representation Funds (ORF), in accordance with AFI 65-603, *Emergency and Extraordinary Expense Authority*. AFI 65-603 specifies the circumstances and the individuals to whom gifts (or "mementos") may be presented.

Key Takeaways

» Trophies, plaques, and other recognition items are not considered gifts to Department of Defense (DoD) employees if provided as part of an established awards program

» Generally, Appropriated Funds (APF) are used to recognize APF employees, and Nonappropriated Funds (NAF) are used to recognize NAF employees, for meritorious performance

» Official Representation Funds (ORF) can be used to purchase mementos and welcoming/courtesy gifts for distinguished foreign and domestic visitors

» ORF-supported events must meet specific ratios (based on the size of the event) of Distinguished Visitors versus DoD employee attendees

---

Impermissible Use of Funds

- Appropriated Funds (APF): May not be used to purchase permanent change of station (PCS) or retirement mementos for either military or DoD civilian personnel. APF cannot be used to purchase trophies and other awards that are used to recognize nonappropriated fund personnel.

- Nonappropriated Funds (NAF): May not be used to purchase PCS mementos for either military or DoD civilian personnel. NAFs cannot be used to purchase trophies and other awards that are used to recognize APF personnel.

Permissible Use of Funds

- NAFs: Special Morale & Welfare Funds may be used in support of a **retirement ceremony** to purchase light refreshments (non-alcoholic) within specified limits for a unit celebration for retiring military and DoD civilian personnel. Likewise, nonappropriated funds may be used to purchase trophies and plaques that are used to recognize NAF employees for mission accomplishment, such as personnel of the quarter awards.

- APFs: May be used to purchase special trophies and plaques that are used to recognize APF personnel for mission accomplishment, such as personnel of the quarter awards. Additionally, a special type of appropriated funds, called Official Representation Funds (ORF), may **potentially** be used to purchase mementos/gifts for distinguished citizens of foreign countries and prominent U.S. citizens who are not DoD employees under certain circumstances.

- Note: Recognition items having minimal cost (e.g., a unit recognition coin) purchased with APFs or NAFs may be used to recognize any employee (APF or NAF) in order for Commanders and Directors to avoid having to use a type of funds they would otherwise have no reason to utilize

Official Representation Funds (ORF)

- ORF is one type of emergency and extraordinary expense fund allowed by 10 U.S.C. § 127. Its purpose is to extend official courtesies of the United States to foreign and domestic dignitaries. Gifts/mementos can be used either for visiting dignitaries or when DAF officials pay official visits to foreign (and domestic) dignitaries when TDY. It is normal for meals to be provided when visiting dignitaries visit DAF installations.

- Use of ORF requires certain ratios of invited attendees to be non-DoD authorized guests. In parties of less than 30 persons, at least 20% of the invitees reasonably expected to attend should be non-DoD. In parties of more than 30 persons, at least 50% of the invitees reasonably expected to attend should be non-DoD authorized guests.

- Only certain individuals will qualify for use of ORF. Examples include members of Congress and Cabinet members, prominent U.S. citizens (retired O-10s are automatically considered prominent U.S. citizens), foreign distinguished citizens, military personnel, and government officials, and the Secretary of the Air Force (SecAF), Undersecretary of the Air Force, Chief of Staff of the Air Force (CSAF), Chief of Space Operations (CSO), Vice Chief of Staff of the Air Force (VCSAF), Vice Chief of Space Operations (VCSO), and certain other Office of the Secretary of Defense (OSD) members.

- AFI 65-603 governs the use of ORF. ORF may be used for meals, receptions and refreshments, reasonable gratuities for services rendered by non-government personnel, recreation events such as sporting activities, sightseeing tours, and concerts for authorized personnel, floral and candle centerpieces for receptions and meals, mementos, modest welcome baskets, and the cost of the gift wrapping, paper or bows, and alcohol at evening events.

  -- The limit on the cost of gifts and mementos is $50 for specified DoD officials and $480 for foreign and domestic dignitaries

- Prohibited uses of ORF: Unless specifically approved by the Office of the Administrative Assistant to the Secretary of the Air Force (SAF/AA), the following uses are **NOT** allowed:

  -- Personal items such as toiletry articles, hair and beauty care, souvenirs, and personal clothing items (unless the article of clothing bears the command or unit logo and is given as a memento)

  -- Personal phone calls or transportation when official duties are not involved

  -- Expenses for support staff (e.g., aides, executive officers, official drivers, and protocol personnel). These individuals are not considered members of the official party.

-- Gifts, flowers, or wreaths for presentation by authorized guests

-- Seasonal greeting and calling cards

-- Cost of music/entertainment for social hours, receptions, and dinners

-- DoD members' (and spouses') cost for recreational activities

-- Membership fees or dues

References

· Emergency and Extraordinary Expenses, 10 U.S.C. § 127

· DoDI 7250.13, *Use of Appropriated Funds for Official Representation Purposes* (30 June 2009), incorporating Change 1, 22 March 2023

· DAFI 65-601, Volume 1, *Budget Guidance and Procedures* (22 June 2022)

· DAFMAN 65-605, Volume 1, *Budget Guidance and Technical Procedures* (31 March 2021)

· AFI 65-601, Volume 1, *Budget Guidance and Procedures* (24 October 2018)

· AFI 65-603, *Emergency and Extraordinary Expense Authority* (29 April 2020)

· AFMAN 34-201, *Use of Nonappropriated Funds* (28 September 2018)

OFF-DUTY EMPLOYMENT

Generally, Air Force and Space Force members may participate in off-duty employment, subject to the limitations and prohibitions stated in the *Joint Ethics Regulation* (JER). The Department of Air Force (DAF) does not currently have an implementing regulation for off-duty employment. Some personnel are required to obtain supervisory permission prior to starting such employment; for all others, it is only necessary to avoid conflicts of interests with the member's official duties.

Key Takeaways

» Financial disclosure filers must receive advance permission from their supervisor before commencing off-duty employment

» Even when advance permission is not required, DAF personnel must avoid a conflict of interest between their official duties and their off-duty employment

» Certain functional areas have additional requirements for advance notice to, or permission from, supervisors

» DAF personnel generally cannot receive compensation for outside speaking, teaching, and writing on matters related to their official duties

Prior Notice and Approval

- Personnel should inform their supervisor prior to engaging in outside employment. Air Force and Space Force financial disclosure filers must request approval of outside activities using DAF Form 3902, *Application and Approval for Off-Duty Employment.*

- Although the Air Force and Space Force does not require civilian employees to seek prior supervisory approval to engage in off-duty employment, it may be required by a local or command policy. Additionally, all Air Force and Space Force civilian employees **MUST** report outside business activity or compensation to their supervisors per DAFI 36-147, *Civilian Conduct and Responsibility.*

- Financial disclosure filers shall obtain prior supervisory approval **BEFORE** working for a prohibited source using DAF Form 3902. Approval to participate in outside employment or business activity will be documented in the Supervisor's Employee Brief. For more information on who is required to file financial disclosures (see Financial Disclosure Forms).

General Concerns with Off-Duty Employment

- Personnel may not engage in outside employment that:

-- Interferes with or is incompatible with performing their government duties or is prohibited by statute or regulation

-- May reasonably be expected to bring discredit upon the government or the Department of Defense (DoD)

-- May tend to create a conflict of interest or create an appearance of impropriety

-- Will detract from readiness or pose a security risk

Outside Speaking, Teaching and Writing

- Personnel are **encouraged** to engage in teaching, writing, or speaking. Such activities must not depend upon information gained from government service, unless available to the public or with approval from the Secretary of the Air Force.

- Generally, federal employees may not receive payment for articles or speeches related to their official duties (see Honoraria). Employees may be eligible to receive compensation or travel related to outside speaking/teaching/writing in an area of professional expertise not directly related to their official duties.

Functional-Specific Requirements

- Certain functional areas have specific requirements for advance notice to, or permission from, supervisors prior to commencing off-duty employment

- Medical providers must consult applicable guidance from the Surgeon General for the Department of the Air Force (AF/SG) (to include AFI 44-102, *Medical Care Management*) prior to engaging in off-duty employment

- Judge advocates desiring to perform off-duty employment should review AFI 51-110, *Professional Responsibility Program*

References

- 5 C.F.R. § 2635, Subpart H
- 5 C.F.R. § 3601
- DoD 5500.07-R, *Joint Ethics Regulation* (30 August 1993), incorporating through Change 7, 17 November 2011
- DAFI 36-147, *Civilian Conduct and Responsibility* (11 January 2023)
- DAF 3902, *Application and Approval for Off-Duty Employment* (11 January 2023)
- AFI 44-102, *Medical Care Management* (17 March 2015), certified current 22 April 2020, including AFI44-102_AFGM2023-01, 5 September 2023
- AFI 51-110, *Professional Responsibility Program* (11 December 2018)

KEY SPOUSE PROGRAM

The Key Spouse Program is a commander's program to enhance unit family readiness. The role of the Key Spouse is designed to enhance mission readiness and resilience and establish a sense of community. The program is a commander's initiative that promotes partnerships with unit leadership, families, volunteer key spouses, centers, and other installation community agencies.

Key Takeaways

» Key Spouses are important volunteers who serve as the commander's representative to unit military spouses and families

» Key Spouses may use government resources in the performance of their assigned duties but must undergo necessary training

» As accepted volunteers, Key Spouses receive many of the same protections and privileges (including recognition for superior performance) as Department of the Air Force civilian employees

» Key Spouses may be able to host Special Morale and Welfare Funds-supported events on behalf of the commander

Commander's Program

- Department of Defense (DoD) components can accept certain volunteer services and the Key Spouse Program falls under such voluntary services

- All Key Spouses should be appointed in writing by the unit commander

- Once appointed, Key Spouses should complete Key Spouse training and sign a DD Form 2793, *Volunteer Agreement for Appropriated Fund Activities & Nonappropriated Fund Instrumentalities*

Key Spouse Responsibilities

- Key Spouses **MAY NOT** serve in a policy making position; supervise paid employees or military personnel; perform inherently governmental functions; obligate government funds; be accountable for the management, quality, financial solvency, and health/safety of an installation program or activity

- Key Spouses are supervised the same way as compensated employees providing like services

- Key Spouses receive Federal Tort Claims Act (FTCA) protections for injuries or damage they may cause when they perform official duties as volunteers

- Key Spouses receive Federal Employee Compensation Act (FECA) protections for injuries they may incur when they perform official duties as volunteers

Key Spouse Training

- Key Spouse members can use government resources and facilities (e.g., office space, computers, email, telephones, supplies, equipment, and vehicles) and may have access to Privacy Act protected information, as needed to perform their assigned duties

- Key Spouse members should complete the same training required of any compensated employee or military member who accesses a particular government resource or facility

    -- Key Spouses should complete any necessary information security training if they will be given access to Air Force and Space Force information technology systems

    -- Training for Key Spouses shall be provided by the Military and Family Readiness Center at least on a quarterly basis, or as requested/needed

Key Spouse Events

- If Key Spouses engage in fundraising (e.g., as a member of a spouses' club), either on or off-base, they must adhere to relevant guidance (see "Private Organizations") and ensure it is clear that they are not acting in their official capacity as the commander's key spouse representative

- Key Spouses may host annual unit New Spouse Orientation Briefs and Key Spouse Program Volunteer Recognition (award) events and use Special Morale & Welfare funds to purchase modest refreshments (non-alcoholic) for these events, subject to typical limits

- Commanders may establish awards and recognition programs to recognize the superior performance and contributions of Key Spouses and other volunteers. Key Spouse Program leaders may present, on the commander's behalf, recognition items to subordinate volunteers.

References

· Federal Employees' Compensation Act, 5 U.S.C. §§ 8101 *et seq.*
· Authority to Accept Certain Voluntary Services, 10 U.S.C. § 1588
· Federal Tort Claims Act, 28 U.S.C. §§ 1346(b), 2671–2680
· DoDI 1100.21, *Acceptance of Volunteer Services in the DoD* (27 March 2019)
· DoDI 1400.25, Volume 451, *DoD Civilian Personnel Management System: Awards* (4 November 2013)
· DD Form 2793, *Volunteer Agreement for Appropriated Fund Activities & Nonappropriated Fund Instrumentalities* (March 2018)
· DAFI 36-3009, *Military and Family Readiness Centers* (4 November 2022)
· DAFMAN 36-2806, *Military Awards: Criteria and Procedures* (27 October 2022)
· AFMAN 34-201, *Use of Nonappropriated Funds* (28 September 2018)
· AFPC Airman and Family Readiness Center Key Spouse Program Guide (4 December 2020)

UTILIZATION OF ENLISTED AIDES

An Enlisted Aide (EA) is assigned to support the assigned general officer (GO) and relieve them of routine duties so that the GO can focus on military duties. They are not assigned to assist the GO's spouse, family, or staff. However, they do generally perform duties from the General Officer's Quarters so a balanced working relationship with the GO's spouse is important.

Key Takeaways

» EAs are important members of a GO's personal staff who can save them time to focus on official duties

» DoDI 1315.09, *Utilization of Enlisted Aides (EAs) on Personal Staffs of General and Flag Officers (GO/FOs)*, provides a comprehensive list of permissible and impermissible duties which may be assigned to EAs

» EAs do not work for the GO's spouse or directly support the general's family, but they do work from the official quarters and must work closely with the spouse

» An important aspect of an EA's duties is to prepare for and assist the GO in hosting qualifying representational events where food and beverages are served

Authorized EA Duties

- Cleaning of common areas in GO quarters (GOQ) and general lawn care

- Care of military uniforms and civilian attire worn for qualifying representational events (QREs)

- Receiving guests at QREs

- Planning, preparation, and conducting QREs, receptions, and parties

- Preparation of daily meals for the GO (and those immediate family members that eat with the GO)

- Packing of uniforms, professional items, and books for a permanent change of station move

- Assisting the GO with errands that have a substantive connection to the GO's official responsibilities (e.g., dry cleaning of uniforms)

Unauthorized EA Duties

- Any form of care for family, personal guests, or pets

- Operation or maintenance of any privately owned vehicle or private recreational equipment

- Personal services or errands for the sole benefit of the GO's family or unofficial guests. The GO may hire an EA, on a truly voluntary basis, outside of normal duty hours, and reimburse the EA at Department of Labor wage rates, to work (e.g., prepare and serve food) at a private or family event.

- Landscaping in areas not used for QREs

- Skilled maintenance of GOQ or cleaning of private family areas

Sharing of EAs between General Officers

- GOs can loan EAs to another GO who is authorized use of EAs to support a QRE

- A GO's spouse can be designated as an alternate host for the purpose of receiving EA support if the spouse hosts a QRE that has direct connection to the GO's official duties. This includes events when the spouse is hosting events attended by spouses of U.S. dignitaries, foreign dignitaries, or foreign military officers when the GO is separately meeting with those individuals. Such QREs normally occur in the GOQ, but this is not an absolute requirement.

Permissible and Impermissible EA Assignments

- DoDI 1315.09, *Utilization of Enlisted Aides (EAs) on Personal Staffs of General and Flag Officers (G/FOs)*, Enclosures 3 and 4, contains examples of permissible and impermissible EA assignments in support of QREs, as well as illustrative examples

- Permissible QREs Include:

  -- Events to honor local government, congressional personnel, and foreign dignitaries

  -- Customary unit morale events such as hail and farewell gatherings and holiday parties

  -- Events to welcome peers and subordinates

  -- Official events in support of family readiness programs

- Impermissible Non-QREs Include:

  -- Purely social events for family, friends, and peers (EAs can voluntarily agree to off-duty employment arrangements with the GO for such events in return for just compensation)

  -- Spouse-hosted social events for unit spouses

References

- DoDI 1315.09, *Utilization of Enlisted Aides (EAs) on Personal Staffs of General and Flag Officers (GO/FOs)* (17 November 2023)
- DAFI 36-2110, *Total Force Assignments*, Chapter 18 (15 November 2021), incorporating through Change 2, 5 October 2023

Page Intentionally Left Blank

OVERVIEW OF THE CIVILIAN PERSONNEL SYSTEM

The area of labor and personnel relations is covered by an assortment of statutes, executive orders, and regulations. It is a complicated area of law which is administered by a myriad of administrative bodies located in a variety of federal departments and independent agencies.

Key Takeaway

» When navigating the civilian personnel system, consult your servicing civilian personnel office and/or the Air Force Personnel Center due to the complex and diverse systems used

The Workforce Structure

- Seven categories offer varying degrees of protection from adverse personnel actions:

  -- *Competitive Service:* Consists of all positions not specifically exempted; most employees enter federal service after passing a competitive exam

  -- *Excepted Service:* Usually excepted from competition by the Office of Personnel Management (OPM) regulations

  -- *Senior Executive Service (SES):* Reserved for federal civilian employees above GS-15 who are considered general-officer equivalents

  -- *Probationary Period Employees:* After 31 December 2022, civilian employees under a competitive or excepted service appointment in their first year of federal employment have limited protections. (Note that employees hired between 26 November 2015 and 30 December 2022 are under a two-year probationary period).

  -- *Term Employees:* Employees hired to fill short-term requirements for a period between one and four years; subject to a one-year "trial period," which is equivalent to a probationary period

  -- *Hybrid Military/Civilian:* Includes National Guard technicians and Air Reserve technicians (ARTs)

  -- *Nonappropriated Fund (NAF) Employees:* Civilian employees typically employed in a morale, welfare, or recreation position and excluded from most laws administered by OPM

  -- *Acquisition Demonstration Project (AcqDemo):* Civilian employees hired under a personnel management system that was designed to increase the ability to attract, retain and motivate highly qualified individuals in the acquisition workforce. Utilizing a three-factor level classification system, the pay is set under a broadband payscale and performance is assessed under the contribution-based system.

Pay Systems

- Appropriated Fund Employees:

  -- *General Schedule (GS):* A nationwide statutory base pay scale divided into 15 grades (GS-1 to GS-15), plus varying levels of locality pay; automatic pay increases for "acceptable" performance

  -- *Executive Schedule:* Statutory basic pay nationwide; potential for merit pay increases

  -- *AcqDemo Broadband Schedule:* A system that does not utilize grades but broadband levels arranged into three or four base pay levels within a career path (NK 1 – NK III / NJ I – NJ IV / NH I – NH IV), plus varying levels of locality pay

  -- *Federal Wage Survey:* Wage Grade/Wage Leader/Wage Supervisor; pay reflects private sector pay rates in locality for the same type of work; manner of computing pay set by statute

- Nonappropriated Fund (NAF) Employees: Pay rates determined by management and may be negotiated with unions; compensated from a NAF instrumentality

Administrative and Adjudicative Bodies

- Merit Systems Protection Board (MSPB):

  -- Hears appeals by certain civilian employees opposing an agency's adverse action—removals, suspensions of more than 14 days, reductions in grade or pay, furloughs of 30 days or less, as well as performance-based removals or reductions in grade, denials of within-grade salary increases, reduction-in-force (RIF) actions, furloughs, OPM suitability determinations and employment practices, denials of restoration of reemployment rights, and certain terminations of probationary period employees

  -- Possesses authority to mitigate or completely reverse agency adverse actions taken under 5 U.S.C., Chapter 75, *Adverse Actions*, but cannot mitigate performance-based actions taken under 5 U.S.C., Chapter 43, *Performance Appraisal*

  -- Adjudicates cases brought by the Office of Special Counsel (OSC), such as whistleblower claims, allegations of mismanagement, requests by SES members for performance deficiencies, and for informal hearings and appeals concerning RIFs

  -- The MSPB also hears appeals based on protections in the Uniformed Services Employment and Reemployment Rights Act (USERRA) brought either directly to the MSPB, or after an employee has filed a complaint with the Department of Labor (DOL) and DOL opted to take no action

- <u>Equal Employment Opportunity Commission (EEOC)</u>:

  -- Adjudicates claims by civilian employees and applicants for civilian employment of unlawful discrimination based on race, religion, national origin, sex (including pregnancy, sexual orientation, and sexual stereotyping), color, disability, or age; claims of unlawful retaliation; and claims of discriminatory hostile work environment. The EEOC also adjudicates claims filed under Genetic Information Nondiscrimination Act which prohibits an agency from using genetic information to make decisions related to any terms, conditions, or privileges of employment (e.g., hiring, firing, and opportunities for advancement).

  -- If discrimination is found, the EEOC may order back pay, retroactive personnel actions, correction of records, reinstatement, promotion, payment of attorney fees, and up to $300,000 in compensatory damages

  -- The EEOC may also adjudicate discrimination claims against the Department of the Air Force made by contractors who qualify as common law employees or where a joint-employer status is found

- <u>Federal Labor Relations Authority (FLRA)</u>:

  -- Administers the interaction between federal agencies, labor organizations, and employees

  -- Decides unfair labor practice cases filed by either the agency or the union

  -- Decides appeals of certain arbitration awards and negotiability appeals

  -- Has authority to direct the Air Force and Space Force to comply with its orders

- <u>Federal Service Impasses Panel (FSIP)</u>: Resolves negotiation impasses between agencies and labor organizations

- <u>Federal Mediation and Conciliation Service</u>: Aids federal agencies and labor organizations in resolving negotiation impasses; provides parties with lists of arbitrators; provides mediators for alternative dispute resolution

- <u>Office of Personnel Management (OPM)</u>: Manages civil service of the federal government such as recruitment, civil service retirement programs, health insurance, examinations, and classification appeals

- <u>Office of Special Counsel (OSC)</u>: Investigates and prosecutes allegations of violations of merit principles; whistleblower complaints; prohibited personnel practices; fraud, waste, and abuse; and violations of the Hatch Act

References

· Merit Systems Protection Board, Office of Special Counsel, and Employee Right of Action, 5 U.S.C. §§ 1201–1204

· Performance Appraisal, 5 U.S.C. §§ 4301–4315

· Employee Classification Act, 5 U.S.C. §§ 5101–5115

· Federal Service Labor-Management Relations Statute, 5 U.S.C. §§ 7101–7135

· Adverse Actions, 5 U.S.C. §§ 7501–7515

· Defense of Defense Personnel Authorities, 5 U.S.C. § 9902 5 C.F.R. Part 1201

· Federal Sector Equal Employment Opportunity, 29 C.F.R. Part 1614

· DoDI 1400.25, Volume 771, *DoD Civilian Personnel Management System: Administrative Grievance System* (26 December 2013), incorporating Change 1, 13 June 2018

· DAFI 36-148, *Discipline and Adverse Actions of Civilian Employees* (27 September 2022), incorporating Change 1, 31 August 2023

· DAFI 36-701, *Labor-Management Relations* (14 November 2019), incorporating Change 1, 10 November 2021

· DAFI 36-2710, *Equal Opportunity Program* (18 June 2020), including DAFI36-2710_ DAFGM22023-01, 20 July 2023

· AFI 51-301, *Civil Litigation* (2 October 2018)

OVERVIEW OF FEDERAL LABOR-MANAGEMENT RELATIONS

The Federal Service Labor-Management Relations Statute (FSLMRS) prescribes the rights of employees along with the rights and duties of federal agencies and labor organizations.

Key Takeaways

» FSLMRS provides employees, unions, and agencies with rights and responsibilities

» Even when management takes action under a right reserved to management, management will have to engage in impact and implementation (I&I) bargaining

» The union must be invited to a *formal discussion* with bargaining unit employees concerning an individual grievance, a personnel policy or practice, or general conditions of employment

» A union representative is entitled to be present during an investigatory interview of a bargaining unit employee if the employee reasonably believes that the examination may result in disciplinary action against the employee **AND** the employee requests representation

» The union is entitled to information "normally maintained by the agency in the regular course of business" that is "reasonably available and necessary" for full and proper negotiation, and not prohibited from disclosure by law

---

Employee Rights

- Under the FSLMRS, employees have certain rights, including:

  -- The right to form, join, or assist any union, or to refrain from such activity, freely, and without fear of penalty or reprisal

  -- The right to serve as a representative of a union and present union views to management

  -- The right to engage in collective bargaining about conditions of employment (COE) through their chosen representatives

- Typically, an employee has limited control over whether they are covered by a bargaining unit. However, it is the employee's decision whether to be a dues-paying union member.

Management Rights and Duties

- The agency has exclusive control over certain decision-making as outlined in 5 U.S.C. § 7106. Those reserved rights include the right to:

  -- Determine the mission, budget, organization, number of employees, and internal security practices;

  -- Hire, assign, direct, layoff, and retain employees or suspend, remove, reduce in grade or pay, or take other disciplinary actions;

  -- Assign work and make decisions on outsourcing;

  -- Promote employees from among properly ranked and certified candidates; and

-- Take whatever actions may be necessary to carry out the mission during emergencies. However, any unilateral action during an emergency should not be taken without consulting the organization's Staff Judge Advocate (SJA).

- Impact and Implementation (I&I) Bargaining: When the agency exercises a right reserved to management, the agency is not required to bargain over the substance of that decision. However, the agency is required to bargain over any legitimate proposals that the union submits concerning the impact or implementation of the agency's decision.

- Formal Discussions: Management has an obligation to invite the union to attend any *formal discussion*. A formal discussion includes a meeting between one or more representatives of the Department of the Air Force and one or more bargaining unit employees concerning an individual grievance, a personnel policy or practice, or general COE. Performance evaluation discussions or weekly staff meetings are normally not considered formal discussions.

- *Weingarten* Rights: In general, agency representatives may not question a bargaining unit employee without union representation present if:

  -- One or more agency representatives are examining (questioning) a bargaining unit employee in connection with an investigation;

  -- The employee reasonably believes that the examination may result in disciplinary action against the employee; and

  -- The employee requests union representation.

Union Rights and Duties

- A union is entitled to negotiate a collective bargaining agreement (CBA) covering all employees in a bargaining unit. Both sides must negotiate in good faith; that is, both sides have a duty to approach negotiations with sincere resolve to reach an agreement.

- Requests for Information: The union is entitled to information "normally maintained by the agency in the regular course of business" that is "reasonably available and necessary" for full and proper negotiation, and not prohibited from disclosure by law. A union is not required to file a request pursuant to the Freedom of Information Act (FOIA) for this information. Undue delay, failing to explain a denial, or failing to advise the union that the information does not exist, may be grounds for an unfair labor practice (ULP) charge.

- Official Time: The FSLMRS provides that certain government employees, as designated by the union, may perform work on behalf of the union at government expense. This time is referred to as *official time*. Official time must be granted to employees representing the union when engaging in collective bargaining. However, official time cannot be granted for internal union business, such as soliciting union membership or campaigning for internal union elections.

Collective Bargaining

- <u>Conditions of Employment</u>: The Department of Air Force (DAF) **must bargain** with bargaining unit employees through their union over all COE, which are defined as personnel policies, practices, and matters affecting working conditions

- The FSLMRS **does not require bargaining** with appropriated fund employees over certain matters, including certain political activities, the classification of positions, matters provided for by federal statute (e.g., pay, vacations, health benefits, holidays, or retirement plans), or proposals that conflict with government-wide rules and regulations or that conflict with "reserved management rights"

- <u>Mid-term Bargaining</u>: Management is not required to bargain over matters already covered in the CBA. To the extent a matter arises concerning a COE that is not covered in the contract, the union can engage management in mid-term bargaining. The union may not engage management in mid-term bargaining if the CBA contains a *zipper clause* that bars such bargaining during the life of the agreement.

- <u>Past Practice</u>: Parties may establish a COE by consistently, over an extended period of time, engaging in a certain practice, and a labor contract clause can be modified or even overturned by such a COE created in this manner (often called a *past practice*). This refers to matters that are already considered COE when the past practice has merely changed the way the COE was originally handled. It is not possible for a past practice to create a COE where the subject matter underlying the practice does not pertain to a COE. A past practice cannot change the term of a CBA.

- If commanders are presented with a demand that a dispute or issue be dealt with through formal bargaining, the safe response is to advise the union representative that the commander will ask the civilian personnel section and SJA to review the request

Unfair Labor Practice

- <u>It is a unfair labor practice (ULP) for agency management to</u>:

  -- Interfere with, restrain, or coerce employees in exercising their FSLMRS rights. Lack of illegal motivation or anti-union animus is not a defense.

  -- Encourage or discourage membership in any labor organization by discrimination in connection with hiring, tenure, promotion, or other COE

  -- Sponsor, control, or assist a union

  -- Discipline or otherwise discriminate against an employee for filing a ULP or testifying in a ULP proceeding

  -- Refuse to bargain in good faith, to include failing or refusing to cooperate in impasse procedures or decisions

  -- Enforce a rule or regulation which conflicts with a preexisting CBA

  -- Otherwise fail or refuse to comply with any provision of FSLMRS

- <u>It is a ULP for a union to:</u>

  -- Coerce, discipline, or fine a union member as punishment to hinder or impede an employee's work performance

  -- Discriminate regarding union membership on basis of race, creed, color, sex, age, handicap, marital status, national origin, or political affiliation

  -- Call, participate in, or condone a strike, work stoppage, or slowdown. Non-disruptive informational picketing is permitted.

- Both the union and the DAF can file ULP charges with the Federal Labor Relations Authority (FLRA). An investigation is then conducted by a regional FLRA attorney/agent. **NEVER** permit management officials to be interviewed without first notifying the SJA.

References

· The Federal Service Labor-Management Relations Act, 5 U.S.C. §§ 7701–7135

· *NLRB v. Weingarten, Inc.*, 420 U.S. 251 (1975)

· Executive Order 14003, *Protecting the Federal Workforce* (22 January 2021)

· DoDI 1400.25, Volume 711, *DoD Civilian Personnel Management System: Labor-Management Relations* (27 August 2021)

· DAFI 36-701, *Labor-Management Relations* (14 November 2019), incorporating Change 1, 10 November 2021

CIVILIAN EMPLOYEE DRUG TESTING

Department of Air Force (DAF) employees must refrain from illegal drug use on and off duty and are subject to drug testing under certain circumstances. The DAF drug testing program is based on federal statutes governing controlled substances and is not affected by any state laws that legalize the use of marijuana or other controlled substances. Failure of an employee to appear for a drug test may be considered a refusal to participate in drug testing and may subject an employee to the full range of administrative and/or disciplinary actions, up to and including removal.

Key Takeaways

» Federal criminal statutes, not state laws, govern the DAF drug testing program

» A civilian employee can be required to provide a urine specimen based on reasonable suspicion of illegal drug use

» Employees that may have contributed to or caused certain safety mishaps or accidents are subject to required drug testing

» A safe haven provision allows an employee to self-identify illicit drug use and avoid disciplinary action if the employee meets certain conditions

» Executive Order 12564 requires supervisors to propose disciplinary action if an employee has taken specific actions

Random Drug Testing

- Only employees in "sensitive positions," also called testing designated positions (TDP), are subject to random drug testing. TDPs include positions that involve work, which impacts national security, public health and safety, protection of life and property, or otherwise requires a high degree of trust and confidence.

- The testing requirement must be identified in the position description and vacancy announcement (if applicable)

Reasonable Suspicion Drug Testing

- A civilian employee can be tested based on reasonable suspicion—a specific and fact-based belief, drawn from specific and particularized facts, and reasonable inferences from those facts, that an employee has engaged in illegal drug use, and that evidence of illegal drug use is presently in the employee's body

- Employees in TDPs may be tested based on a reasonable suspicion of drug use on or off duty. Employees in non-TDPs may be tested based on a reasonable suspicion only when the supervisor suspects on-duty drug use or impairment.

- Examples of evidence that may justify reasonable suspicion include, but are not limited to:

  -- Direct observation of illegal drug use or possession and/or physical symptoms of being under the influence of an illegal drug, including behavior, speech, appearance, and/or body odors of the employee

  -- A pattern of abnormal conduct or erratic behavior consistent with the use of illegal drugs where no other rational explanation or reason for the conduct is readily apparent;

  -- Evidence of drug-related impairment supported by hearsay from identified or unidentified sources supported by corroboration from a manager or supervisor with training and experience in the evaluation of drug-induced job impairment;

  -- A recent arrest or conviction for a drug-related offense, or the identification of an employee as the focus of a criminal investigation into illegal drug possession, use, or trafficking;

  -- Information of illicit drug use provided by a reliable and credible source or independently corroborated; and/or

  -- Evidence that the employee has tampered with or avoided a recent or current drug test.

- A supervisor is responsible for gathering all the information supporting a determination of reasonable suspicion and documenting the information in accordance with AFMAN 44-198, *Air Force Civilian Drug Demand Reduction Program*

- The supervisor's determination must be coordinated with a higher-level supervisor, the civilian personnel section, or human resources office, and an attorney from the installation Staff Judge Advocate (SJA)

- The employee must be notified in writing of the requirement to provide a urine specimen. A sample notification letter is provided in AFMAN 44-198.

Consent Drug Testing

- After consultation with the SJA, a supervisor may ask any employee to consent to provide a urine specimen for testing. A sample consent form is provided in AFMAN 44-198.

- The employee's consent must be knowing and voluntary. A positive test result resulting from a consent-based test does not exempt the employee from disciplinary action.

Accident and Safety Mishap Testing

- Civilian employees are subject to testing for evidence of illegal drug use if the employee's supervisor reasonably concludes an employee's conduct may have caused or contributed to a mishap identified as Class A, B, or nuclear by DAFI 91-204, *Safety Investigations and Reports*

- Similarly, employees are subject to testing if their actions are reasonably suspected of having caused or contributed to an accident meeting the criteria outlined in DoDI 1010.09, *DoD Civilian Employee Drug-Free Workplace Testing Program*. This includes an accident that results in:

  -- Death or personal injury requiring immediate hospitalization; or

  -- Property damage in excess of $10,000.

- Supervisors should consult with organizational personnel, medical, legal, and safety experts in making a determination regarding mishap testing

Rehabilitation Testing

- All employees referred for counseling or treatment for illicit drug use will be subject to unannounced testing for a minimum of one year from the time of initiated rehabilitation services

Personnel Actions

- If an employee who occupies a TDP is found to have used illegal drugs, the employee must be initially removed from the position and assigned other duties pending a decision on the appropriate disciplinary action. Supervisors should also consider whether to suspend an employee's access to classified information (if applicable).

- <u>Safe Haven Provision</u>: An employee who self-identifies as a user of illegal drugs, prior to being notified of testing or being identified through other means, can avoid disciplinary action for previous drug use if they meet specific conditions, including: cooperating with appropriate counseling or rehabilitation; signing a last chance agreement; and refraining from illegal drug use

- <u>Required Actions</u>: Executive Order 12564 requires supervisors to propose appropriate disciplinary action for an employee who:

  -- Refuses to obtain counseling and treatment after having been found to have used illegal drugs;

  -- Alters or attempts to alter a urine specimen or substitutes or attempts to substitute a specimen; or

  -- Fails to complete a medical approved drug rehabilitation program (if mandated or agreed upon).

References

- Anti-Drug Abuse Act of 1988, Pub. L. 100–690, 102 Stat. 4181 (1988)
- Executive Order 12564, *Drug-Free Federal Workplace* (15 September 1986)
- DoDI 1010.09, *DoD Civilian Employee Drug-Free Workplace Testing Program* (22 June 2012), incorporating Change 1, 28 June 2018
- DAFI 91-204, *Safety Investigations and Reports* (10 March 2021)
- AFI 44-121, *Alcohol and Drug Abuse Prevention and Treatment (ADAPT) Program* (18 July 2018), incorporating Change 1, 21 November 2019, Corrective Actions applied on 19 December 2019
- AFMAN 44-198, *Air Force Civilian Drug Demand Reduction Program* (24 January 2019), certified current 5 October 2022

CIVILIAN EMPLOYEE WORKPLACE SEARCHES

The general rule is that a government search of private property is unreasonable and unconstitutional under the Fourth Amendment to the U.S. Constitution unless authorized by a valid search warrant or proper consent. However, the government employer can conduct a limited warrantless search of an employee's workplace for "work-related" purposes.

Key Takeaways

» Employees have a reasonable expectation of privacy in their work area which will prevent searching their work area whenever the employer wishes

» Reasonableness of a search is a case-by-case determination

Workplace Searches

- In the leading case on workplace searches, *O'Connor v. Ortega*, the Supreme Court recognized that government employees may have a reasonable expectation of privacy in their work areas, which may be protected from warrantless searches by a government employer and law enforcement

- However, government searches to retrieve work-related materials, investigate violations of workplace rules, or for a non-investigatory work-related purpose, do not violate the Fourth Amendment. Supervisors are generally not required to obtain a search warrant to enter an employee's desk, office, or file cabinet.

- Supervisors should be able to articulate a legitimate work-related rationale for a search and should tailor the scope of the search accordingly

- Personal handbags, backpacks, and briefcases are **NOT** considered part of the workplace. Therefore, a search warrant or search authorization is generally required before searching such items.

- Consult the Staff Judge Advocate before proceeding with any search and seizure action

References

- U.S. Const. Amend. IV
- *O'Connor v. Ortega*, 480 U.S. 709 (1987)
- *City of Ontario v. Quon*, 560 U.S. 746 (2010)

CIVILIAN EMPLOYEE DISCIPLINE

Disciplinary action or adverse action must be taken without regard to marital status, political affiliation, race, color, religion, sex, disability, national origin, age, or prior engagement in protected equal employment opportunity (EEO) activity. Adverse action based on disability cannot be taken when the employee can perform the essential functions of his/her job either with or without a reasonable accommodation. Disciplinary action or adverse action must be taken to promote the efficiency of the service, and carried out promptly and equitably. Disciplinary actions and adverse actions are personal matters and are carried out confidentially.

Key Takeaways

» Adverse actions can be disciplinary or non-disciplinary for civilian misconduct or poor performance, and may only be taken for the "efficiency of the service"

» Each employment action requires careful consideration of the facts, circumstances, context, and nuance

» Proposing and deciding officials should consult with their Staff Judge Advocate and servicing civilian personnel representative to determine the most appropriate charge and penalty

» Some types of adverse actions are appealable to the Merit Systems Protection Board (MSPB). These include removals, suspensions for more than 14 days, furloughs for 30 days or less, and reductions in grade or pay.

» Due process must be provided to the employee. Due process includes notice and ability to respond to the charge(s) and specification(s) and any factors that aggravate the penalty.

Authority and Requirements

- All Air Force and Space Force commanders and supervisors are authorized to take disciplinary and adverse action when necessary. DAFI 36-148, *Discipline and Adverse Actions of Civilian Employees*, covers all competitive and excepted service employees paid from appropriated funds. AFI 34-301, *Nonappropriated Fund Personnel Management and Administration*, covers nonappropriated fund employees.

- Management may take a disciplinary or adverse action only for such cause as will promote the efficiency of the service, unless the action is being taken for unacceptable performance, in which case different standards apply

- Management may not take an action that would result in a prohibited personnel practice. A prohibited personnel practice is an adverse action taken against an employee for an illegal or inappropriate reason, such as reprisal or discrimination.

Procedures

- <u>Management Procedures</u>: (absent a local collective bargaining agreement that contains other provisions)

    -- Gather the facts and interview the employee if necessary. A bargaining unit employee has rights (called *Weingarten* Rights) to have union representation if the employee believes disciplinary action could result from questioning from his/her employer **AND** he/she requests a union representative.

    -- Consult with the civilian personnel section and the Staff Judge Advocate (SJA) to consider options and determine what action is appropriate

    -- The civilian personnel section will prepare, and the SJA will review, the notice letter of adverse and/or disciplinary action for signature by the "**proposing official**" (normally a first or second level supervisor). The Labor Law Field Support Center (LLFSC) will also review the notice letter if the disciplinary action is adverse and appealable to the MSPB.

        --- The notice must include all aggravating factors considered by the proposing official (e.g., prior discipline, poor performance, seriousness of the alleged offense). There are limitations on what prior discipline may be considered. For instance, reprimands must have occurred within the last two years.

    -- The **employee** gets a reasonable amount of time, but not less than seven days, to answer orally and/or in writing, and to furnish affidavits and other documentary evidence in support of the answer

    -- The "**deciding official**" makes the final decision. This is usually the supervisor one level up from the proposing official (but may be the same person). The final decision is effective no earlier than 30 days after the notice is given to the employee.

        --- The deciding official must document his/her consideration of the *Douglas Factors* governing appropriate penalty selection. The *Douglas Factors* are those factors that management must consider before taking disciplinary actions. They include, for example, the seriousness of the misconduct, the work record of the employee, and other similar considerations (see DAFI 36-148). Consult the civilian personnel section and SJA for assistance in preparing this document.

        --- The deciding official must not consider any information outside of the documentation that was provided to him/her to make the final decision

Air National Guard Technicians and National Guard Employees

- Title 32 Air National Guard Technician and Title 5 National Guard employee discipline is covered under CNGBI 1400.25 Vol. 752. The instruction discusses the procedures for non-disciplinary adverse administrative actions (e.g., letters of counseling, admonition, and reprimand) and disciplinary actions (removal, suspension, reduction in grade, and reduction in pay) for Title 32 Air National Guard Technicians and Title 5 National Guard employees.

Air Reserve Technicians (ARTs)

- ARTs are "dual status" federal civilian employees and members of the Selected Reserve. As a condition of federal civilian employment, ARTs must maintain membership in the Selected Reserve. ART positions within the Selected Reserve span a broad spectrum to include command billets.

- ARTs who are in the military status performing duty for pay/points are subject to the Uniform Code of Military Justice (UCMJ)

- ARTs who are in federal civilian employee status are not subject to the UCMJ. However, they are subject to all civilian employee disciplinary measures discussed in this section. Additionally, an ART in civilian employee status may be subject to military administrative actions such as letters of counseling (LOC), admonishment (LOA), or reprimand (LOR), demotion, and discharge.

  -- Military administrative discharge of an ART will lead to the loss of a condition of employment of an ART's civilian employee position and adverse action is then appropriate

- ART commanders must be in military status when taking certain actions such as preferral/referral of charges pursuant to the UCMJ, nonjudicial punishment actions pursuant to Article 15 of the UCMJ, ordering urinalysis testing, and for actions related to commander directed investigations (CDIs). Consult with your local SJA for guidance regarding actions in which military status is relevant.

References

· Article 15, Uniform Code of Military Justice

· *Douglas v. Veterans Admin.*, 5 M.S.P.R. 280 (1981)

· DAFI 36-148, *Discipline and Adverse Actions of Civilian Employees* (27 September 2022), incorporating Change 1, 31 August 2023

· AFI 34-301, *Nonappropriated Fund Personnel Management and Administration* (24 July 2023)

· AFRCI 36-114, *Procedures on Air Reserve Technicians (ARTS) Who Lose Active Membership in the Reserve* (29 January 2020)

· CNGBI 1400.25, Vol. 752, *National Guard Technician and Civilian Personnel Discipline and Adverse Action Program* (8 November 2021)

CIVILIAN EMPLOYEE INVESTIGATORY INTERVIEW

Civilian employees have a variety of rights during investigatory interviews. The purpose of allowing an employee to seek union representation in an investigatory examination situation is to ensure that the agency can accomplish the purpose of the investigation—to obtain all of the relevant facts and explore all issues regarding the matter under investigation.

Key Takeaways

» Civilian employees have a right to union representation during investigatory interviews if the employee so requests. This safeguard is referred to as "*Weingarten* Rights."

» An agency representative interviewing a bargaining unit employee for arbitration or hearing has a responsibility to comply with a variety of safeguards to mitigate the potential of coercive effects of the situation. These safeguards are referred to as "*Brookhaven* Rights."

Weingarten Rights

- In 1975, the U.S. Supreme Court, in *NLRB v. Weingarten, Inc.*, detailed the right of an employee to have union representation present if the employee believes disciplinary action could result from questioning by his/her employer and if the employee requested the presence of a union representative. These rights are commonly known as *Weingarten* Rights.

  -- 5 U.S.C. § 7103(b)(1) allows the President, by Executive Order, to exempt any agency, or part of an agency, from the Federal Service Labor Management Relations statute if he/she determines that it has a primary function of intelligence, counterintelligence, investigative, or national security work and the application of the statute would be unduly disruptive

  -- Executive Order 12171, *Exclusions from The Federal Labor-Management Relations Program* thereafter excluded *Weingarten* Rights from applying to interrogations by the Air Force Office of Special Investigations (AFOSI) (see para. 1-206(g) which specifically excludes AFOSI)

- Both the union and the employee's right to union representation in connection with an investigation are applicable when four conditions are present:

  -- A meeting is held in which management questions a bargaining unit employee;

  -- The examination is in connection with an investigation (except those conducted by AFOSI);

  -- The employee reasonably believes that discipline could result from the investigatory interview; and

  -- The employee requests union representation.

- The role of the union representative during the interview is to clarify the facts and the questions, help the employee express his/her views, suggest other avenues of inquiry, suggest other employees who may have knowledge of the facts, and ensure the employer does not initiate or impose unjust punishment. There may also be a right for the union representative and the employee to confer in private, but this depends on the nature of the case.

- Agencies must announce this right on an annual basis at all places where employees normally receive employment information

- Individuals being investigated may not serve as representatives for other employees being investigated until their own investigations are completed

- Management cannot tell a union representative to remain silent or not to offer advice. The employer may place reasonable limitations on a union representative's role to prevent adversarial confrontation, but aggressive, unreasonable management behavior interferes with the right to union representation. This may result in an unfair labor practice (ULP).

- Once an employee requests a union representative, management may either grant the request, suspend the interview, or give the employee the choice between having an interview without a union representative or having no interview

- Civilian employees also have a legal obligation to account for the performance of their duties and a failure to provide desired information can serve as a basis for removal under certain circumstances. However, an employee cannot be discharged simply because he/she invokes his/her Fifth Amendment privilege against self-incrimination nor can statements coerced by a threat of removal be used against the employee in a subsequent prosecution. An employee **CAN** be removed for not replying if he/she is adequately informed both that he/she is subject to discharge for not answering and that his/her replies cannot be used against him/her in a criminal case.

  -- Any desire to offer immunity to an employee must be coordinated with the Staff Judge Advocate who will consult with (and possibly get approval from) the Department of Justice

Brookhaven Rights

- A bargaining unit employee also has the right to be advised of the consequences of participating or not participating in an interview for a third-party proceeding (unfair labor practice hearing, arbitration, Merit Systems Protection Board (MSPB) hearing, etc.), and failure to do so can be an ULP by management. These rights are known as *Brookhaven* Rights.

- The employee must be advised of:

  -- The purpose of the interview;

  -- That no reprisal will take place if the employee refuses to participate; and

  -- Participation is voluntary.

- The interview cannot be coercive in nature. Questions must not exceed the scope of the legitimate purpose of the inquiry and cannot otherwise interfere with the employee's statutory rights.

References

· Federal Labor Relations Act, 5 U.S.C. § 7103(b)(1)

· Representation Rights and Duties, 5 U.S.C. § 7114(a)(2)(B)

· Unfair Labor Practices, 5 U.S.C. § 7116(a)(1)

· Executive Order 12171, *Exclusions from the Federal Labor-Management Relations Program* (19 November 1979)

· Executive Order 13760, *Exclusions from the Federal Labor-Management Relations Program* (12 January 2017)

· *Uniformed Sanitation Men Ass'n v. Commissioner of Sanitation*, 392 U.S. 280 (1968)

· *NLRB v. Weingarten, Inc.*, 420 U.S. 251 (1975)

· *Kalkines v. United States*, 473 F.2d 1391 (Ct. Cl. 1973)

· *Internal Revenue Service, Brookhaven Service Center and National Treasury Employees Union (NTEU)*, 9 FLRA 930 (1982)

Chapter 16
OPERATIONS AND INTERNATIONAL LAW

INTRODUCTION TO OPERATIONS LAW

The mission of the Air Force is to fly, fight, and win—airpower anytime, anywhere. To achieve its mission, the Space Force is responsible for organizing, training, and equipping Guardians to conduct global space operations that enhance the way our joint and coalition forces fight, while also offering decision makers military options to achieve national objectives. Respect for the rule of law is fundamental to achieving our objectives.

Key Takeaways

» Department of the Air Force (DAF) service members must conduct operations in accordance with the law of the United Sates and international law

» Respect for the rule of law is a fundamental part of not only who we are as the world's greatest Air Force and Space Force but as a nation. Compliance with the law is a strategic and operational imperative.

» Failure to comply with the law undermines the legitimacy of the United States military operations and can result in mission failure

» Commanders must understand the relationship between adherence to the rule of law and the achievement of operational objectives

» Judge advocate generals (JAGs) must be thoroughly integrated into unit planning and the execution of military operations in order to ensure mission accomplishment

---

Operations Law Defined

- Operations law is the domestic, foreign, and international law associated with the planning and execution of military operations in peacetime or hostilities. The term "operations law" is also used to describe the application of law to a specific mission of the supported DAF unit. Operations law includes, but is not limited to:

  -- The principles of the Law of War/Law of Armed Conflict; Rules of Engagement (ROE) and Rules for the Use of Force; laws relating to security assistance; training, mobilization, and pre-deployment preparation; targeting; overseas procurement; the conduct of military combat operations; counter-terrorism activities; Status of Forces Agreements (SOFAs); operations in the information environment; rule of law operations; air and space law; and international agreements

- Operations law often draws up areas of the law that may affect a commander's ability to plan and successfully execute the unit's mission (e.g., environmental law, contract law, fiscal law, and military justice)

Role of Judge Advocates

- The DAF, like other military services, continue to operate in an increasingly complex environment around the world, demanding nothing less than the very best in legal capability. JAGs who advise on operations law matters are mission-focused and provide commanders with legally sustainable options and recommendations to maximize the commander's options and to enable mission accomplishment.

- Legal support to DAF commanders is critical to mission success because proper legal counsel enhances commanders' decision-making ability. Successful commanders are those who demand close coordination with their servicing Staff Judge Advocate. JAGs must be thoroughly integrated into unit planning and the execution of military operations to ensure mission accomplishment; for example, Chairman of the Joint Chiefs of Staff Instruction (CJCSI) 3121.01B, *Standing Rules of Engagement/Standing Rules for the Use of Force for US Forces*, specifically directs that JAGs be involved in the planning of operations.

References

- CJCSI 3121.01B, *(U) Standing Rules of Engagement/Standing Rules for the Use of Force for US Forces* (13 June 2005), certified current 18 June 2008
- Joint Publication 3-84, *Legal Support* (2 August 2016)
- DAFI 51-101, *The Air Force Judge Advocate General's (AFJAG) Corps Operations, Accessions, and Professional Development* (20 June 2023)
- The Law of Air, Space and Cyber Operations, 4th Ed. (2020)

THE LAW OF WAR

Department of the Air Force (DAF) commanders are responsible for ensuring that their service members know the fundamental precepts of the Law of War (LoW), also known as the Law of Armed Conflict or International Humanitarian Law. Commanders cannot assume that every DAF member is fully aware of all his/her rights and responsibilities and duty to enforce the LoW; personnel must comply with and be trained in the LoW. Proper legal counsel enhances commanders' decision-making ability, aiding in mission success.

Key Takeaways

» It is the Department of Defense (DoD) and DAF policy to comply with the LoW during all armed conflicts, however characterized

» In all other military operations, members of the DoD Components will continue to act consistent with the LoW's fundamental principles and rules, including those contained in Common Article 3 of the 1949 Geneva Conventions and the principles of military necessity, humanity, distinction, proportionality, and honor

» The LoW is the part of international law that regulates the conduct of hostilities and the protection of war victims in both international and non-international armed conflict, belligerent occupation, and the relationships between belligerent, neutral, and non-belligerent states

» One key to success for commanders is to ensure judge advocates are thoroughly integrated into unit planning and execution of military operations so that commanders are aware of their options and recommendations to enable mission accomplishment and compliance with the LoW

The Law of War

- The LoW is the part of international law that regulates the conduct of hostilities and the protection of war victims in both international and non-international armed conflict, belligerent occupation, and the relationships between belligerent, neutral, and non-belligerent states (*jus in bello*). This section will not address the portion of the LoW that regulates the resort to armed force (*jus ad bellum*).

- The LoW has two main sources: (1) treaty law arising from formal written international agreements, which are binding on states that are parties, and (2) customary international law arising from the practice of states followed out of a sense of legal obligation. Customary international law is unwritten and, once formed, is generally binding on all states.

- LoW treaty law is generally divided into two overlapping areas: (1) Geneva Law, named for treaty negotiations held over the years at Geneva, Switzerland; and (2) Hague Law, named for treaty negotiations held at The Hague, Netherlands

Geneva and Hague Provisions

- Geneva Law: Consists of four treaties known as the 1949 Geneva Conventions, which concern the protection of persons involved in conflicts (wounded and sick; wounded, sick, and shipwrecked at sea; prisoners of war (POWs); and civilians)

  -- The Geneva Conventions are supplemented by three additional protocols. The United States is not a party to Additional Protocol I (AP I) concerning international armed conflicts or Additional Protocol II (AP II) regarding non-international armed conflicts, but it accepts certain aspects of AP I and AP II as reflecting customary international law. Advice should be sought from a judge advocate as to the applicable law.

  -- The United States is a party to Additional Protocol III (AP III), which recognizes a red crystal as an additional distinctive protective emblem

- Hague Law: Concerned mainly with the means and methods of warfare and the conduct of hostilities (e.g., lawful and unlawful weapons, targeting)

  -- The Hague Peace Conferences of 1899 and 1907 resulted in bans on certain types of war technology and established a court to settle international disputes; conferences in 1922–1923 to create the Hague Rules of Air Warfare resulted in draft rules that never entered into force, but some draft rules may today be viewed as reflecting customary international law (see para. 19.11, DoD LoW Manual)

DoD Weapons Review Process

- DoD and DAF policy requires a review of all weapons, weapon systems, and relevant cyber capabilities, which are being developed, bought, built, modified, or otherwise being acquired by the DAF, to ensure compliance with domestic and international law, including the law of war. The review must be completed prior to any use in a conflict or other military operation (or for cyber capabilities, where the intended effects of the operation are outside the DoD Information Network) and should be accomplished during the acquisition process.

Military Necessity

- Military necessity is the LoW principle that justifies the use of all measures needed to defeat the enemy as quickly and efficiently as possible that are not prohibited by the LoW

- The principle of military necessity permits attacks on military objectives, such as any objects, which by their nature, location, purpose, or use make an effective contribution to military action and whose total or partial destruction, capture, or neutralization, in the circumstances ruling at the time, offers a definite military advantage. Examples include an adversary's troops, bases, supplies, lines of communications, and headquarters.

Humanity

- Humanity forbids the infliction of unnecessary suffering, injury, or destruction to defeat the adversary or to accomplish a legitimate military purpose. Once a military purpose is achieved, the infliction of further suffering is unnecessary.

- Humanity is the logical inverse of the principle of military necessity. If certain necessary actions are justified, then certain unnecessary actions are prohibited.

Distinction

- Distinction requires parties to a conflict to distinguish principally between the armed forces and the civilian population, and between unprotected and protected objects

- Military force may be directed only against military objectives, and not against civilians or civilian objects. Civilian objects include places of worship, schools, hospitals, and dwellings. However, civilians or civilian objects can lose protected status in certain circumstances.

- The principle of distinction also prohibits attacks against combatants *hors de combat* ("out of the fight")

Proportionality

- Proportionality is the LoW principle that even where one is justified in acting, one must not act in a way that is unreasonable or excessive

- Commanders who plan military operations must take into consideration the extent of expected loss of civilian life, injury to civilians, and damage to civilian objects that will result and, to the extent consistent with the necessities of the military situation, take feasible precautions to avoid or minimize the risk of such casualties and destruction

    -- The expected loss of civilian life and damage to civilian property incidental to attacks must not be excessive in relation to the concrete and direct military advantage expected to be gained

    -- This concept of avoiding or minimizing casualties and destruction does not apply to persons or objects that are considered military objectives. However, individual military personnel may claim a protected status (e.g., chaplains, medics, wounded, sick, shipwrecked at sea, surrendering, or aircrews parachuting from disabled aircraft).

- Feasible precautions are those that are practicable or practically possible, taking into account all circumstances ruling at the time, including humanitarian and military considerations. For example, if a commander determines that taking a precaution would result in a risk of failing to accomplish the mission or an increased risk of harm to his/her own forces, then the precaution would not be feasible and would not be required.

Honor

- Honor (also called chivalry) requires a degree of fairness in offense and defense and a certain mutual respect between opposing military forces. However, honor does allow for lawful ruses, such as camouflage, false radio signals, and mock troop movements.

- Honor forbids treacherous acts such as perfidy. These acts involve misuse of internationally recognized symbols or status to take unfair advantage of the enemy, such as false surrenders, placing anti-aircraft artillery in hospitals, and misuse of the Red Cross, Red Crystal, or the Red Crescent.

References

· Geneva Convention for the Protection of War Victims (12 August 1949)

· DoDD 2311.01, *DoD Law of War Program* (2 July 2020)

· CJCSI 5810.01D, *Implementation of the DoD Law of War Program* (30 April 2010)

· DoD Law of War Manual (June 2015), updated July 2023

· DAFI 36-2670, *Total Force Development* (25 June 2020), incorporating through Change 5, 9 November 2023

· AFI 51-401, *The Law of War* (3 August 2018)

· AFPD 51-4, *Operations and International Law* (24 July 2018)

· The Law of Air, Space, and Cyber Operations, 4th Edition (2020)

RULES OF ENGAGEMENT AND RULES FOR THE USE OF FORCE

This section discusses the Rules of Engagement (ROE) and the Rules for the Use of Force (RUF) for Department of Defense (DoD) operations worldwide and will further consider the differences between both sets of rules, their purposes, and when they apply.

Key Takeaways

» In operations, there are typically mission-specific ROE and RUF that are built upon the Standing Rules of Engagement (SROE) and Standing Rules for the Use of Force (SRUF)

» These standing rules are approved by the Secretary of Defense (SecDef) and are promulgated by the Chairman of the Joint Chiefs of Staff (CJCS) and are contained in Chairman of the Joint Chiefs of Staff Instruction (CJCSI) 3121.01B, *Standing Rules of Engagement/Standing Rules for the Use of Force for US Forces*

» The current SROE provide implementation and guidance on two important issues: (1) the inherent right of self-defense; and (2) the application of force for mission accomplishment

---

Rules of Engagement (ROE)

- *DoD Dictionary of Military and Associated Terms*, and JP 3-84, *Legal Support*, define ROE as "directives issued by competent military authority that delineate the circumstances and limitations under which United States forces will initiate and/or continue combat engagement with other forces encountered"

- ROE govern the use of force in military operations. ROE reflect legal, policy and operational considerations, and are consistent with the international law obligations of the United States, including the law of war. ROE are tools for commanders (e.g., the President of the United States/Commander in Chief, SecDef, combatant commanders) to regulate the use of armed force in military operations and are implemented by those who execute the mission.

Rules for the Use of Force (RUF)

- CJCSI 3121.01B explains that the purpose of the SRUF is to "provide operational guidance and establish fundamental policies and procedures governing actions to be taken by DoD forces performing civil support missions (e.g., military assistance to civil authorities and military support for civilian law enforcement agencies) and routine Service functions (including antiterrorism (AT)/force protection (FP) duties) within U.S. territory (including U.S. territorial waters). The SRUF also apply to land homeland defense missions occurring within U.S. territory and to DoD forces, civilians and contractors performing law enforcement and security duties at all DoD installations (and off-installation, while conducting official DoD security functions), within or outside U.S. Territory, unless otherwise directed by the SecDef."

- Combatant commanders may augment the SRUF as necessary for mission accomplishment, subject to obtaining SecDef approval

- Whereas United States' SROE are fundamentally permissive in nature—allowing commanders flexibility to use any lawful weapon or tactic unless specifically restricted, the SRUF are not permissive and require SecDef approval to use any weapons or tactics not already approved within the SRUF

Purposes of ROE

- ROE serve three main functions: (1) Provide direction on the use of force from the President, SecDef, and subordinate commanders to units conducting military operations; (2) Provide a control mechanism for the transition from peacetime to armed conflict and a return to peacetime; and (3) Provide a mechanism to facilitate planning.

- The three functions all emphasize control, which is necessary for political, operational, and legal purposes

Standing Rules of Engagement (SROE)

- SROE apply to all military operations and contingencies outside U.S. territory (including U.S. territorial seas), as well as to air and maritime (but not land—see RUF) homeland defense missions conducted within U.S. territory (including territorial seas)

- The SROE provide implementation guidance on and distinguish between the inherent right of self-defense and the application of force for mission accomplishment

Self-Defense in SROE

- <u>Inherent Right of Self-Defense</u>: Unit commanders always retain the inherent right and obligation to exercise *unit self-defense* in response to a **hostile act** or demonstrated **hostile intent** and, unless otherwise directed by their commander, individual military members may exercise *individual self-defense*

- Unit and individual self-defense arise in either of two circumstances:

    -- *In response to a* <u>hostile act</u>: A hostile act is an attack or other use of force against the United States, U.S. forces or other designated persons or property. It also includes force used directly to impede the mission and/or duties of U.S. forces (including recovery of U.S. personnel or vital USG property).

    -- *In response to demonstrated* <u>hostile intent</u>: Hostile intent is the threat of imminent use of force against the United States, U.S. forces or other designated persons or property. It also includes the threat of force to preclude or impede the mission and/or duties of U.S. forces (including the recovery of U.S. personnel or vital USG property). Determining the imminence of a threat will be based on an assessment of all the facts and circumstances known to U.S. forces at the time and may be made at any level. Imminent does not necessarily mean immediate or instantaneous.

- National and Collective Self-Defense: The right of a State to defend itself against armed attack (National Self-Defense) is recognized in international law both individually and collectively (i.e., as part of an alliance such as NATO or at the request of another State) and enshrined in Article 51 of the UN Charter. Collective Self-Defense is the defense of designated non-U.S. military forces and/or designated foreign nationals and their property from a hostile act or demonstrated hostile intent. Only the President or SecDef may authorize collective self-defense.

Self-Defense Guidance

- All necessary means available and all appropriate actions may be used in self-defense. However, the following guidelines, which are articulated within CJCSI 3121.01B, apply:

    -- *De-escalation:* When time and circumstances permit, the forces committing hostile acts or demonstrating hostile intent should be warned and given the opportunity to withdraw or cease threatening actions

    -- *Necessity:* Exists when a hostile act occurs or when a force demonstrates hostile intent. When such conditions exist, use of force in self-defense is authorized while the force continues to commit hostile acts or exhibit hostile intent.

    -- *Proportionality:* The nature, duration, and scope of force used should not exceed what is required to decisively respond to the hostile act or demonstrated hostile intent. However, such use of force may exceed the means and intensity of the hostile act or hostile intent. This principle of proportionality should not be confused with attempts to minimize collateral damage during offensive operations.

    -- *Pursuit in Self-Defense:* Self-defense includes the authority to pursue and engage forces that have committed a hostile act or demonstrated hostile intent if those forces continue to commit hostile acts or demonstrate hostile intent

ROE for Mission Accomplishment

- Commanders may tailor ROE for mission accomplishment through supplemental measures from Enclosure I of the SROE. See CJCSI 3121.01B, *(U) Standing Rules of Engagement/Standing Rules for the Use of Force for US Forces*, Enclosure I.

- Declared Hostile Force: SROE permit appropriate U.S. authority to declare any recognized enemy as a declared hostile force. U.S. forces may engage declared hostile forces regardless of whether such forces have committed a hostile act or demonstrated a hostile intent, subject to the LoW and in accordance with prescribed targeting guidance or other ROE provisions. Specific Guidance for U.S. Forces Operating with Multinational Forces.

- U.S. forces assigned under operational control (OPCON) or tactical control (TACON) of a multinational force (MNF) will follow the ROE of the MNF for mission accomplishment, if authorized by order of SecDef. U.S. forces retain the right of self-defense. Apparent inconsistencies between the right of self-defense contained in U.S. ROE and the ROE of the MNF will be submitted through the U.S. chain of command for resolution. While a final resolution is pending, U.S. forces will continue to operate under U.S. ROE for self-defense.

- When U.S. forces are under U.S. OPCON or TACON, operating in conjunction with a MNF, reasonable efforts will be made to develop common ROE. If common ROE cannot be developed, U.S. forces will operate under all applicable U.S. ROE and the MNF forces will be informed of this fact.

Supplemental Measures and Command Guidance

- Although the SROE are fundamentally permissive, commanders at all echelons may issue or request approval of supplemental ROE. The SROE specify the required approval level for certain types of supplemental measures. Supplemental measures are primarily used to define limits or grant authority for the use of force for mission accomplishment.

- Subordinate commanders may issue tactical directives or other forms of command guidance to clarify the application of the governing ROE or RUF for members of their command. However, if a commander's guidance further restricts approved ROE, that commander is obligated to notify SecDef as soon as practical of any imposed restriction.

SRUF Self-Defense

- Outside of military operations, U.S. forces may use force only in self-defense:

  -- Inherent Right of Self-Defense: Unit commanders have an inherent right and obligation to exercise unit self-defense. Unless otherwise directed by their commander, individual military members may exercise individual self-defense.

  -- Unit and Individual Self-Defense: Arises in response to hostile acts or demonstrated hostile intent, and are treated the same in the SRUF as in the SROE

References

· Charter of the United Nations, Art. 51 (26 June 1945)
· Executive Order 11850, *Enunciation of Certain Uses in War of Chemical Herbicides and Riot Control Agents* (8 April 1975)
· DoDD 2311.01, *DoD Law of War Program* (2 July 2020)
· CJCSI 3121.01B, *(U) Standing Rules of Engagement/Standing Rules for the Use of Force for US Forces* (13 June 2005), certified current 18 June 2008
· CJCSI 3370.01D, *(U) Target Development Standards* (8 April 2022)
· CJCSI 5810.01D, *Implementation of the DoD Law of War Program* (30 April 2010)
· Joint Publication 3-84, *Legal Support* (2 August 2016)
· DoD Law of War Manual (June 2015), updated July 2023
· DoD Dictionary of Military and Associated Terms (September 2023)

INTERNATIONAL HUMAN RIGHTS LAW

International Human Rights Law (IHRL) is the body of law focusing on a State's obligation to protect the inherent dignity and inalienable rights of human beings. It is the policy and practice of the United States Government (USG) to respect and implement its obligations under the international human rights treaties to which it is a party. The prevention of mass atrocities and genocide is a U.S. national security interest and moral responsibility.

Key Takeaways

» IHRL imposes obligations on states to protect the life and dignity of individuals

» It is USG policy and practice to act consistently with its obligations under international human rights treaties

» Where provisions of the Law of War (LoW) and IHRL seem to conflict, the provisions of the LoW prevail over IHRL

» Persons who fall under the power of the United States during international armed conflict have fundamental guarantees for the protection of their human rights

» Commanders must prevent human rights violations and punish those who commit human rights violations

Law of War (or Law of Armed Conflict) and International Human Rights Law (IHRL)

- The United States position is that the LoW and IHRL are separate bodies of law. However, to the degree that both can be applied without conflict, the protections of both the LoW and IHRL should be applied during military operations (in peacetime and in conflict).

- In military operations where specific provisions of the LoW and IHRL seem to conflict, it is the Department of Defense's (DoD) position that the provisions of the LoW will prevail over IHRL, including the conduct of hostilities and the protection of persons involved in armed conflict. Advice should be sought from judge advocates about the applicable law.

- Commanders should be aware that some coalition partners may be subject to different IHRL obligations. Coalition partners may be subject to different treaty obligations and may have different interpretations of the law and the scope of its application in military operations.

  -- The European Court of Human Rights (ECtHR) has, for example, ruled that aspects of the European Convention on Human Rights (ECHR) apply to a party's military forces serving abroad and during armed conflict

IHRL Obligations

- The LoW directly incorporates many core human rights protections. DoDD 2311.01, *DoD Law of War Program*, dictates that members of the DoD Components shall comply with the LoW during all armed conflicts.

- The United States acknowledges Article 75 of Additional Protocol I to the 1949 Geneva Conventions as reflective of U.S. policy and practice. This article applies to persons who fall under the power of the United States during international armed conflict, and, at a minimum (unless other LoW provisions offer greater protection), provides certain protections without adverse distinction based on race, color, sex, language, religion or belief, political or other opinion, national or social origin, wealth, birth or other status, or other similar criteria.

Additional Protocol I, Article 75 Prohibitions and Protections

- Prohibits violence to life, health, or physical or mental well-being (in particular, murder, torture of all kinds [whether physical or mental], corporal punishment, and mutilation)

- Prohibits outrages upon personal dignity (in particular, humiliating and degrading treatment, enforced prostitution, and any form of indecent assault), the taking of hostages, collective punishments, and threats to commit any of the above acts

- Guarantees that those arrested, detained, or interned for actions related to the conflict will be informed of the reason for the actions taken; guarantees provisions for fundamental fairness at any court, hearing, or tribunal

- Provides that detained women will be held separate from detained men (other than family members), and will be directly supervised by women

- Common Article 3 of the 1949 Geneva Conventions applies to non-international armed conflicts. It provides similar protections for civilians and those persons no longer taking part in the conflict.

Other Treaty and Customary International Law Protections

- IHRL obligations may arise out of U.S. treaty law or customary international law

- While there is no definitive list of these provisions, the following acts are prohibited: genocide; slavery; murder or forced disappearance; torture or other cruel, inhumane, or degrading treatment or punishment; prolonged arbitrary detention; systemic racial discrimination; hostage taking; punishment without fair trial

Obligations to Prevent or Punish Human Rights Violations

- Commanders have a legal obligation to ensure that forces under their command do not commit human rights violations. Such violations may be punishable under the Uniform Code of Military Justice (UCMJ), the War Crimes Act, or under other federal law.

- U.S. forces should recognize that human rights violations may occur in an area of military operations resulting from adversaries', partner states', or other parties' conduct or actions. If U.S. forces become aware of human rights violations committed by U.S. forces, enemy forces, or other parties, the unit commander must immediately report reportable incidents (as defined by DoDD 2311.01), by operational incident reporting procedures or other expeditious means, through the chain of command to the combatant commander.

- Prior to any forceful intervention to stop IHRL violations, U.S. forces must ensure that their actions are consistent with the rules of engagement (ROE) or rules for the use of force (RUF) for the operation

    -- Under the Standing Rules of Engagement (SROE), collective self-defense of non-DoD persons or the affirmative defense of others would not be authorized unless for the protection of previously-designated persons or groups. Commanders should seek prior authorization before acting.

    -- Under the Standing Rules for the Use of Force (SRUF), the use of deadly force would be authorized when reasonably necessary to prevent an imminent threat of life or serious bodily harm to civilians directly related to the assigned mission. However, the scope of application of the SRUF is narrow.

References

· War Crimes Act of 1996, 18 U.S.C. § 2441

· Executive Order 13107, *Implementation of Human Rights Treaties* (10 December 1998)

· Presidential Study Directive (PSD)-10, *Presidential Study Directive on Mass Atrocities* (4 August 2011)

· DoDD 2311.01, *DoD Law of War Program* (2 July 2020)

· DoD Law of War Manual (June 2015), updated July 2023

· CJCSI 3121.01B, *(U) Standing Rules of Engagement/Standing Rules for the Use of Forces for US Forces* (13 June 2005), certified current 18 June 2008

INTERNATIONAL LAW AND INTERNATIONAL AGREEMENTS

International law consists of rules and principles regulating the conduct of nations (often referred to as "states") and international organizations in their relations with individuals, other international organizations, or other states. States rely on international law in their diplomatic relations, negotiations, and policymaking, and often defend the actions and challenge the conduct of other states by invoking its authority.

Key Takeaways

» In very limited and specific circumstances, Department of the Air Force (DAF) commanders may have authority to negotiate and conclude international agreements in accordance with Department of State (DoS), Department of Defense (DoD), and DAF policy and guidance

» DAF personnel seeking to negotiate and conclude international agreements must first secure approval from the appropriate authority, typically either the major (MAJCOM) or field command (FLDCOM) commander, the Secretary of the Air Force (SecAF), or higher authority

» Commanders should not do anything that might be construed as a negotiation unless they have received advance authority, preferably in writing

» DoDI 5530.03 and AFI 51-403, *International Agreements*, prohibit DoD personnel from making any unilateral commitment to any foreign government or international organization (either orally or in writing), tendering to a prospective party thereto any draft of a proposed international agreement, or initialing or signing an international agreement before obtaining legal concurrence and the required approval to proceed

International Agreements

- The first main source of international law is international agreements, which are a broad category of mostly written, but sometimes oral, agreements entered into by authorized representatives of the parties to the agreement, with each party being either a state or a recognized international organization

- In very limited and specific circumstances, DAF commanders may have authority to negotiate and conclude international agreements in accordance with DoS, DoD, and DAF policy and guidance

- International law does not distinguish between treaties and binding international agreements; any treaty or agreement is binding only on the parties who have agreed to be bound by it

  -- Bilateral agreements involve two parties, while multilateral agreements involve more than two parties

  -- Binding international agreements may be called many names, to include treaty, convention, covenant, pact, protocol, Status of Forces Agreement (SOFA), executive agreement, Memorandum of Understanding (MOU), Memorandum of Agreement (MOA), etc. Whatever their designations, all binding agreements have the same status under international law.

Customary International Law

- The other main source of international law is customary international law, which results from a general and consistent practice of states that is followed by them from a sense of legal obligation (also known as *opinio juris*); the U.S. Supreme Court has long held that customary international law is part of U.S. law, so long as it does not conflict with treaty or controlling executive or legislative act or judicial decision

- Customary international law may take centuries to evolve, or it may be formed very quickly. Examples include:

  -- <u>Outer Space Overflight</u>: Prior to the 1957 Sputnik flight, states had to seek consent before overflying the territory of other states. No state objected to Sputnik's historic space overflight, which evolved into the customary law that a state's space vehicles may pass over the territory of other states while in outer space without seeking prior consent. This custom was ultimately incorporated into the 1967 Outer Space Treaty.

  -- <u>Law of Aerial Warfare</u>: Practices between warring states on land over years evolved into customary principles of the Law of War (e.g., necessity, distinction, and proportionality). States applied the principles to aerial warfare, creating customary rules relating to interception, diversion, search, and capture of enemy and neutral aircraft during armed conflict.

  -- <u>Law of the Sea</u>: Although the United States is not a party to the United Nations Convention on the Law of the Sea, it considers the Convention's provisions on freedom of navigation and overflight as reflecting customary international law and binding upon all nations

DoDI 5530.03, International Agreements

- Under DoDI 5530.03, an international agreement is any agreement concluded with one or more foreign governments, including their agencies, instrumentalities, or political subdivisions, or with an international organization, that:

  -- Is signed or agreed to by personnel of any DoD Component, or by representatives of the DoS, or from other department or agency of the U.S. Government

  -- Signifies the intention of the parties to be bound in international law. An oral agreement that meets the criteria of this definition is an international agreement; DoD representatives who enter into an oral agreement will cause such agreement to be reduced to writing, subject to the requirements of DoDI 5530.03.

  -- A DoD Component's General Counsel or Staff Judge Advocate must be consulted when making a determination as to whether an international agreement or arrangement is binding under international law

- The following may constitute an international agreement: a memorandum of understanding, memorandum of agreement, memorandum of arrangement, exchange of notes, exchange of letters, technical arrangement, protocol, *note verbale, aide-mémoire,* agreed minute, arrangement, statement of intent, letter of intent, statement of understanding, or any other name connoting a similar legal consequence. This includes any implementing agreement or arrangement, annex, project agreement or arrangement, or other subsidiary arrangement to a master agreement or arrangement.

International Agreements in the Department of the Air Force

- AFI 51-403 regulates this area for all DAF personnel, consistent with the obligations set forth in DoDI 5530.03 and delegations established in AFPD 51-4, *Operations and International Law*

- DAF personnel seeking to negotiate and conclude international agreements must first secure approval from the appropriate authority, typically either the MAJCOM/FLDCOM commander or SecAF, or higher authority

  -- Authorized personnel may only negotiate and conclude international agreements on predominantly DAF matters within their authority and responsibility

  -- Until such delegation has occurred in writing, commanders should take great care that their words or conduct do not lead their foreign counterparts to believe that they are authorized to engage in negotiations or to enter into a binding agreement

Reporting

- All international agreements must be promptly reported to the DoS and/or other relevant organizations (e.g., Office of the Secretary of Defense's General Counsel (OSD/GC), Office of the Under Secretary of Defense for Policy (OSD(P)), the Secretary of the Air Force's GC (SAF/GCI), Department of the Air Force – Operations and International Law Directorate (AF/JAO), Defense Intelligence Agency (DIA), or National Security Agency (NSA) for intelligence related agreements), as described in AFI 51-403

References

· Case-Zablocki Act of 1972, 1 U.S.C. § 112b
· Coordination, Reporting and Publication of International Agreements, 22 C.F.R. Part 181
· *The Paquete Habana*, 175 U.S. 677 (1900)
· DoDI 5530.03, *International Agreements* (4 December 2019)
· AFI 51-403, *International Agreements* (8 February 2019)
· AFPD 51-4, *Operations and International Law* (24 July 2018)
· The Law of Air, Space and Cyber Operations, 4th Ed. (2020)

FOREIGN CRIMINAL JURISDICTION

United States service members, Department of Defense (DoD) civilian employees and, in certain circumstances, DoD contractors (collectively "DoD personnel") serving in or deployed to locations outside the United States may be subject to criminal proceedings by both the Host Nation (HN) and the United States for offenses allegedly committed in the HN.

Key Takeaways

» It is U.S. policy to maximize the exercise of U.S. jurisdiction over DoD personnel through applicable Status of Forces Agreements (SOFAs) or other jurisdictional arrangements

» It is U.S. policy to protect, to the maximum extent possible, the rights of DoD personnel who may be subject to criminal trial by foreign courts and imprisonment in foreign prisons

» It is U.S. policy to secure, where possible, the release of DoD personnel to the custody of U.S. authorities pending completion of all foreign judicial proceedings

» This policy also applies to dependents of DoD personnel when those dependents are in a foreign country accompanying DoD personnel

---

Jurisdiction

- Unless an exception has been granted, the HN has criminal jurisdiction under most SOFAs and international law over any person, including another nation's service members, physically within its borders based on territorial sovereignty

    -- Simultaneously, the Uniform Code of Military Justice's (UCMJ) extraterritorial application grants the United States jurisdiction over its service members for UCMJ offenses

- Despite many SOFAs providing a scheme of shared criminal jurisdiction between a receiving and sending state, normally only one nation will exercise criminal jurisdiction against the service member; that nation is referred to as having primary criminal jurisdiction

    -- Primary jurisdiction over an offense is often governed by the terms of any applicable SOFA or comparable agreement with the HN. In certain peace operations, especially those run by the United Nations, a Status of Mission Agreement (SOMA) may be used instead of a SOFA. In this discussion, SOFA will refer to both SOFAs and SOMAs.

DoD Civilian Employees and Dependent Family Members Accompanying the Force

- DoD civilian employees and dependent family members accompanying U.S. Armed Forces abroad are normally considered subject to the terms of the applicable SOFA

- The Military Extraterritorial Jurisdiction Act (MEJA) extends U.S. criminal jurisdiction to cover offenses committed by dependents and other civilians accompanying U.S. Armed Forces if the criminal act, if committed within the special maritime and territorial jurisdiction of the United States, is punishable by at least one year of confinement

    -- This act allows the Department of Justice, not the DoD or Department of the Air Force (DAF), to prosecute the offending civilian. MEJA can also extend criminal jurisdiction over military personnel and contractors' employees, so long as the individual is not a national of or ordinarily resident in the HN.

- Article 2(a)(10), UCMJ, provides criminal jurisdiction over civilians serving with or accompanying U.S. Armed Forces in the field during either declared war or a contingency operation

Violations of Host Nation (HN) Law

- Commanders will make consistent efforts with appropriate officials of the HN to maximize U.S. criminal jurisdiction to the extent practicable and consistent with applicable agreements. If jurisdiction is not waived by the HN, commanders generally have an obligation to place U.S. service members on "international hold" pending resolution of criminal cases within the HN.

- For covered civilians, the Designated Commanding Officer as designated by the appropriate geographic combatant commander, may request the HN waive jurisdiction if he/she determines suitable action can be taken under existing U.S. laws or administrative regulations

- U.S. service members generally are made available to HN officials by commanders in consultation with the local Staff Judge Advocate (SJA). Specific timing of release varies by country. Consultation and cooperation with HN law enforcement agencies is always desirable, but in some HNs, local law enforcement have the right to enter the installation to arrest the member regardless of the desire for consultation and cooperation.

Legal Counsel, Trial Observers, Crime Victims

- When facing HN criminal charges, personnel may request the DAF employ legal counsel and pay counsel fees, court costs, bail, and other expenses incident to the representation. They may also request a Military Legal Advisor (appointed by the SJA) to advise the member on U.S. related matters arising out of the criminal charges.

- A U.S. trial observer will monitor HN criminal proceedings to report whether the trial was fair. If convicted by a HN court, personnel will face HN sentencing, including the possibility of confinement in the HN.

- For personnel in the custody of foreign authorities, DoD seeks to ensure fair treatment at all times. DoD further seeks to assure that when confined (pretrial, during trial, and post-trial) in foreign penal institutions, these personnel are treated appropriately and are entitled to all the rights, privileges, and protections of personnel confined in U.S. military facilities.

- Personnel who are victims of a crime being adjudicated by the HN criminal justice system may request payment of related expenses in accordance with applicable laws

Status of Forces Agreements (SOFAs)

- Many SOFAs contain criteria for determining which country exercises jurisdiction over U.S. personnel for criminal offenses. Within the NATO, Japan and Korea SOFAs, the following provisions exist:

  -- Exclusive jurisdiction belongs to: **U.S.** for crimes under U.S. military or other applicable law that are not violations of HN law (e.g., absent without leave (AWOL), disrespect, and disobeying orders); **HN** for acts that are crimes under the HN's laws but not under U.S. law (e.g., religious crimes, political crimes, and certain negligent acts that, under U.S. law, do not rise to the level of criminal conduct)

  -- Concurrent (shared) jurisdiction occurs when conduct is criminal under both U.S. and HN law. The HN has the primary right to try all concurrent offenses, except when the crime affects only U.S. parties or U.S. property (also known as *inter se*), or where offenses arise out of any act or omission done in the performance of an official duty.

Requests and Waivers of Jurisdiction

- DoD policy is to maximize U.S. criminal jurisdiction, subject to relevant international agreements

  -- With concurrent jurisdiction, when the HN has the primary right to try a case, the United States will normally request a waiver of jurisdiction from the HN

  -- The procedures for and the likely success of a request for waiver vary depending on the HN and, frequently, the individual circumstances and seriousness of the offense, with a waiver generally less likely for more serious offenses

  -- When a waiver is granted, the U.S., pursuant to treaty or other appropriate legal authority, may be required to report to the HN the final result of the action, if any, taken against the U.S. service members, DoD civilian employees, and, in certain circumstances, DoD contractors

- In other HNs not covered by the major SOFAs, there may be other relevant bilateral agreements or diplomatic notes. In the absence of an agreement to the contrary, criminal jurisdiction rests exclusively with the HN. Exercise of jurisdiction over U.S. service members in a HN without HN permission may be considered a breach of its territorial sovereignty.

References

· Article 2(a)(10), Uniform Code of Military Justice, 10 U.S.C. § 802

· *Counsel before foreign judicial tribunals and administrative agencies; court costs and bail,* 10 U.S.C. § 1037

· Military Extraterritorial Jurisdiction, 18 U.S.C. Chapter 212

· Foreign Criminal and Civilian Jurisdiction, 32 C.F.R. Part 151

· DoDI 5525.01, *Foreign Criminal and Civil Jurisdiction* (31 May 2019)

· DoDI 5525.09, *Compliance with Court Orders by Service Members and DoD Civilian Employees, and their Family Members Outside the United States* (23 April 2019)

· DoDI 5525.11, *Criminal Jurisdiction Over Civilians Employed by Or Accompanying the Armed Forces Outside the United States, Certain Service Members, and Former Service Members* (3 March 2005)

· DAFI 51-205, *Delivery of Personnel to U.S. Civilian Authorities for Trial and Criminal Jurisdiction over Civilians and Dependents Not in the United States* (19 January 2023)

· AFI 51-402, *International Law* (6 August 2018)

· AFJI 51-706 (AR 27-50), *Status of Force Policies, Procedures & Information* (15 December 1989)

DEPLOYED FISCAL LAW

Commanders must be aware of the rules regarding the spending of appropriated funds in their area of operations. In a deployed environment, the basic rules of fiscal law still apply. Since statutory authority, threshold amounts, and funding levels can fluctuate from year to year and may be constrained by theater-specific or local guidance, commanders should consult with financial management and legal personnel on fiscal law issues.

Key Takeaways

- » Commanders must have the proper mission authority, funding authority, and type of funds before engaging in security cooperation activities or providing humanitarian assistance
- » Before executing any training of foreign forces, ensure they have not had any human rights violations as necessitated by 10 U.S.C. § 362
- » Coordinate with the Department of State (DoS) and the United States Agency for International Development (USAID) as required before providing any form of foreign humanitarian assistance

Overseas Contingency Operations Funds Discontinued

- While many commanders who deployed over the last decade have likely used a form of Overseas Contingency Operations (OCO) funds before, OCO is no longer a category of funding as of Fiscal Year (FY) 2022

- Instead of OCO funds, the costs of these operations are now incorporated into the base budget of the Department of Defense (DoD) and Department of the Air Force (i.e., Operation and Maintenance (O&M), Procurement, etc.)

Training and Equipping of Foreign Forces

- Generally, the duty to equip, train, or provide assistance to foreign countries rests with the Department of State (DoS). There are two exceptions to the general rule:

-- Training or instruction for foreign forces for the primary purpose of promoting interoperability, safety, and familiarization training with U.S. forces, with the overall benefit being to U.S. military forces. This is sometimes called "little 't' training."

-- Specific authorization from Congress for DoD to obligate defense funding to engage in security cooperation

--- There are a myriad of permanent (10 U.S.C. §§ 127e, 321, 322, 331, 332, and 333) and temporary (Counter-Islamic State of Iraq and Syria (ISIS) Train and Equip Fund (CTEF), Training for Eastern European National Military Forces, and Ukraine Security Assistance Initiative) funding authorities, and this is by no means an exhaustive list

---- *Example 1:* 10 U.S.C. § 333 allows the Secretary of Defense (SecDef), with Secretary of State (SecState) concurrence, to use Defense-wide O&M to provide equipment and training to foreign national security forces to build the capacity of such forces

---- *Example 2:* Section 1236 of the FY2015 National Defense Authorization Act (NDAA), as amended by Section 1234 of the FY2023 NDAA, authorizes SecDef, with SecState concurrence, to use CTEF to provide training and equipment to the Iraqi Government or Kurdish and tribal security forces to counter ISIS

Foreign Humanitarian Assistance and Disaster Relief

- The DoS and USAID are the primary agencies responsible for providing humanitarian assistance and disaster relief abroad. The DoD must have specific statutory authority in order to provide this type of support.

  -- Overseas Humanitarian, Disaster, and Civic Aid (OHDACA) Funds: A series of interrelated statutes, which include 10 U.S.C. § 402 (Relief Supplies Transportation), § 404 (Foreign Disaster Assistance), § 407 (Humanitarian Demining), § 2557 (Excess Non-Lethal Supplies), and § 2561 (Humanitarian Assistance), authorize the use of OHDACA funds. OHDACA supports SecDef and Combatant Commander (CCDR) national and theater strategies to build partner nation capacity and expand and strengthen alliances and partnerships while advancing DoD access, influence, and visibility.

  -- Humanitarian and Civic Assistance: 10 U.S.C. § 401 (Humanitarian and Civic Assistance (HCA) in Conjunction with Military Operations) is a distinct funding authority from 10 U.S.C. § 2561 (Humanitarian Assistance). Rather than using OHDACA funds, HCA uses O&M funds pursuant to Section 8011 of the Consolidated Appropriations Act, 2023. Whereas humanitarian assistance under 10 U.S.C. § 2561 is provided in response to a foreign disaster, HCA allows a CCDR to provide HCA (such as medical care, rudimentary repair and construction of public facilities, etc.) to underserved areas of a county as long as these activities promote the security interests of both the U.S. and the country in which the activities are to be carried out and the specific operational readiness skills of the members of the armed forces who participate in the activities.

General Purpose Funds, Ex Gratia Payments, and Acquisition and Cross Servicing Agreements (ACSA)

- Emergency and Extraordinary Expenses (10 U.S.C. 127): This is funding provided to the Secretaries of the Military Departments for unanticipated emergencies or extraordinary expenses, including unanticipated, short-notice construction. These funds are controlled by the Office of the Administrative Assistant to the Secretary of the Air Force (SAF/AA).

- Combatant Commander Initiative Funds (CCIF) (10 U.S.C. 166a): Enables the Chairman of the Joint Chiefs of Staff (CJCS) to act quickly to support the combatant commanders (CCDR) with: (1) force training, (2) contingencies, (3) selected operations, (4) command and control, (5) joint exercises, (6) humanitarian and civic assistance, (7) military education and training to military and related civilian personnel of foreign countries, (8) personnel expenses of defense personnel for bilateral or regional cooperation programs, (9) force protection, and (10) joint warfighting capabilities. Funds are controlled by the CCDR.

- *Ex Gratia Payments*: Section 1213 of the FY2020 NDAA, as amended by the FY2021 and FY2023 NDAAs, created a means by which authorized commanders may provide nominal monetary payments to friendly civilians as a means of expressing condolence or sympathy or as a goodwill gesture in the event of property damage, personal injury, or death that is incident to the use of force by the U.S. Armed Forces, a coalition that includes the U.S., or a military organization supporting the U.S. or such coalition. Such payments are made from Defense-wide O&M, and the DoD has placed further restrictions on the use of ex gratia payments, as detailed in Department of Defense Instruction 3000.17, *Civilian Harm Mitigation and Response*, dated 21 December 2023.

- ACSA: ACSAs are not funding, but rather bilateral agreements that can be used for reimbursable exchange of Logistic Support, Supplies, and Services (LSSS), such as food, billeting, clothing, petroleum, ammunition, or medical services, with foreign military forces. Before using a pre-existing ACSA with a foreign country, the parties must agree on the reimbursement method to be use and an ACSA warranted officer must approve the transfer. There are three methods of reimbursement: (1) payment in kind, (2) replacement in kind, and (3) equal value exchange. However, this authority does not allow for the transfer of significant military equipment, such as ground combat vehicles or combat aircraft, that are listed on the U.S. Munitions List found at 22 C.F.R. 121.1.

Military Construction Funding Sources

- In addition to the two primary construction authorities, Specified Military Construction (MILCON via 10 U.S.C. § 2802) and Unspecified Minor Military Construction (UMMC via 10 U.S.C. § 2805), there are other important authorities impacting construction projects in the deployed environment

  -- Emergency Construction (10 U.S.C. § 2803): These are unobligated MILCON funds for projects not otherwise authorized. These are for projects that are vital to national security or to the protection of health, safety, or the environment, and are so urgent that they cannot wait until the next MILCON authorization act.

  -- Contingency Construction (10 U.S.C. § 2804): SecDef may authorize MILCON when waiting for the next MILCON authorization act would be "inconsistent with national security or national interest." The expenditure must be within the amount appropriated for such purpose and is normally used on extraordinary projects that develop unexpectedly. In addition, these funds may not be used for projects denied authorization in previous Military Construction Appropriations Acts.

References

· Emergency and Extraordinary Expenses, 10 U.S.C. § 127

· Support of Special Operations to Combat Terrorism, 10 U.S.C. § 127e

· Combatant Commander Initiative Funds, 10 U.S.C. § 166a

· Training with Friendly Foreign Countries, 10 U.S.C. § 321

· Special Operations Forces: Training with Friendly Foreign Forces, 10 U.S.C. § 322

· Friendly Foreign Countries: Provide Support for Conduct of Operations, 10 U.S.C. § 331

· Friendly Foreign Countries: Defense Institution Capacity Building, 10 U.S.C. § 332

· Foreign Security Forces: Authority to Build Capacity, 10 U.S.C. § 333

· Humanitarian and Civic Assistance, 10 U.S.C. § 401

· Transportation of Humanitarian Relief Supplies to Foreign Countries, 10 U.S.C. § 402
  Foreign Disaster Assistance, 10 U.S.C. § 404

· Humanitarian Demining Assistance, 10 U.S.C. § 407

· Cross-Servicing Agreements, 10 U.S.C. § 2342

· Definition of Logistic Support, Supplies, and Services, 10 U.S.C. § 2350

· Excess Non-Lethal Supplies, 10 U.S.C. § 2557

· Humanitarian Assistance, 10 U.S.C. § 2561

· Military Construction Projects, 10 U.S.C. § 2802

· Emergency Construction, 10 U.S.C. § 2803

· Contingency Construction, 10 U.S.C. § 2804

· Unspecified Minor Military Construction, 10 U.S.C. § 2805

· National Defense Authorization Acts (NDAA) for Fiscal Years (FY) 2015–2023,
  (https://whs-mil.libguides.com/dodappropriationslaws)

· DoDD 2010.09, *Acquisition and Cross-Servicing Agreements* (28 April 2003), incorporating
  through Change 2, 31 August 2018

· DoDI 3000.17, *Civilian Harm Mitigation and Response* (21 December 2023)

· DoD Justification Books, (https://comptroller.defense.gov/Budget-Materials/)

· CJCS Instruction 2120.01D, *Acquisition and Cross-Servicing Agreements* (21 May 2015)

· AFI 65-603, *Emergency and Extraordinary Expense Authority* (29 April 2020)

· *The Honorable Bill Alexander*, B-213137, 63 Comp. Gen. 422 (1984)

· ACSA J4 Site, (https://intellipedia.intelink.gov/wiki/
  Acquisition_and_Cross-Servicing_Agreements_(ACSA))

· Security Cooperation Programs Handbook, (https://www.dscu.edu/resources#publications)

· Security Assistance Management Manual, (https://samm.dsca.mil/listing/chapters)

INTELLIGENCE OVERSIGHT

U.S. intelligence activities are highly regulated in an effort to balance the need for intelligence with privacy and civil liberty concerns. In particular, there are numerous legal considerations associated with intelligence collection on U.S. persons. Commanders and their intelligence staffs must be fully cognizant of their intelligence oversight (IO) responsibilities.

Key Takeaways

» IO programs require initial and annual training tailored for units who perform intelligence or intelligence-related activities to understand applicable laws, Department of Defense (DoD), Department of the Air Force (DAF), Air Force, and/or Space Force policy and regulations

» U.S. person information (USPI) must be properly collected, retained, and disseminated (DoDM 5240.01, *Procedures Governing the Conduct of DoD Intelligence Activities*, Procedures 2–4)

» Air Force and Space Force intelligence professionals must know their responsibilities for reporting Questionable Intelligence Activities (QIAs) and Significant or Highly Sensitive Matters (S/HSMs)

» Staff Judge Advocates and legal advisors, in coordination with MAJCOM and FIELDCOM IGs, commanders, and intelligence oversight program managers, are responsible for providing legal advice in QIAs and S/HSMs pursuant to AFI 14-404, *Intelligence Oversight*, para. 2.8.1

» Day-to-day command and control is essential and IO should be incorporated into planning and execution

---

- At various points in our nation's history, Congress has expressed concerns that certain intelligence activities infringed upon the constitutional rights and privacy interests of U.S. Persons. As a result, an oversight regime consisting of statutes, executive orders (EOs), and agency regulations was established to ensure the proper use of intelligence capabilities and the proper conduct of intelligence activities. Subject to the authority, direction, and control of the Secretary of Defense (SecDef), the Secretary of the Air Force (SecAF) is also responsible to SecDef for the effective supervision and control of the intelligence activities of the DAF.

- The U.S. Air Force Intelligence Community Element and the U.S. Space Force Intelligence Community Element conduct these activities and possess an array of intelligence and counterintelligence capabilities designed to provide commanders and national leaders with information on foreign nationals, hostile or potentially hostile forces or elements, and areas of actual or potential operations. Intelligence collection is a specialized mission with tactics, techniques, and procedures that require strict control and oversight.

Intelligence Oversight Governance

- IO is defined as the process of independently ensuring all DoD intelligence, counterintelligence, and intelligence-related activities are conducted in accordance with applicable U.S. law, EOs, Presidential directives, and DoD issuances designed to balance the requirement for acquisition of essential information by the intelligence community (IC), and the protection of constitutional and statutory rights of U.S. Persons. IO also includes the identification, investigation, and reporting of QIAs and S/HSMs involving intelligence activities.

  -- Although the term U.S. Persons includes U.S. citizens, it is broader. It also includes permanent resident aliens, unincorporated associations substantially composed of U.S. citizens or permanent resident aliens, and corporations incorporated in the United States and not directed and controlled by a foreign government (see DoDD 5240.01, DoD *Intelligence Activities*). A person or organization within the United States is presumed to be a U.S. Person, unless specific information to the contrary is obtained. A person outside the United States or whose location is unknown is presumed to not be a U.S. Person, unless specific information to the contrary is obtained.

  -- Per DoDD 5148.13, *Intelligence Oversight*, IO rules apply to the Office of the Secretary of Defense, the Military Departments, the Office of the Chairman of the Joint Chiefs of Staff and the Joint Staff, the Combatant Commands, the Office of the Inspector General of the Department of Defense, the Defense Agencies, the DoD Field Activities, and all other organizational entities within DoD (referred to collectively in DoDD 5148.13 as the "DoD Components"). The IO rules also apply to anyone acting on behalf of a DoD Component when conducting intelligence or intelligence-related activities. A list of DoD and national intelligence organizations is included in Joint Publication 2-0, *Joint Intelligence*. A definition of "Defense Intelligence Components" is included in DoDD 5143.01, *Under Secretary of Defense for Intelligence and Security (USD(I&S))*. (**Note:** Publications have not all been updated with the 18th member of the IC, Space Force Intelligence or new Air Force intelligence organizations (e.g., DoDM 5240.01 does not include SF/S2).

  -- The duties and obligations placed on Defense Intelligence Components arise from the U.S. Constitution; Executive Order 12333 (as amended), *United States Intelligence Activities*; DoDD 5240.01, DoD *Intelligence Activities*; DoDD 5148.13, *Intelligence Oversight*; DoDM 5240.01, *Procedures Governing the Conduct of DoD Intelligence Activities*; and parts of DoD 5240.01-R, Change 2, *Procedures Governing the Activities of DoD Intelligence Components that Affect United States Persons*, and its classified annex. In addition, the DAF has its own governing instruction, AFI 14-404. Careful reading of the rules and definitions is critical when operating and advising within this environment.

- Roles and Responsibilities:

-- IO is a shared responsibility between all DAF members performing intelligence activities, the commander, the Staff Judge Advocate (SJA), and the Inspector General (IG). Airmen and Guardians are the first line of defense and must know the IO standards, comply with them, and report any suspected QIAs or S/HSMs. Commanders should support an active IO program, designate appropriate oversight officials, provide appropriate training, provide reprisal protection for persons reporting QIAs or S/HSMs, and implement corrective action to address substantiated allegations. Guidance and further information are available at the DoD Senior Intelligence Oversight Office (SIOO) website: https://dodsioo.defense.gov/.

-- Servicing SJAs provide advice and counsel on proposed and on-going intelligence activities, interpretations of DoDM 5240.01, and assistance to Intelligence Monitors and IGs as each performs their missions. They also support unit training. Legal support should align to the chain of command of the intelligence unit rather than the location of the unit (i.e., regardless of location, intelligence units get IO support through their command organization). DAF personnel assigned to non-DAF organizations who report QIA or S/HSM to their duty organization are encouraged to also report to their relevant Intelligence Oversight Official or Element commander.

-- IGs conduct inspections to verify that: (1) intelligence personnel understand rules and responsibilities; (2) only Air Force or Space Force Intelligence Elements with assigned intelligence missions are conducting intelligence functions; (3) intelligence activities comply with laws and policies; and (4) reporting procedures are being followed. The IG is also responsible for reviewing every QIA and S/HSM and reporting up to the DoD Senior Intelligence Oversight Office.

- There are only two lawfully assigned intelligence mission sets for the DoD:

-- Foreign Intelligence:

--- Title 50, U.S.C., § 3003(2), defines "foreign intelligence" as "information relating to the capabilities, intentions, or activities of foreign governments or elements thereof, foreign organizations, or foreign persons, or international terrorist activities"

-- Counterintelligence:

--- Title 50, U.S.C. § 3003(3), defines "counterintelligence" as "information gathered, and activities conducted, to protect against espionage, other intelligence activities, sabotage, or assassinations conducted by or on behalf of foreign governments or elements thereof, foreign organizations, or foreign persons, or international terrorist activities"

-- Authority Considerations:

--- DoDD 5240.01 implements EO 12333 and establishes broad responsibilities for officials and offices across the DoD and establishes, as DoD policy, that all DoD intelligence and counterintelligence activities will be carried out pursuant to the authorities and restrictions of the U.S. Constitution, applicable law, EO 12333, and other relevant DoD policies

--- DoDM 5240.01 and the remaining parts of DoD 5240.01-R provide the authority by which DoD intelligence components may collect, retain, and disseminate USPI and also contain the structure for reporting possible violations. DoDM 5240.01 serves as the regulatory foundation for Service, Combatant Command, and along with DoDD 5148.13 outlines intelligence agency IO programs.

Identifying, Investigating, and Reporting QIAs or S/HSMs

- A questionable intelligence activity (QIA) is any intelligence or intelligence-related activity when there is reason to believe such activity may be unlawful or contrary to an EO, Presidential Directive, Intelligence Community Directive, or applicable DoD and DAF policy governing that activity (DoDD 5148.13; AFI 14-404)

-- DAF units within Defense Intelligence Components must submit a quarterly report of all QIAs through the Department of the Air Force Inspector General (SAF/IG) to DoD SIOO, which is presented to the Intelligence Oversight Board

- A Significant or Highly Sensitive Matter (S/HSM) must be reported immediately and is an intelligence or intelligence-related activity (regardless of whether the intelligence or intelligence-related activity is unlawful or contrary to an EO, Presidential Directive, Intelligence Community Directive, or DoD policy), or serious criminal activity by intelligence personnel, that could impugn the reputation or integrity of the Intelligence Community, or otherwise call into question the propriety of intelligence activities. Such matters might involve actual or potential:

-- Congressional inquiries or investigations

-- Adverse media coverage

-- Impact on foreign relations or foreign partners

-- Systemic compromise, loss, or unauthorized disclosure of protected information

- Personnel shall report suspected QIAs or S/HSMs to their chain of command immediately

- If not practicable, personnel may report to their unit's servicing legal office, IG, Air Force Operations and International Law (AF/JAO), Secretary of the Air Force General Counsel (SAF/GCI), Secretary of the Air Force Inspector General (SAF/IG), DoD Office of General Counsel, or DoD Senior Intelligence Oversight Official. Personnel are highly encouraged to additionally report suspected QIAs to their chain of command and Intelligence Oversight Monitors. Generally, IGs investigate QIAs and legal offices advise those conducting the investigation. Specific procedures are found in Section 4 of DoDD 5148.13. Reprisal is prohibited for reporting or even intending to report.

IO Analytical Framework

- Applicability: IO procedures govern the conduct of Defense Intelligence Components and non-intelligence components or elements, or anyone acting on behalf of those components or elements, when conducting intelligence activities under DoD authorities

References

· Combatant Commands: Assigned Forces; Chain of Command, 10 U.S.C. § 162

· Commanders of Combatant Commands: Assignments; Powers and Duties, 10 U.S.C. § 164

· Secretary of the Air Force, 10 U.S.C. § 9013

· National Security Act of 1947, 50 U.S.C. §§ 3001 *et seq.*

· Responsibilities of Secretary of Defense Pertaining to National Intelligence Program, 50 U.S.C. § 3038

· Executive Order 12333, United States Intelligence Activities (4 December 1981), as amended by EO 13284 (2003), 13355 (2004) and 13470 (2008)

· DoDD 3115.18, *DoD Access to and Use of Publicly Available Information (PAI)* (11 May 2019), incorporating Change 1, 20 August 2020

· DoDD 5143.01, *Under Secretary of Defense for Intelligence and Security (USD(I&S))* (24 October 2014), incorporating through Change 2, 6 April 2020

· DoDD 5148.11, *Assistant to the Secretary of Defense for Intelligence Oversight (ATSD(IO))* (24 April 2013), incorporating Change 1, 2 March 2023

· DoDD 5148.13, *Intelligence Oversight* (26 April 2017)

· DoDD 5200.27, *Acquisition of Information Concerning Persons and Organizations Not Affiliated with the Department of Defense* (7 January 1980)

· DoDD 5240.01, *DoD Intelligence Activities* (27 August 2007), incorporating through Change 3, 9 November 2020

· DoD 5240.1-R, *Procedures Governing the Activities of DoD Intelligence Components That Affect United States Persons* (December 1982), incorporating through Change 2, 26 April 2017

· DoDM 5240.01, *Procedures Governing the Conduct of DoD Intelligence Activities* (8 August 2016)

· Joint Publication 2-0, *Joint Intelligence* (26 May 2022)

· AFI 14-404, *Intelligence Oversight* (3 September 2019)

· AFI 14-1020, *Intelligence Mission Qualification and Readiness* (8 November 2017)

· AFI 71-101, Volume 4, *Counterintelligence* (2 July 2019)

· Chief of the National Guard Bureau Instruction (CNGBI) 2000.01D, *National Guard Intelligence Activities* (18 January 2022)

· CNGBI 0700.01A, *Inspector General Intelligence Oversight* (21 December 2018)

· Office of the Director of National Intelligence, *Office of General Counsel, Intelligence Community Legal Reference Book*; https://www.dni.gov/index.php/who-we-are/leadership/general-counsel/ic-legal-reference-book

NATIONAL DEFENSE AREA

Commanders are responsible for the protection of Department of Defense (DoD) resources under their control. When a resource is off a DoD installation, commanders should seek landowner consent and work with local authorities to provide protection. If this is not possible, a commander may establish a National Defense Area (NDA) in an emergency situation to provide military protection of *covered property*.

Key Takeaways

- » Declaring an NDA should only be done as a last resort
- » NDAs are not authorized outside the United States
- » NDAs can only be declared in *emergency situations* and for *covered property*
- » Consult the servicing Staff Judge Advocate before declaring an NDA

Authority – DoD Policy to Protect People and Property

- Commanders at all levels have the responsibility and authority to enforce appropriate security measures to ensure the protection of DoD property and personnel assigned, attached, or subject to their control

- The incident commander (IC) or senior on-scene commander (OSC) may establish an NDA involving any incident where the DoD does not have exclusive jurisdiction of the area containing a covered property, and the property is at an unacceptable risk in an *emergency situation* (e.g., nuclear weapon and related classified components or materiel)

- The DoD IC will typically be the installation commander responsible for the DoD property

Enforcement

- Civilian law enforcement excludes non-DoD personnel from an NDA

- Military personnel may remove NDA trespassers from the NDA or detain them until they can be transferred to civil authorities

- Unless non-DoD personnel pose an immediate threat to life or possess military property, the pursuit of a fleeing civilian by military authorities is limited to the immediate NDA area

NDA – Definition

- An NDA is an area established on non-federal lands for the purpose of safeguarding classified information or protecting covered DoD property

  -- NDAs will be marked with a physical barrier and posted warning signs

-- The landowner's consent and cooperation will be obtained whenever possible, however, military necessity will dictate the final decision

- NDAs cannot be established outside the United States, and such protective areas will be dictated by host-nation agreements

- NDAs off-DoD land will be coordinated with other governmental agencies

Definition – Covered Property and Emergency Situation

- Covered Property: "Aircraft, airports, airport facilities, vessels, harbors, ports, piers, water-front facilities, bases, forts, posts, laboratories, stations, vehicles, equipment, explosives, or other property or places." 50 U.S.C. § 797(a)(4)(c).

- Emergency Situations: Includes crashes of aircraft with sensitive equipment or capabilities, or where aircraft are sent to facilities and unforeseen, inadequate, or uncontrollable civilian security concerns exist. The assets are limited to Protection Level 1, 2, or 3 resources.

Establishing an NDA

- The OSC should immediately secure the site and seek approval from the IC responsible for the covered property before declaring an NDA and posting signage

-- The IC does not need to be physically present to establish an NDA. For example, a subordinate commander to whom responsibility for protecting the property has been entrusted may establish the NDA. A written order authorizing creation of the NDA should follow.

Consent as the Means of First Resort

- Landowner consent and military accommodation of the landowner's concerns are important to reduce unnecessary claims, enhance public perception, and minimize media scrutiny

- Even absent landowner consent, military necessity and capacity to control the site ultimately drive the location, size, and shape of an NDA

- Early consultation with the servicing Staff Judge Advocate (SJA) is important

Marking and Public Notice

- The OSC or senior DoD official is responsible for adequately marking the NDA as required by DAFI 31-101, *Integrated Defense (ID)*

- Use a temporary barrier, such as tape or rope, to mark the NDA. Post Air Force Visual Aid (AFVA) 31-102 at all entry control points.

- The SJA should evaluate whether it is necessary to request that higher headquarters publish notice in the local newspaper and/or Federal Register

Airspace Considerations

- Airspace restrictions may be necessary, including restrictions on small unmanned aircraft systems (sUAS)

- Commanders may request the Federal Aviation Administration (FAA) impose a Temporary Flight Restriction (TFR)

Media and Public Relations

- Public Affairs should be briefed immediately following the establishment of an NDA; ICs and OSCs should be sensitive to interests of the media

- Limit photography as necessary to protect classified information

- Military authorities may use reasonable force to prevent all photography by anyone **WITHIN** the NDA and seize film or video equipment

- If photography is outside the NDA, civilian authorities should handle the matter

- Media representatives should be briefed on appropriate releasable information during an accident or incident, and the procedures to be followed, such as escort requirements

References

· U.S. Const. Art. VI, cl. 2 (Supremacy) and Amend. V, cl. 4 (Takings)

· Use of Aircraft for Photographing Defense Installations, 18 U.S.C. § 796

· Entering Military, Naval, or Coast Guard property, 18 U.S.C. § 1382

· Penalty for Violation of Security Regulations and Orders, 50 U.S.C. § 797

· General Operating and Flight Rules, 14 C.F.R. Part 91

· Security Control of Air Traffic, 14 C.F.R. Part 99

· Executive Order 10104, *Defining Certain Vital Military and Naval Installations and Equipment as Requiring Protection Against the General Dissemination of Information Relative Thereto* (1 February 1950)

· DoDI 5200.08, *Security of DoD Installations and Resources and the DoD Physical Security Review Board (PSRB)* (10 December 2005), incorporating through Change 3, 20 November 2015

· DoDI 6055.17, *DoD Emergency Management (EM) Program* (13 February 2017)

· DoDM 3150.08, *Nuclear Weapon Accident Response Procedures (NARP)* (22 August 2013), incorporating through Change 2, 21 July 2020

· DoDM S-5210.41, Volume 1, *(U) Nuclear Weapon Security Manual: General Nuclear Weapon Security Procedures* (4 May 2022)

· DoDM S-5210.41, Volume 3, *(U) Nuclear Weapon Security Manual: DoD Nuclear Weapon Environment Specific Requirements* (4 May 2022)

· DoDS5210.41-M_AFMAN31-108V1-S, *(U) The Air Force Nuclear Weapon Security Manual* (2 May 2019)

· DoDS 5210.41-M_AFMAN31-108V2-S, *(U) General Nuclear Weapon Security Procedures* (20 May 2019)

· DoDS 5210.41-M_AFMAN31-108V3-S, *(U) Nuclear Weapon Security Manual: Nuclear Weapon Specific Requirements* (20 May 2019)

· DAFI 31-101, *Integrated Defense (ID)* (25 March 2020)

· DAFI 10-2501, *Emergency Management Program* (16 October 2023)

· AFI 31-117, *Arming and Use of Force by Air Force Personnel* (6 August 2020)

· AFI 35-101, *Public Affairs Operations* (20 November 2020)

· AFI 51-306, *Administrative Claims For and Against the Air Force* (14 January 2019), incorporating through Change 3, 5 May 2021

· AFI 51-509, *Appointment to and Assumption of Command* (11 January 2019), including DAFI51-509_DAFGM2023-01, 10 February 2023

· AFVA 31-102, *Restricted Area Sign-National Defense* (13 July 1995) certified current 13 June 2019

· *U.S. v. Aarons*, 310 F.2d 341 (1962)

· FAA Advisory Circular (AC) No. 91-63D, *Temporary Flight Restrictions* (9 December 2015)

POSSE COMITATUS

Punishment for Violations

- Possible criminal sanctions for violating the PCA under 18 U.S.C. § 1385:

  -- Fine and/or two years imprisonment

  -- Suppression of evidence illegally obtained

Posse Comitatus Prohibitions

- <u>Prohibitions</u>: The Army, Navy, Marine Corps, Air Force and the Space Force are precluded by law from enforcing, or assisting local law enforcement officials in enforcing, civilian laws—except as authorized by the Constitution or an Act of Congress

  -- The prohibition applies to the Reserve and to National Guard members while in a Title 10 status (i.e., as Army or Air National Guard of the United States), but not to members of the Title 32 status (i.e., organize, train and equip under the Governor's control) or state active duty status, under the Governor's control at the state's expense

  -- The Act **NEVER** applies to the Coast Guard unless serving in a Title 10 status

- The Act does not apply to off-duty conduct (i.e., good Samaritans), unless induced, required, or ordered by military officials or to Title 10 personnel when they are acting in a private capacity, such as when he/she acts as a private citizen on his/her own volition instead of under the direction or command of a Title 10 or DoD official, even if in uniform and on duty (see *People v. Blend*, 121 Cal App 3d 215, 224 (1981))

- The Act does not apply to civilian employees, unless acting under the direct command and control of a federal military officer

- The Act does not apply to other uniformed services such as the Commissioned Corps of the National Oceanic and Atmospheric Administration or the Commissioned Corps of the U.S. Public Health Service

Exceptions to Posse Comitatus

- <u>Constitutional and Statutory Exceptions</u>: The Act does not preclude support authorized by the Constitution or an Act of Congress

- PCA IS NOT an absolute rule; there are exceptions to this general rule and these exceptions must be "expressly authorized by the Constitution or an act of Congress"

- The Constitutional exception to the PCA is grounded in the President's authority under Articles II and IV of the Constitution

- Section 886 of the Homeland Security Act of 2002 (Title 6 U.S.C. § 455), states the President may exercise this Constitutional exception when he "determines that the use of the Armed Forces is required to fulfill the President's obligations under the Constitution to respond promptly in time of war, insurrection, or other serious emergency" to maintain law and order

- The President can exercise this Constitutional exception in four ways: (1) National Emergency Declaration (*In re Debs*, 158 U.S. 564 (1895)); 50 U.S.C. §§ 1601 *et seq.*; or 6 U.S.C. § 455(a)(5), (2) Inherent Authority to protect Federal property/functions/ personnel, (3) Declaration of Martial Law (32 C.F.R. 501.4), and (4) designating missions/operations as Homeland Defense

- Several statutes also authorize the military to engage in actions that would otherwise violate the PCA

10 U.S.C. § 271

- Allows the military to provide to federal, state, and local civilian law enforcement officials any information collected "during the normal course of military training or operations that may be relevant to a violation of any federal or state law within the jurisdiction of such officials"

- Requires the military to consider the needs of local law enforcement for information when planning and executing military training missions and operations

- Mandates, to the extent consistent with national security, the prompt disclosure of intelligence information relevant to drug interdiction or other civilian law enforcement matters to civilian law enforcement officials

10 U.S.C. § 272

- Allows the Secretary of Defense (SecDef) to make available any equipment, base facility, or research facility of the Department of Defense to local law enforcement for law enforcement purposes although the military may charge for its use (see 10 U.S.C. § 277), it must be in accordance with other applicable laws, and it must not interfere with the military mission

- Loan of "arms, ammunition, tactical-automotive equipment, vessels and aircraft" requires proper coordination

10 U.S.C. § 273

- Allows SecDef to make military personnel available to train federal, state, and local civilian law enforcement officials on the operation and maintenance of equipment, including equipment loaned under 10 U.S.C. § 272, and to provide expert advice related to these matters to such officials

10 U.S.C. § 274

- Allows SecDef to make military personnel available to operate and maintain equipment, including loaned equipment under 10 U.S.C. § 272

49 U.S.C. § 324

- Allows SecDef to detail military personnel to the Department of Transportation under a Memorandum of Agreement, and to perform law enforcement functions for the Secretary of Transportation

Enforcement of Civilian Law on DoD Property

- The military may enforce civilian laws on an installation for a military purpose

- Even on a military installation, the military "detains" civilians before turning them over to civil authorities. Military members do not arrest or apprehend civilians. This is a **CRITICAL** distinction.

- Federal military commanders, heads of DoD components, and/or responsible DoD civilian officials have immediate response authority as described in DoDD 3025.18, *Defense Support of Civil Authorities (DSCA)*. Commanders may exercise this authority in response to a request from a civilian authority for assistance when time does not permit coordination or approval from a higher authority to save lives, prevent human suffering, or mitigate great property damage.

- Actions that would subject civilians to the use of military power that is regulatory, prescriptive, proscriptive, or compulsory are prohibited

References

· Military Support for Civilian Law Enforcement Agencies, 10 U.S.C. §§ 271–277
· Duties: Officers on Active Duty; Performance of Civil Functions Restricted, 10 U.S.C. § 973
· The Posse Comitatus Act, 18 U.S.C. § 1385
· Section 1045 of the NDAA FY2022
· The Homeland Security Act of 2002, 6 U.S.C. § 466
· DoDD 3025.18, *Defense Support of Civil Authorities (DSCA)* (29 December 2010), incorporating through Change 2, 19 March 2018
· DoDI 3025.21, *Defense Support of Civilian Law Enforcement Agencies* (27 February 2013), incorporating Change 1, 8 February 2019
· DAFI 31-118, *Security Forces Standards and Procedures* (18 August 2020), including DAFI31-118_DAFGM2023-0115 November 2023
· AFI 10-801, *Defense Support of Civil Authorities* (29 January 2020)

DEFENSE SUPPORT OF CIVIL AUTHORITIES

Defense Support of Civil Authorities (DSCA) is support provided by military forces to prepare, prevent, protect, respond, and recover from domestic incidents and other qualifying domestic events. The Department of Air Force (DAF) DSCA supports the Federal DSCA mission in response to a submission of Request for Assistance (RFA) to Department of Defense (DoD) from civil authorities or qualifying entities, or as directed by the President or the Secretary of Defense (SecDef).

Key Takeaways

» DSCA is support provided in response to a request from assistance from civil authorities or from other qualifying entities

» Requests for DSCA are generally required in writing and must include a commitment to reimburse the DoD

» Immediate Response Authority (IRA) can be exercised to temporarily engage in activities to save lives, prevent human suffering, or mitigate great property damage within the United States

» Emergency Authority can be exercised to temporarily engage in activities necessary to quell large-scale, unexpected civil disturbances, in extraordinary emergency circumstances

» Title 10 personnel cannot engage in direct civilian law enforcement activities, unless expressly authorized by the President of the United States (POTUS), the Constitution, or act of Congress

DSCA Generally

- DSCA is initiated when civil authorities or qualifying entities request DoD assistance or when assistance is authorized by POTUS or the Secretary of Defense (SecDef)

  -- Unless approval authority is delegated by SecDef, all DSCA requests shall be submitted to the Office of the Executive Secretary of the DoD

  -- DoD federal military forces, civilians, contract personnel, and National Guard (NG) personnel (federalized in 10 U.S.C. status, or as allowed by coordination with State Governors in 32 U.S.C. status) are used to support an approved RFA

  -- AF personnel, equipment, and resources are sourced based on requested capabilities, with regard for impact on national security or readiness

  -- Federal Government support of civil authorities are executed under the Stafford Act, Economy Act, and IRA

Scenarios Requiring DSCA

- Except for immediate response and emergency authority, as well as situations in which the Secretary of Defense (SecDef) has delegated authority to the commanders of U.S. Northern Command (USNORTHCOM) and U.S. Indo-Pacific Command (USINDOPACOM) via the DSCA Standing Execution Order (EXORD), only SecDef may approve requests from civil authorities or qualifying entities for federal military support for:

    -- Response to chemical, biological, radiological, nuclear, and high-yield explosives (CBRNE) incidents

    -- Requests for direct assistance in support of civilian law enforcement agencies to include those responding with assets with the potential for lethality (acknowledging the limited exception provided under emergency authority IAW DoDD 3025.18 for federal military commanders to approve civil authorities' requests in extraordinary emergency circumstances where prior authorization by the President is impossible and duly constituted local authorities are unable to control the situation, to engage in temporary activities necessary to quell large-scale, unexcepted civil disturbances)

    -- Response with potentially lethal assets, which includes: the lending of arms, vessels, aircraft, or ammunition; assistance to the Department of Justice (DoJ) in emergency situations involving weapons of mass destruction; assistance to the DoJ concerning prohibited transactions involving nuclear material; support to counterterrorism operations; and support to civilian law enforcement authorities in situations where it is reasonable to anticipate a confrontation between civilian law enforcement and civilian individuals or groups

Coordination and Requests for DSCA

- There are three broad categories of DSCA operations: (1) domestic emergencies; (2) designated law enforcement support; and (3) other activities

- At the request of a state governor, POTUS may declare a major disaster or emergency under the Stafford Act, 42 U.S.C. §§ 5121 *et seq.*

    -- Federal Emergency Management Agency (FEMA) is generally assigned as the lead federal agency; the DoD supports the lead federal agency through either a SecDef-approved request for assistance or a SecDef-approved mission assignment

- Federal military forces employed for DSCA are to remain under federal military command and control at all times

    -- The Joint Staff, upon SecDef approval of DoD assistance, coordinates with the Services to source the assistance to be provided; based on the capabilities required, DAF assets may be directed to provide assistance

- Per DoDD 3025.18, *Defense Support of Civil Authorities*, requests for DSCA, except requests for support under immediate response authority and mutual or automatic aid arrangements (such as reciprocal fire protection agreements under 42 U.S.C. §§ 1856–1856p and governed by DoDI 6055.06, *DoD Fire and Emergency Services (F&ES) Program)*, must be submitted in writing

Evaluating DSCA Requests

- All DSCA requests for assistance must be evaluated using CARRLL criteria: cost (including the source of funding and the effect on the DoD budget); appropriateness (whether providing the requested support is in the interest of the DoD); risk (safety of DoD Forces); readiness (impact on the DoD's ability to perform its other primary missions); legality (compliance with laws); and lethality (potential use of lethal force by or against DoD Forces)

- Written requests shall include a commitment to reimburse the DoD in accordance with the Robert T. Stafford Disaster Relief and Emergency Assistance Act (42 U.S.C. §§ 5121 *et seq.*), the Economy Act (31 U.S.C. § 1535), or other statutory reimbursement authorities

  -- Support may be provided on a non-reimbursable basis only if required by law or if both authorized by law and approved by the appropriate DoD official

- Domestic use of small unmanned aircraft systems (sUAS) must be executed in accordance with AFMAN 11-502, *Small Unmanned Aircraft Systems,* and DoDD 3025.18

  -- Any domestic use of UAS must be in accordance with Federal Aviation Administration (FAA) regulations and other applicable laws, policies, and memoranda of agreement concerning UAS use in national air space

Matters Not Within Scope of DSCA

- Joint investigations of matters within their respective jurisdictions conducted by military criminal investigative organizations (e.g., Air Force Office of Special Investigations) and civilian law enforcement agencies, where each is using its own forces and equipment are NOT within the scope of DSCA

- Assistance provided by DoD intelligence and counterintelligence components in accordance with DoDD 5240.01, *DoD Intelligence Activities*; Executive Orders 12333 and 13388, DoDM 5240.01, *Procedures Governing the Conduct of DoD Intelligence Activities* (Procedures 1–10); DoD 5240.1-R, *Procedures Governing the Activities of DoD Intelligence Components That Affect United States Persons* (Procedures 11–13); and other applicable laws and regulations are **NOT** within the scope of DSCA

- Support provided in response to foreign disasters (e.g., foreign consequence management or foreign humanitarian assistance/disaster response) are also **NOT** within the scope of DSCA

Immediate Response Authority (IRA)

- Upon request and without SecDef approval, DAF installation commanders may, subject to higher headquarters' direction and/or limitation, temporarily employ resources under their control to save lives, prevent human suffering, or mitigate great property damage within the United States in response to an RFA from a civil authority, under imminently serious conditions. Immediate response authority does not permit actions that would subject civilians to the use of military power that is regulatory, prescriptive, proscriptive, or compulsory. See DoDD 3025.18, *Defense Support of Civil Authorities*, and AFI 10-801, *Defense Support of Civil Authorities*, para. 3.2.4.

  -- For support under IRA, "imminently serious conditions" must be present such that time does not permit seeking approval from higher authority. Air Force and Space Force commanders must consider the impact providing immediate response would have on military mission requirements; commanders must not jeopardize the DAF mission to provide immediate response.

  -- Support provided under IRA is provided on a cost-reimbursable basis, unless nonreimbursement is authorized by law. However, Air Force and Space Force commanders should not delay nor deny IRA support if the requester is unable or unwilling to commit to reimbursing the DoD.

  -- An immediate response ends when the urgent need giving rise to the response is no longer present (i.e., when there are sufficient non-DoD resources available to adequately respond and that agency or department is responding) or when the initiating DoD official or a higher authority directs an end to the response

- DAF commanders acting under IRA must not use military force to quell civil disturbances unless specifically authorized by POTUS in accordance with the Insurrection Act of 1807 or unless permitted under emergency authority

Emergency Authority

- DAF commanders have the authority to temporarily engage in activities necessary to quell large-scale, unexpected civil disturbances, in extraordinary emergency circumstances where prior POTUS authorization is not possible and where duly constituted local authorities are unable to control the situation. Emergency authority is only permissible when such activities are necessary to:

  -- Prevent significant loss of life or wanton destruction of property and are necessary to restore governmental function and public order; or

  -- Protect federal property/federal governmental functions when duly constituted civil authorities are unable/unwilling to provide adequate protection.

References

· Provision of Support for Certain Sporting Events, 10 U.S.C. § 2564

· Prohibited Transactions Involving Nuclear Materials, 18 U.S.C. § 831

· Posse Comitatus Act, 18 U.S.C. § 1385

· Agency Agreements, 31 U.S.C. § 1535

· Robert T. Stafford Disaster Relief and Emergency Assistance Act, 42 U.S.C. §§ 5121 *et seq.*

· Executive Order 12333, *United States Intelligence Activities* (4 December 1981)

· Executive Order 13388, *Further Strengthening the Sharing of Terrorism Information to Protect Americans* (25 October 2005)

· Joint Publication 3-27, *Homeland Defense* (10 April 2018)

· Joint Publication 3-28, *Defense Support of Civil Authorities* (29 October 2018)

· DoD 5240.01-R, *Procedures Governing the Activities of DoD Intelligence Components That Affect United States Persons* (December 1982), incorporating through Change 2, 26 April 2017

· DoDD 3025.18, *Defense Support of Civil Authorities* (29 December 2010), incorporating through Change 2, 19 March 2018

· DoDD 5240.01, *DoD Intelligence Activities* (27 August 2007), incorporating through Change 3, 9 November 2020

· DoDI 3020.52, *DoD Installation Chemical, Biological, Radiological, Nuclear, and High-Yield Explosive (CBRNE) Preparedness Standards* (18 May 2012), incorporating Change 1, 22 May 2017

· DoDI 3025.21, *Defense Support of Civilian Law Enforcement Agencies* (27 February 2013), incorporating Change 1, 8 February 2019

· DoDI 6055.06, *DoD Fire and Emergency Services (F&ES) Program* (3 October 2019)

· DoDM 5240.01, *Procedures Governing the Conduct of DoD Intelligence Activities* (8 August 2016) Secretary of Defense (SecDef) Memorandum, *Guidance for the Domestic Use of Unmanned Aircraft Systems in U.S. National Airspace* (18 August 2018)

· AFI 10-801, *Defense Support of Civil Authorities* (29 January 2020)

· AFMAN 11-502, *Small Unmanned Aircraft Systems* (29 July 2019)

SMALL UNMANNED AIRCRAFT SYSTEMS

As the use of small unmanned aircraft systems (sUAS) by hobbyist/recreational, commercial/ civil, and public (i.e., nongovernment) users increases, so do questions regarding their use on or near military installations.

Key Takeaways

» 10 U.S.C. § 130i authorizes the Secretary of Defense (SecDef) to take certain actions necessary to mitigate the threat of an unmanned aircraft or unmanned aircraft systems that pose an imminent threat to the safety or security of certain assets or facilities of national security significance

» Coordination with the Federal Aviation Administration (FAA) is critical to deconflicting airspace and ensuring successful counter-sUAS (C-sUAS) programs

» At international locations, the host nation generally regulates the use of the airspace above U.S. military bases; Status of Forces Agreements (SOFAs) or other host nation agreements may give installations some rights with respect to airspace control

» Section 848 of the National Defense Authorization Act (NDAA) for Fiscal Year 2020 places restrictions on the operation and procurement of UAS manufactured in or containing critical components made in a covered foreign country

Definitions

- The Department of Defense (DoD) categorizes unmanned aircraft systems (UAS) into five groups based on the weight, altitude, and speed of the system

  -- sUAS generally fall within Groups 1–3 (rotor and fixed wing), while larger, more traditional platforms such as the MQ-1 Predator and MQ-9 Reaper are Groups 4–5

- The FAA considers sUAS to be any aircraft less than 55 pounds and requires registration for all sUASs between .55 and 55 pounds. The FAA has also issued operating rules for sUASs that vary depending on whether the sUAS is flown for commercial or noncommercial uses.

Operation of Non-Governmental sUAS on or over Military Installations

- Airspace within the United States, including airspace above DoD installations, is regulated by the FAA; sUAS operations are subject to FAA regulations and guidance

- Installation commanders generally do not have the authority to further restrict the use of airspace above an installation. They do, however, retain their authority over the installation and its activities and may, therefore, prohibit or limit the operation of sUAS on the installation, to include a sUAS taking off from the installation, a sUAS landing on the installation, and controlling a sUAS from the installation.

- sUAS airspace violations are subject to administrative, civil, or criminal penalties. FAA Notices to Airmen (NOTAMs) contain exceptions for certain sUAS operations, including government or military sUAS operations or other pre-approved flights

FAA Guidance and Regulations

- In 2017, at the request of the DoD, the FAA promulgated Special Security Instructions (SSIs) under 14 C.F.R. § 99.7. The SSIs prohibit any UAS flight within the airspace above most continental United States (CONUS) military installations. The prohibitions extend from the ground to 400 feet above ground level (AGL) and encompass installation perimeters.

- In June 2016, the FAA promulgated the "Small Unmanned Aircraft Rule" (14 C.F.R. Part 107 of the Federal Aviation Regulations), which imposes pilot and aircraft certification requirements and operational restrictions on commercial sUAS

- When flying sUAS for hobby or recreational purposes under the Special Rule for Certain Unmanned Aircraft Systems, sUAS are required to operate in a manner as to not endanger the safety of the U.S. National Airspace (NAS). For example, operators are expected to contact the airport operator and airport air traffic control (ATC) tower (when applicable) if they are planning to operate a sUAS within five nautical miles of an airport.

- Flying a sUAS near or above an installation may be permissible under current FAA regulations, if the sUAS is being used to conduct another activity (e.g., taking photos or videos), additional restrictions may apply

Other Laws Implicated by sUAS Activities

- Installation judge advocates should familiarize themselves with state and local laws relating to sUAS that may be applicable to operations near, on, or over the installation

- Federal laws may also prohibit certain activities, for example 18 U.S.C. § 795, *Photographing and Sketching Defense Installations* and 18 U.S.C. § 796, *Use of Aircraft for Photographing Defense Installations*, criminalize photographing "vital military and naval installations or equipment without first obtaining permission of the commanding officer"

C-sUAS Authorities

- Commanders retain the inherent right of self-defense against sUAS that pose a threat to DoD installations, assets, and personnel consistent with the provisions of CJCSI 3121.01B, *Standing Rules of Engagement/Standing Rules for Use of Force for US Forces*

- DoD has issued additional classified guidance on a commander's authority to counter sUAS. Commanders should consult this guidance and related Department of the Air Force (DAF) guidance before engaging in any C-sUAS operations.

- 10 U.S.C. § 130i authorizes SecDef to take certain actions necessary to mitigate the threat of an unmanned aircraft or unmanned aircraft systems that pose an imminent threat to the safety or security of certain assets or facilities of national security significance. Commanders of such covered assets and facilities should consult their Staff Judge Advocate and the relevant Base Defensive Operations Center sUAS program on the implementation of this authority.

- 10 U.S.C. § 130i only applies within the United States and U.S. territories

Operation of sUAS within the United States by DoD Organizations ("Blue sUAS")

- The 31 October 2023 SecDef memorandum, *Guidance for the Use of Unmanned Aircraft Systems in the U.S. National Airspace*, delegated Military Services the authority to approve domestic use of UASs (also referred to as "Blue sUAS" operations)

- Air Force Special Operations Command is the designated lead command for Blue sUAS operations and coordinates with major commands to develop guidance for the conduct and execution of sUAS operations and training

  -- Units operating sUAS must have a unit-specific installation commander approved concept of employment (CONEMP) when operating on or off military installations

  -- Operation of sUAS must also comply with DoDM 5240.01, *Procedures Governing the Conduct of DoD Intelligence Activities*; DoD 5240.1-R, *Procedures Governing the Activities of DoD Intelligence Components That Affect United States Persons* (Procedures 11-15); AFI 14-404, *Intelligence Oversight*; and applicable Air Force Office of Special Investigations (AFOSI) issuances

- Section 848 of the National Defense Authorization Act for Fiscal Year 2020 places additional restrictions on the operation and procurement of sUAS manufactured in or containing critical components made in a covered foreign country. Section 848 was most recently implemented by the DoD through a 22 December 2021 Under Secretary of Defense for Acquisition and Sustainment memorandum.

International Operation of sUAS by DoD Organizations

- At international locations, the host nation generally regulates the use of the airspace above U.S. military bases. SOFAs or other host nation agreements may give installations some rights with respect to airspace control.

- If no specific rights have been granted in a SOFA, basing agreement, or other host nation agreement, assume that specific permission will likely be needed to operate a sUAS

Conclusion

- The threats posed to the safety and security of DAF facilities and assets are constantly being evaluated. sUAS pose an emerging and unique threat and implicate numerous privacy and communications law.

- Commanders and JAGs should coordinate with their major commands, field commands, and AF/JA – Operations and International Law Directorate (JAO) when sUAS issues arise

References

· Protection of Certain Facilities and Assets from Unmanned Aircraft, 10 U.S.C. § 130i

· Photographing and Sketching Defense Installations, 18 U.S.C. § 795

· Use of Aircraft for Photographing Defense Installations, 18 U.S.C. § 796

· National Defense Authorization Act (NDAA) for Fiscal Year 2020, Pub. L. 116-92, § 848 (2019)

· Special Security Instructions, 14 C.F.R. § 99.7

· Small Unmanned Aircraft Rule, 14 C.F.R. Part 107

· CJCSI 3121.01B, *(U) Standing Rules of Engagement/Standing Rules for Use of Force for US Forces* (13 June 2005), certified current 18 June 2008

· DoDD 3800.01E, *DoD Executive Agent for Counter Small Unmanned Aircraft Systems for Unmanned Aircraft Groups 1, 2, and 3* (21 February 2020)

· DoD 5240.1-R, *Procedures Governing the Activities of DoD Intelligence Components That Affect United States Persons* (Procedures 11–15) (December 1982), incorporating through Change 2, 26 April 2017

· DoDM 5240.01, *Procedures Governing the Conduct of DoD Intelligence Activities* (8 August 2016)

· Secretary of Defense (SecDef) Memorandum, *Guidance for the Use of Unmanned Aircraft Systems in the U.S. National Airspace* (31 October 2023)

· Deputy Secretary of Defense Memorandum 17-00X, *Supplemental Guidance for Countering Unmanned Aircraft* (5 July 2017)

· Deputy Secretary of Defense Policy Memorandum 16-003, *Interim Guidance for Countering Unmanned Aircraft* (18 August 2016)

· Under Secretary of Defense (Acquisition & Sustainment) Memorandum, REVISION 1: *Procedures for the Operation or Procurement of Unmanned Aircraft Systems to Implement Section 848 of the National Defense Authorization Act for Fiscal Year 2020* (22 December 2021)

· AFI 14-404, *Intelligence Oversight* (3 September 2019)

· AFMAN 11-502, *Small Unmanned Aircraft Systems* (29 July 2019)

· ArcGIS FAA UAS Data on a Map, https://faa.maps.arcgis.com/apps/webappviewer/index.html?id=9c2e4406710048e19806ebf6a06754ad

SAFETY AND ACCIDENT INVESTIGATION BOARDS

Safety investigations determine cause(s) and provide recommendations to prevent future mishaps. Their findings, deliberations, and recommendations (and evidence obtained under a promise of confidentiality) are privileged. Accident investigations provide publicly releasable reports and preserve evidence for litigation, claims, disciplinary action, and other administrative action.

Key Takeaways

» Safety investigation boards (SIBs) conduct safety investigations

» The SIB's deliberations, opinions, recommendations, and evidence they receive under promises of confidentiality are privileged and cannot be released outside of DoD safety channels

» Accident investigation boards (AIBs) for aerospace mishaps and ground accident investigation boards (GAIBs) for non-aerospace asset mishaps are legal investigations conducted to provide a publicly releasable report of the mishap

» AIBs/GAIBs must **NOT** receive any safety privileged evidence or information from the SIB, but they receive all other non-privileged information gathered by the SIB

» SIBs have priority of evidence over AIBs/GAIBs, so the legal investigations typically start after the SIB

Safety Investigations

- A Safety Investigation Board (SIB) may be composed of a board of members or a single investigating officer

    -- Conducted solely for DoD mishap prevention purposes; limited use, even within the DoD and the Department of Air Force (DAF)

    -- **NOT** used for disciplinary actions, line-of-duty determinations, flying evaluation boards, litigation, claims, or assessing pecuniary liability

- SIBs may offer a promise of confidentiality to witnesses or contractors if necessary and authorized, but witness statements are not under oath

- Privileged information in a safety report is barred from use in claims and litigation for or against the United States, even if it favors the DAF. The United States Supreme Court has upheld the military safety privilege.

Potential Challenges with Safety Investigations

- <u>Interface with Accident Investigators</u>: The safety investigation has priority over the accident investigation to wreckage, witnesses, and documents. Part 1 of the safety report consists of non-privileged factual information and is released to the accident investigators, along with all other non-privileged information.

- <u>Queries from Next of Kin (NoK) of Mishap Victims</u>: NoK usually speak with the family assistance representative (FAR) appointed by the commander. SIB personnel do not discuss their investigation with anyone, except the convening authority (CA) or the Air Force Safety Center (AFSEC). At an appropriate time once the report is approved, the Accident Investigation Board/Ground Accident Investigation Board (AIB/GAIB) president briefs the report to the NoK and answer questions about the mishap.

- <u>Requests for Information</u>: Requests for SIB reports and information concerning the safety investigation are directed to AFSEC/JA. For AIB/GAIB reports, direct all requests to the convening authority's (CA) major command/field command (MAJCOM/FLDCOM) level Staff Judge Advocate (SJA).

- <u>Appearance of Improper Use</u>: Avoid creating the appearance of improper use of privileged safety information (e.g., for public disclosure, disciplinary actions, flying evaluation boards). Commanders must have clean hands and document the source of information being used to take action.

- <u>Criminal Misconduct</u>: Prosecution may be complicated by a safety investigation preceding a court-martial. The defense may request privileged information, resulting in litigation over its release. Where evidence of criminal misconduct relating to the cause of the mishap is present, the convening authority may delay the SIB and proceed with a legal/law enforcement investigation.

Accident Investigations

- Accident investigations pursuant to AFI 51-307, *Aerospace and Ground Accident Investigations,* are required for all on-duty Class A accidents involving DAF assets, except for (1) Class A accidents in which remotely piloted subscale aircraft and aerial targets are destroyed, (2) when there is only damage to federal government property and no safety investigation is done, and (3) for accidents involving an aerospace asset when the asset is not destroyed

Class A Accidents

- Mishaps where an injury or occupational illness results in a fatality or permanent total disability

- Mishaps where a DAF aerospace asset is destroyed

- Mishaps where the total cost of damages to the government or other property is $2,500,000 or more

Other DAF Mishaps with Mandatory Accident Investigations

- Mishaps with a probability of high public interest, including from Congress or the media

- Mishaps when claims and litigation are anticipated for or against the government or a government contractor because of the mishap

- Mishaps causing significant civilian property damage

- Also, accident investigations not otherwise required may be convened at the convening authority's discretion for any DAF "accident/mishap"

Convening Authority Responsibilities in AIB/GAIBs

- The CA is the MAJCOM/FLDCOM commander who convened, or would have convened, the safety investigation under DAFI 91-204, *Safety Investigations and Reports*. This authority is delegable to the MAJCOM/FLDCOM deputy commander.

- The CA informs the NoK of deceased and seriously injured personnel, through the FAR, of the process and status of ongoing investigations and schedules any planned NoK briefings. The CA also ensures appropriate condolence letters are sent to NoK.

    -- The CA funds costs associated with the accident investigation, determines what information may be released to the public prior to the completion of the AIB/GAIB report, and approves the final report and related public affairs guidance

    -- High-interest AIB/GAIB reports are coordinated and staffed by the CA's SJA through AF/JAO – Aviation & Admiralty Torts Division (AF/JAOA) and AF/JA for review by the Secretary of the Air Force and the Chief of Staff of the Air Force or Chief of Space Operations

Host Installation Commander's Responsibilities in AIB/GAIBs

- Appoint a host installation liaison officer to assist the AIB/GAIB in obtaining accommodations and administrative support, as well as facilitating witness interviews

- Provide in-house facility, communications, supply, photography, and billeting support for the AIB/GAIB

- Remove and store wreckage from the mishap site at the direction of the CA until AF/JAOA or the MAJCOM/FLDCOM SJA releases it from legal hold

- Assist the CA with initial cleanup of the mishap site

- The installation SJA may need to temporarily assume custody of the SIB's non-privileged evidence until the arrival of the AIB/GAIB

GAIB Reports

- Usually do not contain a statement of opinion, unless specifically authorized in advance. Unlike AIBs, the GAIB president's opinion is not statutorily protected and may affect the United States in litigation.

- A thorough GAIB report will allow the facts to speak for themselves

Air National Guard Considerations

- For aircraft accidents involving Air National Guard members, the gaining MAJCOM convenes the AIB/GAIB

- The AIB/GAIB will need to obtain a copy of the orders of any member involved in the mishap

References

· Treatment of Reports of Aircraft Accident Investigations, 10 U.S.C. § 2254

· Aircraft accident investigation boards: composition requirements, 10 U.S.C. § 2255

· *United States v. Weber Aircraft Corp.*, 465 U.S. 792 (1984)

· DoDI 6055.07, *Mishap Notification, Investigation, Reporting and Record Keeping* (6 June 2011) incorporating Change 1, 31 August 2018

· DAFI 91-204, *Safety Investigations and Reports* (10 March 2021)

· AFI 51-307, *Aerospace and Ground Accident Investigations* (18 March 2019)

FLYING EVALUATION BOARDS

When performance of rated duty becomes questionable, a flying evaluation board (FEB) may be convened. This applies to rated officers, career enlisted aviators, non-rated officers, and non-career enlisted aviator enlisted aircrew members. FEBs are administrative, fact-finding proceedings that are closed to the public.

Key Takeaways

» An FEB is convened by a flying wing commander/equivalent or higher

» The member must be notified in writing and has a right to counsel

» FEBs are not a substitute for disciplinary or other administrative action and may occur in conjunction with disciplinary or other administrative action(s)

» MAJCOM/A3T is the final approval authority for boards convened at major command (MAJCOM)-level or below

» Ensure to follow each MAJCOM's supplement to AFMAN 11-402, *Aviation and Parachutist Service,* for FEBs

---

Reasons to Convene a FEB

- Seven bases exist to conduct an FEB: (1) Non-permanent Disqualification; (2) Lack of Proficiency; (3) Failure to Meet Training Standards; (4) Lack of Judgment; (5) Aircrew Requirements; (6) Violations of other Aviation Instructions and Procedures; and (7) Habits, Traits, Characteristics

- Specifics of each basis may vary by MAJCOM supplemental instruction to AFMAN 11-402

Composition of a Flying Evaluation Board

- An FEB is convened by an officer designated as convening authority by MAJCOM/A3T who is the commander of a flying unit at wing level (or comparable-level), or higher

- Three rated voting members, qualified for aviation service in an active aviation service code (ASC) and senior in rank to the respondent, will be appointed and will constitute a quorum

  -- Voting members should be in the same aircrew specialty (e.g., pilot, navigator, or flight engineer) as the respondent. The senior board member is a voting member and final authority regarding conduct at the board.

  -- To the greatest extent possible, at least one voting member should have the same primary duty Air Force Specialty Code (AFSC) as the respondent

- One additional aircrew member is appointed to act as a nonvoting recorder. A judge advocate may advise the recorder but shall not be appointed as an assistant recorder and may not be present during closed sessions.

    -- A recorder prepares the case by presenting the evidence and examining the witnesses in a non-adversarial manner

- A flight surgeon may be appointed as a nonvoting member when a medical problem may be a significant contributing factor in the case

Flying Evaluation Board Procedures and Guidelines

- Notify the respondent in writing, including the reason(s) for the FEB (including the basis for convening the board and all allegations), when and where the board will meet, witnesses to be called, and rights of the respondent

    -- The respondent must reply within 48 hours (two duty days) and may waive an FEB to return to a previously qualified aircraft if enrolled in flying training

- Respondent may submit a request for voluntary disqualification from aviation service in lieu of the FEB (also known as a VILO) within five calendar days of receiving the FEB notification letter. Should such request be submitted, FEB action is suspended until the MAJCOM acts on the VILO request.

- If an Air Reserve Component aircrew member requires an FEB during a formal flying training course with a Regular Air Force unit, the Regular Air Force MAJCOM/A3T will appoint a convening authority for an FEB at the base of training

    -- In these situations, one of the board members must be a rated officer (as appropriate) in the Air Force Reserve or a member of the Air National Guard, preferably from the individual's home unit

Rights of the Respondent at a Flying Evaluation Board

- Assigned military counsel of his/her own choosing (if available) or civilian counsel (at respondent's expense)

- Informed in writing of the specific reasons for convening the board

- Challenge voting members for cause

- Review all evidence and documents to be submitted to the board by the recorder (if practical, this opportunity to review should be accomplished with sufficient time for the respondent to adequately review), and cross-examine witnesses called by the board, call witnesses, and present evidence. The recorder arranges for military witnesses.

    -- Although civilian witnesses may appear, an FEB cannot compel their attendance. Consult with the servicing Staff Judge Advocate (SJA) concerning the procedures for requesting the presence of civilian Department of Defense employees.

- Testify personally and submit a written response. Respondent may not be compelled to testify.

Rules of Evidence

- An FEB does not have to follow the same rules of evidence as courts-martial under the Uniformed Code of Military Justice (UCMJ)

  -- General observance of the same evidentiary rules as those under the UCMJ, however, promotes orderly procedures and a thorough investigation

- The decision about the authenticity of documents rests with the senior board member

Findings and Recommendations

- Findings are made in closed session by voting members only, and each finding must be supported by a preponderance of the evidence

- Findings must specifically include comment on each allegation or point in question

- Recommendations must be consistent with the findings and generally only address qualification for aviation service, not qualifications to remain in the Air Force

  -- If the officer holds more than one aviation qualification, the FEB must make a recommendation as to all qualifications

  -- If the FEB recommends disqualification, it may also recommend whether the officer should be prohibited from wearing the associated aviation badge

- A minority report is appropriate if there is a disagreement among the voting members

Review Process

- The convening authority's SJA reviews for legal sufficiency. This review is limited to sufficiency of the evidence and compliance with procedural requirements.

- The convening authority adds comments and recommendations, but must explain any recommendations that are contrary to those of the FEB

- The convening authority or higher reviewer may reconvene the FEB or order a new board

- The MAJCOM/A3T makes the final determination in all FEB cases convened at the MAJCOM-level or below

Reference

· AFMAN 11-402, *Aviation and Parachutist Service* (24 January 2019), including AFMAN11-402_AFGM2023-01, 14 June 2023

Chapter 17
ENVIRONMENTAL LAW

ENVIRONMENTAL LAWS – OVERVIEW

Failure to comply with environmental laws and regulations may inhibit full mission accomplishment and impact installation resources. Additionally, commanders can be held criminally liable for violations of environmental laws and regulations. Familiarization with this chapter will help a commander minimize negative impacts to the mission and the environment.

Key Takeaways

» The Air Force and Space Force are subject to state and local fines and penalties for violations of environmental requirements related to, but not limited to, hazardous waste, underground storage tanks, drinking water, or lead-based paint

» Most statutes subject Air Force and Space Force personnel to criminal liability for violations of environmental laws and regulations

» There are three levels of enforcement authority: Environmental Protection Agency (EPA), state or local enforcement agencies, and private citizens

» The base has a number of offices with expertise in environmental matters, such as civil engineering, office of the Staff Judge Advocate, bioenvironmental engineering, medical, or safety

Environmental Statutes

- Federal statutes now cover virtually all major environmental issues:

  -- Exemptions from federal statutes and rules are rare because they usually require personal action by the President or the Secretary of Defense

  -- Most statutes subject Air Force and Space Force personnel to criminal liability for violations of environmental laws and regulations

Enforcement Authority

- Three levels of enforcement authority typically apply:

  -- <u>Environmental Protection Agency (EPA)</u>: Retains authority to enforce when it has not delegated that authority to the relevant state or when it learns of violations not being prosecuted or otherwise dealt with by a delegated state

  -- <u>State or Local Enforcement Agencies</u>: Have primary responsibility for taking administrative or judicial action for most violations

  -- <u>Private Citizens</u>: When federal, state, or local enforcement authorities have failed to abate violations, most environmental statutes allow private citizens to initiate civil enforcement proceedings in a federal district court

Assistance

- The base has a number of offices with expertise in environmental matters. These offices typically include civil engineering, office of the Staff Judge Advocate, bioenvironmental engineering, medical, safety, and others.

- To assist commanders in addressing environmental issues, there are required meetings with the installation Environment, Safety, and Occupational Health Council (ESOHC), which is normally chaired by the vice wing commander

Overseas

- Environmental requirements for U.S. forces outside the states, territories, and possessions that comprise the U.S. are determined primarily by treaties and international agreements, Department of Defense (DoD) and geographic combatant command policies, and service and subordinate command directives. Few U.S. environmental laws apply outside the United States, and those that do apply extraterritorially are incorporated into DoD policy for overseas installations and operations.

References

- Environmental Effects Abroad of Major Department of Defense Actions, 32 C.F.R. Part 187
- Environmental Impact Analysis Process, 32 C.F.R. Part 989
- DoDI 4165.69, *Return of DoD Sites Overseas* (20 December 2021)
- DoDI 4715.05, *Environmental Compliance at Installations Outside the United States* (1 November 2013), incorporating through Change 2, 31 August 2018
- DoDI 4715.08, *Remediation of Environmental Contamination Outside the United States* (1 November 2013), incorporating through Change 2, 31 August 2018
- DoDI 4715.19, *Use of Open-Air Burn Pits in Contingency Operations* (13 November 2018)
- DoDI 4715.22, *Environmental Management Policy for Contingency Locations* (18 February 2016), incorporating through Change 2, 31 August 2018
- AFI 32-7001, *Environmental Management* (23 August 2019)
- AFI 32-7020, *Environmental Restoration Program* (12 March 2020), including DAFI32-7020_DAFGM2023-01, 2 February 2023
- AFI 32-7091, *Environmental Management Outside the United States* (13 November 2019)
- AFI 90-801, *Environment, Safety, and Occupational Health Councils* (9 January 2020)
- AFMAN 32-1067, *Water and Fuel Systems* (4 August 2020), including DAFMAN32-1067_DAFGM2022-01, 19 August 2022
- AFMAN 32-7002, *Environmental Compliance and Pollution Prevention* (3 February 2020)
- AFMAN 32-7003, *Environmental Conservation* (20 April 2020)
- AFH 10-222, Volume 4, *Environmental Considerations for Overseas Contingency Operations* (1 September 2012)
- AFH 32-7084, *AICUZ Program Manager's Guide* (2 November 2017)

CONTROLS ON AIR FORCE AND SPACE FORCE DECISION-MAKING: NATIONAL ENVIRONMENTAL POLICY ACT

The National Environmental Policy Act (NEPA) requires federal agencies to evaluate environmental impacts as part of their planning and decision-making process. It also requires public notice of, and involvement in, the process. Failure to follow NEPA planning could result in a court halting the project until the NEPA process is complete. This section is limited to NEPA procedural requirements within the United States and its territories.

Key Takeaways

» Failure to follow NEPA's mandate through the Environmental Impact Analysis Process (EIAP) can result in the action being delayed by litigation challenging the adequacy of the NEPA documentation

» EIAP is required for any "major federal action significantly affecting the quality of the human environment." This includes projects proposed by the Air Force or Space Force and private actions essentially under Air Force or Space Force "control."

Implementation

- Within the Air Force or Space Force, NEPA's mandates are carried out through EIAP, found at 32 C.F.R. Part 989

- A review is required for any "major federal action significantly affecting the quality of the human environment." This includes both projects proposed by the AF and private actions essentially under Air Force or Space Force "control" (e.g., actions requiring Air Force or Space Force permission).

    -- "Major" refers to impact on the environment, not to the size of the project; thus, even a small project can qualify as major

    -- Impacts may be significant, based on context and intensity

    -- The term "human environment" includes the natural and physical environment, as well as the relationship of people with that environment

- Generally, the Air Force and Space Force may not irretrievably commit money or resources for any proposed action until the EIAP is completed

- Failure to follow EIAP can result in the action being delayed by litigation challenging the adequacy of the NEPA documentation

- A reviewing court's focus will be whether the Air Force or Space Force has taken a hard look and made a good faith assessment of potential impacts to the environment and whether reasonable alternatives were considered

Additional Implementing Considerations

- Presence of wetlands or floodplains may require additional documentation and higher headquarters level approval

- Presence of classified information does not exempt the Air Force or Space Force from its NEPA responsibilities, but it may modify the public's right to participate in the NEPA process. Unclassified portions of the required analysis are shared with the public.

- The Air Force and Space Force are prohibited from supporting or taking any action affecting air quality in a nonattainment or maintenance area (e.g., construction, weapon system bed-down, mission realignment, training exercise, etc.) which does not conform to a State Implementation Plan (SIP)

    -- The requirement to conform to a SIP is called "general conformity" and requires the Air Force and Space Force to demonstrate the proposed action will not hinder attainment or maintenance of air quality standards

- Endangered Species Act and National Historic Preservation Act consultation, if required, must be completed prior to completing the environmental review

- Executive Order 14096, *Revitalizing our Nation's Commitment to Environmental Justice for All*, requires federal agencies to deliver environmental justice to all communities with an approach that is informed by scientific research and meaningful engagement

Level of Environmental Review

- Categorical Exclusion (CATEX): Used for actions that do not individually or cumulatively have potential for significant effect on the environment and require no further environmental analysis (see 32 C.F.R. Part 989, Appendix B, for a list of CATEXs)

    -- When application of a CATEX must be documented, an AF Form 813, Request for *Environmental Impact Analysis*, is used

    -- If the proposed action does not lead to a CATEX, the Air Force and Space Force must determine whether to prepare an environmental assessment (EA) or an environmental impact statement (EIS)

- Environmental Assessment (EA): Used for actions that are not expected to have a significant environmental impact

    -- An EA is similar to an EIS in that both consider alternatives and impacts, but an EA is substantially shorter and has fewer opportunities for public comment or participation

    -- Every EA concludes with either a Finding of No Significant Impact (FONSI) or the decision to prepare an EIS

- Environmental Impact Statement (EIS): Required for actions expected to have a significant impact

  -- The heart of an EIS is the identification and analysis of alternatives. A range of reasonable alternatives satisfying the purpose and need of the proposed action must be analyzed, and must include a "No Action" alternative.

  -- An EIS concludes with the signing of a Record of Decision (ROD)

NEPA is a Procedural Law

- The Air Force and Space Force must ensure environmental concerns are given appropriate consideration, but NEPA does not require the Air Force or Space Force to rank environmental concerns above mission goals

- The Air Force and Space Force must ensure all reasonable measures are considered to mitigate adverse environmental impacts associated with an action it has chosen to implement

  -- An EIS or EA/FONSI should clearly identify mitigation measures

  -- A ROD must state whether all practicable means to avoid or minimize environmental harm from the alternative selected have been adopted or, if not, why they were not

  -- If mitigation measures are proposed, proponents must prepare a mitigation plan and submit it to HQ USAF/A4CI for each FONSI or ROD containing mitigation measures

References

· National Environmental Policy Act, 42 U.S.C. §§ 4321 *et seq.*

· Environmental Impact Analysis Process, 32 C.F.R. Part 989

· CEQ Regulations for Implementing the Procedural Provisions of NEPA, 40 C.F.R. Parts 1500–1508

· Executive Order 14096, *Revitalizing our Nation's Commitment to Environmental Justice for All* (26 April 2023)

· AF Form 813, *Request for Environmental Impact Analysis* (August 1999)

ENVIRONMENTAL MANAGEMENT SYSTEM; ENVIRONMENTAL INSPECTIONS; AND THE ENVIRONMENT, SAFETY, AND OCCUPATIONAL HEALTH COUNCIL

Department of the Air Force Environmental Management System (EMS) is a framework for program and process improvement through clearly defined environmental roles and responsibilities, planning requirements, budgeting, effective implementation and operation, and management review. The Environment, Safety, and Occupational Health Council (ESOHC) is a steering group that establishes goals, monitors progress, and advises installation senior leadership.

Key Takeaways

» Environmental inspections are an essential aspect of maintaining compliance with environmental legal requirements

» EMS management is important to identifying needs for funding to ensure mission requirements are supported by compliance with mandatory environmental requirements

» Commanders must ensure implementation of inspection findings to ensure installation compliance with environmental legal requirements

» Inspection documents must be released, if required, but are otherwise internal documents

Environmental Management System (EMS)

- EMS incorporates business processes and business rules for managing and reducing environmental risk. All personnel have a role in their installation's EMS.

    -- EMS drives continuous improvement for all Air Force and Space Force environmental programs

    -- The inspection system uses eDASH, an internet-based document control system maintained by the Air Force Civil Engineer Center (AFCEC), who implements EMS across the Air Force and Space Force

Environmental Inspections

- Installations will conduct EMS compliance and conformance self-assessments and track preventative and corrective actions

Release of Environmental Inspection Documents and Information

- Inspection documents and information must be managed and protected in accordance with applicable laws, regulations, and policies

    -- The Freedom of Information Act (FOIA), DoDM 5400.07, AFMAN 33-302, and DAFI 90-302, govern the release of inspection records

Environmental, Safety, and Occupational Health Council

- The Environmental, Safety, and Occupational Health Council (ESOHC) is the cornerstone of the Environment, Safety, and Occupational Health (ESOH) program. It provides senior leadership involvement and direction at all levels of command, and develops, approves, and monitors ESOH risk-based performance goals and objectives.

  -- The ESOHC reports annually on the progress of ESOH goals, as defined by next higher-level ESOHC, and any issues requiring higher-level assistance or direction until closure

  -- The ESOHC reports annually to the next higher-level ESOHC on the effectiveness of the management systems, evaluate high risk and/or problematic open findings, and track progress to correct validated deficiencies

Figure 17.1. Interaction of EMS, Environmental Inspections, and ESOH Council

Detailed description of chart provided at end of section

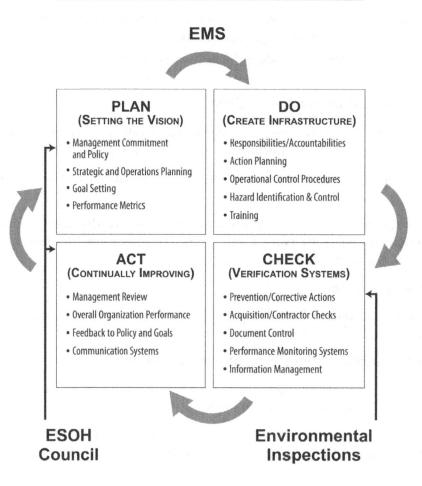

References

· Freedom of Information Act, 5 U.S.C. § 552

· ISO 14001:2015(E), *Environmental Management Systems–Requirements with guidance for use* (15 September 2015)

· DoDD 5400.07, *DoD Freedom of Information Act (FOIA) Program* (5 April 2019)

· DoDI 4715.05, *Environmental Compliance at Installations Outside the United States* (1 November 2013), incorporating through Change 2, 31 August 2018

· DoDI 4715.06, *Environmental Compliance in the United States* (4 May 2015), incorporating Change 1, 31 August 2018

· DoDI 4715.17, *Environmental Management Systems* (15 April 2009), incorporating through Change 2, 31 August 2018

· DoDM 5400.07_AFMAN 33-302, *Freedom of Information Act Program* (27 April 2018)

· DAFI 90-302, *The Inspection System of the Department of the Air Force* (15 March 2023)

· AFI 32-7001, *Environmental Management* (23 August 2019)

· AFI 90-801, *Environment, Safety, and Occupational Health Councils* (9 January 2020)

Chart Detailed Description

Figure 17.1 Interaction of EMS, Environmental Inspections, and ESOH Council: The interaction of the EMS, Environmental Inspections, and ESOH Council is a continuous cycle of 4 stages: Plan, Do, Check and Act. The Plan stage sets the vision addressing: management commitment and policy, strategic and operations planning, goal setting, and performance metrics. The Do stage creates infrastructure addressing: responsibilities/accountabilities, action planning, operational control procedures, hazard identification & control, and training. The Check phase involves verification systems that address: prevention/corrective actions, acquisition/contractor checks, document control, performance monitoring systems, and information management. Environmental inspections come into play during the Check phase. The Act phase deals with continual improvement addressing: management review, overall organization performance, feedback to policy and goals, and communication systems. The ESOH Council is involved in the Plan and Act phases.

INTERACTION WITH THE OCCUPATIONAL SAFETY AND HEALTH ADMINISTRATION

The Occupational Safety and Health Administration (OSHA) establishes occupational safety and health (OSH) standards to ensure safe and healthy conditions in workplaces throughout the United States OSHA enforces its standards through inquiries, inspections, investigations, and issuing citations for violation of OSHA standards.

Key Takeaways

» Federal agencies must comply with OSHA standards

» OSHA standards do not apply to military-unique workplaces

» Air Force installations must respond to OSHA investigations, inquiries, and citations

---

Applicability of OSHA Standards

- Federal agencies must provide safe and healthy working conditions for its employees

- Federal agencies must establish and maintain OSH programs that obey OSHA standards or approved alternate standards

    -- Does not apply to workplaces that use or handle DoD equipment, systems, and operations that are unique to the national defense mission

    -- "Military unique" workplaces and places where only military members work do not have to obey OSHA standards

- DAFI 48-145, *Occupational and Environmental Health Program*, specifies Air Force occupational and environmental health standards that apply to all military and civilian personnel

- DAFI 91-202, *The US Air Force Mishap Prevention Program*, provides Air Force industrial and ground safety policy that implements OSHA standards

Reporting Requirements

- In accordance with 29 C.F.R. § 1904.39, prompt reporting to OSHA regarding specific employee incidents that are the result of a work-related incident is required. Typically, this is accomplished through the installation safety office. The type of incident includes:

    -- Any employee death, which must be reported within 8 hours, or

    -- Any in-patient hospitalization of one or more employees, any amputation, or the loss of an eye, which must be reported within 24 hours

- Under 29 C.F.R. § 1904.31(b)(3), this reporting requirement may extend to certain contractors under the day-to-day supervision of the government. Contact your installation safety office to determine applicability.

Contact from OSHA

- There are three typical contacts an installation may have with OSHA:

  -- Inquiry: Process that occurs in response to a complaint from a non-employee or when a complaint alleges a violation occurred, but there is no present danger to workers

  -- Inspection: On-site evaluation of workplace(s), which can be scheduled ahead of time, or under some circumstances, conducted unannounced

  -- Investigation: In-depth look into a fatality or catastrophe caused by a workplace hazard. A catastrophe is defined as an incident resulting in hospitalization of three or more employees.

    --- The Air Force and Space Force must investigate the incident and, upon request, provide OSHA with a report of the investigation's findings

    --- The OSHA Area Director decides whether OSHA conducts an investigation of the incident and whether to participate in the Air Force or Space Force's investigation

- Citation: Issued using an OSHA-2H Form, *Notice of Unsafe or Unhealthful Working Conditions* (also known as an OSHA Notice)

  -- A copy of the citation must be posted at or near the location of each violation addressed in the citation and a copy of the citation must remain posted until the violation is abated or three working days, whichever date is later

Responses to OSHA

- Inquiry and Citation: The Air Force and Space Force reply should be responsive, respectful, timely, and sincere, answer OSHA's questions, and address OSHA's concerns

  -- If a violation occurred, specify which actions have been taken or which actions will be taken to fix the violation and prevent a repeat occurrence

- Inspection and Investigation: During inspections and investigations, Air Force and Space Force representatives should be cooperative, respectful, and interested

  -- Be open and facilitate site visits, interviews, and document reviews

  -- Provide escorts for inspectors and investigators, take pictures of whatever inspectors or investigators take pictures of, and take samples of whatever OSHA samples

- Ensure the servicing legal office knows about and provides support regarding all OSHA contacts and responses

- Respond to citations after consulting the servicing legal office

State OSH Regulations and Regulators

- Generally speaking, State OSH laws and regulations do not apply to Air Force and Space Force workplaces, except for contractors

    -- Air Force and Space Force contractors are subject to federal and state OSH requirements

References

· Occupational Safety and Health Act of 1970, 29 U.S.C. §§ 651–678

· Executive Order 12196, *Occupational Safety and Health Programs for Federal Employees* (1980)

· Reporting fatalities, hospitalizations, amputations, and losses of an eye as a result of work-related incidents to OSHA, 29 C.F.R. § 1904.39

· Basic Program Elements for Federal Employee Occupational Safety and Health Programs and Related Matters, 29 C.F.R. Part 1960

· Coverage of Employers Under the Williams-Steiger Occupational Safety and Health Act of 1970, 29 C.F.R. Part 1975

· OSHA Instruction CPL 02-00-163, *Field Operations Manual (FOM)* (13 September 2019)

· OSHA-2H Form, *Notice of Unsafe or Unhealthful Working Conditions*

· DoDD 4715.01E, *Environment, Safety, and Occupational Health (ESOH)* (19 March 2005), incorporating through Change 2, 30 December 2019

· DoDI 6055.01, *DoD Safety and Occupational Health (SOH) Program* (14 October 2014), incorporating through Change 3, 21 April 2021

· DoDI 6055.05, *Occupational and Environmental Health (OEH)* (11 November 2008), incorporating through Change 2, 31 August 2018

· DAFI 48-145, *Occupational and Environmental Health Program* (21 September 2022)

· DAFI 91-202, *The US Air Force Mishap Prevention Program* (12 March 2020), including AFI91-202_AFGM2022-01, 12 April 2022

· DAFMAN 48-146, *Occupational Health Program Management* (1 December 2022)

· AFI 32-7001, *Environmental Management* (23 August 2019)

· AFI 90-801, *Environment, Safety, and Occupational Health Councils* (9 January 2020)

· AFPD 90-8, *Environmental, Safety and Occupational Health Management and Risk Management* (23 December 2019)

· AFPD 91-2, *Safety Programs* (3 September 2019)

· AFVA 91-209, *Air Force Occupational Safety and Health Program* (14 October 2016)

ENVIRONMENTAL ENFORCEMENT ACTIONS

Environmental regulators issue enforcement actions (EAs) to notify bases of which environmental requirements were violated, actions to take to become compliant, and whether the base faces fines and/or penalties for the violation. EAs can be serious, costly, and trigger various immediate reporting requirements.

Key Takeaways

» EAs can cost an installation a significant amount of Operations and Maintenance (O&M) funds

» Each EA must be quickly coordinated with the base Staff Judge Advocate (SJA) and the Regional Counsel Office (RCO)

» To prevent noncompliance, certain steps can (and should) be taken, such as self-inspections and thorough record-keeping practices

Receiving an EA

- EAs may be issued by various regulatory bodies at all levels, including federal, state, and local agencies

- EAs may also be called notices of violation (NOV), notices of non-compliance (NON), notices of deficiency (NOD), compliance agreements (CA), or consent orders (CO)

- EAs are commonly issued after an inspection or as the result of a report of noncompliance filed by a regulator. In certain cases, a failure to report (e.g., an effluent limit exceedance, spills, etc.) can also result in enforcement.

- Depending on the nature of the violation, fines and penalties may be assessed and are ultimately paid using installation O&M funds. Additionally, regulators may seek injunctions to shut down operations or pursue criminal charges.

- Installations may face EAs for the actions of non-Air Force and non-Space Force personnel, such as the Army & Air Force Exchange Service (AAFES) employees, contractor employees, property lessees, and other agency personnel

Reporting and Tracking EAs

- The base Civil Engineer, Installation Management Flight (CEI) must timely notify the installation commander, installation SJA, and AFCEC/CZ of any written notice of a non-compliance by a regulatory agency. Overseas locations notify the Air Force Civil Engineer Center's Facility Engineering Directorate (AFCEC/CF). Air National Guard installations notify the National Guard Asset Management Division Environmental Management Branch (NGB/A7AN).

- Base CEIs shall report all written notices, emails, field citations, and other correspondence from regulatory agencies pertaining to non-compliance with applicable environmental requirements within one business day through the EA Spills and Inspections Environmental Reporting (EASIER) database

- The installation SJA or representative shall notify the RCO and installation CEI within one business day of receiving any notice of a non-compliance or obtaining knowledge of any potential non-compliance

- Bioenvironmental Engineers (BEs) must notify the BEs at the major command (MAJCOM) level of any violation of potable water quality sampling within one business day and immediately implement public notification procedures required by the regulator

Responding to an EA

- Coordinate with the installation SJA and the RCO prior to responding to any EA

- Pay careful attention to response deadlines contained in enforcement documentation. Some regulators direct a required response date or timeframe. Continue good communication with the regulator throughout the process.

- Do not assume the base is subject to the rule or law allegedly violated, or that actions laid out by the regulator are required to be taken, such as a penalty or paying a fine. Legal advice must be sought from the installation SJA and RCO to determine the validity of the EA.

- Encourage frequent communication within the unit and the applicable regulator throughout the process

- Preserve evidence and document site conditions for potential EA litigation

EA Process

- The RCO is the lead negotiator for all NOVs and coordinates settlement agreements with regulators. The Environmental Law and Litigation Division (AF/JAOE) Chief must approve settlement agreements, including the payment of fines or penalties, prior to receiving the commander's signature.

- Federal regulatory agencies, like the U.S. Environmental Protection Agency, may attempt to resolve EAs through settlement or by filing a "complaint," which triggers a formal administrative process. In that formal process, the installation must generally file an "answer" within 20 days. Failing to respond to the complaint could be considered an admission.

- State and local agencies often have their own distinct rules an installation should follow when responding to EAs

- Paying civil fines or penalties assessed as part of an EA are normally the responsibility of the installation

Avoiding EAs in the Future

- Stress the importance to unit personnel of complying with all environmental and safety instructions (e.g., Air Force Instructions, DoD regulations, permits, material safety data sheets (MSDS), etc.)

- Be prepared for regulator-led inspections by conducting regular self-inspections, promoting thorough record-keeping practices, and fixing deficiencies on the spot

  -- Select and prepare a knowledgeable and professional escort team to accompany regulators during inspections. Escorts should mirror the inspectors by duplicating any information collected, such as taking pictures of what the inspectors photograph, and creating a copy of the documents they collect. Oftentimes regulators will issue EAs but refuse to provide accompanying evidence, which makes it difficult to defend the installation.

  -- Know the areas most likely to produce violations, such as hazardous waste label practices, personnel training records, and documentation pertaining to hazardous waste management and shipments

Bottom Line

- Preparation is the key to avoiding EAs

- Prompt and cooperative responses are the key to resolving EAs

- Consult with the installation SJA, CEI, and BE immediately upon receiving an EA, especially before signing or paying anything

References

· DAFMAN 65-605, Volume 1, *Budget Guidance and Technical Procedures* (31 March 2021)
· AFI 32-7001, *Environmental Management* (23 August 2019)
· AFI 51-301, *Civil Litigation* (2 October 2018)
· AFMAN 32-7002, *Environmental Compliance and Pollution Prevention* (4 February 2020)

MEDIA RELATIONS AND ENVIRONMENTAL CONCERNS

The Air Force and Space Force develop public engagement programs to build public understanding, trust, and support for Air Force and Space Force missions and people. Public Affairs (PA) activities are to inform and include audiences during critical decision-making windows, and to communicate the Air Force and Space Force's commitment to environmental excellence.

Key Takeaway

» The National Environmental Policy Act (NEPA) requires the public be informed of and involved in the decision-making process; therefore, PA's role is to prepare, coordinate, and distribute timely news releases and other public information materials related to and aligned with the proposal and associated Environmental Impact Analysis Process (EIAP) documents, which is critical to meeting NEPA's mandate

Environmental Impact Analysis Process (EIAP) PA Responsibilities

- Ensure all PA aspects of EIAP actions are conducted in accordance with 32 C.F.R. § 989 and AFI 35-101, *Public Affairs Operations*, Chapter 6

  -- Review and clear environmental documents in accordance with AFI 35-101 prior to public release

  -- Ensure security and policy review requirements are met for all information proposed for public release as noted in Chapter 9 of AFI 35-101 and Chapter 8 of AFMAN 35-101, *Public Affairs Procedures*

- Assist Department of the Air Force judge advocates in planning and conducting public meetings and hearings

  -- Attend and assist in preparation of scoping meetings and other public meetings or media sessions on environmental issues

- Advise the Environmental Planning Function (EPF) and the action proponent on PA activities on proposed actions and reviewing environmental documents for public involvement issues

  -- Advise the EPF of issues and competing general-public and stakeholder interests that should be addressed in the Environmental Impact Statement (EIS) or Environmental Assessment (EA)

- Prepare, coordinate, and distribute timely news releases and other public information materials related to and aligned with the proposal and associated EIAP documents

- Notify the media (television, radio, newspaper) of actions as necessary under 32 C.F.R. § 989.24 and purchase advertisements when newspapers will not run notices free of charge. The project proponent will fund the required advertisements.

Installation Restoration Program (IRP) PA Responsibilities

- Serve as the focal point for PA aspects of proposed IRP actions as noted in para. 6.2.3.9 of AFI 35-101

- Advise on and support the PA aspects of the base's development and participation in the Restoration Advisory Board, a community based advisory board, plus other public information activities

- Ensure all concerned stakeholders, community groups, and governmental entities are in the communication channel

- Prepare an IRP community relations plan and announce the availability and location of information repositories (often called the Administrative Record)

Air Installation Compatible Use Zone (AICUZ) Program PA Involvement

- The Base Community Planner (BCP) generally manages the AICUZ program. PA assists the BCP in preparing for public meetings and releasing and distributing relevant information.

- PA handles noise complaints directly, and provides timely, responsive, and factual answers to maintain good media and community relations. PA also presents the complaints to the appropriate installation meetings or boards. PA will refer all claims for damages to the base legal office.

References

· Environmental Impact Analysis Process, 32 C.F.R. Part 989
· AFI 35-101, *Public Affairs Operations* (20 November 2020)
· AFMAN 35-101, *Public Affairs Procedures* (7 December 2020)

MISSION SUSTAINMENT

Mission sustainment hazards have the potential to directly affect both the ability of Department of the Air Force (DAF) installations to accomplish the mission and the quality of life in surrounding communities. AFI 90-2001, *Mission Sustainment*, aligns installation mission sustainment programs with the Air Force risk management model described in AFI 90-802, *Risk Management*, and DAFPAM 90-803, *Risk Management (RM) Guidelines and Tools*. The Air Force Mission Sustainment Risk Management Program should identify common issues affecting installations while integrating existing foundational programs, such as the Air Force Noise Program and the Air Installation Compatible Use Zones (AICUZ) Program.

Key Takeaways

» If a mission sustainment hazard includes topics sensitive in the local community, critical mission impacts, or is likely to garner negative media attention, elevate the issue to the major command (MAJCOM) level and notify the installation Staff Judge Advocate (SJA)

» Inform the installation SJA when a noise complaint is received

» Installations may show support to state and/or local zoning decisions, but may not imply that if that particular decision does not occur it would directly affect a Base Realignment and Closure (BRAC) decision

---

Installation Mission Sustainment Team (IMST)

- The installation commander establishes an IMST to assist in implementing the Mission Sustainment Program at an installation

- The team is a cross-functional team with representatives from various organizations

- Goals of the IMST:

  -- Address mission sustainment across the Installation Complex/Mission Footprint

  -- Brief the installation commander and MAJCOM Mission Sustainment Team, at least annually, on emerging threats, the status of the program (including information on emerging hazards), the status of control implementation, and recommended focus areas for the coming year

- Installation Complex Encroachment Management Action Plan (ICEMAP):
  A three-volume document (Action Plan, Reference Book, and Community Brochure) addressing current and future encroachment and sustainment challenges facing Air Force and Space Force installations and their surrounding communities

Air Force Noise Program

- While the installation Community Planner generally manages the installation noise program, the installation commander may assign noise program management tasks to another office

- Aircraft overflights, weapon system operations, or munitions use have the potential to produce sound levels that may cause annoyance, speech interference, sleep disturbance, or structural damage

- The Federal Noise Control Act (FNCA) exempts aircraft, military weapons, and equipment designed for combat use from noise regulation

  -- Courts have determined state and local regulation of aircraft noise is preempted by Federal Aviation Administration (FAA) regulations

- The DAF considers the FNCA in its National Environmental Policy Act (NEPA) analyses and complies with the substance of FNCA for stationary noise

  -- The FNCA does not allow the federal government to be sued because it does not contain a federal facility enforcement provision or private right of action against federal agencies

- Inform the installation SJA when a noise complaint is received and retain the complaint, with geospatial data, for a minimum of five years

AICUZ Program

- Local governments ordinarily establish land use regulations. The Air Force and Space Force support and encourage local zoning and other land use controls that ensure land areas surrounding bases, especially private lands adjacent to runways, remain compatible with continued Air Force and Space Force operations.

- DoD established the AICUZ program to assist local governments in establishing suitable land use regulations in the vicinity of installations

- The DAF develops and provides local land use planning authorities recommendations designed to ensure continued compatibility between installations and neighboring civilian communities

  -- The DAF has no authority to implement the land use recommendations set forth in the AICUZ study or to control or regulate off-base land use. An installation simply presents its recommendations to the local zoning authority which may approve or reject them.

  -- Close coordination between the commander, the base comprehensive planner, and local zoning officials is essential. This coordination serves to educate local land use planners regarding noise and safety impacts on private lands.

  -- Air Force and Space Force representatives may not threaten the local community with reprisals if the Air Force and Space Force proposal is not accepted. Air Force and Space Force representatives may not appear to coerce or otherwise unduly influence local zoning officials. For example, reprisal or coercion could include linking acceptance of a proposal to potential BRAC decisions.

-- Constant consultation with the installation SJA minimizes the potential for lawsuits and impacts to the mission

- Congress provided authority to acquire property interests, including restrictive use or conservation easements where necessary to sustain the mission and prevent encroachment (10 U.S.C. § 2684a)

The Military Aviation and Installation Assurance Siting Clearinghouse

- The Military Aviation and Installation Assurance Siting Clearinghouse (Clearinghouse) works with energy production developers (e.g., a wind or solar farm development), to mitigate and sometimes avoid mission sustainment hazards

- When a project is determined to have a potential adverse impact to military readiness, the Clearinghouse establishes a Mitigation Response Team, who collaborates with the developer, base, and agency to identify reasonable and affordable mitigation options

- General adverse impacts from energy projects include radar and military training route interference. These impacts can be mitigated by reducing or removing the proposed turbines and/or panels in an area or lowering the height of the turbines.

References

· Agreements to Limit Encroachments and Other Constraints on Military Training, Testing, and Operations, 10 U.S.C. § 2684a

· Noise Control Act of 1972, 42 U.S.C. §§ 4901–4918

· DoDI 4165.57, *Air Installations Compatible Use Zones* (13 December 2021)

· DAFPAM 90-803, *Risk Management Guidelines and Tools* (22 March 2022)

· AFI 32-1015, *Integrated Installation Planning* (30 July 2019), Corrective Actions applied on 4 January 2021, incorporating Change 1, 13 October 2020

· AFI 90-802, *Risk Management* (1 April 2019)

· AFI 90-2001, *Mission Sustainment* (31 July 2019)

· AFH 32-7084, *AICUZ Program Manager's Guide* (2 November 2017)

CONTROL OF TOXIC SUBSTANCES

The Toxic Substances Control Act (TSCA) (15 U.S.C. §§ 2601–2692) regulates the manufacturing, processing, and distributing of chemicals that pose an unreasonable risk of injury to human health or the environment. The TSCA authorizes the Environmental Protection Agency (EPA) to screen existing and new chemicals to identify potentially dangerous products or uses and to take action.

Key Takeaways

» The TSCA requires special handling and use of the materials located on Air Force and Space Force installations

» Regulated materials are polychlorinated biphenyls (PCBs), asbestos, radon, and lead-based paint (LBP)

Polychlorinated Biphenyls (PCBs)

- The TSCA prohibits the manufacture and distribution of PCBs

  -- Sources of PCBs on installations may include old transformers and capacitors, PCB-contaminated soil from past insecticide spraying, ceiling tile coatings, and certain painted surfaces

  -- Installation personnel should be trained to avoid mixing normal used oil and oil containing PCBs. Managing PCB imbued oil under TSCA is far more expensive than managing used oil under the Resource and Conservation and Recovery Act.

Asbestos

- Asbestos was widely used in thousands of products (e.g., floor tiles, insulation, or sealants) because it is strong, flexible, will not burn, insulates effectively, and resists corrosion

  -- Regulatory requirements cover, among many things, remediation of asbestos hazards, implementation of proper work practices, and training in proper handling methods

  -- Installations are most likely to encounter asbestos when maintaining, repairing, renovating, or demolishing buildings or utilities

Radon

- The TSCA requires studies of federal buildings to determine the extent of indoor radon contamination, but does not require monitoring or abatement of radon

  -- Radon is a naturally occurring radioactive gas that may be found in drinking water and indoor air, and which presents serious health risks, including cancer

  -- Radon in soil under homes is the biggest radon source for indoor air

Lead-Based Paint (LBP)

- The TSCA addresses lead hazards, including requirements for the identification, reduction, disclosure, and management of LBP

    -- Lead, especially LBP, is a major concern on installations; it was commonly used in military family housing and other buildings prior to 1950

    -- Bases must address lead hazards during maintenance, repair, renovation, and demolition of buildings. Additionally, DoD policy requires military installations to comply with disclosure regulations related to LBP in military family housing.

- The TSCA also authorizes established state programs (e.g., California) to establish LBP standards for the reduction of lead in buildings not otherwise covered by the child-occupied target buildings referenced above. Check with the installation Staff Judge Advocate (SJA) to determine if an applicable state program is in effect that could potentially impact the installation.

References

- Toxic Substances Control Act (TSCA), 15 U.S.C. §§ 2601–2692
- Occupational Safety and Health Act of 1970, 29 U.S.C. §§ 651–678
- Clean Air Act, 42 U.S.C. § 7401
- National Emissions Standard for Asbestos, 40 C.F.R. Part 61, Subpart M
- DoDI 4715.05, *Environmental Compliance at Installations Outside the United States* (1 November 2013), incorporating through Change 2, 31 August 2018
- DoDI 4715.06, *Environmental Compliance in the United States* (4 May 2015), incorporating through Change 2, 31 August 2018
- AFI 90-801, *Environment, Safety, and Occupational Health Councils* (9 January 2020)

UTILITY LAW

The Utility Law Field Support Center (ULFSC), embedded within the Air Force Civil Engineer Center's (AFCEC) Energy Directorate at Tyndall Air Force Base, assists continental U.S. commanders in minimizing utility costs. The ULFSC assists installations by supporting contracting actions with utility providers, representing the Air Force and Space Force in utility rate litigation, and advising on energy resilience projects.

Key Takeaways

» Legal offices should contact the ULFSC when they become aware of any type of utility projects on base, such as installing new generators or privatization of base utilities. Regardless of who owns the project (the installation, a tenant, or other), these projects can often have effects on the installation's utility contracts, utility bills, and contractual liability to others.

» Prior to representing the DoD in utility rate litigation, the ULFSC notifies all senior mission commanders at any impacted installation, in accordance with 40 U.S.C. § 501(c), through the appropriate legal office

Methods of Purchasing Utilities

- The contracting methods used by installations to purchase utilities are set forth in 48 C.F.R. Part 41, Federal Acquisition Regulations (FAR); DAFMAN 32-1061, *Providing Utilities to U.S. Air Force Installations* (16 July 2019); and AFPAM 32-10144, *Implementing Utilities at U.S. Air Force Installations* (8 March 2016)

- The General Services Administration (GSA) administers area-wide contracts for energy acquisition

  -- Area-wide contracts are convenient, and are modifiable to address specific base issues

  -- GSA area-wide contracts are found online at https://www.gsa.gov/real-estate/facilities-management/utility-services/areawide-public-utility-contracts

- FAR Part 41 individual installation contracts are the most common method for purchasing utility services

- Installation legal offices are responsible for reviewing utility services solicitations and proposed contracts, including modifications to area-wide contracts, to determine whether they are legally sufficient. The ULFSC is available as reach-back support for all utility contract questions.

- Installation legal offices ensure utility service contracts comply with federal, state, and local laws, including ordinances, public utility commission rulings, court decisions, and opinions of the Comptroller General

Utility Litigation Challenging Rate Increases

- The ULFSC represents the interests of the Air Force and Space Force, as well as all other impacted DoD installations and Federal Executive Agencies, in utility rate cases

- Utility rate cases are triggered by utility companies filing a request for a change in rates with a public utility commission

- In accordance with AFPAM 32-10144, Chapter 10, the base civil engineer should provide all known details regarding an actual or potential rate case to the installation legal office, installation contracting office, and AFCEC Energy Directorate Rates and Renewables (AFCEC/CNR) within 24 hours of rate change notification, which usually comes from the utility company as part of a notice with the monthly bill

- Pursuant to AFPAM 32-10144, Chapter 10, within one week of the date the installation informs AFCEC/CNR of a proposed rate increase, the base civil engineer should provide AFCEC/CNR, the installation contracting office, and the ULFSC, all required information related to the rate change notification via the installation legal office

Energy Resilience Projects

- An Energy Savings Performance Contract (ESPC) is a collaboration between a federal agency and a third-party contractor to improve base-owned infrastructure and equipment in order to produce energy savings

- A Utility Energy Service Contract is similar to an ESPC, but is performed by a local utility service provider

- Under a Power Purchase Agreement (PPA), an installation leases land to an energy generation developer (local utility company or third-party contractor) and contracts to purchase energy produced by the project

- An Enhanced Use Lease involves a land lease to a developer who builds an energy project on the leased land on the installation but, unlike a PPA, the project does not provide the energy to the installation directly

- Utilities Privatization permits the sale of DoD utility systems to private contractors for fair market value. An ability to meet the installation's energy resilience requirements must be considered.

Assistance

- Utility acquisition matters can be very complex. Installations should notify AFCEC/CNR and the ULFSC of utility rate increases and seek assistance on utility matters

- The ULFSC is available at (850) 283-6175/DSN 523-6175 or ulfsc.tyndall@us.af.mil

- The 24-hour AFCEC reach-back support center is available at (850) 283-6995, DSN 523-6995 or AFCEC.RBC@us.af.mil

References

· Services for Executive Agencies, 40 U.S.C. § 501(c)

· Acquisition of Utility Services, 48 C.F.R. Part 41

· DAFMAN 32-1061, *Providing Utilities to U.S. Air Force Installations* (18 August 2023)

· AFPAM 32-10144, *Implementing Utilities at U.S. Air Force Installations* (8 March 2016)

Chapter 18
CYBER LAW

CYBER LAW OVERVIEW

This chapter addresses the legal issues in cyberspace operations, and some operations through cyberspace, that Department of the Air Force (DAF) commanders are most likely to encounter. Among these are (1) criminal law matters such as searching and seizing computers, accessing electronically stored information (ESI), and computer misuse; (2) law of war and international law matters to include defending DAF networks and attacking adversary networks; and (3) the application of privacy law, notably the Freedom of Information Act (FOIA) and the Privacy Act. Most of these discrete areas of the law have their own chapter or section throughout this publication, so this chapter will focus on their cyber-specific aspects of these areas.

Commanders and judge advocates should seek the most current guidance from subject matter experts at the Air Force's Operations and International Law Directorate (AF/JAO), located at the Pentagon, and the 16th Air Force (Air Forces Cyber) (16 AF (AFCYBER)) and 67th Cyberspace Wing (CW) legal offices, both located at Joint Base San Antonio-Lackland, Texas.

Key Takeaways

» There are different roles and responsibilities for cyber operations and cybersecurity that fall under Service authorities, combatant command authorities and statutory authorities. Activities and operations must be properly conducted under the appropriate command and control and legal authority to conduct the operation or activity.

» DoD Cyberspace Operations Forces (COF) are particular units organized, trained, and equipped to conduct offensive cyberspace operations (OCO), defensive cyberspace operations (DCO), and DoD Information Network (DODIN) operations (see DoD COF memo)

» The DAF Chief Information Officer (SAF/CN) has responsibility for information technology, cybersecurity, enterprise data management, artificial intelligence, information management, and information resources management for the DAF, to include the role as DAF/CIO

» Mission Defense Teams are not considered a DoD Cyberspace Operations Force (DoD COF); they are Service retained forces essentially under Service authorities

---

Key Roles and Responsibilities

- U.S. Cyber Command (USCYBERCOM):

  -- In May 2018, USCYBERCOM was elevated to a unified combatant command (UCC). Its responsibilities include, but are not limited to:

    --- Directing operations and defense of the DoD Information Network (DODIN)

    --- Planning and executing global cyberspace operations

    --- Fulfilling the general responsibilities of a UCC

-- USCYBERCOM is the joint force trainer and joint force provider of cyber operations forces, and has limited cyber operations-specific acquisition authority

-- USCYBERCOM accomplishes its missions within three primary lines of operation: secure, operate, and defend the DODIN; defend the nation from malicious cyber activities in cyberspace; and provide cyberspace support as required to combatant commanders

- U.S. Space Force:

  -- Serves as the lead service for DAF enterprise satellite communications operations

  -- Direct United States Space Force (USSF)-assigned mission defense teams (MDT) when agreed between Chief of Staff of the Air Force (CSAF) and Chief of Space Operations (CSO) to manage service-level organize, train, and equip of mission defense teams in support of United States Space Force space mission systems; MDTs are not DoD COF, they are Service retained forces

  -- The USSF does not have a service subordinate command to USCYBERCOM similar to AFCYBER

- Joint Force Headquarter-Cyberspace (Air Force) (JFHQ-C (AF)):

  -- A functional component of USCYBERCOM, with Air Force, Army, and Navy forces assigned

  -- It is one of four JFHQ-Cs established to provide general support to combatant commands for the offensive cyberspace operations mission

  -- It is currently aligned to support the U.S. European (USEUCOM), Strategic (USSTRATCOM), and Space (USSPACECOM) Commands

- Service Cyber Component (AFCYBER):

  -- AFCYBER is the Air Force service component to USCYBERCOM

  -- AFCYBER authority is a separate operational control (OPCON) authority under USCYBERCOM

  -- AFCYBER executes the DODIN operations and defensive cyberspace operations internal defense measures (DCO-IDM) missions on the Air Force portion of the DODIN with assigned forces

  -- USCYBERCOM exercises combatant command (command authority) of the service cyber components including AFCYBER and Joint Force Headquarters-DODIN (JFHQ-DODIN). USCYBERCOM commander exercises directive authority for cyberspace operations (DACO) to issue orders and directives to all DoD components to execute global DODIN operations and DCO-IDM.

-- The USCYBERCOM commander delegated DACO over all Air Force components to the AFCYBER commander (CDRAFCYBER) to effectively implement orders from USCYBERCOM/JFHQ-DODIN and to ensure the timely and efficient security, operation, and defense of the Air Force portion of the DODIN. Delegation of this authority allows CDRAFCYBER to issue orders and directives to non-assigned units (i.e., major commands, field commands, wings, deltas, and communications squadrons) as required to compel unity of action to secure, operate, and defend the Air Force portion of the DODIN.

- The 16 AF Commander also performs the following functions:

  -- 16 AF is the traditional organize, train, and equip (OT&E) function in the administrative control (ADCON) chain through Air Combat Command (ACC) including intelligence, surveillance, and reconnaissance (ISR) activities by service-retained intelligence forces

  -- Integrates multisource ISR, cyber warfare, electronic warfare, and information operations capabilities across the conflict continuum

  -- Oversees signals intelligence (SIGNIT) forces as the Service Cryptologic Component Commander

  -- Oversees intelligence forces as one of the Air Force Defense Intelligence Component Heads

  -- Under separate hats and combatant command authority and OPCON, commands cyber operations forces as the Commander, AFCYBER, and Commander, JFHQ-C (AF)

- 616th Operations Center (OC):

  -- The 616 OC serves two primary and distinct functions: (1) command and control (C2) of cyberspace operations forces assigned to AFCYBER and JFHQ-C (AF) under USCYBERCOM, and (2) coordination of ISR activities and information warfare (IW) capabilities by service-retained forces

  -- The 616 OC also issues orders of the AFCYBER commander to Air Force units operating on the AFIN, many of which are derived from USCYBERCOM and JFHQ-DODIN orders or operations addressing DODIN-wide issues. These orders may flow through MAJCOM Cyber Coordination Centers to subordinate units, or may be issued directly by the 616 OC.

- DAF Principal Cyber Advisor

  -- In accordance with 10 U.S.C. § 392a(c), the DAF Principal Cyber Advisor is responsible for advising the Secretary of the Air Force, the Chief of Staff of the Air Force, and the Chief of Space Operations. This advisor also implements the DoD Cyber Strategy within the service by coordinating and overseeing the execution of the service's policies and programs. This is accomplished through: recruitment, resourcing, and training military cyberspace operations forces; assessment and maintenance of force readiness; acquisition of offensive, defensive, and DODIN cyber capabilities for military cyberspace operations; cybersecurity management and operations; supply chain risk management of the industrial base; and cybersecurity of DoD information systems, information technology services, and weapon systems.

- DAF Chief Information Officer (SAF/CN):

  -- Provides policy and guidance to foster an operationally resilient, reliable, and secure AFIN which meets DoD and DAF requirements; key DAF CIO authorities are pursuant to 10 U.S.C. § 2223, 40 U.S.C. § 11315, and 44 U.S.C. §§ 3506 and 3554

- Chief Information Security Officer (CISO):

  -- Enables the DAF core missions by ensuring the cybersecurity and resiliency of systems, information and staff; reviews and reports IT investment compliance with law, directives and guidance

  -- Defines policy and guides DAF Information programs such as the Freedom of Information Act, Privacy Act, Records Management, Section 508 and Civil Liberties, and Federal Register

- Air Combat Command Commander (ACC/CC):

  -- Serves as lead command for the cyber warfare operations mission area. The duties and responsibilities of the ACC/CC are outlined in para. 3.7 of DAFPD 17-2, *Cyber Warfare Operations*.

  -- Responsible for organizing, training, and equipping Air Force cyberspace operations forces and is the parent MAJCOM of 16 AF (https://www.16af.af.mil/)

References

- Joint Publication 3-12, *Joint Cyberspace Operations* (19 December 2022)
- DAFPD 17-2, *Cyber Warfare Operations* (27 October 2020)
- SecDef Memo, *Definition of "Department of Defense Cyberspace Operations Forces (DoD COF)* (12 December 2019)

LEGAL ISSUES IN AIR FORCE INFORMATION NETWORK OPERATIONS

Air Force Information Network (AFIN) Operations Authority

- The operational chain of command, through the Secretary of Defense (SecDef) and United States Cyber Command (USCYBERCOM), delegated the authority to secure, operate, and defend the Air Force portion of the DODIN to the Commander of Air Forces Cyber (AFCYBER). This authority includes Directive Authority to Conduct Cyberspace Operations (DACO) for the Air Force portion of the DODIN in order to effectively implement orders from USCYBERCOM and Joint Force Headquarters-Department of Defense Information Network (JFHQ-DODIN) and to ensure the timely and efficient security, operation, and defense of the Air Force portion of the DODIN. This authority allows the AFCYBER commander to issue orders and directives to compel unity of action to secure, operate, and defend the Air Force portion of the DODIN.

- Orders issued by the Commander of AFCYBER via the 616th Operations Center (616 OC), are mandatory military orders leveraging SecDef-derived authority. It is important to note that the Commander of AFCYBER also serves as the Commander of Sixteenth Air Force (Air Forces Cyber) (16 AF (AFCYBER)/CC).

- 16 AF (AFCYBER)/CC, acting in his/her role as Commander of AFCYBER or Commander of Joint Force Headquarters-Cyber (JFHQ-C)(Air Force), directs the Department of the Air Force (DAF) cyberspace forces in executing missions and tasks assigned by USCYBERCOM and exercises OPCON over forces assigned/attached to JFHQ-C (AF) USCYBERCOM in support of joint objectives

- There are significant overlaps between the DAF's service responsibility to ensure cybersecurity and interoperability of the Air Force portion of the DODIN (largely vested in Department of the Air Force (DAF) Chief Information Officer (SAF/CN) and the USCYBERCOM authority to secure, operate, and defend the Air Force portion of the DODIN which has been delegated to the AFCYBER Commander. Additionally, SAF/CN has designated 16 AF (AFCYBER) as the Component Cybersecurity Service Provider for the AFIN, thus providing 16 AF (AFCYBER) authority to ensure the AFIN is secure, assured, and interoperable, and that all personnel are appropriately trained.

Computer Monitoring and Stored Communications

- Commanders may have to deal with questions concerning monitoring network user activity (active duty military members, civilian employees, and contractors) or obtaining electronic data stored somewhere on the AFIN. These requests typically come from law enforcement, but they also may be requested by unit commanders, investigative officers, judge advocates, DAF civilian attorneys, safety investigation boards, and similar requestors. The following discussion examines the law in this area, some exceptions, and the process for obtaining these items in the DAF.

-- <u>Fourth Amendment</u>: The Fourth Amendment establishes the right to be free from unreasonable government searches and seizures. This applies to electronic systems and communications. What constitutes an unreasonable search is dependent upon whether an individual has a reasonable expectation of privacy (REP).

--- Determination of a REP on any given piece of information on any given computer or computer system (including servers) depends upon a number of factors, such as the owner of the computer (i.e., personal or business), the relationship of the information to the computer system (i.e., in transit or stored), the nature of the data communicated (i.e., metadata or content), the location of the information, and the information owner's citizenship

--- The DoD and DAF do not recognize a REP on government computers or computer systems. All users are expected to understand and acknowledge the DoD notice and consent banner and sign a user agreement before accessing a government computer or the Air Force portion of the DODIN. The banner and user agreement both make it clear that communications and data stored on the Air Force portion of the DODIN are not private and any security measures (such as passwords) are included to protect the U.S. Government and not for personal benefit or privacy.

- <u>Computer Fraud and Abuse Act (CFAA) (18 U.S.C. § 1030)</u>: Prohibits unauthorized access (or exceeding authorized access) to any "protected computer." A "protected computer" includes any computer involved in interstate or foreign commerce or communications, including a computer located outside the United States that is used in a manner that affects interstate or foreign commerce or communication of the United States. This statute is sometimes referred to as the anti-hacking statute. Article 123, Uniform Code of Military Justice (UCMJ) prohibits the unauthorized access of government computers under a variety of circumstances, similar to the prohibitions found in the CFAA.

- <u>The Electronic Communications Privacy Act (ECPA) (18 U.S.C. §§ 2510 et seq.)</u>: ECPA covers various forms of wire and electronic communications. It includes email, telephone conversations, and data stored electronically. ECPA is broken up into three sections: (1) Title I of ECPA is commonly referred to as the Federal Wiretap Act; (2) Title II is the Stored Communications Act; (3) Title III addresses pen register and trap and trace devices.

- <u>The Wiretap Act (18 U.S.C. §§ 2510 et seq.)</u>: Prohibits a third party to a communication from wiretapping, monitoring, or intercepting that communication in transit. The Wiretap Act covers both telephone conversations and electronic communications, and it grants protection to individuals above what is protected by the Fourth Amendment. However, there are numerous exceptions to the Wiretap Act prohibitions that permit most AFIN monitoring and provide options for law enforcement:

-- *The Service Provider Exception* (18 U.S.C. § 2511(2)(a)(i)): Permits service providers to "intercept, disclose, or use" a communication while engaged in activity necessary to the provision of service or the protection of the provider's rights or property. This authority is broad, but there must be a substantial nexus between the monitoring and the system administrator's duties to maintain and protect the system.

-- *Consent* (18 U.S.C. § 2511(2)(c)–(d)): Just as in other applications, consent to a "search" eliminates a privacy interest in the subject to be searched. The DoD banner, as mandated by the DoD Chief Information Officer, obtains consent to monitoring from any potential user prior to authorized use of DoD computer networks. The consent banner and user agreement are now used universally in the DAF and are a reliable exception to the Federal Wiretap Act.

  --- Federal courts have found that users who clicked on consent banners have no reasonable expectation of privacy, similar to one found on, the DoD Consent Banner. (*United States v. Larson*, 66 M.J. 212 (C.A.A.F. 2008)). Nonetheless, there are policy limitations on the release of certain data and information to balance civil liberties. For example, information obtained from an Electronic System Security Assessment (ESSA) mission will not be used as evidence in a criminal prosecution without approval IAW AFI 10-701, *Operations Security (OPSEC)*, para. 6.5.1.

  --- Authority to monitor communications for ESSA missions is derived from the Federal Information Security Modernization Act, 44 U.S.C. § 3554, and implemented in AFI 10-701. The ESSA mission is an OPSEC program and one of the few areas in which privileged information or PII may be accessed, and thus additional safeguards are established to preserve civil liberties. AFI 10-701, para. 6.3.1.

  --- The DoD notice and consent banner still protects some uses of the content of privileged communications or work product related to personal representation or services by attorneys, psychotherapists, or clergy, to include their assistants. Generally, release of privileged information communications, PII, or disclosure of information identifying a specific individual is not releasable outside of an explicit exception under AFI 10-701 (e.g., threat of death or serious bodily injury) or under another program (e.g., ESI request). However, the reason for restricted release is based on policy reasons and updates to AFIs or other regulations may permit further dissemination.

-- *Pursuant to Foreign Intelligence Surveillance Act* (18 U.S.C. § 2511(2)(e)): This exception will most likely only be used by an intelligence-gathering agency

-- *Communication Readily Accessible to the General Public* (18 U.S.C. § 2511(2)(g)(i)): An intercepted or accessed electronic communication which is readily accessible by the general public (e.g., social media post, status update) is excepted (see DoDD 3115.18, *DoD Access to and Use of Publicly Available Information (PAI)*)

-- *Trespasser Exception* (18 U.S.C. § 2511(2)(i)): An individual acting lawfully is authorized to intercept the communications of a trespasser into a computer system (i.e., hackers). The Air Force Office of Special Investigations (AFOSI) frequently relies on this exception when conducting counterintelligence investigations.

-- *Pursuant to a Court Order* (18 U.S.C. § 2518): Applications for orders authorizing or approving the interception of electronic communications are made in writing to a judge of competent jurisdiction

-- Information obtained through some methods may not considered "content." Radio frequency monitoring systems are increasingly being employed to detect Wi-Fi devices and ensure COMSEC on installations (see DoDI 8560.01, *Communications Security (COMSEC) Monitoring*, 22 August 2018). 18 U.S.C. § 2510(8) defines "contents" as "any information concerning the substance, purport, or meaning of that communication." Data transmitted over Wi-Fi, such as email content, webpage content, URLs that disclose content of the page, and text messages, would constitute communication subject to the restrictions of the Wiretap Act.

--- Basic identifying information about Wi-Fi networks themselves "including the network's name (SSID), the unique number assigned to the router transmitting the wireless signal (MAC address), the signal strength, ad whether the network was encrypted" is not considered contents. *Joffe v. Google, Inc.*, 729 F.3d 1262 (9th Cir. 2013). In contrasts, the contents of an email or text conversation would be considered "contents." Commanders should consult with their JAGs when instituting COMSEC monitoring programs involving Wi-Fi devices.

- Stored Communications Act (18 U.S.C. §§ 2701–2712): The protection in this statute applies to stored communications, rather than in-transit communications covered by the Wiretap Act

-- 18 U.S.C. § 2702(a) limits voluntary disclosure of communications or records by those providing electronic communication services "to the public." The AFIN does not provide electronic communications services to the public. *Bohach v. City of Reno*, 932 F. Supp. 1232 (D. Nev. 1996). Accordingly, the Stored Communications Act does not limit the Department of the Air Force's use of stored communications on the AFIN.

- Pen Register and Trap and Trace Act (18 U.S.C. §§ 3121 *et seq.*): The protection in this statute applies to information about communications, such as a log of telephone numbers called. In cyberspace, this statute is most often applied to proxy logs and network routing data. Like other portions of the ECPA, this statute contains exceptions for service providers.

- Search authorizations for electronically stored information should not be used in most cases. However, if the totality of the facts and circumstances indicate that the subject has a reasonable expectation of privacy, usually because the government property was issued for exclusive personal use, obtaining a search authorization is warranted (see DAFI 51-201, *Administration of Military Justice*).

- Routine use of search authorizations to collect information from government computer systems would contravene the language in the consent banner and could create a reasonable expectation of privacy in government computer systems

Electronically Stored Information Request Process

- Electronically stored information (ESI) may be requested for any official purpose. Common purposes include: court-martial proceedings, criminal investigations, administrative investigations, commander-directed investigations, civil litigation involving the DAF, or retrieving emails of an absent member in support of some military mission or duty.

   -- The DoD notice and consent banner eliminates the need for search authorization from a search authority in almost all cases. The DoD banner and is evidence of implied and explicit consent from all users to monitor their activities and retrieve data under the relevant exceptions of ECPA.

   -- As the Service Cyber Component commander, the AFCYBER Commander is directed and authorized by the SecDef and the USCYBERCOM Commander to conduct DODIN Operations on the AFIN. This mission includes actions taken to operate the AFIN to include ensuring the confidentiality, availability, and integrity of AFIN data. The AFCYBER Commander has the authority and technical ability to provide authorized personnel with AFIN data as required for official purposes.

   -- While AFCYBER has the technical ability to access AFIN ESI, AFCYBER is not the record custodian or record holder for such ESI. Whether to search, how to search, and proper handling and processing of search results is the responsibility of the requestor. Additional information on ESI search responsibilities can be found in AFI 33-322, *Records Management and Information Governance Program*, DAFI 51-201, *Administration of Military Justice*, and AFI 51-301, *Civil Litigation.*

   -- Additionally, the Air Combat Command Headquarters Cyberspace Capabilities Center is available to help coordinate network searches in response to litigation

Freedom of Information Act (FOIA) or Privacy Act (PA) Requests vs. ESI Requests

- ESI requests must be differentiated from requests pursuant to the Freedom of Information Act (FOIA) and Privacy Act (PA), but, at times, may follow similar procedures. The servicing legal office should be the first line of defense in determining whether the request requires processing under FOIA.

- Generally, requests for ESI are those which are not of a personal nature and have an inherent military mission or function for its use. For example, requesting emails pursuant to a commander directed investigation would be an ESI request. Also, requesting emails of a recently deceased member to continue a military duty is an ESI request. A request by an individual not selected for an advertised position for all emails between two other individuals concerning the selection decision would need to be made as a FOIA or PA request through proper FOIA and/or PA channels.

- As part of the FOIA and PA process, FOIA and PA Managers will make the request for the release of ESI using the ESI process. ESI identified is released back to the FOIA and/or PA managers for continued processing.

  -- Approval of the request to retrieve emails or data for FOIA and/or PA requests does not constitute a FOIA and/or PA approval or disapproval. Only FOIA and PA managers and the servicing legal office will ascertain whether information contained in the emails should be released to the third party.

ESI Request Format

- A request for ESI must contain key information for the system and exchange administrators to process it. The ESI request format directed by AFCYBER follows. The ESI request should be sent to the 616 OC Senior Duty Officer (SDO) at 616oc.sdo@us.af.mil. Investigating Officers should include a copy of their appointment letter.

- An ESI request should include the proper authority of the requesting individual (a valid basis to request information) and a sufficiently detailed description of the data requested in light of the basis.

- Contact 616 OC for most current suggested format for email message requests for access to ESI

ESI Request Reviews

- The 616 OC process for administering ESI requests is outlined in Tasking Order (TASKORD) 2021-299-001

- Email requests typically provide **ALL** emails for the period requested. These will require the requestor to perform a content review prior to certain uses of the data. The requestor is responsible for ensuring proper uses of all retrieved data and should seek legal advice from the servicing legal office as appropriate.

  -- Specifically, the requestor's local Staff Judge Advocate's office should be contacted for support for requests likely to contain proprietary information of DoD contractors, or privileged communications between the individual and clergy, health care practitioners, or attorneys

  -- Specifically, the requestor's local Staff Judge Advocate's office should be contacted for support for requests likely to contain proprietary information of DoD contractors, or privileged communications between the individual and clergy, health care practitioners, or attorneys

Computer Misuse

- Seemingly, small incidents of computer misconduct may have large impacts for the AFIN. For example, installing unauthorized software on a single computer may expose the entire network to malware infection and disruption.

- DAFMAN 17-1301, *Computer Security (COMPUSEC)*, includes user responsibilities on the AFIN. Often, violations of these standards are reported to commanders by System Administrators.

- When a commander becomes aware of computer misuse, they should consider disciplinary action when appropriate. Most computer misuse is punishable under the UCMJ. Consult your servicing legal office for more information.

- Common inappropriate uses include: (1) unauthorized personal use including use for personal gain; (2) uses that would adversely reflect on the DoD or the DAF; (3) storing, processing, displaying, sending, or otherwise transmitting prohibited content (i.e., pornography, sexually explicit or sexually oriented material); and (4) knowingly downloading or installing unauthorized software

Personally Identifiable Information (PII)

- Breaches involving PII are a high-level interest issue. PII breaches create personal vulnerabilities for individuals, but can also create AFIN vulnerabilities.

- PII refers to "Information about an individual that identifies, links, relates, or is unique to, or describes him or her, e.g., SSN; age; military rank; civilian grade; marital status; race; salary; home or office phone numbers; other demographic, biometric, or personnel information. All information that describes, locates or indexes anything about an individual including his/her education, financial transaction, medical history, criminal or employment record, or that affords a basis for inferring personal characteristics, such as biometric data including finger and voice prints, photographs, or things done by or to such individual; and the record of his/her presence, registration, or membership in an organization or activity, or admission to an institution" (see AFI 33-332, *Air Force Privacy and Civil Liberties Program*).

- Emails containing PII (e.g., alpha rosters, recall rosters, investigative reports, etc.,) must be digitally signed and encrypted and attachments with PII must be password protected (see AFI 33-332, para. 7.1.4)

  -- Controlled Unclassified Information (CUI), Emails, and Marking: A banner marking must appear at the top of the email. In addition, an indicator ("Contains CUI") can be included in the subject line to notify recipients that the email contains CUI. When forwarding or responding to email containing CUI, be sure to carry forward all applicable markings to the email. (See DoDI 5200.48_DAFI 16-1403, *Controlled Unclassified Information*; CUI Websites: https://www.archives.gov/cui; https://www.dodcui.mil/)

- Misuse of the AFIN or failure to follow directives such as those requiring encryption of PII may result in a suspension of access to the AFIN

References

- Freedom of Information Act, 5 U.S.C. § 552 Privacy Act, 5 U.S.C. § 552a
- Computer Fraud and Abuse Act (CFAA), 18 U.S.C. § 1030
- The Electronic Communications Privacy Act (ECPA), 18 U.S.C. §§ 2510 *et seq.*
- The Wiretap Act, 18 U.S.C. §§ 2510–2520
- The Stored Communications Act, 18 U.S.C. §§ 2701–2712
- Pen Register and Trap and Trace Act, 18 U.S.C. §§ 3121–3127
- Joint Federal Information Security Modernization Act, 44 U.S.C. § 3554
- *United States v. Larson*, 66 M.J. 212 (C.A.A.F. 2008)
- *Joffe v. Google, Inc.*, 729 F.3d 1262 (9th Cir. 2013)
- DoDD 3115.18, *DoD Access to and Use of Publicly Available Information (PAI)* (11 June 2019), incorporating Change 1, 20 August 2020
- DoDI 5200.48_DAFI 16-1403, *Controlled Unclassified Information*, (5 October 2021)
- DoDI 8560.01, *Communications Security (COMSEC) Monitoring*, (22 August 2018)
- Joint Publication 3-12, *Cyberspace Operations* (19 December 2022)
- AFI 10-701, *Operations Security (OPSEC)*, (23 July 2019)
- AFI 17-101, *Risk Management Framework (RMF) for Air Force Information Technology (IT)* (6 February 2020), including AFI17-101_DAFGM2022-01, 10 June 2022
- AFI 17-130, *Cybersecurity Program Management* (13 February 2020)
- AFI 33-322, *Records Management and Information Governance Program* (23 March 2020), incorporating Change 1, 28 July 2021
- AFI 33-332, *Air Force Privacy and Civil Liberties Program* (10 March 2020), Corrective Actions applied on 12 May 2020
- AFI 51-301, *Civil Litigation* (2 October 2018)
- AFMAN 17-1301, *Computer Security (COMPUSEC)* (12 February 2020), including DAFMAN17-1301_DAFGM2023-01, 17 January 2023
- AFMAN 17-1302-O, *Communications Security (COMSEC) Operations* (9 April 2020) 616 OC TASKORD 2021-299-001 (2021)
- Office of Management and Budget Memorandum M-17-12, *Preparing for and Responding to a Breach of Personally Identifiable Information* (3 January 2017)
- Air Force Cyber Law Primer, Lt Col Royal A. Davis III, Jeffrey T. Biller, and Air Force Cyber Primer Team, November 2022, https://www.airuniversity.af.edu/AUPress/Display/Article/3209936/air-force-cyber-law-primer/

LEGAL ISSUES IN CYBERSPACE OPERATIONS

Terminology

- Cyberspace terminology used for cyberspace operations often changes and is not always used consistently. Terminology may also be inconsistent with traditional uses (e.g., the doctrinal definition of "cyberspace attack" is inconsistent with the definition of an attack under the law of war). Consultation and verification of source documents is recommended when drafting documents related to cyberspace operations.

Mission Sets

- There are three basic mission sets for cyberspace operations:

  -- <u>Department of Defense Information Network (DODIN) Operations</u>: Operations to secure, configure, operate, extend, maintain, and sustain DoD cyberspace to create and preserve the confidentiality, availability, and integrity of the DODIN. DODIN Operations include the cyberspace security action.

    --- Does **NOT** include actions taken under statutory authority of a service Chief Information Officer (CIO) to provide cyberspace for operations, including IT architecture development, establishing standards, or designing, building, or otherwise operationalizing DODIN information technology for use by a commander

    --- AFCYBER, the Air Force service component USCYBERCOM, has standing authority to conduct DODIN Operations on the Air Force portion of the DODIN

    --- Using the Directive Authority to Conduct Cyberspace Operations (DACO), the AFCYBER Commander may order any Department of the Air Force (DAF) unit to conduct specific DODIN Operations missions on the Air Force portion of the DODIN

  -- <u>Defensive Cyberspace Operations (DCO)</u>: Missions to preserve the ability to utilize blue cyberspace capabilities and data by defeating on-going or imminent malicious cyberspace activity. DCO has three components:

    --- *DCO-Internal Defense Measures (DCO-IDM):* A defensive cyberspace operations mission in which defense actions occur within the defended portion of cyberspace

      ---- AFCYBER has standing authority to conduct DCO-IDM on the Air Force portion of the DODIN, and may be tasked by USCYBERCOM to conduct DCO-IDM on other DoD networks

      ---- Using DACO, AFCYBER may order any Air Force unit to conduct specific DCO-IDM missions on the Air Force portion of the DODIN

--- *DCO-Response Actions (DCO-RA):* A defensive cyberspace operations mission executed external to the defended network or portion of cyberspace without the permission of the owner of the affected system

---- DCO-RA missions require authority flowing from the Secretary of Defense (SecDef) via military order, and consideration of the Law of War (LoW) and Rules of Engagement (ROEs)

--- *Defense of Non-DoD Cyberspace:* When required under a specific authorizing order, and in full coordination with the Department of Homeland Security (DHS) and other U.S. Government (USG) departments and agencies, DoD cyberspace forces undertake DCO-RA and DCO-IDM missions to defend non-DoD cyberspace segments, like other USG networks, national critical infrastructure networks, defense industrial base networks, or mission partner networks

---- DCO-IDM missions defending non-DoD cyberspace may be ordered as part of Defense Support to Civil Authorities (DSCA) operations. These operations generally require consent of the network owner.

---- DCO-RA missions defending non-DoD cyberspace require authority flowing from SecDef via military order, and consideration of the LoW and ROEs

-- Offensive Cyberspace Operations (OCO): Missions intended to project power in and through cyberspace. All cyberspace operations missions conducted outside of blue cyberspace with a commander's intent, other than to defend blue cyberspace from an ongoing or imminent cyberspace threat, are OCO missions.

--- OCO missions include cyberspace exploitation and/or cyberspace attack actions

--- OCO missions require authority flowing from SecDef via military order, and consideration of the LoW and ROEs

Cyberspace Actions

- Execution of any OCO, DCO, or DODIN Operations mission requires completion of specific tactical-level actions or tasks that employ cyberspace capabilities to create effects in cyberspace. To plan for, authorize, and assess these actions, it is important that the commander and staff clearly understand which actions have been authorized under their current mission order.

National Guard Cyberspace Capabilities

- State assets serve as a first responder for Governors and Adjutant Generals (TAGs) for cyber emergencies. The assets provide surge capacity to national capabilities, but the elements employing the cyberspace capabilities are not deployable units for Title 10 missions.

Domestic Law

- Activities and operations must comply with the U.S. Constitution and with U.S. law

- Domestic laws place considerable restraints on cyberspace operations, particularly within the United States, but also in foreign countries

- Legal analysis is key to determining whether and how domestic laws impact military operations

Policy

- National Security Presidential Memorandum 13 (NSPM-13), U.S. Cyber Operations Policy, as amended by NSPM-21: All DoD offensive cyber operations must comply with NSPM-13, as amended. The document itself is classified.

- USCYBERCOM policy applicable to cyberspace operations is largely classified although Joint Publication 3-12 outlines the doctrinal mission in cyberspace

- DoD Policy applicable to cyberspace is contained in 8000-series DoD instructions, directives, and manuals, mostly promulgated by the DoD Chief Information Officer

- The Chairman of Joint Chiefs of Staff (CJCS) policies applicable to cyberspace is contained in 6000-series instructions, manuals, and other directives

- DAF Policy applicable to cyberspace is generally contained in 17-series instructions, manuals, and other directives

- <u>DAF Policy Regarding Cyber Capabilities</u>:

  -- Section 16.6 of DoD Law of War (LoW) Manual states that "DoD policy requires the legal review of the acquisition of weapons or weapons systems. This policy would include the review of weapons that employ cyber capabilities to ensure that they are not per se prohibited by the LoW. Not all cyber capabilities, however, constitute a weapon or weapons system." The manual provides that military department regulations address what cyber capabilities require legal review.

  -- DAF policy currently requires that cyber capabilities "being developed, bought, built, modified (more than minor modification) or otherwise acquired by the Air Force that are not within a special access program [be] reviewed for legality under the LoW, domestic law and international law." (AFI 51-401, *The Law of War*, para. 2.1.2.2)

    --- Air Force software development units may develop cyber capabilities for non-DAF organizations. The requirement for a legal review may not exist if a capability is being developed for a non-Air Force organization (e.g., USCYBERCOM). The legal review requirements are determined by the receiving organization.

    --- Note that this requirement applies to all cyber capabilities, not just to weapons. However, this requirement is directed for DAF cyber capabilities, and it is not automatically extended to joint operations and capabilities.

--- Air Force cyber capabilities do not include capabilities internal to DoD use or training or solely intended to provide access to adversarial and targeted computers, information systems, or networks and are thus do not require a legal review (AFI 51-401).

International Law and Law of War (LoW) Considerations

- *Jus ad bellum*:

-- The United States has generally treated the terms "use of force" and "armed attack" from the United Nations (UN) Charter synonymously. The issue of whether OCO rises to the level of an armed attack is an important one for ensuring the United States complies with the UN Charter and because of the potential application of the nation's inherent right of self-defense.

-- Currently, there is not international consensus regarding what constitutes a use of force or armed attack in cyberspace

--- However, there is also a growing body of state practice supporting the position that disruptive actions resulting in annoyance or harassment, even if for an extended period of time against many websites, do not amount to an armed attack

-- If OCO rises to the level of an "armed attack," then the state where the action occurs would be justified under Article 51 of the UN Charter to use force in response. Actions taken in self-defense under Article 51 of the UN Charter are not restricted to cyberspace (or any specific domain).

- *Jus in bello*:

-- It is also longstanding DoD policy that U.S. forces will comply with the LoW "during all armed conflicts however characterized. In all other military operations members of the DoD Components will continue to act consistent with the LoW's fundamental principles and rules, which include those in Common Article 3 of the 1949 Geneva Conventions and the principles of military necessity, humanity, distinction, proportionality, and honor." "Even if the LoW does not technically apply because the proposed military cyber operation would not take place in the context of armed conflict, DoD nonetheless applies LoW principles. This means that the *jus in bello* principles continue to guide the planning and execution of military cyber operations, even outside the context of armed conflict." Hon. Paul C. Ney, Jr., DoD General Counsel Remarks at U.S. Cyber Command Legal Conference. Thus, *jus in bello* analysis is done, at times, for policy reasons instead of being strictly required under international law.

- Military Necessity:

  -- Just as for kinetic targets, a legal review will address employment of cyberspace capabilities in both a targeting review (whether it is a valid target) and an operational legal review (whether the method to prosecute that target advance a legitimate military objective)

- Unnecessary Suffering:

  -- The use of arms which are calculated to cause unnecessary suffering is prohibited. Generally, cyber capabilities will not cause such effects, but if such effects are likely, they will be addressed in the operational legal review.

- Proportionality:

  -- Just as with physical operations, cyber operations must take into account potential collateral damage caused to the civilian population, and it must not be excessive in relation to the military advantage anticipated

  -- The commander must assess whether the damage to civilians and civilian property is excessive in relation to the military advantage anticipated by the cyber operation

- Distinction:

  -- Due to the overlapping nature of military and civilian uses of cyberspace, distinction can play a very important role in cyber operations. Depending on the language of the code, cyber capabilities can be developed with specific or generic targets.

    --- For example, a cyber capability designed to only create effects on certain industrial control systems known to be used in an adversary's nuclear enrichment facility would likely be considered a discriminate weapon

  -- While many discuss "dual-use systems" which provide service and capabilities to the civilian population and are also used for military purposes the DoD LoW Manual provides that dual-use is a term sometimes used to describe objects that are used by both the armed forces and the civilian population, **however**, from a legal perspective, such objects are either military objectives or they are not

- Honor:

  -- The principle of honor (or chivalry) permits lawful ruses such as camouflage, false signals, and mock troop movements but forbids perfidious acts

  -- Because the infrastructure allowing for the delivery of cyber effects crosses multiple countries and cyber effects can be created by non-state actors (e.g., independent hackers), attributing a cyber effect to a particular source can be challenging unlike physical attacks, the ability to mislead an adversary as to the source of cyber operations is much greater

-- Disguising cyber effects as normal web traffic or concealing the source of such operations is similar to a permissible lawful ruse and does not violate the principle of honor

- The Tallinn Manual 2.0 on the International Law Applicable to Cyber Operations: The manual, published in 2017, expands on the scope of and replaces the original Tallinn Manual. Where the original manual (Tallinn Manual on the International Law Applicable to Cyber Warfare) focused on cyber operations that constitute a use of force and trigger the right of self-defense, Tallinn 2.0 also examines more common cyber operations and incidents at the sub-use of force threshold. **It is important to note, the manual is not binding international law, but rather represents only opinions of how the law of armed conflict applies to actions in cyberspace.** The DoD LoW Manual represents the legal views of the DoD and is a resource for its personnel—including commanders, legal practitioners, and other military and civilian personnel—on the LoW.

- The DoD LoW Manual, published by the DoD Office of General Counsel and updated in July 2023, includes a chapter on how international law applies to Cyber Operations

References

· Authorities Concerning Military Cyber Operations, 10 U.S.C. § 394

· National Security Act of 1947, 50 U.S.C. § 413b

· Covert Action Statute (CAS), 50 U.S.C. § 3093

· Executive Order 12333, *United States Intelligence Activities*, as amended (4 December 1981)

· Hague Convention No. IV, *Respecting the Laws and Customs of War on Land and Annex Thereto* (18 October 1907)

· Additional Protocol to the Geneva Convention of 12 August 1949 (Protocol I), Art. 52(2) 10 October 1980, 1343 U.N.T.S. 137

· Additional Protocol to the Geneva Convention of 12 August 1949 (Protocol I), Art. 51(2)

· National Security Presidential Memorandum 13 (NSPM-13), as amended by NSPM-21

· Trilateral Memorandum of Agreement Among the Department of Defense, the Department of Justice, and the Intelligence Community Regarding Computer Network Attack and Computer Network Exploitation Activities (9 May 2007)

· Joint Publication 3-12, *Cyberspace Operations* (19 December 2022)

· DTM 17-007, Interim Policy and Guidance for Defense Support to Cyber Incident Response (21 June 2017), incorporating through Change 5, 23 June 2022

· DoDD 3025.18, *Defense Support of Civil Authorities* (29 December 2010), incorporating through Change 2, 19 March 2018

· Department of Defense Law of War Manual (June 2015, updated July 2023)

· AFI 51-401, *The Law of War* (3 August 2018)

· Tallinn Manual On the International Law Applicable to Cyber Warfare (2013)

· Tallinn Manual 2.0 On the International Law Applicable to Cyber Operations (2017)

· Hon. Paul C. Ney, Jr., "DoD General Counsel Remarks at U.S. Cyber Command Legal Conference," March 2, 2020, https://www.defense.gov/News/Speeches/Speech/Article/2099378/dod-general-counsel-remarks-at-us-cyber-command-legal-conference/

· Air Force Cyber Law Primer, Lt Col Royal A. Davis III, Jeffrey T. Biller and Air Force Cyber Primer Team, November 2022, https://www.airuniversity.af.edu/AUPress/Display/Article/3209936/air-force-cyber-law-primer/

Chapter 19
SPACE LAW

SPACE LAW OVERVIEW

Space is recognized by the United States and the Department of Defense (DoD) as a warfighting domain. The United States is becoming increasingly dependent on space-based systems to support military operations and our way of life in the United States and around the world. While space law and policy have existed for decades, their application to military operations has little historical precedent in comparison to other domains. The interpretation of how to apply the legal principles from international space law will be shaped by State practice. Also, the physical environment of space is unique and requires special considerations. Therefore, it is important for commanders to be acquainted with space law and policy and to remain actively engaged with their judge advocates during operational planning to ensure mission success in compliance with international law and domestic law and policy.

Key Takeaways

» The U.S. Space Force (USSF) was established as an independent Military Service under the Department of the Air Force (DAF) in law under 10 U.S.C. § 9081 and is designed to be a lean and agile Service, with few job specialties and two fewer echelons of command than the USAF

» The main principles applicable to military activities in space stem from four United Nations (UN) developed space treaties, the UN Charter, the law of war, and national law and policy

» There is no defined boundary between airspace and outer space under international or U.S. law

» There is no broad prohibition of weapons in space, but there are specific prohibitions including placement of nuclear weapons in space and testing of weapons on celestial bodies

» States are responsible and liable for the activities of their private actors in space

» There is a trend towards developing non-binding standards of responsible behavior in space, at both the international and U.S. national levels, to improve transparency and reduce miscommunication

---

Space Service

- The USSF was established as a Military Service in law under 10 U.S.C. § 9081. With its establishment, there are now two Military Services within the Department of the Air Force (DAF), the U.S. Air Force (USAF) and the U.S. Space Force (USSF).

- As a Military Service, the USSF is responsible for organizing, training, and equipping Guardians (i.e., members of the USSF), and presenting Guardians and space capabilities to the combatant commands (CCMDs) in line with Global Force Management (GFM) principles and policies applicable to all Services. In accordance with the Goldwater-Nichols Act, the USSF as a Military Service is not authorized to conduct warfighting operations.

- As a CCMD, U.S. Space Command (USSPACECOM) is given distinct authorities which allow it to conduct space operations within its area of responsibility (AOR), which begins 100 kilometers above mean sea level. The USSF provides the overwhelming majority of forces and capabilities to USSPACECOM. However, the USSF also provides forces and various capabilities that are terrestrially-based and may be assigned or allocated to other CCMDs.

Organization

- The infrastructure and support functions at USSF installations are provided by USAF personnel under the command and control of the USSF installation commander. USAF lawyers, doctors, civil engineers, chaplains, etc., are assigned to USSF commands to provide functional support to USSF units and missions. Commissioned officers of the USAF and USSF can command organizations and personnel in either Military Service.

- Relative to the USAF, the USSF has two fewer echelons of command in its organizational chain in an effort to remain a lean and agile Service. There are servicing legal offices at each echelon of command, similar to the USAF, and judge advocates are assigned to USSF installation legal offices. The USSF echelons of command are described below:

  -- Field Command: A major subdivision of the USSF that is directly subordinate to the Chief of Space Operations (CSO) at the headquarters. The field command is the USSF equivalent to the MAJCOM and NAF and has General Court-Martial Convening Authority (GCMCA) over its subordinate deltas and squadrons, consisting of both Airmen and Guardians.

  -- Delta: The echelon of command between field commands and squadrons. Deltas are the USSF equivalent of the USAF wing and group. The Commander of a delta has Special Court-Martial Convening Authority (SPCMCA) over its subordinate units.

  -- Squadrons: The basic building block organization of the USSF, similar to the USAF, providing a specific mission or support capability. Squadrons generally report directly to the deltas.

- The USSF reporting chain and echelons of command are depicted and compared to the USAF in the following organizational chart

Figure 19.1 Side-by-side comparison of the USAF and USSF reporting chains

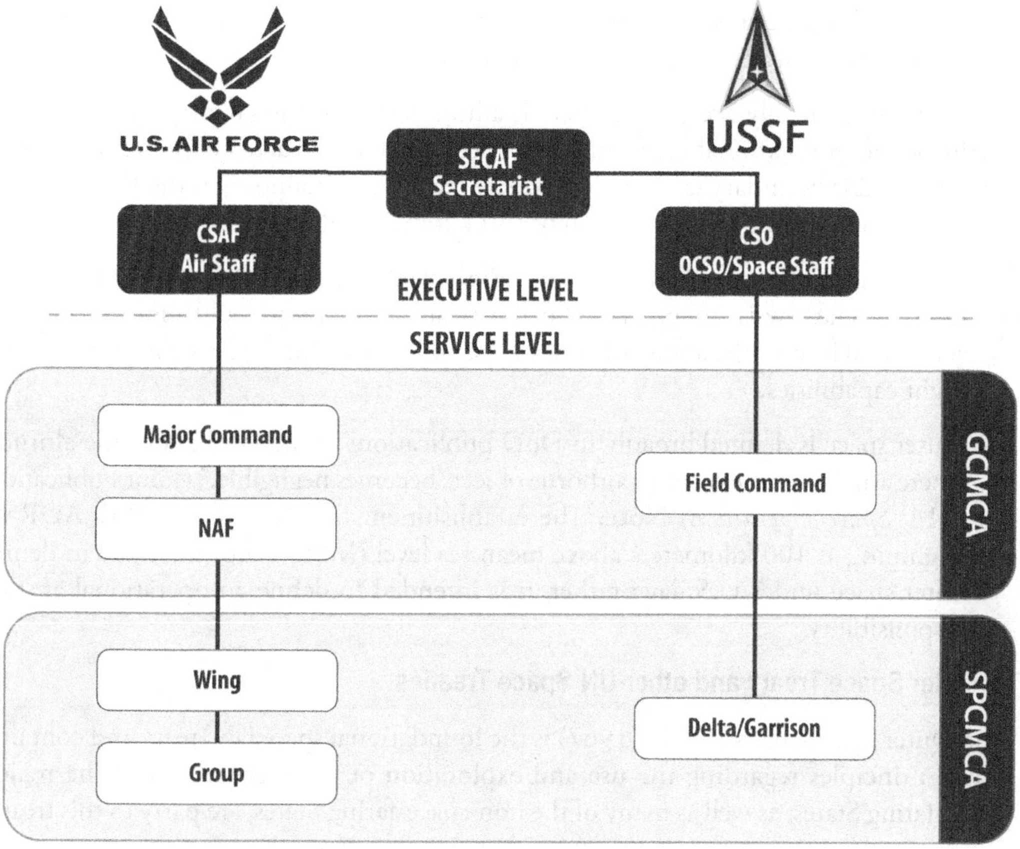

Detailed description of chart provided at end of section

International Law Applicable to Military Space Operations

- The main principles applicable to the use and exploration of outer space stem from four United Nations (UN)-developed space treaties, to which the United States is a party. These include: (1) The Outer Space Treaty (1967), (2) the Rescue and Return Agreement (1968), (3) The Liability Convention (1972), and (4) the Registration Convention (1976). There is a fifth UN-developed Space Treaty, the Moon Agreement, to which neither the United States, China, nor Russia are parties. Further, via Executive Order 13914, the United States specifically rejects the Moon Agreement and formally objects to its contents reflecting or otherwise expressing customary international law.

- With some exceptions, this international body of law provides the DoD wide-ranging freedom and flexibility in the conduct of space activities—from force enhancement to force application

Where Does Airspace End and Outer Space Begin?

- There is no defined boundary between airspace and outer space under international law. This is significant because a nation's sovereignty over its airspace does not extend into outer space and different laws apply in outer space.

- While States generally accept that there is a limit to the sovereign airspace above their territory, the international community has been unable to reach a common consensus over where this boundary is. The most widely recognized boundary is the Karman line, which is at an altitude of approximately 100 kilometers above sea level.

  -- Historically, the United States has taken the view that defining such a boundary under international law is unnecessary. Such a clear delimitation could limit freedom of action and impact the ability of States to exploit new technologies such as hypersonic flight capabilities.

  -- Outer space is defined broadly in DoD publications as the "area above the altitude where atmospheric effects on airborne objects becomes negligible." (Joint Publication 3-14, *Space Operations*) **Note:** The establishment of USSPACECOM's AOR as beginning at 100 kilometers above mean sea level (MSL) is not intended to define outer space under U.S. law; rather, it is intended to define an operational area of responsibility.

The Outer Space Treaty and other UN Space Treaties

- The Outer Space Treaty (OST) (1967) is the foundational space law treaty and contains broad principles regarding the use and exploration of outer space. All of the major space-faring States, as well as many of the non-space-faring States, are party to this treaty.

- Although the OST is over 50 years old and space operations have changed dramatically since the Cold War era, the key principles of the OST are still relevant today. Some of the principles are considered customary international law, meaning they are binding on non-party States to the treaty.

Use of Space for Peaceful Purposes

- The preamble of the OST recognizes that it is in the common interest of mankind to use and explore space for peaceful purposes. Notably, nothing in the binding provisions of the OST declares that outer space generally must be used for peaceful purposes; rather, it only requires that the moon and other celestial bodies be used *exclusively* for peaceful purposes and prohibits military bases, weapons testing of any kind, and military maneuvers on the Moon and other celestial bodies.

- The OST does not define what the term "peaceful purposes" means. The majority view, influenced by the United States, is that peaceful purposes equate to non-aggressive exploration and use of outer space. Therefore, military activities such as intelligence collection, missile early-warning, and the transmission of military communications and navigation signals to, from, and through space all constitute non-aggressive, peaceful purposes.

- Even though there is no overarching requirement that outer space generally be used for peaceful purposes, most countries, including the United States, recognize this principle as a matter of national policy. For example, this concept is incorporated throughout the current U.S. National Space Policy (2020).

Militarization and Weaponization of Space

- There is an important policy distinction between the militarization of space and the weaponization of space. As mentioned above, nothing in the OST prevents the militarization of space, although there are significant limitations on the military use of the moon and other celestial bodies. Space has otherwise been militarized since the beginning of the space age and that development represents nothing new.

- The weaponization of space has become a threat to our national security and space interests, particularly the development of anti-satellite (ASAT) and space-based weapons by U.S. competitors. The OST does not contain a general prohibition on weapons in space, but there are a few specific prohibitions and arms-control provisions.

- Nuclear weapons and other weapons of mass destruction are prohibited from being placed in orbit around the Earth, installed on celestial bodies, or stationed in space in any other manner. Further, as mentioned, no weapon testing of any kind may be conducted on the moon and other celestial bodies. Aside from this, there is no prohibition on other types of weapons, whether kinetic, directed energy, electronic warfare, or otherwise. There is also no express prohibition on launching intercontinental ballistic missiles (ICBMs) which transit through space because ICBMs are not placed in orbit around the Earth or stationed in space.

  -- Although provisions of the OST prohibit harmful interference without appropriate consultations, political sensitivities, rather than law, appear to be responsible for the cautious approach of the United States and other countries towards ASATs and other space-based weapons

- Other arms-control treaties may further limit the use or placement of weapons in space. For example, the Limited Test Ban Treaty (1963) prohibits nuclear weapons testing or any other nuclear explosion under water, in the air, or in outer space.

Freedom of Use and Non-Appropriation Principles

- The OST requires that space be free for the exploration and use by all States, and States should therefore make an effort to avoid interfering with the exploration and use of space by other States. In other words, unless authorized under international law, no State may prohibit another State from accessing space or any areas on celestial bodies.

- Unlike airspace, States have no right to claim territorial sovereignty in space, the Moon, or other celestial bodies. This, with the free exploration and use right noted above, cements the right to navigate, in space, over another State's territory, a legal principle known as the Freedom Principle. However, the right of space objects to pass through foreign airspace during launch or recovery generally requires pre-authorization.

- If military space activities may cause harmful interference with the space activities of other States, "appropriate" international consultations are required by the OST before proceeding. In practice, consultations have rarely, if ever, occurred.

- Outer space, including the Moon and other celestial bodies, cannot be owned or appropriated by a State or other entity. One debated issue is whether this provision allows for the appropriation of extracted resources in space, such as from the Moon, asteroids, or on Mars. This issue has become more prominent with the increasing number of commercial actors in space. U.S. law specifically permits the commercial exploitation of resources in outer space by citizens and private entities.

- The OST requires States to exercise their free exploration and use of outer space with "due regard" for the interests of other States. While due regard is a standard found in other domains, there is no fixed or settled meaning of due regard obligations for space operations.

International Law Applies to Space Activities

- The OST recognizes that international law is applicable in space. Therefore, international law should be considered when planning military space operations, including principles of customary international law (e.g., the inherent right to self-defense), the UN Charter's prohibition against the threat and use of force, and other international agreements. In addition, the applicable law of war principles must be considered during operational planning and targeting processes.

- While it is clear the law of war applies to military space operations, the practical application of the law can be challenging, given the lack of historical state practice in this area and the unique characteristics of the physical space environment

States are Responsible and Liable for the Space Activities of State and Non-State Actors

- A unique aspect of the space domain is that States bear international responsibility and liability for the space activities of both State and non-State actors. For example, if a commercial entity launches an object into space from U.S. territory, the United States will be internationally responsible for any wrongful act(s) committed by the commercial entity. As a result, States must authorize and continually supervise all space activities by State and non-State actors, which is usually accomplished through a national licensing process.

- Space object registration provides one means of determining which State is responsible for a particular space object, by requiring States to establish a national registry to record every object the State launches into space, including military objects. Each State that launches or procures the launch of an object into space and each State from whose territory or facility an object is launched is internationally liable for any damage the launched object causes on the Earth, in airspace, and in outer space.

- Two UN space treaties expand upon these OST principles and are further explained below:

  -- Liability Convention (1972): This convention elaborates upon the OST regarding the liability of launching States for any damage on Earth or in orbit caused by launched space objects. Launching States are absolutely liable for damage caused by space objects on the surface of the Earth or to aircraft in flight; that is, whether there is fault is irrelevant—if damage is caused, the State is liable. For damage caused to objects in space, launching States are liable only if they (or the non-State actor for which they bear responsibility) are at fault. The convention describes the circumstances under which States may be held liable for such damage and sets out procedures to follow in pursuing a claim for damages. The convention is likely inapplicable between Parties engaged in an armed conflict, but may be applicable to harmed third parties.

  -- Registration Convention (1976): This convention expands upon the OST and assists States in identifying responsibility over space objects. It requires a launching State to maintain a registry of objects launched into space and provide certain data to the UN as soon as practicable for every object launched, including military objects. The UN publishes the data in a register available to the public via the Internet at https://www.unoosa.org/oosa/en/spaceobjectregister/index.html.

Astronauts are the Envoys of Mankind

- The OST provides that astronauts shall be regarded as "envoys of mankind in outer space" and requires State Parties to render them all possible assistance in the event of accident, distress, or emergency landing on the territory of another State or on the high seas. The Rescue and Return Agreement (1968) expands upon this principle. The agreement also provides for the retrieval of space objects found outside the territory of a launching State and the return to the launching State, upon request.

- Given that astronauts are often military personnel, it remains unclear whether military personnel would be protected by this agreement and the OST during an armed conflict. Applicability may depend on the mission and the circumstances, to include the developing interpretation of the inter-relation of privileges and obligations of States under the law of war and international space law.

Satellite Communications and the Role of the ITU

- The International Telecommunications Union (ITU) is a specialized UN agency that provides the international framework for the management of international telecommunications (including satellite communications) and administers relevant international treaties, including the ITU Constitution, the ITU Convention, and the Radio Regulations.

- The United States is a member of the ITU and is therefore bound by the provisions of the three governing instruments, which declare the radio-frequency spectrum and the geostationary orbit are limited, natural resources to which all States are authorized equitable access. The overarching goal of the ITU is to prevent harmful radio-frequency interference through the development of international standards and the de-confliction of radio frequencies.

- The ITU allocates satellite orbits and bands of radio-frequency spectrum to different categories of services, allots radio frequencies to countries or regions, and registers radio-frequency assignments at the international level.

  -- The assignment of radio frequencies to satellite operators occurs at the State level. For example, in the United States the Federal Communications Commission (FCC) assigns radio frequencies to commercial satellite operators and the National Telecommunications and Information Administration assigns radio frequencies to federal government operators. Once satellite operators are assigned frequencies, they are entitled to operate without harmful interference.

- For the geostationary orbit, the ITU also allocates physical orbital slots, and satellites must remain within + or − 0.1 degrees of an allocated physical slot. The geostationary orbit is a circular orbit above the equator, which has an orbital period equal to that of the earth. A satellite stationed in this orbit therefore appears stationary above the earth, making the orbit ideal for satellite communication purposes.

- The ITU procedures and rules generally do not apply to military activities, with some exceptions. It is important to consult a judge advocate in any situation where military operations may interfere with the rights of other spectrum users.

U.S. Law and Policy Applicable to Military Space Operations

- Given the permissive nature of international space law for military operations, U.S. military activities and operations in space are largely regulated by national and DoD policy. Military space operations are also guided by joint doctrine, such as Joint Publication 3-14, *Space Operations*. As a matter of national policy, the United States acknowledges that the use of space is for peaceful purposes, in accordance with international law, while also safeguarding U.S. interests in space.

- There are several national laws and policies that may impact or shape how the DoD conducts space activities and operations

U.S. Satellite Interference

- 18 U.S.C. § 1367 makes it a felony to intentionally or maliciously interfere with authorized satellite operations or transmissions without the permission of the satellite operator. While 18 U.S.C. § 1367 specifically exempts authorized law enforcement and intelligence activities, it does not specifically exempt other military and national security activities.

- The law does not apply extraterritorially and there is arguably an implied national security exception for defense activities. Given these sensitivities, consultation with a judge advocate is essential whenever the provisions of 18 U.S.C. § 1367 may be implicated by military space activities and operations.

U.S. Space Domain Awareness

- Space Domain Awareness (SDA) (formerly Space Situational Awareness [SSA]) encompasses the effective identification, characterization, and understanding of any factor associated with the space domain that could affect space operations. In addition to informing military space operations, SDA is essential to avoiding collisions in space and minimizing environmental damage and orbital debris.

- SDA is enabled by the U.S. Space Surveillance Network, which is a network of sensors and radars positioned around the world. As a result of SDA services and information, the United States has established one of the world's most robust and complete catalog of space objects. **Note:** The DAF is transitioning to the use of the term SDA, rather than SSA, now that space is recognized by the DoD as an independent warfighting domain. Not all policy/guidance has been updated to reflect this change; therefore, SSA is sometimes still used in DoD/DAF publications as well as in U.S. law and policy.

  -- Pursuant to 10 U.S.C. § 2274, the DoD is authorized to provide SSA services and information to, and obtain SSA data and information from, non-U.S. government entities, if determined to be consistent with national security. This law authorizes SSA sharing agreements with entities such as the governments of foreign States, political subdivisions of States, and U.S. and foreign commercial entities.

U.S. Global Positioning System

- The U.S.-owned Global Positioning System (GPS) and space-based position, navigation, and timing (PNT) have become essential to both military and civil activities worldwide. In accordance with 10 U.S.C. § 2281, the DoD is responsible for sustaining and operating GPS for both military and civilian purposes. Additionally, under 51 U.S.C. § 50112, Congress encouraged the President to promote GPS as the international standard.

- 10 U.S.C. § 2281, the 2020 National Space Policy, and Space Policy Directive 7 further assert that the United States should provide uninterrupted access to GPS for U.S. and allied national security systems; provide access to GPS on a continuous, worldwide basis free of direct user fees for civil, commercial, scientific uses, and homeland security purposes; and improve capabilities to deny hostile use of any PNT services, without unduly disrupting civil and commercial access

U.S. Orbital Debris Guidelines and Launch Licensing

- Space is becoming more and more crowded, with an increasing number of actors and objects. The number of defunct satellites and other man-made objects orbiting the Earth is continuously on the rise, increasing the odds of potentially devastating space collisions.

- Although there is no express requirement under international law to minimize orbital debris in space, the U.S. government has enacted its own U.S. Orbital Debris Mitigation Standard Practices (ODMSP), which were updated and strengthened in 2019. These guidelines are intended to minimize new and mitigate existing space debris and encourage the implementation of similar standards by other States. All U.S. military launches must follow these guidelines or seek an exception to policy.

- The United States meets its obligations under the OST and other UN space treaties to authorize and continually supervise all space activities and objects through its licensing process. Various U.S. agencies are involved in the licensing process depending on the function and operations of a satellite. These agencies include, but are not limited to, the Federal Aviation Administration (FAA) for commercial launches, the Federal Communications Commission for satellite communication links, and the Commerce Department's National Oceanic and Atmospheric Administration (NOAA) for remote-sensing satellites. The DoD launch mission transitioned to Space Systems Command (SSC) in 2021. Commercial and civilian launch (including contracted DoD) is a rapidly growing and changing area of law, regulation, and policy; therefore, consultation with a judge advocate is essential to ensure compliance with the latest guidance in this area.

DoD Guidelines and Standing Rules of Engagement

- The 2020 U.S. National Space Policy directed the heads of U.S. agencies, in collaboration with the Secretary of State, to: "[l]ead the enhancement of safety, stability, security, and long-term sustainability in space by promoting a framework for responsible behavior in outer space ...." Pursuant to this effort, on 7 July 2021, the U.S. Secretary of Defense directed the DoD to conduct its space operations consistent with the following five tenets of responsible behavior: (1) Operate in, from, to and through space with due regard for others and in a professional manner; (2) Limit the generation of long-lived debris; (3) Avoid the creation of harmful interference; (4) Maintain safe separation and safe trajectory; and (5) Communicate and make notification to enhance the safety and stability of the domain.

- The U.S. Standing Rules of Engagement (SROE) contains a classified annex, Enclosure E, concerning space operations

Major U.S. Policy Efforts

- In April 2022, Vice President Kamala Harris announced that the United States committed not to conduct destructive direct-ascent antisatellite missile testing and that the U.S. sought to establish this as a new international norm for responsible behavior in space. Since that time, 13 countries have made similar unilateral commitments, including Canada, Japan, the United Kingdom, France, Italy, South Korea, and others. This represents a recent significant shift in State practice.

- The U.S.'s Artemis Program is designed to return humankind to the Moon, demonstrate new technologies, conduct lunar research, and eventually send the first astronauts to Mars. A NASA-led civil space project, the Artemis Program seeks broad international cooperation and partnership. In furtherance of this cooperation, NASA and the Department of State established the Artemis Accords, which 32 countries have since signed onto. While not binding on military space activities, these Accords reinforce the commitments of the signatories to some of the foundational principles of the primary international space treaties, as well as best practices and norms of responsible behavior, such as the public release of scientific data or the deconfliction of space activities. Notably, the signatories affirm that the extraction of space resources does not inherently constitute national appropriation under Article II of the Outer Space Treaty.

Non-Binding Standards of Responsible Behavior in Space

- The binding international legal regime in space is unlikely to change in the near future due to a lack of international consensus amongst the space powers, which has driven efforts to develop non-binding standards at both the international and U.S. national levels. One of the stated primary goals of developing non-binding standards is to reach a common understanding of responsible versus irresponsible behaviors in space to increase transparency among States and reduce the chance of miscommunication or miscalculation, which can lead to an escalation of tensions and hostilities.

- In December 2021, UN General Assembly Resolution 75/36 sought the views of UN Member States on the further development and implementation of norms, rules and principles of responsible behaviors. The U.S. Department of State led and coordinated with other U.S. agencies (including the DoD) regarding the U.S. national submission to the UN Resolution. Member State submissions are available at https://www.un.org/disarmament/topics/outerspace-sg-report-outer-space-2021/.

References

· Space Situational Awareness Services and Information, 10 U.S.C. § 2274

· Global Positioning System, 10 U.S.C. § 2281

· The United States Space Force, 10 U.S.C. § 9081

· Interference with the Operation of a Satellite, 18 U.S.C. § 1367

· Promotion of United States Global Positioning Systems Standards, 51 U.S.C. § 50112

· Executive Order 13914, *Encouraging International Support for the Recovery and Use of Space Resources*, 6 April 2020

· *Treaty on Principles Governing the Activities of States in the Exploration and Use of Outer Space, Including the Moon and Other Celestial Bodies*, 27 January 1967, 18 U.S.T. 2410

· *Agreement on the Rescue of Astronauts, the Return of Astronauts and the Return of Objects Launched into Outer Space*, 22 April 1968, 19 U.S.T. 7570

· *Convention on International Liability for Damage Caused by Space Objects*, 29 March 1972, 24 U.S.T. 2389

· *Convention on Registration of Objects Launched into Outer Space*, 14 January 1975, 28 U.S.T. 695

· *Constitution and Convention of the International Telecommunication Union*, 22 December 1992, T. Doc 104-34

· *Radio Regulations of the International Telecommunication Union* (2020)

· *Treaty Banning Nuclear Weapon Tests in the Atmosphere, in Outer Space and Under Water*, 5 August 1963, 14 U.S.T. 1313

· UN General Assembly Resolution 75/36, *Reducing Space Threats through Norms, Rules and Principles of Responsible Behaviours*, 16 December 2021

· The Goldwater-Nichols Department of Defense Reorganization Act, Pub. L. 99-443 (4 October 1986)

· U.S. Government Orbital Debris Mitigation Standard Practices (2019)

· U.S. Standing Rules of Engagement (SROE), Enclosure E

· Joint Publication 3-14, *Joint Space Operations* (23 August 2023)

· Defense Space Strategy (June 2020) National Space Policy (December 2020)

· Space Policy Directive 7, *The United States Space-Based Positioning, Navigation, and Timing Policy*, 15 January 2021

· Space Capstone Publication, *Spacepower*, Doctrine for Space Forces (2020)

· DoDD 3100.10, *Space Policy* (30 August 2022)

Chart Description

Figure 19.1 Side-by-side comparison of the USAF and USSF reporting chains: At the executive level, the U.S. Air Force (USAF) has the Chief of Staff of the Air Force who presides over the Air Staff, and the U.S. Space Force (USSF) has the Chief of Space Operations who presides over the Office of the Chief of Space Operations (referred to as Space Staff). The two service chiefs report to the Secretary of the Air Force (SecAF). At the service level, the USAF units include (from top to bottom) the major command, numbered air force (NAF), wing, and group. The NAF is typically a general court-martial convening authority (GCMCA) and the wing or group is typically a special court-martial convening authority (SPCMCA). The USSF units include (from top to bottom) the field command and the delta. The field command is the USSF equivalent to the USAF major command and NAF and is typically designated by SecAF as a GCMCA. The deltas are USSF equivalents to the USAF wings and groups and typically designated by SecAF as SPCMCAs.

INDEX

E

General (Under Honorable Conditions), 82

J

M

N

O

Q

Questionable Intelligence Activity, 525–526
Quid Pro Quo, 357

R

Radon
 See Environmental Law: toxic substances
Raffles, 375
Random Drug Testing, 248, 482–483
Records Management, 235–236
Redlining, 62
Reenlistment
 See Selective Reenlistment Program
Referral Reports, 56
Religious Freedom Restoration Act, 227
Religious Issues
 accommodation of religious practices, 227
 expression in the workplace, 225
 immunizations, 264
 official communications, 226–227
 outside advocacy groups, 227–228
 prayer, 225–226
 religious displays, 226
Remission, NJP
 See Nonjudicial Punishment: remission
Removal from Base Housing, 329
Rental Vehicle Damage
 See Claims: rental vehicle damage
Reported Offenses, 167–168
Report of Investigation, 128–131
Reports of Survey/Financial Liability Investigation,
 413–416
Reprimands
 See Adverse Administrative Actions
Reprisal, 268, 312, 351, 354, 366, 381, 487, 491, 526
Reservist
 See Air Force Reserve
Retaliation, 310–312
 when reporting a criminal offense, 253
 when reporting a sexual assault, 81, 135–136, 139
Right of Free Expression, 221–223
Right to Remain Silent, 156–157, 172
Rules for the Use of Force, 503–504
Rules of Engagement, 503–506

S

Safety and Accident Investigation Boards, 544–547
 Air National Guard considerations, 547
Safety Investigation
 See Investigations: Safety Investigation Board
Satellite Interference
 See Space Law: satellite communications
Satellites
 See Space Law
Searches, 164–166
Secretary of the Air Force Personnel Council
 administrative separation (Guard and Reserve),
  107–110
 conscientious objector, 281–283
 Disability Evaluation System, 297–301
 dual action processing, 92–93
 officer grade determinations, 305–306
Security Services, 438–439
Seizure
 See Inspections and Searches
Selective Reenlistment Program
 active duty, 48–50
 Air Force Reserve and Air National Guard, 51–53
Self-Defense
 See Rules of Engagement; Rules for the Use of Force
Self-Identification (Substance Abuse), 215–216
Sentencing, 25
Separations
 See also Involuntary Separation of Enlisted
 Air Force Reserve, 107–110
 Air National Guard, 107–110
 drug abuse, 215–216
 dual action processing, 92–93, 300
 general (under honorable conditions), 82
 honorable, 82
 Individual Ready Reserve, 110
 interest of national security, 90
 medical discharges, 92–93
 officer separations, 103–106
  discharge procedures, 105–106
  involuntary separations, 104–105
  resignations in lieu, 106
 probation and rehabilitation, enlisted, 99–102
 under other than honorable conditions, 82
 veteran's benefits, 83
 voluntary separation, 104

Page Intentionally Left Blank

The Judge Advocate General's School
150 Chennault Circle (Bldg. 694)
Maxwell Air Force Base, Alabama 36112-6418
Comm. (334) 953-2802 or DSN 493-2802
AFLOA.AFJAGS@us.af.mil

This publication is available at:
https://www.afjag.af.mil/Library/AFJAGS-Library

Made in the USA
Monee, IL
14 February 2025

12265106R00348